A Companion to
QUALITATIVE
RESEARCH

A Companion to
QUALITATIVE
RESEARCH

Edited by **Uwe Flick, Ernst von Kardorff and Ines Steinke**

Translated by **Bryan Jenner**

S SAGE Publications

London ● Thousand Oaks ● New Delhi

SAGE Publications Ltd
1 Oliver's Yard
55 City Road
London EC1Y 1SP

SAGE Publications Inc.
2455 Teller Road
Thousand Oaks, California 91320

SAGE Publications India Pvt Ltd
B-42, Panchsheel Enclave
Post Box 4109
New Delhi 110 017

British Library Cataloguing in Publication data

A catalogue record for this book is available
from the British Library

ISBN 0 7619 7374 5
ISBN 0 7619 7375 3 (pbk)

Library of Congress Control Number 2003112201

Typeset by C&M Digitals (P) Ltd., Chennai, India
Printed in Great Britain by Bell & Bain Ltd, Glasgow

Contents

Notes on Editors and Contributors

EDITORS

Uwe Flick, is Professor of Empirical Social and Nursing Research (Qualitative Methods) at the Alice Salomon University of Applied Sciences in Berlin, Germany and Adjunct Professor at the Memorial University of Newfoundland at St. John's, Canada. Research interests are qualitative methods, social representations and health. He is author of several books and articles on qualitative research including *An Introduction to Qualitative Research* (Sage, Second edition, 2002) and *The Psychology of the Social* (Cambridge University Press, 1998).

Ernst von Kardorff, is Professor of the sociology of rehabilitation at Humboldt University in Berlin. Research interests are living and coping with chronic illness, the role of partners and volunteer organizations and qualitative methods. Publications include, with C. Schönberger, *Mit dem, kranken Partner leben* (*Living with a Chronically Ill Partner*) (Opladen, 2003).

Ines Steinke, Dr. Phil. works in industry in areas such as market- and marketing psychology and usability and design-management research and teaching in qualitative research, general psychology and youth research. Publications include: *Kriterien qualitativer Forschung. Ansätze zur Bewertung qualitativ-empirischer Sozial-forschung* (*Criteria of Qualitative Research: Approaches for Assessing Qualitative-Empirical Social Research*) (Weinheim, 1999).

CONTRIBUTORS

Bauer, Martin, Ph.D., born 1959, Lecturer, Department of Social Psychology and Methodology Institute, London School of Economics. Research interests: New technologies, qualitative methods, social representations, resistance in social processes.

Bergmann, Jörg R., Prof. Dr., Dipl.-Psych., born 1946, University of Bielefeld, Faculty of Sociology. Research interests: Qualitative methods, new media, communication in everyday life and in complex work situations.

Böhm, Andreas, Dr. phil., born 1955, Federal Office of Health, Brandenburg. Research interests: Epidemiology, children's health, qualitative methods.

Bohnsack, Ralf, Prof. Dr. rer. soz., Dr. phil. habil, Dipl. Soz., born 1948, Free University of Berlin, Faculty of Education and Psychology. Research interests: Qualitative methods, sociology of knowledge, youth research, deviance.

Bude, Heinz, Prof. Dr. phil., born 1954, University of Kassel and Hamburg Institute of Social Research. Research interests: Research on generations, exclusion and entrepreneurs.

Denzin, Norman K., Prof., Ph.D., born 1941, College of Communications Scholar, Distinguished Research Professor of Communications, Sociology, Cinema Studies and Humanities, University of Illinois, Institute of Communications Research. Research interests: Cultural studies, interpretative research, media and ethnic groups.

Eberle, Thomas S., Prof. Dr., born 1950, Sociological Seminar, University of St Gallen (Switzerland). Research interests: Phenomenological sociology, sociology of knowledge, sociology of culture.

Erzberger, Christian,   Dr. born 1956, Society for Innovative Social Research and Social Planning (GISS), Bremen. Research interests: Quantitative and qualitative methods in empirical social research, analysis of sequential patterns, evaluation.

Fischer-Rosenthal, Wolfram,   Prof. Dr., born 1946, University of Kassel, Faculty of Social Work. Research interests: Qualitative case reconstruction (of biographical structures), sociology of knowledge, analyses of interactions (especially of professional activities).

Fleck, Christian,   ao. Univ. Prof., Dr. phil., born 1954, University of Graz. Research interests: Sociology of science, history of empirical social research and of institutions of social sciences.

Gildemeister, Regine,   Prof. Dr. phil. habil., Dipl. Soz., born 1949, Institute of Sociology, Eberhard-Karls-University of Tübingen. Research interests: Mode of social construction of gender, sociology of professions, qualitative methods.

Harper, Douglas,   Prof. Ph.D., born 1948, Duquesne University, Chair and Professor, Sociology Department; Co-Director: Center for Social and Public Policy. Research interests: Visual sociology, sociology of culture, sociological theory.

Hermanns, Harry,   Prof. Dr. rer. pol., born 1947, University of Applied Sciences Potsdam. Research interests: Study reform, especially multimedia-based learning, qualitative methods.

Hildenbrand, Bruno,   Prof. Dr. rer. soc., born 1948, Institute of Sociology, Friedrich Schiller-University of Jena. Research interests: Structure of professional activities (in therapy and in children's and adolescents' services), change of structures in rural areas, case reconstructive methods in social sciences.

Hitzler, Ronald,   Prof. Dr., born 1950, Chair of General Sociology, University of Dortmund. Research interests: Phenomenology, dramatological anthropology, hermeneutic sociology of knowledge.

Honer, Anne,   Dr., born 1951, Faculty of History and Sociology, University of Konstanz. Research interests: Sociology of knowledge and culture, phenomenology, ethnography/qualitative research.

Hopf, Christel,   Prof. Dr., born 1942, Institute for Social Sciences, University of Hildesheim. Research interests: Methods of empirical research, especially qualitative methods, research on socialization, political sociology.

Kelle, Udo,   Dr., born 1960, Institute of Interdisciplinary Gerontology, University of Vechta. Research interests: Methodology of empirical research, sociological theory of action, life course research, especially sociology of ageing.

Knoblauch, Hubert,   Prof. Dr., born 1959, Institute for Sociology, Technical University of Berlin. Research interests: General sociology, sociology of religion and knowledge, qualitative methods.

König, Hans-Dieter,   Prof. Dr. phil., born 1950, freelance psychoanalyst in Dortmund, teaches sociology and social psychology at the University of Frankfurt/Main. Research interests: Psychoanalytic research into culture and biography, theory of socialization, methods of hermeneutic research.

Kowal, Sabine,   Prof. Dr., born 1944, Apl. Professor of General Linguistics, esp. Psycholinguistics, Technical University of Berlin, Institute for Linguistics. Research interests: Conversation analysis, transcription, rhetoric.

Lincoln, Yvonna S.,   Prof., born 1944, Program director of the Higher Education Program, Texas A&M University, Faculty of Educational Administration. Research interests: Higher education administration and leadership, qualitative research methods, program evaluation.

Lindner, Rolf,   Prof. Dr. phil, Dipl. Soz., born 1945, Professor of European Ethnology, Institute for European Ethnology, Humboldt-University of Berlin. Research interests: Ethnology of the city, science research, cultural studies.

Luckmann, Thomas, Prof. Ph.D., born 1927, University of Konstanz, Research interests: Sociology of knowledge, phenomenology, communication.

Lüders, Christian, Dr., born 1953, Deutsches Jugendinstitut, Director of the Department 'Youth and Youth Support'. Research interests: Qualitative research, children's and adolescents' services, social pedagogy.

Marotzki, Winfried, Prof. Dr. habil., born 1950, Otto-von-Guericke-University Magdeburg. Research interests: Qualitative research, theory of education (philosophy of education), Internet research.

Matt, Eduard, Dr. rer. soc., born 1955, lives and works in Bremen. Research interests: Sociology of youth, criminology, sociology of knowledge and culture.

Mayring, Philipp, Prof. Dr., born 1952, Institute of Psychology, University of Klagenfurt/Austria. Research interests: Qualitative methods (content analysis, evaluation), developmental psychology (gerontology), educational psychology (emotion and learning, virtual media), mixed methodologies.

Meier, Christoph, born 1963, Fraunhofer Institute of Work Economics and Organisation, Stuttgart. Research interests: Tele-cooperation, team development in distributed organizations, analysis of (technically mediated) processes of communications, qualitative methods (ethnography, conversation analysis).

Meinefeld, Werner, apl. Prof. Dr., born 1948, Institute of Sociology, University of Erlangen-Nürnberg. Research interests: Epistemology, methods of empirical research, university research.

Merkens, Hans, Prof. Dr., born 1937, Free University of Berlin, Faculty of Education and Psychology, Institute for General Education. Research interests: Youth research, organizational learning and development of organizational cultures, educational institutions.

Métraux, Alexandre, Dr. phil., born 1945, Member of the Otto Selz Institute at the University of Mannheim. Research interests: History of sciences, especially brain and nerves research between 1750 and 1950, epistemology, research on scientific media.

Nadig, Maya, Prof. Dr. phil., born 1946, Professor of Ethnology, Bremen Institute for Cultural Research, Faculty of Cultural Sciences at the University of Bremen. Research interests: Ethnopsychoanalysis, gender relations, cultural identity and transcultural processes.

O'Connell, Daniel C., Prof., born 1928, Prof. of Psychology, Department of Psychology, Loyola University of Chicago. Research interests: Temporal organization of speaking, transcription, dialogue.

Ohlbrecht, Heike, Dipl. Soz., born 1970, Institute for Rehabilitation, Humboldt-University of Berlin. Research interests: Qualitative methods, family sociology, coping with chronic illness in adolescence.

Parker, Ian, Prof., Ph.D., BA (Hons.), born 1956, Professor of Psychology, Manchester Metropolitan University, Discourse Unit, Department of Psychology and Speech Pathology. Research interests: Marxism, language, psychoanalysis.

Reichertz, Jo, Prof. Dr., born 1949, Professor of Communication, University of Essen. Research interests: Qualitative research, sociology of knowledge in the context of text and image hermeneutics, sociology of culture.

Reichmayr, Johannes, Prof. Dr. phil., born 1947, Lecturer in Psychology, esp. Psychoanalysis. Institute for Psychology, Department of Social Psychology at Faculty of Cultural Sciences of the University of Klagenfurt. Research interests: Ethnopsychoanalysis, history of the psychoanalytic movement..

Rosenstiel, Lutz von, Prof. Dr. Dr. hc., born 1938, Institute for Psychology, University of Munich. Research interests: Leadership, socialization in organizations, motivation and volition.

Rosenthal, Gabriele, Prof. Dr., born 1954, Professor of Qualitative Methods at the Georg-August University of Göttingen, Center for Methods in Social Sciences. Research interests: Interpretative sociology, biographical research, sociology of families.

Schmidt, Christiane, Dr. phil., born 1951, University of Hildesheim, Institute for Applied Linguistics. Research interests: Subjective coping with experiences with (networks of) computers, evaluation of Internet-based seminars, qualitative methods of observation and interviewing.

Soeffner, Hans-Georg, Prof. Dr., born 1939, University of Konstanz, Chair of General Sociology. Research interests: Sociology of culture, anthropology of culture (communication, knowledge, media, religion, law).

Willems, Herbert, PD Dr. phil., M.A., Dipl. Päd., born 1956, currently Professor of the Sociology of Culture at the Justus-Liebig-University of Gießen. Research interests: Sociological theories and methods, everyday culture, mass media.

Winter, Rainer, Prof. Dr., born 1960, psychologist (Diplom) and sociologist (M.A., Dr. phil., Dr. habil.), Professor of Media- and Culture Theories, University of Klagenfurt. Research interests: Sociological theories, sociology of globalization, qualitative methods, media and culture analysis.

Wolff, Stephan, Prof. Dr., born 1947, University of Hildesheim, Institute for Social Pedagogy. Research interests: Applied organization research, qualitative methods, cultural anthropology.

Preface

Qualitative research is a growing and ever more diverse field. The continuous development of new approaches, new methods and new techniques results in a wider and wider diversity in the literature – in books, in journals and on the Internet. Students, as well as experienced researchers, will find it increasingly difficult to keep up with these developments and with the range of methodological alternatives available for doing their own research projects. The *Companion to Qualitative Research* seeks to highlight and illustrate connections, common ground and differences in the heterogeneous developments of qualitative research. It intends to give readers a representative overview of the current landscape of qualitative research with its epistemological roots, its main theoretical principles, its methodological bases and the development of its procedures, and also to offer an impression of trends for further development. To achieve this, themes from current debates in the German- and English-speaking worlds have been brought together, so that the *Companion* takes a wider, international perspective on qualitative research with authors from Continental Europe, Britain and North America.

At the outset, the *Companion* presents examples of how *qualitative research* operates *in action,* using descriptions of the research style of various scholars who have had major impacts on this field or are particularly instructive in their way of doing research. This first part of the book is intended to explain the unique contribution that qualitative research has made to the acquisition of achieving knowledge in the social sciences, to theory construction and to methodology.

The *theory of qualitative research* is explained by presenting the most important background theories, which are illustrated using examples from selected areas of interest for qualitative research. Issues of *methodology and qualitative research* are central to the next part of the *Companion*, where issues of research design, epistemology and evaluation of methodological procedures and results are outlined.

The major part of this *Companion* is devoted to the presentation of the most important methods currently used for *doing qualitative research*. Practice in the collection and interpretation of qualitative research data therefore occupies a central place in the book.

The concluding part looks at *qualitative research in context*. Contributions are included on research ethics, on teaching and on the application of qualitative research, as well as critical reflections on the status and future prospects of qualitative research.

This *Companion* is intended for students of a variety of disciplines where qualitative research is applied. For this reason, we have appended a separate part on *resources* which includes recommendations for further reading from introductory works and classic textbooks of qualitative research, and also offers lists of journals and current Internet sources. The *Companion* is also intended for those who teach social sciences and, finally, should also be a useful reference work for qualitative researchers in universities and in professional practice. It is not intended to replace a course book of qualitative research. Nor should it be seen as a 'recipe book' to be used as the sole aid in setting up a concrete piece of research. It seeks, rather, to provide orientation, background knowledge and reflection and to give information about current trends and developments. Each contribution offers suggestions for further reading.

Acknowledgements

We wish to express our warmest thanks to all the authors for their contributions and for their willingness to rewrite and revise them.

Also, we would like to thank the people who have supported the development of this book over the years, especially Michael Carmichael and Patrick Brindle at Sage and Burghard König at Rowohlt.

Uwe Flick, Ernst von Kardorff and Ines Steinke

Part 1

Introduction

1 What is Qualitative Research? An Introduction to the Field

Uwe Flick, Ernst von Kardorff and Ines Steinke

In recent years qualitative research has developed into a broad and sometimes almost confusing field of study. It has become part of the training in empirical research methods in a variety of subjects and disciplines. This broad palette of subjects extends from sociology, via psychology, to cultural studies, education and economics, to name but a few. Alongside the traditional compartmentalized subjects it is receiving growing attention in the rather more applied disciplines, such as social work, nursing or public health. Qualitative research has always had a strongly applied orientation in the questions it addresses and in its methods of procedure, and it now occupies an important place in these areas. In the realm of social sciences there is, in the broadest sense, hardly any area of research in which it is not at least partially used – particularly if one considers the international dimension. Even though there is no shortage of criticism, preconceptions and prejudice about qualitative research, one may still claim that it is now established and consolidated, and that, in the way suggested by Thomas Kuhn (1970), it has now achieved the status of a paradigmatic 'normal science'.

1 INVITATION TO QUALITATIVE RESEARCH

Qualitative research claims to describe life-worlds 'from the inside out', from the point of view of the people who participate. By so doing it seeks to contribute to a better understanding of social realities and to draw attention to processes, meaning patterns and structural features. Those remain closed to non-participants, but are also, as a rule, not consciously known by actors caught up in their unquestioned daily routine. Qualitative research, with its precise and 'thick' descriptions, does not simply depict reality, nor does it practise exoticism for its own sake. It rather makes use of the unusual or the deviant and unexpected as a source of insight and a mirror whose reflection makes the unknown perceptible in the known, and the known perceptible in the unknown, thereby opening up further possibilities for (self-) recognition. The theory and practice of obtaining these perspectives will be briefly illustrated here by looking at four questions that are addressed in classic qualitative studies.

1   How do young migrants affect a local culture? How do they view their life and their prospects? How do they react to their environment and what form of social organization does their group life engender?

2   What are the consequences of living as a patient in a psychiatric clinic, and how can patients preserve their identity under the conditions that prevail there?

3   What are the bases for the possibility of communication and joint action in quite different social situations?

4   What are the concrete results of unemployment, and how are they processed individually and in a local community?

These are a few topic areas from the infinite variety of possible questions that, with the aid of qualitative methods, may be handled particularly well and in a theoretically productive and practically relevant form.

1   William F. Whyte's (1955) classic ethnographic study of a street gang in a major city in the eastern United States in the 1940s offers, on the basis of individual observations, personal notes and other sources, a comprehensive picture of a dynamic local culture. Through the mediation of a key figure Whyte had gained access to a group of young second-generation Italian migrants. As a result of a two-year period of participant observation he was able to obtain information about the motives, values and life-awareness and also about the social organization, friendship relations and loyalties of this local culture. These were condensed in theoretically important statements such as:

> Whyte's gangs can be seen simply as an example of a temporary non-adjustment of young people. They withdraw from the norms of the parental home … and at the same time see themselves as excluded from the predominant norms of American society. Deviant behaviour is to be noted both towards the norms of the parental home and towards the prevailing norms of the country of immigration. Deviant behaviour, even as far as criminality, may be seen as a transient faulty adaptation that bears within itself both the option of adaptation and of permanent non-adaptation. (Atteslander 1996: XIII)

2   From an exact description of the strategies used by inmates to secure their identities, Erving Goffman (1961b), in his studies of psychiatric clinics and prisons, was able to capture general structural features of what he called the 'total institution': when confronted with such depersonalizing modes of behaviour as institutional clothing, the lack of privacy, constant surveillance, a regimented daily timetable and so on, inmates reacted with irony, play-acting, exaggerated adaptation, secret pacts with the staff, rebellion and the like. Through this construction of a 'sub-life' in the institution, they safeguard their survival as subjects. This study may be regarded as one of the great studies of organizational sociology using qualitative research methods. Moreover, it set in train a public debate about the situation of psychiatric patients and prisoners, and provided a stimulus for reform in the appropriate quarters. Even today it still provides the motivation for a plethora of similar studies in other areas, such as old people's homes (e.g. Koch-Straube 1997).

3   From a basic theoretical perspective, Harold Garfinkel (1967a), using so-called crisis experiments, was able to demonstrate the implicit preconditions and rules that govern the production of everyday processes of understanding. This made it possible to describe social integration as a consistent fabric of constructs which participants adapt to situations: if, in an everyday encounter, a person replies to the cliché enquiry 'How are you?' with the counter-enquiry 'Do you mean physically, mentally or spiritually?', this leads to a breakdown in the expected sequence of events. From this it becomes clear that utterances can only be understood in relation to some context and that there is no 'pure' meaning. Shared everyday human activities are more strongly marked by a competent situational application of interactional and communicative rules ('ethnomethods') than by abstract norms, and in these rules knowledge and cultural experience is constantly being produced and activated.

4   In a study that is still regularly quoted in unemployment research, Jahoda, Lazarsfeld and Zeisel (1933/1971) investigated the consequences of unemployment in a small Austrian industrial village at the time of the world economic crisis in the 1930s. Using an imaginative combination of quantitative (for example, measurement of walking speed, income statistics) and qualitative methods (for example, interviews, housekeeping books, diary entries, young people's essays about their view of the future, document analysis and so on) and also some historical materials they developed, with the basic concept (*Leitformel*, see Jahoda 1992) of a 'tired society', a concise

characterization of the life-feelings and the everyday course of events in a community affected by unemployment. At the same time they were able to identify a variety of individual 'behavioural types' in reaction to unemployment, such as 'unbroken', 'resigned', 'desperate' and 'apathetic' – a result that has proved to be of heuristic value in contemporary research (see **2.8**).

Whyte represents a successful example of an ethnographic study (see **3.8**, **5.5** below), and it is in this tradition that community and subculture research, investigations of deviant behaviour and 'cultural studies' (see **3.9**) have developed. Goffman (see **2.2**) provided the stimulus for many institutional analyses, investigations of interactions between professionals and their clients or patients, and also drew attention to strategies for situational presentation of an individual identity in the face of others. Garfinkel's study represents a development in qualitative research that seeks to identify formal rules and structures for the construction of everyday action (see **2.3**). And the complex sociography of Jahoda et al. shows the practical value and socio-politically relevance qualitative research may have (see **2.8**).

2   WHY QUALITATIVE RESEARCH?

What is it, in general terms, that constitutes the particular attractiveness and relevance of qualitative research? In its approach to the phenomena under investigation it is frequently more open and thereby 'more involved' than other research strategies that work with large quantities and strictly standardized, and therefore more objective, methods and normative concepts (Wilson 1970). In replies to questions in a guided interview (see **5.2**), in biographical narratives (see **5.11**), in ethnographic descriptions (see **5.5**, **5.22**) of everyday life or of processes in institutions, a fundamentally more concrete and plastic image often emerges of what it is like, from the point of view of the person concerned, to live, for example, with a chronic illness, than could be achieved using a standardized questionnaire. In an age when fixed social life-worlds and lifestyles are disintegrating and social life is being restructured out of an ever-increasing number of new modes and forms of living, research strategies are required that can deliver, in the first instance, precise and substantial descriptions. They must also take account of the views of those involved, and the

subjective and social constructs (see **3.4**) of their world. Even if postmodernity age is perhaps already over, the processes of pluralization and dissolution, the new confusions that are referred to by this concept, continue to exist. Standardized methods need for the design of their data-collection instruments (for example, a questionnaire), some fixed idea about the subject of the investigation, whereas qualitative research can be open to what is new in the material being studied, to the unknown in the apparently familiar. In this way perceptions of strangeness in the modern everyday world, where 'adventure is just around the corner' (Bruckner and Finkielkraut 1981), can be described and their meaning located. This very openness to the world of experience, its internal design and the principles of its construction are, for qualitative research, not only an end in themselves giving a panorama of 'cultural snapshots' of small life-worlds, but also the main starting point for the construction of a grounded theoretical basis (see **2.1**, **6.6**).

3   RESEARCH PERSPECTIVES IN QUALITATIVE RESEARCH

The label 'qualitative research' is a generic term for a range of different research approaches. These differ in their theoretical assumptions, their understanding of their object of investigation and their methodological focus. But they may be summarized under three broad headings: theoretical reference points may be sought, first, in the traditions of *symbolic interactionism* (see **3.3**) and *phenomenology* (see **3.1**), which tend to pursue subjective meanings and individual sense attributions; second, in *ethnomethodology* (see **3.2**) and *constructivism* (see **3.4**), which are interested in everyday routine and the construction of social reality. A third point of reference is found in *structuralist* or *psychoanalytical* (see **2.5**, **5.20**) positions, which proceed from an assumption of latent social configurations and of unconscious psychic structures and mechanisms.

These approaches also differ in their research goals and in the methods they apply. We may contrast those approaches in which the 'view of the subject' (Bergold and Flick 1987) is in the foreground with a second group whose goal is rather to describe the processes involved in the construction of existing (everyday, institutional or simply 'social') situations, milieux (e.g. Hildenbrand 1983) and social order (such as

Table 1.1 Research perspectives in qualitative research

	Research perspective		
	Modes of access to subjective viewpoints	Description of processes of creation of social situations	Hermeneutic analysis of underlying structures
Theoretical positions	Symbolic interactionism Phenomenology	Ethnomethodology Constructivism	Psychoanalysis Genetic structuralism
Methods of data collection	Semistructured interviews Narrative interviews	Focus groups ethnography Participant observation Recording of interactions Collection of documents	Recording of interactions Photography Films
Methods of interpretation	Theoretical coding Qualitative content analysis Narrative analyses Hermeneutic procedures	Conversation analysis Discourse analysis Genre analysis Document analysis	Objective hermeneutics Deep structure hermeneutics Hermeneutic sociology of knowledge
Fields of application	Biographical research Analysis of everyday knowledge	Analysis of life-worlds and organizations Evaluation research Cultural studies	Family research Biographical research Generation research Gender research

ethnomethodological linguistic analysis: see **5.17**). The (largely) hermeneutic reconstruction of 'action and meaning-generating deep structures', according to psychoanalytic (see **5.20**) or objective-hermeneutic (see **5.16**) ideas (Lüders and Reichertz 1986), is characteristic of the third type of research perspective.

The methods of data collection and processing that are dealt with fully in Part 5 of this book may be allocated to these research perspectives as follows. In the first group, guided and narrative interviews (see **5.2**) and related processes of coding (see **5.13**) or content analysis (see **5.12**) are in the foreground. In the second research perspective, data tend to be collected in focus groups (see **5.4**), by ethnographic methods or (participant) observation and through media recording of interactions so that they may then be evaluated by means of discourse or conversation analysis (see **5.19**, **5.17**). Here we may also include approaches to genre and document analysis (see **5.18**, **5.15**). Representatives of the third perspective collect data mainly through the recording of interactions and the use of photos (see **5.6**) and films (see **5.7**), which are then always allocated to one of the various forms of hermeneutic analysis (cf. Hitzler and Honer 1997).

Table 1.1 summarizes these subdivisions and gives examples of research fields that are characteristic of the three perspectives.

4 BASIC ASSUMPTIONS AND FEATURES OF QUALITATIVE RESEARCH

In all the heterogeneity of the approaches that may be characterized as 'qualitative research', there are certain basic assumptions and features that are common to them all (cf. also, in this context, Flick 2002, chs 1 and 2; von Kardorff 2000; Steinke 1999, ch. 2).

Basic assumptions of qualitative research

First, social reality may be understood as the result of meanings and contexts that are jointly created in social interaction. Both are interpreted by the participants in concrete situations within the framework of their subjective relevance horizons (Schütz 1962, see **3.1**) and therefore constitute the basis of shared meanings that they attribute to objects, events, situations and people (Blumer 1969). These meanings they constantly modify and 'frame' (Goffman 1974, see **2.2**) according to context in reaction to the meanings of others. In this sense social realities appear as a result of constantly developing processes of social construction (Berger and Luckmann 1966, see **3.4**). For the methodology of qualitative research, the first implication of this is a concentration on the forms and contents of such everyday processes of construction more than on reconstructing the subjective views and meaning patterns of the social actors.

Secondly, from the assumption about the constant everyday creation of a shared world there emerge the character of the process, and the reflexivity and recursivity of social reality. For qualitative research methodology a second implication of this is the analysis of communication and interaction sequences with the help of observation procedures (see **5.5**) and the subsequent sequential text analyses (see **5.16, 5.17**).

Thirdly, human beings live in a variety of life situations that may be 'objectively' characterized by indicators such as income, education, profession, age, residence and so on. They show their physical circumstances meaningfully in a total, synthesized and contextualized manner and it is only this that endows such indicators with an interpretable meaning and thereby renders them effective. Statements obtained from subjects and statements classified according to methodological rules may, for example, be described using the concept 'life-world' (see **3.8**). Here subjective or collective meaning patterns (such as 'lay theories', 'world-views', shared norms and values), social relationships and associated incidental life circumstances may be related to individual biographical designs, past life history and perceived possibilities for future action. This process renders subjectively significant personal and local life-attitudes and lifestyles both recognizable and intelligible. From a methodological point of view this leads to a third implication: to a hermeneutic interpretation of subjectively intended meaning that becomes intelligible within the framework of a pre-existing, intuitive everyday prior understanding that exists in every society of meanings which may be objectivized and described in terms of ideal types. This in turn makes it possible to explain individual and collective attitudes and actions.

Fourthly, background assumptions of a range of qualitative research approaches are that reality is created interactively and becomes meaningful subjectively, and that it is transmitted and becomes effective by collective and individual instances of interpretation. Accordingly, in qualitative research communication takes on a predominant role. In methodological terms this means that strategies of data collection themselves have a communicative dialogic character. For this reason the formation of theories, concepts and types in qualitative research itself is explicitly seen as the result of a perspective-influenced reconstruction of the social construction of reality (see **3.4**). In the methodology of qualitative research two fundamentally different reconstruction perspectives may be distinguished:

- the attempt to describe fundamental general mechanisms that actors use in their daily life to 'create' social reality, as is assumed, for instance, in ethnomethodology (see **3.2**);
- 'thick description' (Geertz 1973b, see **2.6**) of the various subjective constructions of reality (theories of everyday life, biographies, events and so on) and their anchoring in self-evident cultural phenomena and practices in places and organization-specific environments.

Investigations of the first type provide information about the methods used by everyday actors to conduct conversations, overcome situations, structure biographies and so on.

Investigations of the second type provide object-related knowledge about subjectively significant connections between experience and action, about views on such themes as health, education, politics, social relationships; responsibility, destiny, guilt; or about life-plans, inner experiences and feelings.

BOX 1.1   BASIC THEORETICAL ASSUMPTIONS OF QUALITATIVE RESEARCH

1   Social reality is understood as a shared product and attribution of meanings.
2   Processual nature and reflexivity of social reality are assumed.
3   'Objective' life circumstances are made relevant to a life-world through subjective meanings.
4   The communicative nature of social reality permits the reconstruction of constructions of social reality to become the starting point for research.

Characteristics of qualitative research practice

The practice of qualitative research is generally characterized by the fact that there is (1) no *single* method, but a spectrum of methods belonging to different approaches that may be selected according to the research questions and the research tradition.

A central feature of qualitative research that is related to this is (2) the appropriateness of methods: for almost every procedure it is possible to ascertain for which particular research-object it was developed. The starting point was normally that the previously available methods were not suited to this specific purpose. For example, the narrative interview (see **5.2**, **5.11**) was originally developed for the analysis of communal power processes, and objective hermeneutics (see **5.16**) for studies of socializing interaction. It is typical of qualitative research that the object of investigation and the questions that are brought to bear represent the point of reference for the selection and evaluation of methods, and not – as often still generally happens in psychology with its emphasis on experiments – that everything that cannot be investigated by particular methods is excluded from the research.

Qualitative research (3) has a strong orientation to everyday events and/or the everyday knowledge of those under investigation. Action processes – for instance, the development of advisory conversations – are situated in their everyday context.

Accordingly, qualitative data collection, analytical and interpretative procedures are bound, to a considerable extent, to the notion of contextuality (4): data are collected in their natural context, and statements are analysed in the context of an extended answer or a narrative, or the total course of an interview, or even in the biography of the interview partner.

In the process (5), attention is paid to the diversity of perspectives of the participants. A further feature of qualitative research is that the reflective capability of the researcher about his or her actions and observations in the field of investigation is taken to be an essential part of the discovery and not a source of disturbance that needs to be monitored or eliminated (6).

Moreover, the epistemological principle of qualitative research is the understanding (7) of complex relationships rather than explanation by isolation of a single relationship, such as 'cause-and-effect'. Understanding is oriented, in the sense of 'methodically controlled understanding of otherness', towards comprehension of the perspective of the other party.

To allow this perspective as much freedom of movement as possible and to get as close to it as possible, data collection in qualitative research is characterized, above all, by the principle of openness (8) (Hoffmann-Riem 1980): questions have an open formulation, and in ethnography observations are not carried out according to some rigid observational grid but also in an open fashion.

Qualitative studies frequently begin (9) with the analysis or reconstruction of (individual) cases (Gerhardt 1995), and then only proceed, as a second step, to summarizing or contrasting these cases from a comparative or generalizing viewpoint.

Furthermore, qualitative research assumes the construction of reality (10) – the subjective constructions of those under investigation and the research process as a constructive act (see **3.4**).

Finally, despite the growing importance of visual data sources such as photos or films, qualitative research is predominantly a text-based discipline (11). It produces data in the form of texts – for example, transcribed interviews or ethnographic fieldwork notes – and concentrates, in the majority of its (hermeneutic) interpretative procedures, on the textual medium as a basis for its work.

In its objectives qualitative research is still a discipline of discovery, which is why concepts from epistemology – such as abduction (see **4.3**) – enjoy growing attention. The discovery of new phenomena in its data is frequently linked, in qualitative research, to an overall aim of developing theories on the basis of empirical study.

5 RELATIONSHIP WITH QUANTITATIVE-STANDARDIZED RESEARCH

Qualitative and quantitative-standardized research have developed in parallel as two independent spheres of empirical social research. Where research questions correspond they may also be used in combination (see **4.5**). But here it should not be forgotten that they also differ from each other on essential points. For example, differences between the two research approaches are seen in the forms of experience that are

BOX 1.2   CHARACTERISTICS OF QUALITATIVE RESEARCH PRACTICE

1   Spectrum of methods rather than a single method
2   Appropriateness of methods
3   Orientation to everyday events and/or everyday knowledge
4   Contextuality as a guiding principle
5   Perspectives of participants
6   Reflective capability of the investigator
7   Understanding as a discovery principle
8   Principle of openness
9   Case analysis as a starting point
10 Construction of reality as a basis
11 Qualitative research as a textual discipline
12 Discovery and theory formation as a goal

considered to be subject to methodical verification and, consequently, admissible as acceptable experience. This impinges in essential ways on the role of the investigator and on the degree of procedural standardization (see **4.1**).

1   In quantitative research a central value is attached to the observer's independence of the object of research. Qualitative research, on the other hand, relies on the investigator's (methodically controlled) subjective perception as one component of the evidence.
2   Quantitative research relies, for its comparative-statistical evaluation, on a high degree of standardization in its data collection. This leads, for example, to a situation where in a questionnaire the ordering of questions and the possible responses are strictly prescribed in advance, and where – ideally – the conditions under which the questions are answered should be held constant for all participants in the research. Qualitative interviews are more flexible in this respect, and may be adapted more clearly to the course of events in individual cases.

Apart from debates in which both research directions deny each other any scientific legitimacy, we may ask more soberly under what circumstances – that is, for what questions and what objects of research – qualitative or quantitative research respectively may be indicated.

Qualitative research may always be recommended in cases where there is an interest in resolving an aspect of reality ('field exploration')

that has long been under-researched with the help of some 'sensitizing concepts' (Blumer 1969). By using such 'naturalistic' methods as participant observation, open interviews or diaries, the first batch of information may be obtained to permit the formulation of hypotheses for subsequent standardized and representative data collection (for example, on the role of family members in rehabilitation; on the lifeworld of mentally ill people). Here qualitative studies are, if not a precondition, then a sensible follow-up to quantitative studies.

Qualitative research can complement so-called 'hard data' on patients (for example, sociodemographic data, the distribution of diagnoses over a population) with their more subjective views – such as perceptions of their professional future in the face of illness, or their degree of satisfaction with the results of particular types of treatment.

Qualitative (case-)studies can complement representative quantitative studies through differentiation and intensification, and can offer explanations to help in the interpretation of statistical relationships.

6   THE HISTORY AND DEVELOPMENT OF QUALITATIVE RESEARCH

Qualitative research can look back on a long tradition that, in most of the social sciences, goes back to their origins. Since the 1960s in the United States and since the 1970s in the German-speaking world it has experienced a renaissance, and since then has become still more widely disseminated (cf. Flick 2002: 10, for the phases in this development). To date, there is no monograph that describes the history of qualitative research.

Its development has always been characterized by the fact that it has been conducted in very different subdisciplines that were each characterized by a specific theoretical background, an independent understanding of reality and an individual programme of methods. One example of this is ethnomethodology, which has distinguished itself by a specific research style (see **2.3**) and theoretical background (see **3.2**), with conversation analysis as its research programme (see **5.17**) that has itself been differentiated into several newer approaches (see **5.18**, **5.19**), and which is altogether characterized by a broad empirical research activity. Corresponding to such developments, we find today that a whole range of qualitative research fields and approaches have been established which are developing independently and which have relatively little connection with discussions and research in the other fields. In addition to ethnomethodology, these fields of qualitative research may be exemplified by objective hermeneutics (see **5.17**), biographical research (see **3.6**, **3.7**, **5.11**), ethnography (see **3.8**, **5.5**), cultural studies (see **3.3**, **3.9**) or (ethno-)psychoanalytic research and deep structure hermeneutics (see **2.5**, **5.20**). This differentiation within qualitative research is reinforced by the fact that the German- and English-language academic debates are, to some extent, concerned with very different themes and methods and there is only a very modest degree of interchange between the two areas.

In conclusion, we should refer again to the fact that discussions on method in the German literature, after a period in the 1970s where the main focus was on debates about matters of fundamental methodological theory, have now entered a phase of increasing methodical consolidation and the broad application of methods in empirical projects. In the Anglo-American debate, on the other hand, the 1980s and 1990s were marked by a new kind of reflection and by the questioning of certain methodical certainties. (The key issue here is the crisis of representation and legitimization brought about by the debates on writing in ethnography: cf. contributions in Denzin and Lincoln 2000; see also **2.7**,

3.3, **5.5**, **5.22**.) Here too, however, there has been in recent years an increased desire to present the canonization of the procedure in textbooks, with at least partial reference to the self-critical debates (e.g. Gubrium and Holstein 1997; see part 7).

7 AIMS AND STRUCTURE OF THE BOOK

The *Companion* will provide a survey, with appropriate 'map-references', of the different versions of qualitative research and a state-of-the-art overview of new trends in the spheres of theoretical and methodological development. In addition, it will endeavour to establish connections and to show common ground and differences in the (sometimes) extremely heterogeneous developments in the basic assumptions in epistemology, the types of classification specific to particular theories, the underlying methodological positions and the way methods have developed in qualitative research. These aims will be met in the following stages. Part 2, *Qualitative Research in Action*, will give the reader some insight into the research practice of a number of leading figures in qualitative research. By means of one or more studies we will show how such research personalities as Anselm Strauss, Erving Goffman, Norman Denzin or Marie Jahoda arrive at their research questions, and what characterizes their typical research designs, their selection of methods, their approach to their field and their procedures for data collection, evaluation and final interpretation. The selected representatives will then be classified according to whether they occupy an important place in either the history or the current practice of qualitative research.

Part 3, *The Theory of Qualitative Research*, first introduces the essential theoretical bases of qualitative research. In the first sections (3.1–3.5) the various *background theories* (such as phenomenology, ethnomethodology, symbolic interactionism) are examined to ascertain their influence on the design of qualitative investigations, their implications for matters of method in general, and for the selection of specific methods and interpretations. In the later sections (3.6–3.12) outlines are given of various object-related *qualitative research programmes* (such as biographical, organizational or evaluation research).

Part 4, *Methodology and Qualitative Research*, deals with questions of epistemology – from abduction and the role of hypotheses, to quality control in qualitative research. In addition, this part is concerned with more general questions of set-up in qualitative research – from the framing of the research design, to possibilities and limitations in linking qualitative and quantitative research, or in the sampling procedure.

Part 5, *Doing Qualitative Research*, introduces the essential methods of qualitative research with reference to the sequencing of the qualitative research process. The chapters are organized in four subsections. 'Entering the Field' outlines ways into the field and obstacles researchers might meet on their way. In 'Collecting Verbal Data' the most important methods of collecting verbal material – interviews and focus groups – are characterized. 'Observing Processes and Activities' introduces approaches to audiovisual data (observation and the use of film and photographic materials). 'Analysis, Interpretation and Presentation' includes chapters on methods for the elaboration (transcription of verbal data) and analysis of interview data, on computer-assisted analyses, content analyses and the most important methods of data interpretation. The final chapters in this subsection deal with questions of the presentation of results and research procedures in qualitative investigations.

In Part 6 we consider *Qualitative Research in Context* from several points of view, again in two subsections. In 'The Use of Qualitative Research', issues of research ethics and data protection, and of how qualitative research is to be incorporated in teaching, and questions of the utilization of findings are considered. The second half of Part 6 focuses on 'The Future and Challenges of Qualitative Research', with reference to its development: what has happened in the past, what is perhaps problematic, what is desirable and what may be expected in the future. Finally, Part 7 presents a selection of *Resources* for the qualitative researcher, which provides information about such matters as relevant journals, the classic literature and manuals, databases, computer programs and Internet sources.

FURTHER READING

Flick, U. (2002) *An Introduction to Qualitative Research*, 2nd edn. London, Sage.

Gubrium, J. F. and Holstein, J. A. (1997) *The New Language of Qualitative Method*. New York: Oxford University Press.

Strauss, A. L. (1987) *Qualitative Analysis for Social Scientists*. Cambridge: Cambridge University Press.

Part 2

Qualitative Research in Action: Paradigmatic Research Styles

Introduction

In this part of the *Companion* a number of scientists are introduced who have made a lasting impact on the present landscape of qualitative research. Their impact results not only from their ground-breaking theoretical ideas, methodological assumptions or methodical innovations. These researchers have also left a very personal imprint through their mode of work. It is this very personal approach to the field, the way of dealing with the people being investigated in their particular environments, the original and searching way of developing methods, courage in theory-building – often cutting directly across established routes – which plays such an important role in qualitative research. Many attempts have been made to standardize and codify qualitative research and to develop traditions of teaching (see **6.2**). However, there is still an immovable 'remnant' that is determined by the persona of the investigator, his or her originality, obstinacy, temperament and preferences – in other words, by an unmistakable individual *style*. The individual character of the researchers introduced in Part 2 – their inventiveness (see also **6.6**), their powers of observation, sensitivity to utterances, sense of situation and 'art of interpretation' (see also **5.21**) – is the key to what makes their works into classics in the field. Such features turn these researchers into giants on whose shoulders we stand, to use the formulation of Robert K. Merton. Seen from this perspective, it may be evident that our selection of examples of paradigmatic theorizing and good research practice should not be taken for invariable recipes, but as guidelines to be developed and adapted for further research. The presentation of different paradigmatic perspectives and research styles in the field of qualitative research will give the reader the chance to compare the specific features and qualities of discovery of the various approaches. We do not want to suggest, however, that students in the field of qualitative research, who decide to follow one of the research styles, are forced to exclude the others. Nor do we want to turn readers into 'pure' 'Goffmanians' or 'Geertzians'. We may find different 'schools', factions or personal disciples of famous researchers in the field of qualitative research, with implications of academic control in 'invisible colleges', but the lines of development in the field tend to transgress paradigms, combine methods and research styles to come to a better understanding of the social realities and the realities of the social. The description of personal ways of doing qualitative research is intended to inspire the reader and inform students about the different ways of doing qualitative research, from which stimulation can be drawn for developing one's own way of researching.

With a number of examples selected from the work of very distinguished qualitative researchers, we want to show 'qualitative research in action'. Our selection is oriented to representatives of qualitative research who, even today, still characterize the mainstreams of qualitative research: they founded their own research paradigms and produced classic studies in their own field; or they achieved results in their work that transcended their own discipline or background; or they made a substantial contribution to the further development of qualitative research in general. Our selection, however, is not intended as a definitive and/or comprehensive canon of 'classics'. Therefore personalities such as Howard S. Becker, Herbert Blumer, Dorothy K. Smith, Arlie R. Hochschild or William F. Whyte, and many others who undoubtedly belong in such a hall of fame, may perhaps forgive us for not including them here.

The first contribution is devoted to Anselm Strauss (see **2.1**). With Barney Glaser, he is the founder of grounded theory in the tradition of symbolic interactionism (see **3.3**). Apart from his major theoretical works and landmark studies in the field of the sociology of medicine, Strauss still exercises a major influence, particularly through his textbooks on concrete procedures – from data selection and collection to evaluation, coding, interpretation and presentation.

Erving Goffman (see **2.2**) is perhaps better known to the general public for his books *Asylums* (1961b) and *The Presentation of Self in Everyday Life* (1959). Even today, his original and individual ideas still influence studies of face-to-face interaction, identity-formation, the day-to-day presentation of self, and the ways in which social interaction is bound up with situations and determined by its organizational features.

Harold Garfinkel is looked upon as the founder of ethnomethodology (see **3.2**). Harvey Sacks is the founder of conversation analysis (see **5.17**). They both (see **2.3**) opened up new perspectives for social research by means of their radical questioning about the foundations of social order and their innovative development of new instruments of investigation, such as sequential text analysis: all of this opened the way for a deep structure grammar of sociality.

Paul Willis (**2.4**), co-founder of the Centre for Contemporary Cultural Studies in Birmingham, made a great contribution to the development of cultural studies with his studies of the popular culture of youth groups, and of the tensions between traditional and new media.

The studies by Paul Parin, Fritz Morgenthaler and Goldy Parin-Matthèy (see **2.5**), together with the investigations of Georges Devereux, belong to the classics of ethno-psychoanalysis, and provide insights into alien worlds, but where familiar and unconscious patterns are still found, concerning in particular the relationship between the individual and society.

With Clifford Geertz (see **2.6**) and Norman K. Denzin (see **2.7**) we choose two researchers who come from very different scientific backgrounds and are now among the great innovators and critical voices in qualitative research. Indeed, on the basis of their extensive experience of the field and their comprehensive empirical work, they believe that there is a crisis of representation, to which they respond in considered, although different, ways.

Finally, Marie Jahoda (see **2.8**) represents in many of her numerous studies on unemployment and prejudice a productive type of qualitative action research and advocacy, inspired by political motives for social change, justice, equal opportunities and anti-discrimination. Furthermore, her work stands for a pragmatic and problem-driven combination of qualitative and quantitative methods beyond ideological debates; at least, in emphasizing the biographical method in analysing social problems she opened the way to bridge the gap between psychological and sociological perspectives.

2.1   Anselm Strauss

Bruno Hildenbrand

1   PRAGMATISM AND SYMBOLIC INTERACTIONISM AS THEORETICAL FOUNDATIONS OF STRAUSS'S METHODOLOGY

In one of their overviews of grounded theory, Corbin and Strauss (1990) cite two key themes that guided the development of this methodology, which was first established by Barney Glaser and Anselm Strauss. The first theme is to do with the concept of *change*, that is to say, it is a matter of discovering certain basic processes that result in change. These processes affect social entities from the individual to the organization; these are influenced by change and, in turn, themselves influence change: in fact they bring it about. The second theme concerns the relationship of grounded theory to determinism. The existence of structural conditions of some action is recognized (cf. Strauss 1993a: 60–65; Corbin and Strauss 1988: 135ff.). But the actors are not powerless in the face of these conditions – they perceive possibilities of choice and on this basis they make their choices.

To put this differently, one could speak of four basic concepts that are derived from pragmatism and guide Anselm Strauss's research: 'To analyze social processes within the frame of a theory of action, means that one has to think automatically interactionally, temporally, processually, and structurally' (Soeffner 1995: 30).

As an additional foundation concept we should also mention the closeness of artistic and scientific works, from the point of view of how artists or scientists deal with their material (such as the subject of a painting or the theme of a research project). There is an intensive interchange in dealing with a research theme, which changes both participants and results in '[a]n order they did not first possess' (Dewey 1934: 65, cited in Strauss 1987: 10). Underlying this is the view of pragmatism (like other philosophical traditions, such as phenomenology): not to accept a division between recognizer and what is recognized, between subject and object, but simply an interaction between the two. Objectivity is not denied by this. It is ultimately the material that drives the research process, and the creativity of the investigator that reveals the structuredness of the material: 'The research process itself guides the researcher to examine all the possibly rewarding avenues toward understanding' (Corbin and Strauss 1990: 420).

2   THE CHARACTERISTICS OF THE RESEARCH PROCESS

Grounded theory as a triadic and circular process

In his research Anselm Strauss does not take as his starting point a set of prior theoretical assumptions that have to be tested. Of course, an exact knowledge of existing theories is

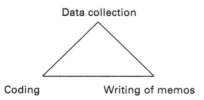

Data collection

Coding   Writing of memos

Figure 2.1.1 Grounded theory as a triadic and circular process

indispensable, but his way of dealing with them is rather lacking in respect (Star 1997: 2). Theoretical concepts which are developed during an investigation are *discovered* in the data and have to *prove themselves* in the data: there are no other criteria. Even at the end of the research process the researcher always returns to the data, and so the analytical process is at the same time triadic and circular (in the sense of the hermeneutic circle) (Figure 2.1.1).

Corresponding to this there is also the process of *inference*. This idea derives originally from the pragmatist Charles S. Peirce. Strauss himself speaks of a link between inductive and deductive types of inference and refrains from substantiating his views on this with any reference to Peirce. In Strauss's work these views only appear 'between the lines'. If he had made this link explicit, it would have been necessary to include abductive inference as the first stage in the inferencing process (see **4.3**).

The whole process looks like this: abductive inferences are used to formulate an explanatory hypothesis in such a way that a consequence can be derived from what went before. Conclusions of this sort are a fundamental principle of conscious recognition in general, and therefore occur in everyday life. At the same time they constitute the main research strategy in the recognition of new phenomena (Grathoff 1989: 281).

Discoveries on the basis of abductive inference come, as Peirce says, like lightning – law and application are recognized simultaneously. A precondition for this is a willingness to free oneself from any preconceptions and to look at the data impartially (see **4.3**). An example of this (from Hildenbrand 1999: 52ff.) is the following.

In a particular study, data from the history of a family – the Dittrich family – were being analysed. The father, as a travelling salesman, was often away from home. Mr Dittrich, the second son, had broken off his further education and gone back to his mother's farm; his elder brother, however, continued at school. Later, after many years of travelling and after the war, Mr Dittrich returned to the farm for a second time, and now, in spite of considerable disputes about the inheritance, he was able to take over the farm. He therefore never detached himself from the farm (nor from his mother), to whom he was an intimate confidant.

If we put this information and related suppositions together, it signifies the following: a close relationship grew up between Mr Dittrich and his mother in the earliest years of his life, from which the father was excluded. It was so close that it restricted the development within Mr Dittrich of any capability to adopt another perspective.

At the second stage of the research, the stage of deduction, the hypotheses that have been gained abductively are transferred to a typologizing schema, which is formulated in the nature of a diagram; that is, an '"Icon", or Sign that represents the Object in resembling it' (Peirce 1960a: 6.471: 321). Here there is an investigation of 'what effects that hypothesis, if embraced, must have in modifying our expectations in regard to future experience' (Peirce 1960b: 7.115: 67). To continue our example: from the abductively formulated hypothesis about the limitations on taking another perspective, we conclude deductively that, from his childhood, Mr Dittrich had a problem with the regulation of proximity and distance that is manifest as ambivalence. We can sketch in a diagram (see Figure 2.1.2) what results we expect for the present pairings and family relationships.

At the third stage in the research, the stage of induction, the investigator's final task is 'that of ascertaining how those concepts accord with experience' (Peirce 1960a: 6.472: 322). Now the research, at the end of the research process, has returned to the data. To return to our example:

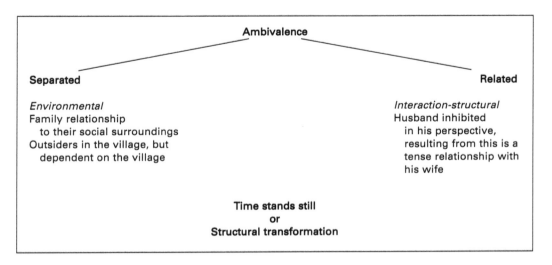

Figure 2.1.2   Expected results

Limited takeover of perspectives shows its subversive power most forcibly when there has been no development in the person concerned. It is for this reason that *'Time stands still' or 'Structural transformation'* is included in the diagram. Therefore the life of the family is being investigated both from environmental (e.g. position of the family in the village) and from interaction-structural viewpoints, focusing on the complex of hypotheses that are sketched in the diagram. This is done after data suited to the purpose have been collected. The question of development is analysed separately: How was it at the beginning of the marriage? What has changed? When and how? And what has remained the same?

Steps in the research process

The process of analysis begins with the investigator collecting a small amount of data and questioning this material. That means, '[i]ncidents, events, and happenings are taken as, analyzed as, potential indicators of phenomena, which are given conceptual labels' (Corbin and Strauss 1990: 420). What is decisive is not to separate the phase of collecting material from that of analysing it, but to bond them together and to collect only as much material as is necessary for the analytical process. Only if this is done can the material drive the analysis. The individual steps are as follows (cf. Strauss 1987: 27–33).

- The investigator asks questions of the material (Strauss calls this process 'coding'), and in this he or she is supported by the *coding paradigm* (Strauss 1987: 27): questions are asked about conditions/interactions among the actors, strategies and tactics, consequences (see **5.13**).
- During the process of coding the investigator develops *concepts*, which are hypotheses captured in ideas, and establishes connections between these concepts. Repeated coding of data leads to denser concept-based relationships and hence to a theory (see **4.2**).
- This emerging theory is constantly checked by means of making contrasts: in a procedure which Strauss calls 'theoretical sampling' and which is driven by the developing theory, examples are referred to that are suitable for checking previous conclusions.
- New data are constantly being coded.
- The successive integration of concepts leads to one or more key categories and thereby to the core of the emerging theory.
- The individual components of the developing theory are processed into theory-memos, are put into a relationship and are, in the process, extended.

- Even in the final phase of theory-development it may seem advisable to collect and code new data – it is always the empirical dimension in which a theory has to prove itself and to which the theory always returns in the last instance.
- This also extends to the framing of the emerging theory. In addition, aesthetic requirements are made of the final report: here the scientist should *write creatively*.

Grounded theory in teaching and research

No presentation of the research style of Anselm Strauss would be complete if it did not include the aspects of research consultancy and teaching. For Strauss 'learning, teaching, working and playing are inextricably combined' (Star 1997: 1; see **6.2**).

Strauss is a good example of the school of thought of the Humboldtian university, and until his death in 1996, shortly before his 80th birthday, he continued to be an embodiment of this type of scholar.

Just as Strauss insisted on the technical detail of the analytical process and resisted every form of intuitive procedure, he also established guidelines for the process of research consultancy, although without publishing these as a form of dogma.

In any case, this would not have accorded with Strauss's image of humanity. Essentially, this is characterized by a great respect for the other party, whose perspective (in the sense of G. H. Mead) Strauss saw as a priority. If, in this respect, the consultant, or supervisor, of a piece of scientific work also has to take on the responsibility for the process of consultancy of supervision, one option consists of formulating guidelines which the recipients of the advice *can* use on their own responsibility. Again, Strauss is guided by the fundamental principles of pragmatism when he requires that the consultant should:

- incorporate the perspective of the person seeking advice not only in the research process but also in the process of the life-history, as far as this is necessary in the interest of the research;
- become involved in the research process of the person seeking advice, above all remain within the frame of reference established by that person, and from this position ask

generative questions, that is, questions oriented to processes and structures;
- suggest, as an option, stepping outside this framework and trying out alternatives, when this seems to be advisable;
- finally, treat as a touchstone for any advice the question whether this advice provides an answer to the problem of the person seeking the advice.

These guidelines are compatible with a theory of professional practice in consultancy and therapy; or – to put it the other way around – from them a theory of this kind could be developed (cf. Welter-Enderlin and Hildenbrand 1996). This demonstrates how close, for Strauss, is the link between theory, methodology and practice.

3 ILLUSTRATION OF THE RESEARCH PROCESS: A STUDY OF THE CHRONICALLY ILL USING GROUNDED THEORY

The questions

Anselm Strauss moved to the University of California Medical Center in San Francisco at the end of the 1950s. After a few months of observation in hospitals, he decided it would be appropriate to investigate how the processes involved in the death of patients were handled.

> This was a logical choice for several reasons: dying was a clinical, managerial and professional problem for hospital personnel; it was significant sociologically as well as professionally; also it fit my interests in the sociology of work, occupations, and organizations. (Strauss 1993a: 21)

This was followed by further investigations in the field of medical sociology, for example, on coming to terms with chronic illness.

Conduct of the investigation

Field research (Schatzman and Strauss 1973), conducted on the continuum from participation as observation to observation as participation, is central to data collection; interviewing, on the other hand, takes on a subordinate role and is carried out only where it is indispensable.

From the beginning of data collection, concepts are being developed and tested. In this a significant part is played by 'microscopic examination' (Strauss 1995a), which can be illustrated by the following example. In their textbook of 1990, Strauss and Corbin present a seminar discussion of a comment from a young handicapped man, which contained the phrase 'Once I'm in the shower'. (This may also exemplify the analytical process within a research project, since Strauss preferred to conduct research in a team.) The expression 'once' is analysed thus.

I = Instructor
S = Student (any student)

I   Knowing the context of the interviewee's action, what might *once* mean?
S   The man felt **independent** once he was in the shower. A *consequence*.
I   Where else might he feel independent, once he was there?
S   In bed and in the wheelchair
I   Where might he feel **dependent** once he was there? Another *consequence*, but related to a variation in activity.
S   When faced with a flight of stairs.
I   What else could *once* mean?
S   A *condition* for what might come next in the interviewee's activity.
I   The end of one action and the beginning of the next. The idea of **phasing** or **sequence** of action. Let's take another situation where the word *once* might be said and compare it to this one. Perhaps by making this comparison it will generate other potential meanings of the word. The situation is a track race. The speaker says: 'Once the gun went off, I forgot all about the months of gruelling training.'
S   Rates of movement through each phase of action. *Property* of time and idea of *Process*.

(Strauss and Corbin 1990: 82)

In this example it may be seen how – using the *coding paradigm* (in this case conditions and consequences) and intellectual variation in the contrast-process of *theoretical sampling* – conceptual horizons are developed and the formation of concepts and theories is advanced. This allows us to see the specific qualities and features of the way in which Anselm Strauss did his research.

- Principle 1: Data are analysed in a research group. The main task of the group's leader is 'to further a creative process by creative minds' (Strauss 1987: 287).

- Principle 2: The most important instrument to start a creative process is what Strauss calls 'microscopic analysis' (1995a). The members of the group are asked to express their everyday understanding of the first word in the text to be analysed. In doing so, they will discover a variety of different meanings for this word and compare them to each other. This procedure will agitate the naive everyday understanding of the word and thus will enable the participants to take an analytical attitude towards the research issue. Analysis is not only interested in the semantic profile of a word but concentrates on the analysis of the 'how' as well, that is, how the word has been placed, spelled out, etc. This procedure allows analysis of the relations between meanings and thus provides a basis for reaching a structural level. This leads to

- Principle 3: The 'microscopic analysis' aims at discovering the meaning between the lines and thus at uncovering the structure of the social object represented in a text. In his previously mentioned work, Strauss (1995a) characterizes this procedure by using the metaphor 'to mine the data' in order to dig 'nuggets'.

- Principle 4: When the structure has been identified in the way just described, the next step is to express this structure by using 'in vivo codes', which means by using the language of the case itself.

- Principle 5: The developed structure is further elaborated in a systematic comparison in order to identify variations of the revealed structure.

- Principle 6: The process of 'microscopic analysis' follows the principle of extensive interpretation of meanings. Practically speaking, this means that analysing the first word in a text may take an hour. Analysing materials according to the style of grounded theory is to reveal a maximum of meaning from a minimum of data and to avoid detaching oneself from the text too quickly and developing theoretical considerations that are not grounded in the data.

Results

Admittedly this example does not tell us anything about the concept to which this analysis makes a contribution. But if one were to consider the study of the chronically ill within the family, the actual study from which this example is taken (Corbin and Strauss 1988), a number of things become clear. Two central concepts are used: the first is the *trajectory*, and the second is *work*. Trajectories are categorized according to their *direction*: there are stable, unstable, ascending and descending curves. Each of these directions indicates a *phase*, and each of these phases requires of the actors (the sick person and the family members) different types of *work* in the different *lines of work*. This is why, in the example above, there was the focus on *action* (as work), and the question about *dependence* or *independence*: according to the phase, the degrees of autonomy of the sick person and the family members are greater or smaller, or rather the *conditions* imposed by the phase require different kinds of activity on the part of the participants.

The italicized words were developed and tested in the study that we have taken as an example, using the procedures of sequential analysis mentioned above. The result is a *substantive* theory about coping with chronic illness, but this can equally be used as the starting point for a *formal* theory (Glaser and Strauss 1967: 79–99), and in this particular case, for a theory of action (cf. Strauss 1993a; on the general theoretical status of the notion of trajectory, see Soeffner 1991).

4   THE PLACE OF GROUNDED THEORY IN THE CONTEXT OF QUALITATIVE SOCIAL RESEARCH

Grounded theory is part of the established canon of qualitative social research. This is demonstrated by the fact that the three authors most closely associated with grounded theory, Glaser, Strauss and Corbin, have the highest number of entries in the list of authors in one of the leading manuals of qualitative data analysis (Miles and Hubermann 1994). In other important textbooks in the fields of symbolic interactionism and phenomenological sociology, grounded theory also has an established position.

During Anselm Strauss's lifetime, processes of differentiation in grounded theory began. Barney Glaser, who had published the principles of grounded theory together with Strauss (Glaser and Strauss 1967), criticizes in his *Basics of Grounded Theory Analysis* (Glaser 1992) that

Strauss increasingly had abandoned grounded theory's claim to be a creative alternative to the established methodologies. Glaser associates this tendency mainly with the book *Basics of Qualitative Research* published in 1990 by Anselm Strauss and Juliet Corbin (Strauss and Corbin 1990). He criticizes the advancing codification of the coding process, aimed at a validation of theories and which is linked to an intolerable approximation to those methodologies from which a clear distinction was originally intended in *The Discovery of Grounded Theory* (Glaser and Strauss 1967). Glaser's critique is mainly directed at Juliet Corbin and Anselm Strauss's intention to make grounded theory fit for practical use in applied sciences such as nursing research and to make it connectable to the mainstream of social science.

Adele E. Clarke has dealt with the further development of grounded theory within the framework of new developments in the humanities (cf. Clarke: forthcoming). In her opinion, grounded theory should be reformulated in the context of the 'postmodern turn'. Starting from G. H. Mead's concept of perspective and from Strauss's writings on social worlds and arenas (1991: ch. V), she emphazises the concept of the 'map'.

However, it might be doubted that there is a direct or necessary link from concepts like perspective and social world to the basic assumptions of 'postmodern' theories. Eagleton, for example, criticizes postmodern theories for their reduction of history to change, or in other words, of structure to interaction (Eagleton 1996). In my view, grounded theory needs development, but not further conceptual dissolution in the area of analysing structures. Instead, it would be important to develop concepts for mediating structure and action.

What role does grounded theory actually play in the methodological canon of qualitative social research? Grounded theory was developed by Barney Glaser and Anselm Strauss in the context of a research project on the death of patients in hospital (Glaser and Strauss 1965b). From this starting point, grounded theory has begun to play an influential role in research in the fields of nursing, education and social work. A methodology that aims at developing middle range theories (Merton 1967) is especially attractive for these disciplines of applied sciences. Beyond this, however, grounded theory today plays a significant role in all fields of social science. Since a growing number of researchers in the grounded theory tradition deal with basic research, the approach is increasingly exposed to competition with the classical research paradigms.

A different question is how close to or how distant from the various efforts of working with grounded theory remain to the original ideas in *The Discovery of Grounded Theory*. A journey through the Internet gives the impression of creative variety, but also of disillusionment. A split between a faction of adherents of Strauss on the one hand and those of Glaser on the other cannot be overlooked. My impression is that the former has stronger ties to academia than the latter. As a consequence, members of the Glaser faction are not compelled to compete as much as those of the Strauss faction, who hold positions in the academic world.

What are the remaining characteristics of grounded theory beyond such internal differences? Chiefly it seems to promise primarily not to *reflect* the research process but to *push it forward*, that is, with a minimum investment in data collection to achieve a maximum of data analysis and subsequent theory formation. This is guaranteed by the use of analysis from the very beginning, by theoretical sampling and by constantly returning to the data.

FURTHER READING

Charmaz, K. (2000) 'Grounded Theory: Objectivist and Constuctivist Methods', in N. K. Denzin and Y. S. Lincoln (eds), *Handbook of Qualitative Research, 2nd edn*. Thousand Oaks, CA: Sage. pp. 509–536.

Glaser, B. G. and Strauss, A. L. (1967) *The Discovery of Grounded Theory: Strategies for Qualitative Research*. Chicago: Aldine.

Strauss, A. L. (1987) *Qualitative Analysis for Social Scientists*. Cambridge, MA: Cambridge University Press.

2.2 Erving Goffman

Herbert Willems

Goffman's methods are determined by his central object, *face-to-face interaction*. In this Goffman sees predominantly – and the whole of his method is marked by this – a world of *implicit knowledge* that actors can barely articulate or 'say' because of its habitual nature. The kind of knowledge he means is manifest, for example, in the equally unconsidered and subtly adapted behaviours of looking, smiling, tactful avoidance or repartee. A result of the 'unconscious' nature of this kind of behaviour (Giddens speaks of 'practical consciousness' as opposed to 'discursive consciousness') is the limited nature of methods that depend on explanations and self-descriptions from the actors under investigation (for example, interviews, or personal biographical evidence). In Goffman's view, laboratory experiments are even more limited in value because they eliminate precisely what ought to be investigated first, the 'social' nature of (interactive) behaviour.

The set of methods that Goffman used in place of what he called 'traditional investigative procedures' (Goffman 1971: XVI) will be listed below.

1 NATURALISTIC OBSERVATION

Goffman developed *interaction ethology* (1971: X). The aim of this methodological framework is to investigate the processes of interaction 'naturalistically', that is, first to *discover* and document them in their 'natural milieu'. In a posthumously published lecture on fieldwork, Goffman (1989) stresses that it is a matter of getting as close as possible to the objects of research, and of subjecting oneself as authentically as possible to the circumstances of their life. Only in this way can the decisive goal be reached, that of a high degree of familiarity with the practice in question and its actors. In this familiarity Goffman sees a preliminary stage of sociological information which is then arranged at a first level when the investigator succeeds in discovering natural behaviour patterns in apparently unordered streams of behaviour.

In his early works Goffman uses *naturalistic observation* primarily to mean 'participant observation' (see **5.5**). Working, in this sense, as an 'ethnologist of his own culture' (Dahrendorf's term), he observes, on the one hand, normal 'everyday life'. On the other hand he invokes particular, remarkable and separate worlds beyond the layman's everyday world. A remote community of peasant farmers, a gaming casino and a psychiatric institution are the best-known examples. Goffman's studies of these (cf. 1959, 1961a, 1961b) show the systematic possibilities that sociological observers have of using their own 'alienness' as a generator of information.

By becoming familiar, as an 'outsider', with the society and meanings under investigation, the researcher may experience their peculiarities as a set of differences from what he/she has taken for granted.

In his later work Goffman sees a special and especially important option for naturalistic observation in the use of audio-visual recording equipment (see **5.6**, **5.7**). With 'recorded' data, they produce, in his opinion, a qualitatively new basis for 'microfunctional study, that is an examination of the role of a bit of behaviour in the stream which precedes co-occurs and follows' (Goffman 1979: 24). From his belief that the 'coincidence of a subject matter and recording technology ... places the student in an entirely novel relation to his data, (Goffman 1979: 24), he does not draw the conclusion, however, that media recordings should be privileged or allowed to play the only central role.

Goffman's basic position on the question of data tends to be 'pluralistic'. He makes use of a range of materials in order to obtain alternative and complementary access routes to his research objects and alternative bases for comparison. It is also important that Goffman relies on the richness of his own primary experience and on newspaper 'stories'.

2 METAPHORS, MODELS, THEORETICAL PERSPECTIVES

From the very beginning Goffman's 'naturalism' means more than simply 'empiricism'. In Goffman we are dealing rather with a 'theoretically oriented empiricist' (Collins 1980: 174). Goffman's full observational, analytical and descriptive strategy therefore consists of using metaphors, concepts and models. For example, Goffman uses theatrical metaphors (1959), a ritual model (1967, 1971, 1979) and the game-theory (1969). On the one hand he is concerned with the generation of conceptual and meaning devices that are applicable, in the sense of a 'strategy of analogies' (Lenz 1991: 57), to the widest range of social practices. On the other hand Goffman aims at sociological information by means of *relative* alienation from social reality, that is, the familiar reality of everyday life. Many of Goffman's 'discoveries' are a result of the reflective and distancing perspective of his 'frames' that give new significance to the obvious and the well-known (cf. Williams 1988: 73). Here it is important that Goffman relies on certain interpretative tools which, like the theatre or games, have their own world of meaning and reality which, however, *resembles* that of the object of investigation. This is the basis of Goffman's 'comparative analysis' which leads – in a systematic and empirically valid manner – to the determination of identities, relationships and also differences.

Goffman practises this strategy in a number of studies which, in terms of the 'interaction order' (Goffman 1983), have the same object of interest, but which are framed from different perspectives. This corresponds to his idea that there is both an unbridgeable gulf between sociological objects and methods of interpretation and also that the different methods of interpretation each have their own relativity. Goffman counters this relativity – that is, the specific blindness attached to every individual perspective in an investigation – with a pluralization of his own perspectives.

3 FROM ABNORMALITY TO NORMALITY

One of Goffman's most important research strategies has been called by Hans Oswald (1984: 212) 'the method of extreme contrast' and by Paul Drew and Anthony Wootton (1988: 7) 'the investigation of the normal through the abnormal'. This refers to the fact that Goffman uses extremes, deviations, crises, instances of anomie and other 'abnormalities' as bridges to the understanding of normal forms.

Ultimately, therefore, Goffman's analyses of strategic interaction aim to shed light on the structural principles of everyday interaction. Similarly, Goffman elaborates the 'negative experience' (1974: 378) in which normality collapses, is broken or never exists. Extreme experiences, such as those of psychiatric inmates, provide Goffman (1961b, 1963a) with a way into what ultimately 'holds normality together'.

Apart from his reliance on 'natural' contrasts or deviations, Goffman's way of using 'artificial' deviations and irritations is totally in accord with other approaches within qualitative social research. There is a kind of 'crisis experiment' (see **3.2**) in his investigation of gender representation in advertising photographs (1979). There he recommends that the gender of the subjects displayed should be mentally interchanged to reveal implicit expectations of normal forms. This 'technique' could rely on the 'vast social competence of the eye and the impressive consensus sustained by viewers' (1979: 25). Here, as everywhere else, Goffman assumes that social scientists may make analytical use of their intuitive (*habitus-*)knowledge because they share this with other members of society.

4   DECONSTRUCTIONS

Goffman also pursues his goal of unveiling social 'meaning mechanisms' and 'mental machination' with a kind of sociological deep-structure hermeneutics that 'deconstructs' such daily-life constructs as that of the speaker and such distinctions as that between truth and falsehood (see, for example, 1959, 1961a, 1971, 1981). Goffman's first monograph, *The Presentation of Self in Everyday Life*, which deconstructs the 'individual' into various dramaturgical functions and elements, was already conceived along these lines and may therefore be understood programmatically.

The systematic high point in Goffman's 'deconstructivist' perspective is, without doubt, his *Frame Analysis* (1974). Goffman's strategy of frame analysis, used to reveal 'unconscious' meaning complexity, corresponds to a complex system of concepts that permits the identification of different classes of frames and the description of logical transformational relationships between different frames. Transcending the level of interaction (and thereby the boundaries of microsociology), Goffman analyses and deconstructs the reflexivity and stratification of various kinds of social meaning.

5   MATERIAL CLASSIFICATIONS, IDEAL TYPOLOGIES, DIFFERENTIATIONS

One variant of Goffman's way of handling phenomena and data may be labelled 'subsumption – logical'. In *Gender Advertisements* he pursues his analytical goal on the basis of arranging and rearranging a variety of pictorial material. He makes the subsumption of 'superficially' diverse data which, on the principle of 'trial and error', he locates hypothetically in one and the same frame (1979: 25). The classification of the materials reveals a kind of form, namely a structural identity, that emerges from the recorded differential contexts. The depth and breadth of the

contextual differences in the materials somehow convey, according to Goffman, 'a sense of structure, a sense of a single organization underlying mere surface differences' (1979: 25).

The logic of this procedure corresponds to Max Weber's notion of ideal types to which Goffman explicitly refers in *Asylums* as his 'method' (1961b: 5). Concepts such as that of the 'total institution' are therefore abstract constructs, incorporating a large number of different phenomena (cf. Manning 1992: 21). Accordingly, Goffman strives to show how the elaboration of significant differences follows from the identification of common features (1961b: 5). For example, when he brings together social structures such as monasteries, concentration camps, psychiatric institutions, barracks and merchant ships and identifies them as 'total institutions', he then – in the next step – deals with the limitations of this frame, deriving from the structural peculiarities of the phenomena in question. Goffman handles every kind of data according to the same principle. For him the search for apparent or real discrepancies of facts and 'exceptions to the rule' is as important, in terms of research strategy, as the procedure of sorting in the search for an (ideal) typology.

6   SEQUENTIAL ANALYSIS

Another of Goffman's range of research strategies is 'sequential analysis', the aim of which is to reconstruct the sequence of events in the process of interaction (cf. 1971, 1981). The procedure of sequential analysis, which ethno-methodological conversation analysis (see **5.17**) and structural hermeneutics (see **5.16**) see as their core, relates to a notion of (interaction-) order that does not only consist of the serial adjacency of two utterances. 'Sequence' rather refers to the specific linking of elements of behaviour to a 'genuine sequential pattern. An utterance, such as a "question", can have "sequential" implications to the extent that it establishes, in respect of the following "turn(s)", by what speaker, through what activity, by what kind of utterance, and so on, it is to be realised' (Bergmann 1991: 310). In the sense of this interpretation, and relating explicitly to ethno-methodological conversation analysis, Goffman also requires the investigator to uncover the sequencing: 'We deal with the sequencing of action in which the move of one participant is followed by that of another, the first move establishing the environment for the second and the second confirming the meaning of the first' (1971: 149).

Admittedly the sequential analysis postulated and practised by conversation analysts, as a pure 'systemic analysis', where 'the process of communication [is] more or less conceptualized as an independently organized system' (Bergmann 1991: 311), was considered by Goffman to be inadequate. What Goffman objects to here is the detachment or denial of the moral-ritual dimension of social practice, defined in culture-specific terms. It is in this dimension that Goffman discovers a *distinctive* and distinctively *sequential* ordering (cf., for example, 1967, 1971).

7 DOUBLE HERMENEUTICS

One of Goffman's most important research strategies seeks to discover implicit meaning patterns and 'world-views' in the practice of everyday life, whether they be common to all members of society or limited to particular social groups. 'One must', he says in *Frame Analysis*, 'try to form an image of the group's framework of frameworks – its belief system, its "cosmoslogy" – even though this is a domain that close students of contemporary social life have usually been happy to give over to others' (Goffman 1974: 27). Frederic Jameson (1976), referring to this essential idea of Goffman's research programme, spoke of his 'theory of theories'. Anthony Giddens (cf. 1984: 12ff.) called Goffman's approach 'double hermeneutics' – 'double' because it is to do with the art of interpreting everyone's 'art of interpretation' (see **5.21**).

This does not only refer to meaning structures and skills of judgement at the level of interaction. Goffman is also rather more concerned with practical constituents of knowledge or types of 'hermeneutics' that more or less correspond to complex life-forms and identities. In this he assumes 'that any group of persons – prisoners, primitives, pilots or patients – develop a life of their own that becomes meaningful, reasonable and normal once you get close to it, and that a good way to learn about any of these worlds is to submit oneself in the company of the members to the daily round of petty contingencies

to which they are subject' (Goffman 1961b: IXf.). In addition to participant observation (see **5.5**), Goffman also relies on a reflexive knowledge of particular classes of actors. As we have already said, Goffman is assuming that the knowledge of 'life-practitioners' is of a predominantly intuitive-unconscious nature (and therefore not testable), but he also believes that extreme or borderline cases, such as stigmatized people, adulterers, spies, kings, or concentration camp inmates, acquire, through their deviation *from* normality, a kind of discursive knowledge *about* normality. Goffman separates this 'para-sociological' knowledge, for example, from cleverness as a type, and uses it simultaneously to make inner social perspectives transparent. In this way, from 'asylums' one can also learn the 'meaning' of how the social world of the clinic is 'subjectively experienced' by the inmates (1961b: IX, cf. von Kardorff 1991: 337).

8 CONCEPT CONSTRUCTIONS

For Goffman the development of a conceptual reference system 'into which a continuously larger number of facts can be placed' (1971: XVI) is a major task for his discipline. Goffman set himself this task in the context of an inter-play of theoretical and empirical work. Instead of forming 'top-down' theories he first imported conceptualization techniques into empirical work. This procedure pursues two principal goals: first, he is concerned with perspectives 'that reorder our view of social activity' (1971: XVI); secondly it is a matter of organizing, or reorganizing, large and diverse quantities of data. What is decisive is that the starting point of Goffman's approach always lies in empirical work, and from its varying particularity he then decides on a guiding analytical perspective, such as the theatre model. Goffman achieves the separation of the different guiding perspectives from conceptual systems of relationships by setting up hierarchies of 'partial constructs'. The development of these is carried out in terms of more or less abstract basic conceptual distinctions, for example the distinction between 'keying' and 'fabrication' (cf. 1974: 40ff.). To this is always attached a network of further distinctions in differing layers of abstraction that come increasingly close to the empirical. All of this always takes place during the processing of, and confrontation with, materials on which the concepts have to prove themselves. (cf. Williams 1988: 71). The final objective of this both inductive and deductive procedure is a formal analytical language that will make it possible to describe the field of face-to-face interaction.

Goffman achieves the highest level of formalization in his 'frame analysis'. There he succeeded in developing a 'meta-schema' for the analytical description of the interaction order which also substantially incorporated his earlier conceptual apparatus. This meta-schema and its precursors in Goffman's work are, as a sociological 'map' and as a theoretical-analytical programme, rather closer to Parsons's sociology than is generally believed. Goffman's critical distance and even opposition to Parsons cannot hide the fact that his approach deserves the title of 'structural-functionalism' that is normally associated with Parsons. And even Parsons's formalism finds, in Goffman's sociology, not an opponent but rather an emulation.

FURTHER READING

Burns, T. (1992) *Erving Goffman*. London: Routledge.

Manning, Ph. (1992) *Erving Goffman and Modern Sociology*. Cambridge: Polity Press.

Williams, R. (1988) 'Understanding Goffman's methods', in P. Drew and A. Wootton (eds), *Erving Goffman – Exploring the Interaction Order*. Cambridge: Polity Press. pp. 64–88.

2.3 Harold Garfinkel and Harvey Sacks

Jörg R. Bergmann

Harold Garfinkel (b. 1917) is widely known today as the founder of ethnomethodology. He gave this research approach its name, and in his early work, which appeared in his 1967 collection *Studies in Ethnomethodology,* he created the theoretical, conceptual and methodological foundations of the approach. The subject of ethnomethodology, according to Garfinkel, is practical everyday action in situations. Its goal is to determine the practices and procedures (or *methods*) that are taken for granted, and by means of which members of a society (or *ethnos*), in their actions, make their own behaviour perceptible and recognizable, and structure and order meaningfully the reality that surrounds them. Unlike the work of Erving Goffman (see **2.2**), which dates from about the same period, Garfinkel's works are much more cumbersome and inaccessible: they are basic in their demands, thoroughly programmatic in character, and for these reasons are often very opaque. In spite of this, or perhaps even because of this, Garfinkel has attracted a large number of followers who made 'ethnomethodology' into a school of its own. In the 1960s and 1970s conversation analysis (see **5.17**) developed out of ethnomethodology, as an independent research orientation that concentrates on identifying the structural mechanisms of linguistic and non-linguistic interaction. In conversation analysis the work of Harvey Sacks (1935–1975), in particular his *Lectures* (1992), was of fundamental importance. For reasons that will be explained below, both Garfinkel and Sacks were very reserved in explaining and setting out the methods of their procedure. It will therefore be all the more revealing to examine the research style of these two scientists more closely.

1 SCIENTIFIC AND HISTORICAL BACKGROUND

Garfinkel's decision to place everyday action at the centre of social scientific interest was not due to a fascination with the exotic nature of trivial matters. It is based, rather, on a theoretical consideration with many underlying assumptions. Garfinkel's starting point is a theme that is known in sociology as the Hobbesian Problem, and relates to the question of how social order is possible when human beings pursue egoistical goals and are therefore constantly in conflict with one another. Garfinkel began with the reflections of Talcott Parsons (1937), his doctoral supervisor, who had set out in his theory of social action a general framework for sociology, and who dominated international sociological debate at that time. Parsons saw the solution of the problem of social order not in utilitarian models of society, but in a way already landmarked by Durkheim and Freud: social order, he claimed, results from the collective adoption and internalization of commonly shared values and norms, and this not only restrains the egotistical tendencies of individuals but also exerts cultural control over the objects of their desires. Garfinkel, however, in his dissertation *The Perception of the Other: A Study in Social Order*, made this kind of solution the target of a theoretically developed critique, supported by an empirical interview-based study. (On the relationship between Parsons and Garfinkel cf., in particular, Heritage 1984.)

In his criticism of Parsons, Garfinkel relies essentially on the works of Alfred Schütz, who was already – in the course of a correspondence with Parsons (Schütz 1978) in the early 1940s – expressing reservations about Parsons's failure in his work to clarify the subjective perspective. This is where Garfinkel also begins. His criticism is that the specific adaptations, interpretations, translations and decisions made by actors are glossed over as irrelevant or neutralized by the model of scientific-rational action. He argues that the solution to the problem of social order can only be found in the elementary processes of the everyday constitution of meaning, that is, by investigating how actors, in their day-to-day activities, transmit cultural norms and values to a situation, agree with others and make them relevant to their actions. Because the interest of ethnomethodology is based, from a theoretical point of view, only in the situational practices of everyday life, it is not surprising that Garfinkel (1991: 11) – in one of his later texts on Parsons's (1937) *Structure of Social Action* – claims that 'Ethnomethodology has its origins in this wonderful book. Its earliest initiatives were taken from these texts.'

Although in preparing his dissertation Garfinkel was looking primarily at Parsons's theory of action and the subsequent development of ethnomethodology was not yet in sight, we already find, in this early work, at least the germ of many concepts and aspects that characterize the style of his later work: the sharp distinction he draws between scientific and everyday rationality; the transfer of meaning constitution from a transcendental or psychological frame of reference to the social events of everyday life; the idea of social order not as a fixable, almost material fact, but as a continuous creation over time; the centring of research interest on the adaptable situational practices of actors; the uncompromising refusal to accept general schemata to explain social action; the bold 'empirical' readings of theoretical texts. To

these characteristics a sharp and sometimes polemical confrontation with conventional 'formal analysis' (Garfinkel 1996) was added in Garfinkel's later work.

In the mid-1950s, Harold Garfinkel and Harvey Sacks met for the first time (at a seminar led by Parsons at Harvard). At that time Sacks was studying law at Yale University, but he was less interested in practising law as an attorney than in discovering how law functioned as an institution (Schegloff, in Sacks 1992). For Sacks's further intellectual development the first thing that was of decisive significance was the continuing interchange with Garfinkel, and the second was the environment in the University of California at Berkeley, where he moved at the end of the 1950s. It was here that, in the following years, Erving Goffman in particular had a strong influence on Sacks and on other later ethnomethodologists (David Sudnow) and conversation analysts (Emanuel Schegloff). Goffman's first book (*The Presentation of Self in Everyday Life*) appeared in 1959 and turned the investigation of face-to-face communication into an independent area of study. From the *Lectures* that Sacks began to give from 1964, and which he had recorded, transcribed and circulated, we may conclude that, in addition to the development of his research interests, he attached great significance to the late work of Wittgenstein, classical philosophy and logic, the ethnographies of the Chicago School and cultural anthropology, generative grammar and the work of Freud. But he used all of these works rather as thought-stimuli and resources and – without being particularly faithful to the original – turned them to his own interests. On the other hand, what remained of central importance to him was Garfinkel's attempt to make the methical nature of everyday action in its situational practices into the primary subject of investigation.

2 DEVELOPMENT OF THE RESEARCH PROGRAMME

Nowhere is a more accessible and convincing representation of the ethnomethodological research programme to be found than in one episode reported by Garfinkel himself under the title 'Shils' complaint' (Garfinkel et al. 1981: 133). In 1954, Fred Strodtbeck of the University of Chicago Law School was appointed to analyse tape-recordings that had been secretly made of the deliberations of jurors. When Strodtbeck suggested using Bales's categories of interaction process analysis for this analysis, Edward Shils warned that 'By using Bales' Interaction Process Analysis I'm sure we'll learn what about a jury's deliberations makes them a small group. But we want to know what about their deliberations makes them a jury.' The fact that Strodtbeck countered this by claiming that Shils would ask the wrong question and Shils then agreed with this claim, was seen by Garfinkel as part of the moral of this story: Garfinkel was convinced that Shils had in fact asked the right question, but that the social sciences are not equipped with appropriate concepts and methods to translate Shils's criticism into investigable phenomena. Shils's question is an exemplary formulation of what ethnomethodology is trying to achieve in its research programme: not to subsume a social phenomenon under a familiar sociological category, but to work out by what practical methods 'something' becomes 'something'.

Garfinkel prescribes for ethnomethodology a constitutive-analytical programme and criticizes traditional sociology and social research for ignoring the question of how a social phenomenon is constituted in the situational practices of actors, and for using – without further clarification – everyday knowledge and common-sense practices as resources, instead of making these into its subject of study. In the early phase of ethnomethodology this was a recurrent theme that Garfinkel reflects in his papers on a range of different phenomena. An example of this is the subject of 'suicide', which is suitable as an illustration of the new-style ethnomethodological way of looking at things because Durkheim had contributed a classical study to this topic that was important for the establishment of sociology as a discipline. In Durkheim's work, the ethnomethodologists argue, we find everyday knowledge about 'suicide' and the use of this category without any more precise clarification. What Sacks holds against this practice (1963: 8) is that 'till we have described the category, suicide, i.e. produced a description of the procedure employed for assembling cases of the class, the category is not even potentially part of the sociological apparatus'. Garfinkel (1967a: 11–18) himself also subsequently showed, in a participant observation, the situational practical procedures used by a coroner to 'confirm' a

suicide and to construct, for a discovered body, an 'account of how a death *really*-for-all-practical-purposes-happened', using particular identifiable clues.

Since ethnomethodology makes into its object of investigation whatever was used in traditional sociology and social research as an unquestioned resource and precondition, its procedures could not simply rely on the established methods of data collection, data processing and theory construction. In the first place, the object of ethnomethodology – the situational practices for generating reality – would be eliminated if social events are methodically processed by coding and numerical-statistical transformation. And in the second place, these practices cannot simply be accessed through an interview. They are, in Garfinkel's words, 'seen but unnoticed' in everyday life. Judgements as to whether everyday actors' statements or declarations are appropriate, relevant, meaningful and so on are always practical judgements, because they are assessed and accepted with the help of situational procedures in respect of practical goals and needs. For this reason, ethnomethodology adopts an attitude of 'indifference' towards them (Garfinkel and Sacks 1970: 344ff.). This implies that ethnomethodology, in realizing its constitutional-analytical programme, cannot simply depend on interview responses (unless there is some enquiry into what, in the behaviour of parties concerned, makes an interview into an interview).

With its focus on the local practices and unvarnished details that constitute a social phenomenon, ethnomethodology seeks, in its own investigations, to collect data in which the events it is looking at are conserved. This obliges the discipline to use a conserving mode of data recording (Bergmann 1985), where social events are preserved in their raw form, irrespective of plausibility or expectations of behaviour. This is the background for the interest of ethnomethodologists, which started in the 1960s, in tape- and video-recordings of social interactions in 'natural' or unmanaged contexts, and in the development of transcription conventions that made it possible to fix a conversation in writing without either orthographic 'normalization' or reduction. Of course, this creation of a method out of an ethnomethodological perspective is not without problems. By its own admissions, general non-object-dependent categories and rules – and methods are in principle nothing more than this – should not be used in the investigation of a social phenomenon, because otherwise there is a risk that the specific generative procedures and 'identifying features' (Garfinkel) of this phenomenon will be lost or prejudiced. It is therefore only consistent that Garfinkel's study of a transsexual person, or the practice in conversation analysis of processing and presenting data by means of transcripts, should themselves be ethnomethodologically deconstructed (cf. Anderson and Sharrock 1984; Rogers 1992).

In the formative years of ethnomethodology and conversation analysis, Garfinkel and Sacks, when dealing with the objectives that characterized Garfinkel's texts in particular, firmly refused every request to make the procedural rules of their approach explicit and to make them binding in the sense of a school of method. (This is perhaps one of the reasons why Garfinkel and Sacks published comparatively little and had more influence through oral forms of academic communication – and here one might also think of Wittgenstein.) For methods of investigation Garfinkel postulated a 'unique adequacy requirement', which means that methods must be so fashioned that they are uniquely suited to their object – but this can only be decided after information about the object of investigation has successfully been obtained, which therefore makes any formalization impossible. Prescriptions and canonizations of particular methods were subsequently developed – particularly in conversation analysis – and even today these still attract criticism from many ethnomethodologists. The representatives of the two positions are, however, united in the conviction that methods should never come before the object of study and in doubtful cases must even be sacrificed.

3 RESEARCH PRACTICE

If one wishes to characterize ethnomethodology and conversation analysis as qualitative approaches, on the basis of the work of Garfinkel and Sacks, and in addition to describe the methods in a systematic way, then on the basis of the properties of these approaches that we have outlined, a very diffuse picture emerges. In data collection ethnographic methods (see **5.5**) are used, and in particular methods of data recording; Sacks and other researchers frequently

also rely on process-generated data – such as tape-recordings of telephone conversations with a 'Suicide Prevention Center'. What is decisive is that social events are documented in their 'natural' context and in their real chronological sequence. Garfinkel, in the 'studies of work' that he inaugurated (see **3.2**), required the researcher to become familiar with the specific competences of the workplace being investigated – an extreme requirement that can only be met in exceptional cases. Conversation analysis, on the other hand, was frequently satisfied with data consisting of simple tape-recordings of conversations, without any requirement for a more profound knowledge of the conversational context.

In accordance with their constitutional-analytical approach, Garfinkel and Sacks viewed questions merely as a global theoretical tool; they only take on their particular relevance when they are faced with the material that has been collected. In interpreting data both ethnomethodology and conversation analysis normally begin with familiar social scenes and intuitively intelligible communicative utterances, and attempt to discover analytically from these the formal procedures by means of which the structures and events of the social world are constituted in the behaviour of the actors. It is mastery of such procedures that makes up the interpretative and interactive competences of the actors, and it is only through them that they become members of a society. Since these competences are largely a matter of routine, however, they do not normally attract attention and are difficult for the researcher to access. But in order to make visible the products of social reality that are concealed in the same social reality, Garfinkel, Sacks and other ethnomethodologists and conversation analysts have always employed certain tricks that are designed to assist in exposing the opaque nature of the everyday world. Three of these tricks will now be outlined:

1 In his dissertation (Garfinkel 1963: 187) Garfinkel already followed the strategy of asking, on the basis of a stable system of action, what one would need to do to create disorder. The motivation behind this was that the same operations that are necessary to evoke anomie and disorganization could also provide the key to understanding how social structures are maintained. The crisis experiments carried out

by Garfinkel and his students indeed managed to bring about confusion and annoyance in the parties concerned. Ultimately, however, they were not very significant from an analytical or revelatory viewpoint, and served rather as a way of demonstrating to non-ethnomethodologists that the everyday world contains hidden structural features that had previously been taken for granted. It should be noted that Garfinkel never abandoned the idea of making heuristic use of critical occurrences where social order breaks down. In his 'studies of work', for example, he therefore examines the presence and effect of 'procedural troublemakers', that is, persons who are blind, confined to wheelchairs, or who suffer from other handicaps, because 'with these "troublemakers", work's incarnate social organizational details are revealed by overcoming their transparency' (Garfinkel 1996: 12). A further example is provided by Garfinkel's student Robillard (1999), who made use of his own disability – he suffers from progressive paralysis and is dependent on technological support to enable him to communicate – to gain insight into the practices that enable us to perceive everyday phenomena as normal and natural (cf. further examples in Schwartz and Jacobs 1979).

2   An opposing and apparently paradoxical movement is characteristic of the methods of ethnomethodology and conversation analysis. This consists of approaching as closely as possible the social event being investigated during the research process but at the same time distancing oneself from it. In conversation analysis this approaching consists of overcoming the fleeting nature of the observed social events by making audiovisual recordings. These are then fixed by precise transcription (see 5.9) in a written form in their smallest and apparently most insignificant details, and the representation becomes progressively more fine-grained and richer in nuance through repeated listening and viewing of the social events being investigated. Conversation analysts therefore put a social object under the microscope and examine it in a way that is not possible in the normal haste of everyday life and which is alien to current practice in the social sciences. At the same time, however, they distance themselves from the social object of their investigation by avoiding the normal everyday practice of making social events intelligible by hurriedly attributing motives to them. In addition they do not replace the recorded utterances and behavioural sequences with condensing and interpretative paraphrases, and they admit knowledge of the context of a social interaction into an analysis only in a highly controlled and measured form. The point of this attitude of conversation analysis, simultaneously approaching and distancing itself from its object of investigation, is to focus the analysts' attention completely on the interaction order of social behaviour and its creation by the participants. The aim is to reconstruct the constructive achievements of the interacting partners, and also to observe their observations, to interpret their interpretations and to find the methods in their (ethno-)methods.

3   Both ethnomethodologists and conversation analysts are committed to using, in their research work, procedures and methods the analysis of which they have selected as the theme of their investigation. In the interpretation of an action or an utterance they have no other choice than to make continual use of their competence as members of society and to employ their intuitive understanding. But ethnomethodology and conversation analysis both seek not simply to use intuition but to take a step back from the analyst's own intuition and to analyse the underlying generative mechanisms of this intuition. In this way Harvey Sacks (1972), in a paper that has now become well known, analyses a story told by a three-year-old girl: 'The baby cried. The mommy picked it up.' First he presents his own intuitive understanding of this story, that the mother who picks up the baby is the mother of this particular baby, even though there is no explicit personal pronoun to mark this kind of relationship. His paper then turns to the problem of reconstructing that led him – and presumably most other people who hear this story – to the intuitive understanding that he describes. (For another ethnomethodological study of the same kind, with a paradigmatic character, cf. Smith 1978.)

To make easier this rather difficult distancing from one's own intuitive understanding, Sacks made use of a trick. One sees a person and intuitively notes that this person is 'angry'. But what is it in the behaviour of this person that evokes the intuition of 'angry'? Sacks directs attention to these fundamental production practices by placing before the intuitively perceived marker of person the phrase 'doing being'. So 'angry' becomes '[doing being] angry', and a person intuitively perceived as being a policeman becomes a '[doing being] a policeman'. Now there is a possibility of breaking down individual intuition into observable production practices (Sacks 1984).

This recourse to individual intuitive understanding is by no means a rule for Garfinkel and Sacks. On the contrary, for both of them it is not intuition and spontaneous understanding but observation that is of fundamental methodological importance. For Garfinkel and Sacks intuitive understanding does not play the role of the final piece of evidence; it is not explanatory but rather, as something created, has to be explained. For this reason those observable states of order in social behaviour that go against intuition must also be investigated to establish the meaningful nature of their production.

4 GARFINKEL, SACKS AND QUALITATIVE SOCIAL RESEARCH

Garfinkel and Sacks have made no explicit pronouncements on questions of qualitative social research. But from their criticism of quantitative research and from their own research practice – their interpretative approach, their orientation towards the subjective perspective of actors, the tendency to use case studies, and so on – it is absolutely clear that in their own minds they associated themselves with qualitative social research, because it gives a better guarantee of preserving the integrity of data. From this it also becomes clear what their specific contribution to qualitative social research consists of. Their work shows that the construction of social reality can be observed in the communicative processes and situational practices of everyday life; they draw attention to the fact that research must analyse its social objects within

the timescale in which life takes place; they demonstrate the enormous gain that can be made for sociology in considering apparently insignificant details; and they encourage mistrust both towards individual common-sense interpretations and towards the scientific categories that scientists all too gladly use in handling data. Helmuth Plessner (1974: 146) once wrote of Husserl's phenomenology that it was characterized by 'the tendency to abolish philosophical theories and "-isms", viewpoints and principles, to dispense with the systematic unit as opposed to the surging wealth of concrete themes, by the will to work and openness to the public, respect for the small, patience with the partial, modesty in face of the immeasurable'. It is this attitude which – mediated by Alfred Schütz – also characterizes the research style of Garfinkel and Sacks. Their unconditional orientation towards the matter in hand and the secondary role of method are perhaps the most important – if rather ambivalent – contribution that ethnomethodology and conversation analysis, by their own example, will make to a more general methodology of qualitative social research.

FURTHER READING

Garfinkel, H. (1967) *Studies in Ethnomethodology*. Englewood Cliffs, NJ: Prentice Hall.

Heritage, J. C. (1984) *Garfinkel and Ethnomethodology*. Cambridge: Polity Press.

Sacks, H. (1992) *Lectures on Conversation,* vols I and II (edited by G. Jefferson with introductions by E. A. Schegloff). Oxford: Blackwell.

2.4 Paul Willis and the Centre for Contemporary Cultural Studies

Rolf Lindner

Paul Willis is considered to be the most important exponent of ethnographic research in the context of the Centre for Contemporary Cultural Studies (CCCS) in Birmingham. His study *Learning to Labour – How Working Class Kids Get Working Class Jobs* (1977) is a fieldwork-based investigation of the transition from school to the world of work. Using the example of an informal group of secondary school students he traces the processes whereby school-leavers see the decision to opt for unqualified jobs in the area of material production as a conscious choice deriving from cultural factors. *Learning to Labour* is now regarded as a classic and equated in importance with such works as William F. Whyte's (1955) *Street Corner Society*.

1 PAUL WILLIS AND THE CCCS

Willis's ethnographic work came out of the CCCS. The CCCS was set up in 1964, on the initiative of Richard Hoggart, at the University of Birmingham Department of English as a post-graduate course and was led by him, unofficially, from 1964 and officially from 1972. His successor was Stuart Hall, under whose leadership the Centre has won international acclaim, with *cultural studies* becoming a trademark for interdisciplinary teaching and research (see **3.9**).

The early Hoggart phase of the CCCS emphasized the enlargement of the discipline of literary criticism to include the products of popular and mass culture such as low-grade literature, soap operas, film, advertising and others. In this it was not a matter of merely changing objective labels (from highbrow to mass literature, from opera to pop music, and so on) but a change of perspective in literary studies which found expression in the title 'cultural studies'. From the very beginning, the interests of cultural studies went beyond basic textual analysis. The central object of interest was rather the relationship between the 'text' in question (book, film, music and so on) and the 'reader' (consumer, recipient). The basic assumption was that this relationship was determined by the 'reader's' way of life. In this context cultural studies came to be understood as a discipline, or rather as a perspective that undertakes the analysis of culture 'as a way of life' (Raymond Williams). This anthropological turn in literary studies also brought the ethnographic approach closer to the field. Only by analysing the elements of an entire way of life is it possible to understand the meaning that is attributed by subjects to particular cultural forms and categories.

2   WILLIS'S STUDY *PROFANE CULTURE* AS A RESEARCH PARADIGM FOR CULTURAL STUDIES

Paul Willis's ethnographic studies *Learning to Labour* (1977) and *Profane Culture* (1978) come under the aegis of Stuart Hall, who was director of the CCCS until 1979. In this period the socio-analytical and anti-authoritarian accent of the Centre's intellectual activity was further strengthened, with the result that the relationship of cultural hegemony and subordinate cultures became the main object of investigation. Willis's study *Profane Culture*, which was based on his doctoral dissertation, can be seen in many respects as a showpiece for the contemporary understanding of cultural studies outlined above. The title already shows a breach with one concept of culture, which sees it merely as an assemblage of canonical (or 'sacred') works. From the viewpoint of classical literary studies, 'profane culture' is a contradiction in terms, and that is precisely the intention of this term: it resists the claims to exclusivity of the 'sacred culture'. This 'resistance' that is already embodied in the title points to a further dimension of *Profane Culture*: a perspective that is directed towards the everyday creativity of the subjects. In order to avoid the image prevalent in manipulation theory of the consumer/recipient as a passive victim of the culture industry, there has grown up in cultural studies a way of interpreting the consumption of mass culture as a creative or even subversive act: today this is increasingly criticized as being 'populist'. But this is precisely the theme of *Profane Culture*: 'that oppressed, subordinate or minority groups can have a hand in the construction of their own vibrant cultures and are not merely dupes' (1978: 1) Furthermore, the study is a good example of the methodological principle underlying cultural studies: to reveal the inner relationship between the object and the lifestyle of a group. This inner relationship is described by Paul Willis, analogously to Claude Lévi-Strauss, as cultural homology.

Two youth subcultures that were paradigmatic for the late 1960s constitute the object of investigation of Willis's study: 'rockers' (or bike-boys) on the one hand, and 'hippies' on the other. On the basis of general observation of 'scenes', participation in group events and individual and group conversations, Willis is able to give a coherent picture of the respective group culture, in which nothing – neither the rockers' preference for singles, nor the hippies' preference for concert albums – is a matter of chance. In a fascinating and impressively concentrated way Willis elaborates the homologies that exist, in the case of the rockers in their dealings with the motor-bike – the core element of group culture – and the rituals of rock'n'roll, and in the case of the hippies in the use of mind-expanding drugs, progressive rock music and aesthetic self-presentation. In an illuminating manner the reader is shown that particular objects in the environment of a social group have close parallels in their views, values and feeling-structures. But these are also decisively marked by the original background. Ultimately both cultural subsets are shown to be generation-specific modifications of their background culture. Paul Willis's study may, in this sense, be seen as a classic example of the analysis of subcultures at CCCS which took youth subcultures to be generation-specific subsystems of class-specific 'parent cultures' (Clarke et al. 1979).

3   *LEARNING TO LABOUR*: THE VIEW OF ACTORS AS A SCIENTIFIC AND CULTURAL CHALLENGE

When Willis is spoken of as a 'minor classic', the reference is to Willis's second ethnographic study, *Learning to Labour – How Working Class Kids Get Working Class Jobs* (1977). Although it appeared earlier than *Profane Culture*, the period when the research took place was later, between 1973 and 1975. This study grew out of a research project funded by the Social Science Research Council (SSRC), entitled *The Transition from School to Work*. As may be seen from the final report, published as a 'stencilled paper', the aim of this project was to overcome the restriction of the research activities of the CCCS to the leisure activities of young people and give greater attention to work-related orientations concerning values and activities. The original title of the project makes clear in what perspective this was to take place; for Willis it was important to analyse the inner dynamics of the process of transition from school to the world of work from the point of view of the actors. Paul Willis's grant application was based on two working hypotheses:

1   Working class school leavers develop their definition of the situation (evidently a reference

to the Thomas theorem) in the first instance not from official sources, but rather from the 'informal culture of work'.

2 The transition from school to work is understood from the perspective of the 'subjective meaning' of the actors rather than from the adoption of the institutional viewpoint (cf. Willis 1975: 3).

The research project included a main study and five small comparative investigations. The latter, with one exception, played only a very minor role in *Learning to Labour*. Willis's interest is clearly focused on a friendship group of 12 boys aged 15 and 16, who all attend a secondary school in the Midlands industrial area. This group, known as 'lads' in the study, were selected by Willis because in their rebellious behaviour they expressed their negative, 'oppositional' attitude to the school as an institution, its representatives and its supporters. On the basis of this selective focusing it also becomes clear why the only relevant comparative study is based on a group of pupils with a positive orientation towards school. These school-conformists, who form the opposite pole in the cultural school landscape, were described by the 'lads' (with an unambiguous allusion) as 'ear'oles', or swots. In this opposition it seems clear, moreover, that we find a repetition of the contrast between 'corner boys' and 'college boys' in Whyte's (1955) *Street Corner Society*.

Willis followed this school class during its final 18 months in school. He sat in on lessons, monitored the careers advice, accompanied the 'lads' in their free time (and continued this in their first few weeks in the workplace), conducted individual and group interviews with pupils, teachers and parents, and in addition to all this analysed other materials such as diaries and careers advice brochures.

The special problems of participant observation in a structured context, such as school as an institution, are manifest not least in the conflict of loyalties – towards the pupils on the one hand and the teachers on the other – in which the researcher is caught up. The power differences between these two groups made it impossible to maintain a close relationship with both teachers and pupils: 'Any tendency towards the staff would have been identified by the lads … as complicity with the school and its authority. You were taken, simply, as staff. That cut off exactly those information flows, and inhibited

those types of behaviour, with which we were most concerned' (Willis 1977: 8). On the other hand, a clear siding with the 'lads' could have been interpreted as a disturbing act and led to the shutting out of the researcher. Willis opted for a 'pronounced lean towards the kids in the situation coupled with a strategy of making clear explanations to staff in private' (1978: 9). Willis's siding with the 'lads' was subjected to fierce criticism, particularly from feminists. It was not only that he apparently took no steps to counter the macho-talk in conversation. He was criticized especially for celebrating the cult of manliness as a kind of resistance, without referring systematically in his analysis to its violent, sexist and racist elements that were a major theme of his work (McRobbie 1980). From Willis's final report it emerges that, on the basis of his sympathetic approach to the young people, he won a kind of 'intermediate' status, neither group member nor teacher, someone who was 'easy to talk to, and most of all (a person) who would not "shop" them' (1978: 9). Perhaps this status, because of its sympathetic elements, is best described as an older 'mate'. The procedure and the narrative are strongly reminiscent of Whyte's contact with 'Doc's Gang' in *Street Corner Society*. One important but rarely mentioned component of fieldwork in youth subcultures seems to consist of investigator and investigated (as with Whyte and Willis in *Profane Culture*) belonging to one and the same age and gender-group, or at least (as with Willis in *Learning to Labour*) not being too far apart in respect of age.

The accusation that he implicitly shared in the machismo of the 'lads' strikes particularly hard, as Willis sees, in the masculinity and toughness of the rebellious school group, the essential elements of cultural self-assertion. To question this would imply disavowing those aspects of working class culture that are critical of the system. In the last resort Willis sees the critical attitude of his protagonists towards capitalism in their distinguishing mental and physical work, in their rejection of the former and their very enthusiastic defence of the latter as the core of a male-oriented ethos. It is the pride in physical work, transmitted from father to son, that becomes, in school, the hallmark of cultural distinction and of the class-cultural alternative to education and mobility-optimism. 'Thus physical labouring comes to stand for and express, most importantly, a kind of masculinity and also an opposition to authority – at least as it is learned in school. It expresses aggressiveness; a degree of sharpness and wit; an irreverence that cannot be found in words; an obvious kind of solidarity' (Willis 1977: 104). But in this we may also see the paradoxical result of this study, combining adjustment to and rebellion against circumstances in one and the same act.

The answer to the initial question about 'how working class kids get working class jobs' can only be: by means of cultural practices. The cultural self-assertion, which sets the informal culture of a group against the illusive (because it affects only a few) chance of advancement in the form of education, leads ultimately to the social disintegration that can even be interpreted as a kind of self-condemnation to a (sub-)proletarian existence. Paradoxically this self-condemnation is understood by the 'lads' as an act of rebellion, as opposition to the (school) authorities and 'creeps' or 'ear'oles'. This encapsulates both the logic and the tragedy of cultural reproduction.

With this diagnosis of a mechanism for self-integration built into the cultural practice of subjects, Willis succeeds – as Mahnkopf (1985: 239) sums it up – in thinking of processes of social reproduction without resorting to deterministic short cuts. As George Marcus (1986: 178) points out, it is rather that the structure of capitalism is reformulated in terms of human relationships. But at the same time there is, in the thesis of self-integration via cultural practice, a danger of concealing one's own kind of cultural determinism. In this respect Willis's theory of cultural reproduction resembles the thesis of the 'Culture of Poverty' (Lewis 1967). In both contexts we are dealing with forms of cultural self-assertion that are based on the transmission of 'deviant' value and behaviour norms between the generations. And in both contexts the refusal to 'play the (exposed) game' is central to these value norms.

4   ON THE ETHNOGRAPHIC RESEARCH PRACTICE OF CULTURAL STUDIES

Although ethnographic research is central to the work of the CCCS, there are in fact few truly ethnographic studies; Willis's harsh judgement that the 'CCCS hasn't really had a genuinely ethnographic tradition' (1997: 187) may seem exaggerated but has a core of truth. Experienced-based

research does indeed belong to the basic principles of cultural studies, with personal experience being given a privileged place (as, for example, in subculture research or in 'women's studies'). But, as far as I can determine, no one apart from Willis spent very long on research activities. For both *Profane Culture* and *Learning to Labour* Willis spent more than a year on fieldwork and so fulfilled the classical criteria. Here the spectrum of methods extends from (often underrated) 'hanging about' in the setting to participant observation in the strict sense of the word (see **5.5**), supplemented and extended with informal conversations, group interviews and diary analysis.

The methodological focal point of the Birmingham School was the sociological 'naturalism' of the 'Chicago School', deriving from William F. Whyte, Howard S. Becker and others (Roberts 1975). Willis also bases himself in this tradition, but at the same time criticizes its covert positivism, which consists of 'objectivizing' the subject of investigation: this is manifest in an insistence on the passivity of the participant observer as a fundamental methodological principle that is intended to guarantee objectivity (Willis 1976). Willis's criticism of traditional fieldwork, of course, goes beyond this claim, which perhaps even then sounded banal. It relates in particular to the inherent 'humanism' of ethnographic research which results in a tendency to consider the culture under investigation – normally a limited entity – as a world in itself 'with centred human beings in some way controlling their own forms' (Willis 1997: 184). Ethnographic investigations often 'lose' themselves in the life-world of their protagonists, without considering the relationship between this world and the predominant system (see **3.8**). In the face of this, Willis insists on the need to involve in the investigation theoretical knowledge that cannot be directly 'extracted' from the field of enquiry, so as to take account of the historically given circumstances within which the subjects are acting. Willis gave to this approach the acronym TIES: *Theoretically Informed Ethnographic Study*. This type of theory-driven research already begins in the selection of the research field: 'Why precisely are you in this locale rather than another?' (Marcus 1986: 172). *Learning to Labour* displays this kind of strategic choice of scenario, but adapts itself particularly well to the transition from school to the world of work, in order to investigate questions of the reproduction of systems from the action perspective of the subjects. It is precisely in the ability to bring more order – whether we call it system or society – into the realm of ethnography where the particular success of Willis's research methods is to be found.

'Learning to Labour is thus the most comprehensive meditation on a trend of experimentation that seeks to adapt the writing of ethnography to take into account larger issues of political economy and broader vistas of representation' (Marcus 1986: 177). In this way ethnography succeeds, in its best moments, in allowing structure to be recognized as a result of human activity, and in the case of the 'lads' as the unintended consequences of goal-directed behaviour. Furthermore, beyond the ethnographer's traditional search for the 'native's point of view', ethnography here becomes a form of cultural criticism which, as Marcus (1986: 180) points out, is 'embodied' in the lives of victims of macro-social systems.

The effects of Learning to Labour are still felt even today, and this is to be seen not least in follow-up studies such as Learning Capitalist Culture (Foley 1990), which pursue the methodological procedures first established by Paul Willis.

FURTHER READING

Marcus, G. E. (1986) 'Contemporary Problems of Ethnography in the Modern World System', in J. Clifford and G. E. Marcus (eds), Writing Culture. The Poetics and Politics of Ethnography. Berkeley, CA: University of California Press. pp. 165–193.

Willis, P. (1997) 'TIES. Theoretically Informed Ethnographic Study', in S. Nugent and C. Shore (eds), Anthropology and Cultural Studies. London and Chicago: University of Chicago Press. pp. 182–192.

2.5 Paul Parin, Fritz Morgenthaler and Goldy Parin-Matthèy

Maya Nadig and Johannes Reichmayr

1 THE PERSPECTIVE OF ETHNO-PSYCHOANALYTICAL QUESTIONS

Paul Parin, Goldy Parin-Matthèy and Fritz Morgenthaler are looked upon as the founders of *ethno-psychoanalysis*. During their research visits to West Africa in the 1950s and 1960s they succeeded, for the first time in the history of linking psychoanalysis with ethnology, in applying the methods and techniques of Freudian psychoanalysis to an ethnological investigation of members of tradition-directed cultures. The Freudian structural model of the psyche (*id*, *ego*, *super-ego*), the ego-psychology and its further developments, formed the theoretical basis and starting point for the investigations of the Zürich research group. They examined the different attempts to apply psychoanalysis in the social sciences. In the field of ethnology the Zürich psychoanalysts used, in particular, the studies by Werner Muensterberger of Chinese migrants in the United States (1970) and the investigations of the American 'Culture and Personality School' (cf. Reichmayr 1995). Their special interest was in the investigation of structural aspects of the organization of the inner-psyche, which can be summarized in the question of whether different laws apply in

different social and cultural circumstances, for example with West Africans who still live in village communities and according to their own traditions, compared to Western Europeans.

2 FIELD RESEARCH IN WEST AFRICA – DEVELOPMENT OF TECHNIQUES AND THEORY CONSTRUCTION

The first trip to West Africa, from December 1954 to April 1955, had no predetermined scientific goals. Curiosity and an interest in understanding and conducting a psychoanalytical investigation of unfamiliar types of experience and behaviour were aroused in the course of this trip and became crucial for later research activities.

The *development* of ethno-psychoanalysis and its methodological approach can be broken down into three stages. On the first two journeys through West Africa (1954–1955 and 1956–1957) data on striking behaviour patterns were collected, systematized and psychoanalytically evaluated, using techniques for interpreting character analyses with regard to the structure and dynamics of the psyche. The purpose of this was to arrive at some more general statements about the personality of West Africans. After completion of the first trip intense ethnological studies began, and henceforth these became a fixed component of the ethno-psychoanalytical research activities. The interpretative techniques of comparative character analysis and the insights yielded by this constituted the first step in the development of a new field of psychoanalytical research.

The use of the main instruments of psycho-analysis, *transference* and *dealing with resistance*, belonged to the next step, where psychoanalytical technique was freed from its clinical setting and applied to an area of ethnological investigation as a research method. This was done for the first time, in the course of conversations to introduce psychoanalyses, with the Dogon people in the West African state of Mali during the third research trip (from December 1959 to May 1960). The Dogon were selected because a sufficient number of them could speak a European language and their ancient way of life, together with their traditional and religious institutions, had largely survived. The study, entitled *Die Weissen denken zuviel: Psychoanalytische Untersuchungen bei den Dogon in Westafrika* [The White People Think too much: Psychoanalytical Investigations with the Dogon People in West Africa] (Parin, Morgenthaler and Parin-Matthèy, 4th edition 1993) was first published in 1963. Unlike the investigations of the first and second trips, the research aim was now only to discover details about the inner life and the unconscious mental structures of the persons being investigated, and 'to test whether the technique of psychoanalysis was suitable for understanding the inner life of people who live in a tradition-directed West African social structure' (Parin 1965: 342), and also for acquiring knowledge of how the *ego* has developed from the *id*: 'The purpose of the investigation is to get Africans to speak to us in this way about how they themselves think and feel, and to enable us to understand them' (Parin et al. 1993: 34).

For this purpose, Paul Parin and Fritz Morgenthaler conducted series of psychoanalytical conversations with 13 Dogon people over a period of several months. Each individual took part in 20–40 sessions, making up a total of 350 hours. Shorthand transcripts of the sittings were taken, and these recorded the 'free associations' of the persons under analysis. To understand this correctly, they considered, in addition to information already available in the literature

on Dogon culture and society, the results of 25 psychiatric investigations and Goldy Parin-Matthèy's Rorschach-table interpretations of 100 subjects as a non-linguistic project collection procedure.

From the experience of applying psychoanalytic methods with the Dogon it may be clearly concluded 'that Western psychology only describes a particular instance of the possible compositions of the human mind' (Parin et al. 1993: 534).

The fifth research field trip to West Africa began in December 1965 and lasted until 1966. Its aim was to carry out an ethno-psychoanalytical field investigation with the Agni, who lived in the tropical rainforest of Ivory Coast. The large quantity of material that the researchers were able to collect in the course of this investigation was published in 1971 in the book *Fürchte deinen Nächsten wie dich sellbst: Psychoanalyse und Gesellschaft am Modell der Agni in Westafrika* [Fear your Neighbour as much as Yourself: Psychoanalysis and Society on the Model of the Agni in West Africa] (Parin et al. 1971). In relation to the research with the Agni there is also a series of shorter publications dealing with questions (of culture shift, psychoanalytic aggression theory and culture-specific forms of the Oedipus complex) for which ethno-psychoanalytical experience with the Agni and Dogon peoples and psychoanalyses within the writers' own culture provided a basis (Parin 1992; Parin and Parin-Matthèy 1988). Unlike the investigation with the Dogon, in which the idea of the psychic structure of individuals was central, particular attention is paid, with the Agni, to the interplay between *individual* and *social structures*, and prominence is given to the study of the individual within the framework of a particular culture.

Proceeding from the intentionally differently selected conditions with the Agni, compared to the Dogon, the researchers came to the assumption that there would also be far-reaching differences in the psychology of the Agni, and they saw in this a 'challenge to the direct application of psychoanalytic method: can it contribute to the understanding of matrilineally organized societies, even though it grew out of the psychology of patrilineal organization and one of its fundamental concepts – the real or assumed Oedipal conflict – derives exclusively from a system of patriarchal family organization?' (Parin et al. 1971: 13).

This question was embedded in a superordinate research aim: with the help of ethno-psychoanalysis with the Agni, it was intended to make a contribution to the relationship between psychoanalysis and the social sciences, by showing the interlocking of individual and social forces using the technical and methodological resources of psychoanalysis. The interrelation between social and individual factors becomes clear if one can consider the historical dimension of mental experiences, establish the connection between the type of economy and psychic structure or compare the nature of individual relationships to social structure.

3   THE RESEARCHER IN ETHNO-PSYCHOANALYTICAL FIELD RESEARCH

One essential dimension of research is connected with the *reflection of one's own role as a researcher*, which is constantly required.

> If one wishes to give a theoretical description of the mental development and its product – the psychical makeup – of the Agni, which we investigated using the equipment and methods of psychoanalysis, one cannot do this comparatively: 'with us it is like this, and with them it is different'. The inevitable involvement of the observer in his/her own psychology, reliance on the values, judgments and prejudices of the home cultural community and class ideology will distort and mutilate what the investigator wanted to discover. It is only the abstract conceptual world of metapsychology, with its theories, hypotheses and conjectures that reduces this difficult and – in its individual and cultural properties – incomparable mental structure to simple precepts. Structures, functions and developmental stages sustain, to be measured against those of different people in a different environment. (Parin et al. 1971: 505)

In the same way as with the Dogon, the need also arose with the Agni of ascribing to the development of the *ego* and *super-ego* certain special functions that were tentatively presented in the terms 'group-ego' and 'clan-consciousness'. Essential differences, compared to experience in European psychoanalytic practice, were also found in the formation of Oedipal conflicts. All modifications took account of the requirement that the research was intended to make use of psychoanalytical theory in order to create better

conditions for a theoretical understanding of the relationship between the individual and society (see **5.20**).

4   ETHNO-PSYCHOANALYSIS IN UNDERSTANDING CULTURES AND SOCIETIES

The ethno-psychoanalytical observations and investigations that were made in West Africa between 1954 and 1971 led to 'insights about previously unknown or undervalued connections between social institutions and unconscious processes' which 'forced themselves upon us' (Parin 1989: 103). The result was that it became clear that, above all, the effects of social forces are manifest and foregrounded in the individual, whereas biological aspects are less important than the cultural conditions. The psychoanalysts' experiences in this tradition-directed culture were the reverse of psychoanalytical activity in their own society. The ethno-psychoanalytical ideas were

> developed among the Africans and, simultaneously and subsequently, with our subjects in Switzerland in the course of direct examinations of individuals. In this we first used, without modifications, the psychoanalytic theory – or metapsychology – of Sigmund Freud, his associates and followers. Only when this theory was simply inadequate to explain our observations did we modify it, add something, omit or change something else. We did not, of course, arrive at a new and watertight theory. But our hypotheses and assumptions had a reciprocal effect on our psychoanalytical attitudes, they influenced our behaviour as analysts and could perhaps assist other analysts to understand better the problems of their subjects. (Parin 1980: 6)

This experience with the Dogon and Agni peoples sharpened awareness of relationships in the researchers' own society. The ethno-psychoanalytical investigations had made totally clear the effect of social forces on the individual. These insights created the distance necessary in psychoanalytical work within one's own culture to grasp complex social processes and to include them in the theory and practice of psycho-analysis. At the theoretical level they took account of these experiences with the model of the adaptation-mechanisms of the *ego*. The adaptation-mechanisms 'relieved the *ego* of the constant dispute with the external world ... just as the defence-mechanisms do when confronted with the demands of rejected impulses' (Parin 1977: 485). Now they examined the functioning of adaptation-mechanisms in their own culture, and this led to 'identification with the ideology of a role' and brought the phenomena of power and dominance under scrutiny. This could be used to approach the social environment, but not as in the past (by Freud and on the model of the psychoanalytic *ego*-psychology) as an immutable mass. It was now possible to study different social and community-based circumstances and structural relations affecting the functioning of the *ego*, and in this way to determine the achievements of the *ego* in an environment that was constantly changing and affecting it. This 'ethno-psychoanalytical' extension of psychoanalysis permitted a broader psychoanalytical investigation of the individual in a society. The obstacles to working out the procedure were not at the theoretical level or in the basic assumptions of psychoanalytic theory, which had always taken account of the effect of social forces in its work. They lay rather in the circumstances under which psychoanalysis was carried out in the home culture:

> The psychoanalytical observer always belonged to the same society and often to the same class as the subject under investigation, and both parties had undergone more or less the same socialization process. The necessary distance for the understanding of social processes could rarely be achieved. At least this one difficulty disappears if one applies the tool of psychoanalysis to members of a different people, especially if one can put oneself beyond what has been called the 'Western cultural circle'. Then the relationship of social institutions and processes to psychic structures and functions emerges far more clearly. (Parin 1976: 2)

The attempt to go beyond the adaptation-mechanisms of the *ego* to the psychoanalysis of social processes distinguishes itself from other experiments of this sort in that it uses the tools of psychoanalysis itself, its methods and theory, while maintaining the drive and conflict model of psychoanalysis. The psychology of the *ego* was so extended that the effect of social processes could be explained in the place 'where they make themselves visible: in the inner life of the individual' (Parin and Parin-Matthèy 1992: 14).

5 OVERVIEW OF ETHNO-PSYCHOANALYSIS TODAY

It is interesting to note that the advances that are being made today in epistemological discussion of constructivist (see **3.4**) and post-structuralist (see **3.3**) concepts are, in scientific terms, very close to the theoretical and methodological positions of ethno-psychoanalysis. This relates, at the methodological level, to the techniques of psychoanalysis, which attach great importance to the unconscious, to subjectivity, to the course of a relationship and to the specific context (frame/setting), which collect and interpret material, using the method of free association, that is bound to sequences of conflict or process, to circumstances specific to particular places and situations and to relationships. The more unambiguously Parin, Morgenthaler and Parin-Matthèy implemented this approach in their ethno-psychoanalytical research, the more precisely they were thereby anticipating a statement of the research postulates of post-structuralism. The systematic use of the techniques of psychoanalysis as a method of field research broke the social science taboo on context, time and place-related interpretation.[1]

From a retrospective point of view, the methodological integration of psychoanalysis into ethnology developed rather slowly. It started in the United States with 'culture-and-personality' research (1930–1960), when ethnologists first found a theoretical orientation in psychoanalysis and organized their classic field studies around psychoanalytic concepts and essentialist cultural theories.

Georges Devereux, in addition to his research in different cultures (1951, 1961), developed a concept of ethnic defence mechanisms (1974) and a method theory to link ethnology and psychoanalysis. He focused on the role and fears of the researcher in the field and showed how 'objective' methods could be used as a defence against these fears of transfer (1967). Among his students in Paris were Tobie Nathan (1977, 1988, 1995; Nathan and Stengers 1995) and Marie Rose Moro (1994, 1998).

A first methodological approximation between psychoanalysis and ethnology was brought about in the period between the 1950s and 1970s, particularly by a group of psychoanalysts trained in the USA, with whom Paul Parin was in contact. Their methodological procedure was a blend of ethnological observation,

Rorschach tests and systematic psychiatric and psychoanalytic interviews with members of an 'alien' culture (e.g. Boyer 1980, 1983). The forum for many of these studies was *The Psychoanalytic Study of Society* (Boyer and Grolnik 1975) This interest in ethno-psychoanalysis has lasted until the present day (cf. Crapanzano 1973, 1983, 1985; Gehrie 1989; Heald and Deluz 1994; Muensterberger 1970; Obeyesekere 1990).

In European ethno-psychoanalysis – mostly inspired by the works of Parin, Morgenthaler and Parin-Matthèy – there were several monographs by psychoanalysts with an interest in ethnology (Nadig 1986; Rodriguez-Rabanal 1990; Tripet 1990; Weilenmann 1992). At the same time ethno-psychoanalytical questions were taken up by ethnologists who underwent analysis or collaborated with psychoanalysts to produce a range of empirical studies (e.g. Crapanzano 1973, 1983; Kayales 1998; Kubik 1993, 1994; Roth 1998; Weidmann 1990; Weiss 1991; and others). According to the conditions under which they lived in the field, they applied the concepts and the methodological approach of 'classical' psychoanalysis in very different ways. The strictest possible monitoring of transference, therefore, became an ever more important requirement.[2]

Theoretical works on ethno-psychoanalysis concern themselves with its history and theory (Adler 1993; Erdheim and Nadig 1983; Hauschild 1981; Heinrichs 1993; Zinser 1984), with the role of the subconscious in the relationship between the individual and society (Erdheim 1982, 1988), and with methodological questions (e.g. Leithäuser and Volmerg 1988; Nadig 1992; Nadig and Erdheim 1980; Saller 1993). A sound overview of the development of ethno-psychoanalysis and its most important literature is given in Reichmayr (1995, 2000). Extracts from the spectrum of more recent work may be found in the series *Ethnopsychoanalyse* (from 1990).

Critical discussions of the relationship between psychoanalysis and ethnology focus on the categorial aspects of psychoanalytic metapsychology that is imposed on the living nature of the data (Reiche 1995), and on the questionability of such typological concepts as the image of women, the notion of homosexuality, and so on. Methodology and technique are irritated by the principle of self-reflection, which may be misunderstood as ethnocentric self-reflection

and navel-gazing, or 'discovering the self in others' (cf., for example, Kohl 1992).

In the history of psychoanalysis an important role has been played by the question of the breadth and transferability of psychoanalytic methodology and, more recently, its techniques. There has been discussion of whether the 'method' (= techniques) can be extended to diagnosis and therapy: many authors have relativized the metatheory and – albeit so far only implicitly – have put the accent, in linking psychoanalysis and social science, on the discovery potential of psychoanalytic techniques. What they see as important are the uninhibited concentration, work with the setting (Morgenthaler 1978) in which encounters take place, and transference. Winnicott (1997) developed the concept of the *'Übergangsraum'* (= 'transitional space') and thereby opened up to psychoanalytic technique a dimension for the unspeakable, the not-yet-language-capable, in the process of individuation and symbol formation; and Bion, in his book *Learning from Experience* (1962), formulated the conditions which the analyst (as enquirer/researcher) must set him/herself to be able to provide a 'container' for the sensations and experiences that cannot yet be understood in the relationship. Roy Schafer (1981) criticized the historic fixedness and bareness of metatheoretical concepts as opposed to the mobility and context-relatedness of psychoanalytical technique as an interpretative process. Or else there is argument as to whether psychoanalysis and the social sciences can be unified at all (Reiche 1995). The scientific application of psychoanalytic techniques – the principle of transference to objects, texts and works of art, the analysis of the unfamiliar structures that reside in cultural products – began with Lorenzer (1981b; see **5.20**). It was continued by Leithäuser and Volmerg (1988) and extended to groups and questions of social psychology (Keupp 1994; Menschik-Bendele and Ottomeyer 1998). Leuzinger (1998) supports the 'packaging' of quantifiable methods with psychoanalytic procedures in psychological research. These methodological links are very similar to the strategies of ethno-psychoanalysis.

At present psychoanalysts who have accumulated experience with migrants are moving in a practice-related ethno-psychoanalytic or ethno-psychiatric direction. Techniques and settings are being developed to accommodate the multiple cultural and often unspeakably traumatic experience of refugees and migrants that will make possible a continuous shared observation of its significance (Bazzi 1996; Möhring and Apsel 1995; Moro 1994, 1998; Nathan 1988, 1995; Ottomeyer 1997; Pedrina 1999; Peltzer 1995). An impressive collection of innovative psychoanalytical and ethnological concepts is to be found in the book *Überlebenskunst in Übergangswelten* [The Art of Survival in Worlds in Transition] (Ninck Gbeassor 1999).

The convergence between the social sciences and ethno-psychoanalysis began with the so-called postmodernist change of epistemological paradigms in philosophy (e.g Kuhn 1970; Lyotard 1993; Toulmin 1990), which questioned the dualist and objectivist concepts of science and opened the way to dynamic, process-based and relational concepts. The social and literary-critical awareness of the problems of generalizing statements and classifications and of the context-relatedness of every discovery was sharpened; the status of qualitative social research was greatly enhanced (cf. Flick 2002). In the context of the debate on 'writing culture' that was carried out in ethnology and cultural sciences it was equally a question of the relativity of ethnographic work, and the fact that ethnologists are only ever able to describe a relationship – the relationship between the researcher, with his/her own provenance, and the alien environment. In the post-colonial crisis in ethnology it was realized that a consequence of a de-territorialized, globalized and interlocking world was a change in the theory and practice of the science. (e.g. Berg and Fuchs 1993; Hall 1994, 1997; Hannerz 1992, 1995; Kuper 1973; and others). Examples of this are the breakdown of the traditional territorial and unified concept of culture in favour of a process-based concept, or the move to analysing the construction of discourses from a variety of perspectives and in a range of contexts rather than 'realities'.

This may be summed up in the following key-words: abandoning the requirement for objectivity, premature generalizations and categorizations; a more dynamic basic concept of culture and ethnicity, and of the essentialist concept is of sex and gender; a critique of dualist thinking that divided up the world in terms of binary oppositions; acceptance of the context-relatedness of every scientific statement; upgrading of qualitative research and the methodological principle of dialogic practice (Dammann 1991), story-telling (Abu Lughod 1991, 1993), thick description and self-reflection (Geertz, 1972, 1973a; Clifford and Marcus 1986; Clifford 1986a,b, 1988a; see **3.3**).

With the post-structuralist paradigm shift, certain principles gained weight in ethnology, literary and cultural studies that ethno-psychoanalytic methodology had already developed and differentiated long before. The methodological viewpoints and the technical tools that other disciplines have benefited from had been developed in psychoanalysis or ethno-psychoanalysis in a process lasting some 10 years. Among these are:

- Predominantly qualitative work in which the representation of case histories and 'story-telling' play an important role.
- Transparency of the research relationship by means of the reflection of transference phenomena and the context-relatedness of relationships.
- Interpretation of situation-specific, subjective or emotional materials, i.e. contextualization and specification instead of categorization.
- Consideration of sequences, i.e. research and research-relationship are seen as processes.

With the increasing concentration on the structure of the discovery process and on transparency of method, so that it can accommodate complexity of culture, a congenial kind of relationship has developed between post-structuralist social science, post-colonial ethnology, and ethno-psychoanalysis and psychoanalysis, which has so far attracted little attention or discussion.

NOTES

1 This claim, that ethno-psychoanalytical research is close to post-structuralist positions on knowledge, relates in particular to its methodological procedure. But this does not exclude the possibility that in the secondary interpretation of conversational data reference may be made to essentialist cultural models, and this would again reduce or remove the process-vitality of the primary data. We are dealing here with two different levels and two different stages in the interpretation (cf. Signer 1994).

2 Apart from the necessary adjustment to the particular field situation (individual or team-research with mutual supervision), what is also important is the fact that by no means all researchers have

training in psychoanalysis or experience of the psychoanalytic approach to perception, or of its methodology. What will be of decisive value for the further development of ethno-psychoanalysis as method and practice will be how training in this discipline can be improved. It is very demanding: ethnological and psychoanalytical competence need to be linked together. Ethnologists rarely have any psychoanalytical competence and psychoanalysts are rarely competent in ethnology. It is in the interest of all three disciplines that there should be intensive work to solve this problem.

In this chapter ethno-psychoanalytical works are mentioned which (1) see themselves as such in their own estimation, or (2) locate themselves in the tradition of the debate between psychoanalysis and ethnology; and (3) which show the most fully developed application that could really be called ethno-psychoanalysis and makes use of the techniques of psychoanalysis (first found in Parin, Parin-Matthèy and Morgenthaler).

FURTHER READING

Boyer, L. B. and Grolnik, S. A. (eds) (1988) *Essays in Honor of George Devereux* (The Psychoanalytic Study of Society, Volume 12). Hillsdale, NJ: The Analytic Press.

Boyer, L. B. and Grolnick, S. A. (eds) (1989) *Essays in Honor of Paul Parin* (The Psychoanalytic Study of Society, Volume 14). Hillsdale, NJ: The Analytic Press.

Parin, P. (1980) *Fear the Neighbour as Thyself: Psychoanalysis and Society among the Anyi of West Africa*. Chicago: University of Chicago Press.

2.6 Clifford Geertz

Stephan Wolff

'Thick Description' is the most literate theater in town! Organizational Mission: ... For us theater is our thick description of the world around us. Target audience: 'crossover audience'. (From the website of the theatre with the same name in San Francisco)

Coming to understand qualitative research by contrasting different research styles is a particularly good description of Clifford Geertz's understanding of science. What is fascinating about his work is not the originality of the methods that he used in his fieldwork in Java, Bali and Morocco, but his *research attitude* that finds expression in this work. It is manifest in a specific way of writing up and describing ethnological facts that he calls 'thick description'. In work on and with descriptions Geertz sees the decisive options for interpretative work in ethnology, a thought that was taken up with great interest by a range of social sciences and humanities.

1 CLIFFORD GEERTZ AND HIS SCIENTIFIC BACKGROUND

Geertz (b. 1923) first studied English literature and philosophy and only turned to anthropology after his BA. He carried out his graduate studies in the Department of Social Relations at Harvard (PhD 1956), which was then completely under the influence of Talcott Parsons's attempts at interdisciplinary integration. Geertz himself emphasizes the enormous influence that Parsons had on him – not least because he introduced him to Weber and Durkheim. Other colleagues who impressed him at this time were Allport, Bruner, Kluckhohn, Krech and Murray.

A legacy of this time – despite all later emphasis on the aspect of action – consists of a clear preference for a systematic rather than a person-centred approach. Geertz adopted from Kroeber and Parsons (1958) the definitive thesis they put forward of a dichotomy between culture and society. This held that *culture* relates to values, ideas and symbols and relates to social interaction only through them. As with Weber, Durkheim and Parsons, Geertz's individuals remain collective and anonymous. With him there is always in the foreground the question of how culture directs and determines actions, rather than how members of society actively, and on their own initiative, integrate cultural forms of expression into meaningful patterns of experience or apply them for practical goals. Geertz also follows Parsons in saying that he views culture as holding a position equal to, or perhaps higher than or even superordinate to, other social function-systems.

At the beginning of the 1970s Geertz formulated his research position in three programmatic articles (1972, 1973b, 1984b) that have become ethnological 'classics'. These works gave an essential impulse to the shift in the focus of interest in (not only) his discipline towards interpretative approaches (Ortner 1984). They resulted in Geertz becoming probably the most frequently quoted ethnologist of modern times. This popularity is admittedly often associated with simplifications and misunderstandings. *Problematic attempts at reception* are, for example, those which try to do one of the following with the 'thick description' form of representation that Geertz developed:

- to reduce it to a *research technique* and fit it into the normal arsenal of methods;
- to monopolize it as a *patent recipe* for a number of quite different disciplines; or
- to *trivialize* it by equating and confusing it with providing detail and colourful descriptions.

Moreover, such questionable tendencies have not ceased, because Geertz has normally left both opponents and supporters to their own devices in their attempts at reconstruction. As a result of this he has become not only an object of reverent admiration but also a popular target for some very varied types of criticism. Some attack him as an 'anything-goes-relativist' who has gambled carelessly with the status of ethnology as an objective discipline, while others attack him as a latent but therefore all the more stubborn realist. Geertz, who, in the 1970s and 1980s represented the ethnographic avant-garde, is today seen almost as a conservative by many of his postmodernist followers. Even among his opponents there was hardly one who would dispute his contribution to moving ethnology from an exotic and highly specialized marginal position to the centre of intellectual debate. Almost no one can escape his influence, and not only in his own discipline; as head of the School of Science, Institute of Advanced Studies in Princeton he also occupies one of the most prominent positions of leadership in the field of international scholarship.

2 THE DEVELOPMENT OF THE RESEARCH PROGRAMME

The basis for his views on *ethnological understanding* is the thesis that after empathy, naïve realism and other supposedly immediate access points to the problem or to reality have been discredited, the problem of conceptualizing the 'native's point of view' in some new way has to be formulated and solved. As Geertz tries to argue in a series of critical commentaries of other prominent ethnological theories (cf. Geertz 1988), this problem cannot be naturalistically glossed over nor psychoanalytically evaded; it cannot be solved by structuralism nor materially trivialized. The job of ethnologists is rather to grasp the *meaning* of social events and to do this on the basis of the *observation of simple actions*. But a detailed observation would, in itself, not yield a meaningful picture of a situation. Instead, it is necessary to unravel the multiple layers of local meanings, in order to arrive at a comprehensive and insightful picture of the social circumstances under investigation.

Geertz never tired of pointing out that an ethnological analysis that can achieve this is a particular *form of knowledge* and not a question of methods or methodology. What really distinguishes the enterprise is a particular mental effort, a complicated act of intellectual daring. To characterize the risky effort, he used the distinction proposed by Gilbert Ryle (1971) between a *'thin'* and a *'thick'* description of a fact. This difference may be clarified with Ryle's own example of describing the winking of two boys in the presence of a third: winking is described 'thinly' if it is reduced to noting a rapid movement of the eyelids. Conversely a 'thick description' of this specific winking may amount to stating that the winker was only pretending to wink to make an uninitiated third party believe that there was some kind of secret agreement.

The 'thickness' of a description is apparently not confined to its wealth of detail or its credibility. It should relate to the conceptual system of what is being investigated ('emic analysis'). Thick descriptions are, in the first place, our (re-)constructions of what the participants construct at the time. Producing them is therefore like the task of an arts critic who has to comment on a performance or interpret a painting. The fact that, precisely for scientific reasons, a procedure of this nature is not only required but also realizable is – in Geertz's opinion – entirely consistent with his *understanding of culture*:

> The concept of culture I espouse ... is essentially a semiotic one. Believing, with Max Weber, that man is an animal suspended in webs of significance he himself has spun, I take culture to be

those webs, and the analysis of it to be therefore not an experimental science in search of law but an interpretative one in search of meaning. It is explication I am after, construing social expressions on their surface enigmatical. (1973b: 5)

Geertz conceives of cultures as systems of symbolic forms. In so far as social action consists of the constant interchange of significant symbols, these symbols are at the same time both the *product* and the *medium* of processes of social action and comprehension (see **3.3**). On the one hand they impart decisive information about life in the particular social setting – *world-view* – and, on the other, indicators as to how a member should live, feel and act there – *ethos*. Together with the meanings with which they are bound up, they form part of a cultural totality of relationships whose components are bound together and refer to each other.

The 'closeness' of this binding can, of course, vary. Geertz (1980) describes an extreme example of coherence in the Balinese Theatre-State of the nineteenth century, where he finds correspondences between the arrangement of major state rituals, the layout of the buildings in the ruler's palace, the geography of Balinese principalities, the relative importance of different status groups and their historical changes, the structure of foreign trade dealings and the settings of dates for the irrigation of fields. In this way the Balinese state is crystallized as a gigantic multidimensional work of art in which all the available levels of signs point to the example of the centre.

3 ELEMENTS OF ETHNOLOGICAL UNDERSTANDING

Ethnological understanding follows a *specific thought movement*: Geertz talks of a constant fluctuation between locally specific details and surrounding structures, of a progressive spiral of general observations and detailed commentaries (1984b: 134). Culture presents itself to its ethnological observers as a publicly performed and, in that sense, *readable* document. They produce different and, if possible, more profound and complex interpretations of these 'performances' (for example, of their interpretations by the members of the culture being investigated) than are available to these members themselves.

Geertz's procedure differs from that of other disciplines concerned with culture (such as

sociology, folklore, literary criticism, history) and from other orientations (such as classical ethnography or phenomenology) in its specific form of ethnographic representation: by its *thick description*. Its special quality consists of its *microscopic* approach, which implies that it concentrates on individual, comparatively small social phenomena.[1] Geertz seeks to isolate those symbolic elements of a culture that express in exemplary fashion the basic modes of experience and orientation of that culture: in his own words this is a process that can scarcely be planned, and which is highly dependent on chance but also on disciplined intuition (cf. Ostrow 1990: 67). Geertz reads these central symbols as 'metasocial comments' on the particular culture.

As a rule these are elaborated situational constellations or rituals (like cock-fights and burial ceremonies in Bali, Javanese neighbourhood festivals or Moroccan markets). But these may also be different terms and their respective semantic fields, such as the concepts of justice in the Malay, Islamic or Hindu cultural circles (Geertz 1966), or even particular paradigmatic persons who are introduced and used as metaphors for a particular culture. (In these cases, for the special kind of spirituality of Islam in Java or Morocco; Geertz 1968.)

The basis and the *first step* for a thick description is a brief portrayal of what happened as it appeared immediately to the observers of the occurrences involved. Geertz begins with the native's understanding of reality (for instance, by using terms for its portrayal that are as close as possible to the experience), but in his subsequent analysis he goes significantly beyond this. Interpretation, in his words, 'consists in trying to rescue the "said" of … discourse from its perishing occasions and fix it in pursuable terms' (Geertz 1973b: 20). In view of the situational contingencies of social action the task of the ethnologist is 'like trying to read … a manuscript – foreign, faded, full of ellipses, incoherences, suspicious emendations, and tendentious commentaries, but written not in conventionalized graphs of sound but in transient examples of shaped behavior' (Geertz 1973b: 10).

Geertz seeks this key to the 'said' not in any causes, conditions or correlations with other variables external to the phenomenon itself but in or by means of the description of the phenomenon. For this purpose he demonstrates, in a *second step*, the *other* descriptions which lie beyond the level of the obvious or which can be additionally developed on the basis of field observations and other knowledge of the culture in question or analogous phenomena in other cultures. In this way, a large number of quite different interpretative documents are accumulated which can allow the particular phenomenon to become transparent from a series of different perspectives. For this assembling of levels of meaning there is no cut-off point: thick description remains *open-ended in principle*.

Geertz notes that the research must leap from one meaning-level to another in order to unify the different representations in a single fabric and again to be able to recognize and make transparent a conceptual pattern in this. The result of this interpretation should then be applied interpretatively to the components to produce, ultimately, a completely new *reading* of the original text. A description gains in 'thickness' to the extent to which the different levels of representation link together and complement one another from an interpretative point of view. 'Thickness' must not be confused with inductive generalization, triangulation or even logical conclusion. The levels of description are not in a derivative relationship with each other but in a relationship of *juxtaposition*. This means that two or more areas of cultural meaning or levels of description can be juxtaposed in text and argument in such a way that they can be simultaneously linked and contrasted with each other. The elaborate nature of these juxtapositions becomes clear when Geertz, to give his readers a feeling for the particular form of the cultural organization of person-awareness in Bali, combines personal names, patronymics, kinship titles, technonyms, status titles and public titles. In a further step he then projects on to these the Balinese concepts of time as these are manifest in the different calendar systems in use there or in an interplay between them. In this way the text gives the impression that the different modes of symbolic structuring of experience in Bali interlock in complex ways, repeat themselves and mutually strengthen one another. On all these social 'stages' and meaning levels the same drama is constantly being performed – namely, the ethos of Balinese culture.

If we are to capture the significance of social forms of expression, the data obtained in interviews and on-the-spot observation will not be sufficient. The ethnologist must become personally active, must read these meanings, possibly supported by the interpretations of 'natives', against the background of prior knowledge, and must in this way *attribute meaning* to them. In this sense thick descriptions inevitably represent fictions ('something produced') for which the ethnologist must accept responsibility – without ultimately being able to appeal to some base of incontrovertible fact. This affects *all* the interpretations made by ethnologists in the light of theoretical assumptions, and these assumptions influence the process of ethnological discovery down to the level of direct experience. Although *key symbols* (Ortner 1972) or *total social facts* (in the sense of Marcel Mauss) seem particularly suited to Geertz's kind of description, it is in fact only the 'thickness' of an ethnographic description that gives objects their 'depth'.

The mode of representation in interpretative ethnology is, however, not limited to thick descriptions. The *third step* consists of drawing analytically substantial conclusions from individual thickly described objects. To create a deeper 'reading' of a cultural phenomenon it is necessary to add its *theoretical specification*. This specification, in the context of the interpretative procedure, corresponds to what classical approaches called 'explanation'. Here it is a matter of establishing what knowledge acquired in this way has to tell us about the *specific* society in which it was obtained. What is also interesting is what may be concluded in respect of answering *more general* questions of social theory that are completely independent of the particular research topic.

These were to be the themes of a collection of essays published in 1983: the figurative nature of social theory, the reciprocal moral effect of contrasting mentalities, the practical difficulties in attempting to see facts as others see them, the epistemological status of common sense, the revealing power of art, the symbolic construction of authority, 'the clattering variousness of modern intellectual life and the relationship between what people take as a fact and what they regard as justice' (cf. Geertz 1983c: 5).

In this way such different 'art-forms' as Balinese cock-fighting, *King Lear* and *Crime and Punishment* may profitably be related to one another: namely, in so far as, in their different ways, they thematize existential challenges – and here Geertz lists death, masculinity, anger, pride, loss, mercy and happiness – and examine their implications. Unlike the traditional understanding, specifications do not aim at the formation of ethnological theories or the testing of hypotheses. On the contrary, for Geertz it is rather a question of ethnographically informed reflection on themes of *more general intellectual significance*. He attempts to make a virtue out of the proverbial provinciality of ethnographers, who have only 'their' respective culture in view. By bringing together, in a state of dynamic tension, the various 'local knowledges' that are accessible to him through his fieldwork, he allows the reader to conceive of a bridging *discourse community between cultures*. Geertz thereby locates the real ethnological object neither in the events that were observed in some remote villages, nor in thick descriptions of these, but, as it were, *between* these two. In essence he is interested in *understanding culture as a whole* using the contrastive description of local cultures.

4 RESULTS AND CRITICISMS OF GEERTZ'S PROGRAMME

Geertz has had many admirers but almost no disciples or followers (Ortner 1997). While Geertz is still in vogue in the humanities and cultural studies, his influence within his own discipline has clearly diminished. This can only be explained to a limited extent by the fact that his empirical claims have met with increasingly critical questioning (e.g. Wikan 1990). What seem to be more important are the following two considerations.

1 The 'interpretative turn' has turned increasingly against itself and this has led to a sometimes crippling and self-centred concentration on and preoccupation with epistemological and political questions of ethnographic representation. (Geertz himself wrote the first ironically critical commentary along these lines in 1988.)

2 As a consequence of *scientific developments* inside and outside of ethnology (such as those in cognitive anthropology, cultural sociology, discursive psychology or ethnomethodology), but also as a result of *changes in world politics* (where the global village increasingly seems to be a 'world in pieces' looking for some order in its differences), the question of an adequate understanding of culture has become distinctly more complex.

Today culture must clearly be conceptualized, located and investigated in *different ways*:

- as fragmented between different groups but also as a construct that is inconsistent in its manifestations: as a subject of disagreement between meaning-relations in regional, social and ideological border-areas;
- as a public performance with its own textual coherence, but one that is constantly being produced and reinterpreted *in situ*;
- as a fragile and continuously developing network of meanings which the most diverse actors join, sometimes in competition with each other;
- as a tool-kit that members of society (can) use to shape and interpret social action *in situ* and with regard to their practical goals (cf. Ortner 1997).

All of this, however, would require a withdrawal not only from the *culture-as-variable* view (which Geertz has done) but also, partly, from the *culture-as-context* view (which he avoids), and above all a fuller consideration of the aspect of *cultural practice*. It is precisely this point that most critical commentaries of Geertz's research programme have attacked.

On the one hand he is accused of *disregarding the level of the 'native'*. Because he regards all attempts to participate in indigenous discourse as predestined to failure, Geertz prefers to adopt the position of a *distant and distinguished observer*. It is not only that his texts contain practically no first-order interpretations: there are almost no second-order interpretations of the sort that observe the observations of natives. As an ethnographer he conducts a kind of 'monologic discourse'. By the elimination of concrete discovery conditions and, in particular, all communicative and interactive instances, the 'native's' view is largely excluded from the ethnographic text. Crapanzano (1986) criticizes the handicap that results from this: it leads to an aura of arbitrariness that diminishes what is convincing in his portrayals and stimulates doubts about the basis of his data. Moerman (1988) complains that Geertz's interpretations are almost totally independent of what the subjects of his investigations actually said and did. Although Geertz argues for the microscopic nature of thick descriptions and a notion of culture that is both scenic and based on action theory, he does not look for culture in communicative action but primarily in words, symbols and rituals. And so Geertz stops at the gateway to interaction. In methodological terms this leads to a one-sided concentration on 'fine data' and 'interesting cases': in other words, to a problematic devaluation of the analytic scope of 'thin' descriptions and of the cultural content-value or methodological usefulness of social phenomena that are presumed to be less 'profound' (cf. Sacks 1992 for an example of an opposing view).

On the other hand, Geertz's preference for setting up elaborate relationships between various meaning levels, or between what is there and how it is there, has led to accusations of *relativism* (cf. Shankman 1984). This is unjustified in so far as Geertz looks upon relativism primarily as a methodological strategy and does not therefore see it in the same way as critics of relativism, as an epistemological position. Even if he might therefore be considered rather as an *anti anti-relativist* (cf. Geertz 1984a), his pluralism, his predilection for cultural differences, contrasts, conflicts and nuances, are nevertheless very strongly characteristic of his work. Unlike most of his colleagues, he compares not only what is there with how it is there, but even different cultures with each other. Taken together with the reflexivity he emphasizes, this sometimes leads him to an ironic and coquettish nonchalance about the standards of empirical work (e.g. Geertz 1995: 17f.).

What is daring but also fascinating about this way of presenting ethnographic information is that when we read it, the borders between here and there, between reality and imagination, between science and poetry begin – if not to disappear – at least to become blurred. A feeling of ambivalence grows in the reader: is what Geertz states really a reconstruction of the meaning that this kind of social action has for the native, or is it only what Geertz induces or reads into it? For the claims that he makes, an empirical foundation is signalled as given ('ethnographically informed'). But Geertz is notorious for omitting more detailed indicators about their justification or even justifiability according to normal scientific criteria. If, as Greenblatt (1997) supposes, the 'seductive power' (Roseberry 1982) of Geertz's work for non-ethnologists lies mainly in the fact that, apart from their literary-aesthetic qualities, they promise 'contact with the factual', then this *quasi-referential style* of Geertz's represents a variant of 'genre blurring' (Geertz 1983a) that is not without danger: what is gained in imagination could easily be offset by a loss of confidence in the 'empirical foundation'.

Geertz sees himself as a master of 'unabsolute truths' (Berreby 1995), as one who provides curative irritations and prevents us from finding easy answers: a highly potent medicine, and not a household remedy for the everyday work of qualitative research.

NOTE

1 Microscopic does not mean *microanalytical*. Microanalytical approaches (such as context analysis, ethnography of communication or conversation analysis) are concerned with how *everyday processes of interaction are organized*, whereas for Geertz it is important to explore the meaning content of a small section of culture. He aims not at more exact viewing (such as that obtained with video recordings) but at more profound interpretations.

FURTHER READING

Geertz, C. (2000) *Available Light. Anthropological Reflexions on Philosophical Topics.* Princeton, NJ: Princeton University Press.

Inglies, F. (2000) *Clifford Geertz. Culture, Custom and Ethics.* Cambridge: Polity Press.

Ostrow, J. M. (1990) 'The Availability of Difference: Clifford Geertz on Problems of Ethnographic Research and Interpretation', *Qualitative Studies in Education*, 3: 61–69.

2.7   Norman K. Denzin: Life in Transit

Yvonna S. Lincoln

1 INTRODUCTION

Perhaps no one has made such profound shifts, or contributed to as many genres – or to the blurring of so many genres – as Norman K. Denzin. In the course of his career, he has embraced two major courses of intellectual action: the ongoing exploration of sociology in everyday life, particularly the cinema's role in shaping contemporary culture (see **5.7**), and the shaping of interpretive method and paradigm for the social sciences. Each of those intellectual 'transits' crosses disciplines, sociological traditions and methodology in the social sciences conceived broadly.

Although it is nearly impossible to sort out the transformations that characterize Denzin's methodological shifts (from classical symbolic interactionist perspectives to postmodern narratives and performance texts) from the disciplinary boundaries he has crossed, some idea of the matrices that intersect in his work will help to sort the evolutionary stages in his thinking. It would be wrong to suggest, however, nor should the reader infer, that Denzin has left behind symbolic interactionist work. Quite the opposite. Influenced heavily by both Blumer and the Chicago School of symbolic interactionism (see **3.3**), he still anchors much of his writing in the search for codes and cultural symbols that act beyond the propositional level to shape communication and meaning in contemporary American life. He still grounds method, writing and narrative practices in 'theor[ies] of the social' (1996b), and consequently, theories of the social and linguistic codes and symbols which both mark and create culture. Indeed, one of the most stable themes of his writing has been the attempt to merge or find important overlaps between symbolic interactionism and other methods, perspectives and currents of thought (cf. interactionism and ethnomethodology 1969; the sociology of emotion and interactionism 1983; semiotics and interactionism 1987; interactionism and cultural studies 1992; and interactionism and the postmodern impulse 1989b). In trying to make the connections between interactionism and other traditions and methods, Denzin has drawn on a variety of disciplines, artifacts (primarily contemporary cinema), material practices (primarily ethnography as a written product of research on social life), and social critiques (Baudrillard, Foucault, Deleuze and Derrida, among others). And even though he crosses and re-crosses borders and boundaries, like the Buddhist in the epigram, he never steps into the same stream twice.

Consequently, 'sorting', as I shall shortly do, is at once a technique to simplify a rich and prolific intellectual life and a complex body of work, and at the same time, a shorthand, and accordingly misleading, way of dealing with the intricate interrelationships between intellectual influences which mark his work. The reader is cautioned to read the subsequent sections as they were intended: for flavor, for some notion of the profound activity of this work, for the 'length and the breadth and the sweep' of thought.

2 THE TRANSIT OF DISCIPLINES: BLURRING GENRES

Clifford Geertz (1983) may have prophesied its coming, but he could not himself blur genres as well as Norman K. Denzin. In the course of some 30 years or more, Denzin has traversed the social sciences – including sociology and anthropology (1971, 1989a, 1990a); the old film and cinema studies and the new film criticism (1986, 1988, 1991b, 1992a, 1993); deviance in social life; alcohol – its social organization, personal destruction and the associated 'industries' and social organizations of recovery (1977); fiction, ethnographic fiction and ethnopoetics (1997); children and families (1985b, 1997); the phenomenology of emotion (1983, 1985a); sex and sexuality in the postmodern era (1985b); *cultural studies* (1991b, 1992, 1997); and method in the social sciences (1971, 1979; Denzin and Lincoln 1994b, 2000).

In a more general sense, the blurring of genres refers to the crossing over between disciplines, borrowing intellectual traditions and illuminative insights from one discipline which might inform the study of another. It also means, in a much narrower sense, the disappearance of strict and rigid boundaries between academic disciplines, and even the eventual collapse of such disciplinary boundaries. Blurring also refers to the creation of new disciplines, for example *cultural studies* (see **2.4**, **3.9**) or communications studies, which are hybrids of intellectual concerns and issues, frequently with borrowed, appropriated, adapted, and *bricoleur-*style methods crafted on the spot for particular analytic tasks.

In seeking, proposing and explicating crossover intellectual concerns, Denzin has provided the intellectual ammunition for young scholars (and those wishing to open new intellectual avenues of study for themselves and others) by demonstrating how it might be done. His most important call for crossover method was probably the *Handbook of Qualitative Research*, which we edited together (Denzin and Lincoln, 1st edition 1994b). In this work, Denzin explicitly calls for qualitative researchers in dozens of disciplines to abandon the project of assigning to any given discipline the rights to any method, philosophy, or analytic strategy, and instead to become *bricoleurs* – jacks-of-all-trades willing to confiscate methods and materials as each was deemed useful, constructive or profitable. 'Traditions' developed within specific academic disciplines were no longer to be considered the property of those disciplines, but rather tools, scraps and raw material from which might be constructed new methods, new analytic strategies, and new understandings of social life. 'Traditions' passed into methodological 'bone-yards', where pieces and structures might be reassembled into more serviceable objects, even while the parts and pieces might be recognizable to other handymen, generalists, or specialists.

In abandoning strict adherence to method, Denzin concomitantly not only proposed movement across the social sciences, he projected (with others) a movement away from the sciences *qua* science, and a blurring of the boundaries between the human sciences and the arts, fiction, poetry, oral traditions such as storytelling, film and performance texts. Like others in cultural studies (see **2.4**, **3.9**), Denzin specifically proposed that virtually any material project – whether art, film, television, advertisements, newspapers, or other media forms – become the subject of study in the modern West. His project is not to create an abstruse body of sociological knowledge; rather it is to create 'ethnograph[ies] which refuse abstractions and high theory' (Denzin 1999), to 'return to narrative as a political act' (1999), and to provide the means to create understanding, empathy and solidarity.

Central to this review is the question of to which fields, subjects and methods Denzin turned his fertile intellect and productive analyses, but additionally, how did he move from 'there' – the beginning of his career – to where his work points today? Are there hallmarks of the transit through intellectual stages and periods? Is it possible, as it might be with Picasso, for instance, to see 'periods', sequences, influences, initiations, closures, in this work? Although a work this brief cannot possibly trace the elements of influence, the books, films, articles and personal introspections that led to where his work is today, some sense of the history of these ideas can be gleaned from a few representative works. It is to that set of transitions I wish to turn now.

3 THE TRANSITION THROUGH METHOD: FROM CLASSICAL SOCIOLOGY TO POSTMODERN PERFORMANCE

A signal shift in the passage from a solely symbolic interactionist perspective to a form of interpretivism can be found in 'The logic of naturalistic inquiry' (Denzin 1971). Many of the early ideas found in this work are repeated, with increasing elaboration and theoretical sophistication, in later works. While he labelled 'this version of the research act *naturalistic behaviorism*', terminology that he would later abandon, nevertheless he begins to create an image of the sociologist's new work and new role. He argues that

> Naturalistic behaviorism places the sociological observer squarely in the center of the research act. It recognizes the observer for what he or she is and takes note of the fact that all sociological work somehow reflects the unique stance of the observer .... The naturalistic behaviorist thus stands over and against the broader sociological community and takes himself or herself seriously. (1971: 167)

In these three sentences, Denzin set the stage for later enrichment and refinement of his ideas concerning the centrality of the researcher in the research and later, writing processes; the pivotal role of a standpoint epistemology; and the role of the sociologist as social critic, advocate, public intellectual and constructor of compelling social images.

It is clear, however, that even as this work foreshadows many of the larger concerns that will occupy centre stage today, he is still grounded in the contemporary sociological norms of the early 1970s. His 'programmatic statement' of what it will take for symbolic interactionists and other sociologists to make their cases persuasive includes, for instance, assessment of the naturalistic 'indicators by the usual canons of reliability, repeatability, and validity' (1971: 167), generalizability (p. 174) and causal analyses (p. 179). Yet even while he suggests for the naturalistic behaviourist the canons of scientific method as a route to scientific respectability, he begins the process of loosening the bonds of that same scientific method. He begins with Garfinkel's dictum of language as a social production (see **2.3, 3.2**); he greatly extends this idea, however, by arguing that the

self is a 'a social production', and that objects and sites provide interactional stimuli and the 'behavioral locus of all joint acts' (p. 172). Consequently, the self is constantly being defined by the language it chooses to use, the 'others' and objects with whom/which it interacts (or chooses not to interact), and the arenas in which it engages in the production of self. Later, these categories would include reflection on the researcher as a producer of one or more selves in the field.

Ruminating on Wittgenstein's ideas that 'what we cannot speak about we must pass over in silence', Denzin moved next to considering notions of time and mind (1982), transversing the distance then again between mind and emotion, emotion and feeling, feeling and the embodied self (1983, 1984, 1985a,b; Charmaz 1985). In 'On time and mind', he specifically and directly calls sociologists to 'set aside ... the tenets of logical positivism ... as the interpretive social scientist moves forward in the construction of a viable, authentic depiction of meaning and human interaction' (Denzin 1982: 43). It is here, too, that he begins a call that extends to work in press today: the plea for a social science enlarged and refurbished by cross-disciplinary and literary and artistic work.

It is a signal *pentimento* that he would, in this cry to leave behind logical positivism, look for a way to construct 'a viable, authentic depiction of meaning and human interaction' (p. 43), then, in 1990, conclude that it is not possible to 'ever get to the personal troubles and epiphanic experiences that fundamentally alter people's lives' (1990a: 2); that we risk the possibility that the 'beliefs, attitudes and experiences, like the subjects who supposedly hold them, are only cultural, textural creations ...[who] have no autonomy outside the texts we (or they) write' (p. 14). The answer, he concludes first, is in 'minimalist theoretical preconceptions' (p. 14), which 'study and write the stories of personal trouble that ordinary people tell one another. We give a voice to these people' (p. 15). But he would later propose (1996a, 1999, 2000a) an ethnography that is 'simultaneously minimal, existential, autoethnographic, vulnerable, performative and critical', a 'sociologist's tale [which] is always allegorical, a symbolic tale, a parable that is *not just a record of human experience* ... [but also] a utopian tale of redemption, a story that brings a moral compass back into the readers' (and the writer's) lives' (1996b: 748; emphases added). The dialectic is between writing stories of minimalist theoretical preoccupation, and understanding that writing itself is a political and theoretical act (cf. 2000), and that those 'who write culture also write theory' (Denzin 1997: xii). One understanding of this dialectic is the growing understanding that minimalist theoretical preoccupation may mean minimalist preoccupation with *a priori* theory, but the construction of new social theories from accounts of lived experience (inductively reasoned theories of social life). An alternative understanding of the dialectic may simply be as a reaction to the elaborate, sometimes overblown, theories of social life constructed by a generation of modernist social scientists in their attempts to create *grande theories* of social phenomena. Whatever the source of the dialectic, the ongoing ability to see and label contradictions, tensions, opposing and paradoxical elements within cultural artifacts (especially film – see, for instance, 1988; see 5.7) was to become a hallmark characteristic of Denzin's work after 1990.

In any event, the natural next step was the postmodern and deconstructive turns. In two review essays in the *Journal of Contemporary Ethnography*, scarcely one year apart, Denzin makes the case for an emerging postmodern ethnography. In 1989, he argues that

> My thesis is simple. Contemporary sociological ethnography must embrace the postmodern impulse in anthropology. It must let go of its pre-occupation with scientific method, qualitative data collection and analysis, writing about writing ethnography, the search for generic principles of social life, and the problems of institutionalized journals. It must become seriously existential. (1989a: 89)

In 1990, he again defined what he believed to be the central point of ethnographic work:

> Written with a minimum of theory, interpretive ethnography erases the conventional boundaries between an objective observer and the worlds he or she has studied. Inscribed in the first person, these accounts use the researcher as a window into the worlds entered. The writer becomes the subject of the text. In such works traditional ethnographic problems fall by the wayside, including reliability, validity, theoretical constructs, distinctions between fact and fiction, and the judgment, or evaluation of experiences … in terms of Western categories of reason, logic, and science. (1990b: 231)

These two works represent a shift in Denzin's thinking which will characterize all the works to follow, including the *Handbook of Qualitative Research*, (Denzin and Lincoln 1994b), and the second edition of the same volume (2000).

Comprehension of what this postmodern moment means is accomplished via the analytic technique of Derridan deconstructive reading, a form of close textual analysis which 'examines how a text creates its own sense of logic, order and presence … [and] examines how a text creates its particular images of society, culture, the other, the subject, structures, and their centers, oppositions, hierarchies, order, rationality and reason' (Denzin 1991b: 35).

Undertaking deconstruction on cultural texts (particularly film) permits an analysis of what is normally 'hidden' from the reader: rhetorical structures that support or deny racism, sexism, classism, or other oppressive structures, forms of control, and cultural hierarchies. Engaging in deconstructive practices (and reading others who do so also) engages the reader in cultural critique and examination of the assumptions undergirding Western, colonial and modernist ideas.

Such deconstructive intellectual activities have led, finally, to the space Denzin occupies today: where he views the possibilities of 'qualitative research and interpretive ethnography as forms of radical democratic practice' (Denzin 2000). No longer is qualitative method merely a set of tools of choice for interpretive practices. Rather, qualitative methods are the framework for enacting a new sociology and a new social science, one which will provide the 'way to undo traditional sociology' (1996b). In a re-imagined sociology, the old epistemologies and axiologies have given way to a new, 'postpragmatist, feminist, communitarian, moral ethic', one possibility of which is 'changing the world' (Denzin 2000). The new social science texts are connected, in Denzin's mind, with what he labels an 'intimate, civic journalism' (2000: 899), performance ethnography, critical race and ethnic studies, and the humanities (see 2000).

A social science for the new millennium will be 'an existential, interpretive ethnography, an ethnography that offers a blueprint for cultural criticism' (Denzin 2000), following Marcus and Fischer's (1986) advocacy for a social science that provides not only cultural description, but also *cultural critique*. Quietly, but with great urgency, Denzin now seeks a future that embodies both a criticism of the 'critical elements of the cultural logics of late capitalism' (1991: 408), and a loving and respectful 'politics of hope' (2000). It is an enriched standpoint from which to seek and see the possibilities for qualitative research and ethnographic writing (see **5.22**).

FURTHER READING

Denzin, N. K. (1989) *Interpretive Interactionism* (Applied Social Research Methods series, Vol. 16). Thousand Oaks, CA: Sage.

Denzin, N. K. (1989) *The Research Act: A Theoretical Introduction to Sociological Methods*, 3rd edn. Englewood Cliffs, NJ: Prentice Hall.

Denzin, N. K. (1997) *Interpretive Ethnography: Ethnographic Practices for the 21st Century*. Thousand Oaks, CA: Sage.

2.8 Marie Jahoda

Christian Fleck

There exist at least two ways of contributing to the development of social research: (1) someone writes programmatic statements and provides methodological considerations about how research should be done appropriately or (2) someone does research, seldom explaining how, why and whose footsteps he or she is following. Marie Jahoda belongs to the second camp. Saying this does not imply that she was unaware of methodological problems, but Jahoda always was convinced that enlarging our knowledge about the social life is more important than debating the fine-graining of procedures and techniques. One could call this attitude instrumentalistic. In Jahoda's case this approach came to life very early in her career, and is rooted in the social, political and scholarly micro-environment in which she grew up.

1 SOCIO-CULTURAL BACKGROUND

Marie Jahoda was born in 1907 in Vienna at a time when the city, for some ten more years, was the metropolitan centre of the increasingly disintegrating Austro-Hungarian Empire of the Hapsburg dynasty. Her family was of middle class background, living there for generations. Her parents were assimilated Jews but did not dissolve their relationship to the Jewish community by converting to Christianity. Jahoda's parents did not object to higher education for her nor for her three siblings, a clear indication of a progressive parental attitude towards gender equality.

The parents' admiration both for the legendary literary critic Karl Kraus, who favoured rigorous attentiveness towards the proper use of language, and for the author of comprehensive practical utopian pamphlets, Joseph Popper-Lynkeus, a relative of the philosopher Karl Popper, was transferred to and adopted by the young Marie Jahoda. The Vienna of Jahoda's youth was also the place where psychology rose to popularity due to the fame but unobtrusive presence of Sigmund Freud and the much higher visibility of his admirers on the one hand and Alfred Adler and his devotees on the other hand. Finally, after the collapse of the old regime, the Austro-Marxists took over power in the municipality of Vienna and established there virtually a laboratory for social reform.

Marie Jahoda and her peers joined the movement and there she started her first career as an aspiring politician. Later in her life she would explain the choice of psychology as her major by saying that she had been completely sure that after the revolution she would become Minister of Education in the first Socialist government, and psychology seemed to her then the best preparation for this dream (Jahoda 1983: 345). She did not succeed with her political aspirations but at the university she familiarized herself with the tools of research. She acquired her sociological frame of reference, however, not in university courses. Jahoda never attended a sociology class and took only few in psychology; she received most of her professional education as a participant of several discussion groups in Vienna's then lively intellectual environment. Besides Austro-Marxism and academic psychology she took part in debates of reform pedagogues, school reformers and neo-positivist philosophers.

Since neither Freud nor his early-collaborator-turned-opponent Alfred Adler taught at the University of Vienna Jahoda had to study psychology under the Bühler couple. Karl Bühler, who was the only full professor there, had developed his own version of psychology before he was called to a chair at the University of Vienna. He combined insights from Gestalt with developmental psychology, creating an early version of psychology of thought and language. His wife, Charlotte, the first woman to receive a *habilitation* in psychology in Vienna and subsequently promoted to associate professor, directed a large group of PhD students. Financial support came from the Rockefeller Foundation. The students observed not only the behaviour of children in a foster clinic but, under the leadership of Charlotte Bühler, they founded a life-span-oriented theory of psychological maturation. Jahoda wrote her PhD about the biographical narratives of elderly men living in an asylum. She finished it the very year her first major contribution to social research appeared in print. *Marienthal: The Sociography of an Unemployed Community*, co-authored with Hans Zeisel and conducted under the guidance of Jahoda's first husband, Paul F. Lazarsfeld, became a classic in qualitative social research. It appeared in print in spring of 1933, the worst time for a study inspired by Marxism and written by Jews.

2   MARIENTHAL

The topic for this study (see Fleck 2002), which started in 1931, seems to be no surprise, given the fact that the Great Depression of 1929 caused mass unemployment world wide. Nevertheless, it was the leading Austro-Marxist theoretician Otto Bauer, with whom the group around Lazarsfeld met regularly, who proposed this theme instead of the one Lazarsfeld preferred. Bauer too pointed the group to the tiny workers' village some 20 kilometres outside Vienna where the only factory had closed its doors recently.

Marienthal is exemplary in three aspects: methodologically because of the combined use of a wide range of research strategies; politically because the authors detected, to their own surprise, that economic deprivation caused apathy instead of an uprising mood and finally because of the group of investigators' devotion not only to produce a sociologically interesting piece of research but to be instrumental to the people of Marienthal themselves during their stay in the field. Today one would call the last aim *action research* and the first *triangulation* (see **4.6**). Given the fact that the group of researchers was inexperienced and very young the quality of the study, a product of only some weeks of investigations, is amazing. Perhaps lack of a research tradition and the non-existence of a school-like dependence of the novices made this success possible. In *Marienthal* one finds a huge number of different research techniques, both obtrusive and unobtrusive, quantitative oriented and qualitative, and numerical as well as verbal data providing 'sociographic' information and life-cycle narratives to the point. Some of the techniques were invented on the spot: for example, when someone from the research team had the impression that men and women walked at a different pace over the village's central square, Hans Zeisel took a watch, placed himself at an apartment window and started measuring people's velocity. Together with other data this was one of the earliest contributions to the then non-existent speciality 'sociology of time'.

Not being part of a distinct scholarly tradition, the Marienthal team was free to find its own way through the field and afterwards through the data (see **5.1**). Fortunately, they succeeded in both endeavours. Before Jahoda et al. entered Marienthal for the first time they were thinking about their project in the terms, concepts and premises of their university teachers Charlotte and Karl Bühler. Since, however, this research was only loosely connected to the Bühlers, the investigators were independent enough to go beyond the frame of reference of their teachers. They abandoned some of Charlotte Bühler's follies and were looking for new keys to make sense out of their field experiences. Not being trained as social anthropologists eased their commitment to the expected length of staying in the field. (Here one should add that all members of the research team were in the field at large – the Austrian labour movement – for a much longer period of time, and therefore they did not experience the shocks of cultural newcomers.)

Politics hindered the continuation of the group's research in Austria. Because of her activities in the socialist underground movement Jahoda was imprisoned in 1936. After half a year in jail she was freed only under the condition that she left the country immediately. She moved from Vienna to London, less than a year before the Nazis took over power in Austria.

3 FIELD RESEARCH AND EXILE POLITICS

During the Second World War Jahoda lived in England, active in the exiled group of Social Democrats, as a radio broadcaster for the Foreign Office, and in refugee aid organizations. Besides these she continued her research efforts. Immediately after her arrival she started a field study in an unemployed miners' community in South Wales where she investigated a self-help scheme, proposed by Quakers. Completely on her own, she tried to use similar research procedures as in Marienthal, but also adopted techniques of field research from the social anthropologist Bronislaw Malinowksi. Jahoda spent weeks in the area, lived with the families of the unemployed miners, ate their meagre meals, and observed the behaviour of those who participated in the subsistence scheme where old-fashioned miners had to do work they thought morally inappropriate for them.

The harsh experiences of doing field research became irrelevant when Jahoda heard that the Nazis had taken over Austria. She interrupted her research to help family members and friends to get out of Austria. One of the Quakers offered her his help, and thanks to the collaborative effort all Jahoda's relatives escaped. She herself returned to her research site, finished the study and submitted a copy of her manuscript to the very man who had helped her family in the weeks before. When he declared to Jahoda that her findings would destroy his life's work she decided to bury her manuscript in her desk. This study appeared in print only decades later, and Jahoda then still

struggled with herself whether the publication might hurt some of the surviving Quakers (Jahoda 1938/1987).

During her stay in England Jahoda did some more field research, for instance when she investigated the experiences of young women during the status passage from school to work. Anthropologists usually go through a period where the deliberate unfamiliarity of the field offers them insights into the world-view of the subjects. Jahoda acted similarly during her early years in exile but did not make use of this technique afterwards. It seems that she was not inclined to follow anthropologists' textbook advice.

4 POLITICALLY RELEVANT SOCIAL RESEARCH

Near the end of the Second World War Jahoda migrated to New York, where she spent the next 12 years. Her first job was with Max Horkheimer's group of mainly European refugee scholars who started studying prejudice in America under a grant from the American Jewish Committee. Jahoda not only contributed a study of her own to the 'Studies in Prejudice' series but acted as a research assistant for the whole project. Together with a New Yorker psychoanalyst, Nathan W. Ackerman, she examined protocols of therapeutic sessions to detect anti-Semitic attitudes expressed by average clients (Ackerman and Jahoda 1950). Later on she edited, together with Richard Christie, a critical examination of the main study of the Horkheimer group, the still well-known *Authoritarian Personality* (Christie and Jahoda 1954). Theodor W. Adorno and Horkheimer were not pleased with the criticism expressed in the contributions to this volume.

Psychoanalysis played a major role in Jahoda's life and research. She herself went through a rigorous analysis with Heinz Hartmann, and later in her career she made studies of the emigration of psychoanalysis to the United States and the contribution of Freud to academic psychology (Jahoda 1977).

Jahoda left the Horkheimer group, which later became well known as the Frankfurt School of critical theory, to join the newly created Bureau of Applied Social Research at Columbia University under Lazarsfeld and Robert K. Merton, notorious for its leading role in developing and establishing mainstream quantitative methodology in social research (see Lautman and Lécuyer 1998). There she collaborated primarily with Merton in a huge study about human relations of ethnically and socially mixed residents in housing projects. In the still unpublished study she examined the differences between statistical averages and what she called 'fit'. The group of people which fits best in a community is not always the majority or the average. To identify the fitting subset one is forced to use methods other than those ordinary sample surveys offer. Identifying patterns of normative and cultural integration is possible only if the researcher looks at real inter-relations and pays less attention to statistically produced correlation (Jahoda 1961).

Two years after coming to Manhattan, Jahoda was called to a chair at New York University, where she also became director of a newly established Research Center for Human Relations, a topic then very much in vogue in different parts of the social sciences. The following decade was the most productive period of her career. She not only published a textbook on research methods but did a lot of research on different topics, mostly in collaboration with other psychologists and sociologists.

The two-volume textbook *Research Methods in Social Relations, with Especial Reference to Prejudice*, edited with her long-time affiliates Morton Deutsch and Stuart W. Cook (New York 1951, second, one-volume edition 1959), is intended to inform different types of users of social research instead of addressing academic apprentices about new procedures. This commitment foreshadows the 'public understanding of science' approach of more recent days. The textbook, one of the earliest of its kind, was widely used in undergraduate courses, reissued four times, and translated into several languages.

Jahoda later left the United States and resettled for private reasons in England, where she lived for the rest of her long life. She started there at Brunel University and was later awarded a chair in social psychology at the newly established University of Sussex. During the 1960s she did some more empirical research and later in her life she returned to her first research topic, the socio-psychological consequences of unemployment. Her main contribution to this field could be seen in her attempt to identify latent consequences of employment. Manifestly paid work contributes to the well-being of the worker; latent consequences of being employed can be seen in the fact that it 'imposes a time structure on the waking day. Secondly, employment implies regularly shared experiences and contacts with people outside the nuclear family. Thirdly, employment links an individual to goals and purposes which transcend his own. Fourthly, employment defines aspects of personal status and identity. Finally, employment enforces activity' (Jahoda 1979: 313).

Jahoda died in April 2001 at the age of 94 at her home in Sussex.

5 JAHODA'S RESEARCH STYLE

In several studies Jahoda demonstrated her own style of doing social research. As she explained later in her life, she always tried to start from real problems instead of those elaborated in university seminars or psychological laboratories (Fryer 1986). The topics of some of her articles illustrate this point of view impressively: prejudices, not only those directed against Jews, interracial and inter-ethnic relations, problems of female students adapting to the mores of a liberal arts college, and others. When the hysteria of the so-called McCarthy era reached its peak Jahoda started several investigations about the consequences of this climate for those who never were targets but feared to be implicated (Jahoda and Cook 1952). Later on she studied blacklisting in the entertainment industry. When other social scientists started downgrading their public profile, eliminating references to suspected authors, and choosing research topics according to the *zeitgeist*, Jahoda took the opposite route, using what she had learned to find out something that might help others to understand the contemporary world.

A second aspect of her style of doing social research could be seen in the complete absence of narrow-mindedness with regard to the selection of research procedures. The question under investigation directed her decision as to which research procedure might be of value and which not. Therefore she sometimes used conventional questionnaires, made use of projective tests, and invented tests of her own. Jahoda never believed in any research practice as a silver bullet. An agnostic in religious affairs, she acted similarly with regard to scholarly holy texts and routines.

Furthermore, Jahoda was never committed to defend convictions or theoretical orientations against empirical evidence. Her roots in Vienna's intellectual micro-environment where explanation and critical examination were favoured over 'school' thinking and defence of undependable claims saved her from being a member of a dogmatic sect of any conviction. In her autobiography, available only in a German translation, she remembers an episode from her early days, when she tried to defend her Marxist convictions against the facts and an exiled Hungarian Marxist made the audience laugh at her. As a corollary of this attitude she labelled most of her research papers 'explorative', 'preliminary', 'case study', etc., and did not think of herself as someone who did work that others could not achieve.

Jahoda's instrumentalistic approach with regard to research techniques offered her the advantage of using insights from several scholarly fields freely. Since she never thought of herself as a member of a narrowly defined discipline, she assembled in her work findings and concepts from psychology, psychoanalysis and sociology.

The most astonishing feature of Jahoda's work, spanning a period of nearly seven decades, can be seen in the continuities she was able to preserve. She never abandoned her basic convictions, neither those that are rooted in a scholarly ethos nor those that are more closely related to political or moral principles.

What we can learn from Jahoda's life and work is that the main obligation of social scientists lies in the explanation of hidden patterns, developments not visible to untrained observers.

There exist more than one mode of learning and those who commit themselves to a qualitative approach in the social sciences should not seek for an algorithm to solve our research problems, but perhaps make use of a more complex model, and therefore stick to basic qualitative insight. There is some agreement that one successful way of learning is by looking closely at role models. Marie Jahoda is certainly one.

FURTHER READING

For biographical and bibliographical information see: http://agso.uni-graz.at/lexikon/klassiker/jahoda/24bio.htm.

Fleck, Christian (2002) 'Introduction to the Transaction edition', in M. Jahoda, P. F. Lazarsfeld and H. Zeisel, *Marienthal: The Sociography of an Unemployed Community*. New Brunswick, NJ: Transaction Books. pp. vii–xxx.

Fryer, D. (In press) 'Marie Jahoda: Community and Applied Social Psychologist', Special Issue (guest edited by D. Fryer), *Journal of Community and Applied Social Psychology* (in press).

Jahoda, M., Lazarsfeld, P. F. and Zeisel, H. (1971) *Marienthal: The Sociology of an Unemployed Community*. Chicago: Aldine–Atherton.

Part 3

The Theory of Qualitative Research

Introduction

Qualitative research cannot be reduced to data collection and interpretation procedures, methodological principles or detailed and exotic descriptions of life-worlds. Methods and methodologies are not, for this kind of research, an end in themselves. They are based on theoretical considerations and should, in turn, serve in the formulation of theories. The precise description of life-worlds ought to contribute to a better understanding of specific cultural phenomena and forms of action, to assist in the recognition of structures and patterns of their social reproduction and their particular rationale.

A common starting point for the different individual theoretical traditions within qualitative research is the day-to-day action of members of society in differing situations and under varying cultural conditions. But what is important in the detailed descriptions of these is not a duplication or a 'portrait' of reality. It is rather that their character itself is a central theme of theoretical endeavour in qualitative research. To capture social reality in a theoretical form it is first necessary to make a reconstruction and analysis using a variety of ethnographic procedures, derived from interviews and documents. Secondly, the knowledge gained in this way has then to be incorporated into a set of general theoretical relationships – perhaps as a contribution to the basis of a constitution of sociality, a theory of social order, or a theory of culture or regional cultures.

Part 3 consists of two subsections: the first focuses on the most important background theories of qualitative research, whereas the second subsection addresses examples of qualitative research programmes with specific theoretical frameworks.

The first group of contributions includes: phenomenological life-world analysis (see **3.1**), ethnomethodology (see **3.2**) and symbolic interactionism (see **3.3**), as well as the constructivist (see **3.4**) and hermeneutic (see **3.5**) theoretical perspectives. The second group addresses *research programmes* and theoretical developments *for specific issues*: biographical (see **3.6**) and generation research (see **3.7**), approaches like ethnography (see **3.8**), cultural studies (see **3.9**), or gender studies (see **3.10**) have developed their own theoretical discourse. Research in organizations (see **3.11**) and qualitative evaluation research (see **3.12**) confronts the empirical work with specific theoretical demands.

BACKGROUND THEORIES (PART 3A)

The first chapter (see **3.1**) gives an overview of phenomenological life-world analysis as developed by Alfred Schütz following the ideas of Edmund Husserl. Here the bases of the constitution of meaning for social science analysis are developed. In this theoretical perspective we see the existing social reality, which we take for granted, as a preconditional 'social construction' (Berger and Luckmann 1966) of members of a given society (see **3.4**).

Ethnomethodology represents an independent theoretical development within qualitative research (see **3.2**). It shares with phenomenological analysis the question of the routine foundations of everyday action and its formal mechanisms. Within the tradition of sociology it picks up the question first posed by Durkheim concerning the preconditions of social order and directs its attention to the 'productive achievements' of members of society that bring about social order as an arrangement of communication and interaction.

Symbolic interactionism (see **3.3**) has its roots in pragmatism and is governed by a humanist perspective. In its basic assumptions it stresses the importance of the subject in the creation of social reality, it indicates the processes of joint situational negotiation of lines of action and the role of settled cultural and symbolically transmitted norms, which only become a concrete action-reality for participants in the course of an interaction. In its most recent developments under the conditions of postmodernism and the influence of the crisis of representation, the constructivist aspects of the approach have been more fully elaborated.

We are concerned here (see **3.4**) with certain approaches to a constructivist perspective that belong not only to qualitative research but which have led to particularly intensive discussion and further developments in this area. Here, in addition to methodological considerations, there is also some treatment of epistemological questions concerning the character of social reality; this involves discussion of the links with a theory of science deriving, on the one hand, from system-theory and, on the other hand, from literary studies, with regard to their importance for theory construction in qualitative research.

Hermeneutic approaches constitute, after phenomenology and symbolic interactionism, the third major tradition within qualitative research (see **3.5**). Qualitative data such as protocols, memos, interview transcripts, photographs or films do not speak for themselves; in qualitative research they are viewed as texts that have to be read (in the sense of interpreted) and related to available research results. In the different hermeneutic approaches there is a broad tradition of transforming these interpretative endeavours into theory-driven methodologies.

RESEARCH PROGRAMMES AND THEORETICAL PERSPECTIVES FOR SPECIFIC ISSUES (PART 3B)

Qualitative biographical research (see **3.6**) and qualitative generation research (see **3.7**) are closely related: how are individual interpretations interrelated, which also always means the creation of new or reconstructed personal biographies in the light of historical constellations and events, which members of a given generation have both undertaken and suffered, and how do new configurations and lifestyles emerge from these constellations? It is also in the context of an everyday history of the modern world that new perspectives in qualitative theory provide scope for new discoveries.

Life-world analysis reconstructs the inner view of the actor in a variety of local environments, 'meaning-provinces' and special worlds, in order to achieve a better overall understanding of participants and their life-world(s) (see **3.8**). The investigation of these is not only manifest in the diversity of modern forms of life. In its methodological perspective on the artificial alienation of the habitual and apparently familiar it opens up, as a reflection, a view of general principles and processes in the social construction of life-worlds. Cultural studies (see **3.9**) – an interdisciplinary field between sociology, ethnography, media science and literary studies – is interested in the following questions: how are cultural symbols and traditions used and altered in the context of social change, under specific power relations and in states of social conflict between participants? To what extent are actors in this process marked by the traditions, fashions and temporal misalignments of (popular) culture?

Theoretical aspects of qualitative research have also made an impact on modern gender research (see **3.10**). This is concerned both with the processes involved in the social construction of gender and with the qualitative analysis of communication and interaction within and between the genders. It is a particular theoretical challenge to analyse, for example, pieces of interaction analysis as an expression of the socially unequal treatment of the genders.

Organization analysis and development (see **3.11**) and evaluation research (see **3.12**) are examples of two central applications of qualitative research. They are of theoretical interest in that the application of qualitative procedures to organizational development and evaluation makes visible both the necessary and the obstructive mechanisms in changing and redefining social constructions. This enables qualitative research to provide insights into the microstructures and preconditions of social change.

Part 3A

Background Theories of Qualitative Research

3.1 Phenomenological Life-world Analysis

Ronald Hitzler and Thomas S. Eberle

1 THE IDEA OF A LIFE-WORLD PHENOMENOLOGY

The variant of life-world phenomenology, which was developed by Alfred Schütz on the basis of ideas derived from Husserl and re-imported to Europe from the USA by Thomas Luckmann, is today without question one of the most important background theories of qualitative research (cf. also Brauner as early as 1978). The main objective of this mundane phenomenology is to reconstruct the formal structures of the life-world.

From a historical point of view, Husserl's diagnosis (1936) of the crisis in European scholarship forms the scientific background to this focus on the life-world. For him, the crisis consisted of the fact that the scientific protagonists have (or at least had) forgotten that all science is rooted in the life-world. For Husserl, the explanation of the life-world essence of science therefore provided the only way to overcome the crisis in science. For when the 'meaning-basis' of the life-world is (again) revealed, scientific idealizations will – in Husserl's opinion – no longer be reified, and science will be able to achieve an 'adequate' methodological self-awareness.

Life-world, in Edmund Husserl's sense, is the original domain, the obvious and unquestioned foundation both of all types of everyday acting and thinking and of all scientific theorizing and philosophizing (cf. also Welz 1996). In its concrete manifestations it exists in all its countless varieties as the only real world of every individual person, of every *ego*. These variations are built on general immutable structures, the 'realm of immediate evidence'.

Alfred Schütz adopted this idea of Husserl's and attempted to discover the most general essential features of the life-world, in respect of the particular problems of social as opposed to natural sciences (cf. Schütz and Luckmann 1973, 1989).

The general aim of life-world analysis, oriented to the epistemological problems of the social sciences, is therefore to analyse the understanding of meaning-comprehension by means of a formal description of invariable basic structures of the constitution of meaning *in the subjective consciousness of actors*.

Unlike the normal objective and inductive understanding of science, phenomenology begins with experience of the individual and develops this in a reflexive form. The mundane phenomenology of Schütz and his followers, therefore, is not a sociological approach in the strict sense of the word, but a *proto*-sociological enterprise that underlies actual sociological work (cf. Hitzler and Honer 1984; Knoblauch 1996a; Luckmann 1993). It is therefore interested in the *epistemological* explanation of the 'foundation' of the life-world, which is on the one hand a point of reference and on the other hand an implicit basis for research work in the social sciences.

Nevertheless both 'normal' science and mundane phenomenology – in the extended sense of the term – proceed *empirically* (cf. Luckmann 1979). Of course, the specific 'difference' in *phenomenological* empiricism consists of the researcher beginning with his/her own subjective experiences. Whatever phenomenological 'operations', and on the basis of whatever epistemological interests, are then carried out, it is the personal subjective experiences that are and remain the only source of data, because they alone are evident. On the basis of this 'special' type of data, phenomenology advances towards controlled abstraction formulations of the basic layers of the processes of consciousness and reveals the universal structures in subjective constitution-behaviour.

But Schütz not only analyses the life-world in respect of how it is constituted meaningfully in the subjective consciousness: he also sees it as *produced* by the actions of people (cf. also Srubar 1988). This also explains the high level of compatibility of phenomenological life-world analysis with many of the problems of interpretative sociology in general and with the theoretical perspective of American pragmatism (cf. particularly Schütz 1962, 1964).

2 FROM MEANING-CONSTITUTION TO UNDERSTANDING THE OTHER

Throughout his life Schütz worked on the problem of a sound philosophical basis for interpretative sociology. As his starting point he selected Max Weber's definition of sociology as a 'science that seeks to interpret social action and thereby provides a causal explanation for its sequencing and its effects' (Weber 1972: 1). According to Weber, what has to be understood is the 'subjectively intended meaning' that

actors relate to their actions. Consequently, Schütz recognizes the principal problem of a methodological basis for the social sciences in analysing the processes of meaning-creation and meaning-interpretation together with the incremental constitution of human knowledge. In other words: mundane phenomenology, in the methodological sense, is 'constitution analysis'. All meaning configurations – according to Schütz's main thesis (1932) – are constituted in processes of meaning-creation and understanding. To explain social phenomena from the actions of participating individuals therefore implies referring back to the subjective meaning which these actions have for the actors themselves.

In this process of reconstruction, Schütz builds on the transcendental phenomenology of Edmund Husserl: the meaning of experiences is determined by acts of consciousness. A meaning-relation arises when (individual) experiences are brought together to form a unit by syntheses of a higher order. The total coherence of the experience then forms the quintessence of all subjective meaning-relations, and the specific meaning of an experience arises from the way in which it is classified within this total coherence of experience.

Actions are experiences of a particular kind: their meaning is constituted by the design that anticipates the resulting action. For this reason Schütz keeps acting and action strictly apart. The meaning of acting is determined by the meaning of the projected action. The goal of an action is the 'in-order-to' motive of the action, while the stimulus or the reasons for the action-design form the 'because' motive. Weber's 'subjectively intended meaning' is, in this respect, nothing more than a self-explanation on the part of the actor of his/her own action-design. This self-explanation always derives from a process of 'now and in this way', and therefore necessarily remains 'relative': interpretations of meaning vary, according to the time when they occur, according to the momentary situational interest in the explanation, and also according to the underlying reservoir of knowledge specific to a particular biography and marked by typological and relevance structures.

In *analysing* the understanding of the other Schütz departs from the level of transcendental phenomenology: with his (everyday) 'general thesis of the *alter ego*' (Schütz 1962) he presupposes the existence of the fellow human and analyses the way we understand the other from a quasi-natural perspective. His basic question is: how can other human beings be understood if there is no direct access to their consciousness? His analysis shows that the *alter ego* can only be understood in a 'signitive' way, that is, through he signs and indications. The act of understanding therefore always consists of a self-explanation on the part of the interpreter on the basis of a biographically determined reservoir of knowledge, adapted to his/her situational relevance system. In consequence of this, no more than fragmentary excerpts of the other's subjective context are ever accessible to the interpreter. Every meaning-interpretation can therefore be no more than an approximation, the quality of which depends on the degree of familiarity with, and the 'temporal proximity' of, the particular *alter ego* in the consciousness of the interpreter.

Unlike (transcendental) phenomenology, the social sciences are therefore obliged to take account, in methodological terms, of the semantic pre-constitution of the social world. This means that the theories and methods of social science are 'second order' constructs which (must) derive from 'first order' everyday constructs. Schütz expresses this in the form of two methodological postulates: the postulate of subjective interpretation, and the postulate of adequacy.

The *postulate of subjective interpretation* requires social scientific explanations to relate to the subjective meaning of an action. From the point of view of theory-construction this means that on the basis of typical patterns of an observed sequence of actions a model of an actor is constructed to whom an awareness of typical *in-order-to* and *because* motives is attributed. The *postulate of adequacy* requires that the social scientist's constructs be consistent with the constructs of the everyday actor. They must therefore be comprehensible and give an accurate explanation of acting. Complete adequacy is achieved when the concrete meaning-orientation of actors is captured accurately. In this way we explain the subjective perspective of the individual actors at truly the ultimate reference point for social science analyses, because 'holding on to the subjective perspective' offers, according to Schütz (e.g. 1978), the only really sufficient guarantee that social reality is not replaced by a fictitious non-existent world constructed by some scientific observer.

As Schütz has shown, however, the perspective of another actor can only be captured approximately. Complete adequacy therefore remains an unachievable ideal for interpretative social sciences.

3 ON THE SOCIOLOGICAL RELEVANCE OF LIFE-WORLD ANALYSIS

If one sees phenomenological life-world analysis as both *proto-* and *para*-sociological epistemology, it then appears to be of immediate relevance to any kind of sociology based on the notion that our *experience* rather than 'objective' factual content is decisive in the way we define situations: we are, to use Schütz's (1962) term, 'activity centres' of our respective situations and thereby also capable of subjective definition – and, in our relation to one another, alternating between high-level agreement and crass opposition.

Accordingly, if our everyday world consists not simply of 'brute facts' but of (manifold) meanings, then the essential task of *sociology* is to understand, in a reconstructive way, how meanings arise and continue, when and why they may be described as 'objective', and how human beings adapt interpretatively these socially 'objectivized' meanings and recover from them, as if from a quarry, their 'subjective' significations, thereby collaborating in the further construction of 'objective reality' (cf. Berger and Luckmann 1966). The empirical programme of phenomenology therefore includes, from the point of view of research practice, the *systematic reconstruction of multiple qualities of experience* (see **3.8**).

In this sense the life-world is in no way a *marginal* theme in the social sciences, but their systematic central problem: since perception, experience and action constitute an original sphere that is only 'really' accessible to the perceiving, experiencing or acting subject, the so-called factual realities are only truly evident as phenomena of the subjective consciousness. Of course this experience can always 'deceive' in the face of an 'objectively' defined factual content. Nevertheless, it may be said to determine our behaviour 'objectively'. For not only is our consciousness necessarily intentional ('about something'), but also the correlates of this intentionality – at least in everyday experience – are meaningful (cf. Schütz 1967 for further discussion).

Because the life-world reveals at every moment fundamentally more experiential possibilities than an individual can truly bring into any thematic focus, the individual is constantly and inevitably selecting from the total of possible experiences available at any given moment (cf. Esser 1996). It is not generally important to us that, in consequence, our experience and action is always the result of elective procedures, because we are constantly concerned with completing our actual experience meaningfully or with creating a structure for every selected perception. This means that in respect of the meaningfulness of experiences we distinguish, according to our respective subjective relevances, between the important and the unimportant, or between the relevant and the irrelevant.

This meaningfulness can be distinctly situation-specific and short-term, but it can also be (almost) completely independent of situation and permanent; it can be of purely subjective or of general social 'validity' (to an extent that always has to be determined). This is because all individual human beings live in their own life-world as the sum total of their concrete world of experience. However, all concrete manifestations of life-world structures also have intersubjective features. To come to terms with our normal everyday life we make use of a large number of shared meaning schemata, and our various subjective relevance systems overlap at many points.

Shared beliefs first of all facilitate and determine our everyday life, which is always a matter of *living together*. To a certain extent the subject 'shares' his/her respective concrete life-world with others. To put this more precisely: the correlates of an individual's experience correspond to the correlates of the experience of others in ways that may be typologized. From this, meaning schemata may be created, which are shared by different subjects and are therefore intersubjectively valid, and these correlate to a greater or lesser extent with individual, biographically conditioned, meaning structures. To put this rather differently: human social practice is – inevitably – a practice of *interpretation*, of decoding signs and symbols, and essentially of *communication* (cf. Luckmann 1986, 1989).

In this sense, writers such as Werner Marx (1987) understand the life-world as a plurality of sometimes clearly defined, and sometimes undetermined, purposive individual worlds. Marx argues that Husserl distinguishes the life-world

from individual worlds by virtue of the fact that the former are pre-determined and not intentionally constituted, whereas the latter are goal-directed (for example, the world of the employed person, of the family member, of the citizen, and so on). Every immediate experience, every present world, according to Marx (1987: 129), has 'the content of an individual world'.

For a variety of reasons, Hitzler and Honer (e.g. 1984, 1988, 1991), following Benita Luckmann (1970), prefer the term 'small social life-worlds', but in a broad sense are referring to the same phenomenon: a small social life-world or an individual world is a *fragment* of the life-world, with its own structure, within which experiences occur in relation to a special intersubjective reservoir of knowledge that is obligatory and pre-existent. A small social life-world is the correlate of the subjective experience of reality in a partial or temporally restricted culture. This kind of world is 'small', therefore, not because it is concerned only with small spaces or consists of very few members. A small social life-world is described as 'small' rather because the complexity of *possible* social relevances is reduced within it to a *particular* system of relevance. And a small social life-world is called 'social' because this relevance system is obligatory for successful participations. Empirical examples of the analysis of small social life-worlds may be found in Honer (e.g. 1994a), Hitzler (1993, 1995), Hitzler et al. (1996), Hitzler and Pfadenhauer (1998) Knoblauch (e.g. 1988, 1997) and Soeffner (e.g. 1997).

Therefore, while, in principle, every person is indeed given his/her own and unique life-world, from an empirical point of view the individual subjective life-worlds seem only relatively original, because human beings typically refer back to socio-historically 'valid' meaning schemata and concepts of action in the process of orientation within their own world.

Particularly in modern societies, small social life-worlds are therefore the subjective correspondences to cultural objectivizations of reality showing multiple social diversity, as is manifested, for example, in divergent language and speaking environments (cf. Luckmann 1989; Knoblauch 1995, 1996b). The most important result of this is that the relevance structures of different members of society can only be the same in a very conditional and 'provisional' way. Moreover, in connection with the developing division of labour, the proportions of generally known meanings and those of factual contents currently known 'only' to experts are diverging: the quantities of specialist knowledge are increasing; they are becoming ever more specialized and are increasingly remote from general knowledge (cf. Hitzler et al. 1994). It follows from this that contexts can be divided between what everyone knows and what is known by relatively few people. If, however, as Schütz and Luckmann (1973: 318) affirm, 'in a borderline case, the province of common knowledge and common relevances shrinks beyond a critical point, communication within the society is barely possible. There emerge "societies within the society".'

This is again a very significant insight in respect of the repeatedly postulated need for an ethnological attitude on the part of the sociologist towards his/her own culture; for it means that under such conditions, for every type of grouping, for every collective, even within a society, different kinds of knowledge and, above all, different hierarchies of knowledge types are or at least might be relevant.[1] And as the manifold life-worlds and the small social life-worlds of other people become the object of scientific interest, the problem of how and how far one can succeed in seeing the world through the eyes of these other people (cf. Plessner 1983), and in reconstructing the subjectively intended meaning of *their* experiences, becomes virulent not 'only' from a methodological viewpoint but also, and more particularly, in terms of *method*.

Admittedly Schütz himself was never concerned with the *methods* of empirical social research. Such implications of life-world analysis are already to be seen, however, in the works of Harold Garfinkel in particular (1967a; see **2.3**) and Aaron V. Cicourel (1964). In Germany, Schütz's matrix is most often used for the systematic analysis of the way social scientific data come about (cf. Luckmann and Gross 1977), for the analysis of communicative genres (see **5.18**), for the explanation of hermeneutic reconstruction procedures (see **3.5**, **5.16**) and to provide a theoretical base for ethnographic sociology (see **3.8**).

Against the background of the above outline it becomes increasingly evident that the epistemologically relevant antagonism in social research is not between qualitative and quantitative, nor even between standardized and non-standardized, investigations, but between hermeneutic and scientistic methodologies and methods.

NOTE

1 In contrast, the testing of hypotheses in the deductive-nomological explanatory model presupposes – quasi-implicitly – that human beings under the same conditions will act in the same way. In societies with a predominantly traditional orientation this is indeed often the case, but in modern societies, only in the area of routine actions. As modern societies are marked by de-traditionalization, an increase in options and individualization (Gross 1994, 1999), and actors frequently re-interpret their situations, so their knowledge and behaviour becomes more contingent, the prognostic capability of 'if–then' statements becomes more disturbed and exploratory-interpretative research design becomes more necessary (cf. also Hitzler 1997, 1999b).

FURTHER READING

Knoblauch, H. (2002) 'Communication, Contexts and Culture. A Communicative Constructivist Approach to Intercultural Communication', in A. di Luzio, S. Günthner and F. Orletti (eds), *Culture in Communication. Analyses of Intercultural Situations*. Amsterdam: John Benjamins, pp. 3–33.

Maso, I. (2001) 'Phenomenology and Ethnography', in P. Atkinson, A. Coffey, S. Delamont, J. Lofland and L. Lofland (eds), *Handbook of Ethnography*. London: Sage. pp. 136–144.

Psathas, G. (1989) *Phenomenology and Sociology: Theory and Research*. Washington, DC: Center for Advanced Research in Phenomenology and University Press of America.

3.2 Ethnomethodology

Jörg R. Bergmann

1 SCIENTIFIC AND HISTORICAL BACKGROUND

Ethnomethodology (EM) is the name of a sociological approach to investigation that sees social order, in all the ramifications of everyday situations, as a methodically generated product of members of a society. It is the goal of EM to determine the principles and mechanisms by means of which actors, in their action, produce the meaningful structure and ordering of what is happening around them and what they express and do in social interaction with others.

The name and programme of EM derive from Harold Garfinkel (1967a), who, in the 1950s and 1960s, examined the work of Talcott Parsons (1937) and Alfred Schütz (1932), and applied himself to the old and, for sociology, key question of how social order is possible (Hilbert 1992). In Talcott Parsons's structural functionalism the problem of social order was considered to be solved by referring to a normative consensus; with the existence of socially identical internalized cultural value systems the solution to the problem of social order was seen as guaranteed. Harold Garfinkel countered this with the argument that between, on the one hand, rules and values that could only be formulated generally and, on the other hand, the inevitably particular situation of current action, there is an epistemological hiatus (Heritage 1984, 1987).

General rules, in Garfinkel's opinion, must necessarily be transmitted into the current interactive process; they must be situated, in order to be relevant to an action. This transmission, however, must be achieved by actors through interpretation of the rules and the situation; rules, values and situation can only be harmoniously related by means of meaning attribution and interpretation.

In coining the term *ethnomethodology* Garfinkel (1974) relied on the concept of 'ethnoscience' developed in North American cultural anthropology. The research orientation of 'ethnoscience', which subsequently developed into a 'cognitive anthropology' (D'Andrade 1995), was concerned with 'the ordering of things in the heads of people' (Goodenough 1964). Its goal, using special techniques of semantic analysis, is to determine individual cultural orientation schemata from the vocabulary used in a language community. 'Ethnomedicine' therefore refers to the reconstructed system of knowledge and ideas in a single language community about sickness, causes of sickness and curative procedures. Garfinkel was also interested in what members of a society know, think and do in dealing with everyday circumstances; in the term 'ethnomethodology' this is expressed in the prefix 'ethno-'. But unlike the cognitive anthropologists, Garfinkel's aim was not to determine the structure of patterns of orientation and experience specific to particular domains. The problems he addressed were of a more fundamental nature. His interest was in the operational basis of that meaningful ordering that is taken for granted in everyday action, that is to say, in the techniques and mechanisms – or ethno-methods – of its production.

Compared to the 'cognitive consensus' proposed in Parsons's theory (cf. Wilson 1970), Garfinkel advances the idea that members of a society are not passively subject to their socialized need-systems, internalized norms, social pressures and so on, but rather that they are continuously producing and actively developing social reality in interaction with others as a meaningful action-context. This actor-model was not 'politically' motivated, but it did have great affinity to the social emancipation movements of the 1960s. While the normative-consensual character of Parsons's system of categories was increasingly felt to be inadequate, if not unreal, against the background of political, social and generation conflicts in American society, approaches that emphasized the constructive and negotiational character of social reality were much more in keeping with the spirit of the age (Gouldner 1971). This is a significant – if extra-scientific – reason for success, from the 1960s onwards, of EM, symbolic interactionism, the treatise of Berger and Luckmann (1966), or the works of Erving Goffman (Widmer 1991), which fed on sources with, in some respects, a different conceptual history but which united in emphasizing the active, creative role of the individual in social interaction (Arbeitsgruppe Bielefelder Soziologen 1973). Garfinkel himself points out in many places that explanatory approaches that ignore the interpretative and constructional accomplishments of actors are, in his opinion, working with an actor-model in which actors appear as *judgmental dopes*.

The developmental history of EM was first determined by the fact that it was perceived almost exclusively as a critique of the predominant structural-functional theoretical model and as a critique of the accepted methodical canon of empirical social research. This was particularly true in the German-speaking world, where Jürgen Habermas (1970) very quickly drew attention to the ethnomethodologists' criticism of the unconsidered preconditions of social science research practice, and where the reputation of EM as a methodologically critical

enterprise was secured through the success of Aaron Cicourel's (1964) book. It was realized only with some delay that EM also had its own research programme.

2 THE REALITY MODEL OF ETHNOMETHODOLOGY

It is characteristic of EM that it operates with a model of reality that differs sharply from the 'real knowledge' idea, deriving from Durkheim, that social facts as an objective reality are the object and legitimization of sociology. In the introduction to his book *Studies in Ethnomethodology*, which rapidly became the foundation text of EM, Garfinkel writes (1967a: VII)

> In contrast to certain versions of Durkheim, that teach that the objective reality of social facts is sociology's fundamental principle, the lesson is taken instead, and used as a study policy, that the objective reality of social facts as an ongoing accomplishment of the concerted activities of daily life, with the ordinary, artful ways of that accomplishment being by members known, used, and taken for granted, is, for members doing sociology, a fundamental phenomenon.

Garfinkel does not deny that social facts are experienced as an objectively determined reality, but he decisively rejects the idea of making this experience of certainty in everyday life the basis of a science of social phenomena. Instead he proposes observing 'the objective reality of social facts as an ongoing accomplishment of the concerted activities of daily life', which means not proceeding from the existence of social facts, but rather conceiving their objective reality as an ongoing accomplishment or product that is accomplished in and through the activities of everyday life. In this reality model the following conditions are of particular importance.

1 For EM what actors observe and deal with in their everyday activity as given social facts, as a reality existing without their being involved, is only created as such in their actions and observations. Social deeds acquire their character of reality exclusively through interactions that take place between people. It is only in social interaction that the objectivity of 'objectively' perceived events, the factual nature of 'factually' valid phenomena, is created.

2   This process of creating reality is, in principle, not completed at any given moment: it is continuously carried out in the finely matched social actions of actors. Social reality is understood by Garfinkel as an 'ongoing accomplishment', as a reality that is created 'locally' by interactants at every moment and in every situation (Mehan and Woods 1975). Unlike social science theories with a resolutely normative and objectivist view of reality, EM proceeds on the basis that the nature of reality in social facts is not a property inherent to them; social facts acquire their type of reality exclusively in interactions between people; it is only in everyday practical action that social reality is *real*-ized.

3   In the continuous process of creating reality, everyday knowledge, routines and interpretations play an important part. And yet the ethnomethodological representation of the genesis of meaningful order in everyday practice cannot be 'cognitively' curtailed and restricted to the question of how the meaning of an action is produced in the subjective perception of participants. In the accomplishments of order that EM sees as its object of investigation it is rather a matter of meaning-indications and revelations that actors, in their utterances, give to their partners in interaction as clues along the way.

4   EM is guided by the idea that everyday actions are, in their performance, made recognizable as 'evidences-of-a-social-order' (Garfinkel): two people who are walking together make it clear to others that here 'two people are walking together' (Ryave and Schenkein 1974). Because it is shared by all competent members of society, this process of creating a meaning-related reality cannot take place in a subjectively random fashion: it is, on the contrary, *methodical* (Weingarten et al. 1976), which implies that it displays individual, formal and, therefore, describable structural features. For everyday actors this process of the methodical production of reality is uninteresting, and is taken for granted. For EM, however, this generative process is of central importance: what is taken for granted in everyday life becomes, for EM, a problem (Wolff 1976).

From this characterization it may be recognized that the ethnomethodological model of reality was influenced by the phenomenological technique of epoché described by Husserl – the bracketing of belief in the existence of the world (Eberle 1984; Filmer et al. 1972). Garfinkel also pursues an interest in constitutive analysis, although it is not his aim to appropriate the stream of consciousness with its cogitations and intentional objects, and he is not interested in the transcendental status of this operation of bracketing and reduction in phenomenological philosophy (see **3.1**). Garfinkel suspends his belief in the given nature of social facts in order to gain some insight into how social facts become social facts in the acts of members of a society. This transfer of a constitutive-analytical perspective from the world of philosophy into the world of social sciences is undoubtedly problematic, and for that reason it has often been criticized (Eickelpasch and Lehmann 1983; List 1983); but it is an original achievement of Garfinkel and has set in train a high degree of innovation and creativity amongst generations of social scientists.

To illustrate and explain the ethnomethodological model of reality nothing is more appropriate than a case study by Garfinkel (1967a) of the transsexual 'Agnes'. Just as the distinction between man and woman in the everyday world is taken for granted as a social fact, in sociology and social research membership of one gender is presupposed as a unit of description that is taken as a variable in every kind of data collection. Using the example of 'Agnes', Garfinkel demonstrates that gender distinction and its natural self-evidence quality is in no way a natural fact. Agnes was born with male sexual characteristics, was first raised as a boy, changed her own appearance, lived as a young woman, and at the age of 19 underwent an operation to change her gender. She taught Garfinkel that to be a woman meant to be perceived and treated by others as a 'woman', which again requires making oneself perceptible to others, by various methods, as a 'normal, natural woman'. In this way the fact of gender-membership becomes a continually self-fulfilling and continually presented accomplishment that is interactive and perceptive (cf. also the investigations of Kessler and McKenna 1978 and Hirschauer 1993 that complement Garfinkel's Agnes study). In the view of EM a concrete immutable fact becomes an event that takes place over time and that can change and develop in an unexpected way.

3 CENTRAL CONCEPTS AND PROGRAMMATIC STATEMENTS

Since Garfinkel does not see the problem of how meaningful social order arises between people as being solved by reference to uniform internalized value systems, for him the question of the 'how' in the constitution of meaning takes centre-stage. 'This thesis', begins Garfinkel's PhD dissertation (1952: 1) – supervised by Talcott Parsons – 'is concerned with the conditions under which a person makes continued sense of the world around him'. This concern with the question of meaning constitution permeates EM from its beginnings down to its most recent past. But Garfinkel gives this question a new direction that marks the special character of EM compared to other interpretative research approaches. For him, the process of meaning endowment in everyday life is not something that can be separated from the action itself and removed into the heads of people. Instead, he assumes that 'meaningful events are entirely and exclusively events in a person's behavioral environment. ... Hence there is no reason to look under the skull, for nothing of interest is to be found there but brains' (1963: 190). This decision of Garfinkel's to conceptualize, for the purposes of investigation, the process of subjective allocation of meaning not as an inner 'private' act of consciousness, but from the outset as a social, 'public' event, is of central importance for EM and has far-reaching consequences for its research practice. (For an ethnomethodological discussion and critique of mental concepts and cognitive theories, cf. Coulter 1989.)

EM is not concerned with the reconstruction of a silent internal understanding in the sense of reconstructive hermeneutics, but with observing and describing the structural principles of the process of understanding and making oneself understood that is documented in action itself. Garfinkel (1967a: VII) incorporated this aim in a definitive description of EM in which various concepts appear that are of crucial importance for the understanding of EM: 'Ethnomethodological studies analyze everyday activities as members' methods for making those same activities visibly-rational-and-reportable-for-all-practical-purposes, i.e. "accountable", as organizations of commonplace everyday activities.' The concepts contained in this definition may be set out as follows.

1 The place where for EM the meaningful construction of reality takes place is the social event, because actors, in carrying out their actions, employ techniques and procedures to make these actions recognizable, understandable, describable and accountable. 'Account' in this context means more than 'understand': it means the observable forms and representations in which a perception, an interpretation or an explanation materialize. This externalized character of *accounts* is shown with particular clarity where Garfinkel (1967a: 1) writes 'When I speak of "accountable" ..., I mean ... observable-and-reportable, i.e. available to members as situated practices of looking-and-telling.' Other paraphrases of the term *accountable* that are scattered through Garfinkel's work include *recordable*, *countable*, *picturable*, *tellable*, *storyable*, *representable*.

2 Garfinkel's definitive description of EM also shows that these *accounts* should not be understood as discrete linguistic events that are produced or perceived outside the current event; they are, rather, an integral component of the social event to which they relate. For example, in the particular way in which two people speak together, we may recognize that in this talk we are dealing with a conversation between a doctor and a patient; and at the same time their utterances are only understandable if one hears them as utterances in a doctor–patient conversation. *Accounts* therefore possess a fundamental *reflexivity*: while on the one hand they serve to create and make recognizable the order and meaning of a social event, on the other hand they are themselves a part of this event and obtain their meaning and intelligible content only with reference to this social order.

3 This reflexivity of *accounts* is manifest primarily in the fact that utterances and actions constantly relate to the context in which they occur and thereby inevitably take on an *indexical* character. They point continually to the situation and the context in which they are produced, and to understand their content and meaning recipients must continually take account of the environment of the event. But since in the course of an event the situational and contextual circumstances are constantly changing, every social encounter possesses something unique and particular. The indexical-particular character of all social events is an inconvenience for scientific observation, which looks

for typology, formalization and generalization. Attempts to overcome this inconvenience by de-indexicalizing – by replacing indexical expressions by objective expressions – will only lead to unreal solutions, since indications of context cannot be avoided even in scientific discourse. But if, in view of this situation, one proceeds to represent social interaction simply by actualization and invoking abstract describable behaviour patterns (roles and so on), one is denying exactly its essentially context-dependent quality. Garfinkel therefore decided to dedicate the investigative programme of EM totally to the question of how social order can possibly arise out of inevitably indexical utterances and actions that are dependent on situation and context. 'I use the term "ethnomethodology" to refer to the investigation of the rational properties of indexical expressions and other practical actions as contingent ongoing accomplishments of organized artful practices of everyday life' (Garfinkel 1967a: 11). What does Garfinkel mean by saying that indexical expressions have rational properties?

4 It is a premise of EM that the reflexive context-dependency of meaning-generation and the indexicality of everyday utterances and actions cannot, in principle, be removed (Garfinkel and Sacks 1970). This means, however, that the conditions under which people act in everyday life, develop projects for action or take decisions are always unclear and can only be explained in advance to a very limited extent. But under such conditions, how is appropriate and efficient behaviour, communication and cooperation at all possible? For Garfinkel, however, this question is already wrongly worded because it proceeds from the model of scientific-rational communication, according to which everyday communication must appear defective. And yet in everyday life – and this is what the remark about the rationality of indexical expressions relates to – communication can only take place because of the fact that terms are not clearly defined in an interaction, but are defined vaguely; meanings are not fixed once and for all, but are used fluidly; themes and meaning-contents are not formalized and freed from contradictions, but are kept open and ambiguous. 'What a stir it would cause in the world if the names of things were turned into definitions!' observed Lichtenberg (1983: 450) once in his *Sudelbücher*, and it is in precisely this sense that Garfinkel is interested in stressing the special rationality of everyday action as opposed to scientific rationality.

For EM the sense of linguistic utterances in socially organized action contexts is structurally uncertain. The vagueness and the elliptical character of statements are not seen in everyday life as 'errors'; they are, rather, sanctioned as situationally appropriate behaviour. The partners in communication, guided by pragmatic action motives, rely on the fact that the other will always understand what was meant by a particular utterance, and that what was not immediately understood has a meaning that will be clarified in the further course of the conversation. To put this more pointedly: EM assumes that the structural uncertainty of meaning in everyday interactive events is a constitutive condition for certainty of meaning, that is to say, for meaningful experience and action. In this way EM, in respect of the character of everyday rationality, arrives at a similar assessment to that of Ludwig Wittgenstein (1958: 63), who – coming from a totally different theoretical tradition – formulated this paradox as follows.

> On the one hand it is clear that every sentence of our language is 'in order, as it is' means that we are not looking for an ideal: as if our normal vague sentences had as yet no completely unflawed meaning and we still have to construct a complete language. On the other hand it seems clear: where there is meaning there must be complete order. ... The most perfect order must also be hidden, therefore, in the vaguest sentence.

Everyday discourses are characterized, for EM, by their provisional nature, vagueness, incompleteness or ambiguity, but these characterizations, which suggest some deficiency, cannot hide the fact that communication and understanding in the everyday world can only be achieved in this way. It is only in comparison with the scientific model of understanding that relies on unambiguity, completeness and objectivity of statements that these features of everyday communication have to be seen as deficiencies. At this point it becomes clear that EM as a critique of the scientistic procedure of the traditional social sciences, and EM as a programme for investigating the special rationality of the world of everyday life, are two sides of one and the same undertaking. (On the relationship of EM to canonical social sciences and humanities, cf. Button 1991.)

4   DEVELOPMENTS AND PERSPECTIVES: 'STUDIES OF WORK'

In the initial phase of EM the works of Garfinkel (1967a) were totally directed to the task of proving that in the everyday world an unknown field of research lay before the eyes of the social scientist, and that this was worthy of investigation. Garfinkel did this, in the first place, by showing how – for example, in coding a questionnaire – social science research practice was continually but unknowingly influenced by everyday elements that needed urgently to be clarified in accordance with the methodological and statistical requirements of empirical social research (see also Cicourel 1964). Alternatively, he showed that medical records from a psychiatric clinic, which seemed, to an external social scientific observer, to be defective sources of data, immediately lost their 'deficits' when put into the context of their clinical application; there are, therefore, as Garfinkel pointed out, 'good organizational reasons for bad clinic records'. Garfinkel has become best known for his unconventional crisis experiments, in which individual features of the everyday world – such as its characteristic vagueness – can be made clear and a matter of conscious awareness if they are confronted systematically, for instance if the use of indexical expressions is criticized or the clear meaning of a term is demanded. The collapse of normal communication makes visible its everyday world foundation.

Inspired by the works of Garfinkel, many studies, in the early days of EM, dealt with the question of how 'facts' are produced in various organizations. In a law court how is a clear order of events reconstructed in the face of contradictory information (Pollner 1987)? In a clinic how does a patient who has died become a dead person in the actions of the staff of the clinic (Sudnow 1967)? In a corrective institution how is the difference between inmates and supervisors created and maintained (Wieder 1974)? In a social welfare office how is it decided whether a client has a legitimate claim (Zimmerman 1974)?[1]

Garfinkel himself has been concerned, since the mid-1970s, with a particular development of EM that has become known under the label 'studies of work' (Garfinkel 1986). This will be described briefly below. Research done in this area concentrates on describing the practical competences that underlie the performance of specific types of professional activity. In the first instance this is a matter of tracing the unique quality of a particular professional activity that cannot be subsumed under a general category. Here a focus is provided by the analysis of (natural) scientific work (Lynch et al. 1983) in which it becomes clear why the ethnomethodological 'studies of work' of previous years received and discussed primarily in the sociology of science (Knorr-Cetina and Mulkay 1983; Lynch 1993).

The formulation and definition of the 'studies of work' approach (Garfinkel 1991, 1996; Garfinkel and Wieder 1992) should be understood to a certain extent as a reaction to the development and success of conversation analysis, which also has its roots in the original programme of EM and was able to consolidate itself to a large extent as an independent research approach (see **5.17**). 'Studies of work' as the latest version of ethnomethodological research, on the other hand, do not offer such a clear picture, and this is not least a result of the complexity of the area of 'work' (Heritage 1987). While conversation analysis had restricted itself to the limited aspect of linguistic and non-linguistic interaction, 'studies of work' include everything to do with the carrying out of working activities – even over an extended period of time – and this included not only episodes of linguistic interaction, but also matters of the technical handling of instruments, the manipulation and spatial organization of objects, or the pictorial and written documents that were produced in the course of work.

A central theorem of early EM claims that actors, in carrying out actions, employ numerous techniques and procedures to make these actions portrayable and accountable, and that in this way they produce the reality of social facts. In this respect 'studies of work' go a step further and, in their own estimation, radicalize the idea of the meaningful creation of reality. They reject the division implicit in this conception between description, portrayal and explanation on the one hand and objects, facts and circumstances on the other. Instead they insist on the indivisibility and irreducibility of the local production of social order in, and as the embodied practices of, the actors. The meaning and reality of social objects are no longer viewed as the result of the application of distinguishable representation practices: instead object and representation are understood as a unit, as a totality that realizes itself in the performance of sensory and bodily activities.

Here it becomes clear that the 'studies of work' approach was formulated under the influence of Maurice Merleau-Ponty's investigations of the phenomenology of the human body. By analysing work performance, the 'studies of work' attempt, from a sociological perspective, to continue his endeavours to overcome the distinction between the body as a self-contained mechanism and consciousness as the essence for itself. Their focus of interest is the embodied knowledge that is materialized in the natural mastery of skilful practices and that is constitutive for the successful execution of a particular piece of work. With this they aim to provide an empirical analysis of competence systems that are characteristic of a particular type of work and give it its identity.

These competences cannot be depicted in handbooks or training manuals, and are ignored by traditional occupational and professional sociology. Between the training manual representations – the official rules for a particular kind of work which can provide only model versions of the working process – and the factual, practical performance of work at a particular situational moment, there is a fundamental gap, which everyday experience sees as the difference between theory and practice. In spite of fundamental theoretical training, every type of work – from driving a tractor, to playing the piano, right down to carrying out a mathematical proof – must first be learned as a practical activity. In this process the practitioner acquires the ability to recognize and adjust to contingencies, to take decisions about the course of work, not schematically but moment by moment, and, in association with situational imponderables and local constellations, somehow to manage the observable adequacy and efficiency of his or her activity. This 'somehow' had long been omitted in the descriptions of both practitioners and sociologists. 'Studies of work' make precisely this 'somehow' their primary focus, by asking 'how exactly' the specific nature of a particular type of work is constituted in the skilled physical performance of practical activities, in the details of their performance.

For the 'studies of work' approach some of the investigations that started in the 1970s have a paradigmatic value. This applies to studies that concerned themselves with the discovery activity of astronomers in an observatory (Garfinkel et al. 1981), with the laboratory activity of neurobiologists (Lynch 1985), with mathematicians' performance of proofs (Livingston 1986), with concealed educational activity of introductory scientific texts (Morrison 1981), with improvisation activity while playing the piano (Sudnow 1978) or keyboard work (Sudnow 1979). In these studies it is demonstrated that even producing the 'demonstrability' of a mathematical proof, which is normally assumed to be independent of context, is anchored in the local situational sequences of actions of the mathematician performing with chalk on the blackboard. Moreover, a pulsar is defined as a 'cultural object' in that it is shown that it only begins to exist because of a series of embodied work-activities by the astronomer during a sequence of sets of observations.

More recent investigations in the 'studies of work' tradition are concerned, on the one hand, with the local situational practices of professionalized work (cf. for example Travers 1997 for a study of the work of lawyers and defence counsels), and on the other hand – and this applies to the majority of current research in this area – with situational work practices in dealing with technology, and in particular information technology. 'Studies of work' are indeed aiming not at developing general schemata for the description of the use of machines and computers, but at determining the 'identifying features' (Garfinkel) of this work from the situational details of the use of objects and information (for example, on a computer screen). This precise attention to local practices in the use of objects and in the execution of work-tasks makes 'studies of work' attractive and applicable to research in the field of human–computer interaction (HCI) and computer-supported cooperative work (CSCW), as the work of Lucy Suchman (1987), in particular, has impressively shown.

The programme of 'studies of work' has also had a strong influence on the development of the so-called 'workplace studies' (Knoblauch 1996c), which are concerned with the analysis of complex work-tasks, particularly in the area of information technology (for an overview cf. Button 1993). An important aspect of this type of working context is that specialization, division of work and concentration on a computer screen lead to the necessity for actors to apply particular skills of coordination and anticipation with regard to the behaviour of their colleagues. Checking, observing, thinking, recognizing and so on often do not happen in these contexts as an impersonal psychic procedure, but are imparted to colleagues as part of a person's own communicative behaviour in highly distinctive and implicit ways. Because ethnomethodological 'studies of work' have always made this embodied, communicative form of knowledge and recognition their special theme, fascinating new links to cognitive science have resulted that do not reduce the processes of cognition to cerebral physiological processes, but which localize them as 'distributed cognition', manifest in the communicative ecology of working and learning contexts (cf. Engeström and Middleton 1996).

5 CRITICAL EVALUATION AND PROSPECTS

Tensions between conversation analysis and 'studies of work' have permeated the discussions of recent years and have frequently led to marked differences of opinion. These differences cannot be written off as an internal battle between two ethnomethodological camps, since they concern a point of general relevance – particularly for qualitative research. Conversation analysis pursues the goal of determining the mechanisms that are principally relevant for the organization of 'talk-in-interaction'. For many ethnomethodologists (cf., for example, Pollner 1991), Garfinkel's original programme is being diluted by this procedure to the point where it is no longer recognizable. They fear that in the formalization and linguisticization of conversation analysis the idea that interaction is always locally bound, that it inevitably has an indexical character, and is subject to a process of reflexive meaning-constitution, will become unimportant. Garfinkel himself (1991, see also Lynch 1993, ch. 7), in his programmatic works, has spoken consistently of the 'haecceitas' of the social world (see below) and has singled this out as the focus of ethnomethodological interest. This term (whose origin Garfinkel does not indicate) is intended to express that everything social only exists as a unique, individual manifestation – a feature that is eliminated if the social is described in general terms and subsumed under predetermined theoretically derived categories. This

confronts the fundamental problem of determining the level of generality at which pieces of qualitative research should treat their respective social objects of investigation.

However, insisting on the 'haecceitas' of all social objects, which should not be damaged in scientific observation, will ultimately handicap every analytical endeavour and will lead, through an ever-deepening multiplication of detail, to a descriptive duplication of the object. The term 'haecceitas' was originally coined by the mediaeval scholasticist Johannes Duns Scotus to characterize the 'here-and-now' nature of things. What he meant, in the formulation of Heidegger, who studied Duns Scotus's early works, was 'what really exists is an individual thing. ... All that really exists is a "such-here-now"' (Safranski 1997: 84). But this miracle of the singularity of the real is a nominalist construct, since human reason always operates in a comparative, linking and ordering fashion between the respective unique individual manifestations – and the social scientist does the same with a systematic intent. However, Garfinkel's reference to the 'haecceitas' of everything social should not be seen merely as a provocation of model-building social sciences, but as a warning that, in the course of all necessary formalization and generalization, the local, reflexive constitutive process of the social should not be lost from sight. If ethnomethodological 'studies of work' succeed, with a measure of generalization, in gaining access to what situational demands, practical and embodied knowledge contribute to professional work, then its discoveries could have a lasting influence in many areas.

NOTE

1 Information about further ethnomethodological studies on these and similar themes can be found in the collections of Douglas (1970), Turner (1974), Psathas (1979), Helm et al. (1989), Coulter (1990) Watson and Seiler (1992), Have and Psathas (1995), Psathas (1995). An extensive bibliography on ethnomethodology up to 1990 may be found in Fehr et al. (1990). Surveys and critical discussions of the further development of ethnomethodology since its foundation by Harold Garfinkel are in Attewell (1974), Sharrock and Anderson (1986), Atkinson (1988) and Maynard and Clayman (1991). Further presentations are in Fengler and Fengler (1980) and Patzelt (1987).

FURTHER READING

Fehr, B. J., Stetson, J. and Mizukawa, Y. (1990) 'A Bibliography for Ethnomethodology', in J. Coulter (ed.), *Ethnomethodological Sociology*. Brookfield: Edward Elgar. pp. 473–559.

Heritage, J. C. (1984) *Garfinkel and Ethnomethodology*. Cambridge: Polity Press.

Hilbert, R. A. (1992) *The Classical Roots of Ethnomethodology: Durkheim, Weber, and Garfinkel*. Chapel Hill, NC: University of North Carolina Press.

Sacks, H. (1992) *Lectures on Conversation*, Volume I and II (edited by G. Jefferson with introductions by E. A. Schegloff). Oxford: Blackwell.

Turner, R. (ed.) (1974) *Ethnomethodology: Selected Readings*. Harmondsworth: Penguin.

3.3   Symbolic Interactionism

Norman K. Denzin

Symbolic interactionism is that unique American sociological and social psychological perspective that traces its roots to the early American pragmatists, James, Dewey, Peirce and Mead. It has been called the loyal opposition in American sociology, the most sociological of social psychologies. Only recently has this perspective entered the discourses of the other social sciences, including anthropology, psychology and science studies, where the works of Mead have been joined with the theories of Wittgenstein, Vygotsky and Bakhtin (1989). Harré, for example, places 'symbolic interactions' at the heart of psychology, showing how selves, attitudes, motives, genders and emotions are 'discursive productions, attributes of conversations rather than mental entities' (Harré 1992: 526).

Other social scientists are adopting an interactionist informed approach to the study of lives, identities and social relationships (see Dunn 1998; Holstein and Gubrium 2000; Musolf 1998; Wiley 1994). A relatively new journal, *Mind, Culture, and Activity*, publishes work that connects the symbolic interactionist tradition with science studies, cultural psychology and the Soviet tradition represented by the works of Vygotsky and others. The journal *Symbolic Interaction* and the research annual *Studies in Symbolic Interaction* routinely publish work by symbolic interactionists, and members of the Society for the Study of Symbolic Interaction. Interactionism has had a tortured history in American sociology (see Fine 1993). Many times its death has been announced, and its practitioners maligned, but the perspective refuses to die. Today it is alive and well, thriving in its journals and at its annual meetings and symposia.

1   BASIC PRINCIPLES OF SYMBOLIC INTERACTIONISM

The term *symbolic* in the phrase symbolic interaction refers to the underlying linguistic foundations of human group life, just as the word *interaction* refers to the fact that people do not act toward one another, but interact with each other. By using the term interaction symbolic interactionists commit themselves to the study and analysis of the developmental course of action that occurs when two or more persons (or agents) with agency (reflexivity) join their individual lines of action together into joint action.

2 THEORIES OF AGENCY AND ACTION

The concepts of action and agency are central to interactionist theories of the self and the inter-action process. Action references experiences that are reflexively meaningful to the person. Agency describes the locus of action, whether in the person, in language, or in some other structure or process. At issue is the place of an autonomous, reflexive individual in the construction of meaningful action. That is, do persons, as agents, create their own experience? Or, is experience created by a larger entity, or agent? Are agency, meaning and intention in the actor, in the experience, or in the social structure? Do persons, as Karl Marx argued, make history, but not under conditions of their own making? If history goes on behind people's backs, then structures, not persons as agents, make history. If this is the case, then the real object of interactionist enquiry is not the person, or a single individual. Rather, external systems and discursive practices create particular subjectivities, and particular subjective experiences for the individual. Interactionists reject this interpretation, arguing that experience, structure and subjectivity are dialogical processes.

Following Giddens's theory of structuration, and his concept of the duality of structure, it can be argued that 'the structured properties of social systems are simultaneously the *medium and outcome of social acts*' (Giddens 1981: 19; emphasis in original). Further, 'all social action consists of social practices, situated in time-space, and organized in a skilled and knowledgeable fashion by human agents' (1981: 19). Thus does Giddens's interactionist model overcome the false opposition between action, agency, meaning and structure. Giddens's formulation is consistent with symbolic interactionist assumptions. Every individual is a practical social agent, but human agents are constrained by structural rules, by material resources, and by the structural processes connected to class, gender, race, ethnicity, nation and community.

3 ROOT ASSUMPTIONS

In its canonical form symbolic interactionism rests on the following root assumptions (see Blumer 1981).

1 'Human beings act toward things on the basis of the meanings that the things have for them' (Blumer 1969: 2).
2 The meanings of things arise out of the process of social interaction.
3 Meanings are modified through an interpretive process which involves self-reflective individuals symbolically interacting with one another (Blumer 1969: 2).
4 Human beings create the worlds of experience in which they live.
5 The meanings of these worlds come from interaction, and they are shaped by the self-reflections persons bring to their situations.
6 Such self-interaction is 'interwoven with social interaction and influences that social interaction' (Blumer 1981: 53).
7 Joint acts, their formation, dissolution, conflict and merger constitute what Blumer calls the 'social life of a human society'. A society consists of the joint or social acts 'which are formed and carried out by [its] members' (Blumer 1981: 153).
8 A complex interpretive process shapes the meanings things have for human beings. This process is anchored in the cultural world, in the 'circuit of culture' (du Gay et al. 1997: 3) where meanings are defined by the mass media, including advertising, cinema and television, and identities are represented in terms of salient cultural categories.

The basic task of the mass media is to make the second-hand world we all live in appear to be natural and invisible. Barthes (1957/1972: 11) elaborates, noting that the media dress up reality, giving it a sense of naturalness, so that 'Nature and History [are] confused at every turn.' The prime goals of the mass media complex are to create audience members who: (1) become consumers of the products advertised in the media; while (2) engaging in consumption practices that conform to the norms of possessive individualism endorsed by the capitalist political system; and (3) adhering to a public opinion that is supportive of the strategic polices of the state (Smythe 1994: 285). The audience is primarily a commodity that the information technologies produce (Smythe 1994: 268). A final goal of the media is clear: to do everything it can to make consumers as audience members think they are not commodities.

Herein lies the importance of cultural narratives and stories that reinforce the epiphanal nature of human existence under late twentieth-century capitalism. These stories give members the illusion of a soul, of structural freedom and free will. Thus do the circuits of culture (production, distribution, representation) implement this system of commodification.

4 RACE AND GENDER

All human experience is racially gendered; that is, filtered through the socially constructed categories of male and female. This system privileges whiteness over blackness. It reproduces negative racial and ethnic stereotypes about dark-skinned persons. It regulates interracial, inter-ethnic sexual relationships. The gendered categories (male and female) of the racial self are enacted in daily ritual performances, in the conversations between males and females, and in media representations (see **3.10**).

These gender categories are performative, established in and through the interaction process. This process of performing gender produces a gendered social order. In these performances there are no originals against which a particular gendered performance can be judged. Butler argues that each person constitutes through their interactional performances a situated version of a heterosexual, or non-heterosexual identity. Every performance is a masquerade, a copy of the real thing, an imitation of an imitation. Butler elaborates, 'If heterosexuality is an impossible imitation of itself, an imitation that performatively constitutes itself as the original, then the imitative parody of "heterosexuality" … is always and only an imitation of an imitation, a copy of a copy, for which there is no original' (1993: 644).

5 EPISTEMOLOGICAL AND CONCEPTUAL ASSUMPTIONS

The symbolic interactionist perspective may be clarified by outlining the empirical and theoretical practices interactionists value and do not value.

1 Interpretative (and symbolic) interactionists do not think general theories are useful.
2 Interactionists reject totalizing, grand theories of the social; interactionists, like many post-structural (Foucault) and post-modern (Lyotard) theorists, believe in writing local narratives about how people do things together.
3 Interactionists do not like theories that objectify and quantify human experience. They prefer to write texts that remain close to the actual experiences of the people they are writing about.
4 Interactionists do not like theories that are imported from other disciplines, like the natural sciences or economics (for example, chaos or rational choice theories).
5 Interactionists do not like theories that ignore history, but they are not historical determinists. They believe that persons, not inexorable forces, make history, but they understand that the histories that individuals make may not always be of their own making.
6 Interactionists do not like theories that ignore the biographies and lived experiences of interacting individuals.
7 Interactionists do not believe in asking 'why' questions. They ask, instead, 'how' questions. How, for example, is a given strip of experience structured, lived and given meaning?

These are the things that interactionists do not like to do. This means they are often criticized for not doing what other people think they should do, like doing macro-studies of power structures, or not having clearly defined concepts and terms, or being overly cognitive, or having emergent theories, or being ahistorical and astructural (see Musolf 1998). Too often these criticisms reflect either a failure to understand what the interactionist agenda is, or the fact that the critics have not read what interactionists have written.

6 ORIGINS: COOLEY, JAMES, MEAD, DEWEY, BLUMER

I now turn to a brief discussion of the origins of this perspective in American social theory (see also Musolf 1998: 20–92; also Holstein and Gubrium 2000: 17–37; Wiley 1994). Interactionists are cultural romantics. Often tragic and ironic, their vision of self and society stands in a direct line with the Left romanticism of Ralph Waldo Emerson, Karl Marx and William James. From the beginning, interactionists have been haunted by a Janus-faced spectre. On the one hand, the founding theorists argued for the interpretative, subjective study of human experience. On the other hand, they sought to build an objective science of human conduct, a science that would conform to criteria borrowed from the natural sciences.

Pragmatism, as a theory of knowing, truth, science and meaning, is central to the interactionist heritage. For Mead, James, Peirce and Dewey, truth is defined in terms of its consequences for action. What is true is what works. Pragmatism became a form of cultural criticism for Dewey and James. Dewey's pragmatism celebrated critical intelligence, implemented through the scientific method, as the proper mode of scientific enquiry. This pragmatic tradition, in its several forms, continues to the present day (see Denzin 1992: 131; Strauss 1993b). It remains one of the most viable interpretative philosophical positions now operating in the human disciplines.

Cooley contended that the self of the person arises out of experiences in primary groups, especially the family. Modern societies are shaped by the media. Governmentally regulated competition is the best mechanism for maintaining the democratic values of a society like the United States.

James argued that the state of consciousness, or stream of consciousness, is all that the field of psychology needed to posit. The self, in its principal form of knower or subject (the 'I'), is at the centre of the person's state of consciousness. In experience the 'I' interacts with the 'me', or the self as object. For James the person has as many selves as he or she has social relationships.

Mead turns Cooley and James on their heads. For him the self is not mentalistic. Self and mind are social and cognitive processes, lodged in the ongoing social world. Self is a social object which lies in the field of experience. It is structured by the principle of sociality, or the taking of the attitude of the other in a social situation. The self can be scientifically studied, like an object in the physical sciences. Rejecting introspection because it is not scientific, he argued for a view of the self and society which joins these two terms in a reciprocal process of interaction. His key term was 'the act', which replaces James's concept of stream of experience.

Blumer (1969) turns Mead into a sociologist. Offering a view of society that derives from Mead's picture of the social act, he introduced the concepts of joint action and acting unit to describe the interactions that extend from dyads to complex institutions. His self is an interpretative process, and his society (after Park and Thomas) is one built on the play of power, interest, group position, collective action and social protest. He applied Mead and Park to the study of fashion, film, racial prejudice, collective behaviour and the industrialization process.

With Mead, and Blumer's extension of Mead, the interaction tradition decisively moves away from the interpretative and phenomenological suggestions of Cooley and James. It enters a confused phase, as noted above, which attempts, though unsuccessfully, to become naturalistic, subjective and scientific. (In 1974 in *Frame Analysis* Goffman attempted to reclaim and then refute the neglected James and phenomenological tradition; see **2.2**.)

7 VARIETIES OF INTERACTIONIST THOUGHT

Symbolic interactionism comes in multiple varieties. These include: pragmatic, feminist, phenomenological and constructionist varieties. Diversity is not just theoretical. At the methodological level, interactionists employ a variety of interpretative, qualitative approaches, including autoethnographies, narratives of the self, structural, articulative, semiotic and practical ethnographies, grounded theory, the biographical, life history method, performance and feminist ethnographies, more traditional interviewing and participant observation practices, creative interviewing, the interpretative practices hinted at by Blumer, conversation analysis, ethnographic and laboratory searches for generic principles of social life, and historical studies of civilizational processes.

Substantively, interactionists have made major contributions to many areas of social science. An incomplete list would include the fields of deviance, social problems, collective behaviour, medical sociology, the emotions, the arts, social organization, race relations and industrialization, childhood socialization, fashion, film, the mass media, family violence and small groups. In short, there are many styles and versions of symbolic interactionism and these variations are displayed across the fields of sociology and social psychology.

8 RECENT DEVELOPMENTS: THE NARRATIVE TURN

Contemporary symbolic interactionists emphasize the reflexive, gendered, situated nature of human experience. They examine the place of language and multiple meanings in interactional contexts (see Holstein and Gubrium 2000). This reflexive, or narrative concern is also evidenced in other points of view, from phenomenology (see **3.1**), to hermeneutics (see **3.5**), semiotics, psychoanalysis (see **5.20**), feminism (see **3.10**), narratology (see **5.11**), cultural, discursive and dialogical psychology (see **5.19**), interpretive sociology and cultural studies (see **3.9**).

This narrative turn moves in two directions at the same time. First, symbolic interactionists (and other theorists) formulate and offer various narrative versions, or stories about how the social world operates. This form of narrative is usually called a theory, for example Freud's theory of psychosexual development (see **5.20**). On this, Charles Lemert reminds us that sociology is an act of the imagination, that the various sociologies are 'stories people tell about what they have figured out about their experiences in social life' (Lemert 1997: 14). This is how interactionism is best understood: various stories about the social world, stories people tell themselves about their lives and the worlds they live in, stories that may or may not work.

Second, symbolic interactionists study narratives and systems of discourse, suggesting that these structures give coherence and meaning to everyday life. (A system of *discourse* is a way of representing the world.) Systems of discourse both summarize and produce knowledge about the world (Foucault 1980: 27). These discursive systems are seldom just true or false. In the world of human affairs truth and facts are constructed in different ways. Their meanings are embedded in competing discourses. As such they are connected to struggles over power, or regimes of truth; that is, to who has the power to determine what is true and what is not true (Hall 1996c: 205).

9 EXPERIENCE AND ITS REPRESENTATIONS

It is not possible to study experience directly, so symbolic interactionists study how narratives, connected to systems of discourse (interviews, stories, rituals, myths), represents experience. These representational practices are narrative constructions. The meanings and forms of everyday experience are always given in narrative representations. These representations are texts that are performed, stories told to others. Bruner is explicit on this point: representations must 'be performed to be experienced' (1984: 7). Hence symbolic interactionists study performed texts, rituals, stories told, songs sung, novels read, dramas performed. Paraphrasing Bruner (1984: 7), experience is a performance, and reality is a social construction.

The politics of representation is basic to the study of experience. How a thing is represented involves a struggle over power and meaning. While social scientists have traditionally privileged experience itself, it is now understood that no life, no experience can be lived outside of some system of representation (Hall 1996d: 473). Indeed, 'there is no escaping ... the politics of representation' (Hall 1996d: 473; see **5.22**).

Symbolic interactionists are constantly constructing interpretations about the world. All accounts, 'however carefully tested and supported are, in the end, authored' (Hall, 1996a: 14). Interactionist explanations reflect the point of view of the author. They do not carry the guarantee of truth and objectivity. For example, feminist scholars have repeatedly argued (rightly we believe) that the methods and aims of positivistic social psychology are gender-biased, that they reflect patriarchal beliefs and practices (see **3.10**). In addition, the traditional experimental methods of social psychological enquiry reproduce these biases.

10 ASSESSING INTERPRETATIONS

The narrative turn and the feminist critique lead interactionists to be very tentative in terms of the arguments and positions they put forward. It is now understood that there is no final, or authorized version of the truth. Still, there are criteria of assessment that should be used. Interactionists are 'committed to providing systematic, rigorous, coherent, comprehensive, conceptually clear, well-evidenced accounts, which make their underlying theoretical structure and value assumptions clear to readers ... [still] we cannot deny the ultimately interpretive character of the social science enterprise' (Hall 1996a: 14).

Interpretive interactionists (see Denzin 2000) seek an existential, interpretive social science that offers a blueprint for cultural criticism. This criticism is grounded in the specific worlds made visible in the research process. It understands that all enquiry is theory- and value-laden. There can be no objective account of a culture and its ways. The ethnographic, the aesthetic and the political can never be neatly separated. Qualitative enquiry, like art, is always political.

A critical, civic, literary form of qualitative enquiry is one that should meet four criteria. It must evidence a mastery of literary craftsmanship, the art of good writing. It should present a well-plotted, compelling, but minimalist narrative. This narrative will be based on realistic, natural conversation, with a focus on memorable, recognizable characters. These characters will be located in well-described, 'unforgettable scenes' (Ford 1998: 1112). Second, the work should present clearly identifiable cultural and political issues, including injustices based on the structures and meanings of race, class, gender and sexual orientation. Third, the work should articulate a politics of hope. It should criticize how things are and imagine how they could be different. Finally, it will do these things through direct and indirect symbolic and rhetorical means. Writers who do these things are fully immersed in the oppressions and injustices of their time. They direct their ethnographic energies to higher, utopian, morally sacred goals.

The truth of these new texts is determined pragmatically, by their truth effects, by the critical, moral discourse they produce, by the 'empathy they generate, the exchange of experience they enable, and the social bonds they mediate' (Jackson 1998: 180). The power of these texts is not a question of whether 'they mirror the world as it "really" is' (Jackson 1998: 180). The world is always already constructed through narrative texts. Rorty (1979) is firm on this point. There is no mirror of nature. The world as it is known is constructed through acts of representation and interpretation.

Finally, this performative ethnography searches for new ways to locate and represent the gendered, sacred self in its ethical relationships to nature. An exploration of other forms of writing is sought, including personal diaries, nature writing and performance texts anchored in the natural world.

11   DISPUTES OVER TRUTH

There are many in the interactionist community who reject the narrative turn (as outlined above) and what it implies for interpretive work. These critics base their arguments on six beliefs:

1   The new writing is not scientific, therefore it cannot be part of the ethnographic project.
2   The new writers are moralists; moral judgements are not part of science.
3   The new writers have a faulty epistemology; they do not believe in disinterested observers who study a reality that is independent of human action.
4   The new writing uses fiction; this is not science, it is art.
5   The new writers do not study lived experience which is the true province of ethnography. Hence, the new writers are not participant observers
6   The new writers are postmodernists, and this is irrational, because postmodernism is fatalistic, nativistic, radical, absurd and nihilistic.

These six beliefs constitute complex discursive systems; separate literatures are attached to each. Taken together, they represent a formidable, yet dubious critique of the new interactionist project. They make it clear that there are no problems with the old ways of doing research. Indeed, the new ways create more problems then they solve. These beliefs serve to place the new work outside science, perhaps in the humanities, or the arts. Some would ban these persons from academia altogether. Others would merely exclude them from certain theory groups, that is from symbolic interactionism.

12   CONCLUSION

To summarize, symbolic interactionism offers a generic theory of action, meaning, motives, emotion, gender, the person and social structure. This theory has relevance for all of the human disciplines, from psychology, to sociology, history, anthropology and political science. Thus do interactionists study the intersections of interaction, biography and social structure in particular historical moments.

FURTHER READING

Holstein, J. A. and Gubrium, J. F. (2000) *The Self We Live By: Narrative Identity in a Postmodern World*. New York: Oxford University Press.

Musolf, G. R. (1998) *Structure and Agency in Everyday Life: An Introduction to Social Psychology*. Dix Hills, NY: General Hall, Inc.

Strauss, A. (l993) *Continual Permutations of Action*. New York: Aldine de Gruyter.

3.4 Constructivism

Uwe Flick

1 INTRODUCTION

The construction of social reality is booming as a topic. For almost all areas of social scientific research there are monographs or collections in which a constructivist approach is selected: on socialization (Grundmann 1999), health and illness (Gawatz and Nowak 1993; Lachmund and Stollberg 1992); on technological change (Flick 1996); or transsexuality (Hirschauer 1993) to name but a few. Scientific findings are also generally treated as social construction (e.g. Latour and Woolgar 1979), which has led to bitter controversies (cf. the debates resulting from Sokal 1996). Hacking (1999) desperately asks 'the social construction of What?'. With regard to qualitative research, constructivist ideas (such as Schütz 1962 or Berger and Luckmann 1966) have been the basis for a variety of methods. Over the course of time, however, little attention has been paid to these ideas in qualitative research. At present interest in constructivist ideas is again on the increase (e.g. Flick 2002: ch. 4; T. Sutter 1997).

2 WHAT IS CONSTRUCTIVISM?

A number of programmes with different departure points are subsumed under the label 'Constructivism'. What is common to all constructivist approaches is that they examine the relationship to reality by dealing with constructive processes in approaching it. Examples of constructions are to be found at different levels.

1 In the tradition of Jean Piaget (1937), cognition, perception of the world and knowledge about it are seen as constructs. Radical constructivism (Glasersfeld 1995) takes this thought to the point where every form of cognition, because of the neurobiological process involved, has direct access only to images of the world and of reality, but not of both. Luhmann (1990a) relates these ideas to systemic perspectives in order to use them as the basis for a social theory (1997).
2 Social constructivism in the tradition of Schütz (1962), Berger and Luckmann (1966) and Gergen (1985, 1999) enquires after the social conventionalizations, perception and knowledge in everyday life.
3 Constructivist sociology of science in the tradition of Fleck (1935/1979), the present-day 'laboratory-constructivist' research (Knorr-Cetina 1981; Latour and Woolgar 1979), seeks to establish how social, historical, local, pragmatic and other factors influence scientific discovery in such a way that scientific facts may be regarded as social constructs

('local products'). (On the distinctions between these different variants of constructivism cf. Knorr-Cetina 1989.)

Constructivism is not a unified programme, but is developing in parallel fashion in a number of disciplines: psychology, sociology, philosophy, neurobiology, psychiatry and information science. In what follows we shall deal briefly with the first two of the three levels we have presented here from the point of view of what is relevant to qualitative research. The empirical programme of (laboratory)-constructivism has not so far been applied to qualitative research. The following sections are guided by the idea that constructivism is concerned with how knowledge arises, what concept of knowledge is appropriate and what criteria can be invoked in the evaluation of knowledge. For qualitative research this is doubly relevant since, like all research, it engenders knowledge and therefore (at least very often) looks empirically at specific forms of knowledge – for example, biographical, expert or everyday knowledge.

3 EPISTEMOLOGICAL ASSUMPTIONS ON THE NATURE OF SOCIAL REALITY

Alfred Schütz has already claimed that facts only become relevant through their meanings and interpretations:

> Strictly speaking there are no such things as facts pure and simple. All facts are from the outset selected from a universal context by the activities of our mind. There are, therefore, always interpreted facts, either facts looked at as detached from their context by an artificial abstraction or facts considered in their particular setting. In either case, they carry along their interpretational inner and outer horizon. (Schütz 1962: 5)

A considerable part of the criticism of constructivism is devoted to the questions of the approach to reality, and it is for this reason that Mitterer (1999: 486) insists 'no kind of constructivism is of the opinion that "everything is constructed"'. Glasersfeld (1992: 30) underlines the point: 'radical constructivism *in no way* denies an external reality'. On the other hand, the various types of constructivism, from Schütz to Glasersfeld, do question whether external reality is *directly* accessible – that is to say, independent of perceptions and concepts

that we use and construct. Perception is seen not as a passive-receptive process of representation but as an active-constructive process of production. This has consequences for the question whether a representation (of reality, a process or an object) can be verified for its correctness against the 'original'. This form of verifiability, however, is questioned by constructivism, since an original is only accessible through different representations or constructions. And so the different representations or constructions can only be compared with one another. For constructivist epistemology, and empirical research based on it, knowledge and the constructions it contains become the relevant means of access to the objects with which they are concerned.

4 CONSTRUCTION OF KNOWLEDGE

Taking three main authors we may clarify how the genesis of knowledge and its functions may be described from a constructivist viewpoint.

1 Schütz (1962: 5) begins with this premise: 'All our knowledge of the world, in common-sense as well as in scientific thinking, involves constructs, i.e. a set of abstractions, generalizations, formalizations and idealizations, specific to the relevant level of thought organization.' For Schütz, every form of knowledge is constructed by selection and structuring. The individual forms differ according to the degree of structuring and idealization, and this depends on their functions – more concrete as the basis of everyday action or more abstract as a model in the construction of scientific theories. Schütz enumerates different processes which have in common that the formation of knowledge of the world is not to be understood as the simple portrayal of given facts, but that the contents are constructed in a process of active production.

2 This interpretation is developed further in radical constructivism, whose 'core theses' are formulated by Glasersfeld (1992: 30) as follows.

1 What we call 'knowledge' in no sense represents a world that presumably exists beyond our contact with it. ... Constructivism, like pragmatism, leads to a modified concept of cognition/knowledge. Accordingly knowledge is related to the way in which we organize our experiential world.

2 Radical constructivism *in no sense* denies an external reality. ...

3 Radical constructivism agrees with Berkeley that it would be unreasonable to confirm the existence of something that can/could not at some point be perceived. ...

4 Radical constructivism adopts Vico's fundamental idea that human knowledge is a human construct. ...

5 Constructivism abandons the claim that cognition is 'true' in the sense that it reflects objective reality. Instead it only requires that knowledge must be *viable*, in the sense that it should *fit* into the experiential world of the one who knows ... .

Seen in this way, knowledge organizes experiences that first permit cognition of the world beyond the experiencing subject or organism. Experiences are structured and understood through concepts and contexts that are constructed by this subject. Whether the picture that is formed in this way is true or correct cannot be determined. But its quality may be assessed through its *viability*, that is, the extent to which the picture or model permits the subject to find its way and to act in the world. Here an important point of orientation is the question of how the 'construction of concepts' functions (Glasersfeld 1995: 76–88).

3 For social constructionism the processes of social interchange in the genesis of knowledge take on a special significance, and in particular the concepts that are used. In this sense Gergen formulates the following 'assumptions for a social constructionism'.

> The terms by which we account for the world and ourselves are not dictated by the stipulated objects of such accounts ... . The terms and forms by which we achieve understanding of the world and ourselves are social artefacts, products of historically and culturally situated interchanges among people ... . The degree to which a given account of the world or self is sustained across time is not dependent on the objective validity of the account but on the vicissitudes of social processes ... . Language derives its significance in human affairs from the way in which it functions within patterns of relationship ... . To appraise existing forms of discourse is to evaluate patterns of cultural life; such evaluations give voice to other cultural enclaves. (Gergen 1994: 49ff.)

Knowledge is constructed in processes of social interchange; it is based on the role of language

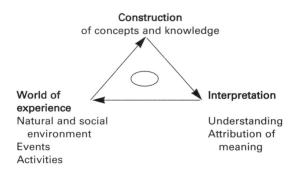

Figure 3.4.1 Construction and interpretation as means of access to the world of experience

in such relationships, and it has above all social functions. The eventualities of the social processes involved have an influence on what will survive as a valid or useful explanation.

In accordance with these three constructivist positions, our access to the world of experience – the natural and social environment and the experiences and activities it contains – operates through the concepts constructed by the perceiving subject and the knowledge deriving from these. These are then used to interpret experiences, or to understand and attribute meanings (see Figure 3.4.1).

The ideas of radical and social constructivism relate to cognition and knowledge in general but not (or only in specific ways) to scientific cognition. In particular, for radical constructivism there is as yet no translation of the basic ideas into a conceptualization of empirical research (the first guidelines were presented by Schmidt 1998). Here the focus should be on the importance of constructivism for research, and especially qualitative research. What remains to be clarified is the relationship between knowledge and research (see section 5) and the links between the world of experience and constructs, between constructs and interpretations, and between interpretations and the world of experience (see section 6).

5 SOCIAL SCIENTIFIC KNOWLEDGE AS A SOCIAL CONSTRUCTION

For the social sciences Schütz assumes that their knowledge starts from everyday understanding: 'The thought objects constructed by social scientists refer to, and are founded upon, thought objects constructed by the common-sense thought of man living in his everyday life among his fellow men' (1962: 6). Social scientific knowledge is developed on the basis of pre-existing everyday knowledge and socially constructed through this developmental process. The main idea is the distinction that Schütz makes between constructs of the first and second degree: 'the constructs of social science are, so to speak, constructs of the second degree, that is, constructs of the constructs made by the actors on the social scene'. Accordingly Schütz holds that 'the exploration of the general principles according to which man in daily life organises his experiences, and especially those of the social world, is the first task of the methodology of the social sciences' (1962: 59). For Schütz, everyday knowledge and cognition become the basis on which the social scientist develops a more strongly formalized and generalized 'version of the world' (Goodman 1978). Schütz (1962: 208ff.), therefore, assumes 'multiple realities', of which the world of science represents only one, which is, in part, organized according to different principles compared to the everyday world. Social scientific research becomes a kind of research that, on the basis of pre-existing everyday constructs, constructs another version of the world. Its results – the knowledge and objective meanings that it produces – are social constructs in the everyday world that is under investigation and, by extension, constructs in scientific analyses. Schütz's ideas were further developed for sociology by Berger and Luckmann (1966) and have subsequently exerted a strong influence, particularly on biographical research (see **3.6**, **3.7**, **5.11**) and on the development of ethnomethodology (see **2.3**, **3.2**, **5.17**).

Scientific knowledge as text

Social scientific analyses are increasingly using the medium of text for their constructs: data are collected as text (for example, in the form of interviews, see **5.2**), and processed and interpreted as such (see **5.10**, **5.21**). Ultimately, all discoveries are presented in textual form (see **5.22**). In concrete terms text is already partially used as a metaphor or a concept: from the 'world as a text' in general terms (Garz and Kraimer 1994a) to the city as a text (Darnton 1989); life as a story (Bruner 1990) to people and identities as texts (Gergen 1988; Shotter and

Gergen 1989). A similar direction is taken by ideas that there is no fundamental difference, at the level of modes of experience, between interpretations of texts, persons and artefacts (Dennett 1991), or that cognitive processes should first be analysed through the analysis of discourses, rather than memory and experiment (Edwards and Potter 1992; see **5.19**). In all these approaches the contexts being investigated and the modes of action and experience are presumed to be in texts or are investigated in them. Social scientific constructs therefore often become textual constructs, linked in part to the idea that everyday constructs are textual constructs. This approach has found particular favour in the context of the postmodernist debate and is related to the most recent developments of symbolic interactionism (see **3.3**) and the work of Denzin (see **2.7**, **5.7**). If this thought is pursued further, it may be asked what processes of construction (Schütz's first or second degree) or of world-making (Goodman) are going on in the transformation of modes of action and experience into texts or at least text-like constructions. To answer this question we shall refer to the concept of mimesis (cf. Gebauer and Wulf 1995), which will also give pointers for a social science working with texts.

6 MIMESIS AND WORLD-MAKING IN TEXTS

Mimesis is concerned with the representation of worlds – and in Aristotle this originally meant natural worlds – in symbolic worlds. In Blumenberg (1981) this is discussed as 'the imitation of nature'. In the critical theory of Horkheimer and Adorno (1972) and Adorno (1973), the term was used as a counter-idea to the rationality of conceptual thinking in the context of an increasingly scientized world-view (cf. also Wellmer 1985). At present growing interest may be detected in a broader understanding of mimesis: 'Mimesis can therefore be used in a comprehensive way to mean representation' (Reck 1991: 65). As an example, the representation of natural or social contexts in literary or dramatic texts or stage performances is often discussed: 'in this interpretation mimesis characterizes the act of producing a symbolic world, which encompasses both practical and theoretical elements' (Gebauer and Wulf 1995: 3). Current interest also focuses on this concept outside literature and the theatre. The debate thematizes mimesis as a general principle that can be used to demonstrate understanding of the world and texts: 'the individual assimilates himself or herself to the world via mimetic processes. Mimesis makes it possible for individuals to step out of themselves, to draw the outer world into their inner world, and to lend expression to their interiority. It produces an otherwise unattainable proximity to objects and is thus a necessary condition of understanding' (Gebauer and Wulf 1995: 2–3).

In applying these considerations to the production and functioning of social science and its texts mimetic components can be identified in the following places: in the translation of experiences into narratives, reports and so on by those under investigation,[1] in the construction of texts on this basis on the part of researchers, in their interpretation of such constructs and, finally, in the reflux of such interpretations into everyday contexts. This reflux of science into everyday life is discussed more fully in the theory of social representations (Moscovici 1984) or Matthes (1985). This means that social science has already contributed to determining and constructing the world it is investigating by means of its results – so long as these, as individual results, can attract to themselves the attention of a broader public (cf. also Gergen 1973 for further discussion of this). In this way its interpretations and modes of understanding again feed back into the modes of everyday experience. The fact that in this process such interpretations are not accepted one-for-one but are transformed in accordance with the rationalities of the everyday world has been shown by Moscovici (1961), on the reception of psychoanalysis, and utilization research (cf. Beck and Bonß 1989, see **6.3**) in a number of different case studies.

Mimesis as a process

A fruitful starting point to illustrate mimetic transformation processes in the production and reception of social scientific texts may be found in the ideas of Ricoeur (1981a, 1984). He breaks down the mimetic process, 'playfully yet seriously', into the steps of mimesis$_1$, mimesis$_2$ and mimesis$_3$:

> Hermeneutics, however, is concerned with reconstructing the entire arc of operations by which practical experience provides itself with works,

authors, and readers. … It will appear as a corollary at the end of this analysis, that the reader is that operator par excellence who takes up through doing something – the act of reading – the unity of the travel from mimesis$_1$ to mimesis$_3$ by way of mimesis$_2$. (Ricoeur 1984: 53)

The understanding of texts – and by extension of social reality – becomes an active process of producing reality in which not only the author of texts, or versions of the world, is involved but also the person for whom these are produced and who 'reads' or understands them. For Ricoeur the three forms of mimesis are distinguished as follows.

The mimetic transformation in the 'processing' of experiences from the social or natural environment into textual constructs – into concepts, knowledge or everyday stories to others, into particular types of document during the production of texts for research purposes – is always to be understood as a process of construction. According to Ricoeur, mimesis$_2$ is taking place here:

> Such is the realm of mimesis$_2$ between the antecedance and the descendance of the text. At this level mimesis may be defined as the configuration of action. This configuration is governed by a schematization which is historically structured in a tradition or traditions, and it is expressed in individual works that stand in varying relationships to the constraints generated by this schematism. (Ricoeur 1984: 53)

The mimetic transformation of such texts in modes of understanding by transformation takes place in processes of the everyday understanding of narratives, documents, books, newspapers and so on, and in the scientific interpretation of such narratives, research documents or texts. Ricoeur refers to this as mimesis$_3$. It 'marks the intersection of the world of text and the world of the hearer or reader' (1981a: 26).

Finally, in the reflux of such everyday and/or scientific interpretations into modes of action via prior understanding of human action and social or natural phenomena, mimesis$_1$ plays a role:

> Whatever may be the status of these stories which somehow are prior to the narration we may give them, our mere use of the word story (taken in this pre-narrative sense) testifies to our pre-understanding that action is human to the extent that it characterises a life story that deserves to be

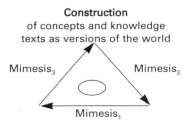

Construction
of concepts and knowledge
texts as versions of the world

Mimesis₃ ... Mimesis₃

Mimesis₁

World of experience
Natural and social
  environment
Events
Activities

Interpretation
Understanding
Attribution of
  meaning

Figure 3.4.2   Process of mimesis

told. Mimesis₁ is that pre-understanding of what human action is, of its semantics, its symbolism, its temporality. From this pre-understanding, which is common to poets and their readers, arises fiction, and with fiction comes the second form of mimesis which is textual and literary. (Ricoeur 1981a: 20)

According to this view, which Ricoeur formulated to handle literary texts, mimetic processes can be found at the following points in social scientific understanding as an interplay of construction and the interpretation of experiences (see Figure 3.4.2).

Gebauer and Wulf (1995) explain that understanding as a constructive process, by involving the person who understands, extends to understanding as a whole in social scientific research. They base this on Goodman's (1978) theory of different modes of world-making and the versions of the world that derive from this as a result of cognition: 'knowing in terms of this model is a matter of invention: modes of organization "are not found in the world but built into the world"' (Gebauer and Wulf 1995: 28). Gebauer and Wulf discuss mimesis in processes of cognition in general terms. Ricoeur develops this concept for processes of understanding in relation to literature in a manner that emerges without the narrow and strict idea of the portrayal of a given reality, and without the corresponding narrow concept of reality and truth: 'Mimesis in this sense is ahead of our concepts of reference, the real and truth. It engenders a need as yet unfilled to think more' (1981a: 31). This interpretation of mimesis can extend the process of the social construction of reality – in

knowledge, in texts and generally – and can complement the conceptions of radical constructivism and social constructionism.

7 CONSTRUCTIVISM AND QUALITATIVE RESEARCH

From this point of view, mimesis may be used to provide a conception of understanding in the social sciences that takes account of the fact that material to be understood should be dealt with at various levels as something that is constructed and presented: mimetic processes can be found in the processing of experiences in everyday practice. They also take place in interviews and thereby in every construction of textualized and textualizable versions of the world which are thus rendered accessible to social science. Finally, they also play a role in the production of texts for research purposes – for example, transcripts, reports or interpretations.

This idea of the mimetic process can also be applied to a type of design (see **4.1**) that is widespread in qualitative research – the reconstruction of life-histories or biographies (see **3.6**, **3.7**) in interviews (see **5.2**). In this, narratives (see **5.11**) are considered to be the appropriate form for the representation of biographical experiences. Ricoeur (1981a: 20) supports the 'thesis of the narrative or pre-narrative quality of experience'. With regard to the mimetic relationship between life-histories and narratives Bruner explains:

> that the mimesis between life so-called and narrative is a two-way affair: … Narrative imitates life, life imitates narrative. 'Life' in this sense is the same kind of construction of the human imagination as 'a narrative' is. It is constructed by human beings through active ratiocination, by the same kind of ratiocination through which we construct narratives. When someone tells you his life … it is always a cognitive achievement rather than a through the clear-crystal recital of something univocally given. In the end, it is a narrative achievement. There is no such thing psychologically as 'life itself'. At very least, it is a selective achievement of memory recall; beyond that, recounting one's life is an interpretive feat. (Bruner 1987: 12–13)

Seen in this way the biographical narration of one's own life is not a portrayal of factual sequences. It becomes a mimetic representation of experiences that are constructed more generally in one's knowledge and more specifically for this purpose – in the interview – in the form of a narrative. On the other hand, the narrative provides a general framework within which experiences are ordered, represented, evaluated and so on – in short, within which they are experienced. The object that qualitative research is investigating (here) already has, in everyday life, the form in which it seeks to investigate, construct and interpret it. In the interview situation these everyday modes of interpretation and construction are used to allocate these experiences to a symbolic world – that of science and its texts. The experiences are then interpreted from within this world.

Through reconstructing life by means of particular questions a version of the particular experiences is constructed and interpreted. The extent to which the life and experiences actually occurred in the form reported cannot be checked, but it can be established what construction of both the narrating subject is presenting, and also which version arises in the research situation. These experiences and the world in which they happened should ultimately be presented and seen in the representation of the results of this reconstruction in a specific way – perhaps in the form of a (new) theory (see **2.1**, **5.13**, **6.6**) with claims of validity. Mimetic processes create versions of the world which can then be understood and interpreted through qualitative research. Ricoeur's different forms of mimesis and Schütz's distinction between everyday and scientific constructs provide further content for the framework that was set up by Goodman with his assumption of different versions of the world created by everyday, artistic and scientific modes of construction.

For qualitative research constructivist assumptions become relevant for the understanding of collected data – for example, biographies as constructs (cf. Bude 1984 for discussion). Here we must ask whether qualitative research succeeds in gaining access to the constructs of the interview partner or the members of a research area.

As may be shown in the case of objective hermeneutics (see **5.16**), constructivist assumptions also become relevant for the critical analysis of procedure and methodological requirements (cf. Flick 2000a for an application to this process of the idea of mimesis outlined here), or in the sense of some further development (cf. T. Sutter 1997 on the linking of this approach or conversation analysis (see **5.17**) to constructivism in the sense given in Luhmann 1990a).

In more general terms we may ask, in the sense of social scientific constructivism, what processes of decision-making belong to the qualitative research process (see **4.1**) and how they influence the process of cognition and the desired results (cf. Flick 1995, 2002 for further discussion).

Finally, constructivist assumptions may be used as a starting point for the debate on the question of justifying the validity of qualitative research (cf. Steinke 1999, and **4.7**) – in particular, because the validity of knowledge and its determination are a major problem for radical constructivism which has to be dealt with under the key-word of the viability[2] of knowledge, models, theories or discoveries (cf. Glasersfeld 1995).

NOTES

1 Here the understanding of mimesis which Bruner develops, with reference to Aristotle and Ricoeur, becomes relevant: 'mimesis was the capturing of "life in action", an elaboration and amelioration of what happened' (Bruner, 1990: 46). 'Mimesis is a kind of metaphor of reality. ... It refers to reality not in order to copy it but in order to give it a new reading' (Ricoeur 1981b: 292–293). Mimetic processes can then be understood as a principle of the representation in everyday language of modes of action, events and situations, 'brought' by the latter into a communicable and intelligible version – for the subject and for others.

2 Viability means that knowledge or other constructions must show themselves to be useful and sustainable (capable of life) in the particular context of use – they must fit and allow the individual to act and survive in the particular environment. This does not mean that constructions must be true or contain correct depictions: neither of these can be checked since they cannot be directly compared with the original.

FURTHER READING

Flick, U. (2002) *An Introduction to Qualitative Research,* 2nd edition. Thousand Oaks, CA: Sage.

Gergen, K. J. (1994) *Realities and Relationships. Soundings in Social Construction*. Cambridge, MA: Harvard University Press.

Glasersfeld, E. von (1995) *Radical Constructivism. A Way of Knowing and Learning*. London: The Falmer Press.

3.5 Social Scientific Hermeneutics

Hans-Georg Soeffner

In the course of its history the teaching of the interpretative procedure known as hermeneutics has undergone many changes, seen many extensions and – as a self-reflective mode of discovery – has contributed critically to its own modification. From a historical and systematic viewpoint it is bound up with the principle of the written nature of phenomena, then with the recording of language (or texts), but then – by logical extension – with the recorded nature of 'data' in general, that is to say, with the fixedness and implicit tendency to infinitely repeated recursivity (or 'discursivity') of both linguistic and non-linguistic documents: these include human utterances, actions and productions, or human objectivizations of every kind.

The general questions with which hermeneutics is concerned, however, have also been subject to supplementation and change. Whereas in the past it was concerned exclusively with the 'value' of understanding, today – particularly in those procedures that may collectively be referred to as social scientific hermeneutics – it is interested to an ever-growing extent in the 'how'. It is therefore interested in the understanding of understanding itself, in procedures, 'rules', 'patterns', implicit premises, modes of meaning and understanding that are communicated as part of the socializing processes of adaptation, instruction and the passing on of traditions.

1 PHENOMENOLOGY OF UNDERSTANDING

We can give the name *understanding* to the process that gives meaning to an experience. The name *understanding the other* we can give to the process by means of which we give meaning to an experience in such a way that it relates to some event in the world which has already been given a meaning by the *alter ego*.

Understanding, as a process related to the achievements of my own consciousness, is on the one hand *logically* at the root of the understanding of the *alter ego*, and on the other hand self-understanding is *empirically* a product what, in the tradition of symbolic interactionism (see 3.3) since Charles H. Cooley (1902), has been called the 'looking-glass self': a transference of the understanding of others to my own consciousness. Self-understanding is, in principle, continuously and fully possible, since experiences have no immediate meaning in themselves. It is, rather, the subjective consciousness which constitutes meaning by relating an experience to other phenomena. This act of meaning-making contains in essence what is meant by understanding as self-understanding. Conversely, other-understanding – and this is crucial for the problems of understanding in general – takes place according to *perspectives of interpretation*. This means that other-understanding is only possible in a discontinuous and partial manner. Self-understanding is, in principle, an unquestionable act; other-understanding is, in principle, a questionable act.

Other-understanding is based on *my* experiences of the *alter ego*. Every meaning that I ascribe to it can deviate from the meaning that the *alter ego* itself gives to its experiences. I always grasp only fragments of its actual experience. And I always understand possibly only its actual subjectively intended meaning. The consciousness of *alter ego* is available to me only through signs and tokens. These demonstrate three layers of meaning (cf. Eberle 1984): (1) an objectivized, inter-subjectively valid meaning; (2) a subjective meaning; and (3) an occasional meaning. If I wish to understand the *alter ego*, then, hypothetically, I have to display its subjective motives and reconstruct the objective, subjective and occasional meaning of its denotations. In this way it becomes plausible that understanding of the meaning of the 'other' can only be achieved in an approximate way.

Unquestionably, the *ego* does not have a monopoly on the interpretation of the world in everyday life but empirically is always to be found in a world that has been pre-interpreted by others. In the everyday world the maxim applies that the viewpoints of the one and the other are, in the main, interchangeable, and that what is valid for the one would also be relevant for the other, if he were in the same place, and that this is and always will be the case. This means that other-understanding in everyday life is not difficult in itself but a matter of unquestionable routine. While, from an epistemological point of view, the problem of other-understanding also consists of explaining how this is at all possible, in everyday opinion it represents a rather banal achievement of the consciousness: for human beings it is 'normally' so normal that it is not a matter of everyday interest.

Human behaviour, as an observable form of human action – be it linguistic or non-linguistic – is interpretable by and for human beings because, in addition to many other properties, it always displays that of being (proto-)symbolic. From the gesture to the 'significant' symbol, from the token and symptom to the constructed and unambiguously defined mathematical sign, from the body and facial expression to clothing, from the natural impression to the human product, we attribute to ourselves and our environment the qualities of signs, and with these we

constitute the human interpretative horizon (Wundt 1928; Bühler 1934; Mead 1934). Here the different types of signs and their varying semantics and associations also correspond to different interpretative procedures (cf. Schütz and Luckmann 1989: 131–147).

Understanding is therefore not at all an invention of the human and social sciences. Furthermore, it does not initially happen in a particular theoretical perspective, but is a constantly practised everyday routine for human beings. The permanent problem of hermeneutic scientists therefore consists of giving a plausible explanation of what makes their activity into a scientific undertaking, even though it is based explicitly on a completely everyday competence that is common to all human beings.

2 PARTICULAR FEATURES OF SOCIAL SCIENTIFIC UNDERSTANDING

Every social scientist, before he or she dares to make prognoses, is concerned with the description and analysis of those constructs that relate to the actions and plans of members of society in an everyday, pragmatic perspective: constructs of the 'first degree' (Schütz 1962: 3–47) of everyday socio-historically based types, models, routines, plausibilities, forms of knowledge, contents of knowledge and (often implicit) inferences. This means above all that the 'data' of the social scientist, unlike those of the natural scientist, are pre-interpreted, that his constructs are constructs of constructs. The social scientist develops constructs "of the second degree". These are controlled methodically tested and testable, interpretative reconstructions of constructs "of the first degree"'.

The scientific interpreter is doing, in principle, nothing different from what humans do in their daily life: he or she is interpreting perceptions as evidence of a meaning that underlies them. But unlike the ordinary person, the scientific interpreter seeks to create clarity through the preconditions and methods of his or her understanding. For it is in this way, and only in this way, that interpretation becomes a scientific method. And it is only through this that interpretation becomes systematically teachable and learnable.

Between constructs of the 'first degree' and of the 'second degree' there is therefore a logical difference (cf. also Carnap 1928), and also more than this alone. The action to which reconstructions relate is, by the time these begin, long past, gone for ever and unrepeatable. If it can still be at all accessible to understanding, it must be represented in particular 'data' (or traces), and it 'presents' itself in the data as a completed action. Because they are concerned with testable, that is, intersubjectively and rationally feasible, reconstructions, social scientists cannot hope either to replicate these actions congenially, or to enter empathetically into the souls and minds, the thoughts and feelings of the (original) actors: instead they are subject to 'reconstructive-hermeneutic' models of possibility for the courses of action *and* the actors.

The understanding of the social scientist, therefore, takes place according to a special rather than an everyday perspective, which Schütz calls a theoretical sub-world of meaning. This is a perspective of fundamental doubt in a taken for granted social reality. It is characterized by the fact that it discounts concern about one's own existence and is only interested in seeing reality clearly and in recognizing the 'truth' (that is, the make-up) of social reality. In this perspective there is no presence of the social world, no being-in-situation, no living people, but only idealized models of social phenomena and artificial beings constructed by the social scientist. Social scientific understanding differs from everyday understanding in that interpretative achievements do not happen here with reference to everyday understanding but with reference to extensively activated knowledge and in reliance on a reservoir of specialist professional knowledge. This kind of understanding is, unlike everyday knowledge, not related to the pragmatic needs of daily living but to the relevance system of a pragmatically disinterested observer (Schütz 1932/1967: 220–241).

Social scientific understanding has as its goal the discovery of the constitutive conditions of 'reality' and the demystification of social constructs. It has to reconstruct phenomena on which the scientist is focusing in a manner that corresponds to the meaning, is adequate to the problem and logically consistent. It must also make it possible to explain them in a way that is 'adequate to meaning' and also 'causally adequate', in the sense of Weber (1949a). The practical social value of this enterprise lies in making human beings aware of the circumstances, contexts and rules that are not normally prominent in everyday understanding but within which their life is conducted (cf. Luckmann 1983).

Social scientific understanding, therefore, is always essentially an understanding of understanding, an understanding 'of the second degree'.

3 HERMENEUTICS AS A SELF-REFLECTIVE ENTERPRISE

Most human interpretative achievements are carried out, as we have already said, in a manner that is not methodically controlled, but is rather unquestioning – and perhaps incidentally – against the background of an implicit knowledge of the 'here and now' and of what has to be done. To what is implicitly known, always indicated and involved in the interpretation of actions, we must add what, in phenomenologically oriented social-philosophy or 'proto-sociology', is known as the 'daily life-world' (Luckmann 1983, 1990), and in social research as the 'milieu' (Grathoff 1989) or 'small social life-world' (e.g. Hitzler and Honer 1984, 1988; Luckmann 1970; see **3.8**): the human being's concrete environment, the totality of all that humans experience as having an effect on them, irrespective of the question of what affects them 'objectively' (Gurwitsch 1977/1979: 60).

For a social science of the forms of social orientation, action, production and knowledge the same is true as for phenomenological philosophy: 'environment' is a concept that 'has its place exclusively in the spiritual sphere' (Husserl 1936/1978: 272), that is, a concept that represents the specifically human forms of denotation, symbolically organized perception, interpretation and action, 'behind' which human beings cannot look. Accordingly, it is unreal to describe the natural environment or the non-spiritual world as something alien to the spirit and 'to buttress humanistic science with natural science so as to make it supposedly exact' (Husserl 1936/1978: 272).

The human environment, or life-world, therefore cannot be described either by a model of 'external/internal' or 'subject/object' or with the aid of spatial measurements and territorial demarcations. For us it is not something opposed, it is neither a cage nor an unlimited space but, rather, a horizon of perception, orientation and action. It moves with us, when we move, it changes us – and our action – when we change it. It does not exist without us, and we do not exist without it. But we *are* not our environment:

we *have* it. Our relationship to it and to ourselves – if we agree with Plessner (1970: 41f.) – is determined by our 'eccentric positionality', by the 'ambiguous character' of our existence, which represents two distinct but overlapping orders. Empirical milieu-analysis, or life-world analysis, represents an attempt to describe the concrete forms of orientation, action and organization of individuals in and with their environment, and to interpret concrete action against this background.

Descriptions of milieux or 'small life-worlds' therefore document – in addition to spoken and transcribed texts – the modes of orientation of a human being in space, in the concrete environment, in the time lived in, to the personal physical essence and to other human beings: in this sense they document the largely non-linguistic production and reproduction of a social interactive structure, the singularity of which is translated into the collective semantic types of language and which must therefore also be interpreted.[1] At the same time, however, there arises the fundamental problem of recording and describing milieux and/or situations: putting non-linguistic phenomena into language.

Beyond the sensually perceptible world – to order, classify and interpret it – a separate world of collective signs and symbols is constructed (Cassirer 1953–1996; Langer 1957), both in language and in action and orientation (see Berger and Luckmann 1966: 97–146). Small life-worlds, milieux and the actions which take place within them and which form them are constituted symbolically: life in social order and in milieux as components of this order means life in symbols and symbolically organized referential contexts. To this extent linguistic and milieu-analysis are also the analysis of symbols, and to this extent the symbolic context as a whole also determines the forms and typology of human action. Accordingly, science as the analysis of symbols consists of the attempt to reconstruct the symbolic total context of the forms of human action, orientation and knowledge. (Concrete examples of this are in Soeffner 1997.)

Beyond (linguistic) texts and, in scientific hermeneutics, often underlying them, the universal interpretative claim of hermeneutics becomes recognizable together with this change of focus to the milieu or everyday life-world: for hermeneutics there are no *materia nuda*, no 'brute facts'. Instead, the problem of the delimitation of texts and/or meaning objects now becomes visible; this is, in other words, the problem of context, of the embedding of the meaning horizon of signifier, meaning and objects of meaning (see also Bühler 1934). From this it follows that (1) hermeneutics is, in terms of this claim, *universal*, as an interpretative human approach to the world and human existence within it which is carried out in everyday life (and which is therefore also scientifically reconstructable and capable of methodological definition); (2) because signifier, interpretation and objects of meaning, however, are independent of their respective embedding in milieux, history, narratives and meaning-communities, the various results of hermeneutic interpretation are *relative*. They exist in relation to a given socio-historical context of meaning and acquire their validity relative to this.

This relativity is not in any sense arbitrary, for – in scientific hermeneutics – it does not exclude rigorous processes of checking: these checking processes focus on the relationship between interpretation and its specific surrounding conditions, and this relationship can be made plausible intersubjectively. By taking conscious account of the principle and the actual instance of relativity, the claim to intersubjectivity of the procedure and of the results is maintained and implemented: arbitrariness is excluded by linking relativity and intersubjectivity to each other in a controlled way.

From a perspective of milieu theory and life-world analysis, which makes visible an objectively operating layer of meaning of subjective orientation prior to the historical perspective, the whole scope of what is perceptible is determined by the cultural relevances of the observer. The approach to intersubjectively possible understanding must therefore fulfil the following (Scheler 1923; Srubar 1981):

1 conscious and controlled abstraction on the part of the interpreter from his or her own cultural certainties and historical perspective (reflection of personal prejudice);
2 reconstruction (as far as possible) of the structure of the 'alien' milieu and the historical linking of a transmitted document or 'record', and of the 'other' life-world of the producer (getting the 'other' to speak);
3 allocation of one's own and the other's experiential structure and interpretation, and the object of meaning, to a scientific 'universe of discourse' of objectively possible (that is,

intersubjectively realizable) milieux, contexts and meanings (location in semantic space).

4 PROBLEMS OF METHODOLOGICALLY CONTROLLED UNDERSTANDING

Social scientific interpretations are essentially sample case studies. They are carried out at two levels: (1) in seeking, testing and fixing the rules of interpretation and procedures; (2) in reconstructing a particular case-structure in which they make visible the conditions and constitutive rules of social phenomena and objects in their concrete manifestation, their concrete effect and their mutability. In this process, on the one hand, the case in its particularity and the conditions of its individualization should be made visible (see, for example, Soeffner 1997: ch. 1). And on the other hand, this typicality and comparability should be developed and 'explained' from the analysis of the forms and structures involved in the development and changing of types.

The interpretation of a case requires objectivity in two directions: (1) with regard to verifiability, that is, clarification of the interpretative procedure and the prior knowledge that informs it, as well as the related obligation to verify which interpreters impose on themselves and other scientific interpreters; (2) with regard to the direction and goal of the procedure: the analysis of what is from a social viewpoint 'objectively' effective – to the social institutions and their historically valid meaning as determinants of an action, and to the meaning-structure of the action, which is possibly hidden, or 'latent', for the actor (Oevermann et al. 1979).

The goal of analysis is the concise reconstruction of an objectivized type of social action from its concrete, case-specific manifestations. This objectivized type is an 'ideal type' in so far as it is constructed on the one hand with the aim of falsifying empiricism to the extent that it gives an unreliable reproduction of what is specific in a particular case; and on the other hand to help justify the individual case precisely because it highlights what is historically particular against the background of structural generality (Schütz and Luckmann 1973: 229–241; Weber 1949b: 89–101).

The reconstruction of an objectivized type of social action is built up from (extensive) single-case studies via case comparison, description and reconstruction of case-transcending patterns, to the description and reconstruction of case-transcending and, at the same time, case-generating structures. The type that is reconstructed in this way encompasses and illuminates the structural difference of evolutionary and historically changing structural formations, on the one hand, and their concrete historically and culturally specific defining characteristics, on the other.[2]

In this way single-case analyses assist in the gradual discovery of general structures in social action, while the single case itself is interpreted as an historically concrete response to a concrete historical (problem-)situation and formation of structure: with the individual phenomena the development of structure is advanced, and with the single-case analyses the development of theory is updated.

The route from interpretative understanding to 'causal' explanation of the sequence and the effects of social action therefore passes through a construct of a *conceptually pure type* of the actor or actors thought to be acting as a type and the meaning subjectively intended by them (Weber 1972/1978: 1–10), that is to say, a construction of the 'second degree' (Schütz 1962). Then and only in the world of these ideal-typical, purposive-rational constructs can it be decided how the actors would have behaved and acted in a case of 'ideal purposive-rationality' (Esser 1999). Only with the assistance of these ideal-typical constructs, which achieve their terminological, classificatory and heuristic purpose better the more 'alien' they are, can comparisons be made with the action that has been documented. And only then is it possible to give a 'causal' explanation of the 'distance' between action in this ideal-typical purposive rationality, on the one hand, and the documented action, on the other hand, so that one can name the elements that, in the case being studied, have interfered in the 'pure purposive-rationality' and infiltrated these with other features.

The concrete single case is therefore causally explained exclusively with regard to its distance and difference from the conceptually 'pure' and purposive-rational ideal type. The single case is not interpretatively understood through this causal explanation of difference, but rather the reverse: through interpretative understanding of social action one arrives at a construct of ideal types which for their part make the single case visible and help it achieve its goal. In so far as they clarify its difference from the ideal type, they assist in the understanding of its singularity and concrete manifestation.

Interpretative social science is, in this sense, the progressive reconstruction, the progressive interpretative understanding of social action which takes seriously the single case and thereby human beings, their norms and their history. Scientific 'constructs of the second degree', the historical-genetic ideal-types, are seeking precisely this historical understanding of the single case and, equally, the understanding of history.

NOTES

1 At a clear distance in time from the related research activities in the USA, an everyday ethnography, in the sense given here, has developed in the German-speaking world since the 1980s (see **3.8**). Examples of this are to be found in studies of the agricultural milieu (Hildenbrand 1983), of the small life-world of the body-builder (Honer 1985) and the water-diviner (Knoblauch 1991a), of the labour situation (Knorr-Cetina 1981, 1989), of punk culture (Lau 1992), of police work (Reichertz 1991a) and of the making of donations (Voß 1992). See also the relevant contributions in Soeffner (1988).

2 As a 'famous' example we may refer here to the hospital studies of Barney Glaser and Anselm Strauss, in the context of which the so-called 'grounded theory' – the principle of abstracting a theory step by step on the basis of single-case studies – was developed (Glaser and Strauss 1965b, 1967, 1968; Strauss 1987; see **2.1**, **5.13**, **6.6**).

FURTHER READING

Denzin, N. K. (1989) *Interpretive Interactionism*. Newbury Park, CA: Sage.

Dewey, J. (1934) *Art as Experience*. New York: Menton, Balch & Co.

Psathas, G. (ed.) (1973) *Phenomenological Sociology*. New York: Wiley.

Soeffner, H.-G. (1997) *The Order of Rituals. The Interpretation of Everyday Life*. New Brunswick, NJ: Transaction Books.

Strauss, A. (1991) *Creating Sociological Awareness. Collective Images and Symbolic Representations*. New Brunswick, NJ: Transaction Books.

3.6   Qualitative Biographical Research

Winfried Marotzki

1   BIOGRAPHY AND THE HISTORY OF EDUCATION IN A TIME OF SOCIAL CHANGE

The questions how human beings learn and what education means should also be considered with reference to the *intellectual situation of the time*. What is characteristic of contemporary social development is the rapid introduction of new information processing technologies. If one also considers the areas of genetic research and research into artificial intelligence together with the public discussions they have unleashed, then the question of the place of human beings within the whole structure of modern socio-technical systems becomes ever more urgent. We are obliged to rethink our understanding of mankind to be able to give information about the significance of learning and education in highly complex societies. To deal with this question it is helpful to make use of a research direction that has grown in popularity both in the social sciences and in education over the past 15–20 years: qualitative biographical research

(see also **3.7**). Human development is approached, from the perspective of this research direction, as a lifelong process of learning and education, so the question 'What can we know about a human being today?' (Sartre 1981: 7) can in essence be handled through the study of patterns of learning and educational profiles in their biographical dimensions.

Although in the tradition of educational studies the theme of biography can also display a tradition as autobiography – for example, in Wilhelm Dilthey's pertinent reflections – the true motivation for the development of a research programme comes from the development of the so-called interpretative or qualitative paradigm (Hoffmann-Riem 1980) in the social sciences. With this, in addition to a predominantly quantitative approach to educational and biographical research (Leschinsky 1988), a type of biographical research has arisen that is oriented to the standards of qualitative social research (Marotzki 1995a; see **3.7**).

Its bases consist of assumptions that have been elaborated in such differing disciplines as the sociology of knowledge, symbolic interactionism (see **3.3**), ethno-theory, ethnomethodology (see **3.2**) and conversation analysis (see **5.17**). One central methodological assumption consists of establishing social facts according to the meaning attribution of the actors. Here we apply the 'premise of the interactional conditionality of individual meaning attributions' (Hoffmann-Riem 1980: 342) that has been particularly developed in symbolic interactionism (Blumer 1969). The interplay between the individual and society is seen as an interpretative process which is played out in the medium of significant symbols (such as language). The human being becomes acquainted with the world and him/herself primarily in interpretations that are mediated by, and bound to, interaction. Qualitative biographical research accepts that the biography of an individual can always be understood as a construct, but not only as that. The main focus of its observation lies in studying individual forms of the processing of social and milieu-specific experience. Individual forms can, of course, be those that are projected on to individuals during socialization and which they accept. But not every case can be treated as an acceptance. Individual variation or even the creation of new structures of experience processing, as an emerging and in part also a contingent process, cannot be derived from social models. Individuality and the problems of emergence and contingence are interrelated.

Emergence, in this context, means that human decisions are never completely programmable by environmental factors. Biographical decisions, which always contain an element of freedom, cannot be reconstructed as an ethical algorithm. *Contingence* means the existential experience of the finite and the coincidental, which cause humans to be thrown back on themselves. If it was said at the outset that the question of how humans learn must always be viewed within a temporal diagnostic framework, then we must also point out here that an increase in contingence is indeed a feature of the development of modern society. In this sense Peukert writes:

> What is characteristic of the new age is a matter of debate. The least controversial claim is that it is based on a radicalized experience of the finiteness and coincidental nature of everything that happens: it is coincidental and finite, that is 'contingent', to the extent that it could also be different

or not happen at all. The contingency of facts is no longer captured by an intuitively comprehensible order of being. (Peukert 1984: 130)

Accordingly, it becomes increasingly difficult to describe or predict *normal biographies*. It becomes increasingly questionable to describe and expect any development as *normal*. Human forms of reaction and processing are diverse. The increased distinctions between worlds of social meaning are accompanied by an increasing diversity of individual lifestyles and values. Discovery movements and experimental forms of existence seem for many people not to be restricted merely to crisis situations in their lives but to be taking on the nature of a permanent way of living. In other words, the question about subjective meaning content implies that it means something different from merely what an individual is offered in the way of social models. In this perspective subjectivity is not understood just as the simple result of social intersubjectivity, but as its condition. Qualitative biographical research sees its opportunity in the fact that it confronts the complexity of the individual case. Two aspects of this, which are decisive for the constitution of biographies, will be developed below: processes of meaning-production, and processes of the creation of self-images and world-images.

2 PROCESSES OF SENSE- AND MEANING-MAKING

Wilhelm Dilthey (1852–1911), in his *Foundations of the Humanities* (1968b), opened a way of understanding the course of human life that has hitherto scarcely been used. He opposes mechanistic, technocratic and reductionist concepts of mankind and, on the basis of the now famous dictum 'we explain nature; we understand mankind', he developed a concept to make it possible to understand mankind through its manifestations. By human manifestations he means both artistic products and every kind of ordered activity and behaviour in social contexts. He sees the methodological starting-point for this kind of concept of understanding in that internal experience in which reality is presented to us. For him understanding is closely linked to the tradition of hermeneutics, which concerns itself with the interpretation of texts and communicative situations. From a methodological point of view human objectivizations and manifestations are conceived in the broadest sense as *text* (see Blankertz 1982: 219), which has to be interpreted in the process of understanding.

For Dilthey the task of the humanities consists of understanding socially interrelated individual *life units*, that is 'to re-experience them and capture them in thought' (Dilthey 1968b: 340). These life units are first described as individual persons and as their forms of expression, their words and actions. These single individuals, however, are not understood as isolated atomized subjects but, as we would put it today, as mediated by socialization. This means that they are embedded in social units such as families, groups, society, humanity. On the one hand they are characterized by these in a particular historical situation; and on the other hand the individuals influence these units to a greater or lesser extent. No concept, in Dilthey's opinion, can capture all of the content of these individual units:

> Rather the multiplicity of what is apparently contained in them can only be experienced, understood and described. And their enmeshing in the course of history is a singular event that is inexhaustible for human thought. (1968b: 341)

Conceptual thinking therefore, if we pursue Dilthey's idea, is only conditionally capable of understanding humans in their individual incarnations. It is an *essential* element of the process of understanding, but not a *sufficient* one.

Sense-making as the production of coherences

Sense is produced, in Dilthey's opinion, with the aid of the mechanisms of coherence-creation. The category of coherence, for him, is a *central category of life*.

> The course of a life consists of parts, consists of experiences that are related together in some internal coherence. Every individual experience relates to a self of which it is a part; it is bound in coherence through its structure with other parts. Everything intellectual contains coherence; therefore coherence is a category that arises from life. We understand coherence by virtue of the unity of consciousness. (1968c: 195)

The creation of coherence, in Dilthey's work, is therefore seen as an achievement of consciousness which constantly produces links between parts and the totality and then checks or modifies them in new biographical situations. In this way life-history shows itself to be a construct produced by the subject and which, as a unit, organizes the wealth of experiences and events in the course of a life into some coherence. The creation of this kind of coherence of experiences is achieved through an act of meaning attribution. From the present meaning is given to past events. The memories that a person can call up of his or her life are those that seem globally meaningful and through which that person structures his or her life. It is only when these meaning-coherences set up by the subject are available that development is possible (cf. Dilthey 1968a: 218).

In summary, therefore, it must be said that the concept of *biographization* characterizes that form of meaning-ordering, sense-creating behaviour of the subject in conscious awareness of his or her own past life. A meaning-giving biographization is only possible when the subject is in a position to produce retrospective coherences that allow him or her to organize events and experiences within them and to create relationships between them and also to a totality. In this way we are constantly working at making our life consistent, at drawing lines in the *material of our past*, which will order it and create coherence. Lines separate, make prominent, show contours and give directions. They represent indications of relationship and orientation. If we fail to enter lines into our biography then we say, in colloquial terms: 'I can't work it out'. If this kind of line-drawing and coherence-creation fails, we may legitimately speak of a crisis, an existential crisis of sense. Human plans bear the mark of the individual and are only generalizable under certain conditions:

> Every life has its own meaning. It is to be found in a meaning context in which every memorable present has a counter-value, but at the same time, in the context of memory, it has a relation to a meaning of the whole. This meaning of the individual being is completely singular, inseparable from recognition, and yet, in its way, it represents – like Leibniz's monad – the historical universe. (Dilthey 1968c: 199)

The *perspective of individual sense and meaning-making* leads directly to the approach of modern biographical research. An approach to understanding that sees itself as concerned exclusively with the realm of social interaction does not meet the target. The problems of subjectivity cannot be replaced by the problems of intersubjectivity. In no way does this mean that intersubjectivity should be excluded; it means, rather, that intersubjectivity is an essential but not a sufficient condition of understanding. In this it is not only the question of the intersubjective conditions of subjectivity that are of interest, but also that of the subjective conditions of intersubjectivity. The consistent perspective of the individual leads to the category of biography.

This position of modern biographical research may be further illuminated by certain thoughts of Jean-Paul Sartre. In his critique of Marxism, he required that the attention of hermeneutics be directed to the individual. Contemporary Marxism, he claimed, has driven the exile of man from human knowledge. Sartre opposed this with his famous definition: 'The object of existentialism – because of the failure of the Marxists – is the individual in the social field' (1983: 106). Sartre demands that individuals be understood by studying the forms they use to process reality. Against any kind of finiteness of knowledge, against unambiguity in the understanding of meaning, he sets up multiplicity and multi-dimensionality: 'It is necessary to insist on the ambiguity of past facts' (1983: 100). Marxism displays a degree of anaemia; it has driven the exile of man from knowledge. The rediscovery of a knowledge of the individual is Sartre's goal. For this reason, *biography* is consistently a central category for him. With hermeneutic intention he follows the traces of the individual. In a number of existential and hermeneutically designed extensive interpretations of particular cases (for instance on Flaubert, Genet, Baudelaire) he showed – from a philosophical perspective – the way of modern biographical research, which sees itself as the qualitative interpretation of individual cases.

The reflections on Dilthey in this section have essentially brought forth the idea that the making of sense and meaning are characteristic of human existence. The processes of biographization are an immediate expression of these dimensions. In this way the thesis of the interpretative paradigm that we reviewed at the outset, with mankind as an interpreting, world-designing and reality-creating creature, has been clarified from a particular point of view. The production of sense and meaning represent the creative centre of human existence.

An understanding of learning and education cannot ignore this, but becomes possible only when one comes to understand processes of learning and education as specific ways of interpreting oneself and the world. This viewpoint will be developed in the next step in the argument.

3 PROCESSES OF SELF-CREATION AND WORLD-MAKING

Here it is appropriate to refer back to Alfred Schütz's position on the sociology of knowledge, which is in the tradition of phenomenologically oriented theory-building. His name is associated with the endeavour to base the social sciences essentially on the ideas of Edmund Husserl through explaining the processes of meaning-constitution in the life-world (see **3.1**, **3.8**). In Schütz's work questions are dealt with which seek to clarify how the social world is meaningfully constituted and how a scientific analysis of these processes of meaning-creation is possible. Schütz developed his field of enquiry in the course of his debate with Georg Simmel and, in particular, Max Weber. In this the question of how one can understand the subjective meaning of the behaviour of others came to be a central theme of his thinking. He assumes that humans can construct different internal attitudes to themselves and to the world. He provides a polymorphy of such approaches. These are not reducible to one another. A human being cannot be understood from a single form (cf. Srubar 1988: 49, for discussion), but only from an ensemble of varied forms of the approach to himself and the world. This is the central nucleus of Schütz's position.

From 1928 onwards Schütz began the preparatory work on *The Phenomenology of the Social World*, which appeared in 1932. In this work he establishes an essential link between meaning constitution and social action and its sociality. After his emigration to the United States he worked, from 1939, on a synthesis of action theory and life-world theory, which he described as *pragmatic life-world theory*. To characterize it he used the term *cosmion*, which refers to the symbolic self-interpretation of a society. When a human being interprets the world meaningfully he or she makes it into his or her life-world, or cosmion. In this cosmion there are different realms of reality. The assumption of the multiplicity of levels of reality was developed by Schütz in his *Theory of Multiple Realities* (1962), in which he attempts to justify the inter- and intra-cultural multiplicity of human reality. The recognition of the life-world basis of human action leads him to the conception of a plurality of finite areas of meaning, and this marks the broad boundary of his so-called life-world. The pluralization of areas of meaning corresponds to a pluralization of areas of rationality, since every area of meaning is characterized by a particular attitude towards the world and oneself.

It was William James who, in his *Principles of Psychology* (1890), drew attention to the fact that such worlds are in principle created subjectively. Schütz develops this idea, for example in his work *Don Quixote and the Problem of Reality*:

> The whole distinction between real and unreal, the whole psychology of belief, disbelief, and doubt, is, always according to William James, grounded on two mental facts: first that we are liable to think differently of the same object; and secondly, that when we have done so, we can choose which way of thinking to adhere to and which to disregard. The origin and fountainhead of all reality, whether from the absolute or the practical point of view is thus subjective, is ourselves. Consequently, there exist several, probably an infinite number of various orders of reality, each with its own special and separate style of existence, called by James 'subuniverses'. (Schütz 1964: 135)

The spectrum of possible worlds extends from the everyday world and the world of science, to the world of dreams and fantasy, the insane world of psychosis, and the world of intoxication with hallucinogenic drugs such as LSD; finally, we must also include today the world of virtual reality in which many computer freaks operate. Each of these worlds has its own limits and is real in its own way (see **3.8**). In every area of reality there are meaning patterns that do not need to be mutually compatible with each other. But we have the ability to switch between them. It is perhaps constitutive for humans that they are *world-migrants*, that they can reside in a variety of worlds and then return to their own everyday world. This last-named ability is both an essential and a sensitive criterion of the ability to live communally: the everyday world is the indispensable referential framework for such migrations. Migrating into other worlds is a diversion from daily life, in confidence that it will be possible to return there. These other worlds call

into question what is taken for granted in the everyday world, threaten it directly or indirectly, and therefore frequently create anxiety. Communities, therefore, develop forms (traditions, conventions) to allow for other worlds, and for calling-into-question the everyday world. Any calling-into-question or exceeding the boundaries of the everyday world may often bring about a crisis which leads, as a rule, to specific processes of biographization:

> If his life [the life of a human being] (or what he considers to the meaning of his life) seems threatened, he must then ask himself whether what just seemed so urgent and important is still so urgent and important. The relevancies that had previously operated so matter-of-factly are then subjected to an explicit interpretation in the light that the present crisis casts on his previous life and on his future life (which has been put into question). What results from his interpretation is another matter: the relevances can, as the case may be, turn out to be void or still remain valid. The person can hold on to the results of his reflections as a *memento mori* for his further course in life, or else forget them as quickly as possible (especially after the crisis has faded away). (Schütz and Luckmann 1989: 128)

Humans then begin to ask questions of themselves and the world. This can result in a restructuring of subjective relevances and thereby in a transformation of the behaviour of oneself and the world. Humans then see both themselves and their world differently. It is just these processes that are of interest in biographical research: can we understand such migrations from a single case? Can we make statements about conditions and consequences? Therefore, although the everyday world takes on a pragmatic character, the other worlds are not rejected: they represent an internal enrichment. The individual is deprived if, as a world-migrant, he or she settles in only a single world. For crossing borders means that everyday life loses the focus of its reality in favour of another. On the other hand human beings see themselves exposed to the danger of dissociation if the everyday world, as the Archimedic point of the existence as organization, is put out of action. From this viewpoint human life is a constant process of creation and maintenance of worlds. We are world-migrants, frontier-crossers, aliens and home-comers. A fragility of identity is the hallmark of our existence.

From the Schützian position further links to modern biographical research can be set up: it is a matter of becoming acquainted with a large number of the forms of human beings' approach to themselves and to the external social reality. Knowledge of a broad phenomenology of such approaches ought to be a fundamental component of social-scientific thinking. It might be said that a typical feature of modern biographical research is that it has moved from the question of *what* and *why* to consider *how*. The question of *how* is concerned with forms and performances; it could be called a morphological question. The analysis of the biography-making processes documented in the form of a narrative interview serves the purpose of clarifying the forms of these attitudes to self and the world. The results of such analyses are often micro-logically exact descriptions of the formation process, which represent a morphology, and – to a certain extent – a genealogy of the empirical educational profiles. Biographical research in this sense is concerned with determining figures of education. It carries out what W. Benjamin and T. W. Adorno have called micro-logical analysis (Marotzki 1997a). The interest in possible forms of attitudes to self and the world works on the premise that these are produced by individual people in interactive contexts, but that they cannot be derived from these. The making of sense and meaning means, above all, that a person's behaviour to self and the world is being developed. Worlds are not pre-determined, but have to be created and maintained by action, communication and biography-making. We are constantly developing ourselves and the world in processes of biography-making from the viewpoint of a particular way of being that is unique to ourselves. It is legitimate to use the term 'education' to approach this behaviour to self and the world. Modern qualitative biographical research (with educational intent) is therefore interested in concrete educational profiles, their origin and their transformations (Marotzki 1997b).

4 FINAL REMARKS

In this chapter the phenomenological aspect has been stressed because the everyday life-world is understood here as a fundamental dimension. Here it is not – as, for example, in the tradition of Habermas – a matter of an opposition between life-world and system. Nor is it therefore a matter of finding systemic bridging designs of the life-world to protect them from one another. Biographical research in the phenomenological tradition (see 3.1) should not, therefore, be equated with a lyric of affliction or a new subjectivism. This must be emphasized because it is only in this way that the accusation of turning the processes of learning and education into a therapy can be avoided. Qualitative biographical research, which concentrates on the interpretation of single cases, can be associated with the tradition of micro-logical analysis (Benjamin, Adorno) and in this sense does not see itself as necessarily being in opposition to social theory approaches, of which it has often been accused.

At the beginning of this chapter we enquired about the place of mankind within the scenario of socio-technical systems. Technical systems, particularly new technologies, relieve us of routine activities. As a rule these are carried out more rapidly and reliably with the help of technical systems. Mankind can now devote more attention to its creative, innovative and expressive ways of problem-solving. Because of problematic social situations these are more in demand than ever. To release this potential, to develop and promote it, requires suitable scenarios for learning and education. The decisive insight consists of not only understanding the problem-solving potential as a cognitive capacity. There are, in particular, biographical resources that represent, in a comprehensive way, a potential for order. One of the main tasks of qualitative biographical research is to explore these. It is therefore concerned with exchanging new-style perspectives and meaning contexts, with learning how human beings perceive and process unambiguous *facts* differently, and what meaning they attribute to them. In this there are no right and wrong ways of looking at things. It is rather a matter of systematically considering and recording the concrete experiential world of humans as an independent sense and meaning-context for processes of creativity and problem-solving. The flexibility needed for this cannot be achieved through a similar flexibility in definition of self and the world.

FURTHER READING

Alheit, P. and Bergamini, S. (1995) 'Biographical and Life History Research as a New Qualitative

Approach in Social Sciences and Education. An Introduction', in S. Papaioannou et al. (eds), *Education, Culture and Modernisation*. Roskilde: RUC. pp. 203–228.

Chamberlayne, P., Bornat, J. and Wengraf, T. (eds) (2000) *The Turn to Biographical Methods in Social Science. Comparative Issues and Examples*. London: Routledge.

Yin, R. K. (1994) *Case Study Research: Design and Methods*, 2nd edn. Thousand Oaks, CA: Sage.

3.7 Qualitative Generation Research

Heinz Bude

With the loss of a society of large groups the concept of generation today offers one of the last reference points for a we-concept of the individual (Bude 1997). Now that 'class' and 'nation' are no longer automatically available as obvious collectivization entities, 'generation' is coming to be preferred as a category of social embedding, and this seems to be unencumbered either by political ideology or by national history. The generational community of experience and memory emphasizes a horizontal identity of seeing and coming to terms with the world beyond the vertical solidarities of feelings of provenance and willingness to associate (Nora 1996). What makes proximity of year of birth into a generation is a feeling of being identically affected by a unique historical and social situation. In this way reactions of completion and thematic merging in everyday conversations create a unique proximity between people who in other respects are alien to one another (cf. Bahrdt 1996). The generational coherence that is, in this way, becoming thematic is the focus of comparison between the life of an individual and others of the same age, and in this the experience of contingence of biography is anchored in relationships of collective experience. Individual life-history is judged in respect of the life-course of members of the same generation: what can be expected, what constituted happiness and where there was failure.

1 AN EXPRESSION OF THE MODERN EXPERIENCE OF TEMPORALIZATION

The present popularity of the concept of generation in social and sociological self-description can indeed lead one to ignore the fact that the problem of generations has occupied sociology since its beginnings and that the concept of generation belongs to the fundamental historical concepts of the modern experience of temporalization of social relationships (see Koselleck 1978). Admittedly the methodological use of the term is relatively underdeveloped. Despite the classical reference to Karl Mannheim's article (1952b), there is no agreement on questions of how generations are formed, how they are to be identified and what socializing effect they have on the lives of their members. A structural weakness in the concept has been postulated, and although this does permit a reformulation of retrievable obvious facts of everyday life, it does not allow for a controlled structuring of anonymous data. Alternatively, one can refer back to methodologically tighter concepts, but with these the essential informative content of the concept of generation is lost. It is therefore essential, for a justification of interpretative generation research, to make a number of conceptual statements and methodological clarifications, so that it is not always necessary to start again at the beginning when one could long since have made progress.

2 THE CONCEPT OF GENERATION RATHER THAN COHORT

The move from cross-sectional to linear descriptions that was so vital for the understanding of social change, and the related insight that well-founded statements of trends can only be derived from the systematic comparison of the life-situations and life-balances of different birth cohorts (cf. Mayer 1990 for an outline), has incidentally led to a replacement of the historical concept of generation by a chronological concept of cohort. Although cohorts, according to Norman B. Ryder's (1965) open definition, refer to an aggregate of individuals who have shared the same experience in the same time-frame, in research the concept normally denotes a year-group (on the genesis and application of the term cohort, see Sackmann 1998: 29–63). Birth cohorts, however, do not in themselves constitute a generation: it is rather a matter of the possible relation to a common experience that marks and influences, and from which there arises evidence of something shared, despite differences of provenance, religion or ethnic affiliation. Where this evidence is missing, then we are not dealing with a generation, even when years of birth coincide. But where this feeling of participation in a common way of experiencing and reacting does exist, it cannot be countered by a contradictory chronology. For generations are collective formations and it is only they which make possible a meaningful adding together of individual year-cohorts. We are beginning at the wrong end, as Richard Alewyn (1929: 522) saw long ago, if we compare the courses of individual lives and seek to harmonize them. From this, instead of constructions of generations, we shall achieve only catalogues of cohorts, which always make too many conceptual promises and always contain too little information about forms of behaviour and meaning-patterns.

It is not a matter of contesting the argument advanced by representatives of the cohort-approach to demography and, by extension, to mobility and socialization research, that objective life-chances are determined solely by year-group strength (Easterlin 1980), or by the chance structure encountered by same-age groups in the transition from education to employment (Müller 1978). It is simply that the constituted generational situation needs a context of generation which constitutes it, and which creates – from diverse effects – a socially attributable unity. Here we may see the methodologically demanding implication of the concept of generation: the fact that it makes intelligible the gradual definition of a generation entity which is only the initial framework for the aggregation of individual birth cohorts into the totality of people of the same age. Without this interpretative element generation research would lose itself in a process of random distinction and comparison that would miss the phenomenon of a society that renews itself with every generation.

The concept of generation does not embrace the simple variation in living circumstances within the simultaneity of that which is non-simultaneous, but the constant new application of predominant formations which give expression to a new approach to facts and new kinds of distancing from tradition. The way in which generations act, either as desired by themselves or expected by others, cannot be captured by the concept of cohort. With all necessary caution in the face of a corresponding reductionism, one cannot ignore the truth that the periodic emergence of generations is based on the biological facts of our limited existence. Nothing sociological can be derived from this biological basis, but the phenomenon is missed if no account is taken of this relationship between the fact of a limited life-span and the projects of generational self-assertion. It therefore makes a decisive difference in the mode of procedure, whether one is looking at social alterations in the sequence of cohorts or at the vital moments in the change of generations.

Here the theorists of generation and cohorts are pulling in the same direction, when it is a question of abandoning assumptions of constancy and slowness in their observation of social development. Modern generations are characterized not by smooth transitions but abrupt mutations, as may particularly be seen in the political history of the twentieth century. The generation of youth movement at the beginning of the century, the generation of political youth of the inter-war years, the sceptical generation of the post-war period, or the protest generation of the welfare society (Schelsky 1981) demonstrate about-turns and new beginnings in social self-understanding, and these can hardly be made to fit a process of collective learning or gradual audience development. The genealogical concept of the family generation, in particular, presupposes links with tradition in which some new access to accumulated culture is sought. The processes whereby the social status of the family of origin is inherited from one generation to the next must also be distinguished from the changes between generations in collective behaviour, passions and memories. Generation is not a concept of updating but one of interruption (see Riedel 1969 on the history of the concept).

3 PRINCIPLES OF RECONSTRUCTION

Self-determination from the setting of differences

From this follows the first principle of an interpretative method of generation research: generations define themselves by their difference from other generations. One cannot always immediately say which generation one belongs to, but one can definitely state the generation one is not associated with. From this form of self-determination by difference, spontaneous generational attributions can be both extracted and also reconstructed. Here, as always, help is available from the structuralist doctrine of relationism, according to which the individual thing can only be defined through its relationship to some other. Colloquial patterns of identification can then be related to public formulae in order to measure the degree to which the meaning of some term has been adopted (see Bude 2000). For example, there is the expression the '89 Generation' (Leggewie 1995), and this comprises a multiplicity of meanings and attributions which first of all need to be checked for their place in our lives before they can be used to give an informative description of society.

Polar unit

A generation is indeed a problem unit and not a unit of solutions (Jaeger 1977). Generations reproduce themselves in both external and internal opposition. Not only are there always different patterns of individuality (see Popitz 1972: 15 on this term) within one generation, but, in

particular, contradictory consequences are drawn from the shared experience of the same situation. For this reason Mannheim (1952b) distinguishes between the 'generation-situation', which requires interpretation, the horizon-forming 'generation-relationship' and the polarized 'generation-units'. In the 'auxiliary-generation'[1] of German reconstruction after the Second World War (Bude 1987), for example, an influential critical fraction of protest and rejection stood in opposition to a dominant passive faction of 'communicative keeping quiet' (Lübbe 1983). The polarity of Luhmann and Habermas, or of Walser and Grass, is constitutive of the social and intellectual physiognomy of this generation. The systematic consideration of such polar forms of dispute over the same social and historical involvement may be taken as a second methodological principle of generation research.

Avant-garde and receptive groups

This involves a third principle of reconstruction which concerns the interplay of *avant-garde* and receptive groups in the formation of a shared meaning-horizon. It is always a few people who set the tone for the totality of their contemporaries and who coin the keywords. In Germany, the active core of the movement of 1968 consisted of about 10,000 people who provided the majority of what was subsequently known as the 68-generation with their atmosphere and their material (see Bude 1995: 40f.). It is possible to trace the process of retrospective multiplication of the 68-generation through the 1970s, 1980s and 1990s, which presents itself as a paradoxical case of intensification of experience through dissipation of the experience. It becomes ever less relevant what actions one really took part in: what is most important is the we-feeling of common origins and shared motives. The generational narrative community is open to alternative versions and histories that go further back, and becomes ultimately only a resonance chamber for matching associations.

Leading, suppressed and redirected types

Finally the adaptive relationship of biography and history is changed with the history shifts of emphasis in the context of generation. Julius Petersen (1926) coined the distinction between 'leading', 'redirected' and 'suppressed types of generation', to account for the different forms of establishment and development of the constitutive basic intentions and formative tendencies of a generation (cf. Mannheim 1952b). While the 'leading type' of generation accepts the opportunities and demands of a social and historical situation as a realization of dispositions and tendencies contained within itself, the 'redirected type' feels itself obliged by a certain existential indecisiveness to cling to dominant themes and styles. The 'suppressed', on the other hand, sees itself as pushed into a position where it can either surrender to the spirit of the age or can confront its age in isolation.

How in 1989 the balance was distributed between the heroes of the civic movement, the sceptics from the official opposition and the 'people' of the change, cannot yet be said. But it is beyond question that the age of 'leading generation types', like Bärbel Bohley or Sascha Anderson,[2] is over. Now other forms of self-fulfilment are required in which the members of a generation can see their opportunities and measure their risks. For generations there exists, therefore, the experience of the historical moment where decisions are made between forerunners, pathfinders, distinctive figures of the age, independent talents with no major significance, dependent fellow-travellers, lone runners and fashionable talents. But then, in the very next moment the original 'leading type' may turn out to be an exaggerated and extravagant figure full of self-deception and false attitudes, and the formerly 'suppressed types' are remembered, who have anticipated, in their resistance and obstinacy, what is now required. The fourth methodological principle of generation research is connected with these alternating relationships between biography and history through which the generation becomes a reality of constant re-interpretation and re-modelling. Every total reconstruction must therefore become aware of its own position in respect of the ageing of a generation, so that what actually counts as a primary experience is not simply repeated.

At any event, with all the reflexivity in the life-long self-formation of a generation there remains an 'a-problematic life-source' which causes the feeling of fateful closeness amongst contemporaries. It is this basis, in the non-reflexive and the unavailable, which brings about the historical-social unit of a generation. It is encountered when the question has been found to which the reconstructed form of a generation is the answer.

4   RESEARCH PERSPECTIVES

Measured against these interpretative principles qualitative generation research is comparatively underdeveloped. The mixing of the concepts of cohort and generation is responsible for the proliferation of methodologically uncontrolled definitions of generation that are attached partly to the fashions of popular culture (Diederichsen 1993) and partly to the changes in lifestyle or value-orientations of the younger generations (Jugendwerk der Deutschen Shell 1985). To this must be added the dominance of a genealogical concept, relatively unconnected with cycles of public thematization, which is used to determine a succession of generations who are coping with the past: according to this we have now reached the Third Generation – the grandchildren – of the victims and agents of National Socialism (Kohlstruck 1997). A new generation that would make its claim for a definition of reality is, according to this research, nowhere to be found.

One may view this situation as an expression of some modality of historical time that promotes an exhausted blurring rather than a sharp differentiation between young and old. But wherever possible we are experiencing a phase of groundbreaking changes in the educational processes and developmental dynamics of generations. It is no longer wars and their consequences, but the welfare state and its transformations that characterize the life-chances and life-views of neighbouring year-groups (Leisering 1992). Nowadays politically mobile generation conflicts are breaking out in the interpretation of the 'Generation Contract' in the provision of pensions (Stiftung für die Rechte zukünftiger Generationen 1998). How these kinds of institutionally created relationships between generations relate to ideas of historical generations is, of course, recognized as a research problem (Kaufmann 1993). So far, however, it has not been solved, either conceptually or methodologically, by generation research.

NOTES

1 'Auxiliary-Generation' = the male cohorts born between 1926 and 1929 that were drawn as anti-aircraft fighters from the highschools in the last months of the Second World War.
2. Bärbel Bohley was a leading figure in the critical civil movement of the former GDR, Sascha Anderson a then well-known poet.

FURTHER READING

Elder Jr, G. H. (1974) *Children of the Great Depression*. Chicago: University of Chicago Press.

Mannheim, K. (1952) 'The Problem of Generations', in K. Mannheim, *Essays on the Sociology of Knowledge*. London: Routledge & Kegan Paul. pp. 276–320.

Nora, P. (1996) 'Generation', in P. Nora (ed.), *Realms of Memory – The Construction of the French Past. Volume 1: Conflicts and Divisions*. New York: Columbia University Press. pp. 499–531.

3.8   Life-world Analysis in Ethnography

Anne Honer

If we make the experiential correlates of other people into the object of our scientific interest we are faced with a methodologically crucial problem of how and how far it is possible to see the world – approximately – through the eyes of these other people (cf. Plessner 1983), which means to reconstruct what is typically called the subjective meaning of *their* experiences.

Alfred Schütz (1962: 138, footnote 20) relied on the fact that the scientist 'constructs (obviously, according to quite definite structural laws) the pertinent ideal personality types with which he peoples the segment of the social world he has selected as an object of his scientific research'. However, this concerns only the theoretical *reflection* of data already analysed, but in no sense the *collection* of data. Data collection, in the first place, rather requires the use of methods whose quality criterion is whether, and to what extent, they are suitable for discovering and reconstructing the relevances of the *other*. And the *analysis* of the data requires, in turn, careful and hermeneutically reflected interpretative work in order to understand, beyond the idiosyncrasies of both the other and the researcher, the *ideal* types of world experience (cf. Honer 1993; 89–116; Reichertz 1991a; see **3.5, 5.16**).

Relying on phenomenology, therefore, in the sense of Alfred Schütz, will clarify in the context of this area of research interest the social scientist's own approach to reality – in the sense of a reflexive reconstruction of his (or her) own modes of experience and consciousness procedures – in the study (by whatever means) of the particular (sociological) object of research (see **3.1**; cf. also Eberle 1999; Hitzler 1999b).

In general terms, this research approach may therefore be characterized as 'ethnographic life-world analysis' or 'life-world analysis in ethnography'. Its purpose is the interpretative description of small social life-worlds, of socially (co-)organized extracts of individual world experiences, since – according to Thomas Luckmann (1989: 34) – 'the primary task of social scientific methodology is the systematic reconstruction of "meaning"' (cf. also Honer 1999). Seen in this way, ethnographic life-world analysis complements in a relatively unproblematic way other ethnographic research programmes, such as that of 'thick description' (see **2.6, 5.5**).

In simpler terms 'thick description' as a research programme means discovering and developing the meaning schemata of the cultural fields being studied, or particles of such fields, which constitute a kind of 'meaning-web' of more or less hierarchically ordered 'semantic fields'. From these access may then be gained to the culture, knowledge and habitual behaviour of the people under investigation. 'Thick description' aims at the explanation of 'explanations' (in a cultural field) in relation to the totality of this cultural field.

1 THE NATIVE'S POINT OF VIEW

With this orientation, the ethnologist Clifford Geertz (see **2.6**) gave an essential impetus to the placement in the ethnological tradition of the ethnographic interest in the (small) cultures of modern societies, which is outlined below. This was due, in particular, to his plea for the reconstruction of 'the native's point of view' (1984b) – using, as it were, all available means. To this extent the approach shows many links with the kind of journalistic tradition that finds its classical expression in Robert E. Parks's method of 'nosing around' (cf. Lindner 1990). These kinds of reportage-style studies (cf. also Hartmann 1988) are in most cases not only highly entertaining and instructive but also extremely productive from a sociological point of view. At the same time we need to clarify the technical consequences for research that are or should be produced by the general 'embellishing' claim of this kind of reportage that it is reconstructing extracts from life 'as it is lived'.

Unlike what happens in the ethnography of foreign peoples, the ethnographer in his 'own' society must first rediscover the strangeness of what is well known and familiar by an artificial change of attitude (see **5.5**). From very close proximity he has to discover that strangeness which the ethnological ethnographer generally experiences almost 'existentially' because, and by virtue of the fact that, his everyday routines in the field are often rather violently disturbed. He must learn that he cannot assume 'that his interpretation of the new cultural pattern coincides with that current with the members of the in-group. On the contrary, he has to reckon with fundamental discrepancies in seeing things and handling situations' (Schütz 1964: 16). The sociological ethnographer, deliberately rejecting the unquestionable 'reciprocity of perspectives', must therefore always reckon with the possibility that – in the sense of Pascal Bruckner and Alain Finkielkraut (1981) – 'the adventure begins *just around the corner*', and that 'just around the corner' it is indeed the *adventure* that begins (cf. Hirschauer and Amann 1997; Knoblauch 1991a, 1995).

It is only through a 'stranger's view' of the phenomenon that is of interest that the sociological ethnographer can be in a position to make explicit his own unquestionable (background) knowledge and, if necessary, to clarify where this knowledge comes from, in what typical situations it was acquired, so that it can then be modified or suspended for methodological reasons. It is not a matter, therefore, of forgetting one's own knowledge but of recognizing its relativity and taking this into account in an interpretation. It is a matter of looking for the 'strange', as opposed to the certainties of 'thinking-as-usual', or 'and-the-like', or 'the interchangeability of viewpoints' to which general everyday understanding (including that of many sociologists) normally allocates everything that appears to be reasonably familiar or even simply known (cf. Adler and Adler 1987a; Soeffner 1985: 111).

Ethnography, therefore – like every non-standardized type of social research, if it wishes to meet the conditions of unequivocal basis research – must now and, above all, in the longer term be marked by a fundamental scepticism about the quality of data provided by others. At the very least it seems questionable whether information received from others about social phenomena should count as data of the phenomena themselves. In the first place, and without question, they are simply data of communication, data about how a fact (whoever it comes from) is represented situationally (cf. Bergmann 1985; Reichertz 1988). This basic dilemma – that the subjective knowledge of other people is not 'really' directly accessible, but is nevertheless the most important data-base of social scientific research – cannot of course be solved. Ideally, however, it can be compensated for by the fact that the researcher in the field is trying to acquire a high degree of familiarity with the world being investigated. Ideally this is done by becoming 'immediately involved in practice' (Garz and Kraimer 1991: 13), which implies acquiring something like a temporary membership; and under less ideal circumstances it is achieved through a very flexible and sensitive use of exploratory and interpretative procedures.

'Life-world analysis' therefore means a methodological attempt to reconstruct the world seen, as it were, through the eyes of an ideal type of (some) normality. Because:

> only this methodological principle gives us the necessary guarantee that we are dealing in fact with the real social life-world of us all, which, even as an object of theoretical research, remains a system of reciprocal social relations, all of them built up by mutual subjective interpretations of the actors within it. (Schütz 1964: 16)

Normality, in the general sense of the term, however, can only be recognized abstractly – if at all – in modern societies: perhaps in such phenomena as a 'bricolage existence' (cf. Hitzler 1994; Hitzler and Honer 1994). From an *empirical* viewpoint, however, only thematically limited, goal-directed normalities, specific to a sub-culture, milieu or group (i.e. relative), can, as a rule, be identified.

The implications of this insight for research technique are that we, as 'vital' ethnographers (Geertz 1988) of the world 'around us', must shut out most of the usual questions that are normally considered to be significant in sociological research, and must ask instead what is of importance to the object being investigated – as a type – or what he (or she) experiences as 'his world'. Only on the basis of the things that he finds important do we go on to ask for the most exact information possible about what is important, and perhaps we also ask how it comes about that other things are unimportant to him, because 'before one explains phenomena from factors or interprets them according to purposes, an attempt ought to be made in every case to understand them in their original world of experience' (Plessner 1982: 229).

2 EXISTENTIAL COMMITMENT

While 'thick descriptions' in this way serve essentially the reconstruction of the typical forms of understanding of a given culture and society, its ethno-hermeneutics, life-world analysis aims ultimately at the translation of the 'historically objectivized meaning-structures of a culture and society … into a "universal" human hermeneutics that bridges all component cultures, all complete cultures and all historical epochs' (Luckmann 1989: 35). This means that the significance of life-world analysis consists above all of the fact that we can use it to increase the chance of at least approximately reconstructing a world (or worlds) as experienced by people, rather than the world as it appears in the opinion of sociologists. The world of sociologists can, of course, also be of interest, but then precisely as the world of sociologists – not an apparently 'objective' world.

Alfred Schütz's postulate for life-world analysis recommended that the scientist should make a cognitive move out of existential worries and reflect in isolation and complete disinterest,

from a pragmatic viewpoint, and from a purely theoretical perspective. This is, admittedly, often misinterpreted, to the effect that not only data analysis but equally also field data collection could or perhaps even should take place from a 'worldless position'. This sort of idea, however, is in direct opposition to Schütz's dictum that the scientist is never in a social environment, that he is never concerned with real living other people but rather with *homunculi* in a model-world which he constructs, in a secondary fashion, out of pre-interpreted data from previous and parallel worlds (cf. Schütz 1964: 3–54). This means that social scientists, so long as they are working empirically and collecting data themselves, can never lay claim to a higher or – in any sense – 'objective' perspective (cf. also Hitzler 1999a).

Field researchers act in a practical way in a social environment. They must, therefore – and more explicitly than Geertz – also reflect their concrete viewpoint as participants in social phenomena and give an account of where and how they are to be located in the network of social relationships. But because the relationship between the social scientist and the object of study is a 'special case of the link between cognition and action, between symbolic mastery and practical operation, between the logical (i.e. equipped with all the accumulated instruments of objectivization) and the *universally pre-logical logic of practice*' (Bourdieu 1982: 40f.), it is in fact advisable, in the longer term, to develop a 'theory of the meaning of nativeness'.

In the short term the fact that explanatory knowledge is of a different quality than action knowledge has two consequences for ethnographic work: on the one hand, in research practice one must make a clear distinction between the process of data collection in the field of everyday action and the process of data interpretation from the theoretical viewpoint. On the other hand, in dealing with data constituted in everyday practice a clear distinction must be made between action data (obtained by means of active participation and observation) and self-presentation data (obtained in conversations or interviews), which ideally represent action-directing knowledge (cf. Honer 1994b).

Bourdieu agrees that the social researcher has better chances of understanding the perspective of his object of investigation the more he or she is in command of not only the symbolic logic of scientific theory but also the logic of everyday practice (as it applies in his particular field of research). The person who, in this sense, has developed a particular set of procedures but can also put them at a distance – through the 'objectivization instruments of science' or controlled scientific reflection – will gain access to a particular kind of data that is hard to obtain in any other way. And in this we find the *phenomenological* contribution to the accessing and reconstruction of the object of research that is essential to life-world analysis.

In life-world analysis it is not a matter of using the phenomenological method in place of the canon of field-adequate modes of data collection, as defined, in particular, in the framework of the so-called 'interpretative paradigm'. Nor is it in any sense a question of using 'introspection' (and, in consequence 'picture-book phenomenology') rather than practical field research – that is, looking at people, looking over one's shoulder, talking to people and studying their 'documentation'. The only important thing is that what phenomenology does, namely reflect its own experiences, should be more strongly integrated into empirical social research. According to this interpretation 'life-world analysis in the ethnography' therefore implies a research procedure that seeks to integrate different possible methods of data collection and to apply methods each specifically adapted to its task. The ideal basis for this is to acquire practical membership in the phenomenon to be investigated and thereby to obtain an existential inner view (cf. Douglas 1976: 197ff., Schütz 1962: 17).

What seems to be indispensable, if we are to be able to speak of an ethnography oriented to life-world analysis, is that we describe phenomena from the perspective of a (typical) participant, check our comments for what kind of relevance systems they relate to, and reflect our analyses as products of a theoretical standpoint. But since one can only reflect on experiences that one has had, one must always consider what (kinds of) experience – in relation to a particular theme – one has really had.

With many subjects it is only possible in a very limited sense, or even completely impossible, to reach the 'inner view' of a participant. It is therefore only possible to become truly acquainted with the world in question from the outside, from some different perspective, and this means, above all, that it is only mediated through the representations, through the (symbolic and symptomatic) objectivizations and representations of what was really experienced there. For an inside experience can only be had, at least in the strictly phenomenological sense, if one is (also) personally involved in a subject.

In the framework of this sort of membership a variety of 'natural' observations can then be made. Communications from other people can be better evoked and organized, on the basis of an intimate knowledge of the field, and communicated data can be more reliably evaluated.

3 RECONSTRUCTION OF SOCIAL CONSTRUCTS

Ethnographic life-world analysis, the connection between participation and observation, between hermeneutics and phenomenology, essentially consists in the first place of capturing and making interpretatively available as many, and as varied, as possible current and sedimented forms of utterance and behaviour from some (partial) reality that is to be reconstructed. Secondly, it consists of understanding and reproducing, at least approximately, the 'inside view' of the normal participant in some cultural phenomenon (cf. in this connection Geertz 1984b). For '[s]afeguarding the subjective point of view is the only, but sufficient guarantee that social reality will not be replaced by a fictional non-existing world constructed by some scientific observer' (Schütz 1978: 50).

To reach the life-world as the basis for sociological reconstructions of social constructs of realities implies neither a folkloristic kind of explanation nor the combination of research and practical interests. To penetrate into the 'jungle of the life-world' (cf. Matthiesen 1983) means describing the correlates of our action, our experience and our suffering and translating into second-degree constructs the postulates formulated by Alfred Schütz (1964: 49ff.) of logical consistency, adequacy and subjective interpretability.

It is precisely from this 'professional schizophrenia', from this deliberate "leaping" from the sub-worlds of meaning, that we arrive at the position of the "marginal man"' (Stonequist 1961) that is analytically so useful.

The objectivity of the marginal man that leads to multiple viewpoints is neither a result of indifference (in the sense of a position above party interests) nor is it born of an attitude of self-criticism that leads him to doubt the apparently obvious. The more profound reason for the objectivity of marginal man is rather ... in recognizing the limits of 'thinking as usual'. He has become alienated and because of this socio-cultural alienation he has the opportunity for clear vision. (Lindner 1990: 206)

This 'marginal man' is capable of insights that are closed to the 'native', who neither knows nor sees, nor is ready to countenance, any alternatives (cf. Park 1950; Schütz 1962: 53–69). Here it is important to stress that the marginal man has the opportunity for clear visions and that he is not compelled 'to reflect on cultural differences and cultural change' (Stagl 1986, cited in Lindner 1990: 203). The 'perspective of the stranger' is a complex 'heuristical trick' in research into one's own culture. 'The field researcher is, accordingly, an *experimental* marginal man' (Lindner 1990: 210).

For a sociological ethnography this experimental basis is indispensable as a knowledge-generating attitude at the theoretical level; for 'there may be people who are so completely committed to being professional sociologists that they can never escape the thought that they are sociologists. If so, they shouldn't be field researchers' (Douglas 1976: 120). From the point of view of research ethics, therefore, this means, for ethnographers oriented to life-world analysis, that they must be ready for unexpected experiences and must be prepared to allow themselves to be confused, to experience shocks, to shut out (at least temporarily) their moral convictions, to acknowledge and give up their prejudices: in short, they must be maximally prepared to understand the other meaning *in the way in which* it was intended. To put this more ambitiously: in the reflected interchange of frames of reference, relevance systems and world-views, the fundamental duality (in the sense of Plessner 1985) of humans comes into effect from a methodological point of view. The problem here is that with this attitude one never emerges, even 'privately', from any field exactly as one entered it (cf. Lévi-Strauss 1978: 400).

From a programmatic point of view the epistemological interest inherent in an ethnographic life-world analysis is more 'existential'

than that of a 'thick description'. But it is not in the least 'postmodern', if postmodern ethnography really means: 'such writing goes against the grain of induction, deduction, hypothesis-testing, analytic schemes, generic principles, grounded theory, coding schemes and well-kept field-notes ... . Gone are terms like data, reliability, and validity. ... Interpretations are eschewed' (Denzin 1989a: 91). The genuinely sociological quality in handling field material does not consist of leaving it as it 'grew', nor of spreading the researcher's idiosyncrasies in dealing with it, but of examining the theoretical interest of this material during the interpretative phases and 'putting into words' its scientifically relevant implications. In the course of this 'transformation' from one level of typology to another the inherent interpretative operations are made explicit – in the sense of social scientific hermeneutics (cf. Hitzler and Honer 1997; Schröer 1994; Soeffner 1989; see **3.5**, **5.16**).

Even life-world analysis is ultimately nothing more than a method of supplementing the canon of proven methods of recording human ethnomethods, described as 'thickly' as possible, together with their intended and unintended sediments and consequences, in order to understand the meaningfulness of concrete phenomena, processes and events in their typical manifestations.

FURTHER READING

Denzin, N. K. (1997) *Interpretive Ethnography: Ethnographic Practices for the 21st Century*. Thousand Oaks, CA: Sage.

Douglas, J. D. and Johnson, J. M. (eds) (1978) *Existential Sociology*. Cambridge: Cambridge University Press.

Duneier, M. (1999) *Sidewalk*. New York: Farrar Straus & Giroux.

Gubrium, J. and Holstein, J. (1997) *The New Language of Qualitative Method*. New York: Oxford University Press.

3.9   Cultural Studies

Rainer Winter

1   THE CULTURAL STUDIES PROJECT

Cultural studies is an interdisciplinary project which uses qualitative methods to subject the cultural forms, practices and processes of contemporary societies to critical investigation and analysis. There is not a single version of cultural studies; different variants have come about in a range of academic disciplines, in different countries at different times. Although the various context-specific expressions of the project make it difficult to define cultural studies in a precise and uniform way, it is possible to identify in its history a number of common questions, a specific approach to social reality and an intellectual centre. At the Birmingham Centre for Contemporary Cultural Studies (CCCS) this concept was first used in the 1960s, and the characteristic features of theoretical and empirical research were developed that are today still definitive for the project all over the world. The 'invention' of cultural studies depends on the recognition that culture is of central importance in the present day and that it can only be appropriately analysed in the context of power and politics. The stimuli for research projects are often, therefore, social and political problems or questions. The methodological procedure of cultural studies can best be described as 'do-it-yourself'. For a particular research project theories and methods are selected, combined and applied from a range of fields of science according to pragmatic and strategic points of view. If the research question so requires, new theories and methods are 'put together' or developed from what is available (see 2.4).

Cultural studies relates not only to such different theories as culturalist or (post)-structuralist approaches. Even in the methods there is a great diversity, ranging from semiotic text analysis to participant observation (see 5.5), narrative interview (see 5.2) and focus groups (see 5.4). In this, as Stuart Hall – for many years director of the CCCS – claims, cultural studies always seeks 'to enable people to understand what [was] going on, and especially to provide ways of thinking, strategies for survival, and resources for assistance' (Hall 1990: 22).

2   SCIENTIFIC AND HISTORICAL BACKGROUND

The CCCS was founded in 1964 by the literary scholar Richard Hoggart. His aim, building on the synthesis of literary-critical and sociological approaches, was to analyse popular culture. The stimulus for this orientation was provided by a number of different publications and ensuing debates within the British New Left after the end of the 1950s. Hoggart himself, in his book *The Uses of Literacy*, which appeared in 1957, analysed the influence of social change, particularly the negative influence of commercial mass culture, on working class cultures in his exhaustive descriptions of their daily practices and cultural forms. Raymond Williams, in his book *Culture and Society 1780–1950*, which appeared the following year (Williams 1958), provided a full discussion of English literature and literary criticism from the eighteenth century on, and identified, compared and systematized the different meanings of the word 'culture'. On the one hand reactions to and criticisms of modernity intensified under this label, and on the other hand a holistic concept of culture in the English context was developed which views it as a 'whole way of life'. Culture is not defined as an area shut off from everyday life but 'as ordinary'. In his critique of Williams, the historian Edward P. Thompson (1961) stressed the importance of noting that in every 'complete way of life' there are contradictions, social conflicts and disagreements. In *The Making of the English Working Class* (1963), he demonstrated that the working class had taken an active part in the cultural process of their own origins.

These were the starting points for the work in Birmingham, which may initially be described as a search movement. Particularly under the leadership of Stuart Hall, questions of sociology and cultural theory were of central importance. In a move away from the structural functionalism and its integrationist concept of culture that was dominant at the time, the members of the CCCS were concerned with alternative theories which themselves were intensively concerned with the productive role of culture. For example, the German tradition of cultural sociology (M. Weber, G. Simmel), with its interpretative approach to social reality, symbolic interactionsism (H. Becker, see **3.3**), sociology of knowledge (P. L. Berger and T. Luckmann) and French structuralism (R. Barthes, C. Lévi-Strauss, L. Althusser) all helped to provide the resources to push ahead the cultural studies project. Looking back at this time, Hall pointed out that cultural studies in Birmingham developed in the interface and debate between the culturalist and the structuralist paradigms: 'Whereas, in "culturalism" experience was the ground – the terrain of the "lived" – where consciousness and conditions intersected, structuralism insisted that "experience" could not, by definition, be the ground of anything, since one could only "live" and experience one's conditions in and through the categories, classifications and frameworks of the culture' (Hall 1996e: 41).

Finally, an intensive preoccupation with Gramsci's hegemony theory (1991), and subsequently with Foucault's analysis of power (1978), led to culture being defined as a field of social inequality where battles and struggles for power are played out.

Against this theoretical background, a variety of research projects was carried out, proceeding from social problem situations (such as the erosion of the working class, the spread of a consumer lifestyle) and present-day questions (such as media definitions of social disagreements and problems). The studies of youth sub-cultures (Hall and Jefferson 1976; Hebdige 1979; Willis 1977, see **2.4**) and on the analysis and reception of media (Hall 1980; Morley 1980) have become very well known. Since the 1980s, as a result of the activities of students and migrants, there has been a process of international growth in cultural studies, which was pursued first in Australia, Canada and the United States, but today on a world-wide scale.

3 BASIC PROPOSITIONS OF CULTURAL STUDIES ANALYSIS

The difficulty of defining cultural studies should not lead to a situation where every analysis of culture, in particular popular culture, is equated with cultural studies. For example, a semiotic analysis of a Hollywood film or the ethnographic investigation of cultural worlds with no mention of the relation between culture and power do not belong to cultural studies. Cultural studies has as its goal the investigation of cultural processes in their contextual link to power relations. The determining and characteristic influence of these on cultural practices has to be established. For this purpose, in the tradition of Williams, a comprehensive concept of culture is employed which includes both cultural texts and experience and practices. The traditional distinction between high and popular culture is itself understood as an expression of social power relationships. The true object of cultural studies does not consist, therefore, of discrete cultural forms observed in isolation from their social or political context. On the contrary, proceeding from concrete questions, cultural processes in their varying forms are analysed in contexts limited in space and time. As Lawrence Grossberg (1995: 13) writes, a hallmark of cultural studies is a radical contextualism: 'To put it succinctly, for cultural studies, context is everything and everything is contextual.' For this context is not merely a framework that influences and determines social practices that take place within its borders. It is rather that the practices and identities first constitute the context within which they are practices and identities. For analysis this means that 'understanding a practice involves theoretically and historically (re-)constructing its context' (Grossberg 1992: 55). Theory and context, in the framework of cultural studies, therefore condition each other reciprocally: any knowledge gained is always context-specific, and in this contexts are never fully represented but can only be constructed under differing perspectives. It is the goal of cultural studies to understand economic processes better, using whatever theoretical resources and empirical investigations are available, and then, as a second step, to contribute to a change in their contexts. This implies setting up symbolic disagreements, the struggle for meanings and forms of 'resistance', and making 'knowledge' available so that participants can understand these processes better.

Cultures, for cultural studies, only exist in the plural. In contrast to monolithic and essentialist notions of culture it emphasizes the multiplicity of cultures and values that are determined in the course of ongoing changes in contemporary societies – cultures of class, gender, ethnic groups, sexual and political subcultures, fringe cultures, special cultures transmitted by the media. Against the background of the de-traditionalizing and dissolution of stable identities, cultural studies proposes that culture is a battle for meanings, a never-ending conflict about the sense and value of cultural traditions, practices and experiences. Particularly in ethnographic studies, it shows that alongside the dominant ideas of mainstream culture created by the culture industries there are also 'deviant', residual and emergent ideas and values (Williams 1977). Here one of the central insights is that one cannot determine, on the basis of the most erudite and refined interpretation of a cultural text, ideology or discourse, how the cultural forms will *actually* be interpreted, used or

learned in the everyday world by different persons and social groups. In the reception and learning of symbols and media, in the making of styles of self-presentation out of pre-existing resources, or in the efforts to create and maintain a resilient identity in institutions, cultural studies demonstrates the creativity and productivity of cultural processes. This art of obstinacy, which is displayed in everyday contexts, may be interpreted as a critique of power (Winter 2001). This has been very clearly elaborated by John Fiske.

4 AN EXAMPLE FOR QUALITATIVE RESEARCH: THE ANALYSIS OF THE 'POPULAR'

In his analyses of the popular in the present day, Fiske follows closely Foucault's (1978) distinction between power and resistance. In specific historical situations 'resistance' can arise in the relation of discursive structures, cultural practice and subjective experiences. Fiske understands the everyday as a continual struggle between the strategies of the 'strong' and the guerrilla tactics of the 'weak' (cf. 1989: 32–47). In using the 'resources' that the system makes available in the form of media texts and other consumer objects, everyday actors try to define their own living conditions and to express their own interests. Fiske is not interested in the processes of learning that contribute to social reproduction, but in the secret and hidden consumption that is, in the sense of Michel de Certeau (1984), a fabrication, a product of meanings and pleasures, in which consumers become more aware of their own circumstances, and which can (perhaps) make a contribution to gradual cultural and social transformation (Fiske 1993).

In his analyses Fiske deconstructs in a clear-sighted and original way a wide variety of popular texts, ranging from Madonna to 'Die Hard' to 'Married with Children' with the aim of showing their range of meaning potential, which is differently received and transformed by onlookers according to their own social and historical situation. He demonstrates the inconsistencies, the vagueness, the contradictory structure or the polyphony of media texts, and shows from this how closely popular texts relate to social reality and articulate social differences. The reception and the learning of texts becomes a contextually anchored social practice in which texts are not predetermined as objects but are produced on the basis of social experience. In this way Fiske shows the uniqueness and significance of cultural practices which are realized in a particular place and at a particular time. He sees culture, which he understands as a 'whole way of life', as practice, as a series of sense-patterns and meanings that change and compete with each other and which are in conflict: 'I understand culture, then, to encompass the struggle to control and contribute to the social circulation and uses of meanings, knowledges, pleasures and values. Culture always has both sense-making and power-bearing functions' (Fiske 1993: 13).

5   NEW TRENDS AND PERSPECTIVES

Apart from Fiske's work, the tradition of cultural studies offers a wealth of qualitative studies investigating the processes of reception and learning in everyday life, not forgetting the power relations that shape them. David Morley (1980), in a trend-setting investigation, was the first to show how complex the reactions to media texts can be. They are dependent on the interplay of social, cultural and discursive positions (such as class, ethnic affinity, age or gender) which point to the unequal distribution of power in society and in the cultural coding of texts. This was followed by a large number of ethnographically oriented studies of everyday contexts of media reception (Nightingale 1996). For instance, Mary E. Brown (1994) discovered, in an ethnographic study of conversations between women on the subject of soap operas, that the series are used to express critical attitudes towards the dominance exercised by men. Even though most of these series are designed from a masculine perspective, this is used subversively by women in their conversations, for example, when they laugh together about the behaviour of men in the series. Talking about soap operas becomes a rebellious pleasure. This was supplemented by studies of 'fans', which showed that they use media products in a productive and creative way and that they read them 'against the grain' (Winter 1995).

The context that has become topical in many more recent projects in cultural studies is, on the one hand, globalization, involving Western consumer goods and media texts (cf. Morley 1991), and on the other hand the migration of ethnic groups. One central question is the related transformation of cultural identities and the fashioning of new forms of ethnicity (Hall 1992). A first ethnographically based investigation of this context was carried out by Marie Gillespie (1995). She shows how television and video are used as communicative resources by families from the Punjab (Hindus and Sikhs) and by young people in Southall in West London, to negotiate new identities in the diaspora. Taking the example of Coca-Cola advertisements and the way young people address them locally, Gillespie (1995: 191–197) is able to show that a transnational product can open up an imaginary space in which one's own culture can be redefined: 'media are being used by productive consumers to maintain and strengthen boundaries, but also to create new, shared spaces in which syncretic cultural forms, such as "new ethnicities", can emerge' (Gillispie 1995: 208).

In reaction to the growing criticism of their intensive preoccupation with the 'consumption' of media texts, that have led to an accusation of 'cultural populism', the adherents of cultural studies have devoted more attention to investigating the processes of 'production', for example, to the analysis of its cultural dimension (Du Gay 1997; McRobbie 1998), or to the production of 'media events' (Fiske 1994b). To be able to analyse a cultural text or an artefact appropriately, the cultural processes of representation, production, consumption and regulation should be investigated together (Du Gay et al. 1997). Only in this way can the 'circuit of culture' be understood and, from this, the central role of culture in the postmodern period.

6   THE SIGNIFICANCE OF CULTURAL STUDIES FOR QUALITATIVE RESEARCH

Cultural studies is distinguished by the qualitative analysis of cultural processes in a range of social contexts that are marked by power relations, change and conflict. Both in its youth studies and its media research it has been innovative in resisting the dominance of quantitative procedures and developing new theoretical and methodological alternatives. For example, its original linking of semiotic text analysis with ethnographic reception analysis was taken up in other research traditions, such as the 'benefits-and-gratifications approach' (= 'Nutzen- und

Belohnungsansatz'), with its communication science orientation (Liebes and Katz 1990). Cultural studies carries out qualitative research within the framework of comprehensive analyses of culture and society. Its strength is therefore in the production of connections that transcend the locations of individual experiences, and this demonstrates that culture is 'a whole way of life' in the sense of Williams (cf. Fiske 1994a). Its theories and methods, and also its questions, are not universally valid or constant: they are developed, rather, in response to the social problems and questions of specific contexts.

With all the required pragmatism and eclecticism of methodological procedure which make it clear that qualitative social research is bricolage (Denzin and Lincoln 1994a), it would also be sensible for cultural studies to develop criteria for the evaluation and analysis of its own work, in terms of both its data collection and 'the art and politics of interpretation' (Denzin 1993; see **2.7**, **3.3**, **5.21**). Of course, it would not be sensible to borrow and apply positivist and post-positivist criteria (see **4.7**), as critics have tried to do (Ferguson and Golding 1997), since cultural studies has a constructivist orientation, (see **3.4**) in the creation of contexts, and a critical orientation, in its analysis of power relationships. Its critical constructivism is capable of giving a further innovative impulse to qualitative research. A distinct emphasis on the constructivist character of the research process and, in particular, of the role of the researcher may also highlight and augment the reflexivity and interpretative character of both cultural studies and qualitative research.

FURTHER READING

Denzin, N. K. (ed.) (1996) *Cultural Studies. A Research Volume*. Greenwich, CT: JAI Press (has appeared annually since 1996).

Du Gay, P., Hall, S., Mackay, H. and Negus, K. (1997) *Doing Cultural Studies. The Story of the Sony Walkman*. London: Sage.

Storey, J. (Ed.) (1996) *What is Cultural Studies? A Reader*. London: Arnold.

3.10 Gender Studies

Regine Gildemeister

1 SCIENTIFIC AND HISTORICAL BACKGROUND

Gender studies developed against the background of women's studies, which, as a 1970s women's movement, made a scandal in the scientific world concerning the centuries-old exclusion of women from science and research. One consequence of this close link between research and political movement was that women's studies always aimed primarily at making a practical contribution to reducing discrimination against women, so that forms of mobilizing social research (see **3.12**) were highly valued. But even when it saw itself as 'partisan', women's studies was essentially heterogeneous: there was neither a unified theoretical approach nor an agreed methodological foundation. In the *public* debate, however, what was increasingly important were attempts to define 'womanhood' and to see 'women's studies' as a perspective specific to women derived from this 'womanhood'. This made increasing reference to presumed substantive differences between the sexes or generally to concepts of 'difference' (e.g. Irigaray 1987). What emerged as a problem for research was that it took as its starting point what was actually the result of its analyses: that women and men were different in physical, psychical and social respects, and that women's

defining characteristics and abilities were not adequately recognized or valued.

Gender studies developed partly in parallel but partly also with a clear critical rejection of the concepts of identity-politics and the rooted tendency to positivize and essentialize the difference of genders (Knapp 1988). Equally, however, 'gender studies' is not linked to any unified theoretical approach, and there is no clear distinction from women's studies, so that reference is often made to 'gender and women's studies'. Unlike the case with distinction theory approaches, it is consistently pointed out here that gender is a *social* category, and that it is always, in some fundamental way, a question of social *relationships*. For this reason the focus is no longer made to deal with difference as a matter of substance or essence, but on analysing gender relationships under aspects of their hierarchical arrangement and social inequality.

2 LOGICAL AND EPISTEMOLOGICAL ASSUMPTIONS

The division of human beings into men and women is normally viewed as an 'extra-social' fact derived from the world of 'nature'. At the same time, however, a brief glance at the history of science will show 'a human being' or rather 'human beings in general' constitute the basis for all discipline-specific observations and that (bi-)sexuality is *not* a matter of importance. It only receives specific attention when in dealing with a topic like reproduction sexuality inevitably has to be addressed – and in particular with some consideration of 'woman'. In whole areas of the history of science one gets the impression that *only* women are sexual beings, but that 'general humanity' is apparently superior to gender-membership. In this there is normally an unquestioning equation of the 'general human' to the 'masculine' (de Beauvoir 1993). At the same time, this equation – as Georg Simmel pointed out as early as 1902 – is not made explicit. The question of what consequences this identification of the general with the masculine has had in science and research is, from the outset, one of the basic questions for women's studies and gender studies.

In the feminist critique of science the disagreement with the claim to rationality, objectivity and universality of the traditional understanding of science came to occupy a central position. Initially it was 'only' a matter of demonstrating the multiple breaches of the universality and objectivity requirement in the topic areas of women, femininity, gender difference and so on, and of showing that science, by excluding women, was fulfilling functions of legitimizing dominance. Many research results that were accepted as 'gender-neutral' were also shown to be ideologically suspect (Hausen and Nowotny 1986). During a second phase it was much more fundamentally a matter of questioning the principles of rationality, objectivity and universality themselves. They came under the suspicion not only of being capable of abuse by indirectly reinforcing dominance but of embodying in themselves an intrinsic claim to dominance (Klinger 1990: 28). In some sectors of women's studies this led to a rejection of the methodical approach and to attempts to break it down into such areas as involvement, encounter and sensory experience (e.g. Modelmog 1991).

This step was not followed by gender studies. Here there was more emphasis on the assertion that feminist approaches both to cultural critique and to the radical questioning of the understanding of science did not stand alone, but could align themselves with a range of critical traditions within science. In gender studies references of this kind (cf. section 4) have meanwhile become more explicit. In the way in which its position is defined it also becomes clear that rejecting the natural-science ideal of knowledge does not mean that a common epistemological position has to be formulated. The spectrum currently stretches from the dialectic theory of society to radical constructionism (see **3.4**).

What is common to the various approaches, however, is the fact that they are increasingly less concerned with simply adding research on women or (increasingly) on men (cf. Meuser 1998) to a body of science that is otherwise still blind to questions of gender. Instead of naively postulating the existence of a naturally determined (bi-)sexuality, we find much more frequently that the scientific constitution of gender as an object of research, informed by social scientific theories, is viewed as a fundamental category of social order.

3 BASIC PROPOSITIONS OF GENDER STUDIES

At present two poles seem to have become engraved in gender studies in the way in which the object of research is constituted: gender as a *structural category* and gender as a *social construct*. Both positions are engaged in a struggle to argue their case.

Particularly in the context of *research in social inequality* gender is seen as a 'social structural category', comparable to such other categories of social structuring as class/level, ethnicity or age (e.g. Frerichs and Steinrücke 1993). What is of central theoretical importance is the question of the social organization of the *gender relationship*: this term is concerned with the totality of institutionalized arrangements by means of which women and men confront each other as 'social groups' (Becker-Schmidt and Knapp 1995). The demarcation between the genders, for this line of argument, derives from the historically created dominance of the area of production over that of private reproduction. It is only from this imbalance that hierarchies have developed in the gender relationship, and men have been able to dominate in both areas, because their professional work also determines the circumstances of life in the 'private' area. Women, on the other hand, are the principal actors in private reproduction, and their professional work is not rewarded in the same way. The much-quoted 'problem of combining profession and family' essentially consists, for women, of their 'double socialization', as Becker-Schmidt calls it: they commute between two social spheres and are confronted with contradictory behavioural demands.

In another variant 'gender' is presented as a 'social construct', which means that it is investigated in strict opposition to any kind of naturalization that looks socially at the *production* of precisely the kind of order that we only encounter in the *result* as 'gender difference', as 'femininity' and 'masculinity'. It is precisely this assumption, that there are two and only two genders, that has become the object of these analyses. Unlike 'gender as a structural category', this is not concerned with social structural effects but with the question of how the binary mutually exclusive classification into two genders comes into being, and which then takes effect as the ubiquitously relevant background assumption in all social situations and implies the formation of a hierarchy. In this gender is understood as a *generative* pattern for the production of social order (Gildemeister and Wetterer 1992). In this context the analysis of *interaction processes* takes on a core value. For gender-membership from this point of view is not only a 'feature' borne by an individual, but something that is perpetually recreated in interactions, and in which the partners in an interaction are jointly involved ('doing gender', cf. West and Zimmermann 1991).

In this argument the normal English language distinction between 'sex' and 'gender' is essential: 'sex' normally refers to the biological or physiological features of gender, while 'gender' itself refers to the social and cultural attributes. In this distinction an implicit line of separation is drawn between 'nature' and 'culture', where 'nature' counts as the 'basis' of the characterization at the level of 'culture'. The implicit biologism that becomes visible here in the 'sex–gender' configuration has become, in the various theories of 'social constructs', the starting point for criticism (e.g. Nicholson 1994). From this perspective what is important is not to start from a single point, but to shed light on the interface between multidimensional, mutually interdependent frames of reference.

The background for these kinds of theory consists of historical and comparative cultural investigations. They demonstrate impressively that images and concepts of the biological body are not 'naturally given', but that they are the products of historical, socio-cultural interpretation

(cf. for example Honegger 1991 and Laqueur 1990 on the historical dimension; and on the comparative cultural dimension, Douglas 1973; Kessler and McKenna 1978; de Valle 1993). The physical body is only social relevant when *perceived*.

4 DIFFERENTIATIONS IN THE THEORETICAL POSITIONS

Within this broad field of gender studies there are extensive controversies and differences in terms of theory, methodology and, not least, the relationship between science and politics.

On the one hand these are the result of the tension between the 'group rights' of women that result from practices of social attribution and allocation, and on the other they derive from the desire to make 'bi-sexuality' itself into a topic and thereby to stimulate thought models which transcend simple binary oppositions. Furthermore, there are serious differences between the respective scientific traditions with regard to both their epistemological bases and their view of their subject. For example, very different starting points are adopted by social-historical reconstructions of the meaning change in the term gender (Frevert 1995), and epistemological and historiographical studies which show how the various images of a two-gender social order were transferred to the analysis of 'nature' (e.g. Haraway 1995; Schiebinger 1993). Even the approach to the term 'gender', with the increasing differentiation in research, provides less and less of an unquestioning framework within which the design of research questions and perspectives would develop 'automatically'. Instead, different stances on theoretical traditions developed in the 1990s, and out of these research questions were generated. Very widespread attention was also given to analyses of the 'double socialization' of women which relate to the tradition of 'critical social theory' and which often incorporated psychoanalytic approaches (e.g. Becker-Schmidt and Knapp 1995). Bourdieu's sociology has had great influence on gender studies as it opens up the possibility both of making connections with social theory and, at the micro-level, of working with the notion of 'play' or 'construct' (e.g. Dölling and Krais 1997). The idea of construct is also central to approaches inspired by system theory (e.g. Pasero 1995) and by discourse theory, in the latter case related to the political requirement for 'deconstruction' as a scientific strategy (e.g. Butler 1990). In the complex of analyses belonging to the sociology of knowledge (including ethnomethodology, e.g. Hirschauer 1994; Meuser 1998; see **3.2**), the idea of 'social construct' also plays an important role, although here it is not related to the requirement for 'deconstruction', but to the demand for a methodologically driven *re*construction of social sequences (Hirschauer 1995).

From this brief list it is already clear that the term 'construct' is given different meanings according to theoretical context and that the label 'constructivist gender studies' is more confusing than illuminating. This label assumes a common epistemological base to the various approaches, which does not exist. It is rather that the division into multiple 'variants of constructivism' (Knorr-Cetina 1989) occupies a very different position in respect of the core question as to the status of 'reality' in knowledge, as a precondition and as a consequence.

However, all of the approaches mentioned here do have one common basis: they have marked themselves off from the mainstream of the natural science ideal of discovery, which proceeds on the basis of a clear distinction between 'subject' and 'object', between the discoverer and what is discovered, and in which the object area is removed from its historical context. In this sense we may also understand the high value that is placed, or has always been placed, on qualitative procedures, compared to other types of social science research.

5   NEW TRENDS AND PERSPECTIVES

It is particularly in approaches based on constructionist theory, and above all the sociology of knowledge, that the *structural-generative* meaning of the category of gender is emphasized. Here there is a central focus on the fact that social situations are produced in this way and not some other way, and because we start out from a world with two (and only two) genders, a 'culture of bi-sexuality' can develop which has become fixed and objectivized on the basis of institutionalization. The modes of this institutionalization do not reflect and elaborate a pre-existing gender difference: rather, it is only through them that the specific meanings

attached to the categories of gender are produced ('institutional reflexivity'; cf. Goffman 1977; see **2.2**).

If gender as a 'generative model of the production of social order' is becoming a research area, then the focus of empirical analysis is tending to shift from the individual actor to the interactive practice of 'doing gender' that is typical in particular situations. The question of 'gender' or 'gender-membership' is thereby displaced a little from the individual and his/her psycho-physical 'sexuality'. The perspective shifts from the concern with individuals to the analysis of social patterns (of interaction, communication, interpretation and meaning-structure).

This does not mean abandoning the investigation of 'inner representation', gender identity, biographical history or the development of habitus-formations. Such work is not done, however, under a normative precondition (for example, 'complete', 'correct', 'mature' identity), but makes forms and types of learning into an empirical question (on biographical history cf. Dausien 1996).

The *interactional* deep structure in the social construction of gender has been particularly well illustrated by trans-sexual research (for an overview see Hirschauer 1993; Lindemann 1993). This type of research investigates, at the breakdown point of normality, how bi-sexuality is constructed in everyday practice and methodologically, because in the change from one gender to the other the processes involved in 'doing gender' can be analysed as if in slow motion. The research results make it clear that by postulating a binary gender classification in practically any interaction one can rely on a reaction potential that still has to deal with irritations. The extension of this basic research to present-day contexts brings with it a range of problems. In 'normal' empirical work we still find men and women – social reality is bi-sexually structured (Goffman 1977). In the research field investigators and those investigated always have one gender; they are recognizable as men and women and as such are always present in the research-related interpretations and analyses. To this extent the use, in the sociology of knowledge, of a 'social construct of gender' is very remote from experience. It is based on the fact that one must systematically 'act stupid' in confronting the content of one's own knowledge (see **3.1**, **3.8**). One adopts a perspective of artificial alienation, or 'alienates' one's own culture. Moreover, in this research stance one is relieved, in a purposive way, of all pressure to act in the research field. What is stressed is the difference between science and life practice, rather than any applicability (see **3.8**).

From a positive point of view this means developing a research culture that systematically avoids only reproducing (and therefore reifying) familiar figures (and stereotypes) of gender difference. In this it is helpful:

- to avoid comparing 'men' and 'women' with each other as blocks in an essentialist manner or using 'gender' as an unquestioned research resource;
- to check everyday knowledge concerning the difference in developing questions, for example by sometimes making it explicit and sometimes hiding it in a targeted way;
- to space out research phases in time and, at certain stages in the analysis, to 'de-sexualize' the material; in other words to delete indications of the gender-membership of speakers in a text, so that forms classified as 'male' or 'female' are (or must be) based on the statements and not on the persons;
- to investigate 'cross-gender activities' and spaces, to open one's mind to variety, contradictions and ambiguities of everyday practice and analyse for oneself the practice of distinction.

If premature polarizing gender categories can be avoided, and research as a discovery procedure can be emphasized, then gender studies set up in this way will come very close to qualitative and, more particularly, hermeneutic methods (see **3.5**, **5.16**). It does not involve any exclusion of quantifying procedures, but – in the first instance – only the requirement of openness in the research findings against the background of a scientific (and theory-driven) constitution of the object of research.

6 CRITICAL EVALUATION

Gender and women's studies have recently been confronted to a considerable extent by the effects of their own work on science and society, for example in the contribution they have made to a comprehensive topicalization of gender relationships. What is particularly important is what Giddens called 'double hermeneutics' in the social sciences: on the one hand the object area itself is constituted by social actors, and the social sciences reconstruct and reinterpret its frame of reference with their own theoretical concepts. On the other hand, there is a progressive 'sliding' of the terms created in sociology into the language of those whose actions and behaviour are 'actually' supposed to be analysed with those very terms. This 'sliding' could lead to a situation where these terms define essential features of the behaviour that is to be analysed (Giddens 1993: 199). This has happened with concepts from women's studies and is at present particularly happening with an almost inflationary use of the term 'construction'. It is being increasingly detached from its theoretical contexts and prefaced with the adjective 'mere' to indicate a freedom from all social pressures, which are then no longer analysed. This process reflects, on the one hand, important aspects of a general social change in gender relationships. It cannot, for example, be overlooked that with or in the categories of 'masculine' and 'feminine' it is no longer possible to create a singularity of meaning – the codings have become brittle. One indicator of this is the pluralization of 'femininities' and 'masculinities' in the literature. And on the other hand, the 'nature of bi-sexuality' has not given up its 'self-evident' and unquestionable nature. In the research findings of recent years it has become abundantly clear that the social inequality of the genders, in spite of the topicalization, is still reproducing itself locally, and that topicalization is by no means followed by habitualization.

Gender studies will therefore not be able to rid itself quickly of either its object of study (differentiation according to gender) or the relevance of this to inequality (Gildemeister and Robert 1999). And so the perspective of gender studies is of importance in practically every field of action. It becomes all the more important to develop procedures where the interactive creation of gender is linked to the analysis of orders of gender in modern society. Hitherto there has been little effort to link structural and process analyses to each other, or – to put it another way – to analyse social inequality with a focus on 'social construction'. This, however, clearly remains one of the fundamental and largely unsolved questions in the general discussion of methods within qualitative social research. From this it follows that there neither is nor can be, in gender studies, an ideal way, an outstanding single method. At the same time, it also follows that it may contribute significantly to the development of methods.

FURTHER READING

Kessler, S. J. and McKenna, W. (1978) *Gender. An Ethnomethodological Approach.* New York: John Wiley & Sons.

Thorne, B. (1993) *Gender Play. Girls and Boys in School.* New Brunswick, NJ: Rutgers University Press.

Warren, C. A. B. and Hackney, J. K. (2000) *Gender Issues in Ethnography.* Thousand Oaks, CA: Sage.

3.11 Organizational Analysis

Lutz von Rosenstiel

Social sciences that have examined the phenomenon of the organization, and in particular employment in organizations, have almost always – as disciplines oriented to applications – started with the complexity of the object of their investigation, namely the human beings in a complex they have themselves created. For this reason the degree of openness to different methodological approaches was greater here, as a rule, than in basic social scientific research. We have therefore always found – not only in the social sciences of the organization in the narrow sense, or the psychology of work and organizations, and in industrial sociology, but also in related fields such as economic or political science – not only quantitative but also qualitatively oriented methods that focused on a differential description of the phenomenon and sought to interpret it from the viewpoint of the acting subjects. Single case studies were accepted as a source of information, and often there was no attempt to formulate generalizable or mathematically expressed rules. In history and ethnology, insofar as these disciplines addressed the phenomenon of the organization, qualitative research methods have dominated. Today, in the social scientific treatment of organizations, quantitative and qualitative methods are found side by side, and in this the sometimes lesser weight of qualitative research approaches has again increased. Without any claim to completeness or even representativeness, we shall discuss a number of basic considerations and present some sample strategies of qualitative types of research.

1 ON THE CONCEPT OF THE ORGANIZATION

Organizations to be described, explained, predicted and controlled by social science (Zimbardo 1988) are often located in commerce and administration. These are often defined, in relation to their environment, as open systems that exist over a period of time, pursue specific goals, are composed of individuals or groups, and have a particular structure to coordinate the individual activities which – as a rule – are characterized by the division of labour and a hierarchy of responsibility (Gebert 1978; von Rosenstiel 2000).

The experience and action of people in organizations is extremely diverse. Members of organizations play political games there (Neuberger 1995b), they tell jokes about them (Neuberger 1988b), form friendships (Refisch 1997), fall in love with colleagues and live out an open or secret erotic relationship (Mainiero 1994), or else plague one another in a form of mobbing (Leymann 1993). Depending on their work situation, they torment their partners and bring up their children in a particular way

(Grüneisen and Hoff 1977); in an extreme case their intelligence is reduced (Greif 1978). But organizational scientists have only taken a marginal interest in all of this. The aspect of human action within organizations that is of primary interest is their work (Gebert and von Rosenstiel 1996; Ulich 1994). Accordingly, within psychology this particular specialist area, with its applied focus, is normally characterized as the psychology of work and the organization (Greif et al. 1989). In industrial sociology (Lutz et al. 1996) or in organizational sociology (Türk 1992) the structures within which work is carried out are also of central interest.

Images and observational perspectives

Organizations are phenomena created by humans and are therefore components of a culture. Their existence depends on people, they fulfil particular functions in human life, are therefore subject to social change and should, accordingly, be observed historically. Organizations can only be observed from without in a limited way, if the research results are to have any claim to relevance. It must therefore also be made clear what significance they have for the individual, how they are interpreted and what image people have of the organization.

Organizations, as extremely complex entities within which people, tasks and technologies are coordinated within the framework of particular structures in a goal-directed and purposeful way, are well-suited to the selective and focused scientific analysis of a number of quite different scientific disciplines – and, as multifaceted objects, are predestined for interdisciplinary research. But those who, as members of an organization, spend part of their lives within it or are affected by it in some other way, will also have their images of the organization (Neuberger 1989b; Morgan 1986). Here, in the classical organizational sciences – and in no sense only in those with a basis in engineering – the metaphor of the machine is dominant. One cog interlocks with another; if the whole thing revolves slowly, this leads to a considerable acceleration of the small parts; if one component becomes unserviceable it must be either repaired or completely replaced. Since a machine of this kind also wears out, sometimes a completely new construction – 'business re-engineering' – becomes

necessary. If one takes this sort of view of an organization, it is clear that strict assumptions of causality will apply, the attempt to find general regularities and their expression in mathematical formulae will predominate, and the science will be determined by research methods based on procedures with quantitative goals.

There are, of course, a number of quite different metaphors of an organization, different spectacles through which it is observed. For instance, the owner of a moderate-sized concern will often regard it as a family, an ambitious manager as a political theatre where the important thing is to gain influence, a climber who values importance will see it as an arena for 'impression management'. Others again will interpret the organization – focusing on the analogy of a living being – in terms of evolution theory and view it as a garden in which different plants compete with one another, where some plants flower beautifully in the shadow of others, while others wither there. But the image of the organization as a plant that opens in accordance with inherent laws, and is subject to self-regulation, is also frequently encountered. Social scientists often view the organization as a network of self-stabilizing interpersonal relationships. The range of images could be continued, many other metaphors could be cited, but only one more, which has recently found high favour in the science, will be discussed here: the metaphor of culture.

2 THE ORGANIZATION AS CULTURE

In 1951 Jaques had already referred, in a very modern-sounding way, to the culture of a factory, but it was only in the early 1980s that the culture-specific study of the organization won broad general interest through the much-quoted and controversial work *In Search of Excellence* by Peters and Waterman (1982). The authors believed that in their comparative studies of companies they had discovered that the so-called soft factors, such as the social qualification of managers, manner of filling vacancies, style of leadership or company atmosphere, were more important than such hard factors as strategy, organizational structure or systems of direction and control.

The culture of an organization can here be defined in the following way, using the schema of Schreyögg (1992), which builds on the work of Allaire and Firsirotu (1984).

- It is an implicit phenomenon, which characterizes the organization's own image and definition of itself.
- It is 'taken for granted' and, as a rule, is not reflected.
- It relates to shared value-orientations, makes organizational activity unified and coherent.
- It is the result of a learning process in dealing with conditions that exist within and beyond the enterprise.
- It gives meaning and orientation in a complex world and thereby unifies the interpretation of it and contains action-programmes.
- It is the result of a process of socialization that leads to the practice of acting from a cultural tradition, which means that it does not have to be consciously learned.

In this sense it is not a matter of seeing something in the individual elements of the organization that has to be interpreted as a cultural component ('the organization has culture'), but rather that the organization as a whole is seen as a culture ('the organization is culture' – Smircich 1983; Neuberger and Kompa 1987).

Seen in this way, everything that can be observed in the organization may be interpreted as an expression of specific underlying convictions and values. This is true of verbal utterances, interpersonal interactions and artefacts, such as the technology used in the organization, the architecture of the headquarters, or the porters' uniforms. In every case it may be asked what these mean as a symbol of the underlying cultural values.

In this way one point of view is true of almost all descriptions of organizational culture: that it ought to be represented with reference to different levels. Schein (1984) distinguishes three such levels.

- Basic assumptions, which are mostly unconscious, such as fundamental beliefs about the environment, truth, human nature or interpersonal relationships.
- Norms, standards and value orientations, which are quite capable of being conscious and which are used as behavioural guidelines for members of the organization.
- Artefacts, which on the one hand have a clear function in terms of purposive rationality, but at the same time may be interpreted as an expression of the predominant basic assumptions in the enterprise, which applies to everything visible and observable within the organization (Kaschube 1993).

3 THE ORGANIZATION AS A SOCIAL PROCESS

If someone is attempting to gain a rapid understanding of a specific organization, he/she will normally enquire as to its purpose and ask to see some representation of its structure – its organogram. It is all too easy, in such cases, to confuse this graphic representation with the actual structure. In reality, what can be observed in the organization does not correspond to the organogram. This may be interpreted as a plan, as an idea of 'what-should-be', which may or may not correspond to observable reality. In the widely discussed distinction between the formal and the informal organization (Roethlisberger and Dickson 1939), this emerges in a way that may be misunderstood (Irle 1963). The social scientific study of the organization has paid particular attention to these relationships, which may be interpreted as interpersonal relationships. In this sense Kahn (1977) sees the structure of an organization as residing in the stabilized relationships between its members. Now if relations between members of the organization constitute both the structure and operation of the organization, any permanent change in them will also be an organizational change. On this rests the concept of organizational development, which is clearly inspired by social sciences. It goes back to Lewin (1947), and its development is presented in French and Bell (1977).

The Society for Organizational Development (= *Gesellschaft für Organisationsentwicklung*, GOE 1980) defines organizational development 'as a longer-term whole-organizational process for the development and change of organizations and the people working in them. Its goal is a simultaneous improvement in the achievement potential of the organization (efficiency) and the quality of the work-climate (humanity).'

These are some normatively defined features of the process of organizational development.

- Assistance with self-help: this means that external experts do not implement the process but enable those concerned to initiate the process of change themselves.
- Involved parties become stakeholders: this means those concerned formulate and develop further the organizational regulations that affect them. This also involves:
- Democratization of life in organizations: this means that those affected implement the measures themselves, rather than higher levels in the hierarchy or external experts.

It is clear that behind a concept of this sort there is a quite different metaphor from that of the machine. Within the organization a self-regulating social system is ultimately to be seen (Jung 1987).

4 METHODS OF OBTAINING KNOWLEDGE

If one perceives, in a given branch of science, a system of knowledge from a particular object area, the question may be asked how this knowledge is obtained and how it may then be related to the system. Organization as an object is not independent of the observer, but is always a result of his/her observational perspective. Whoever approaches an organization with the machine metaphor in mind will prefer different methods of data collection and different theoretical ideas for organizing knowledge compared to someone who sees in an organization a self-organizing social system, or someone who sees it as a culture. But the question whether, from a general point of view, it is more a matter of diagnosis or intervention, or specifically of organizational analysis or construction, is important for the choice of adequate methods. The juxtaposition of quite different methods of organizational analysis is therefore crucial from this point of view, and in particular the fact that both quantitative and qualitative procedures may be used.

If one considers, in a piece of research oriented to application, that the goals are to describe, explain or understand the object area, to formulate prognoses and introduce design measures (Zimbardo 1988), then one can accordingly dispense with epistemological approaches, devoted to the description, explanation and comprehension of the object area – even in empirical organizational research (Kieser and Kubicek 1977).

If knowledge is the primary goal, then use will be made of both falsification strategies, mostly used in quantitative methods, and exploratory strategies, where a qualitative procedure is more important (Müller-Böling 1992). This predominance of qualitative approaches is also true in the case of construction strategies, which assist in the development of scientifically based ideas for change. Here there are frequently concrete single case studies, or else one may analyse organizational projects whose findings are then generalized (Szyperski and Müller-Böling 1981). The techniques of data collection used in all of these cases correspond to the methods generally used in empirical social research. Questions are asked, orally or in writing, standardized or non-standardized, observation is carried out, covert or overt, participatory or non-participatory, systematically or unsystematically (see 5.5), or the procedures of content analysis (see 5.12) are employed, and in these the data collection can be carried out in case studies or comparative field studies, but also in the context of experiments or within action research (Müller-Böling 1992).

Within this broad spectrum qualitative methods also play a considerable role, and especially if one thinks of specific social scientific modes of procedure (Brandstätter 1978; Bungard et al. 1996; Büssing 1995; Kühlmann and Franke 1989). Examples of all the qualitative methods and techniques listed in Lamnek (1995) can be found within the framework of organizational analyses, and in some cases in a very central and prominent fashion.

One often comes across single case studies or comparative presentations of cases in the field. Examples of this are analyses of company communication in a Bavarian bank, which is interpreted as a condition of success (Wever and Besig 1995), or the presentation of the value-oriented personnel work of a Bavarian car producer that was developed from a theoretical base (Bihl 1995).

What has become very widespread is the use of different forms of qualitative interviews (see 5.2), which is sometimes also carried out in written form with open questions. An early example of this was the questioning of about 8,000 workers by Levenstein (1912). His accompanying letter to those questioned included the following:

Dear Friend,

We make an important request of you. I would like to know something of your feelings and thoughts, what effect work has on you, what hopes and wishes you have ... I address the same request to your wife. Write direct from your heart. No name will be mentioned ...

These are examples of some of the questions:

18 Do you think during your work – and what do you think of – or is it completely impossible for you to think there?
20 What affects you more, the small salary, or the fact that you are so dependent on your employer, that you have so few prospects of advancing in life, that you can offer your children nothing at all?
25 Do you often walk in the forest? What do you think of when you lie on the forest floor, surrounded by complete solitude?

The breakthrough, however, came with the qualitative interview in the Hawthorne studies (Roethlisberger and Dickson 1939), and here it was particularly within the so-called interview programme. The aim of this was to ascertain how the employees perceived their situation, in order to derive from this, on the one hand, suggestions for improvement and, on the other hand, to create a basis for leadership training. For this, 21,000 people were questioned and in the course of method developments it was possible to move from a directive type of procedure to qualitatively oriented methods of questioning and analysis. In this the limitations and the risks of falsification in the context of structured written questionnaires were highlighted. Within the selected indirect approach those questioned were expected, in the framework of the questions, to select the topic of conversation themselves and the interviewer was expected to adjust to the subjects chosen by the interview partner. The interviewer was required to listen amiably and patiently, not to give advice or instruction, not to contradict and to ask direct questions only in exceptional cases. As a basis for the subsequent analysis it was necessary to record, if possible, the entire conversation. The transcripts were then the basis for the development of relevant categories for the analysis.

Qualitative interviews – although in this case structured written mass-questionnaire surveys – are also used in the measurement of job satisfaction (Neuberger 1985), in the analyses of organizational practices, in the investigation of the selection and induction of new employees (von Rosenstiel et al. 1991), in the analysis of the effects of organizational leadership training (Schönhammer 1985), in the description of enterprise culture (Schein 1985) and in many other component areas.

Less frequently, one comes across group discussions (see 5.4) in the context of organizational analysis, where specifically selected members of an organization, advisers or customers of the organization discuss freely topics relevant to the organization. The discussions are often recorded on tape or videotape, and if necessary transcribed (see 5.9). On the basis of these transcripts categories are developed, and then the analysis takes place, usually in an interpretative manner. Group discussions of this kind have considerable importance for procedures focusing on structure in the framework of organizational development processes, particularly when the data are reported back to those concerned, are analysed together with them and transferred to the planning of measures to be taken (Gebert 1995).

Content analyses (see 5.12) are also encountered fairly frequently in empirical research, when, for instance, there is an analysis of the guidelines for a company, the principles of management or other documents specific to the organization (see 5.15) (Dierkes and Hähner 1993). This is also true when the contents of preservice, in-service and further training are being studied (Pawlowsky and Bäumer 1993) or when one is trying to draw conclusions about the culture of an organization from in-house jokes (Neuberger 1988b).

Participant observation (see 5.5) is occasionally applied to varying extents within organizational analysis. One piece of work that became well known in this context was that of Zavala, Locke, Van Cott and Fleishmann (1965), who – in setting out to study the flying of helicopters – acquired this skill themselves and documented their experiences of this in a work analysis. Even more highly regarded was the much-quoted study by Mintzberg (1973) on the analysis of the everyday action of managers in organizations. Admittedly this did not fulfil all the criteria for participant observation. Mintzberg had five high-ranking managers of different functional areas monitored for several days, and the observers recorded all the activities of these managers.

The biographical method is only rarely encountered in organizational research, although a number of approaches of this kind – particularly with a psychoanalytical orientation – may be found (Mertens and Lang 1991). One example of such a biographical orientation was suggested by Kets de Vries and Miller (1986), who postulated five different biographically conditioned forms of neurotic personality structure and outlined their possible effects on an organization. They found, for example, that obsessive personalities in positions of leadership tend to have control-fantasies and erect a distinctly autocratic organization around themselves that seeks to prescribe and monitor every action of their subordinates. Without explicitly invoking concepts of depth psychology, Klein (1991) sought to derive the structures and practices of enterprises from the value orientations and attitudes of employers.

Qualitative methods are therefore to be found – and this must be made absolutely clear – in practically all areas of empirical organizational research, but this is particularly marked in those dealing with organization-culture and organizational development. Both of these will be illustrated with examples.

Methods of organization-culture research

If the scientist looks upon an organization as a culture, then it seems appropriate also to use those methods that are conventionally applied in cultural research, particularly in ethnology (Helmers 1993). This is especially true if the investigator identifies with the metaphorical approach ('the organization is a culture') and tends accordingly to interpretative explanatory approaches. It is less true if he/she adheres to the variables approach ('the organization has a culture') and explains organization-culture from a functionalist perspective, for example with reference to successful organizational approaches to the solution of problems in the past (Schein 1990). In the first of these senses, Turner (1977) proposed looking at complex organizations like 'indigenous tribes' and to use structuralist interpretative approaches – as recommended by Lévi-Strauss (1981) – to investigate them. There are a number of attempts, therefore, to discover and analyse ceremonies in an organization, such as Christmas parties or works outings (Kieser 1988; Rosen 1988), or to interpret rituals within the organization, such as workshops in a quite specific framework with a fixed place, time and duration (Trice and Beyer 1985). To an increasing extent organizational or company myths are being sought (Westerlund and Sjöstrand 1981); in this, stories handed down about the company's founder or other central personalities in the company are particularly suitable for the creation of myths that symbolize values (Kubicek 1984; Neuberger and Kompa 1987).

Taboos are also a feature of particular organizations. There are, therefore, words that can never be spoken, or subjects that can never be discussed, such as salary in many commercial organizations: there is, indeed, said to be a 'salary taboo' (Neuberger and Kompa 1987).

In addition, tribalism, which in ethnology refers to the tendency to prefer contacts with members of one's own cultural group, is also used in organizational research for purposes of analogy, such as in the analysis of social networks, and this is extended to questions of coalition-formation within micropolitics (Neuberger 1995a) or – with negative evaluation – in analysing sets of 'followers'. Here it is characteristic of cultural research – including the investigation of organization-culture – that the observable facts cannot be described objectively, but that they have already been selected and interpreted. This kind of research is therefore to be seen as systematic interpretation.

The attempt that has occasionally been made, in research into the organization-culture of business management, to record the facts 'objectively' and free from any context (Hoffmann 1989; Taubitz 1990) has not proved to be particularly successful. If one chooses the perspective of culture, this means understanding the observable facts in the sense of a surface structure and deriving interpretatively the deep structure of the programmes to be created (Neuberger 1995b). Here it is scarcely possible to embark upon the interpretation with pre-existing rules: these must again be developed in context-specific ways and possibly also together with members of the organization, and they must be communicatively validated (see 4.7). Neuberger (1995b) shows that this was attempted with toilet graffiti, conversations in work-breaks or company logos. For many of these utterances or objectivizations, which may be interpreted as symptoms of a culture, there have been investigations into stories, myths and legends, language rules, jokes, company reports and principles of leadership, community events, dress regulations, status symbols or the architecture

Table 3.11.1 Symptoms of organizational culture

Verbal	Interactional	Artificial (objectivized)
Stories	Rites, ceremonies, traditions	Status symbols
Myths	Parties, banquets, jubilees	Insignia, emblems
Anecdotes	Conventions	Gifts, banners
Parables	Conferences, meetings	Logos
Legends, sagas, fairy tales	Visits of the boss, or auditor	Prizes, certificates, incentive-trips
Slogans, mottos, maxims,	Organizational development	Idols, totems, fetishes
Principles	Selection and induction of new	Dress, external appearance
Linguistic rulings	employees	Architecture, conditions of work
Jargon, slang, taboos	Promotion	Posters, brochures, company
Songs, hymns	Downgrading, dismissal, voluntary	newspaper
	resignation, retirement, death	Systems fixed in writing (e.g. wage
	Complaints	agreement), ranking, promotion
	Magic actions	
	(selection of employees,	
	strategic planning, etc.)	
	Taboos	

of the company headquarters. Neuberger (1989b) shows the sorts of symptoms of an enterprise culture – verbal, interactive, artificial – that may come to mind in this context (see Table 3.11.1).

Methods of organizational development

Those types of research that are interested in formation deal with processes of organizational development. They have transferred the classical subject–object relationship of traditional social research into a subject–subject relationship in the sense of action research (Lewin 1947, 1948; Sievers 1977). In simple terms it may be said that organizational development is an application of action research in organizations. 'Deed-research' (Lewin 1947) is at the core of all organizational development processes in operation today, in the sense of the survey-feedback approach which may be traced back to Lewin. In this, after informing all involved members of the organization about goals and methods of procedure, data are first collected. This can be done on the basis of structured or unstructured questionnaires, through qualitative interviews, in the context of group discussions with the support of moderating procedures or on the basis of spontaneous depictions of one's own situation (Comelli 1985, 1994), impromptu

theatre sketches reflecting the relationships within the organization, and so on. The summarized results of this data collection, mostly in an appropriately visualized form, are then played back to those concerned, and not exclusively to the upper management or external advisers (feedback). The findings are discussed and diagnosed, using methods that involve moderation. In this interactive process attention can be drawn to the social relationships between participants that become visible. The discussion leader, in the role of process-adviser, can intervene supportively, while avoiding any allusion to ideas of content. It is exclusively the participants who, at the practical level, work out strengths and weaknesses, and then – in the context of action plans from individual participants or members of the project team – an attempt is made to implement the proposals for improvement that have been elaborated jointly.

In addition to the survey–feedback approach there is a range of further methods of organizational development (Gebert 1995; von Rosenstiel et al. 1987). In the sense of goals formulated by the involved parties themselves, what seems to be particularly successful is a procedure where, on the one hand, a survey–feedback method is combined with process-advice (Friedlander and Brown 1974; Gebert 1995), and, on the other hand, particular framing conditions are defined (von Rosenstiel 2000), particularly support for the process by the upper management: a culture within which open communication and a modicum of trust are guaranteed, as well as a willingness not to think in terms of short-term results, but to be open to longer-term processes.

5 CONCLUSION

Organizations are systems created by people which gain significance for their members by virtue of their perception and interpretation. If one desires to comprehend this scientifically, qualitative procedures are particularly well suited to the task. It is therefore not surprising that such procedures play an important role within empirical organizational analysis.

FURTHER READING

Argyris, C. (1993) *Knowledge for Action: A Guide to Overcoming Barriers of Organizational Change*. San Francisco: Jossey–Bass.

Dierkes, M., Berthoin Antal, A., Child, J. and Nonaka, I. (2001) *Handbook of Organizational Learning and Knowledge*. Oxford: Oxford University Press.

Schein, E. H. (1985) *Organizational Culture and Leadership: A Dynamic View*. San Francisco: Jossey–Bass.

Weick, K. L. (1995) *Sensemaking in Organizations*. Thousand Oaks, CA: Sage.

3.12 Qualitative Evaluation Research

Ernst von Kardorff

1 TASKS OF EVALUATION RESEARCH IN THE SOCIAL CONTEXT

In modern scientific communities (Stehr 1991, 1994) there is a growing need for scientifically underpinned proof of the effectiveness, efficiency, quality and acceptance of political programmes and measures in all areas of society. The demand is increasing for information relevant to decision-making, aids to planning and evaluations because of a need for social change conditioned by modernization, because of the scarce resources of public budgets which lead to intensified monitoring of efficiency and costs, and because of an increased awareness of quality on the part of a critical public.

Evaluation may be understood as a scientific response to the following requirements.

1 It checks the effectiveness, efficiency and goal-attainment of political, social and ecological programmes, measures, models and laws, of pedagogic and therapeutic types of intervention, of social, cultural and technical innovations and organizational changes in complex and constantly self-regenerating environments.

2 Its results are expected to provide support in decision-making and planning, and – from the point of view of the client – to assist in better monitoring, higher rationality and improved quality of products, and to provide arguments for a legitimate pursuit of goals and interests (von Kardorff 1998a; Madaus et al. 1983; Rossi and Freeman 1993; Weiss 1998; see **6.3**).

3 Evaluation is intended to promote, document and monitor desired social and intra-organizational changes and learning processes (Torres et al. 1996).

4 Finally, in the sense of *exploratory social research*, evaluation should lead to a deeper understanding of the areas under investigation (cf. Chelimsky and Shadish 1997).

2 EVALUATION AS APPLIED SOCIAL RESEARCH

Evaluation (research) is *applied social research*. And applied social research is, to a large extent, evaluation. Because of its area of application it has a number of features that affect both experimentally oriented approaches to evaluation that aim at quantification (e.g. Bortz and Döring 1995; Wottawa and Thierau 1998), and equally qualitative approaches (e.g. Guba and Lincoln 1989; Shaw 1999). For instance:

- It is a commissioned type of task-research that happens mostly outside universities. It can only select its research questions to a very limited extent, and it is tied to strict temporal prescriptions.

• It operates in fields that are characterized by power-constellations and various interest-groups; and so it is inevitably confronted with, and involved in, problematic social situations, trends, policies and their effects.

This also means: evaluation research does not deal with a 'silent' object. On the contrary, its particular 'object' – be it organizations (such as hospitals, schools, authorities), political programmes (such as health promotion, urban development, resocialization), or human behaviour (such as performance in school or profession, deviant behaviour, change of attitude) – shows a *high reactivity* to the process of evaluation itself. In this way evaluation research itself becomes generally a stimulus of change, rather than in the targeted way found in action research or in more recent empowerment approaches (Fetterman et al. 1996; Stark 1996). And here the fact and the processes of evaluation are often of greater significance than the results (see **6.3**). Evaluation comes up against constantly changing interpretations on the part of the individuals and collective actors (e.g. associations) who are affected by programmes, measures and their evaluation. And in this it is often confronted with conflicting reactions to its implementation and its results. This reflexive reactivity on the part of the 'object' means that, for evaluation, interpretative and process-oriented approaches sensitive to this fact become extremely important. They not only have to take account of the 'social construction of reality' (Berger and Luckmann 1966) and its character as a process, but must also make visible the double social construct which arises in the course of the evaluation and which the evaluation itself creates (Guba and Lincoln 1989; Patton 1997).

The majority of the conflicting theoretical debates in evaluation research are to do with paradigms (e.g. Cronbach 1982; House 1994; Lincoln 1994; Stufflebeam 1994), with the role of the evaluation researcher and the participation of those concerned in the evaluation process (Bryk 1983; Fetterman 1994), with the social preconditions and consequences of evaluation (House 1993), with appropriate research design (e.g. from a qualitative viewpoint, Guba and Lincoln 1989, and from a (quasi-)experimental-quantitative perspective,

Wittmann 1985), and with the safeguarding of standards (Cronbach 1983). The practice of evaluation research, however, is marked by a high degree of pragmatism, an eclectic combination of quantitative and qualitative methods (see **4.5**) and by a culture – or lack of it – of operation, little described and often overlooked, at the interface between clients, actors affected by the evaluation, the demand for scientific seriousness and the expectations of the general public (cf. also Freundlieb and Wolff 1999).

3 TOWARDS QUALITATIVE EVALUATION RESEARCH

Guba and Lincoln (1989) who, with Patton (1990, 1997), are among the most prominent exponents of *qualitative evaluation research* in the United States, view the development of evaluation research as consisting of three phases or 'generations', to which they oppose a 'fourth' generation. This is – or should be – characterized by a constructivist paradigm, a naturalistic research methodology, and a consistent practice of negotiating goals, by means of strategies of consensual validation (House 1993; Kvale 1995a; see **4.7**), by means of openness, transparency and fairness towards participants, and a pluralism of values within a democratic society (Guba and Lincoln 1989; House 1993).

In the first *phase of measurement*, from the developmental scales and intelligence tests of Binet at the beginning of the twentieth century until approximately the mid 1930s, questions of quantification, such as school achievement, were in the foreground. In the second *phase of description*, which lasted until the late 1950s, the main concern was with the design and effect of programmes (programme-evaluation), after which differences of individual achievement could be measured statistically. In the third *phase of assessment*, that was bound up with political programmes of social and educational reform in the United States, evaluation became a scientifically supported source of political consultancy. Not only results, but even goals now had to be evaluated, sequences had to be judged according to foreordained standards, and effects assessed not only with reference to the programmes themselves but also with reference to the relevant environments.

From this outline of developments it becomes clear that qualitative process-oriented procedures, and those oriented to communication and participation, in addition to quantifying and summative evaluation studies, are growing in significance. This is used by evaluation research,[1] which in all modern societies, and particularly in the United States, has developed into an independent research industry, to react to crises and deficits. In this the following critical points are of relevance.

- Clients and participants frequently criticize the limited practical value and often legalistic use of results (cf. Legge 1984).
- The organizations and people affected by evaluation and measures for quality assurance are dissatisfied, from ethical and political standpoints, with the lack of attention to the concerns, opinions and demands of 'stakeholders' and their limited opportunities for influence and participation.
- Scientific critics have raised an objection – now corrected – to the so-called summative evaluation that relates only to results rather than the 'formative' evaluation that follows sequences of events. From the point of view of concepts they complain about the lack of a systematic involvement of subjective theories, discourses and practices of those concerned with or addressed by the measures under evaluation, because in these the good and bad reasons for resistance and for unforeseen developments might find expression. Another group of critics point to the lack of communicative responsiveness of the procedures (Stake 1997), to the strategies used by those being investigated in dealing with programmes and measures, or to the distanced perspective of accompanying research. This seems to give an objective description and to demonstrate how programmes fail, only giving reasons for this after the event, rather than intervening in the role of guide (cf. von Kardorff 1988) and instigating learning processes (Patton 1998). A further objection concerns a lack of independent discovery questions which would contribute to social scientific understanding and theory (Chelimsky and Shadish 1997).

Qualitative evaluation claims to respond to several of these criticisms and thereby to open up a new general perspective for evaluation research.

4 FEATURES OF QUALITATIVE EVALUATION RESEARCH

Background assumptions, principles and theoretical perspectives

If one takes as a guideline Guba and Lincoln's *Fourth Generation Evaluation* (1989), as the most broadly developed characterization of qualitative evaluation research, the following normative and conceptual principles may be defined.

1 Under normative aspects, evaluation research is *value-bound research*, if for example it is looking at increases in the performances of employees, or more health-conscious behaviour among patients, or crime prevention. According to Guba and Lincoln, it should embrace such democratic values as transparency, participation, the emphasis on free will, social responsibility, rectitude and a humanistic perspective. At any rate it should declare and publish the values that underlie its work.

2 If one understands social reality as a social construct, the 'addressees' of measures are not only 'objects' reacting to interventions, but acting subjects who incorporate interventions in their environment into their everyday theories, interpret them in particular ways and develop meaningful strategies (creative reinterpretations, resistance, ironic submission, counter-proposals, and so on) in dealing with them.

3 For this reason, evaluation research – and in practice it has no alternative – must be carried out as a process of communicative debate. It does not only fulfil service functions and is not merely an aid to implementation and/or an agent of acceptance or legitimization for the client; it is also indebted to the programmes and those affected by measures, since their interests, areas of activity and quality of life are impinged upon by the measure under evaluation. Evaluation research itself inevitably plays an active role in changes; it therefore acts as a 'change-agent' – even though its real influence should not be exaggerated (Freundlieb and Wolff 1999). From this it follows that evaluation should see itself less as a scientific authority in socio-technical concerns, but should rather cooperate openly in the resolution of conflicts of interest and

prospects of action, in negotiating goals and forms of implementation. This it can do by taking on moderating functions and providing scientific expertise (such as drawing attention to consequences unforeseen by participants), by seeking a consensus that clarification of goals be included in the formulation of the programme and measures during implementation, and that this is approached flexibly, but also by bringing to light irreconcilable differences and disagreements. The results of evaluation then tend to take on the character of reflexive and orientational, rather than technical and instrumental, information.

4 The way in which evaluation research understands reality is basically constructivist (see **3.4**). Social reality is understood as the result of communicatively and interactively negotiated structures that are realized in meaning patterns, discourses, social representations and action patterns. The reflexive and ongoing nature of reality is demonstrated in qualitative evaluation research from the point of view of the different roles and positions of participants. Here the scientific interpretation itself becomes part of the reconstructive discovery and creation of that social reality which is the object of the change brought about by the measure being evaluated. In short – qualitative evaluation research pursues the 'interpretative paradigm' (Wilson 1970).

Methodological principles

Unlike the kind of evaluation research based on the normative paradigm, a qualitative perspective is concerned not with statistical representativity, but rather with a selection of units of investigation that can generate some theory: for example, those that are guided by hypotheses (see **4.2**) in accordance with principles of 'theoretical sampling' (see **4.4**). Instead of foreordained times for measurement it is concerned with observed turning-points, crises and objections in the course of the project, and these are taken as meaningful and significant data. Instead of comparisons with control groups it is concerned with the systematic comparison of contrasting cases (Stake 1995), whose characteristics are examined in detail. In place of a summary observation of reactions to standardized data-collection instruments and tests, the focus is on the reconstruction of

differing patterns of justification and action strategies. And instead of testing model assumptions using prescribed categories it is interested in the communicative negotiation of purposive and mutually accepted criteria for success on the basis of project experiences.

Secondly, process-orientation ('formative') takes precedence over outcome-orientation ('summative') because it provides important guidelines – about the learning processes of implementation, about gaining acceptance and the analysis of failures and objections – for assessment and also for the further development of the measures that are being investigated. Patton (1998) has spoken aptly in this context of the discovery of 'process use'. In this sense narrations of particular events, or observations and feelings, take precedence over generalizable properties, because they are a more sensitive indicator of relevant project developments, of unexpected results and side-effects, and because they reveal patterns of observation and interpretation. These may then be checked for their dominance in the context of the investigation and, furthermore, for generalizable elements that transcend the particular project.

Thirdly, qualitative evaluation research aims at specificity and not necessarily at generalizability; and so in the research design an important role is played by local historical aspects, the various professional environments and networks of the project team and the target groups, local power cartels, particular features of local history and traditions, the influence of local dignitaries, and so on. This does not exclude a transferability of the measures in question, but does bind them to the particular special conditions for implementation. For qualitative evaluation research, therefore, it is not primarily a matter of developing general theories, but of producing project-related, often locally restricted, but scientifically well-founded statements and responses to questions of practical common-sense in situations that are negotiable, but also structurally bound, asymmetric, power-driven and determined by interests.

Finally, the research design (see **4.1**), as a recursive learning and teaching process (Guba and Lincoln 1989), is provided with many feedback loops, for example, using group discussions (see **5.4**), moderated discussions of goals and results, external audits, and so on. Unlike basic scientific research, evaluation research is only open to a limited extent. It is determined by the goals and framework conditions set by the client, and is under both pressure to achieve results and pressure of time. This means that the programmatic postulates can only be implemented approximately and that the need for very time-consuming evaluation of interviews, for example (see **5.2**), or for participant observation in evaluation groups, with peer-reviewing, can rarely be met. In practice, therefore, many 'short-cut strategies' (see **4.1**) and pragmatic compromises have to be used.

Methods

Qualitative evaluation research prefers a 'responsive' procedure (e.g. Stake 1995) that incorporates the reactions of subjects of the investigation. It therefore relies on the whole range of procedures used in other types of qualitative research: different forms of interview (see **5.2**), problem-based group discussions (see **5.4**), participant observation (see **5.5**), network maps, sequence-documentation, document analysis (see **5.15**), field research methods (see **5.5**), as well as personal records made by the investigator, and so on. Quantitative methods of data collection are also used, and in particular descriptive statistics. In the context of evaluations that focus on shared learning and organizational development, use is also made of innovative methods from citizens' movements (such as future workshops, workplace conversations, simulations) and from organizational consultancy (such as map-questioning, mind-mapping, or Delphi-techniques).

Interpretation and validation

Here a decisive role belongs to the process of communication with participants: checking that their views have been correctly recorded, evaluating the course of the project, possibly changing the project goals and initiating further learning processes. These processes of *communicative validation* (Kvale 1995a) are supplemented by external 'audits' by experts, in order to obtain a multi-faceted picture of the measure being monitored and to develop it further as an orientation for action with the stakeholders and clients. Because of the complexity and the dynamics of evaluating measures and programmes the possibilities offered by a triangulation (Flick 1992b; see **4.6**) of the results should be used to achieve a multi-perspective validation (see **4.7**). Cronbach's (1983) '95 Theses and

Criteria for Programme Evaluations' (cf. House 1980 and Sanders 1999) are still a useful orientation for the quality control of evaluation studies.

Presentation of results

A particular problem for evaluation research is the presentation of results, which, in commissioned research, are legally the property of the client. Because their results impinge upon socially and politically controversial fields (such as drug distribution, the confinement of mentally ill criminals, risk prevention, government reform, and the like) clients often have an interest in a particular presentation of results, where, for example, mistakes are expected to be exposed or kept quiet, small successes glorified or acceptance taken for granted. Apart from the obligation to scientific integrity and replicability, data protection, agreement to participation and responsibility to subjects (see **6.1**), we are concerned here with questions of fairness, openness and the obligation to the public, but also with aspects of advocacy of interests in the programme that were not considered, among subjects with little negotiating power (such as those on social assistance, the unemployed, the handicapped, the under-employed and so on). In this respect the role of the participant researcher becomes a difficult balancing act, which begins when he or she first enters the field and attempts to build up an accepted relationship of trust, and which only ends with negotiations about the content and form of the presentation.

The presentation of results from evaluation studies can and should be understood (House 1993) as a process of argumentation with participants (normally only with the clients) about the 'issues' in the investigated field. Useful guidance about forms of presentation, which allow the presentation of results to become an opportunity for 'reflexive application' (see **6.6**) and thence a stimulus for further learning processes, are to be found in Torres et al. (1996).

5 VARIANTS OF QUALITATIVELY ORIENTED APPROACHES IN EVALUATION RESEARCH

Evaluation research is closely related to social change. To this fact there have been reactions from *action research* (for an overview see

Gstettner 1995; Moser 1995), user-oriented concepts based on 'empowerment' in citizens' movements and clients (Fetterman 1994; Fetterman et al. 1996) and consultative and communicative approaches to 'better practice' (Everitt and Hardiker 1996) under the label of *practice research* (Heiner 1988a; von Kardorff 1988). Under the term *self-evaluation* (Heiner 1988b) or *practitioner research* (Fuller and Petch 1995) concepts focusing on aspects of a 'learning organization' (Heiner 1998; Torres et al. 1996) have developed, especially in the psycho-social area and in the field of social work (Shaw and Lishman 1999).

6 PROSPECTS

The developmental opportunities for an independent qualitative type of evaluation research are very difficult to assess. The political and administrative demand – particularly in the crisis confronting the welfare state – is mostly for answers to pre-defined questions and, as far as possible, for quantifiable 'hard' data (that is, data capable of numerical presentation) for proof of effects and for quality and cost control. Furthermore, there is a demand for quality assessment using criteria and standards defined by experts and for reports agreed with experts before publication that seem more suited to purposes of legitimization than a type of evaluation which is open-ended, critical, participatory, determined by conflict-ridden negotiation processes and focused on socio-communicative learning processes. On the other hand, the crises in application (see **6.3**), in acceptance and the significance of evaluation (Kraus 1995; Legge 1984) have increased willingness to see evaluation more as a research accompaniment and development, or as a process of experiencing and learning that goes with social change. In general, this means that there is a desire to reach more satisfactory models of practice, where subjective views and interests, or popular and expert theories and practices, are more strongly

expressed. In this way greater importance will be attached to a *problem-related practical type of reasoning* (Chelimsky and Shadish 1997; Guba and Lincoln 1989; House 1993; Shaw 1999). In pedagogy, in social work, in psycho-social care and public health as well as in local ecological projects where more attention is given to the meaning of subjective theories (cf. Flick 1998b) and to the reinforcement of private initiative, responsibility and self-determination – in all of these areas developments will continue to be characterized by empowerment approaches (Fetterman 1994; Stark 1996), supportive consultancy and monitoring.

In summary, we may claim the following as both description and challenge: qualitative evaluation sees itself as a joint enterprise or type of social research that seeks to discover social reality, to probe its capacity for change and to test its boundaries, and on that seeks to change and create social reality. For this it must also come to terms with its social accountability.

NOTE

1 This is illustrated by the number of specialist journals, such as *Evaluation Review*, *Evaluation Studies*, *Evaluation Quarterly*, *Evaluation Practice*, etc., as well as a vast number of large and small private research institutes.

FURTHER READING

Chelimsky, E. and Shadish, W. R. (eds) (1997) *Evaluation for the 21st Century. A Handbook.* Thousand Oaks, CA: Sage.

Guba, E. G. and Lincoln, Y. S. (1989) *Fourth Generation Evaluation.* London: Sage.

Shaw, I. F. (1999) *Qualitative Evaluation.* London: Sage.

Part 4

Methodology and Qualitative Research

Introduction

Qualitative research is balanced between a variety of theoretical approaches (see **3.1–3.12**) and a broad spectrum of concrete methodological procedures (see **5.1–5.22**). The methodology of qualitative research is concerned with theory, method and conceptualization of procedures in empirical studies, beyond the concrete details of methods and data collection or analysis. The resulting methodological questions are, in varying degrees but also in general terms, relevant to each of the methodological alternatives and theoretical backgrounds.

The discussion in the various chapters of this part revolves around questions of *research design and planning* (see **4.1**), the relationship between qualitative and quantitative methods (see **4.5**) or between different qualitative methods (triangulation, see **4.6**). The question of the selection of cases or case-groups is generally treated under the heading of 'sampling' (see **4.4**).

Beyond these problems, which tend (also) to be relatively technical matters related to the execution of qualitative research projects, this part also includes questions that rather belong in the field of *epistemology*. In recent years the role and application of hypotheses (see **4.2**) in qualitative research has again attracted more attention. Accordingly, for various methods the relationship between theory and empirical data is treated with reference to the concept of 'abduction'. That is to say, in a particular concrete case it is ultimately a flash of intuition on the part of the investigator that leads to some recognition and theoretical development, and not necessarily systematic work in the sense of induction and deduction (see **4.3**). One problem for qualitative research that remains unsolved is the matter of quality criteria that are appropriate to its procedures (see **4.7**).

4.1 Design and Process in Qualitative Research

Uwe Flick

1 ON THE ROLE OF DESIGN IN QUALITATIVE RESEARCH

In quantitative research there is a comprehensive literature on various forms of research design, such as cross-sectional and longitudinal designs, experimental versus non-experimental research, on the use of control groups or so-called double-blind trials in pharmaceutical studies. 'Data collection designs are a means to the end of collecting meaningful data' (Diekmann 1995: 274). The decision to use one of the types of design mentioned is often intended to control, minimize or exclude the influence of the research or the researcher on the data-collecting situation. In qualitative research little importance is attached to this aspect, which leads Miles and Huberman (1994: 16) to point out that 'Contrary to what you might have heard, qualitative research designs do exist.'

In more general terms, in both areas the question of the planning of an investigation is addressed with the keyword of research design: how should the data collection and analysis be set up, and how is the selection of empirical 'material' (situations, cases, persons) to be made, so that the research questions can be answered and this can be achieved within the time available, using the available means? This is in agreement with the definition given by Ragin (1994: 191):

Research design is a plan for collecting and analyzing evidence that will make it possible for the investigator to answer whatever questions he or she has posed. The design of an investigation touches almost all aspects of the research, from the minute details of data collection to the selection of the techniques of data analysis.

The (not very comprehensive) literature on research design in qualitative research (cf. LeCompte and Preissle 1993; Marshall and Rossmann 1995; Miles and Huberman 1994; and see Flick 2002: chs 5–7) deals with the subject in two ways: either particular basic models of qualitative research are contrasted, and the researcher may choose between for his or her concrete study (e.g. Creswell 1998), or else the components from which a concrete research design is put together are listed and discussed (e.g. Maxwell 1996).

The components that play a role in the construction of a research design and must therefore be considered are:

- the goals of the study
- the theoretical framework
- its concrete questions
- the selection of empirical material
- the methodological procedures
- the degree of standardization and control
- the generalization goals and

- the temporal, personal and material resources that are available (cf. section 3 below).

2 BASIC DESIGNS IN QUALITATIVE RESEARCH

The following basic designs in qualitative research may be distinguished (cf. also Creswell 1998):

- case studies
- comparative studies
- retrospective studies
- snapshots: analyses of state and process at the time of the research, and
- longitudinal studies.

Case studies

The aim of case studies is the precise description or reconstruction of a case (for more detail cf. Ragin and Becker 1992). Case is rather broadly understood here – in addition to persons, social communities (e.g. families), organizations and institutions (e.g. a nursing home) could become the subject of a case analysis. In this the decisive problem is the identification of a case that would be significant for the research question, and the clarification of what else belongs to the case and what methodological approaches its reconstruction requires (on this cf. Hildenbrand 1999). If a case analysis is concerned with school problems of a child it must, for instance, be made clear whether it is enough to observe the child in the school environment, whether the teachers and/or fellow pupils should be questioned and to what extent the family and their everyday life should be observed as part of the analysis. Finally, it needs to be made clear what this case represents (cf. Flick 2002: 89ff.).

Comparative studies

In comparative studies, on the other hand, the case is not observed in its totality and complexity, but rather a multiplicity of cases with regard to particular excerpts: the specific content of the expert knowledge of a number of people or biographies in respect of a concrete experience of sickness and the subsequent course of life are compared with each other. Here there arise above

all questions to do with the selection of cases in the groups to be compared. A further problem is what degree of standardization or constancy is felt to be necessary in the remaining conditions that are not the subject of the comparison: to be able to show cultural differences in the views of health among Portuguese and German women, interview partners from both cultures were selected who live in as many respects as possible (big city life, comparable professions, income and level of education) under at least very similar conditions, in order to be able to relate differences to the comparative dimension of 'culture' (cf. Flick et al. 1998; Flick 2000c).

The dimension of single case–comparative study represents one axis according to which the basic design of qualitative research may be classified. An interim stage consists of the interrelation of a number of case analyses which can initially be carried out as such and then compared or contrasted with each other. A second axis for the categorization of qualitative design follows the dimension of time, from retrospective analyses to snapshots and then to longitudinal studies.

Retrospective studies

The principle of case reconstruction is characteristic of a great number of biographical investigations which operate with a series of case analyses in a comparative, typologizing or contrastive manner (see below). Biographical research (see 3.6, 3.7, 5.11) is an example of a retrospective research design in which, retrospectively from the point in time when the research is carried out, certain events and processes are analysed in respect of their meaning for individual or collective life-histories. Design questions in relation to retrospective research involve the selection of informants who will be meaningful for the process to be investigated ('biography bearers' – Schütze 1983). They also involve defining appropriate groups for comparison, justifying the boundaries of the time to be investigated, checking the research question, deciding which (historical) sources and documents (see 5.15) should be used in addition to interviews with the biography-bearers (on this form of triangulation cf. Marotzki 1995b, and 4.6), and how the influences of modern views on the perception and evaluation of earlier experiences should be considered (cf. Bruner 1987).

Snapshots: the analysis of state and process at the time of the investigation

In contrast to this, a large part of qualitative research focuses on snapshots: different manifestations of the expertise that exists in a particular field at the time of the research are collected in interviews (see **5.2**, **5.3**) and compared to one another. Even if certain examples from earlier periods of time affect the interviews, the research does not aim primarily at the retrospective reconstruction of a process. It is concerned rather with giving a description of circumstances at the time of the research.

A range of process-oriented procedures are also strongly related to the present and are therefore not interested in the reconstruction of past events from the point of view of (any of) the participants (cf. Bergmann 1985; see **5.5**), but in the course of currents from a parallel temporal perspective. In ethnographic studies researchers participate in the development of some event over an extended period in order to record and analyse this in parallel to its actual occurrence. In conversation analyses (see **5.17**) a conversation is recorded and then analysed in terms of its sequencing, while in objective hermeneutics (see **5.16**) a protocol is interpreted in a strictly sequential manner 'from beginning to end'.

In these approaches, from the design point of view, there arises the question of how to limit the empirical material. How can the selection guarantee that the phenomenon that is relevant to the research question is actually contained in empirically documented extracts from conversations and processes? Where should the beginning and end of a (conversational or observational) sequence be located? According to what criteria should material for comparison be selected and contrasted: what conversations or conversational extracts, and what observational protocols ought, in concrete terms, to be compared?

Longitudinal studies

The final variant of a basic design in qualitative research consists of longitudinal studies, which also analyse an interesting process or state at later times of data collection. This strategy has rarely been used, at least explicitly, in qualitative research. Exceptions are Gerhardt's (1986) investigation of patients' careers, where an interview partner was questioned again a year

later, and the study by Ulich et al. (1985) on the processing of unemployment among teachers, where the subjects were interviewed seven times in the course of a year. In most qualitative methods there is little guidance on how they could be applied in longitudinal studies with several periods of data collection (see **6.5**). Implicitly, a longitudinal perspective within a temporally limited framework is realized in ethnography (see **5.5**) by virtue of the researcher's extended participation in the field of study, and also – with a retrospective focus – in biographical research (see **3.6**, **3.7**, **5.11**), which considers an extended section of a life-history. The great strength of a longitudinal study – of being able to document changes of view or action through repeated collection-cycles, where the initial state of a process of change can be recorded without any influence from its final state – cannot therefore be fully realized.

Figure 4.1.1 arranges the basic designs in qualitative research that we have discussed according to two dimensions.

3 PROCESSUAL DECISIONS IN THE REALIZATION OF DESIGNS

The process of qualitative research may be described as a sequence of decisions (Flick 1995, 2002). Here researchers, in realizing their projects, can make a choice between a number of alternatives at various points in the process – from questions to data collection and analysis and ultimately to presentation of results. In these decisions researchers realize the design of their study in a dual sense – a design planned in advance is translated into concrete procedures or else, while in process, the design is constituted and modified by virtue of the decisions in favour of particular alternatives.

Goals of the study

A qualitative study may be used to pursue a number of different goals. The model is often the approach of grounded theory development in accordance with the model of Glaser and Strauss (1967; see **2.1**, **5.13**, **6.6**). The form of openness essential for this goal has long been a feature of the debate about qualitative research in general (e.g. Hoffmann-Riem 1980) and lies behind a number of methodological approaches (e.g. theoretical sampling as a principle of case

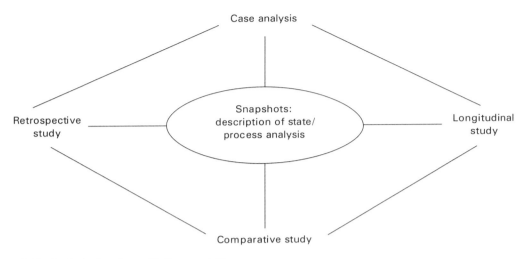

Figure 4.1.1 Basic designs in qualitative research

selection, see **4.4**). In this context, it must be borne in mind that the requirement of theory development is an excessive burden for many types of qualitative studies: to force this goal on graduation theses is as unrealistic as it is incompatible with the intentions of many of those who commission qualitative research projects (see **6.5**). Here what is required are detailed descriptions or evaluations of current practice. In the case of a stage that seeks to provide an exact description of sequences of events in institutional or everyday practice, some of the methodological tools of Glaser and Strauss (for example, theoretical sampling) may be applicable, but do not necessarily have to be. The question of the extent to which a hypothesis-driven or hypothesis-testing study can be realized by qualitative methods (see **4.2**) has not yet been adequately answered, but will be of practical relevance in a number of different contexts: for example, in objective hermeneutics hypotheses will be set up in the course of the interpretation, and these will be tested and falsified during the analysis of further material (see **4.7**, **5.16**). These examples will demonstrate that there are different types of objectives for qualitative studies: description, testing of hypotheses, theory development. At the level of objectives, Maxwell (1996: 16) makes a further distinction between studies that pursue primarily personal goals (for example, a graduation thesis or dissertation), those that pursue practical goals (discovering if and how a particular

programme or product functions) and those that pursue research goals (and are more concerned with developing general knowledge of a particular subject).

Formulation of the research questions

The research question of a qualitative investigation is one of the decisive factors in its success or failure. The way in which it is formulated exerts a strong influence on the design of the study. On the one hand, questions must be formulated as clearly and unambiguously as possible, and this must happen as early as possible in the life of the project. But on the other hand, in the course of the project questions become more and more concrete, more focused, and they are also narrowed and revised (cf. Flick 2002: 64). Maxwell (1996: 49) is representative of the viewpoint that questions should be less the starting point and rather the result of the formulation of a research design. Consequently questions may be viewed or classified according to the extent to which they are suited to the confirmation of existing assumptions (for instance in the sense of hypotheses) or whether they aim at new discoveries or permit this. Strauss (1987: 22) characterizes the latter as 'generative questions'. By this he means: 'Questions that stimulate the line of investigation in profitable directions; they lead to hypotheses, useful comparisons, the collection of certain classes of data, even to general lines of attack on potentially important problems.'

Research questions may on the one hand be kept too broad, which means that they would then provide almost no guidance in the planning and implementation of a study. But they may also be kept too narrow and thereby miss the target of investigation or block rather than promote new discoveries. Questions should be formulated in such a way that (in the context of the planned study and using the available resources) they are capable of being answered. There have been a number of attempts to establish a typology of research questions (cf. for example, Flick 2002; Lofland and Lofland 1984). Maxwell (1996), with an eye on research design, distinguishes between generalizing and particularizing questions, together with questions that focus on distinctions, and those that focus on the description of processes.

Generalization goals and representational goals

In setting up a research design it is advisable to take into account what generalization goals are bound up with the study: is the target a detailed analysis of as many facets as possible, or is it a comparison or a typology of different cases, situations and individuals, and so on? In comparative studies there is the question of the principal dimensions according to which particular phenomena are to be compared. If the study is restricted to one or very few comparative dimensions, based on some theory or on the research questions, this will avoid the possible compulsion to consider all possible dimensions and include cases from a large number of groups and contexts. Here it is important to check critically the extent to which classic demographic dimensions need to be considered in every study: do the phenomena being studied and the research question really require a comparison according to gender, age, town or country, East or West, and so on? If all these dimensions have to be considered, then a number of cases have to be included for each of the manifestations. Then such a large number of cases rapidly becomes necessary that it can no longer be handled within a project that is limited in time and personnel. It is therefore preferable to clarify which of these dimensions is the decisive one. Studies with a sensibly limited claim to generalization

are not only easier to manage but also, as a rule, more meaningful (for an example of this, cf. Hildenbrand 1983).

In qualitative research a distinction must be made between numerical and theoretical generalization. A very small number of projects claim either to want or to be able to draw conclusions from the cases investigated about a particular population. What is more informative is the question of the theoretical generalizability of the results obtained. Here the number of individuals or situations studied is less decisive than the differences between cases involved (maximal variation) or the theoretical scope of the case interpretations. To increase the theoretical generalizability, the use of different methods (triangulation, see **4.5**, **4.6**, **4.7**) for the investigation of a small number of cases is often more informative than the use of one method for the largest possible number of cases. Here it must be decided whether the triangulation of methods can or should be applied to the case or to the set of data.

For the development of a typology, for example, it is necessary not only to use the target selection of cases, but to include counter-examples and to undertake case-contrasts in addition to case-comparisons (cf. Kelle and Kluge 1999: 40ff.).

Under aspects of generalization it is also necessary to attend to the question of what additional gain may be expected from triangulation with qualitative (see **4.6**) or with quantitative methods (see **4.5**), and how this may be reconciled with the available resources.

Finally, it needs to be considered what presentation goals (see **5.22**) are involved in a qualitative study: is the empirical material the basis for the writing of an essay (Bude 1989), or rather for a narrative presentation that would give it more of an illustrative function? Or is it a matter of providing a systematization of the variation found in the cases investigated?

Degree of standardization and control

Miles and Huberman (1994: 16ff.) distinguish between tight and loose research design and see indications for both variations in concrete cases according to the research question and conditions: tight research designs are determined by narrowly restricted questions and strictly determined selection procedures, where the degree of openness in the field of investigation and the empirical material is relatively limited. These designs are seen by the authors as appropriate when researchers lack experience of qualitative research, when the research operates on the basis of narrowly defined constructs, and when it is restricted to the investigation of particular relationships in familiar contexts. In such cases they see loose designs as a roundabout route to the desired result. Tighter designs make it easier to decide what data or extracts from the data are relevant to the investigation and what is not relevant, and they also make it easier, for example, to compare and summarize data from different interviews or observations.

Loose designs are characterized by somewhat broadly defined concepts and have, in the first instance, little in the way of fixed methodological procedures. Miles and Huberman see this type of design as appropriate when a large measure of experience is available of research in different fields, when new fields are being investigated and the theoretical constructs and concepts are relatively undeveloped. This second variant is clearly oriented to the methodological suggestions of Glaser and Strauss (1967; see **2.1**, **5.13**), which are characterized, for example in their handling of theoretical sampling, by great openness and flexibility.

Even though qualitative research often sees itself as indebted to the principle of openness (Hoffmann-Riem 1980), it is sensible for many questions and projects to consider what degree of control is necessary: to what extent must there be constancy in the contextual conditions in which the comparative differences between two groups are manifested (see above)? What degree of control or comparability should be provided in the conditions under which the various interviews in a study are carried out?

Selection: sampling and formation of groups for comparison

Selection decisions in qualitative research focus, on the one hand, on persons or situations from which data are collected, and, on the other hand, on extracts from the material collected, from which novel interpretations are made or results are presented as examples (cf. Flick 2002: 65–72). In this, theoretical sampling is considered to be the royal way for qualitative studies. Frequently, however, other selection strategies are more appropriate (cf. for

example the suggestions in Patton 1990), if the goal is not to do with theory development but rather with the evaluation of institutional practice.

One essential component of the decision about data selection (in comparative investigations) is the formation of groups for comparison. Here it must be clarified at what level the comparisons are to be made: between individuals, situations, institutions or phenomena? Accordingly, the selection should be made in such a way that several cases are always included in a single group for comparison (see **4.4**).

Resources

One factor that is frequently undervalued in the development of a research design is the available resources (time, personnel, technical support, competences, experience and so on). In research, proposals are frequently based on an unrealistic relationship between the planned tasks and the personnel resources that can (realistically) be asked for.

For realistic project planning it is advisable to make a calculation of the activities involved, which assumes, for example, that an interview of around 90 minutes will need as much time again for locating interview-partners, organizing appointments, and travel. With regard to the calculation of time for transcribing interviews (see **5.9**), the estimates will diverge widely – depending on the precision of the system of transcription to be used. Morse (1994: 232f.) suggests that, for fast-writing transcribers, the length of the tape containing the interview recording be multiplied by a factor of 4. If checking the finished transcript against the tape is also included, the length of the tape should be multiplied by a total of 6. For the complete calculation of the project she advises that the time allowed be doubled to allow for unforeseen difficulties and 'catastrophes'. In planning a project that will work with transcribed interviews, a high-quality tape recorder should always be used for the recordings, and a special instrument with a foot-operated switch is essential for transcription. Sample plans of how to calculate the time parameters of empirical projects are to be found in Marshall and Rossman (1995: 123ff.). The time needed for data interpretation is difficult to calculate. If a decision is taken to use computers and programs such as

ATLAS.ti and NUD*IST (see **5.14**; Part 7) for data interpretation, then it is essential to include in the plan sufficient time for technical preparation (installation, removal of errors, induction of team-members in the use of the program, and so on).

In the process of approving a project the equipment asked for is sometimes reduced and additional methodological stages, such as an additional group for comparison or phase of data collection, may be required. At this stage, if not before, it becomes essential to check the relationship between tasks and resources, and short-cut strategies in the methodological procedures should, if necessary, be considered.

4   SHORT-CUT STRATEGIES

Many of the qualitative methods in current use are connected with a high degree of precision and an equally high investment of time – in data collection (here we might mention the narrative interview, see **5.2**), in transcription (see **5.9**), and in interpretation (for example, the procedures of objective hermeneutics and theoretical coding both require a great deal of time, see **5.16, 5.13**). In externally funded projects and commissioned research, but also in graduate theses, this need for time is confronted with a very tight deadline within which the research questions have to be answered (see **6.5**). Under the label 'short-cut strategies' (justifiable) deviations from the maximum requirements of precision and completeness are discussed. For instance, the suggestions of Meuser and Nagel (1991) on the setting up of interviews with experts provide guidance that deserves to be taken seriously on the framing of qualitative interviews with interview partners who are under great pressure of time. The same is true of the suggestions made by Strauss (1987: 266), O'Connell and Kowal (1995a, see **5.9**) and others that only parts of interviews be transcribed, and only as precisely as is actually required by the questions of the particular investigation. The non-transcribed sections of interviews can be kept within the research process, for instance by means of summaries or lists of topics, to be transcribed if necessary. After phases of open coding (see **5.13**) there is often an excessive quantity of codes or categories. In addition to simplifying the administration and ordering of such categories through computer programs such as ATLAS.ti (see Part 7; **5.14**), it has often

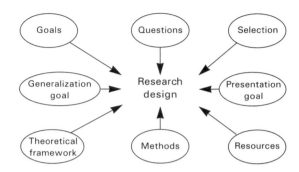

Figure 4.1.2   Components of qualitative research design

proved useful to draw up lists of priorities related to the research questions that make it possible to select and reduce the categories. The same may be said of the selection of textual contexts, based on the research question, which are required to undergo a process of intensive interpretation.

5   SUMMARY

Research designs may ultimately be described as the means of achieving the goals of the research. They link theoretical frameworks, questions, research, generalization and presentational goals with the methods used and resources available under the focus of goal-achievement. Their realization is the result of decisions reached in the research process. Figure 4.1.2 summarizes again the influential factors and decisions that determine the concrete formulation of the research design.

FURTHER READING

Flick, U. (2002) *An Introduction to Qualitative Research,* 2nd. edn. Thousand Oaks, CA: Sage. esp. chs 5–7.

Marshall, C. and Rossman, G. B. (1995) *Designing Qualitative Research,* 2nd edn. Thousand Oaks, CA: Sage.

Maxwell, J. A. (1996) *Qualitative Research Design – An Interactive Approach.* Thousand Oaks, CA: Sage.

eses and Prior Knowledge in
tive Research

einefeld

he particular
often insist
ration from
at aims at
In view of
ed state of
iis is not
n is not
oncerns
iill also
nition
qual-
on by
results
oy the
litative

and the unavoidable selectivity of every kind of research. In the first place it is considered obligatory to reveal the researcher's prior knowledge and thereby to control it. Secondly, an explicit link is made to the state of available knowledge and a contribution is made to the integration and cumulation of this knowledge. And thirdly, the time-sequencing, and the separation of data collection and data analysis, require a *prior* elaboration of the theoretical framework, since this defines and restricts the stages in the research and also means that no correction of operational procedures is possible during the data collection, because of the strict phasing of the research process.

Although in qualitative methodology the fact of theory-driven observation is also unquestioned, there is a predominant rejection of hypotheses formulated in advance: precisely because there is an awareness that knowledge influences observation and action, researchers wish to avoid being 'fixed' by the hypotheses on particular aspects that they can only obtain 'in advance' from their own area of (scientific and everyday) relevance, but whose 'fit' with the meaning patterns of the individuals being investigated cannot be guaranteed in advance. In place of the requirement to reveal prior knowledge in the form of hypotheses, therefore,

GY:

logists the
eginning of
ie means of
ie inevitable
of observation

in qualitative methodology there arises a requirement for a suspension of this prior knowledge in favour of the greatest possible *openness* to the particular meanings and relevances of actors – an openness that is seen as being endangered by the prior formulation of hypotheses.

The basic problem – the influence of prior knowledge on observation – is therefore seen from both sides, but the chosen strategy for solving it is aiming in a different direction, since the implications associated with it are constantly being given a different weighting. If, in quantitative methodology, the need for *control of the researcher* and *the conscious structuring of research activity* are in the foreground (while the agreement of the theoretical categories with the meaning patterns of actors is seen as relatively unproblematic), qualitative methodologists require primarily a guarantee of the *appropriateness* of the categories used by the researcher and an *openness* to the potential 'other' of the research field (and see control of the investigator by means of methodological rules as a false 'solution').

2 DOING WITHOUT HYPOTHESES AS A RESULT OF THE PROFILING OF METHODOLOGICAL POSITION

The programmatic opposition that we have sketched of these two responses to the fundamental epistemological problem appears, from a historical viewpoint, to be less 'naturally given' than a result of the growing competition between two methodological approaches.

In the classic studies of empirical social research we find no explicit treatment of the problem of checking prior knowledge nor even of the problem of prior formulation of hypotheses (cf., for example, the studies of William I. Thomas and Florian Znaniecki, William F. Whyte, Howard S. Becker or Paul F. Lazarsfeld).[1] As far as practice in dealing with 'prior knowledge' and 'hypotheses' is concerned, it is clear to what a great extent the research activity was oriented particularly to the theoretical but also to the everyday knowledge of the researchers, and how greatly these ideas determined the results of their work, by first making possible the collection and structuring of the data material. Conversely, it may

be shown that a formulation including specified hypotheses at the beginning of such studies would often have been completely impossible; Whyte and Blanche Geer, for instance, point out explicitly how completely their research question changed after the 'first days in the field', and how they had to adapt it to the peculiarities and possibilities of their object of investigation (Whyte 1955: 317ff., 320ff.; Geer 1964: 340).

With regard to making this prior knowledge explicit in the form of hypotheses, in the course of working out these two methodological positions – which see themselves as alternatives – during subsequent decades a growing process of contrast and reciprocal delimitation may be distinguished in the methodological procedures that are felt to be necessary and sensible. These then resulted in the opposing research strategies which we sketched in the first section. On the side of qualitative methodology the programmatic work of Barney G. Glaser and Anselm L. Strauss (1967), *The Discovery of Grounded Theory*, is of particular significance. Here the authors expressly require that researchers free themselves voluntarily of all prior knowledge and even dispense with prior reading of theoretical and empirical studies in their subject area, in order to embark upon the research field in as unprejudiced a way as possible. According to this approach, the task of empirical research is not (or at least not primarily) to subject to empirical testing the hypotheses that are systematically derived from 'grand' (armchair) theories, since such theses often did not 'fit' the situations that were to be investigated in concrete cases; empirically based general theories are rather only to be expected when researchers personally derive their categories from the data (see **2.1**). The formulation of a sociological theory, therefore, should take place not at the beginning of the research process but at the end: the overriding goal of social research is not the *testing* but the *generation* of theories (1967: 1–18).

The position developed by Glaser and Strauss in deliberate rejection of the 'mainstream' in empirical social research (see **2.1**) showed itself in the reception of qualitative methodology – over and above the grounded theory approach – as extremely influential: a number of authors saw the requirement for doing without hypotheses as a precondition for an interpretative type of social research and elevated the 'openness' of its methodology to a core belief in qualitative research (e.g. Hoffmann-Riem 1980: 345f., Lamnek 1995: 22f., 139f.). With this shift of attention from *ex-ante* hypotheses to those arising during the research process, the fundamental epistemological problem of checking the prior knowledge which the researcher brings to the job was relegated to a background position. It was believed that this aspect could be overlooked, not least because the very openness of the methods made possible a correction 'by the field': 'unsuitable' prior knowledge would be exposed as such in the course of the study. But even if one concedes the different degree of openness of the various methods, this argument overlooks the fact that even the *first* setting up of data is already an active undertaking on the part of the researcher and is based on the individual's research interest and prior understanding. The requirement for as 'unconditional as possible' an entry into the field conceals precisely this basic setting up of the field in accordance with the researcher's 'available prior knowledge' at this particular moment. Discoveries about social phenomena do not 'emerge' on their own: they are from the outset constructs of the researcher. The idealization of the 'unprejudiced nature' of the researcher that is sometimes to be found in qualitative methodology, and the idea of a 'direct' record of social reality, are therefore untenable from an epistemological viewpoint (cf. Meinefeld 1995: 287–294).

If we consider this from a distance, it is striking that this methodological idealization is both in contradiction to one of the core theoretical principles of qualitative research ('the interpretation of a situation depends on knowledge') and also not a true reflection of research practice. Glaser and Strauss, in their study *Awareness of Dying*, which appeared in 1965, openly acknowledge their reliance on prior knowledge of this subject area (1965b: 286ff.).[2] One explanation for this discrepancy between theoretical insight, practical research and methodological norm might be sought in the concern to establish as sharply defined an alternative as possible to the prevailing standardizing methodology. Horst Weishaupt, for example, offers the following as a result of his analysis of qualitative research reports: 'The impression emerges that the methodological

debate is determined by concerns about demarcation which are of subordinate interest for the practice of qualitative social research' (1995: 94). And in a case study in the sociology of science, Jean Converse demonstrates the mixing of methodological and research-policy arguments in the conflict about open and standardized interviews in the United States during the Second World War (1984).

3 RECENT DISCUSSION

The impetus for a critical methodological discussion, free from the commitment *against* *ex-ante* hypotheses, was provided by Christel Hopf (1983, 1996). Using two empirical studies as examples, she sought to demonstrate that, on the one hand, the question to be investigated could indeed require a qualitative procedure, but on the other hand, because of the availability of previous studies, there was a focus on content that made the formulation of *ex-ante* hypotheses unavoidable.

If hypotheses are rejected in principle, then on the one hand there is no consideration of the very different aims of the hypotheses, and these differ sharply – in terms of their claim to validity and object – in their suitability for qualitative questions. (For example, do they relate to universal laws or to singular facts; do they make claims about the relationship between variables, or are they interested in social processes and meaning patterns? Hopf 1983: 48–50; 1996: 11f.). On the other hand, experience from research practice would speak against an unconditional openness in data collection: the pressure – resulting from the absence of selection criteria – to *extensive exploration* of all aspects that are *possibly* of interest conflicts with the *intensive meaning-discovery* that is characteristic of interpretative research, and in this situation overburdens the investigator (1983: 50–52). A general rejection of *ex-ante* hypotheses would therefore endanger the realization of genuinely qualitative research goals: it is 'dogmatic and not open to discussion' (1983: 49).

Other authors, in their plea for an unprejudiced approach to both the need and the possibility to reflect prior knowledge in qualitative social research, draw attention to the identical effects (from an epistemological viewpoint) of hypotheses and prior knowledge in relation to the structuring of subsequent research activity, and therefore demand that this 'gap' in qualitative methodology be closed. Here we see, in the first place, the simple necessity of accepting the general state of epistemological discussion and not laying oneself open to the accusation of requiring an epistemological special status for qualitative methods, with this demand for 'unprejudiced' observation; and secondly this question, which every form of social research must confront, opens up the possibility of reconsidering the relationship between qualitative and quantitative methodology and redefining both the differences and the common ground (Böttger 1998; Meinefeld 1997; Strobl 1998).

4 STARTING POINTS FOR A RE-ORIENTATION OF METHODOLOGICAL POSITIONS

How could these apparently contradictory expectations be resolved? On the one hand we have to meet the epistemological requirement to include prior knowledge in methodological control, and on the other we should not abandon the sociological *a priori* of allowing the sociological analysis to proceed from the genuine meaning attributions of actors and should not, in the act of interpretation, impose the categories of the investigator on the actions.

One precondition for the solution of this dilemma is, first and foremost, a recognition of the fact that the latter requirement can only be met in an approximate way. It cannot simply be a question of opposing a 'pure' reconstruction of the view of the actors to a recording of social reality in the categories of the investigator: it is only possible, in all cases, to understand the categories of others on the basis of one's own categories (on this point see also Schütz's thoughts on the observation of one's fellows, 1932: 287ff.). Here is precisely the misunderstanding of a *sociological* idea of understanding, for example on the part of Theodore Abel (1948) or Hans Albert (1985), who saw (and therefore rejected) 'understanding' as a direct recording of subjective meaning on the basis of individual sensibility, whereas it can only mean identifying

the actions of others as belonging to a particular meaning pattern available in the knowledge of the social group in question and subsuming them in this meaning pattern *in the way in which, and to the extent that, it is familiar to the person understanding* (on this cf. Meinefeld 1995, ch. 1). We have to accept the fundamental restriction that every observation only takes on meaning in respect of one's own meaning schemata, and so prior knowledge inevitably gives structure to our observations and must therefore be seen as the foundation of all research. In this way, however, the opposition of categories is transformed into a difference of degree, and the fundamental problem exists for all researchers in the same way.

A second step towards the resolution of this opposition might be found in distinguishing research questions according to the nature and extent of the knowledge already available of the area under investigation. If we consider the situation of the classic studies mentioned above, it becomes clear that in these cases a pre-formulation of content-based hypotheses is out of the question. On the other hand, if anyone wished to investigate interaction with the dying today they would scarcely be able to avoid taking note of the prior work of Glaser and Strauss and setting up their own research under consideration of the events reported there.

This does not necessarily mean, however, that one should no longer be open to new observations. If we can learn to distinguish between the principled *methodological* openness and the explicitness with which prior *knowledge* is reflected and expressed, it will be possible to reconcile the formulation of hypotheses with the reconstruction of object-specific meaning contents. The openness to new matters does not depend on our not taking account, at the level of content, of the old and the familiar, but on the how, in methodological terms, we set up the search for the new. Logically, these two levels are independent of one another – the question of putting prior knowledge into concrete terms and selecting the methods to be used to obtain new knowledge are only related (at the concrete practical level) when, for example, a standardized questionnaire is unable to provide information from beyond the dimensions the researcher considers important because there was no room for it in the chosen instrument. In the first place, however, this does not mean that the result has been predetermined, as critics sometimes claim: it is only the framework of the dimensions involved in the investigation that has been fixed, but not their concrete manifestations of content. We could indeed find surprising results as to content using this route (Opp 1984: 65f.). In the second place, it does not mean that the choice of (more) open methods (such as participant observation, see 5.5, or interviews, see 5.2) will *per se* guarantee an openness *of content*: prior knowledge that remains implicit, even using these methods, will lead to selective observation and interpretation, because the recognition of whether something is new or not lies with the researcher and not with the individuals under investigation. The openness required in qualitative methodology to the potentially special nature of the field of investigation is therefore not helped by failing to make prior knowledge explicit, but by a conscious use of methods that permit the recognition and recording of a 'deviation' in the field of study from what was expected. This does not mean, however, that there is a conscious awareness of such an expectation.

As far as the *possibility* of reflecting prior knowledge is concerned, it should be noted that this can take a number of different forms.

1 In every case we have at our disposal an *everyday prior knowledge* on which, however vague and uncertain it may be, we are forced to rely in the absence of better information in order to be able to carry out any kind of initial orientation in the research field. This prior knowledge can only partially be made explicit, because ultimately an infinite regress is possible here. But it is at precisely this level that the basic but not otherwise reflected nature of the research object is decided, and what may be taken for granted from a cultural viewpoint remains fixed, so that its reflection becomes a (frequently irredeemable) desideratum (for an example cf. Bourdieu et al. 1991: 44ff.).
2 Furthermore, every researcher, in his or her approach to the research field, has recourse to a corpus of *general theoretical concepts* which similarly contribute to the researcher's basic definition of the object. Although these are to a large extent conscious, they too cannot be made fully explicit, but the requirement for a conscious reflection may be made with a greater prospect of success.
3 Finally, there are a range of *object-related concepts* which permit the researcher to focus on particular aspects of content in the research area under investigation, and which, even in the context of qualitative research, can therefore facilitate and perhaps require the formulation of *ex-ante* hypotheses.

With regard to measuring the effects of this prior knowledge on the research process, it should be remembered that this does not begin only when hypotheses are formulated or when one 'enters the field' without hypotheses. If the *total* research process is to be reflected methodologically, then a fixation on the formulation of *ex-ante* hypotheses (positive in quantitative and negative in qualitative methodology) is not tenable: the development of the researcher's attention begins earlier and in a more fundamental way. In any case, in thinking about the control of this pre-structuring of limitation, one should be aware that this reflection – at least at the present time – can scarcely be standardized. How it is to be dealt with in the future should be tested in empirical research practice, before any methodological pronouncement is made.

5 CONCLUSION

In the process of self-assurance of having an independent methodology, the decision against *ex-ante* hypotheses has indeed led to a consolidation of the qualitative position as distinct from quantitative methodology, but it has also led to a claim that is epistemologically untenable, and has restricted the applicability of qualitative research. Experience in research practice, however, has shown, on the one hand, that the majority of quantitative research studies also fail to follow the norm of *testing* hypotheses (cf. Meinefeld 1997: 23f.), and on the other hand the examples from Hopf cited above support the view that in a qualitative research programme the testing of hypotheses may also occupy a legitimate place. The deciding line about how and to what extent prior knowledge should be made concrete does not follow the 'quantitative–qualitative' boundary, but is clearly dependent on other factors. It would be highly desirable if this fact could be ratified methodologically and if an uninhibited way of dealing with the problem of structuring research activity could be achieved in both qualitative and quantitative social research.

NOTES

1   The actual methodological procedure at this phase of justifying modern empirical research may be captured very aptly in an observation, where Marie Jahoda relocates the retrospective overemphasis of methodological reflectiveness that characterized the preface to the new edition of Lazarsfeld's *The Unemployed of Marienthal*, published 27 years after the first edition – a study which even today is seen as a model of exemplary empirical research: 'If [this explanation] should give the impression that these principles were available to us during the study, this would be misleading. We had no clear plan, in terms either of content or method. ... The methods grew out of concentration on the problem, not for their own sake' (Jahoda 1980/81: 139). Furthermore – to complete the picture – it seemed legitimate to use, as a research strategy and method, whatever procedure promised to make it possible to obtain interesting data for the research question (see **2.8**).

2   It is of course true that in later publications (1987: 10f. and passim; Strauss and Corbin 1990: 48–56) Strauss recognizes prior knowledge as an important source of theoretical sensitivity; but since Strauss (and Corbin) insist on 'discovery' as a primary goal of qualitative research, they hedge this direction with a renewed warning of the risk of 'constraint' that affects the openness to new matters (1990: 32f.) because of categories known in advance – and in this way they essentially adhere to the normative demand of the position formulated earlier. Even more explicitly, Glaser insists upon dispensing with all prior knowledge (cf. Kelle 1994: 334f., and also the excellent presentations of the positions of Glaser and Strauss in Kelle 1994: 283ff.).

FURTHER READING

Bourdieu, P., Chamboredon, J. C. and Passeron, J. C. (1991) *Craft of Sociology: Epistemological Preliminaries*. Berlin: de Gruyter. Pt III and ch. 2.

Chalmers, A. F. (1982) *What is This Thing Called Science?* Queensland: University of Queensland Press. ch. 3.

Glaser, B. G. and Strauss, A. L. (1967) *The Discovery of Grounded Theory. Strategies for Qualitative Research*. Chicago: Aldine. esp. pp. 1–43.

4.3 Abduction, Deduction and Induction in Qualitative Research

Jo Reichertz

1 ABDUCTION – A RULE-GOVERNED WAY TO NEW KNOWLEDGE?

Social researchers who take an interest in the fluctuation of their own professional vocabulary have been able, for more than a decade, to witness the flourishing of a concept that is around 400 years old: it is a matter of the term *abduction*. The boom has been so vast that we sometimes hear talk of an 'abductive turn' (Bonfantini 1988; Wirth 1995).

First introduced in 1597 by Julius Pacius to translate the Aristotelian *apagoge*, abduction remained quite unnoticed for almost three centuries. It was C. S. Peirce (1839–1914) who first took it up and used it to denote the only truly *knowledge-extending* means of inferencing (so he claimed) that would be categorically distinct from the normal types of logical conclusion, namely *deduction* and *induction* (1976, 1986, 1973, 1992). But several decades were to pass before Peirce's ideas were systematically received and also adopted (Anderson 1995; Apel 1967; Fann 1970; Hanson 1965; Reichertz 1991b; Tursman 1987; Wartenburg 1971).

Today the term 'abduction' has become something of a password within social research (but not only there): educationists, linguists, psychologists, psychoanalysts, semioticists, theatre-scientists, theologians, criminologists, researchers in artificial intelligence and, of course, also sociologists announce in their research reports that their new discoveries are due to abduction.

The great success of abduction, in my opinion, may be traced back to two particular features: first to its indefiniteness and secondly to the misjudgement of the achievements of abductions that derive from this. For frequently the use of the idea of abduction has led in many of its users to one particular hope, that of a *rule-governed* and *replicable* production of new and *valid* knowledge. This hope is found, above all, in artificial intelligence research and in a number of variants of qualitative social research.

All these approaches have in common that they stress both the *logical* and also the *innovative* character of abduction. For abduction is no longer treated as a traditional, classical means of drawing conclusions, but as a new method that is not yet incorporated into formal logic. However, it is, in every sense, a means of inferencing. It is precisely in this quality of being a 'means-of-inferencing' that we find the secret charm of abduction. On the one hand it is a *logical* inference (and thereby reasonable and scientific), and on the other hand it extends into the realm of profound insight (and therefore generates new knowledge). This sort of concept of abduction associates its critique of with a kind of positivism capable only of tautology, with the hope of a new kind of social research which will understand sociality more reasonably and therefore better. Abduction is intended to help social research, or rather social researchers, to be able to make new discoveries in a logically and methodologically ordered way.

This hope is directed against Reichenbach (1938) and Popper (1934), who, by separating the logic of discovery from the logic of justification, 'drove' the first into the realm of psychology, and allowed only the second into the realm of serious science. This separation should be reversed: the unfortunate disjunction of contexts of discovery and justification should be removed by means of abduction. A rethinking of this kind promises a great deal: liberation from the 'chance of a good idea' (Habermas 1971: 147), and (it is hoped) 'synthetic inferences *a posteriori*' (cf. Oevermann 1987).

Because of this hope, many social scientists have treated, and still do treat, abduction as a magic formula – always applicable when the cognitive basis of the process of scientific interpretation is being investigated. In my opinion, however, this hope is the result of a widespread misunderstanding of Peirce's position, namely the misunderstanding that there are no differences between 'hypothesis' and 'abduction' as forms of inference. From the modern point of view it is beyond question that up to about 1898 Peirce combined *two* very different forms of inference under the name of 'hypothesis'. When he became aware of this unclear use of the term 'hypothesis', he elaborated a clear distinction in his later philosophy between the two procedures, and called the one operation 'qualitative induction' and the other 'abduction' (for more detail see Reichertz 1991b, and also Eco 1981).

Many social scientists, with reference to the *achievements* of abduction, refer to Peirce's later work (in my view wrongly), but with reference to its *form* and *validity*, and to his work on hypothesis. It is only on the basis of this 'hybrid meaning' that they succeed in designing a logical operation that produces new knowledge in a rule-governed way.

2 DEDUCTION, QUANTITATIVE AND QUALITATIVE INDUCTION, ABDUCTION

The social order on which humans (often but not always) orient themselves in their actions is constantly changing and is, moreover, 'sub-culturally fragmented'. The different order(s) therefore possess only a localized validity and are continually, and – since the advent of the 'modern' – with increasing rapidity, being changed by these human beings who previously (up to a point) adhered to them. Moreover, it is a fact that both the form and the validity of this order are bound to the meaning attributions and interpretations of the acting subjects. Social science explanations of actions aim at the (re-)construction of the order that is relevant to the acting subjects. Admittedly this kind of order can no longer be derived from proven grand theories, first because these are, as a rule, not sufficiently 'local', and secondly because they have frequently already been overtaken by constant social change. Because this is the case, 'fitting' new views of the make-up of social order must constantly be generated. For this reason it is highly sensible to examine as closely as possible the life practice that is to be understood, and – on the basis of these data – to (re-)construct the *new* orders.

If we are now to make a serious attempt, in (qualitative and quantitative) research, to evaluate collected data, in other words to typologize them according to particular features and orders of features, the question very soon arises of how we may bring a little order into the chaos of the data. This is only to a very small extent a matter of work organization (sorting of data) and much more a question of how the unmanageable variety of the data may be related to theories – either pre-existing or still to be discovered.

In this undertaking (if one pursues the ideas of Peirce) we may, in ideal terms, distinguish *three* procedures, and in what follows I shall subdivide the second procedure into two subgroups – but not because there are fundamental differences between the two, but rather because in this way the difference we have already spoken of between *abduction* and *hypothesis* or *qualitative induction* can be made clearer (for fuller discussion of this see Reichertz 1991b).

1 One type of data analysis consists of the procedure of *subsumption*. Subsumption proceeds from an already known context of features, that is from a familiar *rule* (for example, all burglars who steal from a medicine chest are drug addicts), and seeks to find this general context in the data (for example, the unknown burglar has robbed the medicine

chest) in order to obtain knowledge about the individual case (for example, the unknown burglar is a drug addict). The logical form of this intellectual operation is that of *deduction*: the single case in question is subordinated to an already known rule. Here a tried and trusted order is applied to the new case. New facts (concerning the ordering of the world) are not experienced in this way – merely that the unknown burglar is a drug addict (knowledge that may be quite useful to the police – if the rule is true). Deductions are therefore *tautological*, they tell us nothing new. But deductions are not only tautological but also *truth-conveying*: if the rule offered for application is valid, then the result of the application of the rule is also valid.

2.1 A second form of analysis consists of extending, or *generalizing*, into an order or rule the combinations of features that are found in the data material. Proceeding from the observation that 'in the case of burglaries a, b and c the medicine chest was robbed', and the case-knowledge that 'Mr Jones committed burglaries a, b and c', the inference is drawn that 'Mr Jones always robs the medicine chest when he breaks in'. The logical form of this intellectual operation is that of *quantitative induction*. It transfers the quantitative properties of a *sample* to a totality, it 'extends' the single case into a rule. *Quantitative inductions* therefore (strictly speaking) are equally tautological but not truth-conveying. The results of this form of inferencing are merely *probable*.

2.2 One particular variant of the inductive processing of data consists of assembling certain qualitative features of the investigated sample in such a way that this combination of features resembles another (that is already available in the repertoire of knowledge of the interacting community) in essential points. In this case one can use the term that already exists for this combination to characterize one's 'own' form. The logical form of this operation is that of *qualitative induction*. From the existence of certain qualitative features in a *sample* it infers the presence of other features. (For example, at the scene of a crime I see a particular set of clues. In very many respects these agree with the pattern of clues of

Mr Jones. Conclusion: Jones is responsible for the clues.) The observed case (*token*) is an instance of a known order (*type*).

In brief: if *quantitative induction* makes inferences about a totality from the quantitative properties of a *sample*, qualitative induction – in contrast – supplements the observed features of a sample with others that are not perceived. It is only in this sense that this form of induction transcends the borders of experience – that is, only the experience of the sample in question. This inference only extends knowledge to the extent that it proceeds from a limited selection to a larger totality. *Qualitative induction* is not a valid but only a probable form of inference – although it does have the advantage of being capable of operationalization (albeit with difficulty). Qualitative induction is the basis of all scientific procedures that find, in collected data, only new versions of what is already known.

3 The third type of data processing (apparently similar, but in fact totally different) consists of assembling or discovering, on the basis of an interpretation of collected data, such combinations of features for which there is no appropriate explanation or rule in the store of knowledge that already exists. This causes surprise. Real surprise causes a genuine shock (and not only in Peirce's opinion) – and the search for the (new) explanation. Since no suitable 'type' can be found, a new one must be invented or discovered by means of a mental process. Sometimes one achieves a new discovery of this sort as a result of an intellectual process, and if this happens, it takes place 'like lightning', and the thought process 'is very little hampered by logical rules' (Peirce 1931–35, vol. 5: 117, CP 5, 188).

An order, or a rule, in this procedure must therefore first be discovered or invented – and this has to happen with the aid of intellectual effort. Something unintelligible is discovered in the data, and on the basis of the mental design of a *new* rule the rule is discovered or invented and, at the same time, it also becomes clear what the case is. The logical form of this operation is that of *abduction*. Here one has decided (with whatever degree of awareness and for whatever reasons) no longer to adhere to the conventional view of things.

This way of creating a new 'type', that is the relationship of a typical new combination of features, is a creative outcome which engenders a new idea. This kind of association is not obligatory, and is indeed rather risky. *Abduction* 'proceeds', therefore, from a known quantity (= result) to *two* unknowns (= rule and case). Abduction is therefore a cerebral process, an intellectual act, a mental leap, that brings together things one had never associated with one another.

3 TWO STRATEGIES FOR PRODUCING ABDUCTIONS

If one is to take seriously what has been outlined above, one would have to come to the conclusion (pessimistic though it might be for everyday scientific practice) that abductive discovery of new things is dependent on pure chance, a benevolent God, a favourable evolution, or a particularly well-endowed brain. Science as a *systematic* endeavour would, according to this definition, seem doomed to failure. 'Anything goes.'

However – even if one cannot *force* lightning to strike in an algorithmically rule-governed way – could there perhaps be ways of proceeding and precautions that would make it easier for the (intellectual) lightning to strike? Because even lightning is not entirely unexpected. To extend the metaphor, it happens only as a consequence of a particular meteorological situation. In a storm one can look for the oak tree or seek out the beeches or even go to the top of the church tower. None of these steps will make it likely that lightning will come and strike; but the likelihood is none the less very much greater than with someone who only loves the sunlight, who always takes refuge in a cellar during a storm and who – if they do happen to find themselves in a storm – always tries to find out where the nearest lightning conductor is. In short, if discovery is truly related to accidents, then one can either give accidents a chance or deny the possibility.

Peirce himself cites two *macro-strategies* that are particularly well-suited to 'enticing' abductive processes or at least to creating a favourable climate for their appearance. One can be derived from the story where Peirce talks retrospectively about his talents as an amateur detective (Peirce 1929). In this Peirce tells how, during a voyage at sea, his overcoat and his valuable watch were stolen. He was very alarmed, because the watch was not his own property. He therefore decided to recover the watch, by any means and as quickly as possible. He had all the crew called together and asked them to form up in a line. Then he walked along the line and addressed a few apparently inconsequential words to each of them.

> When I had gone through the row, I turned and walked from them, though not away, and said to myself: 'Not the least scintilla of light have I got to go upon'. But thereupon my other self (for our own communings are always in dialogues) said to me, 'But you simply *must* put your finger on the man. No matter if you have no reason, you must say whom you think to be the thief.' I made a little loop in my walk, which had not taken a minute, and I turned toward them, all shadow of doubt had vanished. (Peirce 1929: 271)

Peirce named one person as the culprit and subsequently, after a great deal of confusion (see Sebeok and Umiker-Sebeok 1985 for a full description), it emerged that the man suspected by Peirce was indeed the thief.

The stimulus for this individual initiative in matters of 'detection' was therefore provided by *fear* – and not the fear of losing 350 dollars, which was the value of the watch, but the fear of an expected 'life-long professional disgrace' (Peirce 1929: 270). The body went into a state of alarm, but clearly this was not enough. When, after the first conversations with the crew, he could not name a suspect, he increased, by an act of will, his pressure to do something. In this partially self-induced emergency situation the abductive lightning struck.

Of course, abductions cannot be forced by a specific procedural programme, but one can induce situations (and this is the moral of this episode) in which abductions fit. According to Peirce, the presence of *genuine doubt* or *uncertainty* or *fear* or *great pressure to act* is a favourable 'weather situation' for abductive lightning to strike.

Peirce, however, develops another possible way of creating situations in which new knowledge may more frequently be obtained. For this to work the investigators – as Peirce advises – should let their mind wander with no specific goal. This mental game without rules he calls 'musement', a game of meditation, or day-dreaming. How one achieves the condition of day-dreaming may be seen in the following formulation of Peirce:

> Enter your skiff of musement, push off into the lake of thought, and leave the breath of heaven to swell your sail. With your eyes open, awake to what is about or within you, and open conversation with yourself: for such is all meditation! ... It is, however, not a conversation in words alone, but is illustrated, like a lecture, with diagrams and with experiments. (Peirce 1931–35, vol. 6: CP, 315)

To do this requires leisure; that is to say, freedom from an immediate pressure to act is a fundamental condition, without which the skiff will not be able to embark. This apparently contradicts quite vehemently the preconditions for successful abductions which Peirce sets out in his detection example.

Admittedly, the contradiction is resolved if one looks for what is typical in the two 'abduction-friendly' settings. For in both cases the procedures mean that the *consciously working mind*, relying on logical rules, is outmanoeuvred. Peirce-the-detective allows no time for the calculating mind to busy itself with the solution of his problem, and Peirce-the-daydreamer switches off his power of logical judgement by entrusting himself to the 'breath of heaven'.

All measures designed to create favourable conditions for abductions, therefore, always aim at one thing: the achievement of an *attitude* of preparedness to abandon old convictions and to seek new ones. Abductive inferencing is not, therefore, a *mode of reasoning* that delivers new knowledge, and neither is it an *exact* method that assists in the generation of *logically ordered* (and therefore operationalizable) hypotheses or some new theory. Abductive inferencing is, rather, an attitude towards data and towards one's own knowledge: data are to be taken seriously, and the validity of previously developed knowledge is to be queried.

4 RESEARCH RESULTS – RECONSTRUCTION OR CONSTRUCTION?

Abductive efforts seek some (new) order, but they do not aim at the construction of *any* order, but at the discovery of an order that *fits* the surprising facts; or, more precisely, one that

solves the practical problems that arise from these.

The refuge for this selective attention (which targets a new order) is not the greatest possible closeness to reality or the highest possible rationality. The refuge is, above all, the *usefulness* which the 'type' that is developed brings to the question of interest. On the one hand it brings order and the means of linguistic representation, and on the other hand these new 'types' are indispensable tools if it is necessary to be able to make predictions about the future on the basis of a past that is hypothetically understood because it is ordered. In other words, they are indispensable when it is a matter of producing answers to the question of 'What to do next?'. New orders, therefore, are also always oriented towards future action.

An abductive discovered order, therefore, is not a (pure) reflection of reality, nor does it reduce reality to its most important components. Instead, the orders obtained are *mental constructs* with which one can live comfortably or less comfortably. For many purposes particular constructs are of use, and for other purposes different constructs are helpful. For this reason the search for order is never definitively complete and is always undertaken provisionally. So long as the new order is helpful in the completion of a task it is allowed to remain in force; if its value is limited, distinctions must be made; if it shows itself to be useless, it is abandoned. In this sense abductively discovered orders are neither (preferred) constructions nor (valid) reconstructions, but *usable* (re-)constructions.

Abduction (as we have already said a number of times), when faced with surprising facts, looks for meaning-creating rules, for a possibly valid or fitting explanation that removes what is surprising about the facts. The end-point of this search is a (linguistic) hypothesis. Once this is found, a multi-stage process of checking begins.

If the first step in the process of scientific discovery consists of the finding of a hypothesis by means of abduction, then the second step consists of the *derivation of predictions* from the hypothesis, that is, of a deduction, and the third step consists of the *search for facts* that will 'verify' the assumptions, which is an induction. If the facts cannot be found the process begins again, and this is repeated as often as necessary until 'fitting' facts are reached. With this definition Peirce designed a three-stage discovery procedure consisting of abduction, deduction and induction.

Finding and checking are, in Peirce's opinion, *two* distinct parts of a *single* process of discovery, or research. If the finding stage is largely a result of a conscious and systematic approach, checking takes place according to operationalizable and rule-governed standards that are controlled by reason.

Certainty about the validity of abductive inferences, however, cannot be achieved even if one subjects an abductively developed hypothesis to extensive testing, that is to say, deduces it from its consequences, then seeks to determine these inductively, and then repeats these three steps many times. Verification in the strict sense of the word cannot be done in this way. All that one can achieve, using this procedure, is an intersubjectively constructed and shared 'truth'. In Peirce's opinion even this is only reached if *all* members of a society have come to the same *conviction*. Since, in Peirce's work, 'all' includes even those who were born after us, the process of checking can in principle never be completed. For Peirce, absolute certainly, therefore, can never be achieved, and so 'infallibility in scientific matters seems to me irresistibly comic' (Peirce 1931–35, vol. 1: X 1.9).

FURTHER READING

Eco, U. and Sebeok, T. (eds) (1985) *The Sign of Three. Dupin, Holmes, Peirce*. Bloomington, IN: Indiana University Press.

Ketner, K. L. (ed.) (1995) *Peirce and Contemporary Thought*. New York: Fordham University Press.

Ochs, P. (1998) *Peirce, Pragmatism, and the Logic of Scripture*. Cambridge: Cambridge University Press.

4.4 Selection Procedures, Sampling, Case Construction

Hans Merkens

According to Flick (2002: 62), decisions about selection in the research process are taken at three different levels:

- during data collection (case selection, case-group selection),
- during interpretation (selection of material and selection within material), and
- during the presentation of results (presentation of material).

To ensure the intersubjectivity of research, criteria are essential that guide the decisions, so that other researchers using the same procedure can arrive at a similar result or so that the outcome of case construction can be subjected to rational criticism. For this reason what follows is devoted above all to a discussion of the relevant criteria. Between the three levels there is a high degree of interdependency, which is also an important focus in some selection procedures. In the first section we shall consider selection problems concerned with the case or the case-group. The second section focuses on aspects of the selection of material, and the final section deals with aspects of case interpretation.

1 CASE SELECTION

Selection procedure

A first decision concerns the selection of the particular case: classical qualitative investigations are interested in what is special. In that sense no special attention was paid to selection procedure, because what was special about a particular case was already determined by the choice of object. This seems to hold true, for example, in ethnology, when a particular tribe is being investigated. But even here there is a need for a research question, as, for instance, Mead (1958) formulated it, which seeks an answer to the problem of whether the distribution of gender roles between man and woman has biological or social causes.

Selection procedures are also needed if one wishes to investigate a problem such as the psychic consequences of unemployment: the consequences of unemployment will most probably be different among the long-term unemployed than among people who have recently become unemployed. One must therefore determine, in respect of unemployment, what features the unemployed in the sample are expected to have: the case of the psychic consequences is constructed before the investigation is started. Problems that arise in this initial construction have been demonstrated by Merkens (1986) in the re-analysis of a field study that was carried out on the subject of 'Turks going shopping'. The difficulty consisted of identifying Turks as Turks, because Turks encountered in the field were supposed to be observed shopping. This required that indicators be set up to identify, amongst the shopping population, those who were Turkish.

Dilthey (1968a,b, 1996) had also formulated criteria for the pre-construction of cases for the humanities, when he declared that, in order to understand a particular era, it was a sound method to use analyses of the biographies of prominent people. This approach was guided by the idea that historical epochs are shaped by culture and that culture is shaped by its leading representatives. Here there was a need to identify witnesses.

Accessibility

In the same way as in quantitative studies, significance is attached to the accessibility of the events, activities or individuals that form the object of the investigation (Burgess 1991; see **5.1**). With individuals this problem can be characterized by their willingness to be reached: it is often the case that groups of people who are to be investigated, or individual members of these groups, refuse to cooperate. If this aspect is not dealt with – was it possible to include all the desired events, activities or individuals in the investigation? – it becomes impossible for an outsider to judge the extent to which the case has been investigated. Refusals or obstacles become important because they are often of a systematic nature. If this should be the case, then not including them distorts the results in a particular direction in relation to the totality of the case. In qualitative studies the stimulus for empirical data collection often consists of guaranteeing accessibility to a particular case or a particular group or institution. Then it is not particular selection procedures that are in the foreground, but rather that the selection is constituted by accessibility.

In this context *gatekeepers* play a particular role in qualitative studies. In the investigation of organizations (see **3.11**) there is often no reference to who the gatekeeper was and what additional gatekeepers within the organization had to be or could be won over. Normally, for instance, in the investigation of an enterprise one of the top managers has to be won over as a gatekeeper. But in addition the company board also plays a central role when it comes to selection of more interview partners. Information about the gatekeepers is important for evaluating the results achieved and the question of transferability, because gatekeepers often link an element of self-interest with their willingness to open one or more doors.

Morse (1994) has divided the importance of accessibility into primary selection – where the cases in the investigation are selected in a targeted way – and secondary selection from some other perspective. The latter occurs when, in a particular investigation, the 'cases' are invited to apply by means of an advertisement or some other appeal. In the second case accessibility is subject to certain restrictions: the participants in the investigation must activate themselves. The first type always occurs when individuals, events or activities are deliberately included in a sample. Since the researchers must often choose a personal means of access to the field, some aspects of the secondary type of selection will frequently play a role.

In qualitative studies attention is often directed to another point that tends to be of interest as a validity problem (see **4.7**): by virtue of the fact that the investigator is the reporter of events, activities or individuals, his information seems to be authentic. Authenticity is therefore claimed as a feature of such studies. This has a tradition that may be traced back to Dilthey (1968a), who claimed that it was an essential feature of the humanities that they were based on experience. Experience, however, is authentic for the one who experiences. The claim to authenticity allows one to overlook the fact that the selection of events, activities or individuals must meet certain criteria if it is to succeed in producing findings that are not only true for the case being investigated.

These problems may be illustrated with a fictitious example: in the social sciences at present investigations of right-wing extremism are a popular subject. For qualitative investigations at least three problems arise in this connection.

1 Are the persons involved in the present study right-wing extremists?
2 Is the spectrum of right-wing extremism appropriately depicted, or are there types of right-wing extremist of which those being investigated are not typical?
3 Are the activities, events and persons that may be encountered in right-wing extremism appropriately represented by the individuals included in the investigation?

Here a circle suggests itself: the selection of the group takes place according to the aspect of accessibility and is not independent of the prejudices of the investigator. The conduct of the investigation remains influenced, within certain limits, by the investigator's prior knowledge and the accessibility of the case. Case construction takes place within the limits fixed in this way. An extension would require a larger sample, but this – on the basis of the particular investigation – would yield no great advantage, because similar members of the group would be included. For this reason a study set up in this way can only give glimpses of the attitudes and activities of right-wing extremists. It requires supplementation by means of further investigations, but these would probably be under similar restrictions. Comparability of results cannot be the object of studies of this sort. It is rather the case that further studies must be selected like supplements to a puzzle: a sample of investigations is needed. The case is expanded into a case-group.

Case-groups

Case-groups may be composed and selected for at least two different reasons. In the first place, it may be a matter of attempting to supplement or complete one's knowledge in the way just described. And in the second place, it may be a question of an attempt at replication (Bourgeois and Eisenhart 1988: 818). This type requires a certain homogeneity of cases on which the general applicability of the evidence obtained may be tested. The selection criteria are characterized by assumptions about the similarity of the cases under investigation.

2 SAMPLING

Sampling techniques

To achieve a systematic approach to data in qualitative studies, two conditions must be fulfilled: first there must be a clear idea of the case to be investigated, and secondly there must be documentation of feasible techniques in the taking of samples of individuals, events or activities. Patton (1990: 169ff.) provides an overview of this. It is surprising that even the most recent handbooks on qualitative methods include no articles on this problem, but merely contain the observation that little value is attached, in qualitative studies, to determining the framework of

a particular sample (cf., for example, Denzin and Lincoln 1994c: 200).

In quantitative methods the totality is known, if findings are to be made there about the distribution of features. The sample is normally made before data collection begins, or else it is completed during the collection process using identical criteria. With qualitative methods the totality, represented by the case or case-group under investigation, can often only be described at the end of the investigation. From this difference there derive differing goals to be pursued both in the investigation and also in the sampling procedure. Whereas in many quantitative studies it is statistical representativity that is sought, with qualitative studies generalizability of results is frequently the target, and this can be achieved when the sample, in terms of content, represents the case being investigated (Merkens 1997: 200). It is not a question of representing the distribution of features in totalities, but rather of determining what is typical of the object under investigation and thereby ensuring its transferability to other, similar objects (Hartley 1994: 225).

What is a problem with quantitative investigations – sampling – is transformed in qualitative investigations into a problem of content and interpretation: the definition of the totality for the case. With this, criteria for sampling become visible (Merkens 1997: 102): it must be guaranteed that the case is represented with as many facets as possible. Patton (1990) proposes for this particular techniques covering sampling of extreme cases (169f.), sampling of typical cases (173f.) and sampling of critical cases (174ff.). For example, in organizations not all of those interviewed should come from the same level in the hierarchy or belong to a single department, if the culture of an organization is being investigated (Morgan 1988: 42). In addition, the investigation should involve not only favourable cases that confirm the existing state of our knowledge, but also unfavourable or critical cases, and apart from the management perhaps also the board, or the parents and pupils as well as the teachers in a school, to give but two examples. In sampling the maximal possible variation should be sought (Patton 1990: 172f.).

In sampling there are two different modes of procedure: on the one hand the sample, before the start of the investigation, can be set up with reference to particular features, that is to say, every element in the sample is included on the basis of a set of criteria. On the other hand the samples can be extended and supplemented on the basis of the particular level of knowledge achieved (theoretical sampling). The concrete technique of sampling in the latter case may therefore be modified during the investigation in line with considerations of relevance (Flick 2002; Wiedemann 1995).

Johnson (1990: 21ff.) undertakes, for the first case, an assessment of the advantages and disadvantages of particular methods of sampling by comparing random sampling – even with qualitative methods he sees the possibility of representative sampling – with sampling where different criteria have been applied, such as the fact that informants in ethnographic studies should occupy key positions in social networks (cf. Bernard 1988). Samples of this sort are often taken purposefully and not according to the principle of randomness (Miles and Huberman 1994: 36). Flick (1996), in an investigation of the social representation of technological change, took a stratified sample in which profession, gender and nationality were used as defining features of the layers. Similarly, Blank (1997: 37f.), with 60 selected interviewees, initially used the demographic variables of 'gender', 'age' and 'old versus new (German) federal states', and for 22 subjects interviewed later he used the additional variable of 'social commitment'. Samples can also be differently stratified according to functions, when investigations within organizations are involved.

In the investigation of an organization at least different samples must be taken: one of employees and one of events, because in organizations employees take part in events. Meetings are examples of such events. For this reason a different rationale applies in the taking of samples: the researcher asks about events and expects from this that the relevant information about a suitable selection of events can be obtained (Hornby and Symon 1994). Here the different activities that are to be encountered in an organization should be included. The differentiation according to activities, events and individuals should not be understood in an either/or sense: it is rather a matter of different aspects that must be borne in mind in taking the sample. If, in respect of events, one were to combine participant observation (event sample) and interrogation of participants (sample of individuals), then there would be an intersection between the two varieties of sample. This is a special case

of triangulation (see 4.6), which has hitherto rarely been presented in this way. In the sense of research economy and the validation of results such combinations of samples are desirable. Huberman and Miles (1994: 440) require that, in addition, processes, events, locations and times are adequately represented in the sample. From a technical point of view we are dealing in such cases with stratified samples.

Apart from features that help in the description of the sample, procedures and criteria can also be formulated which guide the taking of a sample and describe the quality of the content of the sample. For the taking of the sample itself, in many cases where, at the outset of the investigation, there is no fixed sampling plan, there is a procedure based on the snowball method (Burgess 1982; Hornby and Symon 1994: 169f.; Patton 1990: 176f.): those who have been interviewed are asked who else they could recommend for an interview (cf. also Herwartz-Emden 1986). This procedure leads to clustered samples, because nominations take place, as a rule, within a circle of acquaintances.

At different hierarchical levels in the field of investigation a decision has to be taken, according to what is possible, for either a 'bottom-up' or a 'top-down' procedure. In the last few years studies of this type have been carried out with the aim of describing organizational cultures. Here, in the first phase of the investigations, the process has been limited to the involvement of 'top management' in the research. It was clearly a leading assumption that cultures are influenced by managers. In small and medium-sized companies it was possible to include all the managers. More precise investigations of enterprise culture also had to incorporate employees from lower levels in the hierarchy. To achieve this two different procedures are available: on the one hand it must be guaranteed that the different areas within the organization are represented. For this purpose a sample is taken according to the organigram (Johnson 1990: 40ff.). On the other hand it must be guaranteed that different viewpoints are represented and that the informants show themselves to be well informed (Bergs-Winkels 1998). With the techniques outlined above the question must be asked, 'When is a sample large enough?' Kvale (1996: 102) proposes a rule whereby one can cease to conduct further interviews when no new information would be obtained from new interview partners (theoretical saturation).

In taking a sample other criteria may also play a part, such as the quality of informants (Spradley 1979). Hornby and Symon (1994), for example, concentrate on key informants in their investigations of information flows in organizations. In Morse (1994: 228) we find a characterization of this kind of informant:

- they have available the knowledge and experience that the investigators need;
- they are capable of reflection;
- they are articulate;
- they have time to be interviewed;
- they are willing to take part in the investigation.

In addition, selection takes place according to one further criterion: on the one hand information is related to function and the knowledge associated with it; and on the other hand it may be obtained in a particular dense fashion from individuals who occupy a key position in networks. The requirement to select particularly those informants who are especially knowledgeable presupposes that the researcher has some prior knowledge of the case to be investigated.

Single-case

The single-case may be an individual, a group or an organization. In a single-case study, with regard to selection, there must be a justification of why this particular case was chosen. Here a valid reason might be either the special case – the artist whose life-story is being prepared because it seems to contain something typical – or the general case – the steel-worker whose daily routine is being pursued to present what it contains that is typical of a situation. Frequently a series of single-cases are presented, such as those of the Shell Studies (Jugendwerk der Deutschen Shell 1981, 1985, 1991, 1997). The aim here is to look at what is typical of a life-situation of the youth in Germany. For this reason criteria for the selection must be set up.

With a single-case, in addition to selecting the case, a framework of criteria for the selection of events must also be developed, which will guide the collection of data and the description of the case. If, for example, a daily routine is to be represented it would not be possible, either through outsider-observation or by means of a self-report, to achieve a complete account of the

events (Kirchhöfer 1998). It is through selected sections and segments that we can construct what is typical in a particular case. In this way it becomes apparent that there must be some basic understanding of the case before the events are selected. Here a kind of circle becomes clear that is typical of this sort of sampling. The selection of events for description takes place on the basis of prior knowledge. Then the case is reconstructed.

Theoretical sampling

At this point a further distinction must be added. According to Blumer (1969), a distinction can be made, in empirical investigations, between the phases of inspection and exploration. In principle only procedures for investigations with the goal of inspection have so far been outlined. With these a certain level of knowledge of the case is already present, and this makes it possible to undertake a provisional construction at the start of the investigation. Many qualitative studies are carried out in this tradition. But when sampling has been reported, in principle only a single method has been presented, which is oriented, in Blumer's (1969) sense, to an exploratory procedure, because it has only been established in the course of the investigation what individuals, events and activities are to be included in the investigation. Compared to the procedure so far described, the order has been inverted.

Exploratory studies are a special case, because what is characteristic of them is that the case is not yet known but is only constructed in the course of the investigation. A procedure is recommended that is oriented to the premises of grounded theory (Glaser and Strauss 1967; see **2.1, 5.13, 6.6**). Johnson (1990) describes this type as having a framework that only emerges in the course of the investigation. Schatzmann and Strauss (1973: 38f.) had called it 'selective sampling' and justified this description on the grounds that choices have to be made during the taking of samples. These choices are made in the tradition described here in the sense of deliberate selection. They have distinguished between the dimensions of *time*, *place*, *individuals*, *events* and *activities*, and have thereby pointed to a multi-perspectivity that should be borne in mind in sampling in this tradition. Strauss (1987: 16ff.) refers to this method as *theoretical sampling* (cf. Glaser and Strauss 1967). In this he distinguished three stages: data collection, coding and the formulation of theoretical memos. On the basis of both coding and the formulation of memos it may become necessary to collect new data. On the one hand this can be caused by the fact that one needs confirmation of what has been discovered, and on the other hand it can assist the researcher to check what has already been discovered by means of a broadening of the database with reference to the general applicability of the result. In theoretical sampling a decision is taken on the basis of previous analysis as to what groups or subgroups of populations, events and activities should next be included in the investigation. Strauss and Corbin (1990: 181) even go so far as to say that only events should be selected; in other words individuals should be included in relation to events. Events are what constitute the basis of the investigations.

Eisenhardt (1995: 72) points out, in addition, that the selection of individual cases in the tradition of this theory might well be possible according to the principle of chance, but that this would make no sense. Here, with reference to a further aspect, he again underlines the significance attached to the goal-directed selection that must be applied not only in sampling but also in the selection of cases.

On this basis we find another type of sequence in an investigation: after a first phase of data collection hypotheses are formulated, which are then tested with the aid of further data, and further cycles may follow this. With each of the interim stages it must be considered what a supplementary sample would have to look like, given the present state of our knowledge, in order to check or support the level of knowledge so far attained. It must therefore be decided in every case what new or supplementary sample would be of greatest value. Schwartz and Jacobs (1979) add that a promising way forward would be to include in the investigation totally different groups, who go through the same process, in order to test what is right or wrong in respect of ideas about structural uniformity. In a similar vein, Miles and Huberman (1994: 37) describe the research process in qualitative studies as contrast, compare, repeat, catalogue and classify. This makes it clear that with *theoretical sampling* the critical testing of the case is already part of its construction. This is an essential difference from the other techniques of sampling described here. But because such great

importance is attached to these aspects, an exact description of all the additional parts of the sampling procedure, and of the expectations associated with this expansion, becomes very important.

With *theoretical sampling* one of the decisive differences compared to other sampling techniques lies in the fact that the ideas about the case at the beginning of the investigation are still vague and only crystallize in the course of the investigation. In that sense no case can be constructed at the beginning: the construction of the case is shifted to the research process itself.

3 CASE CONSTRUCTION

Ragin and Becker (1992) ask provocatively in the title of their book: 'What is a Case?' In the course of the above, some indication has already been given of what a case is, but some additional clarification is needed. A first variant is provided by the example already mentioned, of the investigation of right-wing extremists – cases are simply found (Harper 1992). The case is discovered as a particular empirical entity (Ragin 1992: 9). From this we must distinguish other empirical examples in which this natural quality cannot be assumed. Cases may also be seen as objects; they are discovered on the basis of studies of the literature (Vaughan 1992). In this variant we are dealing with empirical entities that represent general concepts (Ragin 1992: 9f.). In a third variant cases are constructions (Wieviorka 1992). Theoretical constructions are produced on the basis of these cases (Ragin 1992: 10). With a fourth type cases are related to conventions (Platt 1992). General assumptions about the cases are constructed in this fashion (Ragin 1992: 10f.). In spite of these differences general rules may be formulated, except in the fourth type. At the end of an investigation the case in question must be constructed. As a first step in this process there must be a formulation of preliminary assumptions that led to the selection of the particular case and guided the sampling during the investigation. Through the preliminary assumptions and these criteria intersubjectivity can be established in respect of these steps. As a second step there should be a description of whether the samples were based on primary or secondary selection. Thirdly, the role of the *gatekeepers* should be assessed; and fourthly, the quality of the samples should be described. At the same time – if the sampling criteria were established before the start of the investigation – a distinction should be made between representative, stratified and clustered samples. If only occasional sampling is used, this should also be characterized.

In the further course of the investigation there must be a description of the stages where the case took on a particular form and of the particular methods of sampling used in response to this. Here it is a matter of including cases that support the currently held view, in the sense of a replication of individual cases, but it also concerns the search for critical cases that might serve to contradict this view. Lastly, the database of the investigation must be described, and it must be shown how this relates to the results that have been achieved. In this way both the particular and the general features of the case can be elaborated. On the one hand this process exposes the verifiability of the case construction, which is an important precondition for the intersubjectivity of scientific knowledge. On the other hand it makes it possible to verify the case in further investigations. By means of describing the framework that has been set up in this fashion the generalizability of the results can also be ensured, because the setting of the case or case-group, and from these the case context, become clear. But we can only generalize within the particular context.

FURTHER READING

Flick, U. (2002) *An Introduction to Qualitative Research,* 2nd edn. Thousand Oaks, CA: Sage.

Patton, M. Q. (1990) *Qualitative Evaluation and Research Methods*. Newbury Park, CA: Sage.

Strauss, A. and Corbin, J. (1990) *Basics of Qualitative Research*. Newbury Park, CA: Sage.

4.5 Qualitative and Quantitative Methods: Not in Opposition

Udo Kelle and Christian Erzberger

1 INTRODUCTION

There is a strong tendency to locate qualitative and quantitative methods in two different methodological paradigms and, in so doing, to draw attention to their different philosophical roots. Already the use of the term paradigm allows one to think that we are dealing with fundamentally incompatible ways of thinking and looking at the world.

However, the frontier between qualitative and quantitative research does not need to be quite so impenetrable. There have long been a number of studies which have attempted to develop a basis in both technical methods and methodology for integrating the two approaches (cf. Barton and Lazarsfeld 1955; Denzin 1978; Fielding and Fielding 1986; Flick 1992b; Erzberger and Kelle 2001; Kelle 2001). Independently of this, in research practice interpretative 'qualitative' procedures (such as focus groups, see **5.4**, or non-standardized interviews, see **5.2**) are more and more frequently being linked with standardized 'quantitative' methods for the purpose of joint research designs (cf. Freter et al. 1991; Nickel et al. 1995).

In this process, admittedly, methods themselves are rarely combined (for example, by first analysing textual data interpretatively and then with the aid of statistical methods, cf. Kuckartz 1995, Roller et al. 1995), but as a rule qualitative and quantitative stages of data collection and analysis are carried out in parallel in a research project, each having their own data sets, and the resultant research outcomes are then related to one another (cf. Erzberger 1998; Erzberger and Prein 1997; Prein et al. 1993).

In what follows we shall discuss questions of the integration of qualitative and quantitative research results and shall draw attention not only to the advantages of an integration of methods, but also to possible incompatibilities, difficulties and problems.

2 MODELS OF THE INTEGRATION OF METHODS

In methodological discussions of the integration of methods two different concepts may be distinguished: on the one hand quantitative methodologists frequently speak of a *phase-model*, in which qualitative methods would be used to generate hypotheses and quantitative methods for hypothesis testing. Qualitatively oriented writers, on the other hand, often support an approach in which the union of qualitative and quantitative methods would shed light on the same object from direct perspectives and in different ways, thereby giving a more comprehensive and valid picture: for this kind of procedure the term *triangulation* (see **4.6**) is often used.

The phase-model

In their approach, which has now become a classic, Barton and Lazarsfeld (1955) propose the use of qualitative studies for the generation of hypotheses that will subsequently be tested in quantitative investigations. The authors see as the main virtue of qualitative procedures the possibility of exploring relationships that have in the past received little theoretical attention. Because the results of qualitative studies were normally based only on small numbers of cases, often following an unsystematic procedure, the qualitatively developed hypotheses and theories (see **2.1**, **6.6**) had to be tested, using procedures that allowed a precise measurement of variables defined in advance. Although in the understanding of the two authors quantitative research is clearly superior to qualitative research in respect of the validity of the results, qualitative methods still have a more than marginal significance in the research process: they can provide the investigator with hypotheses that could not have been arrived at in any other way.

The approach of Barton and Lazarsfeld differs in this respect from the hypothetical-deductive concepts that constitute the *standard view* in many textbooks of methods (e.g. Diekmann 1995; Schnell et al. 1999). The idea that hypotheses should be developed on the basis of an empirical foundation is alien to such concepts – the development of hypotheses is understood as a creative rather than a methodological undertaking. So long as textbooks of methods in the social sciences adhere to such views and, at the same time, a phase-model of integration of methods, they are arguing inconsistently: on the one hand they recommend, in the context of discovery, the carrying out of qualitative preliminary studies, but on the other hand they claim that it is impossible to methodologize these, and that, for this reason, they have no confidence in the results of such studies (e.g. Friedrichs 1973/1983: 52ff.; Mayntz et al. 1969: 93). From the point of view of research pragmatics, however, it remains unclear why researchers should take the trouble to carry out field observation and interviews, if the only result of this is arbitrary hypotheses, and why they do not rather simply sit at their desks waiting for intuitions or pulling hypotheses out of a tombola.

The weak point, from a theoretical point of view, of a one-sided hypothetical deductive approach lies in the fact that it does not deal with the question of whether the *context of discovery* can be (at least partially) rationalized or incorporated into a method. If the researcher does not have available any procedural rules for the generation of hypotheses any strategies developed for the testing of hypotheses will also fail. Ultimately these can only use such hypotheses as derived from what the researcher already knows. All other facts remain obscure and, accordingly, cannot appear in the hypotheses. 'They are therefore not tested and are consequently missing from the scientific picture of this area of reality. If such facts are constitutive of the area under investigation, the scientific representation remains disconnected from reality – even when it can rely on empirically confirmed hypotheses' (Gerdes 1979: 5).

The methodological one-sidedness of many methodologists who are otherwise oriented to the natural sciences is also surprising in view of the fact that it is precisely the natural sciences that give examples of how a methodically controlled discovery of relevant phenomena in a quantitatively measured field of investigation must, of necessity, take account of certain aspects of these phenomena. For example, in analytical chemistry the quantitative analysis of certain substances regularly has, as its precondition, a qualitative analysis of these substances. Moreover, the current theory of science debate, with its critical–rational character, in which questions of the methodological and rational character of the *context of discovery* and the value of 'rational heuristics' have been vigorously discussed for the past 30 years (for an overview of this debate see Kelle 1994), has been given insufficient attention in the literature of quantitatively oriented methodology. Barton and Lazarsfeld take account, at least implicitly, of the existence of such a rational heuristics, because ultimately it can only be sensible to carry out a qualitative preliminary study to generate hypotheses if this at least helps to narrow the spectrum of possible hypotheses in some reasonable way, that is, if in principle the hypotheses generated in this way are better than just 'any hypotheses'.

The triangulation metaphor

In the use of the term 'triangulation' (see **4.6**), which is borrowed from navigation and land-surveying and in those disciplines refers to the determination of a location by measuring from two known points, we see an expression of the idea that although qualitative and quantitative procedures are different, in certain respects they are of equal methodological value. The concept was originally developed in the context of quantitative methods, where the use of differing instruments of measurement (Campbell and Fiske 1959) or of different methods (Webb et al. 1966) was believed to increase the validity of the results of an investigation. When Denzin took up this term in 1970, to justify a methodological integration of qualitative and quantitative procedures, he initially used it to refer to a procedure for the reciprocal validation of methods and research results: 'methodological triangulation involves a complex process of playing each method off against the other so as to maximize the validity of field efforts' (Denzin 1978: 304).

Starting with the idea that qualitative and quantitative procedures bring premises from different *theoretical* traditions to the research process, a number of authors set this view against another concept of triangulation, according to which qualitative and quantitative methods are less suited to reciprocal validation than to complementing each other (e.g. Fielding and Fielding 1986: 33; Flick 1992b). These debates reveal the limits of the concept of triangulation as well as its systematic ambiguity: the term 'location of a place', readily intelligible in the context of land-surveying, is not precisely defined in empirical social research. Here the 'calculation of the location of a place by measuring from different points' may mean that:

1 the *same social phenomenon* is treated by different methods, or
2 it is used to treat *different aspects of the same phenomenon* or even *different phenomena*, the representations of which may add up to a unified picture.

This distinction is in no sense a linguistic trick, since it is only when different methods are applied to the same object that they may be used for reciprocal validation of their findings. If, in contrast, different methods deal with different aspects of the same object, or even with different objects, then of course different results are to be expected without this being able to provide the key to their lack of validity.

We have, therefore, two readings of the triangulation metaphor: triangulation as a cumulative validation of research results, and triangulation as an enlargement of perspectives that permit a fuller treatment, description and explanation of the subject area. Here, in more recent literature, the aspect of complementarity, or the enlargement of perspectives as opposed to the validation aspect, is emphasized: 'Triangulation is less a strategy for validating results and procedures than an alternative to validation ... which increases scope, depth and consistency in methodological proceedings' (Flick 2002: 227).

3 THE INTEGRATION OF QUALITATIVE AND QUANTITATIVE RESEARCH RESULTS

General models for the integration of methods are mostly developed at an abstract methodological level. If one confronts them with experience from research practice (Erzberger and Kelle 2001; Erzberger and Prein 1997; Kelle 2001; Prein et al. 1993; Tashakkori and Teddlie 1998) it becomes clear that the relationship between qualitative and quantitative research results cannot be determined on the basis of a single model. One can assume neither that the results of qualitative and quantitative methods are fundamentally convergent and may therefore be used for reciprocal validation, nor that qualitative and quantitative results achieved under different conditions can be combined to give an appropriate general picture. The parallel use of qualitative and quantitative procedures in a common research design may lead, rather, to three types of outcome. Qualitative and quantitative research results may:

1 converge, that is, tend to agree;
2 constitute a complementary relationship, that is, reciprocally supplement each other; or
3 diverge, that is, contradict each other.

Convergence

The fact that qualitative and quantitative procedures for data collection and analysis may relate to the same object may be used not only for the application of the classical phase-model, that is, for the validation of qualitative results by quantitative studies, but also for the validation of quantitative instruments. This latter process may take place, for example, in pre-test studies (using, perhaps, test questions or by means of 'thinking aloud') if the investigator is checking the extent to which interviewees understand test items in the way intended by the constructors of a questionnaire. In this process qualitative material is used to establish how far the items in question actually 'measure what they are supposed to measure', that is to say, to what extent they are *valid*. To achieve this the qualitative and quantitative data cannot, of course, be in a complementary relationship, which means that they cannot reflect different facts that would together produce an appropriate overall picture. Instead they must relate to the same phenomena, such as the evaluation of a particular fact by the interviewee.

A convergence of qualitative and quantitative results, however, may also be used in the context of qualitative questioning. Qualitative guided interviews used in biographical studies may, for instance – if in the same sample biographical data are collected by means of standardized instruments – be structured with the help of information from the quantitative part of the investigation. An example of this would be when the qualitative interviews are carried out using graphic material that portrays the stages in a biography (Erzberger 1998: 183f.).

Complementarity

Using qualitative investigations subjective interpretations of 'relevance limits' and the action-orientations of actors may be discovered in the empirical material about which the investigator had no prior theoretically based assumptions, and which therefore cannot be taken into account in constructing the data-collection instruments. Qualitative investigations, therefore, often yield this type of information, which could not easily have been obtained using a quantitative research design (cf. Kelle 1994: 44ff.).

Qualitative results, in this sense, often lead to (sociologically) profitable explanations where quantitative studies can, at best, describe relationships on the basis of socio-demographic variables.

In biographical research statistically demonstrable differences between particular professional groups may only be explained on the basis of additional qualitative material: it was shown, for example, in a quantitative study of the occupational history of young skilled workers at the beginning of the 1990s (cf. Kelle and Zinn 1998), that young fitters had the greatest interest in further professional training irrespective of school-leaving age, compared to other professional groups. The analyses of structural variables gave no indication of any connections with the labour market, because the tendency for members of this professional group to leave the professional field and seek further formal qualifications in the educational system could not be accounted for as a reaction to poor job opportunities in the profession for which they had trained. This statistical fact, which at first sight was not easy to understand, could only be explained by means of qualitative guided interviews which gave information about professional cultures: the fitters who were interviewed had, on the one hand, developed a pronounced specialist consciousness in the course of their training, and on the other hand their aspirations to further qualified specialist employment in their training place after qualification had, as a rule, met with disappointment. Before accepting the offer of employment requiring a lower level of qualification, these young specialists often preferred to devote themselves to further (often expensive) training.

Qualitative procedures can therefore often help to fill gaps in explanations using 'sociological variables' where statistical relationships are explained by additional assumptions after the event. Quantitative procedures are able to show super-individual structural relationships which are not consciously observed by the individuals and which therefore cannot easily be obtained with qualitative interviews. In both cases the procedures complement one another and give a more comprehensive picture of the object under investigation. A precondition for this complementarity is, of course, that there is a theoretical framework within which the individual results can be meaningfully related to one another.

Divergence

From these considerations we cannot derive a general 'complementarity model' for the integration of qualitative and quantitative methods, because contradictions between the results of quantitative and qualitative partial investigations are not an uncommon phenomenon: in qualitative interviews the interviewees frequently interpret their biographies differently from the way they appear to the empirical social researcher in an aggregate statistical observation. Whilst, for example, in a quantitative study of female employment biographies the first occupation for which women have trained may appear as the decisive variable in the explanation of differences between the careers of the interviewees, in qualitative interviews subjects often explain their own professional biographies largely in terms of events or influences from the family domain (cf. Born et al. 1996). Such contradictions can, in principle, be explained in two ways: as a consequence of *methodological errors*, or as an indication of the inadequacy of the *theoretical concepts* employed. In the case in question it was only after all the possibilities of (qualitative and quantitative) methodological artefacts had been excluded that a modification to the theoretical framework was able to reveal the divergences: here processes of inter-partner negotiation (that is, family influences) on the basis of professional resources (first profession) were identified as the decisive causal factor for differences in the occupational biographies.

Divergences between qualitative and quantitative results, therefore, can motivate the revision and modification of initial theoretical assumptions or even stimulate the development of new theoretical concepts. In a procedure of this sort, however, care must be taken not to immunize existing theoretical assumptions by means of supplementary assumptions that are introduced *ad hoc*. This means that concepts newly developed on the basis of the divergences between qualitative and quantitative results can only be trusted when they have been subjected to additional empirical verification.

4 STRATEGIES FOR THE INTEGRATION OF METHODS

The use of qualitative procedures is particularly indispensable when investigators have no *a priori* access to the typical meaning patterns and action orientations in the subject area being investigated. Depending on how much these action orientations and meaning patterns are influenced by social structures, the linking of qualitative and quantitative methods may serve to illuminate different aspects of social phenomena. Using quantitative methods the meaning of social-structural factors of context can then be investigated, and qualitative methods may be used to study the way in which these contextual factors are interpreted by the actors.

Unlike many quantitatively oriented methodologists, Barton and Lazarsfeld (1955) do stress the need for qualitative research in the process of social scientific investigation, but ultimately attribute a marginal role to qualitative procedures. The concept of triangulation comprises many possibilities for the integration of qualitative and quantitative methods, and the different functions of methodological integration in the research process are even better. Of course, triangulation can be understood in different ways, depending on the research questions, research design and research results: the reciprocal validation of results on the one hand, or the supplementing of different viewpoints to form a unified picture of the object of investigation on the other hand. A unified concept of methodological integration, which allots a particular logical or theoretical status to qualitative and quantitative research results on an *a priori* basis – perhaps in the sense that qualitative and quantitative results would have to complement each other – cannot therefore be derived from these different functions and applications of methodological integration. The results of qualitative and quantitative studies may converge, complement or contradict one another, and each of these possibilities can be beneficial to the research process: for example, a divergence of results enforces the formulation of more powerful theoretical models, with greater explanatory power and validity, which would never have been developed if the investigators had relied on only one of the two methodological strands.

It is a fundamental shortcoming of general models of methodological integration that they frequently attempt to formulate methodological rules for methodological integration without formulating a relation to any theoretical ideas about the nature of the subject area under investigation. The right 'mix of methods', however, is always dependent on the nature of the subject area under investigation and the theoretical concepts employed.

FURTHER READING

Alexander, J. C., Giesen, B., Münch, R. and Smelser, N. J. (eds) (1987) *The Micro–Macro Link*. Berkeley, CA: University of California Press.

Kelle, Udo (2001) 'Sociological Explanations between Micro and Macro and the Integration of Qualitative and Quantitative Methods', *Forum: Qualitative Social Research* (on-line journal), 2 (1). Available at: http://qualitative-research.net/fqs/fqs-eng.htm

Tashakkori, A. and Teddlie, C. (1998) *Mixed Methodology. Combining Qualitative and Quantitative Approaches* (Applied Social Research Methods Series, Volume 46). London: Sage.

4.6 Triangulation in Qualitative Research

Uwe Flick

In social research the term 'triangulation' is used to refer to the observation of the research issue from (at least) two different points.

This is most often realized by means of applying different methodological approaches. As a strategy for the validation (see **4.7**) of the procedures and results of empirical social research triangulation has been given special attention, particularly in the more recent publications on qualitative methods (cf. Marotzki 1995a; Schründer-Lenzen 1997). Triangulation is currently also being used in the debate about the relationship between qualitative and quantitative research (Jick 1983; see **4.5**). In this chapter, however, we are primarily concerned with triangulation within qualitative research, which has been the subject of serious discussion in recent literature (e.g. Flick 1998c; Seale 1999a,b; Steinke 1999).

1 TRIANGULATION AS A VALIDATION STRATEGY

The idea of triangulation was imported from land surveying into the methodological literature of the social sciences – admittedly in a rather metaphorical sense. Blaikie (1991) explains, for example, that its original use in the social sciences has little in common with the way it is used in surveying. The debate about non-reactive measurement procedures (Webb et al. 1966) and the 'multi-trait multi-method matrix' approach of Campbell and Fiske (1959) constitute the starting point for the general methodological discussion of the concept. Greater attention within qualitative research has been given – even in the present day – to the suggestions of Denzin (1978), who initially understood triangulation as a validation strategy and distinguished the following four different forms.

- *Triangulation of data* combines data drawn from different sources and at different times, in different places or from different people.
- *Investigator triangulation* is characterized by the use of different observers or interviewers, to balance out the subjective influences of individuals.
- *Triangulation of theories* means 'approaching data with multiple perspectives and hypotheses in mind … . Various theoretical points of view could be placed side by side to assess their utility and power' (Denzin 1978: 297).
- Denzin's central concept is *methodological triangulation* 'within-method' (for example, the use of different subscales within a questionnaire) and 'between-method'.

The goal of this last strategy is described by Denzin as follows: 'To summarize, methodological triangulation involves a complex process of playing each method off against the other so as to maximize the validity of field efforts' (1978: 304).

2 CRITICISMS OF TRIANGULATION

In a number of contexts there have been critical discussions of triangulation as a strategy for validation in the sense which we have outlined: too little attention is paid to the fact that every different method constitutes the issue it seeks to investigate in a specific way (e.g. Bloor 1997: 39). If this aspect is neglected, triangulation is faced with the accusation of 'extreme eclecticism' (Fielding and Fielding 1986: 33). Silvermann (1985: 21) feels that 'This casts great doubt on the argument that multiple research methods should be employed in a variety of settings in order to gain a "total" picture of some phenomenon ... . Putting the picture together is more problematic than such proponents of triangulation would imply. What goes on in one setting is not a simple corrective to what happens elsewhere – each must be understood in its own terms.' Fielding and Fielding (1986: 33) sum up their criticism of Denzin's ideas in the following terms: 'We should combine theories and methods carefully and purposefully with the intention of adding breadth or depth to our analysis but not for the purpose of pursuing "objective" truth.' Blaikie (1991) complains that the combination of different methods pays too little attention to the respective theoretical backgrounds of the individual methods.

In his more recent work (e.g. Denzin 1989c: 246; Denzin and Lincoln 1994a: 5), Denzin has taken up these criticisms and now understands triangulation as strategy leading to a deeper understanding of the issue under investigation, and thereby as a step on the road to greater knowledge, and less towards validity and objectivity of interpretation. Triangulation is now seen less as a validation strategy within qualitative research and more as a strategy for justifying and underpinning knowledge by gaining additional knowledge (Denzin and Lincoln 1994a: 5; cf. Flick 1992a,b).

3 FORMS OF APPLICATION

The four forms of triangulation suggested by Denzin may be used – even bearing in mind the criticisms we have listed – as starting points for the realization of this strategy.

Triangulation of data

In addition to verbal data – interviews (see **5.2**) and group discussions (see **5.4**) – visual data are currently receiving considerable attention in qualitative research. Apart from the emphasis on (not only participant) observation (see **5.5**), video-recordings and photos (Becker 1986a; see **5.6**) are being used with increasing frequency, and also the analysis of cinema films (Denzin 1989c; see **5.7**). As a result of this, new perspectives in the triangulation of data are emerging: apart from their use in interviews (cf. Flick 2002, chs 8–9; Fuhs 1997), visual data may be triangulated with verbal data as an independent source of information (Harper, in **5.6**, gives an example of the linking of photos and interviews). Completely new types of data, such as electronic data (see **5.8**), are opening up further possibilities of triangulation with traditional types of data.

Investigator triangulation

Current implementations may be found in the proposals that interpretations of collected data should only be carried out in groups, so as to expand, correct or check the subjective views of interpreters. In the context of objective hermeneutics (Oevermann et al. 1979; see **5.16**), this has long been required. Different ideas about research workshops (either in the sense of Strauss 1987 or as they are used in biographical research and objective hermeneutics, see **6.2**) are also indebted to this idea.

Within-method triangulation

This principle may be clarified using the example of episodic interviews (Flick 1996, 2000b): there some research issue (for example, technical change in everyday life) is explored by means of invitations to narrate, focusing on experiences in concrete situations. These are combined with questions that focus more on definitions and general answers. In this, questions are asked, for example, about the concept of a computer, which the interview partner has developed over a long period of time ('What do you associate today with the term "computer"? What types of equipment does it include?'). Before this the interview partner is asked to talk about the situation in which he or she was confronted with a computer for the first time ('Could you describe for me the situation in which you first got an idea of what a computer is?' or 'Under what circumstances did you first come into contact with a computer? Could you tell me about that situation?') or situations in which the computer has a special influence today in everyday life. In this way, an attempt is made in such an interview systematically to unite the methodological approaches of the semi-structured interview and the narrative, using their respective strengths. On the one hand, this is intended to open up complementary perspectives on the research issue through the interviewees' mode of experience: as for the particular process-perspective that becomes clear in (situational) narratives ('When I first encountered a computer … '), the abstract description of a state ('a computer for me is … ') works in a complementary way. On the other hand, it is intended to clarify the different facets of the subjective approach to the research issue. For example, a female French information technologist, at an abstract level of more general concepts, regularly talked of the gender-specific obstacles that generally make it more difficult for women to handle computers or technology. In the particular situations that she recounted, on the other hand, what became clear was a consistent success story of overcoming difficult equipment and situations (cf. Flick 1996).

Between-method triangulation

Its is the combination of different methods, however, that is most strongly associated with the keyword triangulation, and in this different emphases are given: on the one hand this refers to the linking of qualitative and quantitative methods (cf. Engler 1997; Flick 2002, ch. 21; see **4.5**) in different research designs. On the other hand, Marotzki (1995b) proposes the combination of reactive procedures (for example, narrative interviews, see **5.2**, **5.11**), in which the

investigators are part of the research situation, and non-reactive procedures (analysis of available materials such as documents, photos, diaries and the like, see **5.15**), that is to say, data that were not set up for the investigation. In this process, the boundaries of both methodological approaches are transcended. Moreover the triangulation of different approaches makes it possible to capture different aspects of the research issue – such as concrete examples of professional activity and knowledge of one's own modes of action and routines.

In a study of trust in counselling relationships (Flick 1989), subjective theories of consultants about confidence were collected in semi-standardized interviews and triangulated with conversation analyses of consultation talks which the interviewees had had with their clients in their everyday professional life. While the first approach shed light on more general experiences and ideas on the part of the consultants about preconditions and essential prerequisites for the creation of confidence, the second approach made it possible to show how these ideas could successfully be translated into concrete action, or how and why this failed to happen.

Methodological triangulation is of particular current interest in ethnography. In Lüders's opinion (1995: 321), 'ethnography is turning into a research strategy which embraces every conceivable and ethically tenable option for collecting data'. Here the methodological approaches necessary to realize such options are triangulated with each other, even when the term is not always mentioned explicitly. The end-result is less a reciprocal validation of the discoveries made using the individual methods but an extension of the possibilities of discovery about the aspect of life under investigation. Since different methods, such as observation or interviewing, tend to be combined in a rather *ad hoc* way in a situation of extended participation (see **5.5**), it is also possible to speak of *implicit* triangulation in ethnography (Flick 1998c).

Explicit triangulation occurs when ethnographic methods of extended participation and field observation are deliberately combined with the use of (career-biographical or episodic) interviews with individual actors at individually agreed times. For example, in an ongoing project (cf. Gebauer and Flick 1998), regular ethnographic observations in fields where such new sports as inline-skating are practised are being triangulated with episodic interviews conducted separately with individual athletes. The first approach makes it possible to analyse the modes of action and communication, whilst the second clarifies the meaning of the sport and the 'scene' for the participants.

If the concept of triangulation is taken seriously, it is characteristic of all of these variants that they see the procedures they combine as being of equal value and that they do not begin by regarding one procedure as central and the others as preliminary or illustrative.

Triangulation of theories

In combining different methods it must be borne in mind that each of them was developed against a different theoretical background. In concrete situations of triangulation the partially incompatible epistemological assumptions about the research issue, or about (qualitative) research in these different theoretical backgrounds, are carried over by the methods.

This problem may be clarified with reference to one of the examples mentioned above. The reconstruction of subjective theories proceeds from an explicitly subject-oriented understanding of knowledge and action (summed up by the keyword of the reflexive subject, Groeben 1990). Conversation analysis, on the other hand, rests on a more situation-oriented view of action (summed up by the keyword of the conversational machine) that largely dictates to the individual participant how he or she can or should react to particular utterances of their interlocutor (see **5.17**). This becomes a problem if such differences are not taken into account in the way the research issue is understood. As a solution, a number of alternatives have been discussed: Blaikie (1991: 129), for instance, suggests only combining methods within a single research approach, and points to the example of Cicourel (1975) who combined different methods with one another ('indefinite triangulation') within an ethnomethodological approach. As an alternative to this, Fielding and Fielding (1986) require that these theoretical perspectives be included in the analysis of the data obtained, of the convergence and divergences which the methods produce. Finally, Denzin (1989c) feels it is important to look at data from different theoretical angles, in order to uncover new facets of the theories in the data.

4 SYSTEMATIC TRIANGULATION OF PERSPECTIVES

The proposal of 'systematic triangulation of perspectives' (Flick 1992a,b) leads in a similar direction. Here different research perspectives within qualitative research are combined with one another in a targeted way, to complement their strong points and to illustrate their respective limitations. This approach can be related to the four types of application discussed above, but will be outlined here as an example of the inter-relating of different methods, using the example already cited where consultants' subjective theories of trust in relation to clients are reconstructed with interviews and communicative validation (using the ideas of Scheele and Groeben 1988 and Kvale 1995a; see **4.7**), and triangulated with conversation analyses and counselling conversations. Here a number of different research perspectives are applied: the first approach focuses on subjective views (of the consultant), whereas the second approach targets descriptions of everyday routines.

In this way it was possible to realize two of the research perspectives of qualitative research that were distinguished by Lüders and Reichertz (1986). Using a different set of terminology (Bergmann 1985), in the first approach a reconstructive procedure is applied and, in the second approach, combined with an interpretative procedure (for examples see Flick 1992b). This approach explicitly combines triangulation of methods and data with a triangulation of theoretical perspectives.

5 PRACTICAL PROBLEMS OF TRIANGULATION

Case triangulation

The most consistent variant is to apply the triangulated methods to the same cases: counseling conversations by the consultants who are being interviewed are collected and analysed, and the persons being observed in a particular field are (all) interviewed. This procedure makes possible a case-related analysis of both types of data and also makes it possible to compare and interrelate, in the context of a single-case, the different perspectives opened up by the methodological approaches. In addition, these

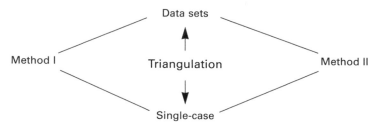

Figure 4.6.1   Starting points for triangulation of methods

comparisons and interrelationships can also be undertaken at a higher level: systems that emerge from a comparison of one type of data (for example, sequential patterns in counselling conversations) can be set against patterns from the comparison of other types of data (emphases and blind spots that may be determined in respect of all subjective theories or specifically for particular professional groups). Sampling decisions (see **4.4**) are only taken once, because the same selection of cases is used for both types of data.

The disadvantages are, first, that the load for an individual participant in an investigation is often unreasonably large: to be ready for an interview and in addition to provide a counselling conversation is, if measured against the normal requirement of taking part in a study, a comparatively heavy burden. Secondly, the danger of dropout rises markedly. Everyone who refuses to provide either an interview or a counselling conversation is 'lost' to the entire investigation that seeks to triangulate on the basis of the particular case.

Triangulation of data sets

Finally, in observations on open spaces (such as sport 'scenes') there is a problem that so many people have to be observed that not all of them can be interviewed. For that reason, case triangulation is not possible, and so it should be implemented at the level of data sets.

The individual methods are initially applied independently of each other, which produces a set of observations and a series of interviews. Both are analysed to assess what they have in common and where they differ. Triangulation then relates in practical terms to the results of

both analyses and puts them in relation to each other. As a practical problem the question arises here of how comparability of the samples, where the different methods have been applied, can be guaranteed. In addition it must be clarified whether the different methods can be applied at the same time or whether, because of project planning and resources, the empirical steps have to be conducted sequentially – first the observational data are collected and analysed and then the interviews are conducted and analysed. In this case possible influences of the different times on content should not be forgotten.

6   PERSPECTIVES: TRIANGULATION BETWEEN CONVERGENCE AND DIVERGENCE

The aim of the triangulation of different approaches and perspectives at both levels (cf. Figure 4.6.1) should be less a matter of obtaining convergence in the sense of confirmation of what has already been discovered. The triangulation of methods and perspectives is particularly useful for theory-development, when it can elucidate *divergent perspectives*, when – to take up the above example again – the action of the consultant is different from what his or her subjective theory about confidence would lead us to expect.

Then we have a new perspective that requires theoretical explanations. From this kind of understanding of triangulation we may make connections to the idea of 'theoretical sampling' and the theoretical saturation of Glaser and Strauss (1967). In accordance with this, Glaser and Strauss (1967: 68) maintain that 'a theory generated from just one kind of data never fits, or works as well, as a theory generated from diverse slices of data on the same category'. In the process of theoretical sampling (see **4.4**), further methods are also consistently used if the level of knowledge can thereby be increased. If the inclusion of new data no longer delivers new knowledge then theoretical saturation has been reached. Where the use of further methods can 'only' confirm knowledge that we already have, in the sense of validating it, then triangulation comes up against the border of theoretical saturation. Accordingly, triangulation should be understood as a means of extending our knowledge of the research issue.

We therefore have *three modes of application for triangulation*: as a validation strategy, as an approach to the generalization of discoveries, and as a route to additional knowledge.

FURTHER READING

Denzin, N. K. (1978) *The Research Act,* 2nd edn. Chicago: Aldine. (3rd edn. Englewood Cliffs, NJ: Prentice Hall, 1989.)

Flick, U. (1992) 'Triangulation Revisited – Strategy of or Alternative to Validation of Qualitative Data', *Journal for the Theory of Social Behavior*, 22: 175–197.

Seale, C. (1999) 'Quality in Qualitative Research', *Qualitative Inquiry*, 5: 465–478.

4.7 Quality Criteria in Qualitative Research

Ines Steinke

How can the quality of qualitative research be determined? What criteria should it satisfy? The question of what criteria can be used to measure the scholarly value, quality and validity of qualitative research is frequently asked, but the responses in the corresponding articles, text-books and manuals are either very general or unsystematic. The further establishment of qualitative research in the overall landscape of empirical social research will depend essentially upon defining appropriate criteria for its evaluation. In this chapter a critical overview is given of the heterogeneous literature on quality criteria for qualitative research, and this is summed up under three basic positions. Then core criteria are formulated for the evaluation of qualitative research together with ways of safeguarding and testing it.

1 BASIC POSITIONS FOR THE EVALUATION OF QUALITATIVE RESEARCH

In discussions of quality criteria for qualitative research three positions may be distinguished.

Quantitative criteria for qualitative research

It is characteristic of this first position that criteria from quantitative research are transferred to qualitative research. The main criteria are objectivity, reliability and validity from experimental–statistical and hypothesis-testing research and from psychometrics (tests, questionnaires, scales and so on). Behind these is the widely used concept of 'unity-criteria' according to which all research has to be evaluated. Criteria from quantitative research are adapted here to qualitative research by being reformulated and operationalized (such as 'inter-coder reliability', suggested by Kelle et al. 1993; Kirk and Miller 1986; Lincoln and Guba 1985; Mayring 2000b). Here we must also include the proposal of Miles and Huberman to incorporate qualitative criteria (such as credibility) into the well-known schema of quantitative criteria (objectivity, reliability, validity):

- Objectivity/confirmability of qualitative investigations
- Reliability/dependability/auditability
- Internal validity/credibility/authenticity
- External validity/transferability/fittingness
- Utilization/application/action orientation. (1994: 278–280)

Independent criteria of qualitative research

Adherents of the second position have funda-mental doubts about the transferability of quan-titative criteria to qualitative research. Unlike the representatives of the first position, they take the particular theoretical, methodological and procedural character of qualitative research as a starting point for the formulation of appropriate criteria. The following aspects are often discussed.

1 *Communicative validation* (Kvale 1995b; Terhart 1981, 1995): data or events from the research are presented to the subjects of the investigation with the aim that they assess them in respect of their validity. In the English-language literature this is referred to as 'member check'.

2 *Triangulation*: the use of complementary methods, theories, data or investigators in the research is intended to compensate for any one-sidedness or distortion that may result from an individual method, theory, database or researcher. Triangulation was initially regarded as an instrument of validation (Denzin 1978), but today it is discussed as a methodological technique that leads to a broader and deeper understanding of the research issue (Denzin 2000b; Flick 2002; see **4.5**, **4.6**).

3 *Validation of the interview-situation*: interviews and their sequencing (see **5.2**, **5.3**) are analysed with regard to whether the interviewees are talking 'truthfully' or sincerely. In concrete terms, what is being checked is whether there are indications that a working relationship between researcher and interviewee has *not* been established (Groeben et al. 1988; Kvale 1996; cf. Legewie 1987). This relationship should be characterized by openness, trust, willingness to collaborate and the lowest possible power-difference between researcher and informant.

4 *Authenticity* (Guba and Lincoln 1989: 254ff. Manning 1997). This criterion for qualitative evaluation research relates to domains such as the following. Was sufficient care taken with the statements of interviewees and the underlying value-structures during the research process? Were the multiple constructs of informants collected appropriately during the research process, were they related systematically to one another, and were they tested for their validity, by 'member check' with the informants? Are any new orientations for the informants being initiated during the research process? Is the research for decision-making purposes or as a stimulus for action?

Postmodern rejection of criteria

Those who hold this third position generally argue against the possibility of formulating criteria for qualitative research.

1 From a postmodern perspective it is postulated that it is impossible to relate criteria to a fixed referential system (e.g. Richardson 1994: 552; J. K. Smith 1984: 383).
2 Shotter (1990: 69) argues, from a social-constructivist viewpoint (see **3.4**), that the assumption that the world is socially constructed is incompatible with standards for the evaluation of epistemological claims, because this would involve abandoning the basis of social constructivism.
3 Denzin (1990b: 231) defines postmodern ethnography as being characterized in part by the fact that researchers write their texts in the first person singular, thereby overcoming the division between the observer and observed reality and no longer asking themselves questions about reliability and validity (see **2.7**, **5.22**).

2 STARTING POINTS FOR THE FORMULATION OF CORE CRITERIA

In contrast to this we shall suggest in section 3 core criteria for the evaluation of qualitative research against the background of the following considerations.

1 *Qualitative research cannot exist without evaluation criteria.* The rejection of criteria in accordance with the third position conceals the risk of randomness and arbitrariness in qualitative research. This can result, not least, in problems for the further recognition of qualitative research beyond its own narrow *scientific community* (see **6.5**). On the very basis of constructivist assumptions it is not obligatory to dispense with criteria. Postmodern and constructivist social researchers are confronted, rather, with the problem of convincing others of the value and quality of their investigations and results (cf. Lincoln and Guba 1985: 290). Furthermore, the increasing tendency to treat qualitative research more as a *Kunstlehre* (art) (cf. Denzin and Lincoln 1994b) or a 'research style' (Strauss 1987, 1995b), and less as a procedure

capable of formalization, does not exempt the researcher from the use of evaluation criteria. Indeed, these should be able to cope with such developments in qualitative research. In particular, constructivist approaches are a suitable platform for the formulation of a consistent epistemological and methodological framework for the development of quality criteria for qualitative research. (cf., for more detailed discussion, Steinke 1999: 81ff.) The results of qualitative studies are treated and evaluated as products of different decisions and constructions within the research process (cf. also Terhart 1995: 375).

2 *Quantitative criteria are not suited to the evaluation of qualitative research.* Quantitative criteria were developed for completely different methods (such as tests or experiments), which are based, in turn, on corresponding methodologies and scientific and epistemological theories. Since their basic assumptions are hardly compatible with qualitative research, it is unjustified to expect that the latter can or should conform to the criteria of quantitative research. In particular, quantitative criteria cannot be directly transferred to qualitative research, because of its comparatively low formalizability or standardizability. There are, however, many incentives to formulate evaluation criteria coming out of the debate about quantitative criteria (cf. Steinke 1999: 131ff.).

3 For qualitative research criteria must be developed that take account of its own profile, that is to say, its particular features, goals, scientific and methodological starting points (see Part 1). It is therefore less a matter of formulating individual criteria, as has often been done, but rather more the case that a system of criteria is needed that covers as many as possible of the necessary aspects for the evaluation of qualitative research. This must also include ways of operationalizing criteria so as to make it possible actually to check them.

For the criteria of qualitative research, the terms 'objectivity', 'reliability' and 'validity' are not used here for two reasons. First, these criteria have differing definitions. Validity in particular is rather differently understood in qualitative research than in the discussion of quantitative research (cf. Steinke 1999: 203). Literature from the English-speaking world on qualitative criteria (Kvale 1989: 73; e.g. Lincoln and Guba 1985: 292) sometimes interprets reliability and validity with reference to the everyday

meaning of these words: reliability, for instance, is equated with trustworthiness or dependability and predictability. The deliberate omission of the terms 'objectivity', 'reliability' and 'validity' is intended to guarantee that meanings in the following proposed core criteria will have their own profile. Secondly, many forms of objectivity, reliability and validity were developed for standardized research and are therefore only transferable to qualitative research under certain conditions. The use of these terms could result in different and partially unjustified expectations in respect of the criteria discussed below.

3 CORE CRITERIA FOR QUALITATIVE RESEARCH

A *conclusive* discussion of criteria can only be conducted with reference to the respective research questions, method, specific features of the research field and the object of the investigation. The object-, situation- and milieu-dependent nature of qualitative research (cf. Lüders 1995: 319f.), the many different types of qualitative research programmes and the severely restricted standardizability of methodological procedures in this area are in contradiction with the idea of formulating a universal and generally binding catalogue of criteria. This contradiction may be presented as a two-stage procedure.

First, the following formulation of central and broadly conceived *core criteria* for qualitative research and of procedures for checking them defines a catalogue of criteria according to which qualitative research may be oriented. Secondly, the criteria and checking procedures to be used need to be specified, modified and, if necessary, supplemented by other criteria, in a way that is *specific to the investigation*, that is, according to the research question, the issue and the method being used.

Inter-subject comprehensibility

For qualitative research, unlike quantitative studies, the requirement of inter-subject *verifiability* cannot be applied. An identical replication of an investigation is impossible, if only because of the limited standardizability of procedures in qualitative research. What is appropriate in qualitative research is the requirement to produce an inter-subjective *comprehensibility* of the research process on the basis of which an evaluation of results can take place. The guaranteeing and checking of comprehensibility may be carried out in three ways.

Documentation of the research process is the principal technique. With this an external public is given the opportunity to follow the investigation step by step and to evaluate the research process and the results which derive from it. With this technique account can be taken of the unique dynamic that obtains in every qualitative study between the issue, the research questions and the methodological plan (cf. also Mayring 1999: 104; Terhart 1995: 383). One advantage of the requirement for documentation of the research processes lies in the fact that readers wishing to evaluate an investigation are not tied to criteria that are either predetermined or already applied in the particular study, but are free to assess the study in the light of their own criteria. The creation of inter-subjective comprehensibility by means of documentation may therefore be regarded as the principal criterion or as a precondition for the testing of other criteria. But what, in concrete terms, should be documented (see **6.5**)?

- The necessity of documenting the researcher's *prior understanding*, his or her explicit and implicit expectations, results from the fact that these influence perception (for example, in observations), the choice or development of the methods used, and thereby the data collected and the understanding of the issue. The presentation of prior understanding makes it possible to decide whether the study really did lead to any new discovery – that is, whether it was only seeking to confirm *ex-ante* hypotheses (see **4.2**) or whether there was also some attempt to upset this prior knowledge.
- Documentation of the *collection method* and the *collection-context* includes precise specification of the particular procedure used (such as the semi-structured interview) as well as information about how it was developed. Information about the context in which the interview takes place makes it possible to assess the credibility of interview statements, which, perhaps because of a lack of openness or trust on the part of the interviewee, might be limited.
- Documentation of *transcription rules* (see **5.9**) allows one to determine what information

should (not) be transcribed, how unified the transcription is and also whether the prescribed rules have been followed.
- One use of documentation of *data* is to determine whether a particular type of interview has been correctly carried out.
- Documentation of *methods of analysis* and of texts (verbal statements of those investigated and sometimes also documents) permit an evaluation of the interpretation and a check as to whether procedural guidelines have been adhered to (Scheff 1994: 8).
- A precise documentation of *information sources* (Bryman 1988: 77; Kirk and Miller 1986: 57f.; Silverman 1993: 146f.; Spradley 1980: 69f.) includes precise specification of the sources from which information was obtained:
  - Verbal statements of interviewees
  - Record of the meanings of interviewees' statements
  - The context in which the statement occurred
  - The investigator's observations
  - Hypotheses and interpretations on the part of the investigator

- On the basis of these indications it becomes clear what data underlie the interpretations. They are a help to a reader who is seeking to reconstruct the perspectives of those investigated.
- Documentation of *decisions and problems* includes considerations of sampling and choice of method, and documentation of contradictions that appeared in the analysis and have not been solved.
- Finally, the *criteria* that the study should satisfy should also be documented.

Secondly, *interpretations in groups* are a discursive way of producing inter-subjectivity and comprehensibility by dealing explicitly with data and their interpretation. Such interpretations are recommended, for example, in objective hermeneutics (Garz and Kraimer 1994b: 13; Oevermann et al. 1979: 393; see **5.16**) and by Strauss (1987) within grounded theory (see **5.13**; see also Kvale 1989; Mishler 1986). An approach that goes one step further is 'peer de-briefing' (Lincoln and Guba 1985: 308), where a project is discussed with colleagues who are not working on the same project.

Thirdly, the *use of codified procedures* derives from traditional ways of creating inter-subjectivity: the unification of the methodological process. Although qualitative research is difficult to standardize it seeks, nevertheless, to find rule-governed strategies and codification of research techniques, which means explanation and systematic analysis of the process with the aim of a logical formulation of methods (Barton and Lazarsfeld 1955: 321, 359; Bohnsack 1999). Nowadays, for example, various codified procedures are available in the form of the narrative interview (see **5.2**), in objective hermeneutics (see **5.16**), in the methods of grounded theory (see **5.13**) and so on. If codified procedures are used, the reader of a given publication has access to information that facilitates checking or replication of the investigation. If no codified procedures are adopted, it is essential to give explicit information and detailed documentation about the steps in the analysis.

Indication of the research process

Appropriateness to the research issue not only is a feature of qualitative research (see Part 1), but can also be taken as a criterion as to whether this requirement has been met. The criterion of indication has wider implications than the requirement of appropriateness to the issue, since it is not only the appropriateness of the methods of data collection and evaluation but the whole research process that is being judged in respect of its appropriateness (indication). Here we must make a number of distinctions.

1 Indication of the *qualitative procedure* in view of the research questions (see **4.1**). Do these suggest a qualitative approach, or would other procedures be appropriate? For example, if the goal of the investigation is representativity or distribution of the phenomenon over the population or if it is merely to test hypotheses, then use should be made of the appropriate quantitative methods.

2 Indication of the *choice of method(s)*. Are the methods of collection and analysis appropriate to the research issue? In more detail:

- Are the methods appropriate to the issue? Does the particular research issue correspond to those for which the selected method was designed? For this it is important to know the areas of application and the limits of qualitative methods (for a typology cf. Flick 2002). If use cannot be made of pre-existing methods for the issue in question, then methods appropriate to the particular issue must be developed.

- Is there sufficient room for the statements and meanings of interviewees in view of the research issue? Are the informants' subjective perspectives, everyday modes of action and meanings shown to best advantage, with reference to the research issue, and are they not too severely constrained or pre-structured by methodological rules? Are the issues being investigated in everyday contexts of the informants?

- Do the procedures in use make it possible to immitate prior knowledge? The procedures for collection and analysis should be set up in such a way that invitations to the investigator's prior knowledge are possible. For this an abductive stance is required (see **2.1**, **4.3**, **5.21**).

- Did the investigator spend a long time in the field (see **5.5**)? In particular, if the investigator is unfamiliar with the life-world of the informants, his or her presence in the field should extend over a lengthy period of time.

3 Indication of *transcription rules*. How precise should the transcriptions be? As a current consensus in the social sciences on the matter of appropriate transcriptions of spoken discourse Bruce (1992: 145, cited in O'Connell and Kowal 1995a: 96) proposes the following features:

- manageability, that is, easy to write (for the transcriber)
- readability, easy to learn and interpret (for the people, or computer, responsible for processing; see **5.9**).

4 Indication of *sampling strategy*. To what extent is there an indication of such things as the cases and situations being investigated? Morse (1994: 228) gives guidance on who makes a good informant. Is the sampling goal-directed, and have informative cases been selected? (For an overview of this, with 15 different sampling strategies, cf. Patton 1990: 169ff.) (see **4.4**).

5 Indication of *individual methodological decisions in the context of the whole investigation*. Do the methods of collection and analysis fit with one another? To what extent is the research design indicated with regard to the available resources (time, size of project team? (See **4.1**).

6 Indication of *evaluation criteria*. Are the quality criteria applied to the study appropriate to the particular issue, the methods and the research question(s)?

Empirical foundation

The formation *and* testing of hypotheses or theories in qualitative research should have an empirical foundation (or grounding), that is, it should be based on the data. *Theory-formation* should happen in such a way that there is a possibility of making new discoveries, and questioning or modifying the investigator's prior theoretical assumptions. Theories should be developed close to the data (for example, the informants' subjective views and modes of action) and on the basis of a systematic data analysis. For *theory-testing* implications or prognoses are derived deductively from the theories, and these are verified or falsified on empirical data. While verification looks for confirmation of the theory with the data, falsification – as a tougher criterion – tests the theory by attempting to reject it (on the latter, cf. Seale 1999a: 73ff.). The following are suitable ways of testing the empirical foundation.

1 The use of *codified methods*, such as objective hermeneutics (see **5.16**) or grounded theory (see **5.13**), is a guarantee of empirical foundation.

2 Is there sufficient *textual evidence* for the theory that has been developed? How were contradictions and deviant or negative cases, situations and settings handled?

3 *Analytic induction* (Bühler-Niederberger 1985, 1991) is a method of theory generation that simultaneously permits falsifications. A theory developed as fully as possible will be tested on a case. If the theory does not work, then the phenomenon will be redefined or the case will be excluded from the theory. 'Cases are studied until the phenomenon is redefined or the hypothesis reformulated, until a universal relationship is established; every negative case calls for a redefinition or reformulation' (Bühler-Niederberger 1985: 478).

4 From the theory generated *prognoses* may be derived and tested with regard to their occurrence in the text (interviews, observations, etc.) (see **5.16**).

5 *Communicative validation* (see above) makes it possible to relate the theory developed in the research process back to the informants. Communicative validation is inappropriate if the generated theory is beyond the informants' ability to agree. This latter is particularly true in objective hermeneutics, which reconstructs objective meanings beyond a subjective-intentional level (see **5.16**).

Limitation

This criterion serves the purpose, in the sense of 'testing the limits', of determining and testing the area of application, or generalizability, of a theory developed during the research process. For this purpose there must be an analysis of the further conditions (contexts, cases, investigated groups, phenomena, situations and so on) where the research results – developed under specific research conditions – may apply. If all of the (very specific) conditions of the investigation must be fulfilled for the results to be transferable, then the results can hardly be claimed to be transferable. There must also be a clarification of what conditions must be fulfilled, as a minimum, for the phenomenon described in the theory to occur. At the same time, aspects that are incidental, and – from the point of view of the theory – irrelevant, are filtered out. This can be discovered particularly through the introduction, omission and varying of conditions, contexts, phenomena and so on that are relevant to the creation or influencing of the research issue. For this, the following techniques are useful.

1 In *contrasting of cases* maximally and minimally different cases are identified and analysed in relation to the theory. This contrastive comparison of cases makes it possible to identify elements, causes, conditions and so on, shared by similar cases and essential to the theoretical phenomenon.

2 Explicitly seeking out and analysing *deviant, negative and extreme cases* follows the idea of

finding evidence about the meaning of the varied concepts by keeping constant as many aspects as possible and maximally varying individual aspects in a concept-driven way.

Coherence

The theory developed during the research process should be internally consistent. Accordingly, the following two points need to be checked. Is the generated theory coherent? Have any contradictions in the data and interpretations been processed? Unsolved questions and contradictions should be disclosed.

Relevance

The judging of theories with regard to their pragmatic usefulness is particularly important in qualitative research, which is located outside action or evaluation research (see **3.12**). For this purpose the following questions may be asked of the research process and the theory generated within it:

1 Is the *research question* relevant?
2 What *contribution* is made by the theory developed?
3 Does it make new interpretations available? Does it contain any explanations concerning the phenomenon in question?
4 Does the theory facilitate the solution of problems?
5 Can the results be generalized?
6 Is the presentation of the theory comprehensible?

Reflected subjectivity

This criterion tests the extent to which the constituting role of the researcher as a subject (with his or her research interests, assumptions, communicative styles and biographical background), and as a component of the social world

that he or she is investigating, is incorporated into formation of the theory in a way that is as far as possible reflected in the methods. Here there should be a consideration of the following questions.

1 Is the research process accompanied by *self-observation*? This will help determine whether any disturbing facts lead to barriers to understanding or to the elimination of such aspects from the theory.
2 Are *personal preconditions* for the exploration of the issue reflected? Is the personal methodological behaviour of the researcher appropriate? A researcher who is not happy with open situations, for example, is not really suited to a narrative interview.
3 Is a relationship of trust between the researcher and the informant a precondition for the collection of data appropriate to the culture and the research issue?
4 Are there any *reflections during entry into the field* (see **5.1**)? The unpleasantness and irritation that may arise provide important clues about what is peculiar to this field.

For the evaluation of a study the use of one or two of the criteria suggested here is not sufficient. On the basis of several of these criteria it should be possible to decide whether the 'best possible' result has been achieved.

FURTHER READING

Flick, U. (2002) *An Introduction to Qualitative Research,* 2nd edn. London: Sage. chs 18 and 22.

Kvale, S. (1995) 'The Social Construction of Validity', *Qualitative Inquiry*, 1: 19–40.

Seale, C. (1999) *The Quality of Qualitative Research*. London: Sage.

Part 5

Doing Qualitative Research

Introduction

The researcher embarking on *doing qualitative research* is confronted by a wide proliferation of available alternative methods. Whilst this variety of methods gives researchers more options as to how to do their research, it also confronts them with a need to decide on the appropriate method. The spectrum of qualitative research methods has expanded considerably in the past few decades. In the search for explanations for this proliferation, there are various reasons, or at least a series of trends, that we may refer to, these being:

- New debates on the theoretical status of qualitative research within the social sciences
- Differentiation of methodological procedures
- Inclusion of new types of data
- Different developments in the discussions in German- and English-speaking countries, which are now paying increasing attention to one another.

To structure the field of qualitative research methods as presented in this part of the *Companion*, we can allocate the individual methods to four larger subsections.

Entering the field (Part 5A) and the different *ways into the field* the researcher may take have quite an impact on which methodological steps the researcher may take next, so that they are already part of the methodology applied in a project. Access to the field (see **5.1**) is often not only a technical problem. The difficulties and obstacles that researchers encounter here are frequently already suggestive of a considerable part of the discoveries that may be made about the particular field and the actors concerned, and also touch on the specific role of the researcher in the field.

Collecting verbal data (Part 5B) becomes increasingly important in the day-to-day practices of qualitative research. The spectrum of interview procedures (see **5.2**) has continuously expanded, but it is still located in the controversial area between semi-structured and open forms, as the narrative interviews. This expansion is a result of the recognition that for different research questions, mixed forms might be appropriate or particular types of collection procedure are necessary. In any case interviewing confronts the researcher with an uncommon social situation with which he or she has to cope professionally (see **5.3**). The group discussion, or 'focus group', has recently flourished at the international level (see **5.4**), especially in the areas of market and media research and in 'cultural studies' (see **3.9**).

Observing processes and activities (Part 5C) is still and once again a prominent way of doing qualitative research. Participant observation as a method has increasingly been accepted as part of the more general strategy of ethnography (see **5.5**, **3.8**) and has thereby become part of a complex procedure that is strongly determined by questions of access (see **5.1**), and the presentation of results (see **5.22**). Apart from data collection oriented to the spoken word and the textual medium, and beyond observation in the field, new media are becoming increasingly important as data: photos (see **5.6**) and films (see **5.7**) have for some time played a growing role, particularly in the international debate. The new forms of electronic communication via email and the Internet make possible completely new forms of analysing communicative processes, characterized above all by the particular quality of the data (electronic traces) (see **5.8**).

Analysis, interpretation and presentation (Part 5D) are often seen as the core activity of the qualitative researcher. In this context, transcription (see **5.9**) has long ceased to be looked upon purely as a burdensome technical stage, where tape-recordings are transformed into readable texts. Today there is increasing recognition of the constructive contribution of this procedure and its rules to the representation of processes, which may then be interpreted. Similarly, the constitutive part played by the production of field notes in participant observation and ethnography will also be discussed in the respective chapter (see **5.22**). With regard to the analysis of data, a number of developments may be discerned. In general, we may distinguish between procedures that use coding and develop categories, either in the tradition of Anselm Strauss (see **5.13**) or of content analysis (see **5.12**), from those that are in the hermeneutic tradition (see **5.16**, **5.18**, **5.20**, **5.21**). These procedures stand alone and may – with certain differences – be applied to all types of data.

In the case of interview studies we may ask how the available analytical procedures may be used for the data obtained. Concrete proposals have been made for semi-structured interviews (see **5.10**) and narrative-biographical interviews (see **5.11**), the former being more strongly oriented to a coding-categorizing procedure and the latter more to hermeneutic understanding.

The use of computers in the analysis of qualitative data (see **5.14**) has become more and more widespread, and at present they are used particularly frequently in coding types of analysis.

In German-speaking countries there is a growing differentiation among hermeneutic methods (see **3.5**): from objective and sociological hermeneutics, hermeneutic theoretical sociology (see **5.16**) has developed. Out of conversation analysis (see **5.17**) has come genre analysis (see **5.18**). In this latter case, the term 'communicative genres' again comprises a broader understanding of data. Similarly, out of conversation analysis has grown discourse analysis (see **5.19**), which has attracted particular attention in Anglo-American psychology.

The role played by the presentation of results (see **5.22**) and procedures in qualitative research has recently been treated as a decisive step, in particular in Anglo-American discussion in the field of ethnography. This has led at the very least to growing awareness of the importance of modes of presentation of the results. Ultimately the making of discoveries in empirical science is often not only the result of a consistent and rule-governed application of methods. The art of interpretation (see **5.21**) sometimes also involves the use of chance and openness to the unexpected as well as methodologically transparent and controlled theoretical speculation.

In general terms, the individual chapters contained in Part 5 of the *Companion* are ordered following the steps a researcher runs through in the process of doing research – from entry into the field, to data collection and transcription and ultimately to analysis and writing. On the other hand, there are an increasing number of integrated methods – for example, ethnography, film analysis or genre analysis – that cannot be unambiguously assigned either to collection or to analysis. In cases such as these, the collection and interpretation of data will be treated together in a single chapter.

5.1   Ways into the Field and their Variants

Stephan Wolff

1   FIELD ACCESS – TERMINOLOGY AND OBJECTIVES

It would be an error in dealing with the 'way into the field' to think in terms of a fixed boundary, the crossing of which provides the researcher with an open and unrestricted view of the interior of the field. For that reason, in what follows we shall speak not of 'entry' but 'access' to the field. This term not only makes more prominent the activity or process quality of the event in question, it also succeeds in avoiding a strict inside–outside distinction. By 'research field' we understand here naturally occurring social fields of action, as opposed to artificial situational arrangements deliberately engineered for research purposes.

Research fields may be public places, groups, social milieux ('scenes') but also organizations or tribal groups. For each of these research fields there are, from the researcher's point of view, *two fundamental questions*.

1   How can the researcher succeed in making contact with the chosen research field and in stimulating the informants to cooperate? If research is to become in any sense a social event, the involved representatives of the field should be ready, of their own volition, not only to take account of unfamiliar *demands*, which might include:

- making available time for conversations;
- partially giving up control of physical space;
- enduring embarrassment;
- facing up to communicative pressures (such as those that arise in narrative interviews);
- limiting one's own communicative needs (if they are subordinate to a semi-structured regime); and
- accepting the questioning of what has always been taken for granted;

But also *display a wide range of their own activities*, such as:

- putting themselves in the researcher's position (in order to be able to provide data interesting to him or her);
- informing the researcher about situational relevancies;

- smoothing the researcher's path and suggesting competent interview partners;
- answering questions they have never put to themselves, the meaning of which is initially obscure;
- trusting the researcher without guarantees;
- explaining to themselves and others what the researcher and the project are aiming at; and
- signalling that they are not disturbed, even though they know they are under scrutiny, and so on.

2 How can the researcher *position himself or herself* in respect of the field so as to secure the factual, temporal and social conditions to carry out appropriately the planned research, or at least not significantly inhibit relevant freedom of action?

There are no patent recipes as to how a way into the field should be sought and found. Furthermore, it is not wise either to invoke the illusion that everything can be planned or to complain about the unpredictability of the situation. It would also be a mistake to trivialize the question of access as a technical or psychological ground-clearing problem, with the real research beginning after it has been dealt with. For this reason one should look upon (and set up) the way into the field as a task that is never completed and which must be handled cooperatively, that is jointly with the intended 'objects' of the research. A preoccupation with the way into the field serves not only methodological or research-pragmatic purposes, it also yields insights into structures and sequences in the research as a social event, and into the field of action that is under investigation. The trial paths, detours and false trails that researchers often complain about and feel to be burdensome, and even the failed attempts at gaining access – which are normally carefully suppressed – all then become 'critical events', the analysis of which opens up chances of making discoveries.

2 THE WAY INTO THE FIELD AND ITS THEMATIZATION IN THE SOCIAL SCIENCES

Classic descriptions of access read like epics of heroism in which, after a phase of struggles and irritation, the researcher ultimate attains the 'Heart of Darkness' (*à la* Joseph Conrad) to which he or she aspires. The decisive moment of arrival in the field often takes on a particular stylization: perhaps an abrupt (positive) change in relations with the 'natives', an overpowering emotional feeling of arrival or a sudden revelation, as with the overturning of familiar ways of looking at things. This also defines simultaneously the precise moment at which the actual research can begin (particularly elegantly expressed in Geertz 1972; see **2.6**).

The problem of access is first discussed as a *problem of the researcher* who desires access and who has to cope, in the process, with the resistance of the field, but also with his or her own psychic defence mechanisms in the face of uncertainties and irritations associated with access to a particular situation (cf. Lindner 1981). Proven interactive and/or psychological strategies are looked for that will put the investigator in a position to recognize and effectively neutralize all such problems (as an example of a collection of such recommendations, cf. Gans 1982). The posthumous (1967) publication of the research diary of Malinowski, the celebrated pioneer of participant observation (see **5.5**), dealing with his time with the Trobriand people, led to a permanent lowering of expectations in respect of how far the field-researcher could substantiate 'being-there', and made it unavoidable that the problems of access should henceforth always be more thoroughly confronted – and not only in ethnology.

As a next step, the problem of access is reformulated as a *problem of relations*. Here the relation to *key informants* and their particular characteristics is brought into the foreground (Casagrande 1960).

Many of these key informants have achieved real fame in ethnographic research: among these we find 'Doc', who not only provided William F. Whyte with contacts in the Street Corner Society, but also accompanied him as a sort of coach; 'Don Juan', who apparently initiated Carlos Castaneda in the teachings of Yaqui magic; or Ogotomméli, who functioned as Marcel Griaule's wise conversation partner amongst the Dogon.

A strikingly large number of these key persons occupy the position of social outsiders in their own community, for example because of earlier intensive experience with outsiders or frequently also because of some particular personal quirk of fate. The problems for field access that might be found in the relation to such 'marginal men' was either treated as a transient problem (which would solve itself when the research took on greater depth) or used positively by referring to the particular sensitivity of such persons and their competence as observers.

One further difficulty on the way into the field results from the fact that the *delimitation* of research fields in the areas of both ethnology and sociology seems increasingly questionable. For a long time field researchers proceeded on the basis that they could relate to isolated social entities on the periphery of (world) society or to clearly defined urban scenes, groups and organizations; that is, that the field to which they sought access could not only be identified without difficulty, but also be reconstructed as an independent cultural context. If we look at the true interrelations between these only apparently isolated entities and their environment we see, however, that it is impossible to draw unambiguous borders between them. The ethnographic view is also blurred by the fact that field research has increasingly to do with its *own* culture, and with phenomena that tend to be situated in the area of *social normality* (see **3.8**). The growing *lack of strangeness*, together with an increased awareness of the way in which ethnographic exoticism functions, makes the use of the strategy of 'methodological alienation' (Hirschauer and Amann 1997), which is typical of ethnographic studies, appear to be simultaneously both acceptable *and* questionable. From this there develops an awareness of the fact that with the autonomy and identifiability of a culture we are dealing with a *constructive research activity*. The issue to which one seeks access is only constituted as such in the course of the research – and this already begins with the classifications of groups to be investigated (cf. Moerman 1974) that are incorporated in the scientific questions. If one relates this consideration to the idea of ethnographic authority (Clifford 1983), then it may be concluded that to a certain extent researchers are *seeking access to their own fiction*.

The discussion of access takes on a new quality if – on the basis of their social status and social capital – one considers more powerful groups (such as supervisory boards, the nobility or senior doctors; cf. Hertz and Imber 1997; Saffir et al. 1980) and organizations as research fields, that is to say 'objects' who want and are able actively to control access to their domains. This is particularly true of *organizations* (see **3.11**), which are increasingly becoming the principal point of address for requests for access. They have at their disposal a wide range of practices to keep curious third parties at a distance, to generate information about themselves, to influence it and control its utilization. Even those organizations that are more open to research needs rarely fail to set up obstacles to access or at least to develop access routines. The investigator, therefore, has not only to persuade informal 'gatekeepers', but also to follow official channels – in an extreme case extending to a highly official contract management via a research access monitoring agency set up precisely for this purpose. Many such agencies and procedural routes actually function as research *preventers*.

The question of access takes on a new dimension in view of the fact that the objects of an investigation increasingly have *prior knowledge* about social research, and are sometimes even equipped with sociological models and education. Occasionally this may contribute to greater understanding and receptiveness towards the research. Such knowledge may also, however, be 'utilized paradoxically', that is, to *resist* attempts at access, resulting in extreme cases in the researcher's being sued on the grounds of inadequate research standards (see **6.3**).

In view of developments of this sort, the classical *model of the invisible field researcher*, slipping unnoticed into the field as if invisible under a magic coat and conducting observations totally unnoticed, is no longer plausible even as an ideal. The fear of reactivity, which sees the interactive aspects of field access only as disturbing variables that have to be neutralized, is increasingly giving way to the view that such effects should essentially be evaluated as evidence of the 'naturalness' of an investigation, and that they should be reflected and, in certain cases, even used as sources of information. Field access must be viewed, analysed and designed as an *independent* social phenomenon. If this is done, a range of *fundamental work problems* become clear which all parties (and not only the investigators) have to deal with on their common path into and in the field, regardless of whether or not they make this an explicit issue.

3 STRUCTURAL PROBLEMS OF ACCESS

The field as a social system

Like every outsider, the researcher, from the point of view of the field, is initially *a person without history* who can only adapt with difficulty to the categories that are normal there and whose loyalty remains dubious. If there arise further fundamental difficulties of understanding at the verbal and non-verbal level (vocabulary, communication style, behavioural types), then it will rarely be possible to integrate this outsider and his or her request *without difficulty* into the normal communicative contexts. In order to answer the question of whether one should 'let in' the outsider, what is decisive is if and how his or her person and request can be identified as 'acceptable' or can be made 'acceptable'. In the process of access, what is crucial, therefore, is not the attempt to achieve a cognitive and social *placement* of the researcher and the request, but simultaneously to establish the experience, dramatization and establishment of a *boundary* between the particular social unit and its environment.

As a rule the social *placement* takes place in two stages: first, the basic acceptability is tested. This is to do with the question of whether the recognizable features of the person (gender, age, ethnic group) and his or her request, together with aspects of the organizational world to which the researcher belongs, are compatible with local world-views, interests and events. It is only at the second stage that the allocation or agreement of particular participant roles is agreed (cf. Lau and Wolff 1983). This two-stage process is mostly described in the literature with reference to an opposition between 'getting in' (physically) and 'getting on' (in terms of social access), although what is overlooked is that 'getting in' already implies some social placement.

In the process of field access the field constitutes itself and is simultaneously experienced by both the actors and the observers as *a social unit*, that is, as a communicative context distinct from its environment, where participants are distinguished from outsiders. In the case of organizations, participation requires the taking on of a membership role and the acceptance of the expectations that are attached to it. One of the implications of this fundamental importance of the *maintenance of boundaries* and the *membership role* is that the researcher *qua researcher* cannot become a member of the organization in question. This would only be conceivable if he or she is given a particular functional status for particular purposes within the organization ('our researcher', perhaps in the role of a consultant or legitimizing authority) or when the

researcher personally resolves the difference between him- or herself and the field ('going native').

One form of breaking down distance that is complementary to 'going native' consists of *undercover research*, where the researcher sets up access to a harmless membership role, but can no longer appear as a researcher. Apart from ethical and political objections (see **6.1**), what is against this form of access is that the necessary adaptations that ensue can limit considerably not only the social form but also the quality of data collection.

Much the same is true in the case of access to *simple social systems* (Luhmann 1972). Even when this is a matter of events in public and apparently freely accessible settings, the way in which the presence of the researcher is set up can become a problem. Simply looking in passing at a social encounter may constitute a problem of access, that is to say, a social situation that demands attention. At that moment when those present become mutually aware of each other's presence and address each other, a simple social system inevitably comes into being, even if this is only of short duration. Accordingly, under conditions of mutual perceptibility, a mere absence of involvement is not sufficient to avoid causing disturbance. What is required is rather a socially acceptable form of making oneself invisible, in the active development of which both the observer and those observed can have a share, perhaps by controlling their facial expressions, gestures, spatial locations and so on. Goffman (1971) points out that outsiders, in order to retain this status, would need to display 'polite indifference'.

If this cannot be achieved, the integrity of the person in question, and sometimes even of the interaction system concerned, becomes problematic. The disturbance has to be considered as a question of access in an *independent* interaction system and worked on there – perhaps by means of allocating an acceptable observer role. Many social settings have institutionalized observer roles that may be adopted by researchers for the purpose of making undercover observations.

Classic examples may be found in investigations of deviant 'scenes', such as in the investigation of the porno-scene around Times Square in New York by Karp (1980), or Humphreys's (1970) controversial observations of homosexual 'toilet-dealings'. As with undercover observation in organizations a number of quite delicate circumstances come to light here, where there is always a risk of loss of contact or discovery, where there is an acute need for information control and impression management, and where there are few opportunities for direct communication.

Dealing with 'gatekeepers'

To take care of their border relationships organizations and many groups have 'gatekeepers' (or 'stranger-handlers') of their own (cf. Agar 1996). Astute dealing with such gatekeepers therefore takes on strategic importance within the process of gaining access. Of course, in individual cases it is not always possible to say definitely who it is who has to agree to a request for access or whose agreement actually counts. In respect of organizations as research fields the following rules of thumb may be formulated (cf. Morrill et al. 1999).

In comparatively monocratic organizations it is only the agreement of the senior management that counts, whereas in decentralized organizations there may be a variety of addresses that have to be contacted. It is difficult to decide upon an orientation if there is a high degree of politicization of decision-making policy within an organization. Then the researcher has to seek the agreement of a coalition of decision-makers, and in the worst case of a number of mutually hostile coalitions. Here experience teaches that there are sensitive phases for attempts at access: one should therefore reckon with difficulties, for example, if there has just been a change of management, if the organization is just recovering from a scandal, or if fellow-researchers have recently been there. In organizations with a range of loosely coupled power centres ambiguous situations may arise in which the researcher finds him- or herself between two stools, and where, conversely, no one can rightly say what is valid and who one should refer to. In particular, in cases of high political dynamics in the field of investigation, the question of identifying the current gatekeepers remains a task of constant importance (for a classic example cf. Gouldner 1954). In cases of doubt, it is advisable to follow official channels.

'Immune reactions'

The fields in question react to attempts at access, as far as possible, by relying on familiar

and tested patterns for neutralizing disturbance and dealing with unpleasant or unusual requests. The following are some of the strategies that may be found in the relevant *repertoire of organizations*.

- *Pass upstairs*: the request is first passed to a higher level with a request for examination.
- *Cross-question*: the researcher is repeatedly asked for new presentations of the research goal and procedures.
- *Wait and see*: the matter is referred for re-submission, because experience shows that many enquiries sort themselves out.
- *Make an offer*: the request is basically accepted, but the organization offers its own data or agrees to a mode of collection that was not originally foreseen.
- *Allocate*: times, roles and research opportunities are provided which the organization, from its own standpoint, considers suitable and appropriate.
- *Incorporate*: the organization makes the research and the results into an affair of its own, and attempts to integrate the researcher into organizational matters or disputes with other organizations, or to give him or her some kind of indirect task.

Because researchers, for their part, can and do adjust to such strategies, there are in practice many types of interaction effect that result from this. The specific dynamic of these derives from the degree of unity in the particular field in the face of research endeavours and the transparency of the research intentions (Hornsby-Smith 1993). Particularly difficult constellations may arise in the case of 'upward' research, in the sense that elites contrast their high visibility with a high degree of inaccessibility, and also because it is part of the social status of such people to control their accessibility and to set up a functioning management of their (non-) availability.

Ambivalence

There is a *notorious ambivalence* on the part of the researcher which corresponds to these immune reactions. This quite often takes the form of aggressively expressed fantasies of omnipotence or inferiority in respect of the field. A researcher then oscillates between a feeling of irritation at not being given more than bare facades and a conviction that he or she basically understands the field and its problems better than the informants. What is characteristic of the state of mind of many researchers on their way into the field is the almost unavoidable idea that behind the facades there is a 'true' but maliciously concealed reality. The field research situation – apparently so open – encourages a pervasive *willingness to suspect motives* or the notorious suspicion that the real show is being played out 'behind the scenes'. Interestingly enough, this feeling is repeatedly encountered in *all* participants, that is, not only the informants. Practically all ethnographers, at some point in their careers, must have been looked upon as some kind of spy.

Secrecy and confidentiality

Lee (1993), referring to such ambivalences, describes access to the field as an exercise in the 'politics of distrust'. How this politics of distrust is carried out depends to a large extent on how secrecy and confidentiality are viewed.

Alois Hahn (1997) provides some useful clarifications on this subject: if there is regulation of access to knowledge or to the content of conscious awareness that is not yet shared knowledge ('How wonderful that nobody knows my name is Rumpelstiltskin'), then we are dealing with secrecy, or the attempt to remove information from a particular piece of information. A more relevant case for field research is that of *confidentiality*. Here there is a restriction on the number of people permitted to talk and write about a particular subject, or who – as hearers or readers – may share in the knowledge of a particular communication. Confidentiality relates to what has already been shared, in the sense that, within a group of people who are in communication with each other, something is subsequently and expressly declared to be a secret, with the result that the group is thereby closed to the outside. For this reason confidentiality may truly be used as a productive mechanism, *for the purpose of creating an identity for the particular field and its members*. But it may also happen that a guarantee of confidentiality *precedes* a particular communication, which means that the information in question is only being passed on under an explicit 'cloak of silence'. In this case the sociological meaning of the secret lies less in

the closing of the communicative frontiers of a social group or association than in the selective opening to third parties (as with institutionalized confessional or Hippocratic secrets, or journalistic protection of sources of information) of a communicative opportunity that would otherwise not exist.

Becoming aware of these distinctions allows one not only to avoid hasty subjectivist interpretations and rationalizations of motives (that is, not confusing secrecy with confidentiality), but also to gain a perspective on the paradox of the 'risk' to the researcher that can derive from *initiation* into the secrets of a particular field. In so far as a secret constitutes a difference from the uninitiated, anyone who has been initiated into secrets is in a quandary. Gaining information about insiders can become a problem for the researcher, which confronts him or her with the alternatives of betrayal or self-censure. Goffman (1989: 129) is therefore quite justified in warning the researcher against believing that it is a sign of really being 'in' if one is admitted, without asking, into strategic secrets.

Structural opacity

One remarkable feature of the process of access that has regularly been reported is the fact that informants rarely ask about the content of the research project or what is said about it in the various papers and introductory talks. From the viewpoint of the field, the researcher must succeed, in the manner of his or her presentation, in giving proof that:

- the research project is *serious*;
- the relevant institutions and groups are not threatened with any *harm*;
- one can, within certain limits, *rely* on the researcher's willingness to cooperate, on their solidarity and discretion;
- the researcher will only *disturb* normal daily business in an acceptably limited way;
- one will again *be rid of* the researcher in the foreseeable future.

These questions are not susceptible to any direct testing by the informants; even the researcher has no final answer to them! It is not so much the weight of the research goal or the elaborate nature of the methodological arsenal – the content aspects – but rather the appropriateness of the presentation, the credible signalling of a reputable organizational environment, the nature of the personal approach, or the willingness to accept annoyances and sensitivities pointed out by the field which therefore prove to be the decisive indicators of the acceptability of a request and of the researcher as a person (cf. Lau and Wolff 1983). Apart from this, experienced gatekeepers believe that presentations that appear to be scientifically neutral are produced, polished and beautified, that is to say, 'non-impartial presentations' – which corresponds to their own handling of information (for instance, if they have to produce or read annual reports, job advertisements or applications). Frequently additional information is only requested in order to be able to draw conclusions from possible gaps in particular presentations (cf. Feldman and March 1981).

In the sense that they do not deal with these ambiguities, strict codes of ethics and radical demands for 'informed consent' imply an unrealistic picture of research practice. The process of field access can, in fact, only be set in motion when any possible demands have been met: work can therefore begin in spite of any remaining lack of clarity. This type of work consensus implies a *situation-related dialectic of honesty*, in the light of which the rule of thumb formulated by Taylor and Bogdan (1984), 'be trustful, but vague and imprecise', seems a sensible recommendation. In contrast, any attempt, from whatever viewpoint, to provide complete transparency (such as handing over full research applications) or to insist upon it (for instance, by requiring information about every detail of a research proposal) is a guaranteed way of *not* getting a piece of research off the ground.

Field research as an independent action system

The goal of access work consists only to a limited extent of removing the distance between the researcher and the field, or the differences of interest, information and perspective of the two parties. It would appear to be of at least equal importance to recognize these mutual differences as resources for the epistemological process, to cultivate them and even exploit them. For the researcher this means above all that there is a need always to remain aware of the difference between participation and observation. What is helpful here are agreements about:

- the allocation of an acceptable observer role (such as that of some practitioners);
- the possibility of a temporary withdrawal from the field ('short-term ethnography');
- the researcher's asking 'naive' questions about matters that are actually self-evident.

Informants must not only be prepared to agree to these 'alienations', which appear at times to be quite artificial (Hirschauer and Amann 1997). They should also be capable of accepting that what they take for granted may be 'questionable'. To be able to engage in any kind of conversation with one another, both parties will feel that it is necessary, to a certain extent, to distance themselves consciously from their social and cognitive reference system. Both parties are moving in a border area between their respective reference cultures. Through their working association they constitute, for a particular period of time, a *hybrid system*, the existence and feasibility of which depends not least on the maintenance of these differences.

Often it is the informants who gamble with the recognition and maintenance of differences. Excessively well-adjusted researchers are commonly faced with as much scepticism as those who announce their solidarity or make helpful suggestions without being asked. Conversely, caution is also advised if there is an over-enthusiastic reception by the field, because this may often relate to secret hopes and expectations in advance of what the researcher may wish to set up.

Within this hybrid system there will also develop particular role-relationships, time horizons, forms of communication, rationality criteria and obligations, and these may again have important consequences for the discovery potential of the project: this may influence, for example, the situational acceptability of particular methods (interviews – yes; observation – no), or the problem of what topics are legitimate subjects for questioning, what events the researcher can participate in, and where limits have to be respected. Experienced field researchers will orient themselves according to the options that arise in the framework of this action-system and, in the light of the particular practical circumstances, will reformulate their questions and the steps in their investigation accordingly. What seems sensible is a *progressive field-access strategy*, which begins with relatively diffuse questioning and does not insist upon immediate use of the most demanding collection procedures. With this kind of strategy what is, at least initially, in the foreground is not the accomplishment of the research plan but the *securing and setting up of an appropriate* situational context for the research *process*.

The researcher can offer nothing to the field

Field research relationships are fragile entities. Participants tend to come together by chance, they are linked by only a brief history, and a common future seems unlikely. They embark on a complex process of cooperation, for which there are almost no routines and whose development cannot be foreseen in any detail. Both parties have to adjust to one another, with no proper bases and certainties for trust. In view of this kind of constellation, it may well be understandable if researchers seek to buy their way in with problematic announcements or even promises concerning the expected uses of the project for the field that is under investigation.

This sort of bargaining model, however, not only implies an unacceptable simplification of the relationship between science and the field. It also represents, in view of the triviality of what the researcher is actually able to offer, a form of *bragging*. Behind this the true value for the field is in most cases limited to a short-term interruption of the daily boredom, an opportunity to bring one's cares and complaints to someone, or the chance of doing a good piece of work. Only rarely are representatives of the field willing and able to do something with the results of an investigation. If gatekeepers really do offer the researcher the role of an evaluator, critic or consultant, and therefore require

achievements in return, then caution is advised, not only because this may require more than the researcher's competence can deliver. What is more problematic is that this may lead to the *diffusion of roles* between the participants, and above all the self-limitations and compromises for which the researcher must be prepared in this kind of situation, to balance out the different expectations of representatives of the field and the interests of the researcher (see **3.12**, **6.3**). What conflicts with this insight, however, is the uncertainty of the researcher about whether he or she will really be taken seriously by the field if he of she is unable to display a modicum of expertise.

In view of the temptations, expectations and fantasies that swamp the researcher in the access situation, he or she can easily run the risk of being or wishing to appear too wise too quickly. To counter this risk, it is advisable to exaggerate one's naivety, not only to the field but also to oneself, to be able to exploit methodologically, and for as long as possible, the researcher's (real or imagined) ignorance.

FURTHER READING

Johnson, J. M. (1975) *Doing Field Research*. New York: Free Press.

Morrill, C., Buller, D. B., Buller, M. K. and Larley, L. L. (1999) 'Toward an Organizational Perspective on Identifying and Managing Formal Gatekeepers', *Qualitative Sociology*, 22: 51–72.

Saffir, W. B., Stebbins, R. A. and Turowetz, A. (eds) (1980) *Fieldwork Experience – Qualitative Approaches to Social Research*. New York: St Martins Press.

Part 5B

Collecting Verbal Data

5.2   Qualitative Interviews: An Overview

Christel Hopf

1   INTRODUCTION

In social research, qualitative interviews – semi-standardized or open interviews – are very widely used. In the context of quantitative research projects they are used predominantly in the preparation of standardized data collection and the development of data collection tools. In qualitative research there are many more opportunities for their use. In the first place qualitative interviews play an important role in ethnographic research projects based on participant observation (see **5.5**). One of their uses here is the imparting of expert knowledge about the research field in question, the recording and analysis of the informants' subjective perspective, or the collection of data relating to their biography (see **3.6**). More usual – at least in Germany – are qualitative interviews in research projects for which they are the main empirical base. These include: projects in the area of biographical research, studies on gender-related questions (see **3.10**), studies of the social and political orientations of different population groups, or studies of access to professions and of professional socialization.

Compared to other research procedures in the social sciences, qualitative interviews are particularly closely related to the approaches of interpretative sociology. Because of the possibility of enquiring openly about situational meanings or motives for action, or collecting everyday theories and self-interpretations in a differentiated and open way, and also because of the possibility of discursive understanding through interpretations, open or semi-standardized interviews provide important opportunities for an empirical application of action- theory ideas in sociology and psychology. Together with the establishment of qualitative procedures in social research, this has repeatedly been emphasized as a particular achievement of qualitative interviews – compared to the more restricted possibilities of standardized questioning – frequently relying on the theoretical traditions of phenomenological sociology (see **3.1**). Reference has also been made to Max Weber's idea of an interpretative sociology or to the traditions of symbolic interactionism (see **3.3**). Nevertheless, the link between interpretative sociology and qualitative interviews is not obligatory, as can be explained, for example, with reference to the more limited function of historical or organization-related (see **3.11**) qualitative questioning.

2 VARIANTS OF QUALITATIVE INTERVIEWS

There are an enormous number of different types and procedures of qualitative interviews (for a summary cf. Flick 2002: 76ff.; Friebertshäuser 1997; Lamnek 1995: 35ff.; Spöhring 1989: 147ff.; and for a discussion of analysis, see **5.10**). After a preliminary survey of the different variants of interviews in the next section, I shall then present two of these variants in more detail: focused and narrative interviews. These are given particular prominence because, in my opinion, they are particularly successful compromises between the different demands that are made of qualitative interviews, demands that are difficult to reconcile with one another. They unite a high degree of openness and non-directivity with a high level of concreteness and the recording of detailed information: they are therefore superior to other interview variants.

An overview

Important questions that serve to distinguish between the different variants of qualitative interviews are the following.

1   The question of whether, in conducting an interview, one is oriented by pre-formulated questions, the sequencing of which in the interview may also be prescribed, or whether the interview is conducted on the basis of a number of less rigidly pre-formulated questions or guidelines. The variants of qualitative interviews that are used particularly frequently are between these extremes and may be described as relatively flexibly applied semi-standardized interviews: researchers orient themselves according to an interview guide, but one that gives plenty of freedom of movement in the formulation of questions, follow-up strategies and sequencing.

2   The question of whether one should concentrate in conducting interviews on quite specific constellations, texts, films and the like, and put the discussion of these in the centre – in an extreme case in focused interviews – or whether a broad spectrum of themes, situations and questions should be addressed in the interviews.

3   The question of whether the requirement to narrate is most important in the conduct of an interview – as in the narrative interview – or whether the primary interest is in the collection of more general meanings, political orientations or complex types of argumentation. While in the first case the requirements to tell a story and listen actively are dominant, in the other cases active questioning and probing, careful argumentation and the construction of possible counter-arguments are more relevant.

In what follows a brief characterization will be given of some of the variants of qualitative interviews that are more commonly used in sociological and psychological research.

Structure or *dilemma-interviews*, in comparison to other semi-standardized interviews, are relatively strictly regulated as to their question guidelines and the sequencing of questions (for discussion of this and the following, cf. Colby and Kohlberg 1987 I: 151ff., and Oser and Althoff 1992: 171ff.). They developed as interview variants in the Piaget–Kohlberg tradition and are used particularly to record the different stages in the making of moral judgements. In dilemma-interviews an attempt is made to record the structure of judgements on the basis of reactions to narrative guidelines. In such guidelines problems of decision-making are presented – a particularly well-known example of this is the so-called Heinz-dilemma, which is concerned with the theft of medicines in an emergency situation – and informants are asked to react to these. Using a set catalogue of standardized questions and follow-up questions (cf. Oser and Althoff 1992: 172f.), the particular explanations of the informants are elicited in a sufficiently explicit and distinctive way for the individual explanations to be allocated, in the process of interview-analysis, to different levels of moral judgement.

Clinical interviews originated in clinical and therapeutic practice, where they are used – with varying degrees of structural regularity – in the diagnosis of illnesses (on the subject of clinical interviews at the beginning of psychoanalytic treatment, cf. Argelander 1970). But in non-therapeutic and primarily research-oriented contexts the concept of the clinical interview – or the in-depth interview (cf. Lamnek 1995: 81) – is also quite frequently used. Particularly for psychologists, the idea of the 'clinical interview' is a collective term for semi-standardized or non-standardized modes of data collection, as opposed to procedures such as testing.

Biographical interviews seek to gain access to life-histories. As Fuchs (1984: 179ff.) explains, biographical interviews can take the form of semi-standardized or narrative interviews. Fuchs recommends that these different interview types should be combined with one another. Other authors also suggest a combination of different types of interview. In particular there is a desire for compromise forms between the semi-standardized and the narrative interview. Examples of this are the problem-centred interview (Witzel 1985) or the episodic interview (Flick 2002: 104–110).

In addition to this list of types of more or less structured semi-standardized interviews, there is a range of further variants of qualitative interviews. Among these we may cite the expert interview (cf. Vogel 1995) or the ethnographic interview (cf. Spradley 1979). But this will perhaps suffice as an overview of the many types and applications of the qualitative interview, particularly since it should be remembered that the different variants of qualitative interviews are – in the practice of empirical social research – frequently used in combinations and sometimes without explicitly being named.

Focused interviews

The form of the focused interview was developed in the 1940s, in relation to communication research and propaganda analysis, by Robert Merton, Patricia Kendall and others (cf. Merton and Kendall 1945/6; Merton et al. 1956). What is central to these interviews is the focusing on a subject or topic of conversation determined in advance – such as a film that the informants have seen, an article they have read, a particular social situation they participated in and which is also known to the interviewers, and so on – and the attempt to collect reactions and interpretations in an interview with a relatively open form.

Focused interviews in their original form are group interviews, but they are not necessarily bound to a group situation. In their focus on pre-determined subjects of conversation they resemble the structure or dilemma-interview (cf. above) and because they are characterized by

conversational themes – albeit flexibly used – they could be looked on as a special form of the semi-standardized interview. But in their design they are freer and more open to associative reactions to the subjects of conversation than, for example, structure interviews. It is indeed one of the goals of the focused interview to maximize the scope of the topics and to give interviewees an opportunity to invoke points of view that had not been anticipated.

In their book on focused interviews, which summarizes their experiences with this interview type on the basis of comprehensive interview transcripts, Merton et al. develop the following four quality criteria for focused interviews (cf. Merton et al. 1956: 12 *et passim*):

1 *Scope*: the spectrum of problems addressed in the interview should not be too narrow. This means that interviewees should have maximal opportunity to react to the 'stimulus-situation' (the film, the text, the picture or whatever). This concerns both theoretically anticipated and non-anticipated reactions (cf. Merton et al. 1956: 41ff.).
2 *Specificity*: the topics and questions that occur in the interview should be dealt with in a specified way. For example, after watching a film interviewees should not simply express global assessments and evaluations, but more concrete memories and feelings that relate to particular scenes.
3 *Depth*: in the interview the dimension of depth should be appropriately represented. Interviewees should be supported in presenting the affective, cognitive and value-related meaning which particular situations have for them.
4 *Personal context*: the personal context in which the analysed meanings and reactions are located must be adequately recorded. Knowledge of this is a precondition for the interpretation of any non-anticipated reactions to the communicative contents that formed the basis of the interview (cf. Merton et al. 1956: 117f.).

A more recent variant of the focused interview may be seen in those interviews where description of a daily routine or more complex personal documents become a topic of conversation (cf. Zeiher and Zeiher 1998: 207ff.), or interviews that are carried out in the context of participant observation (see **5.5**), where specific jointly experienced situations – like education – are dealt with (cf. Hargreaves et al. 1981: 59ff.). Focused interview can also be an important aid in the stimulation of personal recollections that are not always easy to represent. It has proved possible to trace this in a research project on the 'subjective meaning to young people of acts of violence represented in films'. Young vocational school students were shown a film (*Romper Stomper*) about a right-wing violence-oriented group of skinheads in Australia. In their reactions to the film the young informants often talked spontaneously about their own experience of violence. The film served to activate memories that would have been more difficult to access in an interview without the stimulus potential of the film.

Focused interviews as described above have a number of advantages, including the possibility of combining a reserved, non-directive management of a conversation with an interest in very specific information and the opportunity for an object-related explanation of meanings. It is admittedly true that in focused interviews there is also still a gap between interview practice and theoretical claims, and this was discussed by Merton and Kendall (1945/6) in a comprehensive and instructive analysis of individual interview sequences.

Narrative interviews

This form of interviewing was developed by Fritz Schütze in the course of a study of communal power structures (cf. 1976, 1977; on narrative interviews cf. also Hermanns 1995 or Fischer-Rosenthal and Rosenthal 1997b: 412ff.; see also **5.11**), and it is used particularly often in the context of life-history-related questions. Here the term 'narrative interview' is defined very broadly in research practice and is sometimes used as an abbreviation for semi-standardized biographical interviews. In its original form, however, this was not intended: the core element of the narrative interview consisted of a free developed impromptu narrative, stimulated by an opening question – the 'narrative-generating question'.

The individual phases of the narrative interview were characterized by Fischer-Rosenthal and Rosenthal (1997b: 414ff.) as follows.

1 The invitation to narrate, which must be formulated in such a way that the conversation

partners are not subject to too much spoon-feeding and, at the same time, are helped to mobilize their memories and to narrate freely.
2 The independently produced main narrative, or – in the case of a biographical-narrative interview – the biographical self-presentation.
3 Narrative-generating enquiries:
    (a) using the key points noted in phase 2;
    (b) external enquiries.
4 Interview conclusion.

It is an important principle in narrative interviews that the main narrative is produced independently by the interviewees, even if in particular cases it is framed rather in the style of a brief report or a piece of argumentation. Initially there should be no intervention, but during the main narrative the interviewers should primarily adopt the role of attentive listener and contribute to the maintenance of the narrative through supportive gestures and non-directive brief comments. Only in the follow-up section do researchers have the opportunity for a more active contribution. Here the first stage consists of taking up any open questions that result from the narrative. In this there are certain important principles: the questions should be formulated in as open a manner as possible and should stimulate the interviewees to further narratives. Fischer-Rosenthal and Rosenthal (1997b: 418), in respect of the biographical-narrative interview, distinguish between three types of narrative follow-up question:

1 Steering towards a particular life-phase: Could you tell me a little more about this time (e.g. childhood)?
2 Steering towards a situation mentioned in the main narrative: You mentioned earlier (the relevant situation) …. Could you give me a little more detail about this situation?
3 Steering a sample narrative towards an argument: Can you still remember a situation (in which your father was authoritarian, in which you lost all belief in being able to succeed, and so on)?

The follow-up questions that relate to the narrative already have the function of a cautious testing of assumptions that have shown up in the interviewees' narrative, but which they themselves cannot clarify (cf. Fischer-Rosenthal and

Rosenthal 1997b: 416f.). This is even more true of 'external' follow-up questions that arise primarily out of interviewers' decisions about relevance. They should be asked as near to the end of the interview as possible. The final section of the interview may be relatively brief and refer particularly to the evaluation of the interview and the interview situation. It may, however, be more extensive. Fritz Schütze, with regard to biographical-narrative interviews, speaks of a balancing section (cf. 1983). Here the interviewees are addressed more as experts and theoreticians, and are asked at an abstract level for generalizations and self-interpretations, in so far as these more abstract self-interpretations have occurred in the narrative section.

In general terms the form of the narrative interview is related to the idea that narratives are more strongly oriented to concrete action sequences and less to the ideologies and rationalizations of the interviewees. Interviewees who narrate freely may, in particular instances, reveal thoughts and memories that they would not and could not express in response to direct questioning. This is explained by means of the 'constraints' to narrate. With reference to this, Schütze makes particular mention of the principles of the compulsion for completion and the compulsion for detail (cf. 1977: 10; for an overview of these and other compulsions in narrating, cf. Kallmeyer and Schütze 1977: 188ff.).

3 SELECTED QUESTIONS ON THE CONDUCT OF QUALITATIVE INTERVIEWS

In the following section a number of problematic or contentious aspects of qualitative interviews will be discussed, although the presentation makes no claim to completeness (see **5.3**). Matters that will not be dealt with include questions of writing protocols (see **5.9**, **6.4**) and the question of extent to which the technical possibilities should be exhaustively applied in every case. Nor shall we discuss problems relating to the cooperation of two interviewers in a single interview, or the practical difficulties of finding interview partners. We shall focus rather on aspects of the planning and execution of qualitative interviews with respect to professional training (see **6.2**).

The ability to conduct qualitative interviews is generally viewed as an independent and relatively

unproblematic component in the qualifications of social scientists. There is almost certainly a relatively broad consensus that such interviews should only be conducted by interviewers who have official responsibilities within a given research project or who are at least sufficiently well-acquainted with the theoretical approach, the questions and the pilot studies to be capable of conducting interviews independently. One implication of this is that they must be capable of assessing when it is appropriate, in terms of content, to depart from the question guidelines, when it is essential to ask more intensive follow-up questions and when it is of particular significance, for the research interests of the project, to ask only very unspecific questions and to arrange for interviewees to have broad opportunities for self-expression.

In addition to the requirement for theoretical competence as to content, there are very few more precise ideas concerning the qualifications for interviewers in qualitative interviews. Some people insist on everyday competence, while others give the impression that competence problems resolve themselves in the course of the narrative (in this general direction, cf., for example, Hoffmann-Riem 1980: 357ff.). This, however, is not the case. In the first place there are also a number of badly conducted narratives, and in the second place not all sociological questions can be tackled by means of narrative techniques of data collection. In social research practice we are still advised to include semi-standardized interviews and to look for ways of improving the relevant interview practice.

Some time ago I criticized this interview practice on the basis of my own interview experience and that of colleagues (cf. Hopf 1978), and I believe that despite the growth in experience of qualitative research many of the problems and 'performance errors' I highlighted then are still to be found today. In part these are faults in planning: faulty assessments of the relationship between interested information sources and the available time. In many projects there are still problems with over-extensive guidelines and, in relation to this, a tendency towards a superficial ticking-off of questions ('Interview guide-bureaucracy').

The performance errors in qualitative interviews are partly connected, however, with shortcomings in training, and these could basically be removed by means of an improvement in training practice in universities and by intensifying the amount of consultancy and supervision within individual research projects. Here are some of the typical problems caused by faulty training and lack of experience, or 'beginners' errors', in carrying out qualitative interviews. They are due, at least in part, to fear of the unfamiliar situation of intensive communication with strangers.

- The tendency to a domineering communication style: the frequency of suggestive questions and suggestive guidelines and interpretations (on this cf. Richardson et al. 1965: 171–197), or the frequency of evaluative statements and comments, mostly intended to be supportive, but in practice distracting and sometimes disturbing.
- Problems with the passive-receptive aspects of interviewing: difficulties and lack of patience in listening and in picking up stimuli for supplementary questions.
- An inflexibility in dealing with an interview-guide that results from fear and uncertainty: the guide is called to mind in a strident fashion ('We had this question before', or 'That completes this section', and so on), it is used as an instrument of discipline ('If we can all be a little briefer, we can finish our questions today', and so on), or it can divert attention from interesting and non-anticipated aspects (cf. Merton and Kendall 1945/46).

It is certainly helpful to analyse and discuss these and similar communication problems and 'performance errors' in interviewing, either during training or later in the context of project-internal discussions, using the examples of concrete interview-protocols, even if this sometimes leads to discrepancies of assessment, as has happened with the assessment of a widely quoted and *verbatim* published interview with a distance-learner (cf. Heinze et al. 1980: part V). Oevermann et al. (1980: 18f.) express the opinion that in this interview 'more or less all the "rules of the art of unstructured interviewing" were broken by an inexperienced interviewer', whereas the publishers of the book containing this interview and a range of interview interpretations promote this interview as one of the more successful – and less schematic and strongly narrative – interviews in their study on the 'Life-world Analysis of Distance Learners' (Heinze et al. 1980: 7f.). In view of the theoretical complexity of the content and social aspects of interviewing it is not surprising that there are differences of assessment and evaluation. It is therefore vital to discuss these in relation to the text of individual interview passages, and this should always be part of the education and training of social scientists who conduct interviews in qualitative research projects.

FURTHER READING

Gubrium, J. F. and Holstein, J. (eds) (2001) *Handbook of Interviewing Research.* Thousand Oaks, CA: Sage.

Merton, R. K. and Kendall, P. L. (1945/46) 'The Focussed Interview', *American Journal of Sociology*, 51: 541–557.

Riemann, G. and Schütze, F. (1987) 'Trajectory as a Basic Theoretical Concept for Analyzing Suffering and Disorderly Social Processes', in D. Maines (ed.), *Social Organization and Social Process – Essays in Honor of Anselm Strauss.* New York: Aldine de Gruyter. pp. 333–357.

5.3 Interviewing as an Activity

Harry Hermanns

The basic principles of the technique of interviewing have often been described (see **5.2**). Here our principal focus will be on the activity of the interviewer in the creation of a social interaction ('How it is done'). 'Every interview (besides being an information-gathering occasion) is an interpersonal drama with a developing plot' (de Sola Pool 1957: 193, cited from Holstein and Gubrium 1995: 14). This impromptu-drama is actively produced by both participants, although the interviewer also has a special task of shaping it. This will be examined more closely here.

1 THE SHAPING OF THE 'INTERVIEW-DRAMA': TASKS, FEARS, PITFALLS

In an interview specific *tasks* must be carried out. In the first place the interviewees have to be found and the place, time and theme of the interview must be fixed; a productive atmosphere for the conversation must be created and agreement obtained to the use of a recorder. It must be explained to the interview partner in what capacity he or she will be addressed, and the task to be achieved in the interview and the expectation of the interviewer must be clarified. Finally, the interview must be carried out methodically and the encounter concluded at a particular point. The demands on the creation

of the 'interpersonal drama' of an interview are therefore manifold, and there are many possible pitfalls.

Particularly for beginners who dare to take on this medium, the activity of the interviewer may be seen as a sequence of tasks that can bring about uncertainties in the interviewer. These uncertainties are related first to the *dilemma of vagueness*: on the one hand the recommendations for the conduct of interviews are often extremely vague, but on the other hand there is a requirement that the interview should make a significant contribution to the research question. A second difficulty may be characterized as the *fairness dilemma*: the task and the interviewer's interest in learning, in terms of content, as much and as many personal details as possible from the interviewee must be set against the interviewee's need for respectful treatment. Finally, from the interviewer's point of view, a *dilemma of self-presentation* may arise: in order to carry out an interview well, the interviewer must refrain from appearing to be as wise and omniscient as he or she believes him- or herself to be.

2 THE 'DRAMA' IS PREPARED

The approach to the field (see **5.1**) by key persons and the choice of interview partners is comprehensively described in the methodological literature (cf. Flick 2002: ch. 6). One aspect that needs to be pointed out, especially to beginners in the business of interviewing, is how to approach *arrangements about the setting* for the interview. Particularly if, in a particular field, interview subjects are hard to find, beginners are inclined to leave the arrangements as vague as possible so as not to turn anyone down. This leads to a set of unfavourable conditions, because, for example, the subjects are short of time and the interviewer comes under pressure of time in the course of the conversation.

A further factor that interviewers often forget to use in a satisfactory way is the recording equipment, that is, the audio- or video-recorder. Taking the example of the recorder, we may clearly present a central problem: the obligation on the interviewer to *stage* the interview.

For inexperienced interviewers the recorder is a problem from many points of view. Such interviewers often dislike hearing their own voice on tape because they are afraid of sounding unprofessional. This fear on the part of the interviewer is often transferred to the interview partner, who is assumed to have some objections to being recorded. The interviewer then asks whether he or she may use a recorder, but in such a way that a refusal to be recorded is anticipated:

> 'I've brought a recorder, one of these cassette-recorders with me, but if you have any objection, I mean, I could understand, you know if you'd rather not, I mean …'

Another way of coping with one's own fear of the recorder is that the interviewer only switches on the machine at the moment when the interviewee is about to talk. This means that not only is the right to speak transferred to the interviewee, but also this person alone is given the task, in the interview-drama, of coping with the 'fear of the recorder', which can result in contributions that are inhibited or reserved. It is therefore the duty of the interviewer to accept responsibility, in the interview-drama, for *managing the feeling* of 'recorder-discomfort', by demonstrating – with the machine running – that, irrespective of the fact that a recording is being made, it is possible to speak in a relaxed and open way, with all the imperfections of the spoken language (cf. Hochschild 1992). This has a rather more convincing effect on the interviewee than if the interviewer – in brief and abrupt terms – urges the interviewee to be 'explicit'. It is the responsibility of the interviewer not only to give the interviewee a clear

task resulting from the particular method used in the interview, but also to create a *climate for conversation* in which the desired mode of presentation is already part of the 'atmosphere'.

3 THE 'DRAMA' CREATES ITS PERFORMERS

'The first minutes of an interview are decisive. The subjects will want to have a grasp of the interviewer before they allow themselves to talk freely, exposing their experiences and feelings to a stranger' (Kvale 1996: 128). In the first few minutes the interviewer has to create a situation that is so relaxed and open that the people in it can lay bare, without fear, a great variety of aspects of their personality and their life-world. The interviewer's main task in the opening minutes of an interview is to *set the stage* so the people involved can find their roles.

But who is the interviewee for the interviewer and how should he or she be addressed? As a resident in a home? As a member of a particular age group? As a man/woman? And does the interviewer represent to the subject someone from the area of social work, who can perhaps have some influence on living conditions? Someone who 'knows Sister Eva well'? Or a young person who, in any case, knows nothing about being old?

The interviewer must take account of these attributions and cultivate a sense of what aspects of the interviewee are addressed by the interviewer's contributions, and in what role, capacity and function he or she is encountering the subject. The interviewer must also create space for the subject to reveal different aspects of personality: a subject must be able to show herself as a refined elderly lady, but also as a cunning old woman trying to avoid being committed to a home. Such changes of role must be made possible interactively in the impromptu-drama of the interview, often prompted merely by small remarks or gestures. A male interviewer can show a female subject that he understands her perspective as a woman, an older, well-dressed interviewer can show a young person that he can imagine himself in that person's youthful crazes. This requirement that the interviewer shows understanding conceals many dangers. As an interviewer one must keep the correct balance in all of this: be interested and attentive, understand, show respect and at the same time avoid giving oneself away by reacting personally to the interview-content ('I used to be like that'), because this constitutes the offer of an 'alliance', which in some sense binds the interviewee.

One essential skill of the interviewer consists of *understanding roles*, of understanding 'as who' he or she is being seen, and 'as who' the counterpart is acting and speaking. A second skill consists of making it possible for the subject to *take on other roles*: the progression of the action must be so 'stage managed' that the interviewee is really able to be sincere in the aspect of self-presentation (cf. Legewie 1987: 141) and to show other aspects of his or her personality and life-world. This stage managing is often achieved by the interviewer 'proving', through a follow-up question, that he or she can really identify with the perspective of the subject and is truly in a position to 'accept the truth as presented'.

While the subject is speaking the interviewer has two tasks to cope with which often seem to be contradictory. The *dual role* of the interviewer may be characterized thus: on the one hand the interviewer shows *empathy* by attempting to become part of the interviewee's presentation, in order to understand how he or she perceives and interprets the world. At the same time, however, the interviewer must develop a different approach to the subject which shows that, although the words are heard, the interviewer is uncertain of the meaning horizon of the terms for the interviewee. The interviewer does not know what are the given pre-conditions which the interviewee relates to the terms used, and must remain aware of the *alien* nature of the interviewee's presentation. The interviewer must project an attitude of *deliberate naiveté* (Kvale 1996: 33) and ask the subject about his or her view of things which the interviewer 'actually' knows. At the same time the interviewer must also project in to the conversation an impression of listening in an interested and relaxed manner.

4   THE DEVELOPMENT OF THE 'DRAMA': AN OBSTACLE COURSE

It has been said that interviewers should be empathetic and this very feature can be the source of a wide range of problems. Interviewers frequently have an intuitive idea of what points in a conversation will be problematic for the subject and would like to offer some protection. This *protective behaviour* may have a variety of causes. In what follows we shall examine two of these: the *fear of embarrassments* in the course of the conversation, and the *fear of injuring intimacy* or of *personality crises*.

Both the course of the interaction and also the facts presented may be a cause of embarrassment. During an interaction silence is often experienced as embarrassing (for a discussion cf. especially Gubrium and Holstein 1997: 127ff., and Lueger and Schmitz 1984: 103ff.). If the *silence* follows a turn handover on the part of the interviewer, then interviewers generally interpret a 'non-response' as a defect in their question and often tend to correct or complete the lack of clarity in their speech which they suppose to be there. For the interviewee, however, silence after a transfer of turn can have a very different meaning: it is to focus his or her thoughts, or else it is a piece of 'dramatic staging'.

Another type of embarrassment that may be experienced by an interviewer is to do with *embarrassment at the content of the presentation* on the past of the interviewees. This may consist of breaches of morality and convention, their own incompetence, some disgrace, matters they find disgusting or terminal illnesses. But interviewers often also engage in protective behaviour if follow-up questions would bring about some *injury to the image of the subject*, for example by casting doubt on the self-image that the interviewee has developed. Protective behaviour is also shown when the interviewer has entered into an *open* or *secret alliance* with the interviewee (such as a bond of solidarity in face of a common enemy), and this could also be endangered by more detailed follow-up questioning.

A further reason for protective behaviour may be the fear that an interviewee would be over-exposed or that if the interviewer pursues the questioning it could even lead to a *personal crisis*. This fear is found particularly in the case of subjects who have personal problems. But even with people who abandon themselves completely to the dynamics of the interview, without wishing to, the interviewer may justifiably be afraid of infringing the *limits of intimacy*, and counter this by interrupting the interviewee and embarking on a different topic.

This behaviour on the part of the interviewer seems at first glance to be very responsible. There is, however, another factor that plays a role in this, and that is the *relationship of the interviewer to his or her own interview activity.* With interviews that probe deeply into the personal experience of the interviewee, one may broadly distinguish two types of attitude on the part of the interviewer towards the activity of interviewing. The first attitude may be described as a *feeling of exploitation.* This is characterized by a latent guilty conscience: for one's own personal benefit (a thesis, dissertation or research project) one is asking someone to reveal intimate matters to a stranger. The interviewer is afraid of using too much pressure, of coming too close to the interviewee, of shamelessly exploiting this person's friendly agreement to be of assistance. The second attitude derives from the idea that there is a fortunate coincidence of two different facts: the benevolent curiosity of the interviewer and the pleasant feeling the interviewee has when he or she can fully explain a personal view of the world in the course of an interesting conversation. This attitude could be called a *feeling of happy coincidence.* The interviewer has an experience of being someone who is able to offer an enriching experience to another person that is otherwise rarely found. The interviewer is making a present: he or she is showing interest – often for hours at a time – in the other person, and is a good listener. It is evident that an interviewer who inclines to the first attitude (fear of exploitation) is at much greater risk of engaging in protective behaviour than an interviewer of the second type. The problem of being protective, therefore, is not only, and perhaps not even mainly, a problem of the subject but rather of the interviewer: frequently an interviewer is protecting not the interviewee but him- or herself. An interviewer relates not only to the interviewee or the required research results, but to his or her own person.

This also becomes clear when interviewers have to interview members of a group to which they themselves belong. In this case there may be problems of putting themselves into the *role of an outsider.* For example, if students in social work interview social workers, then the subjects will assume that they are dealing with colleagues who are familiar with the world of social work. Situations such as these are problematic for the interviewer, because if he or she asks for clarification of some facts that are taken for granted in social work, then that interviewer will no longer count as a group member. An interviewer who is also a student of social work and who asks a social worker, in the course of an

interview, what he or she means by 'street-work' or 'relationship-work', is liable to be suspected of being professionally incompetent. This dilemma between the interviewer's self-presentation and the requirements of the interview often leads to a situation where interviewers engage in protective behaviour towards themselves, and dispense with follow-up questions that are necessary to reveal the life-world and knowledge of the interviewee, in order to prevent damage to their own personal image in the course of the interview.

An interview is therefore truly a drama, the production of which contains many pitfalls, and which requires social skills of its participants – and not merely the interviewer's ability to ask clever questions.

5 STAGE DIRECTIONS FOR CONDUCTING INTERVIEWS

1 Explain the framework to your subject in good time. In a 'briefing', the following points have to be made clear:

- What is the issue (what they will be talking about and why, what the information will be used for, what is behind it).
- How it will be done (who will conduct the interview, who should or can be present during the interview, where it will take place, how long it will last).

2 Create a good atmosphere in the interview:

- Be relaxed (or at least give that impression), and radiate this feeling, even when you switch on the recorder.
- Try to understand the 'message' of your counterpart: he or she is communicating more than pure 'information'.

3 Give your counterpart room to open up:

- Do not attempt to explain your own position, and especially not your agreement with your counterpart ('I'm like that too!'). You should retain an 'independent' interest, whatever the counterpart says.
- Give your subject the possibility of displaying a range of personality traits (the hero should be able to express his helplessness, and the philanthropist his capacity for hatred).

- Do not protect your subject from something that could be embarrassing, but show, through your own attitude, that you are capable of getting at the truth.

4 Give the 'drama' an opportunity to develop:

- Ask short and easily intelligible questions that may stimulate your counterpart to give more detail.
- Research questions are not the same as interview questions: do not ask for theoretical categories ('What kind of motivation influenced your choice of study?'), but ask for concrete facts from your counterpart's life-world.
- Speak your own language, and do not imitate the language of the environment. But use the concrete names and terms that your counterpart uses. If her boyfriend is called Paul, then refer to Paul, rather than to 'your relationship'.

5 In the interview do not attempt to discover theoretical ideas but the life-world of your counterpart:

- Be naive. Let the subject explain concepts, procedures, situations. Do not feel guilty if you ask about things that seem obvious: 'What is street-work?' 'What do you mean by problems in a relationship?' 'What happened?'
- Try, through the interview, to understand your counterpart's life-world so well that you could write a film-script for scenes from this world and could direct a production. Keep the questions going until it is clear to you what happens or happened there.

FURTHER READING

Gubrium, J. F. and Holstein, J. A. (1997) *The New Language of Qualitative Method*. New York: Oxford University Press.

Holstein, J. A. and Gubrium, J. F. (1995) *The Active Interview* (Qualitative Research Methods Series 37). Thousand Oaks, CA: Sage.

Kvale, S. (1996) *InterViews. An Introduction to Qualitative Research Interviewing*. Thousand Oaks, CA: Sage.

5.4   Group Discussion and Focus Groups

Ralf Bohnsack

The changing history of the group discussion procedure is closely linked, in general terms, to the phases in the modern development of (qualitative) empirical research. For instance, the first large-scale investigation of political awareness in post-war Germany, at the beginning of the 1950s, was based essentially on group discussion. More recently, in both Germany and the English-speaking world, there has been a lively interest in this method, which has resulted in a variety of research practices. Admittedly, however, it still has to be tested very precisely to determine whether such procedures can meet the quality criteria of empirical social research.

If procedures in empirical social research are to merit the name 'method' they need to be anchored and justified in sociological traditions with their various theoretical models and conceptualizations. In what follows we shall first identify these kinds of theoretical model for the group discussion procedure.

of the individual isolation of interviewees in questionnaire research. At the Frankfurt Institute of Social Research, under the direction of Horkheimer and Adorno, an attempt was made to reproduce the *public* conversational situation of a meeting of strangers (for example, in a railway compartment) that were considered typical for the discussion of political questions. For 'deeper' or 'latent' opinions only 'become clear, if the individual – for instance in a conversation – feels himself compelled to state and emphasize his viewpoint' (Pollock 1955: 34). In the psychoanalytically coloured type of empiricism found in the Frankfurt School the aim was to look behind 'defence mechanisms and rationalizations'. Regardless of the criticism of the isolation of individual opinions in questionnaire research, in the (quantitative) empirical analysis the individual speech turns were none the less analysed in isolation from one another.

1   THE MODEL OF THE INDIVIDUAL IN PUBLIC DEBATE

When the group discussion procedure first began to develop in Germany there was criticism

2   THE MODEL OF INFORMAL GROUP OPINION

This very problem was taken up by Werner Mangold (1960) in a dissertation he wrote at the same institute in the course of a re-analysis of available material. Unlike the earlier focus on individual opinion, he developed the concept of 'group opinion'. This was 'not a "sum" of individual opinions but the product of collective interactions' (1960: 49). These group opinions – and this is the other decisive change that Mangold brought about in the methodology – are not first produced in the discussion situation, but only *actualized* there. 'In reality they have already been formed among the members of the particular collective' (1973: 240). These 'collectives', in Mangold's understanding, should be considered as 'large groups', or – one might also say – as milieux (for example, of miners or farmers, or even refugees).

Mangold recognized the *empirical* evidence of a collective as that of a voluntary or even euphoric integration of the individual into the discourse that develops through mutual reference. In contrast, the *theoretical* concept of group opinions is based on the (still prevalent) understanding of a collective in terms of the '*faits sociaux*', in Durkheim's sense, that are external to the actors and vested with power, as Horkheimer and Adorno suggested in their foreword to Mangold's study (1960: 7). This incompatibility of empirical evidence and theoretical framework was one of the major causes of the difficulty in accepting Mangold's work in the following stage of theoretical modelling of the concept of group discussion.

3 THE MODEL OF THE INTERPRETATIVE NEGOTIATION OF MEANINGS

Under the influence of the increasing significance of the 'interpretative paradigm' (cf. Wilson 1970), the interactional dependency and the process character of opinions and meaning patterns was recognized, and methods were sought that were capable of taking account of this paradigm in some valid way. However, as is often the case with the interpretative paradigm – that is, interpretative sociology in the tradition of symbolic interactionism (see **3.3**) and phenomenology (see **3.1**) – it now seemed difficult still to find structures in what are essentially processes. The process character of interactions and conversations was reduced to the single aspect of local and situational negotiation, that is, to the *emergence* of meanings. On the basis of

practical research with group discussions Nießen (1977: 67ff.), in view of the constantly changing processes of negotiation, came to the conclusion 'that the assumptions made, on the basis of discussion results, about action in a real situation are not accurate'. For these reasons Volmerg called into question the validity of the procedure: 'if, as a consequence of the use of the "group discussion" research tool, opinions are changed or only then formed, the results are in principle not replicable' (1977: 205). The *replicability* of results, however, is an essential precondition for the reliability of any method. This implies that the group discussion method will only meet the exactitude criteria of empirical research if the same opinions or orientations within a group can be observed in a different research situation. This is also one of the main methodological problems in the present-day debate about *focus groups* within the Anglo-Saxon debate. In their overview article, Lunt and Livingstone deal with the accusation of a lack of 'test–retest reliability': 'Focus groups are unreliable because different conversations would occur if groups were repeated' (1996: 92).

4 FOCUS GROUPS AND GROUP DISCUSSIONS: ON THE ANGLO-SAXON DEBATE

In the Anglo-Saxon debate there are two different strands or traditions in the use of group discussions. Only one of these two strands is closely linked to the term 'focus group'. This was first coined by Merton et al. (1956; cf. also Merton 1987) in the course of developing a new procedure for research on the reception of propaganda broadcasts during the Second World War. Later use of focus groups in market research largely followed Merton's view, according to which this procedure only seems appropriate for the generation of new research questions and hypotheses and for pre-tests. The groups are set up by the investigators by random selection among participants who are not known to one another.

In examining this practice in market research Morgan (1988) and Krueger (1988) in particular attempted to make the procedure useful for sociological research and to enhance its status. Because, however, there was no comprehensive methodological foundation, the procedure was and continues to be essentially limited to the generation of hypotheses (cf. Morgan 1988: 11, 21); and to Morgan and Krueger (1993: 9) it seems less suited to the production of *generalizable* results. In the work of Morgan and Krueger, and in that of their followers, more 'rules of thumb' (particularly in relation to interview techniques) than methodological or theoretical bases (cf. Lunt and Livingstone 1996: 82) are provided. What is missing, therefore, is a general theoretical base, and only this could make it possible to cope with the problems of validity and reliability.[1] Above all, however, the conversational nature of this kind of data production was not considered, and this was Kitzinger's criticism in a survey of 40 published studies using focus groups: 'I could not find a single one concentrating on the conversation between the participants' (1994: 104).

In her survey Kitzinger does not examine the second, quite different, Anglo-Saxon strand in the development of the group discussion procedure, which has its roots in the Birmingham Centre for Contemporary Cultural Studies – on the one hand in Paul Willis's analysis of youth styles (see 2.4), and on the other hand in David Morley's analysis of the use and reception of the media. The groundbreaking work of Willis (1977) in style and milieu analysis is, like his later work (1978, 1990), essentially based on group discussions: 'the basic method we've used to get inside the words and to spell them out has been a loose and general form of ethnography utilizing, in particular, the recorded group discussion' (Willis 1990; see 2.4).

Admittedly Willis was not particularly interested in a methodological reconstruction of the group discussion procedure. Even the fundamental theoretical importance of his work was only made explicit in the subsequent re-analysis – particularly that of Giddens (1984) with reference to the category of 'practical consciousness'.

Morley (1980, 1992, 1996) deals more fully with the methodological foundation of group discussion, the significance of which he places at two levels: in the first place account should be taken of the process nature and the interactive character of sense attribution and the constitution of meaning in the course of media reception. Accordingly, 'the basic units for an analysis of utilization behaviour should be (a) interactions rather than individual action and (b) interactions in their social context' (1996: 41). In the second place, Morley – like Willis – views discussion

groups as *representative* of broader (macro-social) entities, particularly 'classes'. Discussion groups are made up homogeneously according to demographic criteria (profession, education, age), but were not in fact really existing groups. They represent class and milieu-specific 'discursive formations' whose structural expression is the 'interpretative codes' (1996: 112ff.): they are therefore homologous patterns for milieu-specific sense attributions and orientations (see below). Such 'codes' are not initially produced in the discussion groups; they do not *emerge* in situations. It is rather that they are *represented* and updated in discourse, and thereby constantly *re*produced, for as long as those people come together who belong to the same milieu or the same 'interpretative community' (on this cf. the critical discussion with Morley in Schröder 1994). This model is not therefore one of *emergence*, as in the interpretative paradigm, but one of *representation* (cf. also Loos and Schäffer 2000). In this way it is possible to provide a methodological foundation for the replicability of results and thereby also the reliability of the method.

The empirical procedures for the analysis of such 'codes' or deeper meaning patterns have only been approximately worked out in the methodology of *cultural studies* (see 3.9). Broader possibilities were only opened up by more recent procedures for text interpretation which transcend the 'literal' meaning of single utterances, and advance to those deeper collective orientation-structures or *orientation-patterns* (cf. Bohnsack 1998a for discussion of this term) that are only manifested in the interplay of single utterances.

5 THE MODEL OF COLLECTIVE ORIENTATION PATTERNS

Discourses often seem disconnected or relatively random in their sequencing, which means *without structure* and therefore also *non-reproducible* if we only look at what is 'literally' communicated in the individual speech turns, or their *immanent meaning*, as Karl Mannheim (1982) called it. We may illustrate this with an example from a research project on youth migrants of Turkish origin (cf. Bohnsack and Nohl 1998):

Stimulated by a question from the discussion leader as to whether they currently live with their parents, the (male) young people first embark on a range of stories in which they explain that because of 'respect' for their father it is impossible to smoke in his presence. They next describe, supplementing each other's account, how they deal with one another in the male peer-group. Finally one of them describes the situation of a visit to a restaurant with his German girlfriend. There are differences of opinion with her as to who is allowed to pay.

Although the topics diverge from those given by the discussion leader and apparently jump about, the young people evidently *understand* one another, without themselves actually '*interpreting*' the leader's request, which means being conceptually or theoretically explicit about the pattern of orientation that underlies the passage, or being able themselves to define it 'literally'. Their orientation structure is unveiled rather in descriptions and narratives, that is, *metaphorically*. When the researcher interprets the orientation structure on behalf of the informants, he or she is carrying out what Mannheim (1952a; see also Bohnsack 1997, 1999) has called *documentary interpretation*, that is, the conceptual and theoretical explication of the subjects' mutual (intuitive) understanding (cf. also the term 'practical consciousness' in Giddens 1984).

Seen in this way, beyond the apparently rather disjointed discourse process, there opens up a collective meaning pattern that is common to all the individual turns (narratives, descriptions): in the example cited above what is at issue is a *separation of spheres* that is relevant to the young people's everyday practice. Because the convention of respect towards one's father and family of origin requires that essential areas of the *outer sphere* (that is, actions of young people in public and in social institutions) should be kept out of the *inner sphere* (family, relatives and ethnic group) in a controlled fashion, there comes about a strict separation of spheres that does not permit any 'open' dealing with parents about problems of young people relevant to their identity. Both spheres, with their different moral codes (the 'German' and the 'Turkish'), exist without interconnection. This is also true of the relationship with the German girlfriend. In case of conflict between the two moral codes there is not a (meta-) communicative negotiation of the problem but rather a strategic circumvention. As is also shown in the descriptions that the young

people then include in the passage about their peer-group, no mediation between the spheres is achieved there either, which was not the case in other groups that we investigated. The peer-group orients itself according to the conventional (that is, inner sphere) mode of relationships between young men. In other passages from the same group discussion (for example, in those where young people report their experiences of ethnic discrimination) the orientation structure or pattern is expressed, in homologous fashion, with a strict drawing of boundaries between the two spheres: the orientation structure is therefore *reproduced* here.

Since the passage cited here is characterized by a relatively detailed representation ('metaphorical density') and by a relatively involved relationship between the parties ('interactive density'), we may suppose that a well-focused problem of orientation is being voiced here. In passages such as this we refer to *focusing metaphors*.

In this example a number of central components of the *documentary interpretation of collective orientation patterns* are addressed.

- The documentary meaning content must be distinguished from the inherent literal meaning.
- The documentary meaning content is only revealed if account is taken of the discourse process.
- This kind of *process analysis* presupposes, on the one hand, a very precise *reconstruction* that can be made of the way the individual speech turns relate to one another ('discourse organization').
- On the other hand, process analysis means taking account of the *dramaturgy* of the discourse, its high points – that is, identifying the focusing metaphors.

6 VALIDITY AND RELIABILITY: STANDARDIZED, OPEN AND RECONSTRUCTIVE PROCEDURES

Against this background the problem of *replicability of results*, or of orientation structures, takes on a new meaning: they are *process structures* that are reproduced in the discourse process in a homologous fashion, in relative independence of the specific topics. What is constantly reproduced in the course of a discourse is now recognized as constituting the 'structure of the case'. In the sense of reconstructive methodology researchers have to create the right conditions to make it possible for the structure of the case to unfold according to its own typical rules. Unlike *standardized* procedures, where replicability of results and therefore also their reliability – by analogy with experiments in the natural sciences – have to be guaranteed by the researcher's standardization of the sequencing of the procedure, *reconstructive* procedures are based on the structures or – rather casually expressed – 'standards' of everyday communication, on 'natural standards and routines of communication' (Soeffner and Hitzler 1994a: 41). In contrast, *open* procedures (for example, in both Nießen and Volmerg, see above) dispense with any standardization or structuring on the part of the investigator, and cannot achieve any systematic structuring by the informants themselves through process structures and 'everyday methods'.

7 COMMUNICATIVE AND CONJUNCTIVE EXPERIENCE

According to the 'interpretative paradigm', sociality is 'produced' as 'intersubjectivity' by subjects who mutually interpret one another. Ethnomethodology (Garfinkel 1961; see **3.2**) and Habermas's theory of communicative action also proceed on the basis of this kind of model of constant mutual interpretation.

From this we must distinguish another, more fundamental type of sociality, where participants in discourse are connected to one another by 'understanding each other through the medium of what is obvious' (Gurwitsch 1976: 178). This is based on what is shared in their action practice, in their biographical experience, their destiny, or – in general terms – their socialization history. If this form of sociality as 'belonging' (Gurwitsch) remains largely bound up with a direct experience of living together in concrete *groups*, Mannheim (1982) is able to separate analytically the form of collectivity that he calls 'conjunctive space of experience' from the concept of the group. Mannheim (1952b) developed this using the example of the 'generational connection' as a conjunctive experiential space. Those who are bound to one another through a common, generation-specific stratification of experience, and therefore belong to the same generation, are in most cases not in direct

communication with one another. Of course, mutual experience will be most comprehensively *articulated* when those who share it are in one another's presence. The group, then, is not the social location of the *genesis* and *emergence of experience*, but is the *articulation* and *representation* of a generation-specific or, in more general terms, a collective stratification of experience.

Here it must be clarified in an individual case what collective or milieu-specific shared features of the stratification of experience are represented in the discourse or group, and on the basis of what common features it has constituted itself. We therefore make distinctions, in analysing group discussions, between different experiential spaces or milieux, in particular those that are specific to generations, genders or education (cf. Bohnsack 1989), which are described as *types* (see below). Although the group thereby becomes merely an 'epi-phenomenon' for the analysis of different experiential spaces, it gives a valid empirical access to the articulation of collective meaning-contexts. These are articulated in 'ceremonial' or *habitualized* – in the sense of repeatedly reproduced and basically mimetically appropriate – action practices.

The primordial meaning of this social process in its *process-structure* is the subject of sociogenetic or documentary interpretation. This method seeks to analyse meaning structures beyond the literal or referential meaning-content, but also beyond the communicative intentions of the interlocutors (cf. Bohnsack 1992, 1997). In this there are differences from, but also points of agreement with, socio-linguistic conversation analysis (cf. Bohnsack 1999: 72ff.).

8 SOCIO-LINGUISTIC CONVERSATION ANALYSIS AND THE RECONSTRUCTION OF COLLECTIVE ORIENTATIONS

John Gumperz and Jenny Cook-Gumperz, in work of great significance for socio-linguistic conversation analysis, distinguish two basic levels of meaning: one of literal or 'referential' meaning, and the other that can only be uncovered by 'interpretation' (cf. Gumperz 1982: 207). Interpretation, in Gumperz's sense, on the one hand targets the communicative *intent* of the individual speakers. On the other hand, Gumperz points out that 'what is to be interpreted must first be created through interaction, before interpretation can begin' (1982: 206).

The emphasis on the interactive and cooperative nature of the meaning-content, which is the object of interpretations, has a close relationship with the category of the communicative intent of a particular speaker. The empirical studies conducted by Gumperz and Cook-Gumperz look not only at the individual and intentional self-representations, as was the case with Goffman (1974; see **2.2**), but also – and predominantly – at the collective identities. The communicative styles which they investigated, especially the 'contextualization cues', have the function of signalling and negotiating not only individual self-presentations but also membership of groups, collectives or milieux. Particularly in the area of identifying ethnic group membership, Gumperz and Cook-Gumperz observed 'participants probe for common experiences or some evidence of shared perception … . The ability to establish a common rhythm is a function, among other factors, of similarity of ethnic background' (1981: 436). In this kind of 'common rhythm' or 'frame attunement' (Gumperz 1992: 42) there is represented, to use the words of Mannheim (1982), a shared or 'conjunctive' space of experience.

The nature of the interactive reference in which a collective meaning-pattern is constituted is also reconstructed, in our own analyses, in its *formal structure*. We then refer to *discourse organization* (see **5.19**). This depends, at least in part, on whether one is dealing with *shared* or merely *structurally identical* experience, or whether there is no context of shared experience, and therefore no 'group'. The momentum initiated and encouraged by the discussion leader makes it possible to home in on *centres* of experience where the focus of collective orientations can be found. The representations that unfold in this kind of augmented metaphorical and interactive density may be described as *focusing metaphors*. This dramaturgy, together with the formal discourse organization and the descriptions and narratives that permeate it, is reconstructed sequentially, in a more exact textual interpretation, according to the two interpretative stages of 'formulating' and 'reflective interpretation'.

9 REFLEXIVE PRINCIPLES FOR THE CONDUCT OF GROUP DISCUSSIONS

In conducting group discussions, as with all reconstructive procedures, a basic methodological principle is followed, according to which the investigator must create the right conditions for the particular case – that is, the group – to unfold its *own structural identity* as part of a process. This implies, above all, giving a discourse the opportunity of focusing on those experience centres that represent the focused experiential basis for the group's collective orientation framework. In this way the group can determine its own topics. However, a (thematic) comparability of discourses – as a precondition for a comparative analysis – requires a certain degree of standardization, at least in the opening questions. Initially, follow-up questions are only permitted if the discourse grinds to a halt and they are used primarily to re-establish the momentum. Only in a later stage will themes that have not occurred be initiated by an outsider. What is also revealing for an analysis is what does *not* belong to the focused centres of experience, what topics or areas of experience are alien or avoided and why.

On the basis of a reconstruction of the author's personal research practice, the following principles for the conduct of group discussions may be proposed.

1 *The entire group is the addressee of interventions*. The interventions and questions of the discussion leader are addressed not to individuals but to the whole group. This is to avoid the researchers exerting any direct influence on the distribution of turns.

2 *Suggestion of topics, rather than prescription of propositions*. The opening questions and the follow-up questions of the leader are only to initiate topics, not to prescribe propositions,[2] which means that there should be avoidance of any prescription as to how, in what direction or within what framework of orientation the topic should be handled.

3 *Demonstrative vagueness*. The questioning on the part of the discussion leader is deliberately and 'demonstratively' kept vague. In this way a (milieu-specific) alienness and ignorance is shown, which corresponds to the basic methodological requirement for alienness in the sociology of knowledge, phenomenological sociology and ethnography (see **3.8**, **5.5**). This shows respect for the system of relevance and the experiential world of the subjects; at the same time, these factors become responsible for alleviating the ignorance of the investigator by means

of thorough and detailed representations (cf. also principle 5 below). This demonstration of vagueness, together with the generation of detailed representations, may be achieved by 'imprecise' or open questions, but also by the *sequencing of questions* (for example, 'How was it then with the change from school to work? How was it for you at that time?'). The author's experience with sequencing of questions corresponds to observations that have been made within the framework of conversation analysis (cf. Sacks 1992: 561, and Bergmann 1981a: 133ff.; see **5.17**).

4 *No intervention in the allocation of turns.* Ideally follow-up questions only happen after group members have not noticed an opportunity to take over a 'turn'. In the sense of conversation analysis (cf. Sacks et al. 1974: 25ff.), this means that a follow-up question should only occur when a 'lapse' in the discourse has been reached – rather than a 'gap' or 'pause'. The investigators, therefore, do not observe their rights as participants within the 'turn-taking system' and *demonstrate* that they have no intention of so doing. They do not take on, therefore, the function of participants in an everyday conversation, nor that of discussion leader in meetings – that of 'moderator', which would also include the allocation of turns. The reticence required of the leader in a group discussion must give the participants, on the one hand, the opportunity of concluding a topic and, on the other hand, that of organizing for themselves the distribution and allocation of turns.

5 *Generation of detailed representations.* The questions and follow-up questions should be framed in such a way that they are capable of generating detailed descriptions or narratives. With detailed representations it should be possible to access the (reconstructed) action practice and the *modus operandi* that underlies it – the (collective) habitus. This is achieved, in the first place, by asking for direct or explicit 'narratives' or 'descriptions' and/or 'experiences' (for example, 'Could you just tell or describe what happened to you when …?'). But the generation of detailed representations may also be achieved by *sequencing of questions* (cf. the remarks under principle 3), which may simultaneously also be used to show vagueness.

6 *Inherent follow-up questions.* Inherent follow-up questions, which are directed at a given topic and a given framework of orientation, have priority over 'exherent' questions, which aim at initiating *new* topics.

7 *The phase of exherent follow-up questions.* Once the dramatic high point of the discussion has (in the intuitive opinion of the leader) been passed and the topics most important to the group itself (the focusing metaphors) have been worked over, the topics that are most relevant to the researchers, and which have so far not been treated, are introduced by exherent questioning. For this purpose, a list of topical focuses for follow-up questions should have been drawn up in advance in accordance with the epistemological interest of the project and the desired formation of types (see section 10). Principle 6 above is therefore now put out of action, but all other principles remain valid.

8 *The directive phase.* Towards the end of the discussion the fieldworkers refer back to those sequences in the discourse which – in terms of their intuitive impression – seemed to be contradictory or striking in some other way. By relating inherently to these sequences, these contradictions and other striking features are made topical. In this process principles 2 and 3 become invalid, while all others continue to operate.

10 FORMULATING INTERPRETATION, REFLECTING INTERPRETATION, FORMATION OF TYPES

The distinctive methodological characteristic of the author's own analytical procedure (Bohnsack 1989; Bohnsack et al. 1995) is that of *inherent* as opposed to *documentary* meaning content (cf. Mannheim 1952a). This corresponds to Luhmann's (1990b) distinction between 'cybernetics of the first and the second order' (cf. also Bohnsack 1999: 207ff.). It is important to distinguish *what* is said, reported or discussed, that is, what becomes a *topic*, from what is *documented* about the group in what is said. This is the question of *how* the topic is treated, which means in what *framework*. In this process, *comparative analysis* (cf. Glaser and Strauss 1967) takes on a fundamental significance from the outset, so long as the orientation framework is only extracted from it in a clear and *empirically verifiable* way through comparison with other groups (how is the same topic or problem dealt with in other groups?).

The basic structure of *formulating interpretation* is the thematic composition, that is, the thematization of themes, the decoding of the normally implicit thematic structure of texts.

Reflecting interpretation aims at the reconstruction of the orientation pattern or framework. Its basic tool is the reconstruction of the formal structure of texts (beyond that of their thematic structure). In the case of group discussion this means reconstructing the *discourse organization*, that is, the manner in which the participants relate to each other.

In the *formation of types*, on the basis of *common features* of cases (for example, experience common to all students from the education milieu of dealing with the everyday world of work), specific contrasts typical of a particular milieu for coping with these experiences are worked out (for example, between musical groups and hooligans; cf. Bohnsack et al. 1995). The *contrast in common features* is a basic principle of the generation of individual types and also of the structure that holds a whole typology together. The unambiguity of a type depends on the extent to which it can be distinguished from all other possible types. The formation of types is the more valid the more clearly other types can also be demonstrated with reference to a particular case, and the more fully a type can be fixed within a typology.

NOTES

1 This is also true, in the main, of Lamnek's (1998) monograph entitled *Gruppendiskussion* (group discussion), which otherwise relies essentially on the work of Morgan and Krueger.

2 I use the term 'proposition' to relate to the work of Harold Garfinkel (1961). In Garfinkel's sense propositions, that is, ideas or realizations of orientations and attitudes, are implicit in everyday representations and 'descriptions'.

FURTHER READING

Bloor, M., Frankland, J., Thomas, M. and Robson, K. (2000) *Focus Groups in Social Research*. London: Sage.

Kitzinger, J. (1994) 'The Methodology of Focus Groups – The Importance of Interaction between Research Participants', *Sociology of Health and Illness*, 16: 103–112.

Lunt, P. and Livingstone, S. (1996) 'Rethinking the Focus Group in Media and Communications Research', *Journal of Communication*, 46: 79–98.

5.5   Field Observation and Ethnography

Christian Lüders

1   FROM PARTICIPANT OBSERVATION TO ETHNOGRAPHY

Anyone who wishes to make an empirical investigation of human beings, their everyday practices and life-worlds has, in principle, two possibilities. One can hold conversations with participants about their actions and collect appropriate documents in the hope of obtaining, in this way, rich information *about* the particular practice in which one is interested. Or else one looks for ways or strategies for taking part, for as long as possible, in this everyday practice and becoming familiar with it, so as to be able to observe its everyday performance. The second strategy – which is central to this chapter – is that which has long been described in the specialist literature, particularly in German-speaking countries, as *participant observation*; it is only recently that this has begun to be replaced by the term 'ethnography', under the influence of British and American scholarship. This change in the familiar term has also been accompanied by changes in the conceptual emphasis.

2   PARTICIPANT OBSERVATION

Participant observation has its historical roots in anthropology and ethnology on the one hand and in the social reform movements of the late nineteenth and early twentieth centuries in the United States and Great Britain on the other. Both ethnic conflicts and those related to distribution and migration in the urban industrial centres, and the growth of new forms of poverty and impoverishment in the slums of the large towns, mobilized not only social reformers, but also scientists and universities. In the 1920s and 1930s there arose, especially in Chicago, a particular tradition of urban sociology on the basis of extensive participant observation and reporting. The studies of Thomas and Znaniecki, Park, Burgess and others (cf. Lindner 1990) became particularly well known. This tradition was further developed in the 1950s, above all by William F. Whyte's investigation of 'Street Corner Society' (1955), which has since become a classic.

When participant observation again attracted more attention in the United States at the beginning of the 1960s, methodological interest concentrated on the systematic rationalization and the development of the procedure as an independent sociological research method (cf. Lüders 1995). Participant observation was understood by its protagonists at that time as an important route to the sociological description of reality. At the same time they saw themselves as being obliged repeatedly to admit that they had no clear methodological profile, especially compared to the interview and to the primacy of quantifying social research. They sought, therefore, not only to formulate a set of methodological rules analogous to those of established sociological procedures, but to develop a plausible theoretical and methodological foundation for their research practice. This was the main focus of the reader by McCall and Simmons, which appeared in 1969.

If one assesses these and similarly based attempts from a contemporary viewpoint, one may perceive that the discussions concentrate on two aspects in particular: first, there were the participant observers and their relations in and to their field. For example, Bruyn's 'first axiom' runs as follows: 'the participant observer shares in the life activities and sentiments of people in face-to-face relationships' (Bruyn 1966: 13). What this meant in methodological terms was normally spelled out with the help of role-theory. What became clear in this way were the dilemmas, described in countless ways, of participant observers who had to adhere to their scientific standards and tasks as distanced observers, but at the same time had to act in a socially and culturally acceptable way in the particular situations. Bruyn therefore derives from the first axiom the following 'corollary': 'the role of the participant observer requires both detachment and personal involvement' (Bruyn 1966: 14). In point of fact this conflict of roles could not be resolved (see **5.1**). The methodological debate focused, accordingly, on listing the different types of possible constellations in the field and their variables (overt versus covert observation, differing degrees of participation, degree of standardization of observation, and so on). It was hoped that this would make it possible at least to describe a number of characteristic conflicts and to formulate appropriate pragmatic recommendations.

In addition to the observer and role-conflicts in the field the methodological debate concentrated, secondly, on the different stages in the research process. On the basis of divisions into phases that did not correspond in detail, different types of task and difficulty that the participant observer had to face in the field were classified and reflected in the methodology. Among these are the phases of problem-definition, of making contact, of entering the field, of establishing and maintaining a role in the field, of collecting and reporting data, of exiting from the field, and finally the phases of analysis, theoretical processing and publication of results (cf., for example, Hammersley and Atkinson 1983; Jorgensen 1989). Alongside this, distinctions are made between the different phases of observation. Here one proceeds on the basis that after a rather broadly designed descriptive phase, the research focuses more and more narrowly on the research issue (focused observation), in order to investigate only a number of selected aspects in greater detail (selective observation; cf. Spradley 1980).

It is characteristic of the debate in the English-speaking world that a predominantly heuristic *research-pragmatic* function is attributed to these methodological concepts. This not only prevents a too far-reaching standardization and formalization; at the same time, this understanding implies that not all methodological approaches and concepts can claim validity without first proving themselves in research practice in the context of concrete questions. A consequence of this is that the academic literature – particularly in journals such as the *Journal of Contemporary Ethnography* (formerly *Urban Life* or *Urban Life and Culture*), *Qualitative Sociology*, *Qualitative Inquiry* or *Qualitative Studies in Education*, but also numerous readers and edited volumes (cf., for example, Aster et al. 1989; Shaffir and Stebbins 1991; Shaffir et al. 1980) – is still, apart from research-oriented reports, characterized by methodological articles in which the relevant project-specific experiences are appraised. Just some of the topics of discussion include:

- How to build up relationships of trust
- How to shape one's own role while in the field
- How to report: whether open or (part-)standardized, whether to summarize results from memory later or to make notes in the situation to serve as a basis for more detailed reports
- How and when it is best to withdraw from the field to produce reports

- How to behave in delicate and dangerous situations, and how to find informants
- How to use technical equipment and available documents
- How to use different procedures in a particular situation, such as interviews or group conversations
- How to prevent oneself from being overwhelmed by the volume of information and data and losing track of the research question in the vastness or the fascination of everyday life (cf., for example, Fetterman 1985, Grills 1998, and the series *Qualitative Research Methods*; see Part 7).

The academic debate in German-speaking countries long ignored such developments. Participant observation or field research, as it is sometimes known (Friebertshäuser 1996; Girtler 1984, 1989), has led a shadowy existence, has received little methodological discussion and is rarely used as a main research tool. Of course, it has often been used as a collection procedure together with interviews, group discussion and document analysis, but ultimately opinions have been divided over the question of how to standardize the procedure and over its apparently dubious methodological status. For many scholars participant observation was only accorded a supplementary, or sometimes exploratory, role in research (cf. Bohnsack 1999: 146). Researchers who relied almost exclusively on participant observation were deemed to have a high entertainment value but their work was not really accepted as serious research. Even the boom in qualitative research since the late 1970s was long unable to bring about any major change.

A whole range of developments and factors were needed before an attempt could be made to promote aggressively the strengths of participant observation. What helped here was undoubtedly the insight that the original programme could not be fulfilled, because the large number of settings where participant observation was used were not subject to methodological control. The effort to formulate methodological rules independent of context was *de facto* rejected, because clearly its was mainly the situationally appropriate behaviour of the observer, his or her trained view and ability to condense heterogeneous material into a plausible description, that were decisive for the quality of a study. But precisely because countless studies insisted that this strategy could be used to produce interesting and important research results, researchers began, on the one hand, to live with a degree of vagueness in methodological questions, and this was turned into a principle by emphasizing the 'primacy of research practice over "theory" about how to do it' (Hammersley 1990: 1). On the other hand, researchers began to see participant observation in a broader sense as a *flexible, methodologically plural and context-related strategy* that could incorporate widely different procedures. For this view the term ethnography has now become established, and it therefore seems sensible to use it only in this sense. A further extension of the term to cover the whole area of qualitative or reconstructive social research, as is currently fashionable in the United States (cf., for example, Denzin 1997), is rather unwise since it causes one to lose sight of the unique methodological features of the approach.

3 ETHNOGRAPHY

In recent years there has been a considerable increase, in German-speaking countries, in the number of ethnographic studies, but also in methodological and concept-focused work on the topic of 'ethnography'. Terms such as 'ethnography', 'ethnographic procedure' and 'ethnographic writing' are not yet a part of the established repertoire in qualitative research. Here German-speaking countries, compared to the debate in the United States or Great Britain, are still in every respect in a developmental stage. However, with works such as the reader edited by Berg and Fuchs (1993) a start has at least been made on making available, in German translation, a selection of specialist theoretical texts. With the collections by Hirschauer and Amann (1997) and Knoblauch (1996b), the whole spectrum of relevant topics and studies is now accessible. Recently published collections in 'cultural studies' (cf. Bromley et al. 1999; Engelmann 1999) have introduced to a wider audience not only a theoretical perspective but also a field of research where an ethnographic viewpoint is really essential (see **2.4**, **3.8**, **3.9**).

In a first approximation ethnographies may be understood as descriptions of an *ethnos*, or, to use a term from Honer (1993: 14ff.), as descriptions of small life-worlds. Both the use of the term *ethnos* and the allusion to Husserl's concept of life-worlds in Honer's formulation indicate that ethnographies normally focus their attention on a particular culture and the nature and forms of knowledge embedded in it. Unlike traditional ethnology and social anthropology, sociological ethnographies examine primarily their own culture, or – more precisely – the cultures in their own society. Against the background of a highly differentiated and pluralized society where one's own form of existence increasingly seems to be merely one option among countless others and in which experiences of alienness in its many forms have become an everyday matter, not only transmitted through the media, there has been an increase in curiosity and sometimes also a voyeuristic interest in other apparently remote and abstruse forms of existence. But there has also been a demand for serious description and analysis of what is no longer so obvious and of what is new. The ethnography of one's own culture has thus become a medium for social self-observation.

It is therefore not so surprising that ethnographic studies today cover a broad spectrum of issues and topics (see **3.8**). These studies investigate in particular the perspectives of participants, the nature and forms of their knowledge, their interactions, practices and discourses.

At the centre of ethnographic studies is the question – theoretically put – of how the particular realities are 'produced' in practical terms; they therefore look at the means employed in a given situation for the production of social phenomena from the perspective of participants. This kind of epistemological interest is not identical with the everyday view of participants. Whereas they are normally interested in solving their problems by practical action, the ethnographic view concentrates on those aspects of reality that participants, so to speak, take for granted, namely the practices of their 'creation'; it then asks how participants manage to create themselves and others in the face of social facts. It is therefore quite inevitable that ethnographic research 'observes … what is largely familiar as if it were alien; it is not understood in an interpretative way but methodologicaly "alienated": it is brought to the observer from a distance' (Amann and Hirschauer 1997: 12).

Against this background, one may view ethnographies – following Amann and Hirschauer (1997: 20) – as 'mimetic forms of empirical social research', whose 'selectivity and modality … [are] not regulated by external prescriptions and hypotheses about the what, when, where and how of a standardized observation procedure but are expected of a perceptible object', and which begin with the 'apparently trivial and "unmethodical" opening question "What the hell is going on here?" (Geertz)'.

If one now seeks to describe, beyond the multiplicity of topics and approaches, the essential characteristics of ethnographic research, three features come to the centre of our attention: extended participation, ethnography as a flexible research strategy, and ethnographic writing.

Extended participation

If ethnographers are convinced of anything, it is of the assumption that situational practice and local knowledge can only be made accessible to any analysis by extended participation, 'by the lasting co-presence of observer and events' (Amann and Hirschauer 1997: 21). No interviews or focus groups, no matter how thorough, and no detailed analysis of natural documents can replace this. It is precisely the interest in the insider's perspective that forces the ethnographers to put aside all the situational orders and practices that they have ever experienced, to adapt and, in a certain sense, even to subordinate themselves. A formulation of Hammersley and Atkinson encapsulates this idea: 'The ethnographer participates, overtly or covertly, in people's daily lives for an extended period of time, watching what happens, listening to what is said, asking questions; in fact collecting whatever data are available to throw light on the issues with which he or she is concerned' (1983: 2). In reacting to memories, opinions and descriptions that informants provide in interviews, conversations and discussions, that is, in reacting to reconstructions *about* experiences and events, ethnography is relying on participation and the sharing of contemporary cultural phenomena or – to borrow a term from Goffman (1963b) – on co-presence.

One precondition for an extended and informative presence in the research field is that access is secured and that one of the participants takes on an accepted role in the field (see **5.1**). In accordance with this a central role is played in research reports by the presentation of how one succeeded in gaining access to the field in question, what obstacles had to be overcome in the process, how it was possible to build up trust, and what gatekeepers were of particular importance. Because normally the small life-worlds that become the subjects of ethnographies are alien worlds to ethnographers, and also because the development of an outsider's view is one of ethnography's most important tasks, one might describe immersion in research fields as a process of partial acculturation (cf. Amann and Hirschauer 1997: 27).

Experience shows, in this connection, that the manner in which one gains access in most cases already reflects some of the main characteristics of the field. Even in those cases where access (initially) fails, the experience gained from this is crucial because it can provide helpful clues as to the structure of the object of investigation (cf. Lau and Wolff 1983). At the same time the move into the research field is accompanied by a large number of pointers in respect of the researcher's positioning in the field. The ways in which one introduces and presents oneself, and subsequently 'joins in' the game, are stages and processes in terms of which the ethnographer's position in the field of available relationships is negotiated and defined. Research practice shows that there is a broad spectrum of possibilities, extending from the role of an openly observing researcher, known and visible to all, to different forms of camouflage membership (be it trainee, or interested visitor, or supposed customer or colleague) with fluid transitions between them and possibilities of a change in position during the research process (see **5.1**).

Participation over an extended period is a challenge for ethnographers, in that normally they cannot just retreat into the role of distanced and apparently neutral observer. On the contrary: all productive ethnographies are based on the development of relationships of trust and the experience of participation, from which will normally result a variety of relationships, produced by delicate balances between proximity and distance, between immersion in practice and what Amann and Hirschauer (1997: 27) have appositely described as the 'strategic private game of knowledge creation'.

Flexible research strategy

This kind of extended participation is only possible if the ethnographer is in a position to adapt to the particular situational circumstances. This also implies that he or she must be in a position to adapt methodological procedures and to maintain the balance between epistemological interests and the requirements of the situation, for an all too rigid adherence to principles of methodological procedure could, sooner or later, close the access to important information. Research practice therefore shows itself to be highly dependent on milieu and situation, coloured by the participating informants, the forms and circumstances of their lives and the imponderabilities of everyday life. Ultimately one can only subordinate oneself to these factors: the technique consists of 'getting data, it seems to me, by subjecting yourself, your own body and your own personality, and your own social situation, to the set of contingencies that play upon a set of individuals, so that you can physically and ecologically penetrate their circle of response to their social situation, or their work situation or their ethnic situation, or whatever' (Goffman 1989: 125). Admittedly this implies that the methodological debate in this case has to cope with an abstract multiplicity and complexity of data-collection and field situations, which cannot be controlled in advance, and which render pointless any attempts at standardization.

What is characteristic of ethnographic research, therefore, is the flexible use of different methodological approaches in accordance with the particular situation and issue – and here it is not only the utilization of procedures that has to be adapted to the situation, but also, under certain circumstances, the procedures themselves. For example, biographical-narrative interviews, as strictly defined (see **5.2**, **5.11**), are relatively infrequently used, because in the everyday practice that is being investigated, situations rarely arise in which informants can spend two hours talking in a relaxed fashion about their lives. In such circumstances it is more likely that biographies will be discussed in a variety of situations and contexts, in a fragmentary way, concentrated in countless anecdotes, permeated by contradictions and present-day colouring.

It follows from this principle that ethnographic procedure is open to all research methods. In addition to participant observation in many contexts, a variety of types of interview can be conducted, quantitative data may be generated and collected, conversations arranged with naturally occurring groups, historical and contemporary documents of every kind may be gathered, everyday practice may be elicited in different forms of self-presentation, videos may be made, series of photos produced (see **5.6**) and many kinds of enquiry set up. Much of this is reminiscent of journalistic techniques, and it is therefore understandable that – particularly in the United States – the relationship between ethnography and 'new journalism' has regularly been a topic of discussion (cf., for example, Denzin 1997: 126ff.).

Whilst others – as Knoblauch (1994b: 8) once put it polemically – have developed 'almost police-controlled regulations for "a methodologically controlled hermeneutics"', ethnographers therefore speak of the 'art of fieldwork' (Wolcott 1995), or of a *Kunstlehre* (art), and describe ethnography as an opportunistic and field-specific variant of empirical social research (Amann and Hirschauer 1997: 20). Whereas some people focus on procedures, others emphasize 'the subtle manipulation of their personal forms of contact' (1997: 25) and the 'seismographic abilities' of the researchers (1997: 25). It is therefore no longer a question of the (correct or incorrect) utilization of a single method, but of the situationally relevant and appropriate realization of a general *methodological pragmatism*. This expression brings to our attention, first of all, the risk and the unplannable, situational, accidental and individual aspects of the research process. 'The logic of participant observation is nonlinear, its practice requires the researcher to exercise a wide variety of skills, make judgments, and be creative, and many nonrational factors influence most aspects of actual study' (Jorgensen 1989: 9).

Secondly, the *skilled* action of the investigator in a particular situation also becomes more important: 'ethnography involves risk, uncertainty and discomfort … . Not only do researchers have to go into unknown territory, they must go unarmed, with no questionnaires, interview schedules, or observation protocols to stand between themselves and the cold winds of the raw real. They stand alone with their individual *selves*. They themselves are the primary research tool with which they must find, identify, and collect data' (Ball 1990: 394f.). This not only wards off all claims in respect of a formalization, standardization, and methodization of the research procedure: it also takes account of the fact – often forgotten by researchers and methodologists – 'that the social researcher, and the research act itself, are part and parcel of the social world under investigation' (Hammersley and Atkinson 1983: 234). The basis of this is the insight that the ethnographic researcher must not only take part in the life of the field of investigation, in order to gain experience of something, but that – as with all social researchers – for data collection he or she can only use, in ethnomethodological terms, the practices of everyday life.

In the best case the researcher will succeed in refining these. 'However distinctive the purposes of social science may be, the methods it employs are merely refinements or developments of those used in everyday life' (Hammersley and Atkinson 1983: 15). It is only the possibilities of making all aspects of this state of affairs *reflexively* into a topic, without the decision-pressures of everyday life, that distinguishes research (if one disregards its purposes and functions) from everyday action. The ability to penetrate reflexively one's own action, experience and observations in the field, and one's own individual, cultural, social and existential assumptions, therefore becomes the ethnographer's decisive competence (cf. Hammersley and Atkinson 1983).

A large number of ethical and legal questions are bound up with this sort of 'strategic private game'. Seen from a purely formal perspective, ethnographies are based on person-related data and are therefore subject to the terms of the data protection law and the conditions it defines for scientific research. This has a number of consequences: for instance, by law participants in the field must expressly agree to an ethnographic study and to the further use of data for scientific purposes. Moreover, researchers are obliged to render all data completely anonymous, to store them in a way that is safe and, in every respect, inaccessible to unauthorized persons, and later to destroy them in accordance with legal requirements, for example in a shredder. Irrespective of this, decisions must be made case by case, and an ethical basis provided for the particular strategies to be used in the field (see **6.1**).

Ethnographic writing and reporting

Writing up and presenting what has been observed, heard and experienced is an essential feature and, at the same time, a challenge in ethnographies (for concrete suggestions, cf. Emerson et al. 1995). In addition to the many methodological approaches and the active participation of the researcher in the everyday life of the field, it is characteristic of ethnography that – like no other method of social research – it is based on the subsequent reporting of what has been observed and perceived, or, more precisely, what is still remembered afterwards. Unlike audiovisual recording techniques, which preserve in concrete form what has happened interactively, observation protocols are concerned with the result of a 'transformational process which is substituted for a meaningfully structured and contextually organized social event by means of a *post hoc* typologizing, narrative, and interpretative representation' (Bergmann 1985: 308), that is, a 'reconstructive preservation' (1985: 308; see **5.22**).

Observation protocols, as the basis of ethnographies, cannot therefore be treated as faithful reproductions or unproblematic summaries of what is experienced, but should be seen, rather, for what they are: texts written by authors, using their available linguistic resources, to give a meaningful summary of their observations and recollections after the event, to put them in contexts and mould intelligible protocols in the form of texts.

This insight draws attention to the problem of the author, and here there is not always a clear distinction between the production of protocols as the actual database for ethnographies and the production of ethnographic reports on the basis of such protocols (on the second of these points see **5.22**). While great attention has been paid, particularly in Germany, to the question of evaluating qualitative materials, that is the protocols, this aspect has so far played a secondary role in the ethnographic debate in the English-speaking world. Instead, what is mostly discussed here is the writing of ethnographies, and the associated thesis of the crisis of representation has repeatedly been given wide attention, admittedly without achieving any practical results for research practice.

The starting point in this discussion was the discovery of the author as the source of all ethnographies and the insight that even protocols cannot be taken as one-to-one representations of observable reality, but that they are rather the result of complex processes of meaning-creation. This is very true for the writing of ethnographic reports, since these systematize and order the observations contained in the protocols on the basis of analyses – however

conducted – summarize them into findings and then present these as the result of the observations. Particularly in the United States there has been a series of studies that have made ethnographic texts into a subject for analysis, using a meta-theoretical perspective and the methods of linguistic analysis (see **5.22**). The aim of these studies was to reconstruct the patterns and structures, the linguistic formats and conventions and the ideographic markers which are characteristic of the text-type 'ethnographic report' and to distinguish it from other forms of representation – such as travel writing – or which are used by ethnographers to convince their readers of the authenticity and credibility of their presentation (cf. Van Maanen 1988, 1995). Atkinson (1990), for instance, is interested in how ethnographers are able to project authority in their texts and convince the reader that they are representing reality. The representation in textual form of actions (1990: 104ff.) and acting subjects is as much a subject for analysis as the various linguistic means and formats for expression of such differences as distance and irony (1990: 157ff.).

The implications of this kind of analysis are complex. Initially they provide a plethora of individual empirical observations, concerning the way in which ethnographers produce and shape their texts. But normally there is nothing more than this reconstructive listing; the methodological implications do not go beyond a general requirement that one should learn to be aware of the linguistic means that are being used. Beyond this, such analyses undeniably make it clear that not only writing ethnographic reports but research in general is primarily a 'rhetorical activity' (Atkinson 1990: 10), and that the protocol writer and the author of the report are inseparably bound up with this activity. This insight into the rhetorical nature of social research and the reality it describes (Wolff 1980) leads immediately to the epistemological questions of the relation of text to 'reality' and the unpopular debate about the differences or similarities between everyday life, science, literature, between fiction and reality, between analysis and fantasy, or between the role of the author and his or her subjectivity.

Apart from a growth in self-reflection these debates yielded little in the way of tangible or useful results for research practice. Ultimately every ethnographer confronts the dilemma between rhetorical construction and empiricism, from which there is no reliable way out. In particular, there are no recognizable answers to the burning question of how best to produce research protocols, what information they should contain and what structure they should have in order to serve as a basis for analysis. So even today it is still left to the individual ethnographer whether – depending on the particular research question – he or she should record action sequences or action contexts, individual events and situations, verbatim speech or meaningful summaries, and whether he or she should seek to document processes as far as possible in their spatio-temporal development or, in the writing of the protocol, already begin to interpret the content. This openness sometimes goes so far that in some proposals the text-type 'protocol' threatens to become fuzzy. When, in the context of postmodern notions of ethnography, there is talk of multiple voices, 'performances', 'true fictions' and 'dialogic evocation' (cf. Lüders 1995: 330ff. and 1996 for a summary), this leads to forms of language and presentation where the terms 'protocol' and 'report' lose their traditional and familiar meaning. Those who wish to decipher protocols according to the pattern of reflecting crystal balls (cf. Richardson 1994) are opening up the field to a variety of text-types and realms of experience, and will, at the same time, let themselves in for new problems in their analysis.

4 CHALLENGES

The growing number of ethnographic studies and methodological contributions to ethnography should not distract us from the many critical questions and unsolved problems that have been noted. Apart from the familiar open questions of qualitative research (for example, the problem of validity: see 4.7), particular mention should be made of the problem of analysing ethnographic material. The challenge here is that current debate concentrates primarily on the aspect of field participation, but scarcely looks at the question of how an ethnography, that is the description of an *ethnos* in the form of a text or a research report, comes into being. The widely promoted multi-perspective approach, the parallel use of different collection procedures, undeniably provokes the question of how data gained in this way can be *analysed*, interrelated and summarized, so that the end result is a readable ethnography, useful to others.

In more recent discussion in Germany this problem was systematically embodied in the question of how the protocols of participant observation or field protocols could be analysed, and what could be learned from this. While Schneider makes a plea for treating field protocols, like interview transcripts, as structured texts to be analysed using the techniques of sequential analysis (see 5.16) (Schneider 1987: 196ff.), Reichertz argues that 'the presentation of results [is] always bound up with a single form' (Reichertz 1989: 99), so that initially the field researcher's form of presentation will inevitably be foregrounded. If one takes this argument to its logical conclusion, it would mean that one cannot read and interpret field protocols as protocols of events, but must understand them as pre-interpreted, more or less literary summaries of the experiences and meaning-creations of the field researcher. Reichertz suggests a way out of this dilemma by opting for a comparative approach: with the help of field protocols 'the scientific perspective of an event can very well be reconstructed … and compared with others' (1989: 102).

Here possibilities for comparison materialize in two respects: on the one hand a comparison may be made of data obtained using the same approach, that is data on the basis of field protocols from one or more field researchers (triangulation of data). In addition, comparison may also be made between the results of different approaches, such as interviews, focus groups, document analyses, field protocols and so on (triangulation of methods, see 4.6). One hopes that this systematic bringing together of different data and results will enable one not only to produce a fuller and 'thicker' description of a particular life-world, but also to obtain a validation instrument. The somewhat naive belief in background means that if an action is described in a very similar way from different perspectives, there is good reason to trust the descriptions, that is, the field protocols. The problem with this is that one may indeed go a long way with such arguments at the level of everyday plausibility, but arguments of this kind cannot replace a credible analytical strategy and a rationalization of it. In this sense we may hold to the idea that there is still no agreement about how different data can be related to one another and how field protocols can be analysed. The problem has been made more acute in recent discussion where ethnographers are seen as 'personal recording machines' and field protocols as 'inspective data' (Amann and Hirschauer 1997: 21ff.).

An alternative proposal for at least partially avoiding these difficulties is to involve the reader. In this way the accent is shifted from analysis and presentation to comprehension while reading. What is now of central importance is not the question of how data are individually analysed and compared. The decisive quality criterion is whether the text that comes out of this is comprehensible and plausible from the reader's point of view (Reichertz 1992). The responsibility for deciding about the quality of a study is thus transferred to the reader, and under certain circumstances to the discourse of the receivers. This may still be a possible route within the scientific system. For the receivers outside the system, within the general public, the world of politics, administration and professional practice and the whole area of practice-related research, this proposal does not offer a solution, because readers do not normally fulfil the necessary preconditions. Of course, if one considers the everyday actors under investigation to be experts in their own reality, their judgement could be given a degree of importance still to be determined.

One could easily lose one's way with all of these questions, particularly if one wishes to solve them favourably from the point of view of epistemology, theory of science and methodology. However, rather than waiting in vain for favourable solutions or – using powerful fundamental arguments – throwing out the baby with the bath-water (and that would ultimately mean hindering ethnographic research, because it simply cannot fulfil the strict methodological, theoretical and epistemological conditions), there is a great deal to be said for getting on with research and reflecting carefully. Ethnography thrives on participation and the reports about this participation. What is needed now is an intensification of this research and a discussion of the experience it yields.

FURTHER READING

Atkinson, P., Coffey, S. D., Lofland, J. and Lofland, L. (eds) (2001) *Handbook of Ethnography*. London: Sage.

Hammersley, M. and Atkinson, P. (1983) *Ethnography. Principles in Practice*. London: Tavistock.

Jorgensen, D. L. (1989) *Participant Observation. A Methodology for Human Studies* (Applied Social Research Methods Series, Volume 15). Newbury Park, CA: Sage.

5.6   Photography as Social Science Data

Douglas Harper

To write about photography in social science is deceptively difficult. We live in a world most of us see. Sociology is the study of the world we live in. Therefore it would seem natural to record the world visually as part of how we study society. Yet sociologists rarely use photography or even think seriously about the link between visual information and sociological thinking. For anthropologists the record is only slightly better. Only small academic movements in visual sociology and anthropology balance the otherwise dismal rejection of what one would think to be a natural, creative and interesting way to do social research.

There are many ways to approach the subject of photography as data. For a companion to qualitative research my orientation is pragmatic, focused on fieldwork rather than the semiotic analysis of visual texts. I would hope to encourage others to develop experiments a few researchers have begun. Like many aspects of qualitative research, the visual dimension is best understood through practice. It cannot be described or taught as systematically as can survey research or statistical analysis. It is the area of sociology where science is closest to art.

I will describe how specific qualities of the photograph influence how it may be used in social science fieldwork. I will also describe existing forms of visual sociology which will hopefully serve as guidelines for social scientists hoping to expand their repertoire of methods.

1   THE NATURE OF THE IMAGE

While visual sociology could and does use any kind of visual representation, here I am interested in the photograph. Photographs are the most common form of visual sociology, and they are the most peculiar because they have the dual qualities of recording the world seemingly without interpretation, and at the same time with profound subjectivity. There is no other method for recording the world which has this ironic inconsistency, and everything I say about visual methods reflects on the tension between these competing qualities of the image.

A photographic image results when light leaves its trace on an element that has a 'memory'. That element may be chemical, as in the case of traditional photography, or electronic, as is the case of a light-sensitive computer chip. For the image to exist there had to be light reflected off a subject; thus the photograph is the record of the subject at a particular moment. In this way the photograph is empirical; it records what our senses have perceived. So if a fieldworker wishes to record information such as the houses people live in, or the density of traffic on a street, or what clothes people wear who represent different statuses, it is reasonable to take photographs to record that information. The adage the photograph is worth a thousand words is probably appropriate in this case. The photograph gathers an extraordinary amount of information; a photograph of a complex social event or a complicated material reality may be described only with several pages of text.

A text is never equivalent to the image, but images by themselves do not communicate fully. The traditional bridge between these images and lengthy texts are captions, which are just short texts that specifically tie images to other meanings. Many visual social sciences use captions to tie photos to texts, but captions often are part of a process in which images become simple redundancies of text. Other models of word and image integration inspire visual sociology. Two outstanding examples are Agee and Evans's portrait of sharecroppers in the American Depression (1960) and Berger and Mohr's (1975) study of guest workers in Central Europe. Evans's 31 photos (photo series without captions of three families, and a short essay on a southern town) precede 460 pages of narrative text on the three families by James Agee. In this extraordinary juxtaposition of words and images, neither form repeats nor replaces each other. Rather they develop in tandem; here the expressiveness of the text seems to have been born from the spare energy of the images. In Berger and Mohr's masterpiece on the subject of migrant labour during the 1960s in Europe, the balance is reversed: more than 200 images by Mohr develop the often ironic and implied meanings from Berger's complex text.

Using photography to gather information (data) was the first visual sociology and anthropology. The best example is still Bateson and Mead's *Balinese Character* (1942), in which the researchers used 759 photographs (selected from more than 25,000 taken during fieldwork) to support and develop their ethnographic analysis. Sequences of photographs show how the Balinese perform social rituals or engage in routine behaviour. These images are similar to short movie clips (and the researchers did complete several short movies which worked like the photo sequences). The researchers also used images to survey material culture such as houses and agricultural techniques.

Sociologists sometimes use images made by documentary photographers to enlarge their historical understanding. For example, sociologists study Jacob Riis's photographs (1971 [1890]) to see the living conditions in early twentieth century industrializing cities. These sociologists begin with knowledge of how industrialization and the lack of public transportation led to crowding and other social problems. Riis's photographs examine an aspect of these conditions beyond the historical, demographic and structural conditions even to the point of suggesting, by recording people's expressions and gestures, how people in those settings negotiated their realities.

Sociologists still use photographs to study the empirical world. For example, I used aerial photographs to study the structure of a dairy farm neighbourhood (Harper 1997). Photographs I took from a small plane showed that types of farms I had determined through other analyses looked different from the aerial perspective. In this case the vantage point of the aerial photograph showed things the normal perspective would not. These included the layout of the farmstead, building types and even the effect of certain cropping practices. I also found evidence of the evolution of dairy farms to several post-farm uses in aerial photos of several farmsteads. While these images were not entirely unambiguous, they easily led to a typology that could be used to analyse structure and change in other agricultural neighbourhoods. In this case the aerial portrait is a summary of an extraordinary amount of information about history and change.

These examples suggest that visual sociology consists of taking photographs of sociological topics, sometimes fitting those images into textual analysis of the same topic. As such, visual sociology would be relatively straightforward. In fact this form of visual sociology has suffered a barrage of criticism, largely through its association with empirical sociology, and, to a lesser extent, documentary photography.

The essence of the largely postmodern criticism (Bolton 1989; see especially Rosler's 1989; Solomon-Godeau 1991) is that empirical sociology and the photography done in the service of empirical sociology assert the existence of an objective reality and tools that measure that reality. In fact, argue the postmodernists, reality is fundamentally ambiguous, and photographs, like all records of life, are subjective statements rather than objective documents (Clifford and Marcus 1986, among others). More darkly, sociology and especially documentary photography hide their own ideology behind the guise of false objectivism. I believe that this criticism is correct, although for some of the visual sociology movement (myself included) the criticism does not invalidate the premises of an empirical sociology. Rather it completes it. If we are aware of how the photograph is constructed, we can use it more successfully. Thus I proceed with discussion of how social and technical aspects influence the meaning of photographs, and how this might influence social sciences seeking a visual method.

2 SOCIAL CONSTRUCTION OF THE IMAGE

The photograph is socially constructed in the sense that the social positions of the photographer and the subject come into play when a photograph is made. It takes social power to make photographs (Tagg 1988), partly because making photographs defines identities, relationships and histories. A father may photograph the children in ridiculous poses, but the children do not generally have the social power to photograph their parent's arguing (or making love) and to present those images as the 'official' family story (Chaflen 1986). Sociologists and anthropologists have assumed that it is their right to photograph the people they study, and thus to present them as academic subjects (and in ways in which the ideological bases of their relationships are disguised). Edwards's (1992) collection of essays on early British anthropological photography shows us exactly this point: the images are not objective renderings of objects of scientific study, as interpreted by early twentieth century anthropologists. The images are markers of colonial relationships: anthropology was a science of the colonizer and the images made in the service of anthropology defined the native in a way that reified the relationships of superiority and inferiority endemic to colonialism. There are no photographic records made by natives of colonialism (or colonials) but in recent decades prior 'natives' have assumed the right to make their own images and tell their own visual story. This has, of course, called the relationships of traditional anthropology into question.

The social construction of photography is often more subtle than the illustrations noted above. For example, I am using about 110 documentary photographs made just after the Second World War in a study of the evolution of dairy farming in the Northeastern United States. The photographs are part of a large collection which came into existence through the sponsorship of an American company, Standard Oil of New Jersey (SONJ), and directed by a well-regarded photographic intellectual, Roy Stryker. My collection on dairy farming includes about 40 images made by a female photographer, Charlotte Brooks, and about 70 by several male photographers. It was startling to compare the photographs on the basis of the gender of the photographers. For the men, the farmwomen's work was largely invisible. They did not photograph women as productive parts of the farm; nor did they photograph the work of maintaining and provisioning the house (and taking care of children). Brooks's photographs covered many of these excluded topics. The significance of this is that if we regard the photographs as a document of farm life during the Second World War era, we will accept an incomplete portrait as a full record. Indeed the photos, in this case, are a result of the social construction of 'maleness' and 'femaleness' typical of 1940s America (see **3.10**).

Social scientists should be aware of the social construction of the image for several reasons. We need to acknowledge that photography embodies the unequal relationships that are part of most research activities. I can enter into the worlds of the poor by living temporarily on the street, and photograph the worlds I encounter there; but a homeless person cannot infilter and photograph the life of my university president. For many social scientists this realization has led them to abandon photography. For others it is a cautionary awareness which should help us overcome the inevitable power differentials of subject and researcher. Some sociologists have confronted the issue by giving up their own photography in lieu of teaching their subjects to use photography and writing to investigate their cultures and, perhaps, to empower themselves. Wendy Ewald is a leader in this field, for she takes on the asymmetry of adult/child as well as first world/third world power differences. Her first published project on Appalachian children (1985) is a good introduction to this approach. The photographs and writing of her students contradicted the stereotypes long associated with the internal colony of Appalachia. In this method the camera (and often text which expands upon the images) are methods of inspired reflection; not social science in and of themselves, but data that sociologists and others should put to use.

3 THE TECHNICAL CONSTRUCTION OF THE IMAGE

No camera sees exactly as does the eye. The optics of photographic lenses, for reasons which go beyond this argument, are simply unable to put onto film what we naturally see (this has changed with virtual reality computer simulations, see Boccia Atieri 1996). Thus making a photograph is deciding, whether consciously or not, on one interpretation out of an infinite number of possibilities. Few people, sociologists or not, ever think about this. Most people, social scientists or not, use automatic cameras, which make photos through an unimaginative averaging of technical choices. But visual sociologists or anthropologists must confront the incredible possibilities the camera has to interpret reality in order to make self-conscious visual statements. This means, first and foremost, relegating the automatic camera to the waste bin, and learning simple rules about photography and the techniques through which cameras work. More simply said, it involves becoming self-conscious photographers.

Technical influences on the image can be separated into three aspects. The first involves framing.

Humans have two eyes which are positioned horizontally on our heads. Our normal view is an oval made by our eyes working together. Probably because it is technically easier, photographs were initially made as squares and rectangles, and once this convention took hold, few have questioned it. So photographic framing from the beginning radically interpreted human sight. Different film formats and lenses expand the possible interpretations of sight through framing. Panoramic cameras see more approximately what the normal field of vision records, but panoramic cameras can record information beyond the normal range of eyesight. Telephoto lenses allow the photographer to fill a film plane with a tiny part of reality, the way we do with a telescope.

Visual sociologists need to be conscious of framing and how it lends to photographs that address different kinds of sociological questions. In other words, we need to select lenses and cameras that facilitate recording information that will allow us to explore specific questions. I began my book about the before-mentioned rural artisan with an aerial photo which frames his shop from 2,000 feet (700 metres). This photo shows the shop on a rectangle of land filled with objects. It contrasts remarkably with the fields that surround it. Examined closely, the photograph shows old machinery used for parts sitting randomly around the building. The building is a steel hut, a substantial and not inexpensive setting for a rural fixer living well below the poverty range. Other photos throughout the book function like a low-power microscope, examining minute details of work, tools and broken parts being fixed. A photograph with a telephoto macro lens magnifies the fingers of the hand on the chainsaw file, which records the minute details of hand-work. The framing in these two examples parallels analysis from a wide framework (consistent with a structural perspective) and the close-up photographs document the micro-elements of the social setting: the hand-knowledge embodied in tool use, which is the basis of technical expertise. It is all a matter of framing.

The eye records information flowing past like a movie. It is unusual to look for more than a second or two at the same object. Our brain integrates this information into meaningful visual narratives as we negotiate our way through various venues of life. Still photographs capture some of that implied or real movement through a creative application of shutter and aperture.

The camera shutter is a window that allows more or less light to reach the film surface. The lens aperture can be thought of as a means for varying the size of the window, which is being opened and closed. The correct exposure on the film is determined by adjusting the aperture and shutter speed in relation to each other. The decisions as to what aperture and shutter speed to use, however, also affect the look of the image. Shutter speed affects the 'freezing' of action (a photo taken at 1/500 of a second will stop most action; below 1/30 of a second even a person walking will be blurred). The aperture setting determines the depth of focus (for example, at f 1.4 an object is focused on a foot away and only objects a few inches on either side of it will also be in focus; if the aperture is set at f 64, objects from a couple of feet to as far as the eye can see will be in focus). These elements determine the information the photograph will communicate.

For example, I am currently working on a 'repeat photography' (see Rieger 1996) project in Bologna, Italy. My colleague and I hoped to see how parts of the city, photographed 80 or more years ago, had changed in appearance. We were interested not only in what buildings had been built and torn down, but also in how the 'energy of the city' had changed in intervening decades. The old photos we used for comparison were done with slow shutter speeds and small apertures, because cameras at that time did not have fast shutter speeds. To make images that would compare to the old images we mounted our camera on a tripod (thus the buildings and other still elements would be in focus) and used slow shutter speeds (which show people blurred in the foreground) and with small apertures (which produce depths of focus from a few feet to several hundred metres). These decisions create photos that record reality similarly to the old images we wish to study. It is a simple application of technique to make a specific photographic statement.

Thus, being a visual sociologist means using the camera as a kind of editorial process. Controlling technical factors in picture-making allows a photographer to analyse and to selectively present data, not unlike how a quantitative sociologist uses statistical tests and tables to analyse and present numerical data.

The last element of technical construction in photography addresses the manipulation and interpretation of light. Photography, after all, is nothing but recording reflected light. But recording surfaces like photographic films and computer chips do not record light in the way the eye sees it. Film has the capability to reduce colour to black and white (and at different levels of contrast and graininess), and different colour films emphasize different colours and contrast levels. The light perceived by the eye is seldom the light that will appear on a film plate, and so photographers must add or subtract light to create the desired photographic statement. Steiger (1995) outlined how the technical choices in photography lend themselves to different photographic statements, and how those statements tend to one theoretical perspective or another. Much of her discussion involved using sophisticated lighting to make photographs that recreate the light one encounters in a normal, daytime apartment. Her argument reminds us that our reading of the photograph is actually a reading of light, and it is not simple to recreate the light of a normal moment. Steiger's case is a rare exploration of the relationship between technical consciousness and visual sociology thinking. Indeed, my comments on framing, aperture, shutter and light are all a call to use the camera consciously in order to exact the fullest potential of visual sociology.

4 BECOMING A VISUAL SOCIOLOGIST

So far I have suggested that photography has two characteristics: one objective and the other subjective. The objectivity is based on the fact that cameras record light bouncing off the surface of things; and the subjectivity is due to the social and technical constructions of the image. These are informing arguments rather than lessons in how to proceed. How, then, does one become a visual sociologist?

Perhaps the most important idea is to photograph with sociological consciousness. Howard Becker was the first to make this argument, in 1974, and this paper and others that develop these ideas (gathered in Becker 1986a) should be read by all aspiring visual sociologists.

Becker (1998) regards social science theory as a practical way to order information, rather than a complicated intellectual exercise. Yet he admonishes us to think theoretically when we do photography. What does this mean exactly? For Becker, all photography is done from a theoretical perspective, but little of the theory is sociological. Our pre-existing theory (which Becker calls 'lay' theory) tells us where to point the camera and how to use the camera (speaking technically) to make an image. Thus, we photograph to recreate our unexamined perception. But we also interpret sociological topics in our unexamined theorizing, and when we photograph, we do so in a way that presents information which is consistent with our theories of the world. If we are photojournalists (see Hagaman 1996) we learn to present the theories of our newspaper editors and the recent conventions of photojournalism in our work. We do this not only by choosing certain topics and specific images of those topics, but also by using particular lenses (frames), apertures and shutter speeds. If we are sociologists we presumably have theoretical knowledge of our subject, the way Bateson and Mead knew the Balinese before they began photographing. (Bateson and Mead had already completed several books on their subject.) This prior knowledge will tell the researcher: 'there is the enactment of a ritual my subjects have described … it lasts 20 minutes and has four stages … I will photograph it to highlight the transitions and interactions among actors ...'. From this perspective the work of visual sociology is straightforward: we bring it into the research process to extend our knowledge of our subject.

But not all field researchers have the kind of pre-existing knowledge I describe in the case of Bateson and Mead. There are at least two alternatives for visual sociologists. The first is to use the camera as an information-gathering instrument to discover what Glaser and Strauss (1967) called 'grounded theory' (see **2.1, 6.6**). Photographs made during the research experience concretize observations which fieldworkers use to continually redefine their theories. In this way photographs help build theory. In fact, the need to make photographs in the field requires that the fieldworker look at *something*; and these beginning observations can be the starting point in making theory.

A second alternative to using photographs to confirm and develop existing theory is perhaps even more useful. 'Photo elicitation' is a method in which researchers stimulate subjects' interpretations using photographs as a kind of 'cultural Rorschach test'. I used this method in a study of a rural artisan/mechanic (Harper 1987). My subject was the working knowledge of a 'bricoleur' in an industrial setting, and photographs I made during the research of tools, machines and work in process stimulated interviews in which the subject explained his working knowledge, and the social relationships hidden behind the work, the machines and the objects of the work setting.

Researchers may use photos of events people experienced in the past to draw out a memory of their history. Margolis (1998) studied the political consciousness of coal miners, using photos of mine work decades ago to interview elderly miners about events and their interpretations. In this case one senses that the intervening years between the photographs and their interpretation had led to deeper reflection than would normally be associated with the photo-elicitation process.

Other researchers modified the photo elicitation method by engaging subjects in the photography as well as the interviews. Van Mierlo and her colleagues photographed a multi-ethnic Dutch neighbourhood under the direction of five subjects. The researchers then interviewed their subjects with the images made on their earlier 'photo-tour'. Finally, the researchers did subsequent interviews by showing each informant the images made by their neighbours, who were of different age, gender and ethnic background (van der Does et al. 1992).

In all examples of photo-elicitation, the photograph loses its claim of objectivity; indeed, the power of the photo is its ability to unlock the subjectivity of those who see the image differently than does the researcher.

The photo-elicitation interview achieves the collaboration that the postmodern critic seeks in the research process. It is also a humbling means through which the researcher becomes aware of his or her limited knowledge of the subject's worlds. When it works best, the photo-elicitation interview is a means through which the research roles are reversed: the subject becomes the teacher and the researcher the student.

My suggestions for a visual sociology are modest. Most visual sociologists want to find a way to integrate seeing into the research process. A sensitive fieldworker is already nearly equipped to do visual sociology. It helps to understand how the camera records information and it is important to understand the impact of photography on the research process. Finally, it is important to understand how various constructions (technical and social) influence how the photograph is made and interpreted. Beyond this, the only necessary ingredients are imagination and creativity.

FURTHER READING

Grady, J. (1996) 'The Scope of Visual Sociology', *Visual Sociology,* 11 (2): 10–24.

Prosser, J. (ed.) (1998) *Image-based Research: A Sourcebook for Qualitative Researchers.* London: Falmer Press.

Steiger, R. (1998) 'On the Uses of Documentary: The Photography of Ernst Brunner', *Visual Sociology,* 13 (1): 25–48.

5.7 Reading Film: Using Films and Videos as Empirical Social Science Material

Norman K. Denzin

We tend to privilege experience itself, as if [black] life is lived experience outside of representation ... [but] there is no escape from the politics of representation ... it is only through the way in which we represent and imagine ourselves that we come to know how we are constituted and who we are. (Stuart Hall, 1996d: 473)

In this chapter I explore the use of film and photography by sociologists and students of cultural studies (Hall 1996a,b; see **3.9**). A visual sociology, or a sociology that critically interprets visual representations, has recently come into existence (see Flick 2002: 133–164). The empirical materials of a visual sociology include still photography, advertisements, audiovisual recordings, narrative texts, television, documentary films and Hollywood movies. As a method of research, a sociology of visual representation deals simultaneously with the grammars, semantics and syntax of vision, perception and interpretation.

There is a two-part need for analysing the visual representations of a culture. First, humans have no direct access to reality. They live in a second-hand world of meanings, a world shaped by the meaning-making institutions of the society (Mills 1963: 375). Daily life and its realities are mediated by symbolic and visual representations. These representations are not objectively neutral cultural texts. They express and are shaped by ideological, class, national, gender and racial biases. A critical sociology must learn how to read and analyse these systems of representation and interpretation.

Second, these visual representations are interactional productions. 'Pictures do not simply make assertions ... rather we interact with them in order to arrive at conclusions' (Becker l986a: 279; also 1998: 158–159). Accordingly, the visual representations of a society are both methods of research, and resources, or topics to be studied in their own right. These two assertions organize my discussion in this chapter. I will keep asking 'How do these methods represent society?' and 'How may sociologists read, interpret and use them?'

I will begin by offering a brief review of the use of film and photography in the social sciences. Next, using the work of the Vietnamese filmmaker Trinh T. Mi-Ha (1989, 1991, 1992), I will compare and contrast the essential features and visual epistemological assumptions of the classic documentary and postmodern approaches to the visual text. Thirdly, a method of textual interpretation will be presented. Fourthly I will briefly discuss how film and visual representations as research tools can be used to explore and critically examine society. I will conclude with the principles of visual research.

1 PRIOR USES OF FILM

There is a long history of using film and photography in the human disciplines (see Harper 1994, 2000). Educational films have been used for instructional purposes in United States grade schools since l9l8, in high schools since the l930s, and in colleges since the 1960s. Visual sociology and anthroplogy are primarily subfields of their parent disciplines, and related, at the same time, to qualitative and ethnographic research methods (Harper 1994: 403; see **5.6**). Anthropologists, for example, have been producing documentary films and using photography at least since the l940s, when Gregory Bateson and Margaret Mead (l942) produced their famous photographic study of Balinese character.

However, as Harper notes, at the present time ethnography and documentary photography, 'the two sources for visual sociology, are being questioned and recast' (1994: 403). Interpretative ethnography has turned away from classic forms of ethnographic representation, where pictures were used to document a stable reality. Ethnographers now experiment with first-person texts, photo collages and new forms of visual representation, weaving fact, fiction and autobiography together in the same visual text, even using actors as real persons (see Trinh 1992). The work of Trinh elaborates these changes in the field.

2 CINEMA MEETS ETHNOGRAPHY

Trinh is a filmmaker first. She begins by deconstructing the classic documentary film, the ethnographic film which enters the native's world and brings news from that world to the world of the Western observer. Like ethnography, which separated itself from fiction (Clough

1998: 26–27), the documentary film defines itself against mainstream, Hollywood cinema. Not tangled up in the star and studio system, documentary 'takes real people and real problems from the real world and *deals* with them. It sets a value on intimate observation, and *assesses its worth* according to how well it succeeds in capturing reality on the run ... . Powerful living stories, infinite authentic situations' (Trinh 1991: 33; italics in original).

Documentary film starts with the real world, it uses an aesthetic of objectivity, and a technological apparatus which produces truthful statements (images) about the world (1991: 33). The following elements are central to this apparatus (1991: 33–36).

- The relentless pursuit of naturalism which requires a connection between the moving image and the spoken word.
- Use of the directional microphone and the portable tape-recorder.
- Lip-synchronous sound.
- Authenticity – real people in real situations.
- Real time is more truthful than film time; hence the long-take.
- Minimal editing, and no use of montage.
- Few close-ups, emphasis on wide-angle shots.
- Use of the hand-held, unobtrusive camera to 'provoke people into uttering the "truth" that they would not otherwise unveil in ordinary situations' (1991: 34).
- The filmmaker is an observer, not a person who creates what is photographed.
- Only events, unaffected by the recording eye, should be captured.
- The film captures objective reality.
- Truth must be dramatized.
- Actual facts should be presented in a credible way, with people telling them.
- The film must convince the spectators that they should have confidence in the truth of what they see.
- A focus on common experience, by which the 'social' is defined.
- The presence of the filmmaker is masked, hidden.
- The use of various persuasive techniques, including personal testimony, and the talk of plain folks.
- The film is made for the common, silent people; they are the film's referent.
- The film is shot with three cameras: the camera in the technical sense; the filmmaker's

mind; and the generic patterns of documentary film. The film's facts are a product of these three cameras (1991: 39).

These aesthetic strategies define the documentary style, allowing the filmmaker to create a text which gives the viewer the illusion of having 'unmediated access to reality' (1991: 40). Thus naturalized, the documentary style has become part of the larger cinematic apparatus in American culture, including a pervasive presence in TV commercials and news (1991: 40).

Trinh brings a reflexive reading to these features of the documentary film, citing her own texts as examples of documentaries that are sensitive to the flow of fact and fiction, to nuances, to meanings as political constructions (1991: 41). Such texts reflexively understand that reality is never neutral, or objective, that it is always socially constructed. Filmmaking thus becomes a question of 'framing' reality. Self-reflexivity does not translate into personal style, or a preoccupation with method. It rather centres on the reflexive interval that defines representation, 'the place in which the play within the textual frame is a play on this very frame, hence on the borderlines of the textual and the extratextual ... a work that reflects back on itself offers itself infinitely as nothing else but work ... and void' (1991: 48). In such works meaning is not imposed. The film becomes a site for multiple experiences.

A responsible, reflexive text embodies the following characteristics (1991: 188).

- It announces its own politics and evidences a political consciousness.
- It interrogates the realities it represents.
- It invokes the teller's story in the history that is told.
- It makes the audience responsible for interpretation.
- It resists the temptation to become an object of consumption.
- It resists all dichotomies (male/female, etc.).
- It foregrounds difference, not conflict.
- It uses multiple voices, emphasizing language as silence, the grain of the voice, tone, inflection, pauses, silences, repetitions.
- It presents silence as a form of resistance.

Reflexive films seek the truth of life's fictions, the spirit of truth that resides in life experiences, in fables, proverbs, where nothing is explained, but everything is evoked (1991: 162).

3 TRINH'S OCULAR EPISTEMOLOGY

Trinh creates the space for a new ocular epistemology, a version of the cinematic apparatus that challenges mainstream film, and traditional ethnography and its use of realistic documentaries. Reflexive film questions the very notion of a stable, unbiased, middle class gaze (1991: 97–98, 115). It focuses on the pensive image, on representations that do not turn women into versions of the exotic, erotic, feminine ethnic minority other (1991: 115). The pensive image 'unsettles the male apparatus of the gaze, in which men own, articulate, and create the look of woman as either being looked-at ... [or as one who] holds the [male] look to signify the master's desire' (1991: 115). This look makes the camera's gaze visible. It destablizes any sense of verisimilitude that can be brought to this visual world. In so doing it disrupts the spectator's gaze, itself a creation of the unnoticed camera, the camera which invokes the image of a perfect, natural world, a world with verisimilitude (1991: 115).

This ocular epistemology creates the space for a subversive cinema, a cinema that creates new ways of encountering reality and its representations. Thus in the film *Surname Viet Given Name Nam* Trinh deconstructs the interview and its basis in the documentary film. (The film, made in 1989, is a study of Vietnamese women, whose names change and remain constant, depending on whether or not they marry a foreigner or a Vietnamese.) Trinh (1992: 49) has Vietnamese women speak from five places representing lineage, gender and age status, leadership position and historical period. This creates a complex picture of Vietnamese culture (1992: 144). The film is multi-textual, layered with pensive images of women in various situations. Historical moments overlap with age periods (childhood, youth, adulthood, old age), ritual ceremonies (weddings, funerals, war, the market, dance), and daily household work (cooking), while interviewees talk to off-screen interviewers. There are two voice-overs in English, a third voice sings sayings, proverbs, and poetry in Vietnamese (with translations as texts on the screen). There are also interviews with Vietnamese subtitled in English, and interviews in English synchronized with the on-screen image (Trinh 1992: 49). The interviews are re-enacted in Trinh's film by Vietnamese women, who are then interviewed at the end of the film, asked about their experiences of being performers in the film (1992: 146).

In un-doing the interview as a form of gathering information about reality, Trinh takes up the question of truth (1992: 145). Whose truth is she presenting, that of the original interviewer (Mai 1983), that given in the on-screen interview situation, or that of the women-as-actresses who are interviewed at the end of the film? The film allows the practice of doing interviews (see **5.3**) to enter into the construction of the text itself, thus the true and the false (the actresses are not the women interviewed by Mai Thu Van), the real and the staged, intermingle, indeed the early sections of the film unfold like a traditional, realist documentary film (Trinh 1992: 145). The viewer does not know these are actresses re-enacting interviews. Nor does the viewer know that the interviews were conducted in the United States, not Vietnam. (This only becomes apparent near the end of the film.)

In using these interpretive strategies, Trinh creates the space for the viewer to critically appraise the politics of representation that structure the documentary film.

4   READING PHOTOGRAPHS AND FILMS

A film or a photograph offers an image, or set of images, which are interpretations of the real. The real, or the slice of reality that is captured, can never be reproduced, for what is represented can only occur once. Visual documents are records of events that have occurred in the past (Barthes 1981).

Film (and photographs) speak a language of emotion, and meaning. They present a vocabulary and set of framing devices which mediate and define reality for the viewer. Four narrative or meaning structures exist in any film, or set of photographs: (1) the visual text, (2) the audio text, including what photographers say about their photographs, (3) the narrative that links the visual and audio text into a coherent story, or framework, and (4) the interpretations and meanings the viewer (including the social scientist) bring to the visual, audio and narrative texts. No visual text evokes the same meanings for all viewers. In the process of interacting with the text viewers develop readings and interpretations that are uniquely their own.

A film or a picture can be read as having meaning at two different levels. The first is the literal, or 'realist', level. This is a picture of 'X'. A literal reading takes a visual representation on 'face value'. It asks, 'What does this representation say about X?' The second level of meaning is the one that is below the surface. It is the one that suggests that there is more going on here than just a representation of 'X'. Readings at this level are called subversive. They challenge, go beneath, and go beyond the surface, literal interpretations of a text.

Realist readings: A realist reading of a visual document has four characteristics. First it treats a visual text as a realistic, truthful depiction of some phenomenon. Realist readings assume that pictures are windows to the real world. Secondly, a text is viewed as establishing truth claims about the world and the events that go on in it. That is, it tells the truth. Thirdly, the meaning of a photo-visual text can be given through a close reading of its contents, its attention to detail, its depiction of characters, and its dialogue. Fourthly, these readings will validate the truth claims the film or text makes about reality. A traditional realist reading attempts to discover how visual texts speak to the 'universal' features of the human condition.

Subversive readings: Subversive readings challenge realist interpretations. They suggest that the realism in visual texts is always filtered through preconceptions and biases. Hence a work's claim to being a truthful reflection of 'reality-as-it-really-is' must always be challenged. A subversive reading argues that the truth statements that a realist claims for a text are always biased. They reflect, that is, the viewer's point of view.

A film, under a subversive reading, does not speak to the universal features of the human condition. It only speaks to limited versions of human experience; that is, those captured by the photographer, or filmmaker. A close reading of a film or photograph will reveal other features that a realist reading ignores. It will focus on minor characters, not just major characters. It will contrast the positions of men, women and children in the narrative. It will look at how the film idealizes certain key cultural values, like family, work, religion and love. These features will be the ones that will be highlighted in a subversive reading. By illuminating them, the critic then argues that the film's dominant message presents only one view of reality. The goal of the subversive reading is to discover the multiple meanings that can be found in a film's text.

A film creates its particular version of truth by suppressing particular contradictions that exist within its text. These contradictions will appear at those junctures in the narrative when the film (or visual text) answers cause and effect questions. By examining how a film answers these causal questions a subversive reading illuminates the underlying values the text is attempting to promote.

Of course, a subversive reading can be challenged by a realist reading. It should be clear that the second level of meaning in a visual text can only be discovered after the surface, literal levels of meaning have been interpreted. Any text should be read both ways. There is never a correct reading of a visual text. There are only multiple interpretations. It is erroneous to confine interpretations to just the realist, or subversive levels. To do so misses the other layers of meaning that are always present in a text.

5 EXPLORING SOCIETY WITH FILM AND PHOTOGRAPHY

Visual representations reflect and define problematic cultural experiences, including war, divorce, incest, alcoholism, drug abuse, political corruption, love, birth and death. Hollywood films document key historical moments in the life of a society. Films can expose problems and corruption in key social institutions. Hollywood films express and convey political ideology and core cultural values. Frank Capra's social message films of the 1930s and 1940s (*Mr Smith Goes to Washington, It's a Wonderful Life*) recreated an imagined social past in the United States with comfortable homes, close-knit families, friendly neighbourhoods, prosperous communities and bountiful farms located on the edges of a benign wilderness. These films reproduce the gender, race, ethnic and class relations in society. They inevitably place white males in positions of power, locate women in the family, cast racial and ethnic minorities in service, and servant positions, or attach violent, anti-social attitudes and behaviours to them. In so doing, these films create representations that structure reality. They keep alive the myth of the autonomous individual in the modern mass society.

Films and other visual texts create emotional experiences for viewers. Cinema creates viewer identification with characters who embody the central cultural values, often presenting idealized versions of the male–female, lover, husband–wife, intimate relationship. At the same time, visual texts provide interpretive structures for dealing with problematic everyday life events.

In these several ways Hollywood films reveal, illuminate and explore society. The reading and analysis of these films allows the sociologist to see things about his or her society that might not otherwise be seen. By studying these interactional, processual representations, including how they are made, distributed, and given meaning by the viewing public, the sociologist is able to engage in a level of critical cultural analysis that other sociological methods do not allow.

6 THE PRINCIPLES OF CRITICAL VISUAL RESEARCH

It is now necessary to state a number of principles that organize visual research, including the critical analysis of visual documents. The following guidelines are provisional, and should be fitted to the needs of the researcher (see Collier and Collier 1986: 178–179).

1 Phase One: 'Looking and Feeling'

   A Observe the visual documents as a totality.

   B Look and listen to the materials. Let them talk to you. Feel their effects on you. Record these feelings and impressions.

   C Write down questions that occur to you. Note patterns of meaning.

2 Phase Two: 'What Question Are You Asking?'

   A State your research question.

   B What questions does the text claim to answer?

   C How does it represent and define key cultural values?

   D Inventory the evidence, note key scenes, and images.

3 Phase Three: 'Structured Microanalysis'

  A Do a scene by scene, microanalysis, transcribe discourse, describe scenes, take quotes from the text.
  B Form and find patterns and sequences.
  C Write detailed descriptions.
  D How does the text present objective reality, handle facts, represent experience, and dramatize truth?
  E Keep a focus on the research question.
  F Idenfity major moments in the film/text when conflicts over values occur.
  G Detail how the film/text/image takes a position on these values.

4 Phase Four: 'Search for Patterns'

  A Return to the complete record.
  B Lay out all the photographs, or view the film in its entirety.
  C Return to the research question. How do these documents speak to and answer your question?
  D Contrast realist and subversive readings of the text.
  E Write an interpretation, based on the principles of interpretation discussed above.

These steps will aid in the production and organization of a research statement based on visual documents. They will allow your reader to visually enter the visual situations you have studied. He or she can then judge whether or not your interpretations are naturalistically generalizable to their fields of experience.

7 CONCLUSIONS

I have examined how social scientists may use film and photography as research methods. Visual representations are simultaneously a means of communication and a method of enquiry. Films are cultural and symbolic forms and they may be used to reveal and illuminate important features of social life. Visually recorded documents are of use 'so long as we are aware of how and by what rules we choose our subject matter, and so long as we are aware of and make explicit, how we organized the various units of film from which we do our analysis' (Worth 1981: 193–194). I have attempted to clarify some of these rules in this chapter.

FURTHER READING

Bateson, G. and Mead, M (1942) *Balinese Character: A Photographic Analysis*. New York: New York Academy of Sciences.

Harper, D. (2000) 'Reimagining Visual Methods: Galileo to Neuromancer', in N. Denzin and Y. S. Lincoln (eds), *Handbook of Qualitative Research*, 2nd edn. London: Sage. pp. 717–732.

Trinh, T. M. (1992) *Framer Framed*. New York: Routledge.

5.8 Electronic Process Data and Analysis

Jörg R. Bergmann and Christoph Meier

The development of new information and communication technologies and their growth in our life-world have led to the formation of novel interactive situations and forms of communication which were largely unknown until recently and which, even today, are still comparatively unfamiliar to large population groups – particularly in the older generation. Communities, organizations and businesses appear on web pages with their services and offers, and private individuals often engage in imaginative self-presentation on their homepages. Email is increasingly being used instead of written communication, people more often meet one another through electronic contact exchanges such as ICQ (= 'I seek you') or converse through Internet Relay Chat (IRC).

And finally, using respective applications (like Microsoft's NetMeeting) and a sufficiently fast connection to the internet makes collaborative work on documents with simultaneous sound and image connections possible (see Filinski 1998 for a description of different forms of internet-based communication).

Social scientists have also discovered the 'new media' for themselves using email contact with text exchanges and other materials via attachments, literature searches, data on the internet and presentation of their own research interests and publications on homepages. However, social scientists should not restrict themselves these media as if they were natural resources for their own activities, rather they should also make them an issue for social scientific analyses (Garfinkel 1967a). The influences, procedures for communication and maybe the content of these new media remain unclear but may lead to completely new forms and ways of socialization. For methodological and substantial reasons, it is the task of the social sciences to study these new media with respect to their own dynamics and logic, to describe the interaction situations and communicative forms they generate and to demonstrate how processes of socialization are influenced, formed, produced or obstructed.

If we take on this task it rapidly becomes clear that issue-related research cannot begin without preparation. In the first place there are new methodological challenges and problems that cannot simply be overcome by a combination of established procedures in the sense of triangulation (see **4.6**), as Williams et al. (1988: 51) suggested. In what follows we shall demonstrate this under four headings.

1 ELECTRONIC PROCESS DATA

Even if electronically mediated communication processes appear to be especially fleeting and non-material, they do leave traces. These traces cannot, of course, be detected with the naked eye; but they can more easily be read than perhaps many participants would like, and for this reason they contain a quite threatening *potential for social control* (cf. Dern 1997). Long before the sociologists, other professions had discovered these traces as important sources of information. It is now possible, for example, to record the search and access behaviour of members of a company in the use of the World Wide Web. Emails are sent whose attachments contain cartoons and which, after the attachment has been opened, give the observer the (faked) message that the network administrator has recorded a 'non-professional use of the Internet access', and will pass this on to the appropriate location. In addition, the information resulting from surfing the Web which ends up on the user's hard disc in the form of so-called 'cookies' is systematically analysed for market research purposes and the appropriate addition of promotional messages.

At the moment when communication takes place in an electronic format, different types of process-engendered data are simultaneously created. In general, the term *process data* refers to all those data that occur and are collected as records of public or private organizations in the context of their activity (Müller 1977). By analogy, *electronic process data* is used to refer to all data that are generated in the course of computer-assisted communication processes and work activities – either automatically or on the basis of adjustments by the user. In this way our understanding of electronic process data is narrower than the concept of 'computer-monitored data' (Williams et al. 1988: 91f.), which also includes automatic collection of television viewing, for example, or the use of databases. Electronic process data are found in the form of files on local hard discs, or on the servers of computer centres, and they include such things as logs of chat sessions, files with the content of emails and html files (html = hypertext markup language), and the related graphic elements. Electronic process data, of course, are not readily accessible (and at present are in a grey area legally), but they represent an important resource for the investigation of computer-assisted communication processes.

Admittedly, there are two important restrictions here. On the one hand such files usually have to be transformed and prepared for an investigation. (More on this in the next section.) And on the other hand, it must be remembered that the files have a technical functionality of their own, and – since they were not produced for the

purpose of scientific investigation – may seem deficient from a research perspective (cf. Garfinkel 1967b and his analysis of 'good' reasons for 'bad' hospital documents). Therefore, in electronic process data the result of communication and interactive processes is indeed manifested, but the process itself is not reflected. This will now be briefly illustrated, using the example of emails and web pages.

An email that reaches its addressee via the Internet is the end result of prior activities. To understand and investigate how this result comes about, what formulations are first selected and then rejected, and what resources the author relies on in writing an email (for example, earlier mail from the recipient, the automatic spell-check, and so on) other data are needed. To investigate the factual operation of electronic communication media, one needs an *ongoing documentation* of what appears on the computer screen. In addition, some documentation of what is going on in the immediate working vicinity may be sensible. Only in this way can we observe whether muttering, groaning or laughing make the writing or reading of emails appear to be a troublesome or pleasurable matter to colleagues in the same office.

Similar limitations on electronic process data are to be found with communication via web pages. The page consulted may well be identified from the files stored in the cache of the browser, but the underlying communication process can only be reconstructed in an imprecise fashion. Search movements with the mouse, going back rapidly over one or more links, scrolling through long pages, or pausing at particular points in a text cannot be captured in this way.

The process data that arise in the course of electronically transmitted communication have, in addition, properties of their own. This is particularly true in the case of recording visits to different web pages. Such pages normally consist of a wide variety of elements: formatted text, graphics, coloured background, animated illustrations, embedded video-clips and possibly background music merge here into a *hybrid* with different interpretation requirements than a text that is script-based or has a linear construction (for discussion, cf. Kress and van Leeuwen 1996: 181–229; Nickl 1998: 391; Schmitz 1997: 136–147). Since all these elements are integrated into the structure, web pages must be understood as a separate communicative 'genre' (see **5.18**) for which the amalgamation of a wide range of representational elements is constitutive. A procedure that limits itself to separating out and describing individually some parts of the process data that were created in browsing (for example, the sequence of links followed, or the textual or graphic structure of the pages visited) would therefore inevitably result in the loss of the original object. In our view, this problem is common to all sociological approaches, irrespective of whether one is pursuing a quantifying procedure or the particular research logic of qualitative research.

2 DOCUMENTATION

From what we have just argued, we may derive a requirement to develop forms of documentation that preserve for analysis the details of electronically transmitted communication and interactive processes and the nature of process data as technically separate components in a hybrid that was integrated in advance. The strategies that we might pursue here will be illustrated briefly with the example of web page documentation.

When web pages are stored as html documents their text and formatting can indeed be documented. Embedded objects such as graphic elements, however, are omitted and are represented simply as empty spaces. In a paper printout produced in this way the highly contoured landscape of a web page is flattened out and reduced to a bare text. Even the production of 'screen shots' is not a satisfactory solution. It is true that this does produce a copy of what is visible on the screen, but not all areas of web pages are documented in this way, since some of them can only be reached by scrolling downwards. More recent versions of browsers, with inbuilt 'offline functions', provide a good solution here. With them it is possible to produce copies of individual web pages and also complete websites with all the pages that belong to them. But even here there are limitations on the documentation. These offline browsers only function without problems if the web pages to be documented consist of static html pages. On the other hand, dynamic elements (such as password questions, Java applets, sound playback or screen contents brought about through real-time mouse co-ordinates) still cause problems. An overview of 'offline browsers' may be found in Gieseke (1998: 75–197).

For a more detailed analysis of computer-assisted processes of work and communication, what must be reflected, beyond the preservation of the wealth of detail and the nature of the process data as separate components of a pre-integrated hybrid, is the *temporal structure of the event*. This is not only true of cases where a video-medium interaction – such as a video-conference on the basis of web-conferencing software (for example, Microsoft's Netmeeting) – is being investigated. It is generally true of the investigation of PC-supported activities. For example, the cursor, depending on the screen area across which it is currently travelling, may take on a different shape. And in the course of particular inputs and activities, windows, dialogue boxes and commands appear, which then disappear in the course of subsequent actions. One possibility for the documentation of these events consists of 'filming' the PC screen, using special software (such as Lotus Screen-Cam). These 'films' provide a *real-time documentation* of what is happening on the computer screen, and can be repeatedly viewed for the purposes of analysis. The data generated in this way may, of course, become extremely voluminous, and here the size of the film-files will depend upon the quantity of changes to the screen content and a series of technical settings (screen resolution, depth of colour, speed of picture, and settings for sound recording). Further information can be found in sites such as <http://www.lotus.com/home.nsf/tabs/screencam>.

PC-supported communication processes may, of course, be documented by means of an audio-visual recording with a camera. In this case it would be advisable to adapt the familiar practices for video-recording (see **5.7**) to the new environment. To avoid a disturbing 'picture-roll' while filming a computer screen, one needs a high-grade camera where the frame speed may be adjusted to the signal from the PC videocard. Alternatively, there is a possibility of installing in the PC a graphics card that simultaneously emits the picture information as a standard television signal (PAL). A video-recorder can then be connected to this graphics card, so that what happens on the computer screen can be recorded as a video-film. Finally, there is the possibility of installing a picture converter between a PC graphics card and the PC monitor, and again of connecting a video-recorder to this converter (more detail is given in Meier 1998).

3   ANALYSIS

Web pages – as well as other types of electronic process data – are multi-modal hybrids *par excellence*. Their special character must be considered not only in documentation but also in the course of the analysis. What consequences this might have for the logic of interpretative procedures (see **5.16**) cannot yet be predicted. At present there are no established qualitative methods for these kinds of data. It is important, however, to adapt and modify the existing well-tried analytical procedures for the particular character of electronic process data. A procedure of this kind may be found in works such as those of Englisch (1991) or Wolff (1995), who have adapted the procedures of objective hermeneutics or conversation analysis – which developed in dealing with conversation data – for pictures or for texts created in written form.

The adaptation of existing procedures to the investigation of electronic process is a task for future research. This cannot be done here, but we would like to indicate briefly what problems this will produce for the concept of *sequentiality* that is central to conversation analysis (see **5.17**). Here one must indeed ask what role is played by sequentiality in looking at web pages. Can one speak at all of a sequentiality of action? Is it possible that elements that function to catch the eye, and elements that function as vectors and lead the eye on, can produces sequences of activities and reading pathways (cf. Kress and van Leeuwen 1996: 218–219)? Can the sequencing of activities such as the way the eye of the observer travels in any sense be documented (which is a basic precondition for subsequent analysis)? Do hyperlinks to other web pages suggest particular pathways in the Net? Or does hypertext organization imply that one can no longer talk of the 'conditional relevance' of the ensuing steps in an action?

It is not to be expected that the analytical concepts introduced in the course of this kind of adaptation can be taken over and used in a one-for-one way. Moreover, apart from the adaptation of existing procedures, it will be necessary to combine and integrate a variety of procedures. For the case of the *multi-modal process data* discussed here, this means that in any research plan the investigator must be willing to be inspired by composition analysis, picture analysis, sequential analysis, content analysis or even ethno-semantic procedures.

4   PRESENTATION

The development of computer-assisted work and communication technologies not only leads to the development of new interactive situations, new communication forms and thereby also to new research issues. New forms for the presentation of sociological research work have also developed. One example of this is specialist journals that are published online. In addition, it may be argued that the World Wide Web is particularly suited to the representation and explication of issues in sociological research. This is primarily true of issues that are not based on script – for example, collections of pictures, historic sound documents or audiovisual recordings. Interactive situations may therefore be represented in a more intact way, with fewer losses, through excerpts from audiovisual documents than would be possible, for example, by means of transcripts (Slack 1998, sections 4.2 and 4.4). This means, on the one hand, that the Web can be used to make available primary materials on which an investigation is based, and this increases substantially the verifiability of qualitative research results. On the other hand, presentations of results and publications can be made in a multi-modal form. One example of this would be essays or books for which further materials that would be difficult to present in textual form can be called up from web-servers.

It may, with reasonable certainty, be expected that with these new presentation possibilities there will be a substantial reduction in the traditional pressure to record all empirical data in written form. Against this background we may speculate about the long-term effect electronically transmitted communication will have on the processes of qualitative research. It is, for example, thinkable that the investment of time necessary for the various phases in a piece of qualitative research will change. In addition, we may expect some effects on the process of data analysis. Traditionally, for example, the time-consuming transcriptions in the investigation of linguistic and non-linguistic communication were motivated not only by their analytic uses but by the fact that they were necessary for any presentation of results. The declining pressure for textualization will lead to a situation where interpretative work will be carried out less on the basis of transcripts and more on the basis of the source materials. This may lead to analyses being closer to their materials – a highly desirable result for qualitative research. At the same time it also leads to an increase in the risk that such things as audiovisual documentation will naively be treated as something 'given', that is as 'data', and its nature as a set of *methodologically created constructs* (cf. Bergmann 1985: 317) will be lost from view.

FURTHER READING

Dochartaigh, N. O. (2001) *The Internet Research Handbook.* London: Sage.

Mann, C. and Stewart, F. (2002) *Internet Communication and Qualitative Research.* London: Sage.

Williams, F., Rice, R. E. and Rogers, E. M. (1988) *Research Methods and the New Media.* New York: Free Press.

5.9   The Transcription of Conversations

Sabine Kowal and Daniel C. O'Connell

1   THE DEFINITION OF TRANSCRIPTION

Transcription is understood as the graphic representation of selected aspects of the behaviour of individuals engaged in a conversation (for example, an interview or an everyday chat). Transcription involves *transcribers*, a *system of notation*, the product in the form of a *transcript*, and the *transcript readers*. Transcripts are needed to make fleeting conversational behaviour permanently available on paper for scientific analysis. The aim of producing a transcript is to represent on paper as accurately as possible the strings of words uttered (verbal features), but frequently also their acoustic form, for example, in the shape of pitch height or loudness (prosodic features) and any accompanying non-linguistic behaviour (whether it be vocal, such as laughing or throat-clearing – paralinguistic features – or non-vocal, such as gestures or eye movements – extralinguistic features). The result of this is to make visible the characteristics of a unique conversation. Transcripts should be understood as complementary to, rather than as a substitute for, electronic recordings.

Transcription should be distinguished from the *description* of conversational behaviour. For example, an audible intake of breath by one participant may be transcribed as '.hhh' or described as 'BREATHING'. The letter 'h', it is assumed, represents in written form the act of breathing, and the number of letters gives an impression of the duration of this breathing. In a transcription, therefore, an attempt is made to reproduce in written form features of the conversational behaviour in such a way that there is a relationship of similarity between the behaviour and its notation on paper. Conversely, in description there is no relationship of similarity between the behaviour and its notation. Transcript readers learn from the description 'BREATHING' only that somebody breathed, but not how this was done.

Transcription must also be distinguished from coding of verbal utterances, that is, from their classification according to fixed categories. Transcription systems have been developed in a variety of disciplines. Among these are anthropology (e.g. Duranti 1997), linguistics (e.g. Ehlich 1993), sociology (e.g. Atkinson and Heritage 1984) and psychology (e.g. MacWhinney 1995).

2 THE DEVELOPMENT OF TRANSCRIPTION SYSTEMS

The following basic decisions contribute to the development of a transcription system.

1　The selection of the features of behaviour to be transcribed (verbal, prosodic, paralinguistic, extralinguistic); this selection is always determined by the goals and questions of a specific research project.
2　The selection of a system of notation (e.g. the notation of syllable lengthening as 'da', 'da' or 'da='); this is determined by the availability of an appropriate repertoire of symbols and by assumptions about the readability of the transcripts.
3　The selection of the transcription format for spatially ordering, on paper or on a computer screen, the temporal sequence of conversational turns (for example, as a score or in lines).
4　Determining the abilities required of transcribers for the reliable and valid use of the notation system.
5　Determining the abilities assumed for the reading of transcripts by different readerships (for example, lay people, linguists, anthropologists or computers).

Whilst putting verbal utterances into written form has historically always played a role, it is only in the past few decades that different *systems* have been developed (cf. Ehlich and Switalla 1976). This increased interest may be traced back, on the one hand, to technological developments (audio and video equipment as well as computers), and on the other hand to the creation of data-banks that are networked worldwide for the exchange of transcripts (Leech et al. 1995). The oldest transcription systems include, in the English-speaking world, Jefferson's transcription notation for conversation analysis (Jefferson 1972; Psathas and Anderson 1990),

and in German-speaking countries the semi-interpretative working transcription (HIAT = *Halbinterpretativen Arbeitstranskriptionen*) of Ehlich and Rehbein (1976). Since the early 1990s there has been a more intensive interest in transcription and the development of new systems, but also in critical considerations about their theoretical foundations (e.g. Edwards and Lampert 1993, Kowal and O'Connell 2003b).

3 TRANSCRIPTION AS THEORY

For many years the production of transcripts was considered to be a theoretically neutral process that proceeded from primary data (the original conversation) via secondary data (the audio or video recording of the conversation) to the tertiary data (the transcript of the conversation on the basis of the audio and video recordings): transcribers simply put onto paper what was said and done in the conversation, and the readers of transcripts knew from this how the conversation ran. What was overlooked here was the fact that the creation and use of transcripts are theory-loaded constructive processes. Transcripts are actually characterized by a considerable reduction of the almost infinitely rich primary and secondary data (Cook 1990) as well as by the fact that time-restricted conversational behaviour is transformed into a time-free visual product. Transcripts, therefore, are always selective constructions, and this selectivity has an impact on the analysis and interpretation of transcripts (Ochs 1979). This theory-loaded nature affects each of the aspects of transcription mentioned at the outset, since the production and use of transcripts always involves people with their particular goals, capabilities and limitations.

In more recent transcription systems an increasing awareness of this theoretical dependency is seen in the fact that the selection of notation symbols is fixed and justified and that explicit bases are formulated for developing the systems that affect the production and use of transcripts. Ehlich, for example, stresses that the HIAT system has '(a) simplicity and validity, (b) good readability and correctability and (c) minimum of transcriber and user training' (1993: 125). Selting et al. (1998) add that their conversation analysis transcription system (GAT = *Gesprächsanalytisches Transkriptionssytem*) should also include 'extendability and refinability of the notation' (the so-called 'onion principle').

4 THE PRODUCTION OF TRANSCRIPTS

As a rule transcribing begins with secondary data, such as a tape recording. In every transcript the first thing to be put into written form is the words that the participants have uttered. For this four different forms of written representation are possible: (a) standard orthography, (b) literary transcription, (c) *eye dialect* and (d) phonetic transcription. A representation in standard orthography is based on the norms of the written language and makes the tasks of the transcribers easier. But at the same time it fails to take account of peculiarities of the spoken language, such as the omission of individual sounds (elision) or reciprocal effect of adjacent sounds (assimilation). This is particularly true where speakers deviate from the standard language. These deviations are taken into account in a literary transcription as, for instance, in the elision of 'o' in '*don't*' for '*donot*' or in the assimilation of '*ain't*' for 'is not'. The so-called *eye dialect*, which is used particularly in English-language transcripts for ethnomethodological conversation analysis (see **5.17**), deviates still farther from standard orthography in order to represent colloquial language as faithfully as possible in terms of sounds, as, for example, in '*askedche*' for '*asked you*'. Phonetic transcription using the International Phonetic Alphabet (IPA) represents verbal utterances in phonetic-phonological categories, for example '[ge:n]' for '*gehn*'. In conversational research phonetic transcription is seldom used, because it contains too much information and is difficult to use and to read.

The sequencing of turns on the axes of the transcript is represented differently in the individual systems. One transcription format that is frequently used is the linear writing mode (cf., for example, GAT in Selting et al. 1998: 97ff.), which may be demonstrated with the following fictitious example:

Example 1:

```
A:  have you seen him
B:  no why did [you
A:            [oh sure he was [already there
B:                           [hm
```

Immediately following turns always begin here with a new line in the transcript, so that where lines appear below one another this represents turns which follow each other. A's follow-up turn, which begins at the same time as B's turn, however, is shifted horizontally to the right, and the simultaneity of speaking is indicated with square brackets. Instances of listener feedback, such as '*hm*', are also shifted horizontally and marked with square brackets. Another transcription format is the 'score format' used in HIAT (Ehlich and Rehbein 1976).

Example 2:

```
A: [have you seen him     oh sure he
B:                     no why did you
A: ⌈was already there
B: ⌊   hm
```

Score writing differs from the linear format in its so-called simultaneous axis that is indicated on the left hand edge of the transcript by a square bracket of variable size (depending on the number of speakers) that goes across a number of lines. Within the simultaneous axis the horizontal arrangement of turns shows whether these turns follow one another or occur simultaneously. On the vertical axis one line is provided for each speaker, and this is retained even after a change of speaker.

Most notation symbols that are not letters are used to represent prosodic features. Among the frequently recorded prosodic features we find: pauses, emphasis, intonation, lengthening and volume. In fictitious example 3 we contrast the transcription of such prosodic features in the HIAT system (Ehlich 1993) with that found in GAT (Selting et al. 1998)

Example 3:

```
        HIAT                    GAT

A:  have you . seen him   A:  have !YOU! (.) seen
                                  him?
                 <<<<<
B:             no: why    B:  no: <<f>why).
```

In both HIAT and GAT short pauses are represented by '.' or by '(.)'; emphasis is shown by underlining or by capital letters between exclamation marks; rising intonation by '’' or by '?', falling intonation by '`' or by '.'. Syllable lengthening is shown in both systems by ':'; and volume by '<<<<<<<' as a superscript or '<<f>>'.

Paralinguistic features, to which belong non-linguistic vocal phenomena such as laughter, sighing or breathing (but cf. Selting 2000), are either transcribed or described in most current transcription systems. In HIAT, for example, laughter is described by '((Laughter))' (Ehlich and Rehbein 1976: 31), whereas in GAT it is either described with '((laughs))' or transcribed as 'hahaha' (Selting et al. 1998: 100).

Extralinguistic features include numerous visible (for example, direction of gaze, gestures) and audible non-vocal (for example, applause) forms of behaviour, which occur as accompaniments to speech. In some systems they are given no attention at all (e.g. Du Bois 1991), whereas HIAT (Ehlich 1993: 135–140) and GAT (Selting et al. 1998: 109–113) deal with them extensively.

5 PROBLEMS

The decisions mentioned above, which deal with the development of a transcription system and its use, are all interrelated, and with each of them there are problems that have so far not been solved. The selection of the transcribed categories (in particular prosodic features) is frequently not motivated by any research, which means that considerable effort is devoted to transcribing much more material than will be analysed. In practice, the availability of a comprehensive transcription system seems to suggest to users that they have to use the complete system, without limitation, in every single research project.

Within the same system as well as between different systems the same symbol is sometimes found for the notation of different phenomena (cf. the symbol '.' in example 3, which in HIAT marks a brief pause and in GAT low falling intonation), and, conversely, different symbols are used for marking the same phenomenon. The problem here is that notation symbols, and what they represent, cannot be allocated unambiguously.

The most fundamental problems, however, are less at the level of the system itself than at the level of behaviour in the use of the system. For example, in transcribing conversations, the *transcribers*, therefore, have to put on paper verbal phenomena which – as participants in conversations – they have learned to ignore. Among these are slips of the tongue, incomplete words and hesitations such as repetitions ('the … the') or fillers ('er…'). The notation of these phenomena is therefore particularly susceptible to errors. In respect of the transcription of prosodic features, transcribers sometimes have to make perceptual distinctions that exceed their capabilities. This is true of both the length of speech pauses and for the stressing of individual syllables.

Most transcription systems demand good readability of transcripts as a fundamental principle. In practice, however, readability has so far never been empirically checked. It is therefore questionable whether the following transcription of the word 'grandmother', uttered while laughing, is intelligible to *transcript readers*, because the word shape here is broken up by additional symbols: '^gra@ ndmo@the@r' (Du Bois 1991: 87). Similar doubts arise in the case of our example 3 (above). Selting (2000) draws attention to a whole range of further problems.

In view of these problems we wish to formulate (following O'Connell and Kowal 1995a: 98ff.) a number of basic recommendations for the transcription of conversations.

1 Only those features of conversational behaviour should be transcribed which will actually be analysed.
2 To ensure the unambiguity of notations symbols, letters should only be used to represent the verbal features of utterances, and punctuation marks should be used only for their conventional function.
3 The internal shape of a word should not be broken up by additional symbols.
4 Subjective perceptions and/or categorizations on the part of the transcribers should not be noted as objective measurements.
5 A given notation symbol should only be used in a particular transcript for a single feature of conversational behaviour, and no feature of conversational behaviour should be represented by different notation symbols.
6 In a transcript clear distinctions should be made between descriptions, explanations, comments and interpretations.
7 In the analysis of transcripts it should be borne in mind that transcribers, as language-users, frequently transcribe unreliably (cf. Lindsay and O'Connell 1995; O'Connell and Kowal 1994).

6 PERSPECTIVES

In two publications (O'Connell and Kowal 1995a,b) we have provided an overview of the present state of transcription in the social sciences. Where the strong interest in transcription, the development of new transcription systems and the critical discussion of these will lead is currently still uncertain. Some perspective, however, is beginning to emerge: the contribution of modern technologies to transcription will continue to grow (Kallmeyer 1997). This concerns both the production of transcripts using computer programs (cf., for example, Ehlich 1993: 141ff., MacWhinney 1995: vii) and the publication of collections of transcripts in connection with electronic data-bases (e.g. Redder and Ehlich 1994). In the literature on transcription reference is often made to the need for a standardization of systems. Paradoxically, standardization presupposes a willingness to abandon the development of a system of one's own. As is shown by the multiplicity of available systems, this willingness would so far appear to be missing. And in view of the multiplicity of possible research goals, it is questionable whether any kind of standardization is a desirable objective.

Whilst transcription has long been used in various disciplines in a relatively non-reflective way, in recent years an increase in methodological awareness has become noticeable. Smith et al., for example, consider transcription to be an essential methodological basis for the 'new paradigm in psychology' (1995: 3), and in more recent handbooks of socio-linguistics (Richter 1988) and psycho-linguistics (Kowal and O'Connell 2003a) transcription is given a chapter of its own.

We believe that the most important perspectives consist of making the production and the use of transcripts – as special cases of the use of symbols, or as types of human behaviour – a subject of empirical investigation. Such a research programme would include (a) semiotic analysis of the options tenable in terms of sign-theory for the development of notation systems, and (b) the psychological investigation of language users' behaviour types in the production and use of transcripts. These include questions such as the following.

- What abilities and skills must transcribers have to produce transcripts that reflect tape or video recordings as accurately as possible rather than the perceptual limitations of the transcribers?

- Where do deviations typically occur between different transcribers working on the same transcript?
- To what extent do the perceptions of transcribers differ from instrumental analyses (for example, in the analysis of speech pauses or other prosodic features with oscillographic recordings)?
- How must transcripts be fashioned in order to be readable, that is, give readers an appropriate representations of the course of a conversation? This also includes the question of how the density of signs in a transcript affects its readability through cognitive overload, and also the question of whether particular transcription symbols, such as 'eh...', arouse uncontrollable (negative) attitudes towards the participants in the readers of a transcript.

Only when these (and other) questions have been empirically checked will it be possible to determine more precisely the potential and the limitations of transcription as a scientific method.

ACKNOWLEDGEMENT

We are grateful to the Alexander von Humboldt Foundation for their support in the preparation of this chapter within the framework of a Transcoop Project for the period 1995–1998.

FURTHER READING

Edwards, J. A. and Lampert, M. D. (eds) (1993) *Talking Data: Transcription and Coding in Discourse Research*. Hillsdale, NJ: Erlbaum.

O'Connell, D. C. and Kowal, S. (1995a) 'Basic Principles of Transcription', in J. A. Smith, R. Harré and L. Van Langenhove (eds), *Rethinking Methods in Psychology*. London: Sage. pp. 93–105.

O'Connell, D. C. and Kowal, S. (1995b) 'Transcription Systems for Spoken Discourse', in J. Verschueren, J.-O. Oestman and J. Blommaert (eds), *Handbook of Pragmatics*. Amsterdam: John Benjamins. pp. 646–656.

5.10 The Analysis of Semi-structured Interviews

Christiane Schmidt

1 INTRODUCTION

The analytical categories and instruments for a semi-structured interview, designed and carried out in the spirit of qualitative research, are developed in response to the demands of the material collected. An analysis appropriate to the technique of open questioning (see **5.2**, **5.3**) cannot interpret and summarize the material according to a pre-determined catalogue of topics; this can only be partially designed before the data are collected.

There are a range of analytical techniques for the analysis of qualitative interviews (surveys of these may be found, for example, in Flick 2002, chs 15–17; Kuckartz 1997; Lamnek 1995: 107–125; Mayring 1999: 76–101; Mayring 2000b: 51–54; Witzel 1982: 53–65). The analytical techniques that are selected for semi-structured interviews within the framework of an investigation will depend on the goals, the questions and the methodological approach – and, not least, on how much time, research equipment and human resources are available. In what follows an analytical strategy will be presented which has proved itself in the context of research approaches that postulate an open kind of theoretical prior understanding but do not reject explicit pre-assumptions (see **4.2**) and the relationship with theoretical traditions (on such 'theory-oriented approaches' cf. Hopf 1996; on the widespread rejection of explicit pre-assumptions, cf. Glaser and Strauss, e.g. 1965a; cf. also Fuchs 1984: 281ff.; Kelle 1996). Analytical strategy is here taken to mean bringing together different analytical techniques that are suited to the analysis of semi-structured interviews. The short description offered here, which is oriented to the sequence of practical research, is intended to encourage readers to develop their own appropriate modes of analysis.

2 PROCEDURE AND METHODOLOGICAL BACKGROUND

The analytical strategy selected may be presented in five stages: first – in response to the material – categories for the analysis are set up. As a second stage, these are brought together in an analytical guide, tested and revised. Thirdly, using this analytical and coding guide, all the interviews are coded according to the analytical categories. Fourthly, on the basis of this coding, case overviews can be produced; these form the basis, in the fifth and final analytical stage, for the selection of individual cases for in-depth single-case analyses.

The guiding principle in this analytical strategy is the interchange between material and theoretical prior knowledge. This interchange process begins not only when the data are available in a transcribed form, but at the beginning of the data collection – as a kind of interplay between, on the one hand, theoretical considerations in reaction to literature and theoretical traditions, and on the other hand experience and observation during exploration of the research field. In the course of this interchange process the theoretical pre-assumptions may also be refined, questioned and altered.

First stage: material-oriented formation of analytical categories

The determination of the analytical categories begins with an intensive and repeated reading of the material. The term 'material' is used here to refer particularly to fully and literally transcribed interviews (see **5.9**; on the inclusion of field notes and research diaries, cf. Schmidt 1997: 546f.). It is presupposed that the interviews have been transcribed with the required degree of 'accuracy' (cf. Flick 2002: 176–220) and cleansed from transfer errors by 'corrective listening' (cf. Hopf and Schmidt 1993, appendix C: 1–3). It is advisable (at all stages of the analysis) to work with computer support (see **5.14**).

The reading of individual transcripts is similar to study-reading of academic texts (on this, cf., for example, Stary and Kretschmer 1994). The researcher's own theoretical prior knowledge and the research questions guide his/her attention in the reading of the transcripts. The aim is to note, for every single interview transcript, the topics that occur and individual aspects of these which can be related – in a very broad sense – to

the context of the research question(s). For any one text passage it is possible, in this process, to note more than one topic or aspect. To take account of the openness of the interviews, it is important not simply to take over the formulations from the questions that were asked, but to consider whether the interviewees actually take up these terms, what the terms mean to them, which aspects they supplement, which they omit and what new topics, which were not foreseen in the guide, actually turn up in the collected data. The aim is not to find the same topics in all interview texts; in this first approach to the material the interviews should not be considered comparatively. It is, however, useful for the following stages in the analysis to note any marked similarities and differences between the interviews; if this is done, it will then normally be easier to concentrate again on a single case.

The following example is taken – like all other examples used below – from the (theory-oriented) investigation on 'family and right-wing extremism' (Hopf et al. 1995), in which the questions and theoretical assumptions relate to traditions of research into authoritarianism and relationships.

BOX 5.10.1   EXAMPLE FOR CODING

[*Context:* Volker is talking about a young person whom he does not like, and in response to follow-up questions he tells how he and his friends dealt with him in a disco. *Citation from the transcript:* '... in any case, the way he spoke, the way he walked, I couldn't stand anything about him. Particularly the way he danced. And then I kicked him downstairs a few times and so on, we just made a mess of it, he was beaten up all the time.']

Kontext: Volker spricht von einem Jugendlichen, den er nicht mag, und erzählt auf Nachfragen, wie er und seine Freunde in der Disko mit ihm umgegangen sind. *Zitat aus dem Transkript:* '... auf jeden Fall die Art zu sprechen, die Art zu gehen, ich konnte alles an dem nicht ab. Die Art zu tanzen vor allem nicht. Und dann hab ich ihn ein paar mal die Treppe runtergekickt und so, haben wir nur Mist gemacht, der wurde andauernd zusammengeprügelt.' (S. 69)

Topics and individual aspects

(Notes of one of the investigators on reading the transcript)

- A young man who does not conform is rejected and attacked
- Physical force
- Trivializing way of talking
- Group force

An exact and repeated reading of individual interview transcripts is very time-consuming, but it is essential so as not to relate text passages too hastily to the researcher's own questions and not to overlook text passages in which one does not initially see the connection to the question. In an open semi-structured interview the important text passages are not always found in the direct context of the question that was asked; the aspects that the interviewer introduces are frequently only taken up later in more explicit form, or else they turn up (again) in response to a different question within a quite different context. What is important, in reading and note-taking, is not to tailor the material to one's own theoretical assumptions by reducing the analysis to a search for locations in the text that are suitable as a proof or illustration of these assumptions. On first reading one often finds 'neat and fitting quotations' that seem to be ideal for a presentation in a final report, thereby overlooking parts of the text that fit less well with the researcher's own expectations. Repeated reading of the texts and, in particular, conscious and open dealing with these assumptions helps the investigator to notice not only parts of the text that correspond to these prior beliefs, but also those parts that accord less well (on this, cf. Hopf et al. 1995: 24).

On the basis of the topics and aspects discovered the analytical categories are now formulated. Depending on the number of interviews, the available human resources and personal work-style, it is sensible to begin this to some extent in parallel with the reading of the interviews. In response to existing theoretical and empirical concepts, and against the background of theoretical traditions, a number of (initially rather vague) categories will arise out of discussions within the research team or with (specialist) colleagues. These will be corrected and supplemented, in the course of data collection and during the preparation of the analysis, on the basis of observations and experience in the field. The interchange is now continued by contrasting the topics and individual aspects in the interviews with the ideas for categories previously developed. The terms or combinations of terms that develop in this way I shall call analytical categories.

What form these analytical categories take again depends largely on the questions; it may be a matter of content topics and aspects, such as argumentation or argument configurations (cf. Becker-Schmidt et al. 1982: 109ff.); some categories may also relate to the linguistic form of the responses (cf. 'trivializing way of talking' in the example above). Alternative procedures for the formation of categories are described by Mayring (1999, 2000b) in the context of 'summarizing content analysis' (see **5.12**), by Witzel (1996) as a partial stage in the evaluation of problem-focused interviews, and by Glaser and Strauss (1967) as an element in 'theoretical coding' (see **5.13**).

Second stage: assembly of the analytical categories into a guide for coding

The draft analytical categories are now assembled into a guide of analysis and coding (for further discussion cf. also Crabtree and Miller 1992: 95; Lewin 1986: 284). This contains detailed descriptions of the individual categories, and for each category different versions are formulated. With the aid of this guide, the material collected will be coded. Coding – as will be explained more fully in the next section – means relating particular passages in the text of an interview to one category, in the version that best fits these textual passages. The usability of the analytical categories is first tested and evaluated on a number of interviews – optimally in the form of discourse within the research team. In the process, the categories and their variants may be refined, made more distinctive or completely omitted from the coding guide.

Here is an example of the development of analytical categories in an interchange process between theoretical assumptions, field experience and the material collected:

'In the course of our questioning of young people we began to have more and more doubts about whether the concept of authoritarianism, and the link it seeks to make between authoritarian subordination and aggression, was at all appropriate for us as a central analytical concept'. (Hopf et al. 1995: 70)

For instance, our first experience in the field increased our scepticism towards the assumption that young people with right-wing extremist tendencies could be made to fit the classical image of the authoritarian as a cyclist who bows upwards and treads downwards … . During the interviews or while thinking about them afterwards we often did have the impression of 'treading on weaker parties', but we did not often find suggestions of authoritarian subordination. From this a number of ideas developed for a systematic review of the aspects of 'authoritarian aggression' and 'authoritarian obsequiousness'. (Hopf and Schmidt 1993: 58)

In addition to a number of other analytical categories related to these aspects, an analytical category of 'cyclist-variants' was developed for the coding guide, and 'tested and further developed on the basis of the material' (Rieker 1997: 49). After a description of the classical authoritarian as a 'cyclist', a number of different variants of this type were described in the coding guide as five different versions:

1 tendency to classical cyclist: bowing and treading
2 tendency only to tread, related to a tendency to rather rebellious or pseudo-rebellious behaviour in the face of authoritarians/stronger people
3 tendency only to tread, no rebellious ...
4 tendency only to bow
5 neither bowing nor treading
6 non-applicable, not asked, and so on. Relation to one of the categories, despite available information, was not possible.

Third stage: coding of the material

Using the coding guide, each interview is now assessed and classified, by means of classifying the material according to the analytic categories. Every interview is coded according to all the categories in the coding guide. The analytical categories that were established *from* the material in the previous stage of the analysis are now applied *to* the material. In order to be able to compare the cases with regard to dominant tendencies, the quantity of information has to be reduced at this stage of the analysis. This involves accepting a loss of information, but this is correspondingly less the more differentiated the analytical categories and their content features can be in their formulation. The special features and details of individual interviews are considered again in the next stage in the analysis – the detailed case interpretation (cf. Schmidt 1997: 557).

Initially, from each interview those passages are identified which – in the broadest sense – can be allotted to an analytical category, and then *one* description is given to all of these textual locations (such as that given above as number 4: 'tendency only to bow'). If more than one description fits, the dominant one will be chosen. It is very important in this process of categorization that the descriptive labels are formulated very distinctively, so that there is no overlap. As laid down in the coding guide, all categories are applied in succession to one interview at a time. The coding under one category will thereby remain, as far as possible, uninfluenced by the codings under other categories. If, in any one interview, there is no material for a particular category, or too little to be able to decide on a descriptive label, the label 'unclassifiable' is given. If this happens regularly with a particular category, this may suggest that the formulation of this analytical category and its descriptive labels was inadequate and that it should be deleted or revised.

What has proved helpful in coding – in the above-mentioned study of right-wing extremism – is the process of entering in a copy of the coding guide the assessments and classifications per interview, and also noting as 'evidence', in the form of page and line numbers, the textual locations to which the assessment relates.

One variant of coding that may be recommended is consensual coding. In this, at least two members of the research team take part in the coding of a particular case. Initially they work independently of each other on the same interview. Only when they have coded the interview according to all the categories do they compare and discuss their classifications. If there are discrepancies in their classification they cooperate in attempting to negotiate a consensual solution by means of a thorough discussion. New techniques for asynchronic communication and cooperation – such as CSCW systems (Computer Supported Cooperative Working), Internet-based discussion fora or email (cf. Scholl et al. 1996: 31f. and Diepold 1996: 14 for discussion) – are useful ways of supporting a research team in this work.

The coding described here is similar to the content analysis technique of scaled structures (cf. Mayring 2000b: 85ff.) and the coding of questionnaire data (cf., for example, Benninghaus 1994: 30; Bortz and Döring 1995: 305). It must be distinguished from the 'theoretical coding' of Glaser and Strauss. They use the term coding to describe the process of material-based theory development, or 'grounded theory' (cf. Wiedemann 1995: 443f.).

Table 5.10.1   Quantifying survey presented as a table

Subjection to norms: authoritarian subordination/ authoritarian aggression	Subjection to norms tends to be prescribed (more or less clearly manifest)	Tends not to be prescribed or between instrumental-strategic orientation and subjection to norms	Total
Subordination in relation to aggression	–	6	6
Mostly only aggression	–	5	5
...	...	...	...
Total	10	15	25

Extract from the table '"Cyclist"-Mentality and subjection to Norms and Conscience' (Hopf et al. 1995: 72)

Fourth stage: quantifying surveys of material

The next stage in the analytical strategy described here involves the compilation of quantifying surveys of the results of coding. From a technical point of view this entails clear presentation of results in the form of tables. This kind of overview of material consists of indications of frequencies in individual analytical categories. The indications of frequency give a preliminary overview of distributions within the material (see Table 5.10.1). They do not yet constitute the result, but merely give information on the 'database'. From the overview of the material individual analytical categories may be selected and related to one another in the form of cross-reference tables (Brosius 1988: 211ff.). But even these 'combined indications of frequency' do not yet, if considered in isolation, constitute a result.

Quantifying surveys of material are of particular value in the preparation of further analysis; they point to possible relationships that can be pursued in a qualitative analysis. The assumptions relate to individual cases and must be checked for every single case (cf. Hopf 1996). For this, however, total overviews may be helpful, for instance, in the 'targeted search for exceptions' (Bühler-Niederberger 1995: 448).

To contribute to the transparency and verifiability of a qualitative study, it is also sensible to present, for the main analytical categories, a general overview of the results of the coding process for all the individual cases – for example, in the form of a table where each case is presented in a single line, and each column gives the results of the individual analytical categories (cf. Heppner et al. 1990: 45f.; Hopf et al. 1995: 194ff.).

Fifth stage: detailed case interpretations

Detailed case interpretations are the last stage in the strategy presented here. The goals of this stage of analysis might be: to discover new hypotheses, to test a hypothesis on a single case, to distinguish between conceptual terms, to arrive at new theoretical considerations or to revise existing theoretical frameworks. Using the constellations derived from the codings, a motivated selection of cases may be made for more detailed analysis. The selected transcripts are repeatedly read and interpreted precisely with reference to a particular question. The result of the interpretation, which relates to this single case in all its particulars, is recorded in written form. What particular techniques are used in the interpretation will depend on the design of the investigation, and this is normally based on the particular interpretative tradition that is preferred by the investigator – for example, a hermeneutic (see **3.5**, **5.16**) or a psychoanalytic (see **5.20**) tradition.

FURTHER READING

Crabtree, B. F. and Miller, W. L. (1992) 'A Template Approach to Text Analysis: Developing and Using Codebooks', in B. F. Crabtree and W. L. Miller (eds), *Doing*

Qualitative Research. Newbury Park, CA: Sage. pp. 93–109.

Hopf, C. (1998) 'Attachment Experiences and Aggressions Against Minorities', *Social Thought and Research*, 21 (1–2): 133–149.

Ryan, G. W. and Bernard, H. R. (2000) 'Data Management and Analysis Methods', in N. K. Denzin and Y. S. Lincoln (eds), *Handbook of Qualitative Research,* 2nd edn. Thousand Oaks, CA: Sage. pp. 769–802.

5.11 The Analysis of Narrative-biographical Interviews

Gabriele Rosenthal and Wolfram Fischer-Rosenthal

1 THE NARRATIVE AND MUTUALLY SHARED REALITY

How are people who experience things differently as individuals still able to cooperate? If it is quite normal for members of a society constantly to have to deal with the experiences of others that one has not witnessed or shared, how is any certainty of expectation produced in our dealings with one another? How is it possible to create a shared world in which one can move about in an oriented way, and of which one can assume that it is, for all practical purposes, sufficiently 'real' for everyone in the same way?

As absurd as these questions may sound to the person in the street who takes for granted the world and the possibility of social interaction, the answers are equally difficult. If one wishes to understand *how*, in practical terms people produce and continuously sustain this 'obvious' condition. While looking for a theoretical answer to the question of how sociality and society are constituted, one of the factors that researchers encountered was the social function of linguistic communication in general and of narrative in particular.

The narration of an experience seems to be a suitable vehicle for imparting one's own experiences to others, as a result and a process, in such a way that both they and the narrator can reconstruct these experiences and thereby jointly understand them. The *we-reality* that is initially created in this way makes provisionally possible a harmonious joint orientation, and yet it remains *precarious in principle*. It cannot be separated from a permanently ongoing process of interpretation because it must be constantly sustained: this is for the reason that shared reality exists only 'now'. The production of a shared view of events, of the world that 'we' possess and that matters to 'us', can fail at any point in the process of its creation. For both the narrator and the listener there are situationally variable possibilities of arrangement and checking that may lead to a divergent view on both sides and thereby to a falsification of the story. Whether this means an 'untrue story', or whether the 'real' narrative experience is not accepted by the listener because it would constitute too great a threat to the listener's own world, amounts to the same thing, in the sense that it leads to the non-constitution of a shared world. And possibly it has similarly negative consequences in terms of social recognition, credibility and the narrator's self-esteem. Even when there is shared verification, reality is not guaranteed once and for all, nor is it immune to interpretation, because the mutually accepted experience can – from a different observational perspective or at some later time – be rejected as 'not real'. In view of these ambivalent circumstances, how was it possible for story-telling to become not only an object but also a technique for a scientific methodology?

2 THE NARRATIVE INTERVIEW AS A RESEARCH INSTRUMENT, AND ITS CRITICS

Within the social sciences there was, on the one hand, a need for an ongoing process of criticism of objectivistic approaches that seek to observe and represent social reality independently of symbolic-linguistic internal structures, and on the other hand for a methodologically refined understanding of structures and speech performance as resources for social interaction and the construction of society. Only then – perhaps from the mid-1960s – was it possible to analyse something so obvious but so complicated a means of communication as narrative, and then to develop it further as a research instrument.

The epoch-making article of Labov and Waletzki (1967/1997), 'Narrative Analysis: Oral Versions of Personal Experience', offered a theoretical rationale and the first practical pointers for the development of the 'narrative interview', which gradually became a prominent data-collection tool in qualitative research. The question of how the experience of reality is created by means of communication among members of society, and how it may be scientifically reconstructed, seemed to be solved not only from a theoretical viewpoint but also in terms of research practice. In German-speaking countries it was Fritz Schütze in the 1970s (cf. Schütze 1983, 1987) in particular who – in the context of such approaches as 'symbolic interactionism' (see 3.3), phenomenologically inspired sociology (see 3.1) and the sociology of language – developed a theoretical base and a model for the 'evocation' of narrative texts within an interview (see 5.2) and also procedures for their analysis.

The expansion of the 'narrative interview' was accompanied by fundamental critical questions concerning the relationship between reality and text (see 5.22) as well as the further development of research practice. With the growth in its use there arose the problem of multiple variants, not all of which stand up to 'quality control' according to narrativist criteria either in the data collection or in the analysis.

At this point we need to outline two more fundamental bases for criticism (Bamberg 1997; Baugh et al. 1997). They concern first the practice and model of structuralism, and secondly the more fundamental question of a Cartesian approach within the social sciences.

In the debate – apparently specifically linguistic – about the capacity of *structuralism*, what is at issue is whether the continuity of social interactions can be adequately explained with reference to the concept of structure and its bi-polar features (deep and surface structure, manifest and latent meaning, and so on). Within the broadly compartmentalized criticism, one extreme pole is the general rejection of the idea of a covertly operating generative structure and therefore also of the associated scientific programme for the reconstruction of its unfolding. On the other side of the spectrum we may indeed find a far-reaching acceptance of the basic structural assumptions; but the instrumental use of narration becomes problematic if its setting is not at the same time made a subject of study. This latter may be found, for example, in ethnomethodological conversation analysis (cf. Schegloff 1997; see 5.17) which, on the other hand, provides important methodological components for analysing of narrative texts. The *interactive* production of text by speakers *and* hearers, to 'do something particular here and now' by means of communication, is neglected in a one-sided concentration of the interviewee, just as it is quite wrongly presupposed that there is a ready-made pre-existing story in this person's head which needs only to be delivered in the course of communication in a situationally appropriate way (Schegloff 1997: 99f.).

Here we come to the second, predominantly epistemological problem that is expressed in the criticism of a presumption of consciousness and memory (as internal storage and monitoring media) as opposed to an external world independent of these. This accusation of a Cartesian division of the social world into a cognitive and an objective sphere also turns up in different variants of an opposition to narrativist procedures. The narrativist distinction between an 'experienced event' and the symbolic interpretation in the 'narrated event' (Hopper 1997: 78f.) is seen as being as problematic as the concept of memory as a reservoir from which the narrative simply has to be selected (Rosenthal 1995; Smith 1981). In place of this, proposals are made for monistic or dialectical models of real-time linguistic narrative creation at the moment of communication. In this connection it is generally impossible to refrain from reference to a layering of experience in life-as-lived and the embedding of this in dimensions of past and present that are predominantly only linguistic

BOX 5.11.1 THE SEQUENCE OF STAGES IN THE PRACTICAL ANALYSIS (FISCHER-ROSENTHAL AND ROSENTHAL 1997A: 152FF.)

1 Analysis of biographical data (data of events)
2 Text and thematic field analysis (sequential analysis of textual segments from the self-presentation in the interview)
3 Reconstruction of the case history (life as lived)
4 Detailed analysis of individual textual locations
5 Contrasting the life-story as narrated with life as lived
6 Formation of types

resources. The indiscriminate accusation of Cartesianism in the distinction between social reality and semantics is as unproductive as equating narration with reality. Results without perception are not socially relevant, nor can there be any narrations without perception and observation of something. And so we may adhere to the distinction between events and narrations (as further communicative text types) and to the same extent see for ourselves the reality-constituting *unity* of what is distinguished in the process of real-time linguistic communication.

The modifications to narrative analysis that have developed in the past few years may be interpreted as a reaction to the discourse that has been critical of narration. In particular, the relation to the procedures of structural hermeneutics (e.g. Oevermann et al. 1979; see **5.16**) that has been made by a number of sociologists (cf., for example, Hildenbrand 1995; Wohlrab-Sahr 1992) has expanded the theoretical–technical 'reading-tools' of narrative texts. The reconstruction model presented in box 5.11.1 was developed in a variety of research contexts (Rosenthal 1993, 1995, 1998) and links hermeneutic (e.g. Oevermann et al. 1980) and text analysis procedures (Schütze 1983, 1994) with thematic field analysis (Fischer 1982, inspired by Gurwitsch 1964).

3 THE NARRATIVIST METHODOLOGY OF BIOGRAPHICAL CASE RECONSTRUCTION

In very general terms this concerns a kind of analysis which observes the difference between narration and life in the unity of a real-time linguistic self-presentation (in a sociological interview). That is to say, the distinction between life as narrated and life as lived has an important role to play in the reconstruction. The separate stages in the work (see box above) make use of both sides of the distinction and relate to one another in a process-oriented way. This explicitly includes the considered use of further data-sources (archive material, medical reports, documents from professional 'client processing', and so on).

The formulations of results are always of a provisional character; they are only valid 'until further information is available'. They are therefore *hypothetical,* both with regard to the sequential progress of the material and its various technically produced textualizations and also in respect of the development of structures in the real course of the subsequent life. This latter is of particular importance for therapeutic and social-therapeutic reconstructions, as well as those processed in the context of social work, all of which take account of *potential for change* and instances of restructuring. Finally the hypothetical nature of the results also takes account of the fact that the rather narrow scientific audience can and, sooner or later, will undertake modifications. In other words: the result produced by analytical reconstruction sets up concrete expectations and possibilities in the framework of the structure, but these do not necessarily come about; it could also turn out differently.

4 AN EXAMPLE OF CASE RECONSTRUCTION

The method of narrative analysis as *biographical case reconstruction* will be explained below with the help of an example. The example is presented as a problem and a result, against the background of the analytical schema described above.

Elisabeth Liebig (a pseudonym), born in 1921, was asked to tell the story of her family and her own life.[1] She begins with an opening biographical evaluation: '*Nothing is as you imagined it. Everything turned out differently*' and then immediately embarks on the following report: '*The great love of my youth, met my husband at 15 and was engaged at 18 and married at 20 and at 21 had my son (laughing) that was already in '42, when there was already war then.*'

How can the beginning of this self-presentation be interpreted? The meaning of a biographical statement can be explained, in principle, at two different levels of time – the time in one's life and the time of the narration. On the one hand it is a matter of the *biographical meaning* of the experiences described or of a phase in one's life – here, therefore, the course of the marriage and the start of the family – in the sequential context of *life as lived*. In this particular case, with reference to the date, to the fact that her husband is seven years older and at the time they met was a competitor in the 1936 Olympic Games, we could perhaps formulate the hypothesis that Elisabeth was happy then to have won the great love of her youth, but that it subsequently turned out differently than she had hoped.

On the other hand, we could switch to the level of the narrated life story and interpret the *manner of presentation* of biographical experiences and phases of life. For the present example it must be asked what function it has for the self-presentation that the topic of 'young love' comes first. For what reason does she seek to present herself in this way and not in some other way in the present communication? Here a number of different hypotheses are possible, such as that marriage for her is of the highest biographical significance, precisely because later in the interview she will be involved in reporting her divorce in 1949. Or we might assume that her life before the age of 15 seems unpleasant to her and therefore she does not speak of it at the beginning.

To check this and other possible hypotheses at the two levels of analysis we need:

- at the level of the story of life as lived, a meaning-reconstructing ordering of the story of her marriage and the birth of her son in the sequential form of her biography, that is to say including her life-story before the age of 15;

- at the level of the narrated life-story, a meaning-reconstructing ordering of this opening sequence in the sequential form of the main narrative.

What is decisive for the method of biographical case reconstruction is the basic difference between the two levels of the story of her life as lived and her life as narrated, which we shall attempt to cope with in different stages in the analysis within the unity of the case. The sequential form of what is narrated as well as what was actually experienced will be reconstructed. In analysing the story of her life as lived, the temporal sequence of the biographical experiences, and also the meaning these experiences had for the autobiographer at that time, will – as far as possible – be reconstructed. This reconstruction of meaning can take account not only of the layering of the past, but also of expectations – for example, a happy marriage – or schemata of a 'life unlived', which in turn may change with the stream of events and experiences, and which form the essential future aspect in the constitution of biographical meaning. In order to prepare the reconstruction of the case history, a sequential *analysis of biographical data* (cf. Oevermann et al. 1980) is carried out. Initially, the data that barely relate to the biographer's interpretation are analysed in the temporal sequence of events in the life-story. The individual data, taken one at a time, retrospectively and prospectively, within the chronology of the particular life, become a starting point for setting up hypotheses on the structure of the life as lived and testing them in a process-oriented way. This involves excluding any knowledge about the further course of the biography and *initially* without reference to the knowledge that the interpreters have from the narrated life-story.

Here are some further biographical data on Elisabeth Liebig before her 15th birthday. She was born in 1921 as her parents' first child. Her mother married a second time; her son from this marriage died as a small child. Independent of Elisabeth's self-interpretations a number of assumptions may be made in respect of these data. She may, for instance, have been overshadowed in childhood by her dead half-brother. A derivative hypothesis might be that Elisabeth would try to gain her mother's attention through particular types of behaviour. All derivative hypotheses should be checked against further data from her life-story.

Further biographical data are as follows. The mother developed multiple sclerosis; Elisabeth was about 6 years old when the symptoms of this disease first appeared. At the age of 9 she joined a gymnastics club. After several unsuccessful attempts her mother committed suicide in February 1933. Here, too, we may set up hypotheses and derivative hypotheses on the effect of this distressing biographical constellation on the further course of her life. One possible reading might be: Elisabeth views her mother's suicide as disease-related, she develops a great fear of illnesses and engages in sport as a preventive measure.

Before the hypotheses on these data are contrasted with Mrs Liebig's statements, the analysis of the narrated life-story, the *thematic field analysis*, must be carried out. With the reconstruction of the presentation perspective that was valid at the time of the interview we obtain a critical view of the sources that helps to distinguish the biographical significance of events in the past from the present-day perspective. The analysis of biographical data that is carried out before this stage in the analysis serves as a point of reference that permits answers as to what events have been enhanced in the narration, what events cannot, or only with difficulty, be made subjects of interest and what kind of sequencing that is at variance with chronology may be set up. In this way the beginning of Mrs Liebig's opening narrative – using the knowledge of her mother's suicide, three years before she met her husband – may be read in a completely different way from the earlier reading. But it is just these kinds of reading that the biographer did not want to produce: otherwise she would have put her mother's suicide first.

In the *thematic field analysis* the self-presentation is reconstructed by means of complexes of topics, that is to say, by expanding thematic fields in the order of their treatment. The analysis proceeds on the basis that self-presentation cannot – or only occasionally – be intentionally controlled and that the story of experience is manifest in a piece of text production that corresponds to the uninterrupted opening narrative.

In preparation for the analysis the interview text is sequenced in accordance with the chronology of the time of narration. Criteria for determining the segmentation are: speaker-change, text type and change of topic.

In our sample case the first sequence in the self-presentation cited above was annotated as follows:

1/13	Evaluation *'Nothing is as you imagined it …'*
1/14	REPORT – The great love of my youth, met my husband at 15 – 18 engagement; 20 marriage
1/19	– 21 birth of son – '42, when there was already war then.'

The development of hypotheses is oriented to the following questions.

1　Why is this topic – dates of marriage and start of family – introduced at this point? What other possibilities might the interviewee have had to respond to the request for presentation of her family and personal life-story? Why is the whole period before her 15th birthday not mentioned?

2　Which topics are addressed and which are not?

3　Why is this topic presented as extensively or as briefly in this text type (here a report)? Why are the years from 1936 to 1942 dealt with in only four lines?

4　What are the possible thematic fields that this topic fits into? Does Mrs Liebig embed this topic, for instance, into the thematic field: 'everything that did not happen in my life as I had imagined it', and do the listeners then get to hear about such disappointments?

Here the nature and function of self-presentation in the interview are at issue, and not her biographical experience at other points in her life. The interviewee is therefore not asked what significance it had at the time of her marriage in 1941 that she married the love of her youth. What is of greater interest is what function the opening of this presentation has for her 'today', at the time of the interview. In every segment of the text, what is of interest are the inherent pointers to possible thematic fields and the design of potentially related further segments. In the course of the analysis it becomes clear what thematic fields are being developed by the interviewee, what aspects of these fields are not developed, are only suggested, or are avoided. It also becomes clear what topics are not highlighted, even though they are co-present – and indeed independent of the interviewee's self-interpretations.

After this first segment Mrs Liebig continues with a mixture between report and argumentation about her marriage, the return of her husband from captivity and her marital difficulties. In terms of argumentation she presents the reasons why she sued for divorce in 1949. After a short report about her own professional career she then reaches right into the present day. After a quarter of an hour she finishes the opening section of the interview, in which she has not told any story.

The whole of the opening section, concentrated on a brief presentation of the course of her marriage and divorce, may be reconstructed as the thematic field 'my broken marriage'. The style of report and argumentation gives little insight into Mrs Liebig's experience; she remains distanced and oriented to single dates.

It is only on the basis of four further interview questions that the traumatic circumstances of her mother's death come to be talked about. First one of the two interviewers asks Mrs Liebig to tell more of her family history. The resulting text, with many descriptions, is already longer than the first main sequence. One of the consequences of this is that we may abandon the hypothesis that Mrs Liebig was unwilling to talk about the time before she met her husband. What is indicated is rather that for her the story of her marriage is not thematically related to her family history.

At the beginning of this report Mrs Liebig states that her mother had multiple sclerosis, that she attempted suicide on several occasions and 'in 1933 she succeeded, and I was 12 years old then'. Here, too, it is significant what topic follows this. Mrs Liebig immediately continues: 'but I often spent my holidays down with my aunt', and from the sequencing we find a 13-line description of happy memories of these holidays.

In the opening narrative it is already clear in how detached a manner Mrs Liebig speaks about difficult situations in her life. In response to requests to tell something of her mother's illness and the suicide attempts, Mrs Liebig does then produce a detailed 30-line narrative about the day her mother died. The textual structure makes clear the considerable biographical significance of her mother's illness and death for the life she has lived, but the narrator cannot present this so explicitly. In particular, she was not able to embed it in her initial self-presentation, which was not structured by means of follow-up questions. It becomes clear that it is important for the interviewee to report on her life in a detached manner, and that several interventions are needed to help her draw closer to the traumatic experiences she has suffered in the present communicative situation.

Let us now turn to the third analytical stage in the *reconstruction of a case history*. Again at the level of the story of life as lived, the biographical significance of the individual experiences is explored, while the hypotheses concerning the individual biographical data and the course of the life-story are contrasted with the relevant statements of the interviewee. According to the logic of data analysis the biographical experiences are reconstructed in the chronology of the life-story as actually experienced. The preceding thematic field analysis provides important indicators in this stage of the analysis as to the interviewee's present perspective and the functional significance of her narratives for the present-day presentation of her life-story. This preceding stage in the analysis has given us a critical perspective as to data-sources, and has helped us in a number of ways, including:

1   Not naively to take the dominance of the marital history presented as the decisive determining life-experience in the biography, but rather to look for the hidden layers below it.
2   To recognize the separation made in the presentation between the family-history of the family of origin and the history of the family she created as a strategy for the avoidance of suffering with equivalent time-allocation to the presentation of a 'substitute suffering topic'.
3   Not to interpret the detached presentation simply as an adequate form of presentation of a life presumably not greatly affected by suffering.

This stage in the analysis should be clarified with the biographical detail concerning her mother's suicide. Mrs Liebig tells that on that particular day she 'came home late'. She immediately smelt gas, found her mother dead in the kitchen, turned off the gas and fetched her father from work. A *detailed analysis* of this textual location, which will not be presented here, shows that Mrs Liebig is presenting herself, at the overt level, as a competent girl, but at the latent level of meaning there is a rejected feeling of guilt. The 12-year-old girl felt guilty about her mother's death because she did not come home from school in time, and she felt guilty because of her detached relationship to her mother after her death.

If one contrasts the analysis of the narrated life-story with that of the life as it was experienced, one may formulate the hypothesis that the interviewee is processing the loss of her mother and her unconscious feelings of guilt as a substitute for her broken marriage (and that is why such a large part of the argumentation in her opening narrative is devoted to the reasons for her divorce).

The procedure for reconstruction that we have presented seeks to trace the process of formation of both the narrated and the actual life, without losing sight of their reciprocal relationship and their unity in the case. In separate stages of the analysis there is a sharper focus first on one side, and then on the other, so that ultimately the results may be related to each other.

NOTE

1 The interview was conducted by Gabriele Rosenthal and Bettina Völter (for discussion of embedding in family history, cf. Völter 1998).

FURTHER READING

Fischer-Rosenthal, W. (2000) 'Biographical Work and Biographical Structuring in Present-day Societies', in P. Chamberlayne, J. Bornat and T. Wengraf (eds), *The Turn to Biographical Methods in Social Science. Comparative Issues and Examples.* London: Routledge. pp. 109–125.

Rosenthal, G. (1993) 'Reconstruction of Life Stories. Principles of Selection in Generating Stories for Narrative Biographical Interviews', *The Narrative Study of Lives*, 1 (1): 59–91.

Rosenthal, G. (2004) 'Biographical Research', in C. Seale, G. Gobo, J. F. Gubrium and D. Silverman (eds), *Qualitative Research Practice.* London: Sage. pp. 48–64.

5.12 Qualitative Content Analysis

Philipp Mayring

1 GOALS OF QUALITATIVE CONTENT ANALYSIS

The goal of content analysis is the systematic examination of communicative material (originally from the mass media in particular). This does not have to consist exclusively of texts: musical, pictorial, plastic or other similar material may also be treated. What is essential, however, is that the communicative material should be fixed or recorded in some form.

Content analysis is, of course, a technique that derives from the communication sciences. Today, however, it claims to be able to serve for systematic analysis in a wide range of scientific domains. Modern content analysis, moreover, no longer targets only the *content* of verbal material. Both formal aspects and latent meaning content can be also objects of study. The basic idea of a *qualitative* content analysis, then, consists of maintaining the systematic nature of content analysis for the various stages of qualitative analysis, without undertaking over-hasty quantifications.

2 HISTORY AND DEVELOPMENT

Content analysis in its present form was developed, in its essentials, at the beginning of the twentieth century (particularly in the 1920s) in the United States (cf. Lissman 1997; Merten 1983). The principal focus then was the systematic analysis of large quantities of textual data from the growing mass media (radio and newspapers). Initially only quantitative procedures were developed for this: frequency analyses, in which particular textual components were counted (for example, how often particular political parties were mentioned in one newspaper); analyses of indicators, where the frequency of particular textual components was defined as an indicator of a superordinate variable on the basis of theoretical considerations (for example, words such as 'must', 'never', 'is' as an indicator of the degree of dogmatism of a particular text); analyses of valency and intensity that assessed the material according to predefined scales (for example, how strongly the commentaries in a particular newspaper expressed the positions of the current parties in the government); contingency analyses, in which interrelations between different textual components were analysed (for example, how often, in a newspaper, particular politicians were mentioned in a direct context with positive attributes). Very soon, however, these quantitative procedures attracted criticism:

- The procedures were limited to foregrounded textual content, and neglected *latent meaning structures* (Kracauer 1952).

- The analysis ignored the *textual content* that defined and modified the particular textual units.
- The logic of the analysis had too little *linguistic foundation* (Fühlau 1982).
- The claim it made to being *systematic* and *verifiable* could not be substantiated (Rühl 1976).

Subsequently there were repeated attempts to develop a qualitative form of content analysis as an alternative. Jürgen Ritsert (1972) developed a procedure for tracing latent meaning contents, particularly ideological contents, that consists of a step-by-step application and modification of ideology-related theoretical prior understanding – including the use of certain quantitative stages in the analysis (cf. also Vorderer and Groeben 1987). Mühlfeld et al. (1981) proposed a technique of gradual extraction and summarizing for the analysis of open interviews. Rust (1980) attempted to justify, on cultural-sociological lines, a qualitative content analysis preparatory to quantification. Mostyn (1985) developed a qualitative approach to content analysis that was strictly directed by hypotheses. And the approach to the coding of interview material described by Wittkowski (1994) is similar to what is presented here.

The qualitative content analysis of popular literature ('*Landserhefte*') about the Second World War which was critical of ideology (Ritsert 1964, 1972) has, in many respects, remained exemplary even today. Ritsert joined in the public discussion of a possible danger to young people in such cheap war stories at the beginning of the 1960s, and proved that the accusations made (of brutalizing jargon, Wild West style, playing down of war) were superficial and therefore played down the problem themselves. Against the background of Freud's theory of mass psychology and ego-analysis, he derives four dimensions:

- Mechanisms of defence against guilt
- Rationalization of defeat
- Expressions of a sick collective narcissism (nationalism)
- Relics of authoritarian dependency.

In accordance with these dimensions, material was filtered out of the stories in 33 randomly selected wartime storybooks, the frequency of these topics in the stories was determined, and

the motifs of an ideological syndrome were reconstructed. In this way a 'Führer-loyalty myth', characterized by 'father-officers' and the 'comradeship of the front', was crystallized as the ideological core content: 'an amazingly intact reproduction of the old Führer-loyalty mania of fascist provenance' (Ritsert 1972: 76).

3   THEORETICAL BACKGROUND

The following fundamentals determine the analytical procedures of qualitative content analysis.

- The material to be analysed is understood as embedded in its *context of communication* (Gerbner et al. 1969): who is the transmitter (author), what is the subject and its socio-cultural background (sources), what are the textual characteristics (e.g. lexis, syntax, semantics, pragmatics, non-verbal context), who is the recipient, who is the target group?
- The particular *systematic* nature of content analysis consists of its rule-governedness (proceeding from pre-formulated procedural models), its theory-dependency (following theoretically underpinned questions and coding rules), and of its gradual procedure, breaking down the text into single units of analysis, and oriented to a system of categories (cf. Krippendorf 1980).
- Qualitative content analysis also claims to measure itself against quality criteria (see **4.7**) and inter-coder reliability. The requirements are admittedly set somewhat lower (kappa-coefficients of 0.70 are normally sufficient), but the goal remains that a number of content analysts should be able to achieve demonstrably similar results on extracts from materials.
- In this, qualitative analysis does not seek to shut itself off from quantitative analytical procedures, but attempts to incorporate them into the analytical process in a justified way.

4   TECHNIQUES

In what follows a number of concrete procedural methods will be presented that were originally developed in the context of a research project on the subjective coping with unemployment (Ulich et al. 1985; Mayring 2000b).

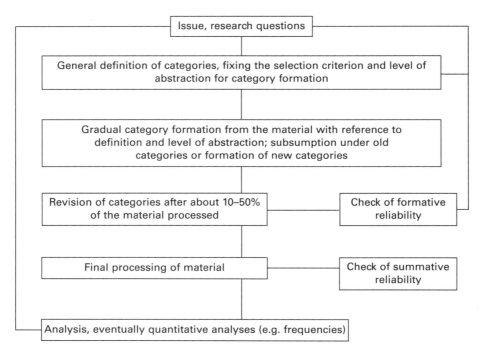

Figure 5.12.1 Flow-chart of procedures for qualitative content analysis with the example of inductive category formation (cf. Mayring 1999)

Here we may distinguish, in principle, four types of procedure.

Summarizing content analysis seeks to reduce the material in such a way that the essential contents are preserved, but a manageable short text is produced. Some use was also made of the psychology of text processing (Ballstaedt et al. 1981; van Dijk 1980), in which a number of individual summarizing (or 'reductive') processes are distinguished (omission, generalization, construction, integration, selection, bundling). Summarizing content analyses are always suitable if one is only interested in the content level of the material and is required to condense the material into a manageable short text.

The basic idea behind *inductive category formation* is that the procedures of summarizing content analysis are used to develop categories gradually from some material. The flow-chart in Figure 5.12.1 clarifies this procedure.

This procedure was used, for example, to analyse open biographical questionnaires from unemployed teachers in the new (i.e. former Eastern) states in the Federal Republic of Germany in order to determine what view of their profession the probationers had developed in the GDR period (Mayring et al. 1996). The most frequent inductively formed categories here were the following:

- Pleasure in being a teacher
- Fulfilling particular functions in the school's organization
- Positive collective experiences
- Interest in the subject
- Recognition, respect
- Implementation of party goals (solidarity, friendship).

These were summarized into two umbrella categories (teachers out of professional pleasure; teachers out of commitment to socialism) and it was further investigated whether these different orientations had any influence on dealing with the experience of unemployment.

Explicating content analysis seeks to do the opposite of summarizing content analysis: for individual unclear textual components (terms, sentences, etc.) additional material has to be collected to make these textual locations intelligible. The basic idea in this is the systematic and controlled collection of explanatory material.

This makes it possible to distinguish between a narrow contextual analysis that only involves the direct textual environment and a broad contextual analysis that collects additional material beyond the text (information about the communicators, subject, socio-cultural background, target group).

Structuring content analysis seeks to filter out particular aspects of the material and to make a cross-section of the material under ordering criteria that are strictly determined in advance, or to assess the material according to particular criteria. This involves formal, content-focused, typologizing and scaling procedures, depending on the type of structuring dimensions that have been developed in accordance with some theory, and these are then subdivided into individual categories. The basic idea in this is the exact formulation of definitions, typical textual passages ('key examples') and coding rules which will result in a coding guide that makes the task of structuring very precise.

5   ACHIEVEMENTS AND LIMITATIONS

The procedures of qualitative content analysis have been utilized in many areas of psychological, pedagogic and sociological research. In this the following have proved to be particular strengths.

- The systematic nature of qualitative content analysis follows, as a rule, established sequential models. This renders the procedure transparent, intelligible, easy to learn and readily transferable to new research questions.
- There is normally a system of categories at the centre of the analysis (as with quantitative content analysis), but this is revised in the course of the analysis by means of feedback loops and is adapted flexibly to the material.
- Its rule-governed procedure also allows for the better implementation of quality criteria and inter-coder reliability.

With qualitative content analysis fairly large quantities of data can normally be processed. Quantitative stages may readily be built into the analysis, and this can make it possible to counter the frequently criticized dichotomy between 'qualitative' and 'quantitative'.

Some restrictions and limitations of qualitative content analysis must, however, be mentioned: if the research question is very open, or the study is of a markedly exploratory character and would also be hampered by an inductive formation of categories or incapable of conclusive theoretical justification, then more open procedures would be more appropriate, such as those found, for example, in grounded theory (see **5.13**). In any case, it is also possible here to think of combinations that bring together, in individual stages of research, both more open and content analytical procedures. The criterion should in no case be simply methodological feasibility, but the suitability of the method to the material and the research question.

6   RECENT PERSPECTIVES

Because of its systematic character, qualitative content analysis is especially suitable for computer-supported research (Huber 1992; Weitzman and Miles 1995; see **5.14**). This is not a matter of automatized analysis (as in quantitative computerized content analysis), but rather of support and documentation of the individual research steps as well as support functions in searching, ordering and preparing for quantitative analyses. In this connection the ATLAS.ti program, developed for the purpose of qualitative content analysis at the Technical University in Berlin, has proved to be of particular value (cf. Mayring et al. 1996).

FURTHER READING

Mayring, P. (2000) 'Qualitative Content Analysis', *Forum: Qualitative Social Research,* 1 (2). http://qualitative-research.net/fqs

Mayring, P. (2002a) 'Qualitative Content Analysis – Research Instrument or Mode of Interpretation?', in M. Kiegelmann (ed.), *The Role of the Researcher in Qualitative Psychology.* Tübingen: Verlag Ingeborg Huber. pp. 139–148.

Mayring, P. (2002b) 'Qualitative Approaches in Research on Learning and Instruction', in B. Ralle and I. Eilks (eds), *Research in Chemical Education – What Does it Mean?* Aachen: Shaker Verlag. pp. 111–118.

5.13 Theoretical Coding: Text Analysis in Grounded Theory

Andreas Böhm

Barney Glaser and Anselm Strauss (1967) created in their *grounded theory* a comprehensive idea of the epistemological and research process in the social sciences (see **2.1**, **6.6**). It extends from the first ideas of a research question to the production of the report on results (see **5.22**). Data collection, analysis and formulation of theory are closely interrelated. The label grounded theory is often used to refer to both the method and also the research result that is sought through the use of this theory. On the basis of empirical research in a particular object area it makes it possible to formulate a valid theory for this area consisting of interrelated concepts and suitable for the production of a description and an explanation of the social phenomena investigated.

1 PROCEDURE ACCORDING TO GROUNDED THEORY

Grounded theory is a *Kunstlehre* (art), and so its procedure cannot be learned in the form of prescriptions. A clear example of the use of the procedure may be found in the chapter by Hildenbrand about Anselm Strauss (see **2.1**). The following summary of the procedure relies in particular on the presentations of Glaser (1978), Strauss (1987) and Strauss and Corbin (1990). The data material here is text in the broader sense of the term (transcribed interviews, field notes, observation reports, and so on). The data collection is oriented to theoretical sampling (see **4.4**): in the early stages as many different people, situations and documents as possible are selected to obtain data covering the complete spectrum of the research question. Subsequently data are sought that will confirm or modify the (provisional) categories of the theory that have already been developed. 'Sensitizing concepts' as guiding principles are the starting point of the research and have the character of open questions ('what happens and how?'). The researchers' own questions, their prior understanding and, related to this, their own prejudices concerning the research issue can be worked out by means of brainstorming and group discussions. The reading of relevant literature also belongs to this (specialist publications, but also journalistic work, novels and stories). The most important intellectual activity in the analytical process consists of *comparison*. This refers less to the search for identical contents than to the search for similarities and differences (Busse 1994). Coding may be described as the *deciphering* or *interpretation* of data and includes the naming of concepts and also explaining and discussing them in more detail. The explanations are reflected in coding notes. The result of coding is then a list of terms as well as an explanatory text. Three types of coding may be distinguished that may be partially considered as phases in the research process – open, axial and selective coding (see below). 'Code' is a technical term from the analytical procedure and signifies a named concept. In the data indicators are sought of the phenomenon being studied. The target of the first analyses is the production of codes that relate *directly* to the data. Initially, concepts always have a provisional character, and in the course of the analysis they become more differentiated, numerous and abstract. The differentiated concepts are known as *categories*.

Writing of memos

Theoretical memos are based on the coding notes mentioned above and on broad interrelations that are gradually revealed by the investigator. The writing of theoretical memos requires researchers to distance themselves from the data, and also helps them to go beyond purely descriptive work (motto 'Stop and memo!'). In the course of the analysis memos can become starting points for the formulation of the final manuscript. Exactly as with theoretical memos, there is a constant process of writing and revision (theoretical sorting). Working in a team of colleagues prevents one-sidedness and can speed up the epistemological process, for which reason working in a team of investigators and (research) supervision have proved to be of value.

Open coding

In open coding data are 'broken down' analytically, and in this the principle of grounded theory shows itself: from the data, that is from the text, a succession of concepts is developed that may ultimately be used as building blocks for the model. As a first step it is advisable to analyse single short textual passages (line by line). Subsequently larger paragraphs or even whole texts may be coded. In order to avoid simple paraphrasing, the following 'theory-generating' questions are asked of the text.

- What? What is at issue here? What phenomenon is being addressed?
- Who? What persons or actors are involved? What roles do they play? How do they interact?
- How? What aspects of the phenomenon are addressed (or not addressed)?
- When? How long? Where? How much? How strongly?

- Why? What reasons are given or may be deduced?
- For what reason? With what intention, and for what purpose?
- By what means? What methods, tactics and strategies are used to achieve the goal?

In coding researchers use their background knowledge about the context of the textual passage being investigated and, in general terms, their knowledge about the area of investigation. The result of the work is an interpretative text which adheres to analytical thinking about the phenomenon and which often contains questions about how the phenomenon might be further investigated (see **2.1** for an example). *Theoretical codes* in the sense of terms from scientific theories should initially be avoided. More profitable are *in-vivo codes,* which, as colloquial interpretations of the phenomena, are taken directly from the language of the field of investigation. In-vivo codes are components of 'theories' formulated personally by the producers of the text in question. Traditional categories such as age, gender, level, and so on, should only be used after a thorough scrutiny of their relevance. The text and the researcher's background knowledge make it possible to specify different aspects or properties of the phenomenon being investigated. Mental comparisons (including false and extreme instances) provide some indication of the possible variation in these aspects or in their characteristics. If a particular aspect or property may be plotted on a continuum, then we are dealing with a dimension.

Open coding is an expanding procedure in the sense that considerable quantities of interpretative text can be added to a small segment of an original text. To retain an overview, the investigator should continually write memos, and sort and weigh up the results of the work. In ordering the interim results it will become clear what concepts are important for the researcher's own question and therefore require deeper analysis, and what results should be discarded and not pursued in greater depth.

Axial coding

This step serves to refine and differentiate concepts that are already available and lends them the status of categories. One category is located at the centre and a network of relationships is

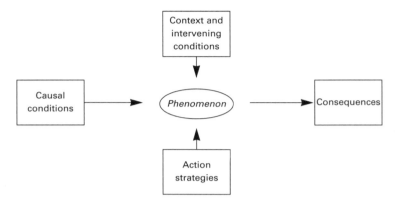

Figure 5.13.1 Coding paradigm for social science research questions

developed around it. Typically, axial coding is used particularly in the middle and later stages of an analysis. In the same way as open coding, axial coding is applied to very short textual segments (in the sense of a detailed analysis), to larger extracts or to the entire text. For theory-formation what is of particular importance is the development of relationships between the axial categories and the concepts that are related to them in terms of their formal and content aspects. The axial category is developed in its temporal and spatial relationships, in relationships of cause and effect, in means–ends relationships and in terms of argumentative and motivational connections. The hypothetical relationships in axial coding must be repeatedly checked in a deductive procedure, using new data material. To explain the relationships between categories that relate to partial aspects of social action, Strauss's coding paradigm has proved to be of value (Figure 5.13.1).

The following example, in which 'pain' has been selected as the axial category, will illustrate the coding paradigm: 'If I've drunk too much (context), I get (condition) a headache (phenomenon/axial category). Then I take an aspirin (strategy). After a while it's better (consequence)' (taken from Strauss and Corbin 1990: 98).

The *phenomenon* denoted by the axial category is, for example, an event or a fact. The actions of an individual as well as interactions between different people revolve around the phenomenon. The following questions make easier the choice of axial category: What do my data refer to? With what are the actions and interactions in the data actually concerned? *Causes* or causal conditions contribute to the occurrence or

development of the phenomenon, for instance, a broken leg (= cause) leads to pain (= phenomenon). It is important here to clarify the properties of the cause. For the example given, this would mean asking: What kind of fracture? Simple or compound? And so on. With causes a distinction must sometimes be made between the subjective view, as it may be presented, for example, as a speaker's perspective in an interview text, and the view of the researcher. *Causes* are normally only valid in a particular set of *conditions*, and here what is of particular importance for the formation of an action-related theory are the conditions that promote or restrict the possibilities for action or interaction. Under *contextual conditions* are included particularly time, place and duration. And among *intervening conditions* we find the social, political and cultural environment and the individual biography. *Actions* and *interactions* have two properties. (1) They are processes and have a sequence, and it is therefore appropriate to ask about sequences and temporal course of action. (2) They are goal-oriented and are often performed for particular and specifiable reasons, for which reason one may refer to (interactional) strategies or tactics.

'Goal-oriented' should not be confused with (conscious) intention. For the purposes of the analysis a functional mode of observation is preferred that disregards intentions. Strauss and Corbin (1990: 104) offer the following example. In an investigation into the self-consciousness of children a field observation was analysed. A child throws a glass of milk onto the floor and is rebuked by its mother in the presence of other children. It was not a conscious intention of the mother that the child's self-consciousness

Table 5.13.1 Coding families (adapted from Glaser 1978: 75–82)

Coding families	Concepts	Examples
The Six Cs	Causes, contexts, contingencies, consequences, conditions	… of pain suffering
Process	Stages, phases, phasings, transitions, passages, careers, chains, sequences	Career of a patient with chronic pain
The Degree Family	Extent, level, intensity, range, amount, continuum, statistical average, standard deviation	Extent of pain suffering
Type Family	Types, classes, genres, prototypes, styles, kinds	Kinds of pain – sharp, piercing, throbbing, shooting, sting, gnawing, burning
The Strategy Family	Strategies, tactics, techniques, mechanisms, management	Coping with pain
Interactive Family	Interaction, mutual effects, interdependence, reciprocity, symmetries, rituals	Interaction of pain experience and coping
Identity-Self Family	Identity, self-image, self-concept, self-evaluation, social worth, transformations of self	Self-concepts of pain patients
Cutting-Point Family	Boundary, critical juncture, cutting point, turning point, tolerance levels, point of no return	Start of chronification in the medical career of pain patient
Cultural Family	Social norms, social values, social beliefs	Social norms about tolerating pain, 'feeling rules'
Consensus Family	Contracts, agreements, definitions of the situation, uniformity, conformity, conflict	Compliance

should suffer from the rebuke (here the interactional strategy), but rebuking can be coded here as a strategy.

Actions and interactions lead to particular consequences. Strauss (1987: 57) recommmends that care be exercised in applying the coding paradigm to linguistic peculiarities in the data: researchers should regard keywords such as 'because', 'since', or 'owing to' as indicators of causal conditions. Consequences of actions are often indicated by means of expressions such as 'as a result of', 'and so', 'with the result that', 'the consequence was', 'consequently'.

As a further stimulus in *axial coding*, an overview of theoretical framing concepts may be used, or so-called *coding families*. The C-family (causes, contexts, consequences, conditions, etc.) corresponds to the coding paradigm described above. For Glaser (1978: 74) this coding family is central to the analysis of social events (the 'bread and butter theoretical code of sociology') (see Table 5.13.1).

Selective coding

In this phase the researcher is particularly active as an author on the basis of the categories, coding notes, memos, networks and diagrams so far developed. As a starting point for establishing the main phenomenon of the analysis it is advisable to look at coding lists, summarizing memos and representations of networks. The main phenomenon is described as the *core category* and is possibly already present in the formulation of the research question of the particular investigation. Admittedly it must sometimes occur in the research process that a different phenomenon than originally assumed will take on central importance for the issue in question. There are indeed such shifts in a research perspective in the course of data collection and interpretation, which lead to new and surprising discoveries. For this reason *grounded theory* recommends asking repeatedly, in the course of an investigation, which phenomena are central and formulating appropriate theory-memos.

If a number of well-worked-out axial categories are available we may assume that the central phenomenon has been captured in its essential aspects – otherwise it is necessary to return to earlier phases in the research process. In the practice of research there are two possibilities. (1) One of the axial categories includes the central phenomenon and is therefore suitable as the core category. The candidate for the core category is characterized by its formal relationships with all the other important categories and occupies a central position in the network of terms. (2) It often proves to be sensible to give a central location to a phenomenon to which more than a single axial category relates. In such a case it is necessary to detach oneself from the axial categories, and to formulate a new category which comes about by means of summarizing or reformulating one of the existing categories.

Frequently investigators experience difficulties in sticking to the central proposition of the investigation because of the 'surfeit of important details'. Here one should ask what 'story' the data tell. The researcher will summarize in a few sentences the results of the investigation for an interested reader. Guiding questions for this kind of record are: What is the issue here? What have I learned from the investigation? What is central? What relationships exist? The main story revolves around a core category, unfolds this in a concise way and shows relationships with other important categories. After determining the core category, its properties and dimensions, other relevant categories are related, systematically and in a schematically oriented manner (for example, in the sense of the coding paradigm), to the core category. Once the relationships to the main categories have been formulated, their particular properties and dimensions may be compared with regard to regularities and patterns.

An example of selective coding

In an investigation of the psychological reaction to the nuclear accident at Chernobyl (Legewie et al. 1989), it was possible to discover the following pattern: in experiencing a threat to one's own physical health and life expectancy what was decisive was whether age was an important constituent in a person's self-image. 'Young' people (not in the sense of biological age, but in the sense of a self-attributed property, or 'subjective age') saw themselves in this respect as far more threatened than 'old' people. This statement could only be made after a systematic comparison of combinations found no evidence of the combinations 'young' + 'no threat' and 'old' + 'severe threat'. The example demonstrates how gaps within a theory (such as defective specification, or defective grounding of the statements in the data) may, through a system-

atic procedure, be discovered, reviewed and ultimately eliminated.

The degree of generalizability of a theory developed in this way depends, at least in part, upon a process of abstraction that permeates the entire research procedure. The more abstract the formulation of the developed categories – in particular the core category – the more widely the theory may be applied. But, in addition, the time and energy invested in its development will also increase, because ultimately the route from the data to the relatively abstract categories must be documented in every detail. A grounded-theory is testable by again confronting the theoretical propositions, as hypotheses, with reality. For social and, in particular, historical phenomena there are limits to this, because the social conditions cannot be reproduced at will nor very precisely.

2 LIMITATIONS OF THE METHOD

The character of grounded theory as a *Kunstlehre* (art) renders its learnability more difficult, and makes particular demands of investigators in respect of their creativity. The requirement – which seems initially to be liberating – that one should distance oneself from existing theories and allow the theory to grow out of the data, often causes insecurity among students. Particularly in respect of decisions about the transition points between the different phases of coding, there are scarcely any fixed rules (Flick 2002: 185). The pragmatic direction, in terms of which data collection and analysis is complete when theoretical saturation is reached (that is, no new aspects can be incorporated into the theory), is hardly adequate for beginners. From this it again becomes clear how important teamwork and research supervision are in the context of this method.

3 DEVELOPMENTS AND PERSPECTIVES

While Barney Glaser withdrew from active research in the 1980s, Strauss developed the approach further and devoted himself in particular to a didactic orientation in order to make the method teachable and learnable (Strauss 1987; Strauss and Corbin 1990). Glaser (1992) accuses Strauss in this respect of having abandoned the original idea of allowing the theory to 'emerge' in favour of 'forcing' theoretical structures. His criticism was particularly directed at the *axial coding* paradigm. In the first comprehensive publication on *grounded theory* it was vitally important to Glaser and Strauss (1967) that the method be adapted to particular questions and circumstances. Adaptations or systematic further developments in the procedure are to be found in Breuer (1996), Flick (1996) and Charmaz (1990). Breuer supplements the grounded theory approach for his own questions by the use of transference and counter-transference in the psychoanalytical sense (see **5.20**). Flick (1996), in his investigation of psychology and technology, proceeds on the basis of Moscovici's (1984) concept of social representations. On the assumption that in different groups different views of technology will be found, groups are pre-selected for investigation. In that way *sampling* is limited to the selection of cases that differ between the groups. Charmaz (1990) takes 'thick' presentation of cases as a starting point for theory development.

A further development of grounded theory is also to be seen in the improvement in practical analysis through the use of specific computer programs (see **5.14**). Programs such as ATLAS.ti (Muhr 1997) support the task of analysis and make quality control possible by ensuring that the analytical process of individual researchers or complete teams can be documented and reproduced in every detail.

FURTHER READING

Glaser, B. G. (1978) *Theoretical Sensitivity*. Mill Valley, CA: The Sociology Press.

Glaser, B. G. and Strauss, A. (1967) *The Discovery of Grounded Theory. Strategies for Qualitative Research*. Chicago: Aldine.

Strauss, A. and Corbin, J. (1990) *Basics of Qualitative Research*. Newbury Park, CA: Sage.

5.14 Computer-assisted Analysis of Qualitative Data

Udo Kelle

1 THE SIGNIFICANCE OF IT-SUPPORTED METHODS FOR QUALITATIVE RESEARCH

The relationship between qualitative researchers and the computer was long characterized less by enthusiasm than by reluctance: IT facilities were looked upon as calculators – necessary for statistical analyses, but of little use for the hermeneutic analysis of texts. Programs for the analysis of text data that have been available since the 1960s, such as *The General Inquirer*, only attracted attention in the area of quantitative content analysis. It was only the introduction of PC-supported text processing that clearly showed the technological potential of IT for the processing, storage, manipulation and archiving of texts. In the 1980s qualitative researchers and research groups – at first independent of one another and for specific research projects – began to develop IT-supported text database systems, and some of these (for example, The Ethnograph, TAP, AQUAD and NUD•IST) were ultimately put on the market. A number of these programs were initially very simple and were cumbersome to use, but they have been developed in successive stages into very comprehensive software packages (such as ATLAS.ti, MAXqda and, as one of the most recent developments, N-Vivo) which meet the requirements of software ergonomics, graphic display and user-friendliness. Currently more than 20 programs dedicated to qualitative research are available, and fierce competition has brought new versions, with a constantly increasing range of functions, onto the market in rapid succession (see Part 7).

The question that is often asked by interested parties and potential users as to 'the best software for qualitative research' will, admittedly, have to remain unanswered here; nor can we offer any comparison of the range of functions and strengths or weaknesses of particular software packages. Because of the rapid technological development in this area, any such comparisons (such as those in Tesch 1990, or Weitzman and Miles 1995) are often out-of-date before they go to press. In addition, the well-known programs (such as MAXqda, ATLAS.ti or N-Vivo) differ very little in terms of the availability of methodologically important basic functions (such as *coding* and *retrieval*, see section 3 below). Differences relate in particular to the levels of user-friendliness and support from the developer. Developments in recent years have also shown that the different software packages are increasingly coming to resemble each other in respect of their range of functions. The question about the program best suited to a particular analytical strategy is therefore very similar to the question as to which table-calculation program is best suited to particular types of calculation (for example, commercial or scientific/technological). A user who has experience of a number of such programs will tend to answer this question by saying that most of the available software packages are suitable for dealing with the kind of problems that normally arise, even though some of the tasks can only be performed in a rather cumbersome way with some of the programs.

What is important here is not only the adaptation of the software to a particular task but also to the (frequently very idiosyncratic) working style of the individual user – the software developers have frequently used different conceptual ideas, metaphors and models for the same tasks and techniques. (In some of the programs a schema of categories is understood as a hierarchical tree with superordinate and subordinate categories, whereas other developers prefer network metaphors, cf. section 3.)

Users who have decided on an IT-supported strategy for the preparation and management of their qualitative data would therefore be well advised not to rely too greatly on the suggestions and recommendations of colleagues or on comparisons in the literature. They should rather assess critically the demonstration versions of the various programs with regard to their usability for the problem in hand and to their own modes of thinking and working.

What might be very helpful here is the information to be found on the website of the *CAQDAS-Networking project* at the University of Surrey (http://www.soc.surrey.ac.uk/caqdas). From this site demonstration versions of a number of different packages may be downloaded on to the investigator's PC, and there are links to various mailing lists and Internet discussion forums where problems of IT-supported qualitative data analysis are discussed, and which the potential user may join in order to obtain help from colleagues experienced in the selection and use of software. But here, too, global questions such as 'What is the best of the available programs?' will receive no other answer than 'That depends on the problem, the goal of the analysis and, most of all, on the investigator's own style of work.'

In the present discussion of IT-supported procedures in qualitative research the term *computer-assisted qualitative data analysis* has become established (cf. Kelle 1995, 1997a; Fielding and Lee 1998). The choice of this term is not without problems since it leads to the mistaken idea that computer programs such as MAXqda, ATLAS.ti or NUD•IST could be used like SPSS statistics software is to carry out statistical analysis. But unlike such statistics program packages, these programs are not tools for *analysis*, but rather for the *structuring* and *organization* of text data. The possibilities for data organization which they provide do have considerable methodological implications for setting up the analytical process and for the validity of the results obtained.

In what follows we shall present, with examples, a number of strategies for the use of IT and discuss their significance for qualitative data analysis, their problems and limitations: *coding* and *retrieval techniques* for a synoptic analysis of textual passages, *schemata of categories* and their *dimensionalization*, together with possibilities for computer-assisted 'testing of hypotheses' and the integration of qualitative and quantitative analytical strategies.

2 METHODOLOGICAL AND TECHNOLOGICAL BASES

Critical information scientists, linguists and linguistic philosophers (such as Dreyfus and Dreyfus 1986; Winograd and Flores 1986) have drawn attention to the fact that there are strict limits to an algorithmic interpretation of texts using automatic data-processing technology. One could therefore advance justifiable methodological objections to the use of the computer in qualitative research. Admittedly in hermeneutic textual interpretation there are a whole range of *mechanical tasks*, particularly when large quantities of text have to be processed. For example, a research project in which more than 30 qualitative interviews are carried out, each lasting one hour, will produce at least 800 and perhaps 1000 pages of textual data. To this must be added written interpretations, theoretical commentaries and researchers' 'memos' (Glaser and Strauss 1967: 108; see **5.13**) which are often scattered in notebooks, on countless manuscript pages and index cards. Dealing with such quantities of text can rapidly become a mammoth exercise of organization, and neglecting it will have serious methodological consequences: the very existence of such quantities of badly organized textual data increases the risk that theoretical conclusions will be supported by a very small number of (perhaps hastily selected) citations and that counter-evidence in the data will be overlooked.

The tool that makes it possible to maintain an overview of large quantities of text was developed in hermeneutically oriented disciplines, such as theology, philology or history, and has already been tested there for centuries. It incorporates the construction of *indexes*, *registers* and *concordances*, the introduction of *cross-references*, to proceed, for example, from one textual location to another. In qualitative research such techniques have also been in use for a considerable time in the organization and management of textual data (cf. Glaser and Strauss 1967: 105ff.; Lofland and Lofland 1984: 134; Taylor and Bogdan 1984: 136). The construction and use of registers and indices of discovery locations using manual methods is admittedly a very time-consuming exercise; the *cut-and-paste* techniques frequently used for organizing textual passages into card indexes also have another significant methodological drawback, namely that textual passages are thereby permanently removed from their context. If the necessary attention is to be paid, in constructing an index of textual locations, to the hermeneutic circle – that textual extracts only acquire their full meaning from their context and are therefore only interpretable in their context – then time-consuming manual work will again be necessary. For this an intact additional copy of the texts has to be preserved so that the location of every piece of text can be noted on the relevant index card.

The construction of an IT-supported organizational system for continuous text may, of course, be achieved with quite simple algorithms and data structures, but these are not normally included in PC standard applications such as text processing programs or conventional database systems. The development of *format-free text database systems* specifically for the requirements of qualitative research, with which one can store the 'addresses' of textual passages together with code words, was the decisive innovation here. Almost all of the currently available software packages for the support of qualitative data analysis are based on this principle. They therefore permit the indexing of textual passages and the search for indexed passages. Moreover, many of the programs contain a variety of additional functions (admittedly with varying scope and configuration – details may be found on the web page of the *CAQDAS-Networking Project*, cf. section 1). Examples are:

1 Functions for the introduction of electronic cross-references (or 'hyperlinks') into the textual data
2 Functions for the storage and management of theoretical commentaries and memos
3 Functions for the construction and graphic depiction of *networks of coding categories*
4 Facilities for defining variables which can be allocated to individual documents and with

which the individual search for text locations can be controlled
5 Facilities for searching for textual passages between which there are particular formal relations
6 Statistical functions for carrying out quantitative content analyses.

The next section, using examples from practical research, will demonstrate how techniques such as these can be used and combined together.

3 TECHNIQUES OF COMPUTER-SUPPORTED QUALITATIVE ANALYSIS AND SAMPLE APPLICATIONS

Computer-supported qualitative data analysis is not an independent qualitative method, but rather includes a number of data organization techniques whose utilization will depend on the particular research issue, the research goals and the methodological orientation of the investigator. These techniques may be integrated into a variety of models for hermeneutic work with texts.

The use of appropriate software programs may be valuable in:

1 the analysis of *differences, similarities and relationships* between passages of text;
2 the development of typologies and *theories*;
3 the *testing of theoretical assumptions* using qualitative data material and the *integration of qualitative and quantitative methods*.

Below we shall discuss the possibilities of IT support in each of these three areas.

The analysis of differences, similarities and relationships between passages of text

The comparative analysis of texts using so-called *synopses* (textual locations that relate to the same topic are kept together and analysed comparatively) is a technique that has long been used, and its methodological significance becomes clear as soon as one looks at the history of biblical commentary. Synopses have been used, since the age of enlightenment, to reveal contradictions between different biblical contexts in order to undermine the dominance of a purely dogmatic interpretation of scripture. For the area of qualitative research the synoptic analysis often actually used by investigators was

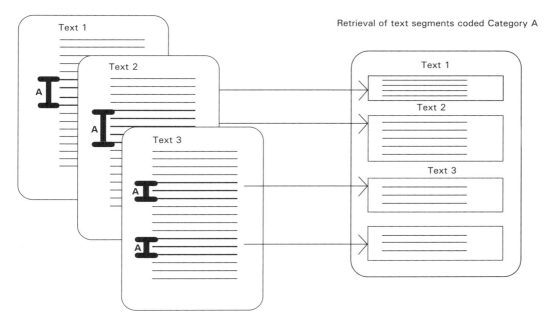

Figure 5.14.1   Coding and retrieval

first explicitly described and discussed by Glaser and Strauss. In the *method of constant comparison* (Glaser and Strauss 1967: 101–116) basic patterns in the text are discovered by a careful and intensive comparison of textual passages. As a precondition of this the data must be *coded*, that is to say, textual passages must be allocated to categories that either are already available in the form of a schema of categories or are developed *ad hoc* in the course of the data analysis (see **5.13**).

Almost all of the currently available software packages that support qualitative data analysis will support the indexing and comparison of textual passages, in that they contain *coding* and *retrieval functions* (Kelle 1995: 4ff.) which make possible the allocation of categories to text segments (= 'coding') and the search for text segments that have been allocated to the same category (= 'retrieval') (cf. Figure 5.14.1.). The function of *selective* retrieval offered by most programs also makes it possible to limit the search for text passages by means of *filters*, with the result that, for example, the search for text passages from interviews can be restricted to interviewees with particular characteristics.

The heavy emphasis on coding and retrieval techniques has led to the long-term neglect of other techniques that also support the comparison of passages of text (cf. Coffey et al. 1996):

the use of electronic cross-referencing, or *hyperlinks*, with which textual passages may be directly interrelated, that is, with prior coding. In view of the rapid developments in this area, it may be assumed that in future an increasing number of the available software packages will contain a function of this sort (at present this applies particular to ATLAS.ti).

The development of typologies and theories

If the comparison of text passages is intended to serve as a basis for empirically based *formation of typologies* and *theory construction* (Kelle 1997a,b), the schema of categories may assume a central role. So as not to limit the formation of types and construction of theory on the basis of concepts and hypotheses developed *ex ante*, the coding categories initially used should restrict the observation of empirical phenomena as little as possible. Two forms of coding categories (see **5.13**) fulfil this condition particularly well:

1   abstract theoretical concepts, or examples of 'theoretical coding' (Glaser 1978), such as *role*, *status*, *meaning pattern*, and so on.
2   concepts from the everyday world (for example, *school*, *profession*, *education*, etc.) such as

1   **Work and Profession**

2   Work and Profession/Aspirations

3   Work and Profession/Realizations

4   Work and Profession/Balancing

(...)

5   **Partnership**

5.1 Partnership/Aspirations

5.2 Partnership/Realizations

5.3 Partnership/Balancing

Figure 5.14.2   Extract From a schema of categories

terms used by the interviewees themselves (so-called *in-vivo* codes, cf. Glaser 1978: 70).

Through the comparative analysis of textual passages both abstract theoretical concepts and also everyday coding categories can progressively be given *empirical content*. An example will serve to illustrate this process.

In a research project that sought to investigate the transition from school and professional training to the labour market, qualitative semi-structured interviews were carried out, which were used to reconstruct the decision-making processes of young people faced with a choice of profession (cf. Heinz et al. 1998). In order to systematize the young people's separate stages of action in choosing their profession the following three theoretical categories were used: *aspirations* included the young people's action goals, *realizations* represented concrete steps taken to implement these, and the category *balancing* related to the assessment of the relationship between action goals and action conditions.

In order to code aspirations, realizations and balancing in respect of concrete areas of life, the theoretical categories ('aspirations', 'realizations', 'balancing') were combined with everyday categories ('work and profession', 'partnership', etc.) to form a schema of categories (cf. Figure 5.14.2).

This schema of categories represents a *theoretical axis* (Strauss and Corbin 1990: 96ff.), or an *heuristic framework* (Kelle 1997a,b), the empirical content of which is supplied by information from the data material. By means of a careful comparative analysis of textual passages aspects or *dimensions* may be identified that will lead to a modification of the schema and to its supplementation through further categories and subcategories, and also to the construction of a typology. This process may be illustrated with a further example from the same research project.

As a first step, in order to investigate the interviewees' orientation to the topics 'marriage' and 'family', textual passages were coded where these two topics were addressed. In a second stage, using selective retrieval, the coded text segments were extracted and interpreted comparatively by interviewees who viewed starting a family as their main life goal, and here three dimensions of the category 'marriage' were identified:

1   some of the interviewees considered marriage as the *only acceptable form of cohabitation between man and woman*;

2   others viewed marriage as an essential *precondition for starting a child-focused family*;

3   others again viewed marriage particularly as a *safeguard*. Interviewees with this orientation quoted (with varying combinations and emphases) three different arguments for marriage, concerning (1) its function as a *financial safeguard*, (2) its significance as a morally binding agreement to a lifelong *bond*, or (3) marriage as a means of fulfilling the *expectations* of the social (and especially family) *environment*.

The comparison of textual passages made it possible to distinguish three different hierarchically structured levels (cf. Figure 5.14.3).

This kind of hierarchical schema of concepts may be described in terms of IT as a *network* or *graph*, and it may be translated into a complex data structure which makes it possible not only to show graphically the relationships between coding categories or the emerging typology, but also to carry out complex retrieval processes, in which the user can take a long pathway along the 'nodes' (that is, the categories in Figure 5.14.3) of the graph or network. Graphs of this kind may be structured in very different ways. ATLAS.ti, for example, allows the user to organize networks with almost random relationships, while other programs (such as NUD•IST) only permit hierarchical 'tree'-structures.

The testing of hypotheses and the integration of quantitative techniques

The strengths of IT-supported data management can be seen when theoretical assumptions developed in the course of the data analysis need to be tested. If the data material has already been

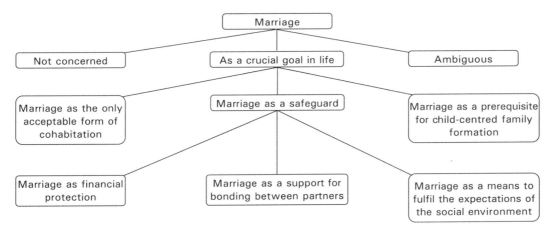

Figure 5.14.3 A hierarchical category scheme as a result of 'dimensionalization'

adequately and exhaustively coded with the relevant categories, it is relatively simple to use IT-support in the search for the text material necessary to test the particular assumption. For example, the hypothesis developed in the course of a qualitative study of occupation-biographical orientations – that gender-specific relationships exist between professional and family orientations – may be followed up by looking for text passages (separate for male and female interviewees) that were simultaneously coded under the categories 'work-orientation' and 'family orientations'. This kind of assumption-testing is supported in most available software packages by complex retrieval functions for the search for *co-occurring codings*, and these make it possible, for example, to find text segments that were coded with particular coding categories and which show a *reciprocal overlap* or a particular *proximity to one another within the text*.

Figure 5.14.4 presents the results of a search for the co-occurring codings 'emo' (= *emotional overload*) and 'cle' (= *critical life events*) in a sample data set, conducted using the AQUAD program. The program yielded as a search result the 'addresses' (in the form of line numbers) for text locations where the text segments coded as 'cle' and 'emo' occur together. From this printout from the program it may be seen that in the interview 'bioss1' the codings 'cle' and 'emo' occur together only once (between line 100 and line 104), whereas in the interview 'bioss2' they appear five times.

It is vitally important here not to overlook the fact that information about the co-occurrence of codings can be used in quite different ways.

1 It can be used to indicate *in which location in the text corpus* relevant information about possible links between *emotional overload* and *critical life events* may be found (giving the appropriate command normally makes it possible to find these locations without difficulty).

2 It may be considered as empirical evidence that the phenomena *critical life events* and *emotional overload* do co-occur or correlate (for example, in the sense that in the life of the first interviewee a critical life event did once occur which led to emotional overload, whereas in the life of the second interviewee it was possible to find this kind of link five times).

The first strategy pursues an essentially heuristic goal, whereas the second strategy corresponds to the normal understanding of hypothesis testing within quantitative approaches, although here it must be verified that the relevant coding categories represent unambiguously and reliably the procedures, facts and events (for example, the fact that an interviewee has indeed experienced a critical life event). For this purpose, the categories must be precisely defined before the coding of the data material (perhaps using key examples), and their reliability would need to be checked by means of a comparison of text passages coded by independent coders. Admittedly, the coding categories used in qualitative studies frequently cannot meet these conditions for obvious reasons: if texts have to be structured and interpreted through coding for a synoptically comparative analysis, it is normally not the *representational function* of the coding categories (that is, the fact that the coding categories depict

```
hypothesis 1/codefile bioss1.cod

100    102    cle    –    102    104    emo

hypothesis 1/codefile bioss2.cod

 24     28    cle    –     26     30    emo
 65     70    cle    –     72     82    emo
110    112    cle    –    111    115    emo
220    228    cle    –    212    224    emo
450    452    cle    –    456    476    emo
```

Figure 5.14.4   Results of a search for co-occurring codings

a particular event) that is highlighted, but rather its *indexical function*. The categories used, therefore, are not intended to represent facts that are defined precisely and *ex ante* in the data material, but to demonstrate that information about a particular kind of more or less precisely defined fact can be found at a particular location in the data on this difference (cf. also Seidel and Kelle 1995). Unlike coding categories which represent clearly defined events or facts, these categories are often kept as general as possible so that they may capture a large class of possible facts and events.

With an open, theory-generating procedure, therefore, it is the *indexical function* of the coding categories used that is foregrounded, at least in the early stages of qualitative analysis: the coding of a passage of text with the category 'cle' does not then represent the *fact* that a critical life event took place, but rather that the *coded passage of text* is in some way related to critical life events. For the application of a classical strategy of 'hypothesis testing', such categories are unusable. Admittedly the categories that a qualitative investigator develops are often not specific and concrete statements about empirical facts, but are provisional, imprecise and sometimes quite vague suppositions about possible relationships. The testing of such assumptions or 'hypotheses' can hardly be compared with a statistically based test of a hypothesis: no use is made of an algorithm that would facilitate a decision about the applicability of a particular theoretical statement – it is rather a matter of collecting textual material, the interpretative analysis of which will help the investigator to support or reject the provisional and initially perhaps general and vague assumptions, and also to modify them and develop them further. The computer-supported search for co-occurring codings can assist this search for

relevant data material and can therefore fulfil some *heuristic purpose* rather than assist in hypothesis testing in the traditional sense.

The methodologically appropriate use of *functions for quantitative data analysis* which are included in many software packages is dependent on whether the *representational* or the *indexical function* of the categories used is foregrounded. For example, the MAXqda program also contains, apart from comprehensive coding and retrieval functions, possibilities for the further development of coding categories for case-related variables and variable-values. The result of this process is a quantitative data matrix which can be analysed with the assistance of standard statistical packages. Of course, the transition this involves from indexical to representational categories requires particular care. The original goal of coding frequently did not consist of producing a quantitative data matrix but of ascertaining that all the relevant data on a particular fact could be assembled.

4 LIMITS AND SCOPE OF COMPUTER-SUPPORTED METHODS IN QUALITATIVE RESEARCH

Since the development of computer programs to support qualitative data analysis began, there has been a discussion about their potential methodological benefits, but also about the methodological risks involved. In this great optimism has been expressed (Conrad and Reinarz 1984; Richards and Richards 1991, 1994), but also notes of caution (Agar 1991; Coffey et al. 1996; Seidel and Kelle 1995).

The following have been emphasized as advantages of the use of IT in qualitative research.

1   Higher efficiency in data organization economizes on time and human resources and makes it possible to *process larger quantities of data* and therefore to *take larger samples* (Kelle and Laurie 1995). Of course, it should not be forgotten here that it is not 'sample size' that is the main criterion in qualitative sampling but 'case contrast' (1995: 22f.), in other words, the possibility of identifying patterns by means of multiple comparisons between deliberately chosen individual cases. A large sample, therefore, does not *per se* result in a higher validity of results, if the desired case selection does not lead to an expansion of the area of interest and an extension of the

analyses. Here, too, there is a danger that the investigator will be overwhelmed by the vast quantity of data that are made available by IT-supported data processing. The amount of time needed to structure textual data by coding should not be underestimated, particularly since this will grow with any increase in the scope of the data corresponding to the extra size of the sample. The increase in the volume of data achieved through larger samples should always therefore be set against the additional costs of data organization in terms of time and effort.

2 IT-supported techniques require the systematization of many research techniques which would otherwise be used in a rather unsystematic fashion, and they therefore support a transparent process of analysis, driven as far as possible by explicit rules.

3 Researchers are freed from burdensome mechanical tasks, and are motivated, on the one hand, to study more carefully the relationships between categories, and, on the other hand, to experiment with the data and to 'play', resulting in more space for creative and investigative aspects of the data analysis (Fielding and Lee 1998).

Concern has been voiced in the discussion, however, that the methodological assumptions that underlie the individual software packages unwittingly influence the analytical process with the result that investigators adopt analytical strategies that do not correspond to their own theoretical and methodological orientations. A further criticism is also directed to the software producers to the effect that they do not take sufficient account in the development of their programs of the pluralism of qualitative approaches. Lonkila (1995), for example, and Coffey et al. (1996) draw attention to the fact that many software packages have a strong link to the *grounded theory* of Glaser and Strauss (see **5.13, 2.1, 6.6**), whilst other methods (for example, procedures more strongly rooted in hermeneutics or discourse analysis) are neglected. In response to this, Lee and Fielding use an analysis of the literature to show that more than two-thirds of qualitative studies that use IT support have no connection to *grounded theory* (Lee and Fielding 1996). On the basis of one of their own empirical studies of software users, these two authors come to the conclusion that fears that computer programs would develop a life of their own in contradiction of the methodological intentions of the users, and that

they would determine analytical practice, find little support in actual research practice: users are more inclined to avoid the use of a particular software package (or even the use of a computer) than to adopt an analytical strategy that would conflict with their methodological orientations.

Further critical warnings in the literature concern the danger that the use of IT will force textual interpretation out of the centre of the analytical process and that it will be replaced by a preoccupation with coding categories (Agar 1991; Seidel and Kelle 1995). In fact, there are considerable risks of producing artefacts, particularly if the user does not attend to the difference between the indexical and the representational functions of coding categories. This is particularly true of the techniques of 'hypothesis testing' and the integration of qualitative and quantitative analytical stages that were discussed in section 3: the move from an indexing of texts to a description and summary of facts is not free from methodological hazards and requires the researcher to give constant attention to the meaning of the complex algorithms which can sometimes be carried out with a single gesture. In this there is a very good parallel with statistical software: here, too, investigators who use, without thinking, the software that is now so easy to handle, and which requires no prior knowledge of mathematical principles, can easily produce artefacts and false interpretations. But when they are used with methodological awareness the modern techniques for IT-supported organization and structuring of data open up many possibilities for a more intensive and systematic analysis of data, frequently also making the tasks a good deal more enjoyable.

FURTHER READING

Fielding, N. G. and Lee, R. M. (1998) *Computer Analysis and Qualitative Research*. London: Sage.

Kelle, U. (ed.) (1995) *Computer-aided Qualitative Data Analysis. Theory, Methods and Practice*. London: Sage.

Kelle, U. (1997) 'Theory Building in Qualitative Research and Computer Programs for the Management of Textual Data', *Sociological Research Online*, 2 (2). http:www.socresonline.org.uk/socresonlione/2/2/1.html

5.15 Analysis of Documents and Records

Stephan Wolff

1 DOCUMENTARY REALITY

Documents, understood here as written texts that serve as a record or piece of evidence of an event or fact, occupy a prominent position in modern societies. A major part of the reality that is relevant to members of modern societies is accessible to them in the form of documents (Smith 1974, 1978). The increase in their significance is due to the secular trend towards the *legalization* and *organization* of all areas of life, and in particular to the development of a modern type of administration characterized essentially by the *principle of documentation*. Literacy, on the one hand, increases the scope of communication, in that it makes it independent of the time and place of the message (cf. Ong 1982). But at the same time it puts its success at risk, since situational pointers for understanding and immediate opportunities for clarification are lost. The insistence on written documents that is typical of organizations as the preferred form for the representation of reality can lead to painful experiences of difference, particularly when people are confronted with official records of events that they have participated in.

An example of this is a legal appeal. In order to judge a breach of law in a court judgment it is *only the text* of the basis of the judgment that is relevant. This alone, but not the recollections of participants, functions as a reference point for the assessment of what was and what was not the case in the main legal proceedings. The formulation 'what is not in the records is not in the world' was already a fundamental principle of the courts of the Inquisition. In clear contrast to this there is the *principle of orality* that obtains during the proceedings; according to this, at least in criminal proceedings, only what was negotiated orally can be used as the basis of a decision (which implies, for example, that written evidence must, as a matter of principle, be read aloud).

Documents are *standardized artefacts*, in so far as they typically occur in particular *formats*: as notes, case reports, contracts, drafts, death certificates, remarks, diaries, statistics, annual reports, certificates, judgments, letters or expert opinions. A major part of official documents, and most private documents, are intended only for a defined circle of legitimate or involved recipients. Official documents also function as *institutionalized traces*, which means that they may legitimately be used to draw conclusions about the activities, intentions and ideas of their creators or the organizations they represented. In view of the elaborate and, on the part of the participants, fully reflective art involved in the production of such records, the element of *fiction*, which is true of all such records, becomes particularly clear.

2 DOCUMENTS IN THE HISTORY OF QUALITATIVE RESEARCH

Qualitative social research developed (in ethnology) in the context of investigating *oral* cultures, that is, those that were not mediated by texts, or (in the so-called Chicago School) in dealing with phenomena outside, or on the fringe of, an organization-based society. Because of this a particular 'bias' developed in favour of verbal communication or verbal data in simple social systems (cf. Atkinson and Coffey 1997). If one does not completely limit oneself to reducing documents to the information they contain, even today any work with them has a predominantly *exegetic character*, which means that they are seen as sources (Hodder 1994; Scott 1990) that point to other underlying phenomena and intentions. Since a close relation is presupposed between the 'declarative force' of a document and its authenticity and credibility, there is, furthermore, a preference on the part of qualitative researchers for private records (such as letters of biographical records; cf. the classic study of Thomas and Zaniecki 1918).

Anyone who reads documents as a basic representation *of something else* is looking at them as a 'window-pane' (Gusfield 1976) through which one is looking at a person, an action or a fact. This window-pane only becomes important when unfortunate or inappropriate formulations distort the 'view', and then one starts on the basis that such obscurities can fundamentally be eliminated (by means of a more transparent representation or more profound interpretation). This leads to a paradox, however, that a document-analysis that begins in this way takes place, in an ideal case, without any analysis of the document itself. However, it seems to correspond much better to the basic idea of qualitative research if we recognize documents as *independent methodological and situationally embedded creations* of their producers (and, in terms of reception, of their readers) and to make them *as such* the object of an investigation. Accordingly, the term document analysis is used not only to characterize a research method but also to denote a specific *mode of access* to written records (which, of course, implies a preference for particular methods).

A more sustained preoccupation with documents as texts that have the independent logic of a textually mediated *documentary reality* only developed in the 1960s. The crucial motivation was a result of the *labelling approach*, whose representatives pointed out that it was only the reaction of society that bestowed the attribute 'deviant' on particular actions or individuals. They therefore tried consistently to look over the shoulders of the relevant agencies in the production of deviant actions. In this way they removed from such data as the statistics of criminality and suicide the image of supposedly natural social facts (in Durkheim's sense) by making visible the processes of definition and documentation necessary for their production (Douglas 1967; Gephardt 1988). Particular importance attaches to the work of Aaron Cicourel, who studied the processes of evaluation and categorization in education and in the way officialdom dealt with youth crime (cf. Cicourel 1968; Cicourel and Kitsuse 1963; Cicourel and Jennings 1974; Kitsuse and Cicourel 1963). Cicourel was particularly interested in the question of how the *translation* of details about people and events, derived from interviews or pre-existing records, into 'official cases' comes about. He discovered that decisions about the allocation to categories are taken in respect of established organizational 'normal cases' and establishment patterns (such as 'broken home') within the framework of informal or institutionalized processes of negotiation (cf. Scheff 1966; Sudnow 1965). The documentary (case) reality, once established, takes on a *dynamic of its own*, and from this the person categorized – but also the bodies subsequently involved – can escape only with difficulty.

Typically the circumstances or the background against which they were produced are no longer visible in the documents themselves. The focus in labelling research was therefore on demonstrating the *rhetorical* character of documents (Gusfield 1976). Documents were unveiled as examples of *institutional display* (Goffman 1961b) or even as a form of *bureaucratic propaganda* (Altheide and Johnson 1980), whose purpose was primarily to engender an appearance of legitimacy, rationality and efficiency in the eyes of relevant organizational environments (Bogdan and Ksander 1980; Meyer and Rowan 1977). What is characteristic of these studies, apart from their revelatory and ironical attitude and their concentration on the aspect of opportunistic information management, is a certain half-heartedness, in that the ideal of a 'correct' portrayal was not really abandoned (Pollner 1987).

A radical change of perspective was then brought about by *ethnomethodological research* in that it consistently dispensed with treating documents as resources – however deficient – and instead made them, or more precisely the socially organized practices of their production and reception, into the real object of investigation. The classic example of an ethnomethodologically set up document analysis comes from Harold Garfinkel (1967b). In the context of a study of patient careers he was struck by the fact that the relevant forms were filled in incompletely and inaccurately. This instance of 'missing data', which was annoying to him as an investigator, strangely caused almost no offence among the staff of the clinic. Since Garfinkel did not wish to attribute this finding to incompetence on the part of the staff, he asked himself whether there were not perhaps 'good reasons' for such 'bad' clinical records. Conducting an information-gathering exercise from the point of view of the staff proves that the situation is, in fact, quite sensible, if account is taken of the time available. In general, this means that one has to be satisfied with doing the job as concisely as possible. Moreover, bearing in mind that records can be used to check on the activity or efficiency of the staff, a certain degree of vagueness in the representation of information is desirable, because in cases of doubt it allows the possibility of an explanation and justification with reference to the practical circumstances. Finally, every competent insider will take account of a *principled discrepancy* between the conditions and factual necessities of the documented activity on the one hand, and the specific requirements for correct fulfilment of professional obligations on the other. The investigator's 'annoyance' therefore becomes, for the participants, a quite rational and comprehensible way of producing documents (cf. Feldman and March 1981). The meaning of the entries in the patient records can only be measured by those who have insight into the typical course of patient contact, the circumstances under which the entries were made, the expected readership, and the relations between them and the producers. Instead of assuming that the patient records would reflect (or conceal) the order of the interaction between participants, it would be more appropriate to say that an understanding of this order is a precondition for a correct reading.

Although in principle different interpretations of the content of such records are always possible, there is, in Garfinkel's opinion, such a thing as a standard reading – at least for the authorized and competent reader. Such a person can always read in such a way as to gain a reasoned impression as to whether and how the work was completed in respect of what might be expected as normal and sensible under the prevailing circumstances.

> The various items of the clinic folders are tokens – like pieces that will permit the assembly of an indefinitely large number of mosaics – gathered together not to describe a relationship between clinical personnel and the patient, but to permit a clinic member to formulate a relationship between patient and clinic as a normal course of clinic affairs when and if the *question of normalizing* should arise as a matter of some clinic member's practical concerns. In this sense, we say that *a folder's contents serve the uses of contract rather than description* .... (Garfinkel 1967b: 202f.)

The 'early' ethnomethodology (see **3.2**) represented by Garfinkel's investigation did achieve a basic clarification of the way documents are socially produced and situationally readable – although this was without coming to terms in any concrete way with the documents as texts. Because of the limited scope of *ethnographic* methods (see **5.5**) there were no attempts at systematic reconstruction of the phenomena contained in the records until the 1980s. Admittedly Garfinkel (1967b: 200f.) himself provided an important starting point by setting up the thesis that documents resembled utterances in a conversation where the participants did not know one another but were none the less in a position to understand allusions and indirect pointers, since they already knew what was being talked about. What also favours a *conversation analysis procedure* is the fact that the ability to read and write texts develops ontogenetically on the basis of interactional and conversational competence. It is therefore reasonable to suppose that the methodological practices that play a role in the production and interpretation of texts also correspond to, or are derived from, those that are used in the production and interpretation of verbal interaction.

3   DOCUMENT ANALYSIS AS CONVERSATION ANALYSIS

These stimuli were taken up by ethnomethodologists working in conversation analysis who, in the course of the 1980s, increasingly began to turn to *institutional* communication and such interactive constellations as jokes, lectures or stories that have a lower degree of 'interactive density'. From this it was only a small step to working with interactions in the written mode (such as exchanges of letters, cf. Mulkay 1985) and ultimately to documents produced in an institutional communicative context, such as scientific articles (Knorr-Cetina 1981; Woolgar 1980), psychiatric reports (Knauth and Wolff 1990) or legal opinions (Wolff and Müller 1997).

Of central importance to document analysis with a conversation or discourse analysis[1] frame of reference are the writings of Harvey Sacks (1972) on the methodological character of descriptions and Dorothy Smith's idea of the 'active text' (1978, 1986). In her study 'K is Mentally Ill: the Anatomy of a Factual Account' (1978) she illustrates the fact that written texts are not passive interpretations of reality handed over, so to speak, to its interpreters but that they actively structure its social readability. The particular achievement of a factual report consists of evoking in the reader the impression of an active and stable reality, but at the same time of making the fact and the mechanisms of its textual mediation invisible. What must first be clarified, therefore, is the procedures that can be employed in making documents in any sense readable as descriptions of reality.

Sacks (1972) developed the methodological toolkit that members of society use in the production and identification of descriptions, using the example of the two sentences 'The baby cried. The mommy picked it up.' Without knowing anything about the concrete circumstances, any competent member of society can understand these two sentences as a story about a crying baby and its mother, who picks it up because it is crying. Alternative readings (such as 'baby' is actually an adult who is addressed by a pet name; the mommy is not the baby's mother; she is picking up some object, and so on) are quite possible, but only if the preferred variant is expressly discounted.

According to Sacks the fact that readers interpret such sentences in largely similar ways depends on the application of particular institutionalized rules of categorization and deduction which he brings together under the heading of *membership categorization device*. The effect of this 'device' becomes clear if one takes account of the fact that the selection of a particular

descriptive category simultaneously implies cross-referring to other suitable categories, and together these constitute a 'collection' (in this particular example: 'family members'). The categorization transcends mere labelling in the sense that particular modes of action that may be socially expected are also bound up with a particular category ('category bound activities'). For example, because one would normally expect of mothers that they take care of small children, the sentences 'The baby cried. The mother watched.' may be heard not only as a description but as descriptive of a piece of *deviant* behaviour. Through the mode of categorization selected, the person undertaking it may adopt a particular relationship to what is being categorized and thereby alter the character of the report: one might imagine that the woman is categorized not as a mother but as a 'patient' or an 'accused'. Analogous effects, such as those deriving from differential identification of individuals (and as implied here: accusations), may also be achieved through the use of conventional implications in the formulation of particular locations (cf. Drew 1978).

Since, in principle, an infinite number of formally correct versions of a fact are conceivable, the concrete form of the description has to be *decided*. The selectivity involved in this is not a problem of information that could, for instance, be removed by means of precision, but one that sets up an inevitable requirement as to formulation. A whole range of structural problems may be postulated with which authors of descriptions are confronted, but whose solution also opens up specific possible modes of expression (cf. Wolff 1995).

Descriptions of any kind relate to a specific (even if only imaginary) audience or may be read as such. To be able to tailor their utterances in a recipient-oriented way, producers of descriptions must take account of conventional assumptions about the identity and prior knowledge of their recipients. They must ask themselves: how can I write a text that can be experienced and understood by my readers as directed at them?

The producers of descriptions also rely on the fact that the appropriateness and validity of their claims is pre-supposed. They then have the problems of *factuality* and of *authorization*. In respect of these one may ask: how do I indicate through my text the extent to which my representations relate to reality? In addition, it is also important to come to terms with conflicting or conceivable alternative versions of the factual content. In this *implicit* descriptive conflicts (when reporting extremely improbable circumstances; cf. Wooffitt 1992) should be distinguished from *explicit* descriptive conflicts (for example, when a supervisor has to express an opinion on the work of his or her colleagues; cf. Knauth and Wolff 1991).

These configurations can only partially be achieved by means of explicit formulations, justifications and explanations: it is better if they are carried *reflexively*, that is to say, through the manner of text formulation, or, so to speak, incidentally. The trick consists of not leaving the interpretation entirely to the reader (in the sense of the reader-response theory), nor of hermetically sealing the text off with instructions against attempts at interpretation. This means making a virtue out of the need for an inevitable vagueness in descriptions. What works to the advantage of text-producers here is the fact that this vagueness is socially sanctioned, that recipients actually expect to be presented with appropriately 'open' texts that require some interpretation. On the other hand, the conventional postulates of the *membership categorization device* are also used. By means of cleverly selected categorizations, attributions, contrasts, orderings and so on, *meaning gaps* and *interpretative puzzles* may be induced, and of these one may assume that a competent reader from the relevant 'interpretative community' (Fish 1980) will decode or solve them in a particular way.

The structuring effect of 'active texts' is therefore found particularly as a result of leading readers in the direction of a particular *conventional mode of reading* (McHoul 1982), that requires of them an *activity of implication* (for analyses in this vein cf. Silvermann 1993, 1998; Smith 1986; Watson 1997).

4 RECOMMENDATIONS FOR PRACTICAL WORK

For practical research work, the following recommendations are offered with regard to the analysis of documentary realities and their mode of production.

In view of the way they are produced, documents may only be used in an extremely limited way as evidence or indications of factual content or decision-making processes that are addressed within them. Documents represent an *independent level of data*. For that reason it is problematic to use statements in documents as opposed to other analytic results (perhaps from interviews or observation) concerning relevant facts that were obtained at other data levels (for example, judgment texts compared to court observation; cf. Wolff and Müller 1997). The current practice of using documents, as it were, as a second front after observational and verbal data should be avoided.

Documents, even those that expressly operate as factual reports, should not be reduced to the function of information containers, but should basically be treated and analysed as *methodologically created communicative features*. Content analysis techniques of paraphrase and reduction, which target only the intended information content, do not grasp this 'independence of meaning' which documents have. Nor is it found in approaches that address the documents with a basic (ideologically) critical or evaluative attitude (such as 'critical discourse analysis'; cf. Titscher et al. 2000. See **5.19**).

It is also advisable, in analysing documents, to adopt the conversation analysis maxim of *order all points*. Even apparent externals (such as layout, line-spacing, colour, quality of paper, order of the various points) or formulations that seem quite obvious (such as modes of address, categorizations or descriptions of sequencing) should not therefore be treated as coincidental or analytically insignificant until the opposite has been proved. Transcriptions of the material (for example, so that they may be processed using text analysis software) should therefore be viewed as problematic, in so far as the nature of the document as a phenomenon is altered. This is unfortunately true of *anonymizations*, which frequently, since they render invisible the relevant forms of referencing, eliminate analytically important material. Whatever the case, there should always be the possibility of checking findings against the original material.

The analysis of conversations is known to be made easier when participants constantly signal mutual understanding or correct supposed errors. In textual communication this resource is available to a greatly reduced extent. In document analysis there is, therefore, a great temptation to invoke *contextual information* to help with clarification in cases of doubt. However, this should be avoided for as long as is possible. In support of this we should remember that the producers or readers of documents are confronted with the same problem. But they can only rely to a limited extent on the necessary contextual information being supplemented by the readers, and are therefore largely compelled to use the internal sequencing and ordering of the text. For this reason the analysis should proceed, in the first instance, from the self-sufficiency of the text and should exhaust the inherent analytical possibilities. Whenever this is possible, in view of the nature of the material, there should also be an analysis of the 'conversation' between the document being investigated and the subsequent or proceeding texts (for example, contradictions, reactions, challenges, cautions).

Since one of the important 'achievements' of documents consists of making the circumstances of their production invisible, the analyst must sometimes have recourse to techniques of alienating the object of investigation (Amann and Hirschauer 1997), in order to get to such structural problems as the local practices of text production. The following have shown themselves to be valuable in this respect.

- The technique of 'reading aloud' the document in question.
- Ethnographic observations of, or narrative interviews about, concrete cases of document production (looking perhaps at the critical incident technique, cf. Chell 1998).
- Comparisons between different groups of text producers (such as psychiatric, psychological and social-pedagogic reports on the same person).
- Contrasting the texts of documents with their oral presentation.

Qualitative document analysis aims at the investigation of *structural problems* and at the methodological toolkit that document producers and their recipients have to come to terms with, and it seeks to make explicit the implications of various formulations and presentation strategies. It is inappropriate to expect of it any guidance for the 'correct' formulation of texts.

NOTE

1 In view of the rapid approximation of empirical discourse analysts to the ideas and methods of conversation analysis (cf. Antaki and Widdicombe 1998; Edwards and Potter 1992; Potter 1996; see **5.17**), we shall not undertake, in this chapter, any contrastive presentation of discourse analysis. (Here we follow the advice of Silverman 1998: 193; for a different emphasis see **5.19**.)

FURTHER READING

Lepper, G. (2000) *Categories in Text and Talk. A Practical Introduction to Categorization Analysis*. London: Sage.

Potter, J. (1996) *Representing Reality – Discourse, Rhetoric and Social Construction*. London: Sage.

Watson, R. (1997) 'Ethnomethodology and Textual Analysis', in D. Silverman (ed.), *Qualitative Research. Theory, Method and Practice*. London: Sage. pp. 80–98.

5.16 Objective Hermeneutics and Hermeneutic Sociology of Knowledge

Jo Reichertz

1 OBJECTIVE HERMENEUTICS

The term 'objective hermeneutics' refers to a complex *theoretical*, *methodological* and *operational* concept that derives essentially from the work of Ulrich Oevermann. In the interim the labels 'structural hermeneutics' and 'genetic structuralism' have also come into use.

Objective hermeneutics, which looks upon itself as a *Kunstlehre* (art), claims to be the fundamental method of investigation for *every* kind of sociological research. Consistently with this, it no longer only interprets protocols of everyday interaction but, in principle, also texts, and here painting, architecture, clues of criminal activity and the like are also understood as texts. The procedure consists of first conceiving and fixing the social action in question as a text, in order subsequently to interpret it hermeneutically with regard to action-generating latent meaning structures.

Initially, the concern was only with the 'reconstruction of *objective* meaning structures' of texts: what the text producers thought, wished, hoped, believed in the creation of their text, that is, what subjective intentions they had, was – and is – unimportant for objective hermeneutics. The only thing that counts is the objective meaning structure of the text in a particular linguistic and interactive community. Later the attribute 'objective' came to relate not only to the area of study: the validity of the findings obtained was also subject to the requirement that they should, with the assistance of the procedure, achieve an objectivity of results.

> Since objective hermeneutics, irrespective of what concrete object it has to analyse, is always primarily directed at the reconstruction of the latent sense structures or objective meaning structures of those expressive forms in which the object of investigation or the question under study is authentically embodied, one can require the same degree of objectivity of its findings or the assessment of their applicability as that which is taken for granted in the natural sciences. This is simply because the meaning structures which are to be reconstructed can be ascertained by means of fundamentally definable rules and mechanisms of a basic algorithmic structure in a precisely testable and complete way in a protocol that is accessible at all times. (Oevermann 1996: 4)

The validity of analyses must be ensured through a strict application of the hermeneutic *Kunstlehre* (art). An *objective reconstruction of objective structures* is understood as a limit that is reached through constant application of the canonical directives of objective hermeneutics.

History of objective hermeneutics

The development of the procedure of objective hermeneutics derives in essence from the 'parental home and school' major research project directed by Oevermann, Krappmann and

Kreppner. This was concerned, from 1968 onwards, with the significance of the restricted and elaborated language codes for school achievement. The investigations were carried out in a purely quantitative way at the beginning of the research process. The inadequacy of the results thus achieved led to a fundamental reappraisal of the methods and to an examination of the Chomskyan competence-performance model, Piaget's learning theory and Freud's concept of traumatization.

Oevermann and the colleagues then working with him (in particular T. Allert, Y. Schütze, H. Gripp and E. Konau) worked on the development of qualitative *data collection procedures* until the beginning of 1970, and subsequently also on hermeneutic *analytical procedures*. The focus of this type of hermeneutics was not the long-standing German discussion of philosophical hermeneutics, but the criticism that had become especially vocal in the United States of the quantitatively focused form of sociological measurement. The new approach was set up, as far as methodology is concerned, with reference to Mead's theory of language, Searle's concept of rules and Peirce's abductive research logic (see **4.3**).

Oevermann's work since 1980 has been concerned less with the further methodological justification of the method and more with theoretical concepts, practical consultancy and current political topics, such as the *theory of professions*, the *concept of structure*, the *organization of the police crime reporting service*, *media criticism*, the *meaning of religion*, the *development of innovation*, and repeatedly with problems in the *interpretation of paintings*. What is methodologically new is Oevermann's attempt to use 'fictional data' (dramas and novels) to reconstruct the structural logic of real actions (Oevermann 1997; see also the interesting debate in König 1996b).

Other authors who associate themselves with objective hermeneutics are, on the other hand, concerned primarily with further case analyses and discussion of the methodological and theoretical implications of the hermeneutic approach (cf. the collections of papers by Aufenanger and Lenssen 1986 and Garz and Kraimer 1994a, and the discussion of these in Schröer 1994 and T. Sutter 1997).

The concept of objective hermeneutics is currently one of the most prominent approaches in qualitative research in German-speaking countries, including Austria and Switzerland, and it figures in all of the more recent methodological handbooks on qualitative research (e.g. Bohnsack 1999; Hitzler and Honer 1997; Lamnek 1995).

Strategies for empirical procedure

Contrary to the erroneous widespread belief, there is not *one single* procedure for objective hermeneutic interpretation of texts. There is merely a kind of basic common understanding that manifests itself in differing and sometimes mutually exclusive variants. What is, of course, common to all variants is the belief that the three major obstacles to an unobscured exposition of meaning must be overcome *before* the analysis begins.

In the first place it is necessary to remove the pressure to act which universally dominates everyday life and which always prematurely interrupts the process of explaining meaning: in a word, it is vital to spend a great deal of time on the analysis. Then it is necessary to make sure that the interpreters are not subject to any neurotic and/or ideological blind spots – although how this is to be done, Oevermann does not make clear. Finally, one should ensure that the interpreters are competent members of the linguistic and interactive community being investigated, and so children are normally excluded.

In looking for the procedure of objective hermeneutics one will admittedly find in the relevant literature that there are to date three variants of text explanation, or more precisely, three forms for the *presentation* of one's own research practice.

1 The *detailed analysis* of a text at eight different levels, in which the knowledge and the external context, and also the pragmatics of a type of interaction, are explained in advance and are borne in mind in the analysis (e.g. Oevermann et al. 1979).
2 The *sequential analysis* of each individual contribution to an interaction, step by step, without clarifying in advance the internal or external context of the utterance (e.g. Oevermann et al. 1979: 412–429). This is the most demanding variant of objective hermeneutics, since it is very strongly oriented towards the methodological premises of the overall concept.

3 The full *interpretation of the objective social data* from all those who participated in an interaction, before any approach is made to the text to be interpreted (e.g. Oevermann et al. 1980). This variant handles the fundamentals of a theory of hermeneutics interpretation very flexibly and uses them in a somewhat metaphorical way.

The first variant initially found many adherents within qualitative research, not only because in its most important elements it is formalized and therefore easy to learn. The second variant now constitutes the real core of objective hermeneutics – texts are interpreted in detail step by step *without* using any knowledge of the case. A clear distinction must be made here between this and the third variant, which places the explanation of the objective case data before the text analysis. This version is particularly used when one seeks to economize the application of objective hermeneutics.

On research logic

In general objective hermeneutics conducts only single-case analyses. Standardized and large-scale data collections are rejected on methodological grounds, since only the collection of non-standardized data and their objective hermeneutic analysis would guarantee valid results. The validity of the analysis derives in particular from the correct application of the hermeneutic *Kunstlehre* (art). The separation between 'logic of discovery' and 'logic of verification' (Reichenbach, Popper) is thereby explicitly renounced: 'truth' results from the correct epistemological procedure, since the correct treatment of a text causes 'the thing to speak for itself' (Oevermann 1984: 11).

Objective hermeneutics proceeds from the singular (reconstruction of the structure of single cases) to the general statement (generalization of structure) by means of the principle of falsification; reconstruction of structure and generalization of structure are conceived of as the outer poles of a targeted research process in which the results of a number of single-case structural reconstructions are condensed into a more general structure. A case structure, once reconstructed, may be used in the interpretation of further examples of the same type as a heuristic to be falsified. The argument goes

approximately like this: in the course of text analysis there is a reconstruction of what structure is to be found in the text under investigation. This description should be as precise and distinctive as possible. If, in the course of the analysis of the text, a location can be found which contradicts the structural description previously spelled out, then the hypothesis may be said to be falsified.

The goal of structural generalization is always the discovery and description of both *general* and *single-case specific* instances of rule-governedness, the so-called generative rules which, according to Oevermann (1999a), have a status comparable to natural laws and natural facts. With the aid of this positive knowledge of the general and the single case soft prognoses for the future of an action system should be set up. Precise deterministic statements are, however, impossible: one can only indicate the scope for transformations.

On actuality

The procedure of objective hermeneutics is currently viewed as one of the most widespread and reflective approaches in German qualitative research. There is, however, no 'school' of objective hermeneutics, but only a range of scientists who have recourse to the procedure of objective hermeneutics in their own research. The *Kunstlehre* (art) of objective hermeneutics can be learned, above all, from Oevermann himself in Frankfurt am Main. He offers regular courses for students and also for practitioners in which one can learn his technique for data analysis (see Part 7). As yet – in spite of all the efforts that have been made – there is no introduction authorized by Oevermann into the principles of objective hermeneutics. Apart from Germany, there are a number of researchers, particularly in Austria and Switzerland, who are exploring the possibilities of objective hermeneutics.

Major debates on the concept of objective hermeneutics have so far been confined to Germany. Reichertz (1986), for example, investigated a whole range of Oevermann's texts using a procedure that relied on objective hermeneutics and thereby reconstructed the development of the approach from a 'distanced inside view'. Liebau (1987), in his study of the socialization theories of Oevermann and Bourdieu, analysed in particular their concept of subject and its effect on a theory of pedagogic action. H. Sutter (1997) brings together, from an insider's view, Oevermann's scattered writings into a unified theory and practice of objective hermeneutics.

2 HERMENEUTIC SOCIOLOGY OF KNOWLEDGE

The term 'hermeneutic sociology of knowledge' refers to a complex *theoretical*, *methodological* and *operational* concept that derives in its essentials from the work of Hans-Georg Soeffner. Initially the name 'sociological hermeneutics' (see **3.5**) was more frequently used. Hermeneutic sociology of knowledge in this form developed out of this, on the one hand as a result of a criticism of the 'metaphysics of structures' in objective hermeneutics (cf. Reichertz 1986) and on the other hand as a result of a debate with the socio-phenomenological research tradition (Schütz, Luckmann; see **3.1**).

This perspective is *knowledge-sociological* in that, beyond constructivism and realism, it investigated the major question of how action subjects on the one hand (have to) locate and adapt themselves in an apposite and socialized way in the historically and socially developed routines and meanings of a particular field of action, and how, on the other hand, they (must) constantly re-interpret and thereby also invent themselves 'individually'. The new (that is, constituted in accordance with the relevances of the action subject) re-interpretations of socially pre-interpreted knowledge, for their part, are then (again as knowledge) fed back into the social action field (cf. Berger and Luckmann 1966; Soeffner 1989).

This perspective is *hermeneutic* in that, in its method-driven analysis of data, it follows the premises of 'sociological hermeneutics' (Soeffner 1989; Soeffner and Hitzler 1994a).

The perspective is *structural-analytical* because the behaviour of individuals is only considered to be understood if the interpreter is in a position both to put the observed behaviour into some relation with the frame of reference that is prescribed and is relevant to the particular type of action, and in this way also to demonstrate that it is meaningful.

Subsequently it is concerned, in reconstructing the action, with making visible (as stored knowledge) the structural and pre-stated problems and possibilities of action which, in working out

the 'egological perspective', can *legitimately be attributed* to the protagonist (cf. Reichertz 1991a). What is central here is admittedly not the reconstruction of the singular perspective that is known to the individuals in question. What is sought, therefore, is the rational *reconstruction* of types of egological perspective (cf. Hitzler 1991; Schröer 1997).

History of hermeneutic sociology of knowledge

'Anyone who knows nothing about the act of interpretation and who does not feel obliged to take account of its premises and sequential structures, will – from the viewpoint of the scientific obligation to check – be interpreting in a simple way, that is on the basis of implicit everyday interpretative routines and plausibility criteria' (Soeffner 1989: 53). Accordingly, the 'understanding of something' naturally also includes the '*description and the understanding of understanding*' (1989: 53). These statements of Soeffner's not only are, in my opinion, essential constituents of any sociological hermeneutics, but they can also (from a historical point of view) be taken as starting points for this research strategy.

In precise terms, these requirements mean that the investigator who wishes to understand his or her observation must also observe *his or her own* action of 'understanding' (that is, his or her 'everyday world of hermeneutics'). Because of this requirement of 'application to oneself', sociological hermeneutics from the outset (and for some time before the arrival of 'radical constructivism'; see **3.4**) was put into the precarious position of having to come to terms with the 'constructivist character' of observation and interpretation. This situation is 'precarious' because the self-application of sociology to the writings of sociologists brings to light the fact that the constructs of scientists may differ in terms of content but not in structure from those constructs which people create in their normal everyday life and which are observed and interpreted by sociologists.

Strategy of empirical procedure

Hermeneutic sociology of knowledge wins recognition exclusively from empirical research. It investigates every kind of social interaction and all types of cultural phenomena. Since its research strategy is not directed towards the discovery of general laws to explain human behaviour but rather the (re-)construction of procedures and typologies that humans use to familiarize themselves with and gain access to a constantly changing world, the systematic 'discovery' of what is new is of particular interest. This is made easier by means of a series of methodological precautions.

For example, in the first phase of a piece of research the investigator should focus on building up an 'abductive attitude' (cf. Reichertz 1991b; see **4.3**). This means that he or she should design his or her research in such a way that 'old' beliefs are seriously tested and, in certain cases, 'new' and more workable beliefs can be developed. This 'programme', however, can only be meaningfully implemented if the collected data are so constituted that their accountability in terms of the existing beliefs is not a foregone conclusion. The data must have the properties of a whetstone, and the interpreter must be forced abductively to grind down, or re-sharpen, his or her existing prejudices.

The most resistant data, in my opinion, are those that are collected in a *non-standardized way*, that is to say, audiovisual recordings and tape-recorded protocols (cf. Reichertz 1991a). Since such data are not produced by informants in response to any particular research question and the collection is not marked by any subjective observation schemata, there is a high probability that they cannot automatically be accounted for by the pre-existing beliefs.

If the collection of non-standardized data is not possible or does not make sense, researchers are obliged to produce the data themselves: they must create observation protocols and conduct interviews – and it would be advisable to do this according to scientifically binding standards. This will then lead to the production of data which, for their part, bear the hallmark of (scientific) standards.

In this the following two collection principles should be observed. (1) Researchers, in respect (*only*) of the facts to be investigated, should enter the field as *naively* as possible and collect data (cf. Hitzler 1991). (2) Particularly in the entry phase it should be ensured that the data collection will be as *unstructured* as possible. The reason for this is that a premature analytical and theoretical permeation of the material, and a data-collection process that focuses on this in the entry phase, would lead to a blunting of the data whetstone on which subsequent theories ought to prove themselves and develop. If investigators apply these two principles in the collection of standardized data, then this will at least open up the possibility that the data will 'set them thinking' and cause them to question 'old' beliefs (cf. Reichertz 1997).

The logic of research

An interpretation of data with the assistance of sociological hermeneutics of knowledge does not stop at the appropriate description of observations or the depiction of subjectively developed and intended meaning. It aims, rather, at the discovery of the *intersubjective* meaning of *actions*. But 'intersubjective' in no way corresponds to 'true' or 'real', but merely that it is a question of the meaning that is engendered by means of a (linguistic) *action* within a particular interaction community. The meaning of an action is thereby (partly) equated with the willingness to react that may be *anticipated* and which is set up by the action within an interaction community.

The interpretation theory therefore relates to the imaginative power of a typologized and typical user of a symbol who has been socialized within a particular interaction community. It does not, however, relate to the concrete content of his or her consciousness.

To put this in brief and placating terms: the meaning of symbolic action does not lie buried in the consciousness of the user of a sign, neither does it manifest itself in some codified reference (that is, it is not to be found in the past). It is rather the case that the meaning of a sign consists of the *willingness to react that may be anticipated* and of the *realized reactions* that the symbol stimulates in the interpreting group (that is, it is to be found in the future).

In methodological terms sociological hermeneutics pursues the following route: in the entry phase the data protocol is subjected to 'open coding' (Strauss 1987; see **5.13**), which means that the document in question is analysed sequentially, extensively and in detail, and indeed line by line or even word by word. What is decisive in this phase is that no (pre-existing) readings are applied to the text, but rather that the investigator constructs as many readings as possible that are compatible with the text. This type of interpretation requires the interpreter repeatedly to break down both the data and the (theoretical) prejudices and assessments, and this creates a healthy climate for the discovery of new readings.

If, in the phase of 'open coding', one is looking for meaning units (which naturally always already contain theoretical concepts or play with and refer to these), then in the second phase of the interpretation one is looking for more highly aggregated meaning units and concepts that bind together the individual partial units. In addition, one may now define good reasons as to why certain data should be collected again or in greater detail. And so in the third phase new data protocols are produced in a more targeted way. In this way the interpretation controls the data collection, but at the same time – and this is more important – the interpretation is falsified, modified and extended by means of the later data collection.

The process is complete when a highly aggregated concept or meaning configuration has been found or constructed, into which all the investigated elements can be integrated in a meaningful whole, and when this whole has been made intelligible (that is to say, meaningful) in the context of a particular interaction community. The question of whether the interpretation achieved in this way actually corresponds to the 'reality in the text' is meaningless, because sociological research is always concerned only with '*social* reality' (examples are in Soeffner 1997).

Current perspectives

Hermeneutic sociology of knowledge is currently taught and practised mainly in German-speaking universities (Konstanz, Dortmund, Essen, St Gallen, Vienna), and yet there is no 'school' of hermeneutic sociology of knowledge. Admittedly a whole range of German, Swiss and Austrian scholars from different sociological disciplines refer explicitly to this research strategy. There is still no 'official' introduction into the procedures of hermeneutic sociology of knowledge, but Soeffner (1989) and Soeffner and Hitzler (1994a) are considered to be the basic texts. In addition, Schröer (1994) provides a source in which research methods in particular are presented and discussed, while the work of Hitzler et al. (1999) gives special attention to an outline of the theory and the methodology.

A first systematic description of hermeneutic sociology of knowledge may be found in Schröer (1997), while Reichertz (1991a) and Knoblauch (1995) present two methodologically well-founded approaches to research. T. Sutter (1997) offers a basic examination of hermeneutic sociology of knowledge.

FURTHER READING

Knoblauch, H. (2002) 'Communication, Contexts and Culture. A Communicative Constructivist Approach to Intercultural Communication', in A. di Luzio, S. Günthner and F. Orletti (eds), *Culture in Communication. Analyses of Intercultural Situations.* Amsterdam: John Benjamins. pp. 3–33.

Soeffner, H.-G. (1997) *The Order of Rituals: The Interpretation of Everyday Life.* New Brunswick, NJ: Transaction Books.

Titscher, S., Meyer, M., Wodak, R. and Vetter, E. (2000) 'Objective Hermeneutics', in *Methods of Text and Discourse Analysis.* London: Sage. pp. 198–212.

5.17 Conversation Analysis

Jörg R. Bergmann

1   OBJECTIVE AND GOALS

Conversation analysis (or CA) denotes a research approach dedicated to the investigation, along strictly empirical lines, of social interaction as a continuing process of producing and securing meaningful social order. CA proceeds on the basis that in all forms of linguistic and non-linguistic, direct and indirect communication, actors are occupied with the business of analysing the situation and the context of their actions, interpreting the utterances of their interlocutors, producing situational appropriateness, intelligibility and effectiveness in their own utterances and coordinating their own actions with the actions of others. The goal of this approach is to determine the constitutive principles and mechanisms by means of which actors, in the situational completion of their actions and in reciprocal reaction to their interlocutors, create the meaningful structures and order of a sequence of events and of the activities that constitute these events. In terms of method, CA begins with the richest possible documentation – with audiovisual recording and subsequent transcription – of real and authentic social events, and breaks these down, by a comparative-systematic process of analysis, into individual structural principles of social interaction as well as the practices used to manage them by participants in an interaction.

2   HISTORY OF ITS DEVELOPMENT AND IMPACT

The beginnings of CA as an independent sociological research direction are to be found in the 1960s and 1970s. Of crucial importance in this were the works of Harvey Sacks (1967), in particular the *Lectures* which he gave at various universities in California from 1964 until his death in 1974. These were devoted to the mechanisms of story-telling, turn-taking in conversations, procedures for the categorization of people, sequencing of utterances, listeners' maxims, the functions of pronouns and a wealth of other topics. For decades these *Lectures* circulated in the form of recording transcripts before they became available in an edited form (Sacks 1992). In addition to the paradigmatically important work of Sacks (cf. Silvermann 1998), it was the studies of Emanuel Schegloff (1968) and Gail Jefferson (1972) that gave CA its particular profiles in the early years.

From a historical point of view, the theory of CA is rooted in Harold Garfinkel's (see **2.3**) ethnomethodology (see **3.2**), and even today its theoretical and methodological self-image bears the essential hallmarks of ethnomethodology (Heritage 1984). In addition, Erving Goffman's work in interaction analysis (cf. Bergmann 1991), the ethnography of speaking, cognitive anthropology and the late philosophy of Wittgenstein (e.g. 1958) have all had a recognizable influence on the development and programme of CA.

Since the beginning of the 1970s, when the first collections containing relevant papers were published (Sudnow 1972; Turner 1974; Schenkein 1978; Psathas 1979), CA has emerged from its initially rather narrow sphere of influence. It was increasingly accepted beyond the United States (cf. Kallmeyer and Schütze 1976 on its impact in German-speaking countries), and found considerable resonance in a number of related disciplines. This is particularly true of linguistics, which had already begun to deal with sociolinguistic questions in the 1960s and had turned to qualitative research methods under the influence of the ethnography of communication (cf. Gumperz and Hymes 1972). Today the concepts and the methodological principles of CA have a fixed place in a branch of linguistics that deals with pragmatic questions (Levinson 1983) and focuses on the dialogical nature of language (Linell 1998).

In contrast, the place of CA within its parent discipline, sociology, was more contentious from the outset. Because of its concentration on the structural level of interaction and its decidedly empirical orientation, it is frequently criticized as empiricist or formalistic, or else it is deemed to be sociologically irrelevant. However, the continuing publication of empirical studies from many different areas of society and the cumulative effect of these studies have made clear to the outsider the epistemological potential of the subject of CA. Today CA is viewed, alongside the 'studies of work' (see **3.2**), as the second distinct analytical direction to have emerged from the ethnomethodological research programme. It is recognized, moreover, as an important micro-sociological approach to analysing the structures of symbolically mediated interaction.

Classic and more recent work resulting from this research approach may be found in a series of collections (e.g. Atkinson and Heritage 1984; Button and Lee 1987; Boden and Zimmerman 1991; Have and Psathas 1995) and in special numbers of particular journals (e.g. Beach 1989; Button et al. 1986; Maynard 1988; Pomerantz 1993). There are also a number of introductory monographs, with explanations of the methodology of CA (e.g. Bergmann 1988; Deppermann 1999; Have 1999; Hutchby and Wooffitt 1998), as well as bibliographies (e.g. Fehr et al. 1990).

3   THEORETICAL BACKGROUND

Ethnomethodology resulted from criticisms of sociological theories with a view of reality that was excessively normative and objectivist. In the 1950s and 1960s Harold Garfinkel (1967a), in a number of studies, was able to demonstrate both theoretically and empirically that one cannot do justice to the specific character of human sociality if one imagines social reality as something concrete which lies behind or beyond the everyday, observable and perceptible actions that actually determine it. Garfinkel sets against this the idea that actors are engaged in the active creation of the realities in which they live, and that what they perceive and deal with as facts that exist objectively and independent of their involvement are only constructed and produced as such by their actions and perceptions. If one assumes that social facts gain their reality only by virtue of interactions between people, the investigation of the structures and properties of these interactions becomes a central theme of the social sciences. It is precisely this to which CA devotes its attention.

For ethnomethodology social reality only 'real-izes' itself in everyday practical action, and it sees social order as the ongoing production of meaning attributions and interpretations. This creation of reality transmitted by meaning is not merely a cognitive process, it is not purely and arbitrarily subjective in nature. It takes place, rather, in a perceptible and 'methodical' fashion, since all competent members of society take part in it: it is this to which the idea of ethno-'methodology' relates (Weingarten et al. 1976). And because the production of reality by action is methodical in nature, it is also characterized by individual formal and structural features that may be described as such.

In general terms, the interest of CA is in the generative principles and procedures by means of which participants in a conversation produce, in and with their utterances and actions, the characteristic structural features and the 'lived orderliness' (Garfinkel) of the interactive events in which they are involved. The area on which CA initially concentrates, and which also gave it its name, consists of conversation of an everyday, normal and self-evident variety, rather than the sort that is determined by conventions and other formal requirements: in other words, simply conversation or chatting. This kind of conversation may be seen as a basic form of interaction – not of course in the sense of a quasi-natural form of social interaction, since the forms of trivial everyday talk also have historical and cultural features (Burke 1993). They serve, however, as the communicative base from which one enters other perhaps ceremonially or institutionally marked forms of communication (religious service, school lessons and the like), and to which one then returns, for example after a court hearing. From the perspective of CA, institutionally specific types of conversation take on their authentic character by virtue of the fact that the structure of the trivial, everyday, extra-institutional type of communication is transformed in specific ways. These other forms of conversation, too, have always been of interest to CA, and it is therefore in no way thematically restricted to the investigation of 'conversation'. For this reason, Schegloff (1988) suggested that 'talk-in-interaction' would be a more appropriate description of its area of interest.

Compared to earlier approaches to interaction analysis (such as that of Bales), CA is characterized by its efforts not to subsume interactive processes under external pre-ordained categories. It is not satisfied with identifying an utterance as a rebuke, a compliment and so on, or with finding a plausible motive for an utterance. Its epistemological goal is rather to capture social forms and the processes of their internal logic, and to determine the methodological resources that are needed to make an utterance recognizable in its meaning content, to tie it into the sequence of a conversation, to match it to a situation, to contextualize and observe it, and reply to it.

One critical point on which discussion repeatedly flares (Hopper 1990/91) concerns the relationship between a linguistic utterance and the context of the utterance. In the view of CA it is not sufficient merely to relate these two entities to one another correlatively, in the sense of adding together utterance analysis and ethnography, and then to construct a plausible connection. At every moment in an interaction, that which might potentially be relevant as an interaction context contains an infinite variety, and it is therefore the task of the analysis to show that a specific contextual fact was relevant to the action for the actors themselves. CA therefore views interactants as context-sensitive actors who analyse the context of their action, interpret with the assistance of their everyday knowledge, match their utterances to this context

and constantly demonstrate their reciprocal contextual orientations (Auer 1986). But it is generally difficult, however, to determine unambiguously the momentary relevance of situational circumstances or of individual personal features of the interactants; it is always *one* specific context that has a predominant importance for the interactants in the course of a social interaction – the sequential context. Every utterance produces a contextual environment for the utterance that sequentially follows it, and this is significant for the interpretation of this following utterance and is therefore constantly referred to by the interactants in the interpretation and production of utterances. Sequential analysis is therefore the typical form of contextual analysis for CA; it is, to a certain extent, modelled on the 'contextual analysis' of the actors themselves.

Beyond sequential analysis CA is also concerned with other principles of the contextual orientation of interactants, such as the principle of 'recipient design', which implies that actors endeavour to tailor their utterances specifically to their particular action partners – and their prior knowledge. The goal of this kind of contextual analysis is to identify the context of the conversation as a context within the conversation. CA therefore has an ethnographic potential to the extent that one of its themes is how the context of an utterance is reproduced in the utterances of the participants.

4 METHODOLOGICAL PROCEDURE

It is a postulate of qualitative research that methods must be appropriate to the particular issue. But the appropriateness of a methodological procedure cannot truly be determined in advance, since at this point too little is known about the issue – indeed, that is why it is being investigated. In principle, it can only be decided retrospectively, when the analysis of a particular phenomenon has led to some factual result, whether a particular method was suitable for the analysis of this phenomenon. Considerations of this kind were central to the criticism of ethnomethodology in traditional social research and they constitute the reason why for a long time ethnomethodology and CA were very reluctant to give their procedures a formulation in general methodological rules. Methods that can be applied in an isolated, generalized, canonized and mechanical way to any kind of phenomena are subject to the great danger that they can at best be used to 'discover' features that are already well-known. New phenomena require new methods – but of course these cannot be constructed in advance (see **5.8**).

With this warning in mind, we shall describe, in what follows, a number of methodological principles which may be distilled from the available studies in CA. When Sacks, Schegloff and their colleagues began to take an interest in everyday conversations, they had at their disposal no methods that could be applied easily. In the light of a large number of theoretical considerations they developed these methods while dealing with sound and video recordings of everyday actions which were left in their raw form; that is, not yet cut or produced from any didactic or aesthetic point of view for instructional or documentary purposes. To accord to materials of this kind the status of sociologically relevant 'data' was very unusual at that time.

Data of this type were novel in the sense that they preserved, in the form of a recording, a social event taking place at a particular moment, whereas a reconstructive mode of conservation – such as numerical–statistical analysis, interview findings or an observer's protocols – was characteristic of traditional types of data. In this kind of reconstruction an irretrievable past social event is captured by means of description, narration or categorization, but in the process the event, in its original sequence, is largely lost: in principle it is already buried by subsequent interpretations, in part highly compressed, and now only available in a symbolically transformed version (Bergmann 1985). It is only the recording type of conservation, which fixes a social event with all the details of its real sequence, that can allow the social researcher to investigate the 'local' production of social order, or to analyse how interactants meaningfully orient themselves to one another in their utterances, and how they cooperate to achieve, in a fixed time and place, intersubjectively determined constructions of reality.

As the material for its analyses CA does not take recollections, imagined examples or experimentally induced behaviour, but rather audiovisual recordings or real interactions, which may be viewed as 'natural' in that they are left in their original habitat and took place without any stimulus from the social researcher and

recording equipment. Imagined examples often constitute idealized and – because they are censored for their plausibility – impoverished versions of social events. Social researchers are therefore obliged to deal, in their observations, with the factual – and frequently improbable – sequence of events, with the possibility that they will be irritated by this.

The attempt to preserve social phenomena as fully as possible for analysis is also characteristic of the following step in the processing of data: the transcription of the recorded interactive events. In the course of transcription no attempt should be made to purge the recorded raw material of apparently irrelevant components, nor to normalize spelling. It should, on the contrary, be preserved in all its details, that is to say, with all the hesitations, slips of the tongue, pauses, utterance overlaps, dialectal colouring, intonation contours and so on. Otherwise the information gain that is possible with audio and video recording would immediately be lost. (For an overview of the transcription symbols normally used in English CA, see Atkinson and Heritage 1984. A new integrated transcription system is proposed in Selting et al. 1998; see **5.9**.)

The attempt to preserve the original events as authentically as possible in the course of data processing is one of the central analytical maxims of CA. In accordance with its ethnomethodological origins CA is guided in its procedures by a premise of order which says that no textual element that turns up in a transcript should be viewed a priori as a chance product and therefore excluded as a possible object of investigation. Every textual element is observed initially – even when common-sense suggests otherwise – as a component of a self-reproducing order and is included in the circle of possible and relevant phenomena for investigation. This 'order-at-all-points' maxim (Sacks 1984) is to ensure that social researchers do not identify possible phenomena for investigation according to a list of preordained questions, but rather deal openly with the investigation material and rely on their observations.

To put this briefly, the methodological procedure of CA consists of reconstructing for an observable and uniform phenomenon the generative principles – or 'the machinery' (Sacks). In detail, this proceeds in such a way that, as a first step, in the recording or transcript of some interactive event one object is isolated as a possible element of order. The nature of this element – be it a particular interaction sequence, an utterance, a formulation, a story, an interjection, throat-clearing or a head movement – is not defined in advance. The subsequent procedure is guided by the assumption that this is a component of some order that is methodically produced by the interactants. Sooner or later, therefore, one will look for other manifestations of this element and thereby assemble, from the data material, a collection of cases in which this object reveals itself – in whatever version that may be.

For the next stage one consideration is central, which is found in both hermeneutic interpretation and in functionalist explanations: the object identified, and its ordering, are understood as a result of the methodical solution of a structural problem – in this case a problem of the social organization of interaction. Here the nature of this problem is not to be found in a set catalogue, but is instead a matter for investigation. For what 'problem' is the normal self-announcement at the beginning of a telephone conversation a 'solution'? What 'problem' does the common form of introduction to a story refer to, when the narrator makes it known that something funny, awful, and so on, happened to him or her? And what kind of problem could be solved by a speaker interrupting his utterance and starting again at the beginning? With questions of this nature CA seeks to reconstruct the practical methods that actors use as solutions to interactive problems, the use of which generates the observable orderliness of an interactive event.

In a procedure of this kind social researchers are inevitably thrown back on their intuition and competence as members of society. But they should not stop at intuition or they will never proceed into the analysis. They must attempt to methodologize this intuitive understanding (that is, work out the formal mechanisms) which makes it possible for them – and the interactants – to interpret meaningfully the documented action sequence.

These formal mechanisms, the reconstruction of which is the goal of CA, have to contain a generative principle that is capable both of reproducing the initial data of the analysis and also of creating new cases and similar phenomena. It is not the description of behavioural uniformities that is the goal of CA but the identification of principles which, in terms of their status, represent to the actors the real orientation dimensions. Here an essential task of the analysis consists of showing in the data material how the interactants take account of these formal principles in their utterances and actions. And since the interactants move in the most varied contextual conditions, these principles must also be seen as formal trans-situational mechanisms, which leave the interactants room, however, for the context-sensitive production of their utterances. (What methods actors use to achieve this particularization of their utterances is itself a topic of investigation for CA.)

Finally, we should look at the question of validity-checking that is generally so difficult for qualitative research. CA practitioners seek to demonstrate the validity of their analyses by bringing together functionally similar phenomena from their data. What underlies this is the belief that these kinds of co-occurrence are found because actors have available not only a single 'method' but an arsenal of formal procedures for the solution of an interactional problem, and therefore they frequently use several of these procedures simultaneously (Schegloff and Sacks 1973). A more rigorous, but often inapplicable, procedure for checking validity consists of looking for 'deviant cases' in the data and using them to prove that the actors themselves look on and treat these cases as breeches of the expected normative orientation pattern, in that they mark them as dispreferred actions or apply corrective measures (Pomerantz 1984). Finally, there is the possibility of checking the validity of an interpretation by referring to a subsequent utterance from one of the participants to the interaction. In this it will be manifested how a recipient understood an earlier utterance, and this demonstration of understanding may be taken up by the social researcher as evidence of the validity of his or her interpretation. This is a further expression of the fact that the methodological principles of CA are directly related to practical everyday methods, that is, to the object of their investigation.

5   SCOPE AND LIMITATIONS

The topic areas that CA research work concerned itself with from the outset, and which are still of interest today, may be grouped as follows.

1 At the centre of attention are the constitutive mechanisms that are responsible for the ordered sequencing and the rule-governed ordering of utterances in a conversation. This is especially true of the organization of 'turn-taking' in conversations (and here the work of Sacks et al. 1974 is of paradigmatic importance) and the sequential organization of speech exchanges that has been determined for many different interaction types – requests, invitations, compliments, refusals, complaints, reproaches, accusations, disagreements, argumentation, story-telling and so on.

2 Since the early work of Sacks on the mechanisms of story-telling in conversations, communicative macro-forms that include more than simple sequences of utterances have been a major topic in CA. (Examples of this are Jefferson's (1988) study of 'troubles talk', or Bergmann's investigation (1993) of gossip.)

3 CA is also interested in the mechanisms that constitute a singular conversation as a social unit, examples of which are the organization of the conversational opening and closure and also the organization of thematic focusing and continuation.

4 The practices of describing and categorization of individuals were one of the early topics of CA that has been neglected for many years and has only recently been taken up again (Hester and Eglin 1997) – for example, in the analysis of the images of foreigners and social stereotypes (Czyzewski et al. 1995).

5 A lasting interest of CA has been in the question of how participants in an interaction produce and secure understanding – or at least a belief in understanding – between themselves, and how the 'repair organization' functions which the interactants activate in cases of comprehension problems.

In its initial phase CA was still totally restricted to investigating the constitutive mechanisms of *linguistic* interaction. One of the justifications for this was that the data material mostly consisted of recordings of telephone conversations. Here – without any intervention from the researchers – the physical presence of the other party and all visual communication are removed, and this brings about an essential reduction in the complexity of the communicative event. This made the task of developing routines and methods for dealing with this kind of material much easier, but of course human beings do not conduct their lives on the telephone – or at least not continuously. On the one hand, there were studies which, in their analyses of non-verbal aspects of communication (Heath 1986; Streeck and Hartge 1992), overcame the limitations of this telephone perspective. And on the other hand, there has been a growth in the number of CA studies that take account of the extra-linguistic context of action and – more particularly – of work in their analyses (Drew and Heritage 1992). Studies of this sort have dominated the literature of CA for a number of years, and it is now almost impossible to gain an overview of the many studies that deal with interaction in legal, medical and psychiatric institutions, or with police interrogations, emergency telephone calls, counselling, psychotherapy sessions, sales talk and political events (for examples cf. Beach 1996; Peräkylä 1995; and for German-speaking contexts Meier 1997; Wolff and Müller 1997).

6 RECENT DEVELOPMENTS AND PERSPECTIVES

CA has heightened the awareness within qualitative research of the linguistic constitution of social reality and of the interactive phenomena within which social structural relations reproduce themselves. Keeping completely to the sociological tradition of Georg Simmel, it has opened up unimaginably small and microscopically molecular forms of socialization as a field of empirical investigation and has made possible a strictly formal qualitative analysis. In this respect it is, of all the 'soft' qualitative methodologies, in some sense the 'hardest'. Its basic analytical and methodological significance derives, indeed, from this rigorous attention to detail, but in the future it will also have to devote greater attention to establishing some relation between the many analyses of single phenomena (for examples, cf. Bergmann and Luckmann 1999; Kallmeyer 1994).

The potential and the vigour of the CA research approach may be found both in the opening up of new research fields and in its promotion of new theoretical endeavours. Over the years many authors have demonstrated that CA, which at first sight appears to be so empiricist, minimalist and purist, can also be used, to a large extent, as a methodology for objective hermeneutic case analyses (Schmitt 1992; see **5.16**) and also for highly abstract sociological theory formation according to system theory (Hausendorf 1992; Schneider 1994). Within linguistics, CA concepts have facilitated a new way of looking at the relationship between interaction and prosody (Couper-Kuhlen and Selting 1996) or grammar (Ochs et al. 1997), and have given an important impetus in the expanding field of the investigation of cultural communication (Günthner 1993). Recent attempts to correct the neglect of communication within psychology and to establish a 'discursive psychology' (Antaki and Widdicombe 1998; Edwards and Potter 1992) are essentially dependent on CA (see **5.19**). And finally, CA has also played an influential role in recent work devoted to investigating communication through the media: there are studies which follow the procedural logic of CA in the analysis of texts constituted in the written mode (Wolff 1995; see **5.15**) or produced by the mass media (Ayaß 1997). In the same way recent research on human–computer interaction (HCI) and computer-mediated communication (CMC) are closely related to CA in terms of their concepts

and methodology (Button 1993; Suchman 1987). In this area, in particular, it may be expected that the proposed combination of ethnography and CA will lead to results that will be of great practical relevance.

FURTHER READING

Have, P. ten (1999) *Doing Conversation Analysis: A Practical Guide*. London: Sage.

Hutchby, I. and Wooffitt, R. (1998) *Conversation Analysis: Principles, Practice and Applications*. Cambridge: Polity Press.

Sacks, H. (1992) *Lectures on Conversation. Volumes I and II* (edited by G. Jefferson with introductions by E. A. Schegloff). Oxford: Blackwell.

Journal

Research on Language and Social Interaction (Mahwah, NJ: Lawrence Erlbaum).

5.18 Genre Analysis

Hubert Knoblauch and Thomas Luckmann

1 BACKGROUND AND AIMS OF GENRE ANALYSIS

Communicative genres have long been an object of interest in rhetoric and poetics, in theology and literary studies, in folklore and linguistics. In sociology and social psychology methods for analysing communicative genres have only been made possible by a certain number of fundamental changes of approach in recent times. Using the analogy of the *linguistic turn* in philosophy, scholars now speak of a change to a communicative paradigm within modern sociology. Whilst this change has sometimes been restricted to the choice of the governing vocabulary, there have, on the other hand, also been empirical approaches that concern themselves with the analysis of communicative events. Among these are the ethnography of communication (see **3.8**, **5.5**), conversation analysis (see **5.17**) and hermeneutic sociology of knowledge (see **3.5**, **5.16**), whose methods also provide a starting point for genre analysis. Finally, technological developments have also played an important role in the development of genre analysis, particularly the availability of rapidly improving audiovisual recording techniques, that is, initially techniques of tape-recording and then of video-recording. The considered use of these devices has made accessible communicative processes that were previously *fluid* (Bergmann 1985).

These developments provide the methodological background for sociological genre analysis, which is related to phenomenologically oriented action theory (Luckmann 1992). Communicative actions reveal the basic structures of a social action that is characterized by reciprocity and the use of signs. Like all other forms of action, communicative action is also subject to becoming routine and institutionalized (processes that arise particularly when actions are repeated and are of great individual or sociological relevance; Berger and Luckmann 1966). Communicative actions of this sort form typical patterns which actors can use as orientation. Communicative genres are considered to be those communicative phenomena that have become socially rooted. Communicative patterns and genres may then equally well be viewed as institutions of communication. Their basic social function consists of alleviating the burden of subordinate (communicative) action problems. They facilitate communication by steering the synchronization of actors and the coordination of stages of action, by means of fixed patterns, into relatively reliable and familiar pathways. Genres are therefore an orientation framework for the production and reception of communicative actions.

Genres differ in terms of their form from 'spontaneous' communicative phenomena in that individuals are guided in a predictably typical way by pre-ordained patterns. This may have the character of a canonical designation of complete action complexes. The pre-ordained qualities, however, may be limited to particular aspects of the action, such as the order of turns (for example, in interviews) or the topics (in conversations about planning). Genre analysis, therefore, does not target only those communicative forms which are fixed as prototypical genres in every respect, and which have a clearly determined structure in terms of situation, function and procedure, as in the laments sung by Georgian women or the genealogical recitations of Bantu kingdoms. Because it is basically interested in the determination of communicative forms and patterns, it also deals with communicative forms that are less fixed and less canonically determined, such as quarrels, instructions and advisory broadcasts on the radio.

2 ON THE METHODOLOGY OF GENRE ANALYSIS

Unlike otherwise related methodological procedures – with a similar emphasis on the 'naturalness' of data and a sequential analytical procedure – genre analysis is not restricted to single illustrative case analyses. It is rather *comparative* in its organization: it compares communicative actions which have been transcribed and which can, in principle, always be recalled, because of the 'frozen' oral nature of a tape-recording. It attempts to discover typical similarities and differences in the 'illustrations'. The texts are interpreted in the context of knowledge of the social and interactively significant background to the communicative actions that are recorded in them. In the same way that this knowledge is a prerequisite for the 'text'-producing actors, it must also be made explicit in the text interpretation.

In detail the procedure of genre analysis may be subdivided into a number of steps.

1 First comes the *recording* of communicative events in natural situations. This may be a matter of chats between neighbours, job interviews, club meetings or party-political gatherings, oral examinations of Internet chats. What is essential is that the data collection concerns itself with the acquisition of ethnographic knowledge about the contexts of these types of communication. In borderline cases of topics that are difficult to

access it may be necessary to carry out conversation-like interviews.

2 The recordings are then transcribed. For this a number of different transcription systems are available (see **5.9**) that extend from the standard written language to linguistic-phonetic and video-analytical systems. The exactness of the transcription depends on the structural level that is central to the analysis (see below). With large data quantities it is advisable to undertake a rough cataloguing of the data, including the thematic, social-interactive, contextual and temporal parameters.

3 The data 'fixed' in this way are then hermeneutically interpreted and subjected to a sequential analysis. This means that an initial attempt is made to clarify the everyday understanding of the texts at the level of the word, sentence and speech-turn. At this level the ethnographic contextual knowledge is essential since it can help in the clarification of context-dependent semantic references of utterances.

4 In the next step a conversation analysis oriented assessment is conducted (see **5.17**), which reconstructs the detailed sequencing and the rule-governed succession of turns and sequences of turns (Bergmann 1981b). The interpretations resulting from the hermeneutic and sequential analyses should, if possible, be carried out according to groups that are not too homogeneous in terms of age, gender, region or social level, in order to be able to refer to the diversity of everyday knowledge, which is the first resource in an interpretation. Varying interpretations should be formulated under the strict obligation that they are based exclusively on the evidence in the texts. Unlike most other hermeneutic methods, particular attention is paid in the analysis to those aspects of the transcribed texts that are anchored in their oral nature (prosody and the like; see **5.9**).

5 In this way structural models are set up that are then tested for their appropriateness with further cases. By looking at comparable or contrasting cases the structural model is supported or modified, until the point where the analysis of further cases brings no further development in understanding.

6 Finally, structural variants are considered which come about as a result of modalization (irony, pejorative forms and so on).

Here it is vital to consider the context of data collection: what is the 'place in life' of the particular communicative form? Does the dialogic genre of the conversion narrative take on a different structure if it is reported as a monologue, if it is reported in the media or if it is collected in the course of a group interview? Do emergency calls to the fire brigade take on a different form if they are dealt with by a voluntary village fire brigade or by the professional fire brigade in a large city? The contextual boundaries of structural variation or fulfilment are, in themselves, one part of the empirical question concerning communicative form. The answers constitute a significant aspect of the results.

3 THE INTERNAL STRUCTURE OF COMMUNICATIVE GENRES

The degree of fixedness of 'whole' communicative structures is established in stages, beginning with the analysis of individual structural features. Because these features vary in their scope they are allocated to structural levels which are analytically rather than 'really' distinct.

The internal structure contains textual features in the narrower sense. Among these are the following.

- Prosody: intonation, volume, speech tempo, pauses, rhythm, accentuation, voice quality.
- Language variety: standard language, jargon, dialect, sociolect.
- Linguistic register: formal, informal or intimate.
- Stylistic and rhetorical figures: alliteration, metaphor, rhythm and so on.
- 'Small' and 'minimal forms': verbal stereotypes, idiomatic expressions, platitudes, proverbs, categorical formulations, traditional historical formulae, inscriptions and puzzles.
- Motifs, topoi and structural markers.

The embedding of such features in superordinate genres is a complex feature of internal structure. Ulmer (1988) provides examples of this in his analysis of conversion narratives. The methods he mentions create a detachment of the time narrated from the time of the narration: a pre-conversion biographical phase, which is presented increasingly negatively and

in a very condensed form, is followed by a conversion phenomenon that is very extended and, above all, paralinguistically prominent. In the light of this the post-conversion biography is then presented.

In the analysis of communicative genres the special features of the medium have to be considered. For example, Keppler (1985) demonstrates that media genres, such as news broadcasts, are marked by the relationship between verbal, musical and pictorial constituents, 'on-' and 'off-text', cartoons and computer animation, colours and lighting. Camera placement, editing, dramaturgy, figures and setting also play an important role in this medium, as Ayaß (1997) demonstrated with the example of the religious television programme *Wort zum Sonntag* (see **5.7**).

4 FEATURES OF THE SITUATIONAL REALIZATION OF COMMUNICATIVE GENRES

Apart from securing the level of internal structure, we also give prominence at this level of structure to those features that relate to the coordination of the communicative actions and their situational context.

At the level of situational realization we also find, for example, rituals of establishing and ending contact, of greeting and leave-taking, of thanking and wishing, of apologizing, of invitation and acceptance or refusal, of assessment and counter-assessment, and so on. In addition to these 'ritual' aspects the level of situational realization also embraces those features which concern the interactive organization of communicative actions. These may be described with reference to models for turn-sequences and adjacency pairs, such as questions and answers, request and compliance with request.

Here we also include strategies of more long-term conversational organization, for example, the announcement of a take-over of a more extended section of a conversation by means of a 'ticket'. As Bergmann's (1993) analysis of gossip showed, the beginning of a gossip-interaction is marked by a pre-sequence in which the actors check whether the appropriate conditions exist for a gossip-conversation: on the one hand these relate to the question whether and in what way the person to be gossiped about is known to the participants and can therefore be made into an object of gossip; on the other hand it is important to ensure that the 'socially respected practice of gossiping is shared by all the participants. For only in this way can the gossip-producer avoid the personally unpleasant situation of being looked upon as a solitary gossip-monger' (1993: 110).

The conversational features of the level of situational realization also include, in addition to insertion, pre- and post-sequences, particular preference structures. Studies of argumentative conversations, therefore, demonstrate that in such communicative events the usual preference for agreement is inverted into a preference for non-agreeing utterances in which the polarity to the preceding statement is actually given prominence. In addition, the specific communicative role of the participants is constituted by means of preference structures: proponents or opponents, teacher and taught, speaker and audience are examples of such roles that are formed through particular preference organizations (Keppler 1994; Knoblauch 1991b).

Finally, the level of situational realization of communicative patterns includes the non-linguistic social context. This embraces the spatial and temporal social ordering of participants as well as the patterns of action that complement speech. The temporally and spatially limited social situations, which are characterized on the one hand by typical communicative patterns and accumulations and on the other hand by a set of people, constitute *social events*. Social events may be informal family mealtimes or groups who meet for pre-arranged activities (Bible-study groups, women's groups and so on), and also those 'key situations' that are crucial for people's careers or for organizationally relevant decisions: meetings, office hours, job interviews (Knoblauch 1995). These are frequently marked by particular utterance formats and a particular choice of communicative patterns.

5 THE EXTERNAL STRUCTURE OF COMMUNICATIVE GENRES AND THE COMMUNICATIVE ECONOMY

The fact that communicative genres are, so to speak, islands in the stream of communicative action may readily be shown if one considers face-to-face situations. They are also related, however, to large-scale social structures. It is evident, for example, that in a variety of institutional contexts not only are particular genres preferred, but they may actually be defined through the use of such genres. One example of this may be seen in religious communication. The specific features of the religious are defined, in essence, by the many frequently very strongly canonized genres such as prayers, sermons, 'sacred words' and sacred texts fixed in written form, but also visual forms (icons, votive images, statues), rituals and liturgically organized social events (Knoblauch 1998). A similar close relation between what is specific to an institution and certain genres is also found in the areas of law, science or politics (Günther and Knoblauch 1996).

Genre analyses are increasingly being conducted in the mass communication media and in electronic communication. For technologically supported communication not only shows particular features at the level of internal structure (such as news as opposed to films, talk-shows as opposed to homepages) and media-specific interaction structures (for example, advice programmes on the television as opposed to chat rooms, or interactive radio as opposed to cinema films), but it is also marked by features of external structure. Between the dissemination, accessibility and utilization of the different media and their particular genres and specific social categories and milieux there may be a dominant close relationship. An example of this is the fact that types of advertising break in which the product is foregrounded mostly correspond to the aesthetic taste of the people to whom the milieu of harmony is attributed, whereas the economically relatively well-off and more highly educated sector of the public – to which the 'self-fulfilment milieu' is attributed – favours the so-called 'artistic spots'. The 'presentation spot', in which the product is tied into an everyday presentation, has to comply with the entertainment milieu.

The parallelism between particular types within the advertising break genre and the social milieux makes it clear that communicative genres are indicators of social categories. But it should also be remembered that institutions, like social milieux, are constituted by means of such forms. This is true not only of locally organized milieux or those framed on the basis of income or education, but also of gender-specific or ethnic milieux, which differ on the basis of varying manifestations of communicative genres (argumentation, job interviews and consultations).

To gain an overview of continuity and change of communicative forms and events within a society and to be able to carry out intercultural comparisons, the term 'communicative economy' is proposed as an overall category: the communicative economy of a society includes all those communicative events that exert an influence on survival and change within a society. It includes genres as well as those 'spontaneous' communicative events that have become important, and both linguistic and non-verbal forms of communication. It is arranged according to situations, institutions and milieux. The communicative economy is the core of what is known as culture. The communicative genres and the more loosely fixed communicative patterns constitute, as it were, the meaning-creating and action-guiding internal architecture of a society. In this sense genre analysis may be viewed as an 'inductive' methodology for the empirical analysis of culture and society.

FURTHER READING

Günthner, S. and Knoblauch, H. (1994) 'Forms Are the Food of Faith: Gattungen als Muster kommunikativen Handelns', *Kölner Zeitschrift für Soziologie und Sozialpsychologie,* 46 (4): 693–723.

Knoblauch, H. and Günthner, S. (1995) 'Culturally Patterned Speaking Practices – The Analysis of Communicative Genres', *Pragmatics*, 5: 1–32.

Luckmann, T. (1995) 'Interaction Planning and Intersubjective Adjustment of Perspectives by Communicative Genres', in E. N. Goody (ed.), *Social Intelligence and Interaction. Expressions and Implications of the Social Bias in Human Intelligence*. Cambridge: Cambridge University Press. pp. 175–189.

5.19 Discourse Analysis

Ian Parker

Discourse analysts study the way texts are constructed, the functions they serve in different contexts and the contradictions that run through them. The term 'discourse' is used because our conception of language is much wider than a simple psycho-linguistic or socio-linguistic one.

Some of the work from socio-linguistics which has explored the semantics and pragmatics – the meaning and doing – of spoken and written texts has been useful in drawing attention to the ways in which a seemingly smooth text can be taken apart, and to the different implications of different types of statement within it (Halliday 1978). However, researchers new to discourse analysis often face problems because many 'introductions to discourse analysis' describe discourse only from a linguistic or sociological point of view. The following sections describe the form discourse analysis takes in psychology and critical psychology before turning to an example to illustrate some concerns of analysts in the critical strand of this new tradition.

1 DISCOURSE ANALYSIS IN PSYCHOLOGY

The version of discourse analysis outlined by Potter and Wetherell (1987, 1998) has been influential among qualitative researchers in psychology in Britain, and has been responsible for defining how many social psychologists here understand 'discourse'. This version of discourse analysis has been acceptable to psychologists partly because of the promise of an alternative 'discursive action model' for the discipline (see Edwards and Potter 1993), which functions to relativize categories that psychology likes to see as essential and unchanging – a positive point, but which (1) contains the work of discourse analysis within traditional psychological categories, (2) evades reference to politics or power, and (3) restricts its analysis to a particular text rather than locating it in wider discursive practices that regulate and police people's understanding of themselves. We then lose sight of the distinctive *critical* contribution of a discursive approach to psychology.

In this version of discursive psychology the 'quantitative–qualitative' debate has tended to mark the point where conversation analysis (see **5.17**) and ethnomethodology (see **3.2**) part company. Ethnomethodology is vehemently opposed to the abstraction of accomplishments that quantification indulges in and it looks to a phenomenological mode of enquiry (Smith 1978; see **3.1**). Conversation analysis, on the other hand, has been happier to play by what it thinks are the rules of the scientific game (Antaki and Widdicombe 1998). Both aspects of discourse analysis here carry the danger of 'essentialism' from mainstream psychology into alternative qualitative methodologies.

Essentialism can be found in contemporary discursive accounts in at least four ways.

The first is where the discourse user is seen as *intentionally* using certain 'interpretative repertoires' or deliberately bringing about certain rhetorical effects (see Edwards 1995). Given psychology's individualistic focus, we should not be surprised if an intentionalist rhetoric creeps into much discourse-analytic description, and the 'functions' of discourse are then traced to the individual speaker. It is all the more important to be aware of individualism, then, in critical work on language. The second is where worry over the determinist language of some discourse-analytic descriptions leads to an attempt to re-introduce some notion of the 'self' (Burr 1994). The third is where claims about the discursive capabilities of human beings are rendered into an account of necessary characteristics of thought, as being 'dilemmatic' for example (Billig 1991). The fourth is where an attempt is made to warrant discursive explanations to a psychological audience by referring to models of quasi-cognition, or even to neurophysiology (Harré and Gillett 1994).

This version of discourse analysis has provided a pole of attraction for writers from 1970s 'new paradigm' social psychology (Harré and Secord 1972), and has helped legitimate qualitative research in psychology departments in the past decade. This has then led to the argument that it is possible to yoke the 'turn-to-discourse' to a 'second cognitive revolution' in which most of the mental machinery will now be seen to have been out in the public sphere all along (Harré and Gillett 1994). Some critical writers in social psychology who had been tempted to turn to the study of rhetoric as an alternative to laboratory experimentation (Billig 1987) and to the study of the way that people handle dilemmas in everyday talk (Billig et al. 1988) would now see their work as 'discursive', and would also make claims, based on that research, that they now know more about the nature of human thinking (Billig 1991). It should be noted that these various elaborations of discourse analysis have also contributed to critical perspectives in psychology, and Wetherell and Potter's (1992; see also Potter and Wetherell 1998) analysis of racism, for example, connects with more radical foucauldian forms of discourse-analytic research.

This chapter focuses on the contribution of foucauldian approaches to discourse analysis that have been influenced by structuralist and post-structuralist theories. These approaches have been explicitly aligned recently to the development of 'critical psychology' (Parker 1997).

2 DISCOURSE ANALYSIS IN CRITICAL PSYCHOLOGY

The linguist Ferdinand de Saussure (1974) suggested a new science called 'semiology', which would study the life of signs in society, and the exploration of semiological patterns of meaning has sometimes been carried out under that heading, and sometimes under the related (US American) heading of 'semiotics' (Hawkes 1977). Although discourse analysts in psychology have tended to focus on spoken and written texts, a critical 'reading' of psychology as part of culture should encompass the study of all the kinds of symbolic material that we use to represent ourselves to each other (Parker and The Bolton Discourse Network 1999). All of this symbolic material is *organized*, and it is that organization that makes it possible for it to produce for us, its users, a sense of human community and identity. Semiology in general, and discourse analysis in particular, leads us to question the way subjectivity (the experience of being and feeling in particular discursive contexts) is constituted inside and outside psychology.

Psychology imagines that it is 'realist', but this is actually often the case only in the empiricist sense of the term. Discourse analysts, on the other hand, challenge the way the discipline studies 'the real' through text. It is possible to analyse the particular qualities of a 'realist' text as something that constructs a sense of the world outside as taken-for-granted without concluding that claims about the world can never be explored and assessed. Some of the analyses of visual texts in film theory (see **5.7**), for example, have been useful in showing how ideology works through re-presenting something on the screen as if it were a transparent window onto the world (McCabe 1974). Psychological reports play the same type of trick when they pretend to provide a transparent window on the mind, and a critical discourse approach links analyses of these written forms with the visual texts that surround us and make the reports seem reasonable and commonsensical.

The organization of discourse through patterns and structures fixes the meaning of symbolic material, and this makes it possible for discourse analysts to take those texts, unpick them and show how they work. The process of focusing on specific texts might lead us to pragmatically treat these as abstracted from culture when we carry out our analysis, and so we have to be aware of the ways in which the meanings we study are produced in their relationship to other texts, the way they are 'intertextual'. When we take a ready-made text or select some material to create a text, we are able to trace connections between signs and to identify regularities that produce certain circumscribed positions for readers. We can then study the ideological force of language by displaying the patterns and structures of meaning. That is, we can identify distinct 'discourses' that define entities that we see in the world and in relationships, and as things we feel are psychologically real in ourselves.

Saussure made a crucial distinction between individual 'speech acts' (Austin 1962) on the one hand and the 'language system' which determined how they may be produced and what sense they would be able to have on the other. Barthes (1957/1972) extended this analysis to look at the way terms in language not only seem to refer directly to things outside language, through 'denotation', but also evoke a network of associations, through 'connotation', and operate as part of an ideological 'second-order sign system' which he called 'myth'. Myth naturalizes cultural meanings and makes it seem as if language not only refers to the world, but also reflects an unchanging and universal order of things. Because it does not make a direct claim to represent the way the world should be, but insinuates itself into taken-for-granted frames of reference, myth is one of the effective ways that ideology works.

Foucault (1980) was suspicious of the term 'ideology' because it may prompt people to find an essential underlying 'truth' that could be counterposed to it, but foucauldian discourse analysis in psychology is now more sympathetic to the ways in which radical literary theorists have struggled with the term and have tried to save it for a reading of texts (Eagleton 1991).

This does not mean that discourse analysts would want to take up the position of 'reader reception theorists' in literary theory however (e.g. Iser 1978). This is because the notion of 'reader reception' invites us back into a cognitivist notion of individuals as having some sort of interpretative paraphernalia inside their heads that helps them to decode what is happening around them. It also presupposes that there could be a position for a reader that was free of discourse, and that this independent reader would be able to analyse what was going on in the text from an objective standpoint (Eagleton 1983). Discourse analysts looking to literary theory are more impressed with some of the other descriptions in Barthes's work of 'readerly' and 'writerly' texts, of different kinds of discourse that either seem closed and only able to be read or seem open to be *written* as well as read, open to be *changed* (Barthes 1977). Readerly texts – psychology textbooks, for example – only allow the reader to reproduce them. Writerly texts are open to the reader to participate and transform the meanings that are offered. There are problems of reading and interpretation here that cannot be addressed by quantitative approaches in psychology.

If we connect our work with the foucauldian tradition in this way, the approach can function as a bridge to a critical understanding of contradiction, the constitution of the modern psychological subject and its place in regimes of knowledge and power. It is then possible for the researcher to break completely from mainstream psychology and to view it as a series of practices that can be 'deconstructed'.

Although researchers in the field of discourse analysis warn against systematizing their approach, because it should be thought of more correctly as a sensitivity to language rather than as a 'method', it is possible to indicate stages that might usefully be passed through in order to identify contradictions, construction and functions of language. Parker (1992) outlines a number of 'steps', for example, of which seven will be mentioned here. The researcher is encouraged to (1) turn the text into written form, if it is not already; (2) free associate to varieties of meaning as a way of accessing cultural networks, and note these down; (3) systematically itemize the objects, usually marked by nouns, in the text or selected portion of text; (4) maintain a distance from the text by treating the text itself as the object of the study rather than what it seems to 'refer' to; (5) systematically itemize the 'subjects' – characters, persona, role positions – specified in the text; (6) reconstruct presupposed rights and responsibilities of 'subjects' specified in the text; (7) map the networks of relationships into patterns. These patterns in language are 'discourses', and can then be located in relations of ideology, power and institutions.

3 A PEDAGOGICAL EXAMPLE

We will take one outstanding example of critical research to illustrate the importance of critical methodological and theoretical debates in discourse analysis.

Walkerdine (1991) analysed the interaction between a female teacher and a little boy in class. The theoretical context for the analysis is elaborated in Henriques et al. (1998). In the brief piece of transcript, the teacher was able to control the boy until he responded with a stream of sexist abuse. She withdrew, and was then unable to reassert her authority.

Psychologists who study power, of course, will usually be tempted to treat it as the deliberate exercise of authority over another who 'conforms' or 'obeys'. However, power in discourse is more complicated, and the notions of 'subject position' and 'interpellation' have been useful in capturing the way in which the 'powerful' and 'powerless' are addressed and recruited. Foucauldians would then look at how the organization of language in a culture provides places for the phenomenon to make sense, and at the 'surfaces of emergence', for certain representations and practices of the self.

Walkerdine explored the way that competing discourses of devalued female sexuality and liberal education theory framed the way the participants in the interaction could relate to one another. The boy was able to position the teacher as a woman, and so silence her, and the woman who had been trained to value the free expression of children positioned herself as a good teacher, and was then unable to silence the boy. History in discourse analysis, then, should not be seen as something that pulls the strings of individual actors: rather, it lays out a field of action in which individuals understand themselves and others. These discourses could only work here, of course, because of the wider systems of power in male–female relationships (see **3.10**) and systems of ideology in education. Power was played out in this classroom in such a way that the woman participated in, and reproduced, her own oppression. An analysis of the rules of discourse that govern any particular social formation must also,

then, be an analysis of how individuals creatively engage with those rules, what forms of power they reconstruct as they participate in them and what forms of resistance it is possible for them to display. The macro-level, then, is something that pervades, constructs and draws sustenance from the micro-level.

Walkerdine does not follow a set procedure or work her way through 'steps' in the analysis, and those examples of discourse analysis that follow steps usually do so for purely pedagogical purposes (e.g. Parker 1994). However, she does identify, for example, the 'subjects' (the particular character of the 'woman', 'boy', 'teacher' and 'child') in the text as objects constituted in the discourse and specify the rights, responsibilities and patterns of power that they are implicated in.

The woman teacher in Walkerdine's study was as much at the mercy of psychology, through her pedagogical training, as of sexism. Psychology itself operates as a kind of 'myth' in commonsense, and it runs alongside a range of exclusionary and pathologizing practices that commonsense justifies as being natural and unquestionable. This is why an analysis of psychological phenomena needs to be undertaken alongside an analysis of practices of psychology in Western culture, and then that analysis must extend its scope to the way in which psychology relays images of the 'self' through its own practices as part of the 'psy-complex' (Rose 1985). It is difficult, then, to appeal to commonsense as an always trustworthy resource to challenge psychology.

Those who are comfortable with the positions language offers them in culture, or who are unconfident about mobilizing their critical awareness of power to focus on what psychology does to them, on the other hand, will trail through handbooks of discourse analysis, and be unable to see the point; for language seems to them to do no more than represent the world as it is and as they think it should be.

There are a number of paradoxes here, for both conservative and critical psychology are part of everyday knowledge outside universities and clinics. It is easier to grasp how this paradox is played out if we focus on the notion of contradiction in discourse, and the way contradictory meanings constitute objects that reinforce or challenge power.

There is no simple line that we could trace through discourse analysis using, for example, the work of Foucault, which would ensure that we would assemble a reliable critical perspective. There is always a struggle over the meaning of terms and what effects they have within regimes of truth (Parker and Burman 1993). We could, for example, see 'discursive psychology' as part of a counter discourse which embeds psychological processes in culture and politics, but it could also be taken and absorbed by mainstream psychology to make the discipline all the more resilient and adept at deflecting critique.

The stuff of mental life lies in discourse, and it then makes sense to say that we are elaborating an alternative 'discursive psychology', but this needs to be argued through theoretically more than methodologically if discourse analysis is to become more than just another method and contribute to the development of critical psychology (Parker 1999).

FURTHER READING

Henriques, J., Hollway, W., Urwin, C., Venn, C. and Walkerdine, V. (1998) *Changing the Subject: Psychology, Social Regulation and Subjectivity* (reissued edition). London: Routledge.

Parker, I. (1997) 'Discursive Psychology', in D. Fox and I. Prilleltensky (eds), *Critical Psychology: An Introduction*. London: Sage. pp. 284–298.

Parker, I. and Burman, E. (1993) 'Against Discursive Imperialism, Empiricism and Constructionism: Thirty-two Problems with Discourse Analysis', in E. Burman and I. Parker (eds), *Discourse Analytic Research: Repertoires and Readings of Texts in Action*. London: Routledge. pp. 155–172.

5.20 Deep-structure Hermeneutics

Hans-Dieter König

1 TEXTS AS A STAGING OF LIFE-PLANS

The deep-structure hermeneutics developed by Lorenzer (1981b, 1986) on the basis of a literary interpretation is a sociological method of psychoanalytic cultural research which investigates the narrative content of texts and pictures by means of their effect on the experience of the interpreter. This may involve both natural protocols such as interviews and group discussions and also artificial protocols such as literary texts or films. The analysis focuses on the conscious and subconscious life-plans that are staged in the social interactions transported via the text or film. An ambiguity of social action sequences is presupposed, according to which the meaning of interactions is revealed at the interface between a manifest and a latent meaning (cf. Figure 5.20.1: Interaction level I).

Whereas the manifest meaning of the interaction is determined by conscious life-plans (expectations, intentions, worries), at the latent level of meaning (wishes, dreams, fears) life-plans express themselves in a way that has hitherto not become conscious or which has been repressed under the pressure of social dominance, so as to have an affect on behaviour behind the back of the subject.

The goal of a deep-structure hermeneutic reconstruction of the manifest and latent meaning of a text or film may be illustrated with the example of Lorenzer's (1990) interpretation of a poem by R. A. Schröder, taken from his cycle *Wintertrost – für S. Stegmann 1941* [Winter comfort – for S. Stegman 1941]. This is the text:

> Wenn dich die Nähe quält,
> Denk an die Ferne,
> Wenn dir die Sonne fehlt,
> Blick in die Sterne.
>
> Einer ist nah und weit,
> Nah wie dein Wille,
> Fern wie die Ewigkeit,
> Denk's und werd stille.

> [If what is near torments you
> Think of far away,
> If you miss the sun,
> Look at the stars.
>
> One is close and far,
> Close as your will,
> Far as eternity,
> Think of this and be calm.]

At the level of the manifest meaning of the poem, this is a matter of 'practical life-consolation' (Lorenzer 1990: 263): the reader is asked to distance him- or herself from a painful reality (the *'quälende Nähe'* = 'tormenting nearness') and to go beyond that by relying on a 'safe world-order' (*'einer ist nah und weit'* = 'one is close and far'). It is irritating that this approach

Research levels of scenic interpretations

Scenic case reconstruction as group interpretation

(I) Scenes from text or film

> **Text or film**
>
> $$\text{Interaction scene} = \frac{\text{Manifest (accepted life-plans)}}{\text{Latent (scorned life-plans)}} \Big\} \text{ inconsistencies}$$
>
> Staging of life-plans

(II) Scenes between text and interpreters (scenic participation)

Effect of text on interpreters

Scenic interpretation of text by interpreters

(III) Scenes in the group

> **Group of interpreters**
>
> Construction of interpretations (readings)
>
> $$\text{Interaction scene} = \frac{\text{Manifest (intellectual understanding)}}{\text{Latent (affective understanding)}} \Big\} \text{ readings}$$
>
> Irritations
> Associations
>
> Experience of text

Figure 5.20.1 Levels of interpretation. Deep-structure hermeneutics investigates the *ambiguity* of the interaction practice arranged in the text or film – a structure of interactive scenes whose meaning is revealed at the interface between a *manifest* and a *latent* sense (I). Discovery of the latent meaning, which is accessed through key scenes that prove to be *inconsistent*, is achieved by means of the interpreter allowing the text or film to affect his or her own experience ('scenic participation') (II). The interpreters, by following the *associations* and *irritations* that occur to them in an attitude of *impartial attentiveness*, gain access to readings that are missed by routine modes of textual understanding. These readings that aim at the discovery of novelty are discussed in a group (III) to grasp the latent meaning that is concealed behind the manifest meaning of the scenically unfolding text or film (I)

to the reader happens in multiple ways: the reader is expected to distance him- or herself from sensory experience (to move from the experience of the 'close' to 'thinking' of 'far away', from experiencing the warmth of the sun to a remote look at the cold light of the stars). The dialogue with the reader is interrupted, moreover, by the preoccupation with the 'one' and by a command ('think of this and be calm'). The overlapping of the manifest and the latent meaning makes it clear how the poem has a discouraging effect on the reader: whilst the manifest meaning aims at 'self-liberation, freedom of thought and self-assurance in agreement with another, the latent meaning asks for "self-assessment" and "abondonment of subjectivity"' (Lorenzer 1990: 272). Just where the reader's resistance to the Third Reich was supposed to be strengthened, his or her subjectivity is taken away because 'abstinence from sensory experience ... relates to the silent isolation of generally refraining from action' (1990: 272). And so it becomes clear what kind of socialization effect the poem can unleash: whilst the manifest meaning which calls for freedom and autonomy may appeal to the reader's reason, the latent meaning takes over, awakening a quite specific emotional reaction behind the back as it were of the reader's conscious awareness: the request to be silent, to withdraw into an internal world and relate to a divinity, invites the reader to abandon the symbolic action that creates subjectivity and to regress to a pre-linguistic narcissistic level of experience where the oceanic feeling of an infinite fusion with the universe may be enjoyed.

2 THE DEVELOPMENTAL HISTORY OF PSYCHOANALYTIC SOCIAL PSYCHOLOGY

Freud (1905) created awareness of the drama of child sexual development, which he understood as 'the nuclear complex of the neuroses' (1905/ 1958: 205), with reference to Sophocles's drama *Oedipus Rex*. Here it becomes clear how psychoanalysis developed at the interface between therapeutic practice and cultural analysis (cf. König 1996c), although initially it was systematically developed only as a method and theory of therapeutic practice. In his works of cultural criticism Freud saw neurotic suffering as a consequence of a dominant 'discontent' within civilization (cf. Freud 1930), which he traced back to the fact that human beings are suffering from a cultural development that is based on the 'suppression of instincts' and its only partially successful 'sublimation' (Freud 1908/ 1959: 186f.).

Important stimuli for the involvement of psychoanalysis in the social sciences came in the 1930s and 1940s from the Frankfurt Institute of Social Research which had resettled in the United States. For example, under the direction of Horkheimer (1932), the problem of how

National Socialism had grown out of civil society was subjected to a social–psychological investigation. The most significant social–psychological contribution from this institute was the study by Adorno and his co-workers (1950) of the authoritarian personality which is susceptible to anti–democratic propaganda.

The dispute on positivism that took place in the 1960s gave the methodological discussion a new impetus. In the context of an examination of analytical–empirical and quantitative social sciences, Adorno developed his method (1969a) of critical social research which decodes individual experience by means of an interpretative fixing of clues and investigates examples of social generalization by means of a reconstruction of single cases. This became the foundation of a theoretical scientific appraisal of psychoanalysis. Following Habermas's (1971) critique of Freud's scientist self-misunderstanding, Lorenzer (1970) reconstructed a way of understanding psychoanalysis as a social science that uses hermeneutic procedures.

3 LORENZER'S UNDERSTANDING OF PSYCHOANALYSIS AS A SOCIAL SCIENCE

On the basis he had outlined, Lorenzer developed a sociological understanding of psychoanalysis in terms of three stages in the research process.

First, in a broader sense the term 'deep-structure hermeneutics', which is used with reference to a characterization by Habermas (1971: 267ff.), denotes Lorenzer's interest (1974: 153ff.) in understanding psychoanalysis as an interpretative social science that aims at the 'reconstruction of a patient's inner life-history' (p. 154). The psychoanalyst is to use what Lorenzer (1970) called a 'scenic understanding', and with the help of this the communications, dreams and memories of the patient may be understood as the staging of conscious and subconscious life-plans. The scenic understanding can bring about conscious awareness of suppressed life-plans, because the analyst decodes the communications of the patient on the basis of the relationship that is scenically established between them, as it unfolds in the interplay of transference and counter-transference.

Second, in order to decode the metaphors of psychoanalytic metapsychology and to remove the blindness to history and society of Freudian conceptualizations, Lorenzer (1971, 1972, 1974) reformulated psychoanalysis as a theory of interaction and socialization. Together with symbolic interactionism (see **3.3**), the psychoanalytical interaction theory that he developed takes the view that actors add a subjective meaning to social interactions and communicate in a tentative way, using the medium of the collective symbolic system of language, about their individual needs, social expectations and norms (cf. Turner 1962). Unlike symbolic interactionsism, however, which reduces the actors' motifs to linguistically articulated conscious reasons for action (cf. Strauss 1968), psychoanalysis is also concerned with subconscious motifs that are hidden behind the linguistically articulated motifs.

Lorenzer seeks to clarify the interaction partners' qualifications for action on the basis of a psychoanalytic socialization theory which reformulates Freudian personality theory in terms of interaction theory. In this the individual, in the course of the early process of family socialization, passes through two different developmental levels of action-plans, which basically correspond to the two forms of social behaviour that Mead (1934) diagnosed in the context of his anthropologically based communication theory: the animal behaviour regulated by an exchange of gestures, and the self-reflexive action of human beings who exchange significant gestures on the basis of their mastery of language. The *id*, which is identified with the structure of *affects* and *drives*, forms a structure of subconscious forms of interaction. These amount to an intra-psychic expression of a sensorimotor interaction, regulated by an exchange of gestures, between infant and primary adult model, in the course of which stimulus–response complexes mesh together. The *ego*, in contrast, shows itself to be a structure of forms of symbolic interaction, which manifest themselves as an intrapsychic expression of an interaction regulated by the exchange of significant gestures and which make thinking possible.

Third, in a narrower sense the term deep-structure hermeneutics is used for the project developed by Lorenzer (1986) of a psychoanalytic analysis of culture (cf. Belgrad 1997; Belgrad et al. 1987; König 1996a,b,c, 1998), which investigates the narrative content of texts and films in a methodologically reflected way. In this way deep-structure hermeneutics differs from a naive

form of applying the subsumption logic of psychoanalysis to culture, which merely illustrates clinical diagnoses with cultural phenomena and so leads to the psychologizing and pathologizing of the sociological research issue. This also ignores the methodological problem that is connected with the application of psychoanalysis to culture. The psychoanalytic terminology, which was developed in therapeutic practice and designed for it, cannot simply be transferred to culture, since here we are dealing with a research field that has quite different and distinct characteristics of its own.

If one wishes systematically to develop Freudian theory as a social science, without directly subsuming, under fragments of psychoanalytic theory, the interaction drama manifest in a text protocol, then the *methodological* problem is to modify the method of psychoanalytic hermeneutics that was developed in therapeutic practice – Lorenzer's 'scenic understanding' (1970) – in such a way that it assists sociological research to discover new things in the context of an independent theory of culture that is still to be developed.

4 RULES TO BE OBSERVED IN IMPLEMENTATION OF THE METHOD

In the context of this chapter we cannot fully explain how deep-structure hermeneutic analysis of culture developed from the therapeutic procedure of scenic understanding (cf. König 1996c; Lorenzer 1986). Nor can we explain here all the rules of deep-structure hermeneutic interpretation (cf. König 1997c). We shall therefore explain only the most important rules of the method. To give an overview of the procedure, the application of these rules will be illustrated using the example of a research project on the media presentation of right-wing extremism in which the Bonengel film *Beruf Neonazi* [=Neonazi by Profession] was scenically reconstructed.

1 The interactive practice arranged in a text or film is conceived as a drama in which different people appear on a stage, equipped with particular scenery and props, in order to represent concrete life-plans by means of an exchange of gestures and language (cf. Figure 5.20.1, Interaction level I). A first understanding takes place

as soon as the events on the stage are so vividly retold in colloquial language that one can imagine them pictorially: when the Munich Neonazi Althans strolls through the Auschwitz memorial, cheerfully whistling under his breath, to find the crematorium, he portrays himself as a curious tourist turning the former death camp into an amusing destination for an excursion (cf. König 1995c).

2   The interpreters, like a theatre audience, allow the drama offered by the text or film to have an effect on their own experience. Irrespective of whether they react with enthusiasm or boredom, emotions are transferred to the text or film on the basis of which one may trace the secret life-plans which the actors on the stage conceal behind the intentions, wishes and worries they openly express, and which they unintentionally express in their interaction.

3   The affective understanding that is realized on the basis of this emotional participation in the text or film can be made productive if one follows Freud's advice for psychoanalytic understanding. This consists, on the one hand, 'in not directing one's notice to anything in particular and in maintaining the same "evenly-suspended attention" in respect of the text' (1912/1958: 111). On the other hand, one adheres to Freud's rule of free association and leaves it to one's own imagination to decide the scenes to which this 'evenly-suspended attention' will be directed and what one wishes to understand: since participants in the seminar were particularly shocked by the two sequences in which Althans reviled a Serbian holocaust-survivor and attempted to destruct Auschwitz, the scenic interpretation began with these two film sequences.

4   Of particular interest are those associations with the text that begin with irritating interaction sequences. The term *irritation* highlights the fact that particular interaction sequences are disturbing because they contradict readings that arise in the course of a routine textual understanding: in the course of interpreting that film sequence where Althans mocks a Serbian holocaust-survivor (cf. König 1995b), the group discussed the fact that the old woman who bursts into tears arouses not sympathy but anger, because she moans as if to order, and someone else added that Althans basically reacts in a 'cool' and 'intelligent' way. A number of variant readings then emerged, which gave access to a latent level of meaning. It then became clear that the audience reacted to Althans's shocking behaviour not only with a feeling of rejection, but also – in spite of their ideals and moral beliefs – with fascination.

5   Understanding the film proceeds on the basis of one's own experience but is normally incorporated, nevertheless, into a group interpretation (cf. König 1993). This defers the intellectual understanding that was subsequently used to interpret Althans's ideology – an orthodox National Socialist attempts to recruit young people to the anti-semitically based world view of fascism. In contrast, in group interpretation one should proceed on the basis of an affective understanding and experiencing of the text or film. Since very personal experiences of the text or film are exchanged, a lively difference of opinion develops about different readings. By discussing whether the Serbian woman is overcome by pain or simply 'moaning', and whether Althans is an evil and cynical anti-semite or a smart and good-looking young man whose right-wing extremism is somehow 'chic', a violent disagreement took place in the group about the most appropriate reading. The conflict stimulated by the clash between competing readings may be understood as a scene developing between the interpreters (cf. Figure 5.20.1, Interaction level III), which allows inferences to be made about the scenic structure of the film. For it is the text and the images which release these kinds of different emotional reactions. The group discussions were recorded and transcribed.

6   Since understanding of the text or film is accessible by means of the effect on one's own experience, it is necessary that interpreters keep a research diary in which they regularly record their own reactions, questions and access to comprehension. In this way one will produce a protocol that captures the different readings that have been used to create one's own access to the text or film.

7   If the seminar participants are guided by their subjective experiences, the attempts at interpretation may be generalized by the fact that they serve the scenic interpretation of the text or film which may be understood as a complex structure of sensori-pictorial scenes. Scenic understanding begins with an interactive scene that attracts an 'evenly-suspended attention' to itself on the basis of associations and irritations. Interpreters may then explain what is disturbing in this scene with reference to other scenes

that are close by, or are in a totally different action-context of the text or film, but have a similarly irritant effect. Such scenes, which on deeper analysis reveal an identical or similar situational structure, may be assembled into different sequences of scenes: the scenes of the Auschwitz sequences are assembled into a series of scenes which is then linked to the film sequence where Althans mocks a holocaust-survivor. The various sequences of scenes, which are compared and combined with one another until they come together in a scenic configuration that illuminates the whole, constitute the different themes of the film which are frequently intertwined in a variety of ways: the rebellion of an angry young man against the older generation; his initiation by the male community of Neonazis visualized in the film sequences with the German–Canadian Zündel (cf. König 1997a); the ordeal by fire of presenting himself in public as a fanatical Nazi who hates Jews; and his successes as a political orator in front of young people (cf. König 1997b).

8   The process of scenic interpretation is the first domain of the *process of hermeneutic understanding* in which one makes use of everyday language. In this a scenic interpretation unfolds at the interface between three levels of interpretation (cf. Figure 5.20.1): the scenic structure of the text or film (I), which is marked with Althans's self-staging, is exposed through the effect it makes on the interpreters; the feelings of powerlessness, anger and fascination with which seminar participants reacted to Althans document the emotional reaction to the drama presented in the text or film; and a scenic participation in a pictorial world (II), which is intelligible through the scenes that come into existence because of the controversy about different readings (III).

9   The second domain in the process of hermeneutic understanding is constituted through *theoretical comprehension* of the case reconstruction. In the same way as the theoretical question which underlay the research project was developed on the basis of knowledge of sociological and psychoanalytical theory, reference is now made to these insights in order to typologize the new discoveries that have been made through the scenic case reconstruction and to bring them under an appropriate conceptual heading. For example, following the scenic interpretation of the Auschwitz sequence, the project conceptualized the way in which the

Munich Neonazi is able to fascinate by presenting himself as a 'Yuppie-Nazi' who is able simultaneously to adjust to authoritarian, consumer and mass-media modes of social conformity.

In the course of a theoretical comprehension of case structure, social and historical references were also established. The analysis showed, for instance, that the director, Bonengel, had created a film which, by virtue of the fact that it tells the story of a Nazi dancing on a volcano, comes close to the spirit of the postmodern age. And finally the project was able to demonstrate that the staging of Althans owed its particular effect to a political climate in which former federal Chancellor Helmut Kohl, using a new jargon of authenticity, attempted to write off the holocaust as a 'bitter experience of history': after Kohl had ensured that one could 'freeze the feelings of shame and guilt ... with which, as a German, one reacts to Auschwitz', a Neonazi like Althans was able 'to evoke quite different feelings in respect of Auschwitz' (König 1995c: 412).

10   *Writing* may be seen as the third hermeneutic domain of deep-structure hermeneutic analysis. In dealing with a text or a film, a text is produced for the readings produced in the group (and these are available by virtue of the reports of group meetings), for the researchers' diaries and for the subsequent thoughts on the theoretical treatment of case structure, and this text seeks to convince the reader and provides a self-critical reflection on the research process.

Between the wide-ranging group interpretation and the concise presentation of the results of the interpretation in a publication, there is the following particular difference: in the context of a group interpretation it is only towards the end, as soon as the text or film material has been scenically set out and is accessible in its deep structure, that the question can be answered of which meaning contexts should be characterized as *manifest* and which as *latent*, and how the relationship between them is to be determined. In contrast to this, the presentation of the interpretation results, which seeks to convince the reader, begins with the easily comprehensible manifest meaning and then, step by step, provides access to the hidden meaning facets of the latent meaning which can only appear plausible to readers in the course of increasing familiarity with the scenic structure of the text or film.

5 DEVELOPMENTAL OPPORTUNITIES FOR A DEEP-STRUCTURE HERMENEUTIC TYPE OF SOCIAL RESEARCH

Deep-structure hermeneutics has been applied in many different ways to aesthetic productions such as literature (cf. König 1996d; Würker 1993), music (Schmid Noerr 1987), film (cf. König 1995a, 1996a), religious and profane rituals (cf. Lorenzer 1981a; Schmid Noerr and Eggert 1986), life-world action contexts (Horn et al. 1983; Leithäuser and Volmerg 1988) and pedagogic, commercial and political interventions in such contexts (cf. Graf-Deserno and Deserno 1998; König 1990; Trescher 1985. Cf. also König 1997c for a summary of these.) The question of how capable the method is of development may be outlined with reference to the problem that Lorenzer (1972) worked out in his action-theory interpretation of Freudian theory in the context of a *materialistic theory of socialization*, in the course of which he developed a criticism of the bourgeois science of psychoanalysis in parallel to the Marxist criticism of political economics. Lorenzer indeed made a link with the insights of symbolic interactionism through his interpretation of Freudian theory as a theory of interaction; but his attempt to mediate between psychoanalysis and sociology remains unsatisfactory, because he was content merely to relate Freudian theory to historical materialism. Social action, however, should not only be understood psychoanalytically as an intra-subjective realization of life-plans and, from a structural–analytical viewpoint, not only as the realization of economic pressures or as the consequence of objective systemic imperatives. It is rather the case that social action, as symbolic interaction, develops, in the context of a life-world, a dynamic of its own which functions as an intermediary between the spiritual life and the social system. Using insights from interpretative sociology and symbolic interactionism (see 3.3), Lorenzer's psychoanalytic theory of socialization may be linked, for example, to Bourdieu's (2000) social–structural theory. From this perspective the subjective suffering of individuals may be seen not only as an expression of unresolved intra-subjective experiences, but also as the result of a struggle for power within a social domain. This mediation of sociology and psychoanalysis is made possible, in particular, by Bourdieu's (2000) *habitus* theory which is open to social–psychological interpretation. According to Bourdieu, *habitus* is produced, in the socialization processes of early childhood, as a system of dispositions by incorporating the external class-specific and social–structural conditions of life. As a kind of second nature, *habitus* subconsciously directs precisely that action-practice which meets the requirements of a social domain. Just as *habitus* may be understood from a sociological viewpoint, in Bourdieu's way, as a 'social instinct' which depends on an internalization of the objective social situation and determines the choice of an appropriate life-style, so from a psychoanalytical perspective it may be determined as the matrix of drives. In Lorenzer's opinion, *habitus* is that structure of subconscious interaction forms which are formed as an internal expression of interactions in early childhood and which correspond to a system of behavioural plans that structures interactions in later life.

How this new bridge between psychoanalysis and sociology may be translated in a deep-structure hermeneutic type of social research has been developed here using the example of biographical research (cf. König 1996a,b. See 3.6, 3.7): in order to investigate the social and psychical constitutive conditions of life-histories, narrative interviews (cf. Schütze 1983) are conducted, and these are then analysed using deep-structure hermeneutics and narrative analysis. By means of the triangulation (see 4.6) of two methods of textual interpretation, the case structure may be reconstructed from two different epistemic standpoints: it becomes clear how biographies develop, on the one hand through dealing with intra-subjective conflicts, and on the other hand through symbolic interaction with others, through the adaptation of specific prior knowledge, and through integration into particular socio-cultural milieux. This example shows how deep-structure hermeneutics can develop as a psychoanalytically oriented method of qualitative research and how it may be combined with other sociological methods.

FURTHER READING

König, H. D. (2001) 'A Neo-Nazi in Auschwitz. A Psychoanalytic Reconstruction of a Documentary Film on Right-Wing Extremism'

[58 paragraphs], *Forum Qualitative Sozialforschung/Forum: Qualitative Social Research* [On-line Journal], 2(3). Available at: http://www.qualitative-research.net/fqs/fqs-eng.htm

Lorenzer, A. and Würker, A. (1989) 'Depth-Hermeneutical Interpretation of Literature', in D. Meutsch and R. Viehoff (eds), *Results and Problems of Interdisciplinary Approaches*. Berlin: de Gruyter. pp. 56–73.

5.21   The Art of Interpretation

Heinz Bude

What Robert Merton (1968), in opposition to the Hempel–Oppenheim schema for scientific explanations, referred to, at the end of the 1940s, as the 'serendipity pattern' in empirical research is essential today for the understanding of post-positivist social research. Empirical research is by no means limited to the testing or verification of hypotheses, but has its own practice of *experimental theorizing*, which results in models for the explanation and terminology for the understanding of everyday social reality. 'Serendipity' means the discovery of unforeseen, non-normal and unspecific data which require a novel view of interpersonal action and embody a different concept of the social universe. Leon Festinger's (1957) concept of cognitive dissonance, Sigmund Freud's (1920–22/1955) concept of the unconscious or Harold Garfinkel's (1967a) idea of suppositions of normality all have their basis in such discoveries.

sociological theorizing when it provides us with ideas, categories and formulae for obscure social facts and unconsidered social relationships which can then be subjected to further theoretical processing and conceptual testing. But this 'serendipity-effect' does not happen automatically. An investigator is always needed to confront the facts and thus overcome the routines of paradigmatic complexity reduction and make interpretation into an art. The term *art* refers here to dealing with ambiguities, handling limitations and mixing separate components (for discussion of this idea of 'art in science' which is inspired by the aesthetics of classical modernism, cf. Clifford 1988b). Of course this is not meant as a mere game or piece of subjective behaviour, but rather as the expression of an experience of truth which exceeds the area of control of methodological legitimization (as formulated by Gadamer 1975: XXVII).

1   AN EXPERIENCE OF TRUTH

In response to a remarkable or superfluous piece of data the hermeneutic dialectic of truth and method becomes effective, making it clear that particular thought habits are taken for granted and particular modes of observation have been forgotten. Empirical research contributes to

2   USING CHANCE AND TOLERATING WHAT CANNOT BE DECIDED

The question about the relationship between art and science serves initially to determine the borders between the forms of artistic intuition and those of scientific scepticism. Even the idea of sociology as a 'third culture' between literature and science (Lepenies 1988) depends on the existing distinction between scientific and literary orientations. The question about the relationship between art and science is not only asked externally with regard to institutional separations but also, for science, from the inside out, if one considers the genesis and validity of scientific knowledge. Here one cannot avoid two fundamental insights: on the one hand the fact that for any discovery quite specific coincidences have to come together to open up the domain of what is 'known' to that of what is 'recognizable'; and on the other hand, the fact that the substantiation of ideas contains some reference to plausibilities that can no longer be substantiated in the context of the same system of ideas. In the first case we are concerned with the scientific–historical insight into the chance nature of discoveries, and in the second case with the philosophical insight into the incomplete nature of explanations. Science is as little capable of capturing the originality of the unknown as the paradoxes of self-explanation. It is therefore part of the art of science to make use of chance and to tolerate what cannot be decided. Those who expect from science only security of method and certainty of explanation are denying themselves in advance the attraction of research, which begins where obedience to method and idealism about explanation are no longer productive.

Art, therefore, makes an impact on science because of the impossibility of methodologizing some research attitude and the circularity of self-reflective consciousness. Because the nature of a case cannot be derived from theories nor generalized from single cases, it requires the practised experience and the purposeful involvement of an investigator who makes him- or herself into the instrument of research. Interpretation is not only an act of self-denial, in the sense that there is always someone who interprets. It is also an act of self-fulfilment, in which there is always some emotion. Where scientific theory presumes a subject of consciousness, in research practice a human being lives. The will for knowledge (Foucault) is therefore an indispensable condition for scientific reality research.

3   THE 'ABDUCTIVE INFERENCE'

Charles Sanders Peirce, in his famous methodology of 'abductive inferencing', saw a way

beyond inductive security of generalization and deductive certainty of derivation: deduction proves that, for logical reasons, something must be the case; induction demonstrates that there is empirical evidence that something is truly so; abduction, by contrast, merely supposes that something might be the case. It therefore abandons the solid ground of prediction and testing in order to introduce a new idea or to understand a new phenomenon (see 4.3).

Peirce was concerned with the procedure for forming a hypothesis, and this for him was more than merely a cognitive act: it was rather an instance of the design of a world.

> The abductive suggestion comes to us like a flash. It is an act of insight, although of extremely fallible insight. It is true that the different elements of the hypothesis were in our minds before; but it is the idea of putting together what we had never before dreamed of putting together which flashes the new suggestion before our contemplation. (Peirce 1960a: 113)

The 'abductive inference' therefore depends on a double movement: on the one hand one must allow the different components of a hypothesis to rotate before the inner eye, and on the other hand one must sum them all up at the right moment in an interpretation. There is therefore such a thing as 'timing' in the interpretative process, according to which one might be too early but also too late: too early because the relevant reference contexts have not yet all been traced, and too late because the associations disperse in a useless infinity (see 2.1, 4.3).

4   THE INTERVIEW AS AN 'OBJECTIVE CHANCE'

What is the significance of these considerations for the various stages in the interpretative research process? What does the art of collecting, analysing and presenting qualitative data consist of? In terms of the naturalistic doctrine in interpretative social research one may be inclined to prefer the preserving instrument of participant observation (see 5.5) to the interventionist one of interviewing (see 5.2). But as far as the encounter with reality is concerned, there is no very decisive difference between these two procedures.

In the introductory self-interview in his *New York Conversations*, Sylvère Lotringer explores the difference between a written work and a recorded interview:

> In writing disappearing is never definitive. Writing means creating a work, or erecting a monument. In addition the trust in one's own immortality or survival is becoming, in my opinion, more and more doubtful in our civilization. The interview, in contrast, is a form which is more fleeting, nomadic and transient. We do not build pyramids but we occupy a corner. We lay no foundations but put up a tent for the night. (1983: 21)

The interviewer resembles a fellow traveller on a train journey to whom one tells one's entire life-history. The limited nature of the contact seems to be a condition for the extraordinary truthfulness of this relationship. As Georg Simmel (1984) put it, we trust the 'passing stranger' – which the interviewer appears to be – with things one would perhaps never say to a close acquaintance. In this way finiteness and distance become structural features of a 'social relationship of a particular kind' (Scheuch 1973: 66), in which the individual emerges for a brief moment out of the anonymous mass as an unmistakable face. Here we are dealing with a chance but extraordinary encounter in which the interviewee can see him- or herself as the singular subject of a statement but at the same time as a categorial representative of some collective consciousness.

The asymmetry of role-distribution between interviewer and interviewee should not, however, conceal what unites the two partners: the reciprocal dealing with the present and the ongoing search for meaning, about which Cicourel (1964) spoke very forcefully. From the very first moments of an interview, when the partners exchange greetings, take their seats and devote a few words to what is to come, the constellation of a relationship is negotiated between interviewer and interviewee (see **5.3**) which determines the whole of the ensuing conversation. Both parties must quickly develop an image of who they are dealing with and how they will get on with one another in the next one or two hours. In this respect every interview is a unique and fleeting encounter that is extracted from the infinite, open and multi-voiced stream of everyday communication. Where is the 'real location' of this talk? What does this chance phenomenon tell us about the social universe of its occurrence? Who does it concern and who is speaking?

From the philosopher Georg Simmel we have the image of a plumb-line that can be sent, from any point on the surface of our existence, into the depths of the soul (1984: 195). The Surrealists spoke of the 'objective chance' of a momentous meeting. It is therefore vitally important for the social investigator who collects data in the form of an 'open interview' to develop significance out of contingency. We are talking to somebody and suddenly we have an entire world in our hands. To remain with Lotringer's image cited above: the interviewer allows the interviewee to occupy a particular corner from where one can glimpse a totality. Where we find ourselves then is a question of provisional suppositions that always remain uncertain and require further scrutiny.

5   SURRENDER TO THE OBJECT AND THE INSPIRATION OF THE CONCEPT

The problem is repeated in the analysis of material in protocols and documents. Where does one begin, and how does one read what is in the transcripts? No research process can begin without the decision of an interpreter who selects a location and understands what he or she reads there. These chance and casual everyday texts can only be talked about as a result of the involvement of a reader who stumbles on some formulation or takes seriously the declarative content of some utterance.

One condition for this kind of reading is the bracketing of one's own judgemental structures which underlie self-preservation motifs. Training in 'methodological stupidity' can transform an acting and experiencing everyday subject into an objective reader who abandons him- or herself to the pleasure of the text. For Roland Barthes (1976: 19), we can then choose between two alternative forms of reading: one goes straight to the expression of the biographical narrative, it looks at the extent of the text and ignores the linguistic games. The other reading omits nothing, it is cumbersome and sticks to the text; it reads, as it were, meticulously and obsessively. Where the first one proceeds rapidly, the other makes no headway. In the first case the pleasure focuses on the worked-out 'total biographical construction', while in the second it is the reconstructed intervals of sensuality. Although Barthes is decidedly of the opinion that only this second cumbersome form of reading is appropriate for modern texts, one would have to say that the type of reading one chooses will show what kind of person one is.

The use of 'methodological stupidity' requires the reader to restrain the affective reactions: these must be transformed into readings that can be tried out and then rejected. But affective reactions cannot be completely switched off, and the testing of readings cannot be infinitely pursued. K. H. Wolff (1976) characterized the tension that leads to an interpretation with the two expressions 'surrender' and 'catch'. One must surrender oneself to the material in order to be able to recognize structures within it. But how does the inspiration of the concept arise out of this surrender to the object? All interpretation depends on the involvement of a self-understanding individual. In the act of interpretation the distanced reader, buried in the text, turns into an engaged *ego* concerned with him- or herself. Hermeneutic philosophy speaks of a *draft quality* of understanding in which the futurity of a self-understanding *ego* may be found. Ultimately no one can be freed from the responsibility for an interpretation, and an investigator who does not dare to make this leap will never be able to grasp a concept.

6   AN OPEN FORM OF THE COMPLEX, THE TEMPORAL AND THE UNSTABLE

We have not only the art of the interview and the art of interpretation, but also the art of presentation. To this, particularly as a result of stimuli from ethnology, an increasing amount of attention has recently been devoted in the discussion of sociological methodology. (Good overviews of this may be found in Clifford and Marcus 1986 and in Berg and Fuchs 1993.) In principle, there is a choice between the systematic form of presentation, based on linear or circular conceptual derivations, the essayistic form devoted to detailed illumination of the essence (Bude 1989), and the narrative form, which follows a historical sequence (Bude 1993). Although in qualitative research narrative presentations are preferred (such as ethnological mystery stories, or a clinical story in the sense of the Chicago School, or a sociological portrait), every presentation requires an author. For writing, despite one or two attempts to develop a

sociological poetics (Brown 1977; Edmondson 1984; Nisbet 1976; or Clifford and Marcus 1986), there are few prescripts to which one could turn for guidance. For this reason writers quickly take refuge in the concept of style (Gumbrecht and Pfeiffer 1986), which, of course, completely obliterates the border between art and science because of its implications of aesthetic genius. For qualitative research a certain formal consciousness of the art of writing is important since the plausibility of research and the generalizability of its results are only manifest through the manner of presentation (see **5.22**).

In addition one must take account of the different purposes of generalization in the social sciences. In its single-case studies qualitative research is concerned with aggregated phenomena from personal life-worlds, organizational developments or social changes, and these cannot be traced back to single aspects of the behaviour of individuals. For this reason the process of generalization is concerned with the analysis of relationships between isolated indicators, but aims rather at the logical reconstruction of the sequential dynamic and the creative logic of social 'formations' and historic 'structures' (Mayntz 1985). The results of qualitative research, therefore, are not general theories with a claim to universal validity, universal applicability and universal relevance, but contextualized explanations which are of limited validity, local applicability and focused relevance (Jahoda 1989 makes this distinction between apodictic theories and casuistic explanations).

What corresponds to this, in terms of presentation, is an openness of form that works with meticulously detailed interpretations, economy of statement and provisional concepts. The author is then no longer a 'generalized other' (Mead 1934) who observes matters from a roving position and looks over people's shoulders, but rather a 'specific other' who is touched by social fault-lines and moved by historical events (cf. Bude 1988 for a discussion of this change of perspective). Because he/she cannot hide behind a theory, every explanation of his/her research object is also a self-explanation which reserves for the reader a place in the text. Contextualistic methodology therefore realizes itself in a strategy for text-production in which the temporal fixedness of the research object, the participatory perspective of the author, and the reader's share in the reception of the text are not merely mentioned as constitutive conditions but are presented as factual aspects.

It is a question of a form which steers attention to the complex, the temporal and the unstable in the social universe, and which moves away from the Cartesian ideal of separation towards the Heraclidean ideal of transformation (for discussion of this, cf. Thompson 1979; see also **5.11**). Freud had the following to say about this 'analytic mentality' (see **5.20**):

Psychoanalysis is not, like philosophies, a system starting out from a few sharply defined basic concepts, seeking to grasp the whole universe with the help of these and, once it is completed, having no room for fresh discoveries or better understanding. On the contrary, it keeps close to the facts in its field of study, seeks to solve the intermediate problems of observation, gropes its way forward by the help of experience, is always incomplete and always ready to correct or modify its theories. There is no incongruity (any more than is the case of physics or chemistry) if its most general concepts lack clarity and if its postulates are provisional; it leaves their more precise definition to the results of future work. (1893–95/1955, vol. XVIII: 253–254)

7 SINGULARITY AND SPECIFICITY

Freud was so aware that this process makes science resemble art that he was afraid his accounts of sickness, which could be read as short stories, would lack the serious stamp of being scientific. But only a thorough presentation of the spiritual events of single cases seemed to him to allow any advance in our understanding of the internal relations between a history of suffering and the symptoms of illness (1920–22/1955, vol. II: 160–161).

Here is the real difference between art and science: the art-form of the short story changes nothing in the scientific form of a case-history of illness. This is because it is not concerned with the case in itself, but with the insight into the operation of the psycho-pathological mechanism.

In the same way, qualitative research is always concerned with individual cases that do not occur twice; but it is not interested in their individuality as such, but rather seeks to understand them. The decisive interpretative step consists of the construction of a category that represents the concrete richness of a case. The feeling that a particular reconstruction provides evidence that defines a form or illuminates a structure derives from this (see **2.1**). Paul Veyne (1984) speaks of a transition from the inexpressible singularity to the captured specificity of a case. Science is not concerned with the mere uniqueness of individuals and events, but with what is simultaneously both general and particular about them. Its goal is the exposure of a case, not the recollection of an individual or an event.

In this way a social research with literary ambitions is not a rival but ultimately an enemy of literature. Art is indeed subject to the attraction of the ideal-typical, but nothing is more damaging to the aesthetic validity of a work of art than the proof that it was entirely congruent with the atmosphere and spirit of an age. There must be some insoluble difference that relates to the non-substitutable characteristics of the work. For literary presentation, unlike sociological presentation, seeks to express not what is specific but what is singular in a person or an event. The secret of the non-identical is missing in science. Roland Barthes (1969: 13) saw the particularity of a work of literature in the fact that it is always more than the sum of its sources, influences and models. It forms an irreducible core in the undecided mass of events, conditions and mentalities.

FURTHER READING

Clifford, J. (1988) *The Predicament of Culture – Twentieth-Century Ethnography, Literature, and Art*. Cambridge, MA: Harvard University Press.

Clifford, J. and Marcus, G. E. (eds) (1986) *Writing Culture – The Poetics and Politics of Ethnography*. Berkeley, CA: University of California Press.

Wolff, K. H. (1976) *Surrender and Catch: Experience and Inquiry Today*. Dordrecht: D. Reidel.

5.22   The Presentation of Qualitative Research

Eduard Matt

One essential activity for a social scientist is the writing of texts: proposals are written, research results and theories are presented, publications are prepared. For these purposes data and analyses have to be 'translated' for the reader into an appropriate form or mode of representation. This (re-)construction of the subject is accomplished by means of the presentation of results (Redfield 1948). For the textual representation of reality there is no one procedure that may be absolutely canonized.

It is possible to distinguish a number of inter-related aspects of writing and textual discussion: the concrete writing difficulties of the scientist; the manner in which the research subjects are put in words in the scientist's texts and the question of how one can avoid objectivizing the other; writing for a particular purpose and for a specific audience. Writing shows itself to be an interaction between theoretical assumptions, the (re-)construction of the research issue, rhetorical strategies and the recipients. At the same time scientific texts themselves may be analysed in respect of their construction. The presentations of data, explanations and theories indicate both epistemological assumptions and strategies for the production of credibility and plausibility.

1   HISTORY OF THE DEBATE

The problems of presentation are a subject of current discussion in anthropology and ethnology under the heading 'the crisis in ethnographic representation'. The works of Clifford Geertz in particular (see **2.6**; Fröhlich and Mörth 1998; Wolff 1992) demand a reconsideration and re-formulation of the relationship between observation, interpretation and textual representation. The crisis arose out of discussions about the validity of studies and about post-colonialism. The unveiling of falsifications, plagiarisms, 'pure fiction', the admission that very different results were achieved in replications of studies, stimulated doubts about the authenticity and reliability of individual observations and complete studies, and about the authority of ethnography (cf. Duerr 1987). There was additional criticism of 'cultural imperialism', which takes the meaning patterns and life-forms of the Western world as being valid, exemplary and standard for the whole world.

For sociologists the description of one's own culture is not without problems (Hollander 1965). In qualitative research there is also an attempt no longer to subordinate the reality of others to theoretically derived categories but to take account of the historical milieu-specific and/or gender-specific features of particular situations. The attempt to understand the 'other', to do justice to the particular structure of a case and to (re-)present this with appropriate textual constructions presents the various disciplines, in different ways, with a common task.

2 THEORETICAL BACKGROUNDS

What is central to qualitative research is the concept of 'reality as text'. The result of the objectivization of meaning, the fixed representational patterns of reality, are themselves characterized as text (Latin *textus* = fabric). The particular quality of social interaction, its fleetingness accompanied by meaning production, can only be subjected to analysis if it is first put into the form of a text. The written text is considered to be the inscription of a meaning structure that has to be reconstructed. Fixing it in this way also frees it from the specific action context. In this way action gains autonomy, and can only then be interpreted beyond the specific individual interpretation and intention of the participants (Ricoeur 1981b). To reconstruct the modes of producing reality, the resources and strategies that are socially, culturally and historically applied in varying ways, means that the social scientist has to abandon objectivist assumptions and adopt a hermeneutic position (Geertz 1973b; Soeffner 1989).

Of course, cultural action is fixed in the form of objectivizations, but a text of this sort cannot be read easily: reality should not be thought of as a homologous structure but should be characterized with reference to its ambiguity, complexity and inconsistency (Geertz 1973a,b). Reading means 'decoding, developing a reading', that is to say, the production and preparation of a toolkit of concepts and categories with which the available 'texts' acquire a meaningful interpretation. To create this interpretative framework, to construct the relevance of an event, is the task of the researcher. The description of an event takes place from this perspective, and thereby determines which data, and how much of the data, are presented. Every explanation is selective, and represents a selection from an infinite number of descriptive possibilities (Sacks 1963). Every narrative 'as it really was' is a construction for specific purposes and for a specific audience, and never a mere reproduction (Bergmann 1985). To construct means neither to depict nor to reproduce a reality, but to discover how a meaning (and what kind of meaning) is established and created on the basis of what resources, and how reality (and what kind of reality) is produced in and through situations, symbols and objectivizations. At the same time we have the principle of reflexivity: questions of constituting an object and questions of capturing the constitution of an object refer to one another (cf. Pollner 1991).

This confronts the investigator with a practical problem of how to analyse data and present results with, or on the basis of, these data. In this different foci may be distinguished, such as single-case orientation, description of milieu, an emphasis on typical structures or a generalization of structures. Each of these emphases leads to a different analysis, interpretation and presentation of the data; they may be used as documentation of authenticity, as evidence or merely as an illustration. The route that is selected depends on the epistemological interest of the investigator, but equally on the data themselves: what problems, constitutive features or structures do they document? The variability of analyses is not an argument for randomness in qualitative research but an expression of a recognition of the unique structural nature of the research field and of the different epistemological interests.

The presentation of reality is always a simultaneous construction of reality. The way in which data, evidence and results are organized also sets up a corresponding interpretation of the world. The appropriateness and authority of the descriptions are simultaneously expressed in specific textual forms. The freedom of movement in a presentation, however, is not arbitrary. The 'construction of reality' by sociologists has its effects and its limitations in socio-historical knowledge.

Todorov (1989) discusses the question of the success of descriptions in relation to 'truth and fiction' using the example of how America got its name. It was not the discoverer, Columbus, but his navigator, Amerigo Vespucci, who became the patron of the New World. Todorov relates this to their different descriptions of the discovery. Columbus preferred a rather scientific, documentary and factual style that was characteristic of medieval thinking (emphasis on the wealth discovered, character of paradise, presence of spirits and monsters). His addressee was the Spanish royal household, and his aim was to obtain money for further expeditions. Amerigo Vespucci, on the other hand, cultivated a literary style; he wrote for a broad public whom he sought to entertain. For him it was a matter of fame rather than truth. Correspondingly in his work there are many exaggerations, and the curious is highlighted. His explanations are an expression of the contemporary European conception of the others as savages (cannibalism, sexual perversion, heathenism). Columbus, in his illustrations, is rooted in traditional drawings. Vespucci, in contrast, also attempts to reproduce in his drawings what is specifically 'American', in other words, to translate into pictures his imaginings. The success of his mode of presentation played a role in linking his name to the newly discovered continent.

3 LIMITATIONS AND SCOPE OF THE DEBATE

With the recognition of the constructive activity of the subject, the style of realism (naturalism), with its assumption of a 'real, true' world beyond our recognition and representation, loses conviction. In competition with this, two continuing discourses have developed: postmodernism and social constructivism (see **3.4**).

According to the 'postmodern' (cf. Clifford and Marcus 1986; Marcus and Fischer 1986; Clifford 1988a; *kea* 4/1992; Berg and Fuchs 1993; Bachmann-Medick 1996) it is no longer possible to find any overall meaning in the world. Texts can no longer create unity or order; only fragments, incomplete discourses, or different versions can be represented. Since everything is interpretation, the representatives of postmodernism dispute the possibility of capturing reality. They concentrate on the analysis of aesthetic dimensions, such as stylistic analysis which can succeed without reference to the truth content of what is represented. It is no longer necessary to test (or validate) the relation of a text to reality, its theoretical force, its new discoveries about the world, but rather its written style, its production of authority and authenticity (see **3.3**).

In contrast to this, in the social constructivist debate (see **3.4**), which is of greater consequence in qualitative research, what is of interest is precisely the modes of construction, the socio-cultural knowledge, the interpretations of the world and the power relations that underpin this 'reality of constructions' in a society. But even here it is not a matter of the truth content of statements but of their social creation and location. The reconstruction and analysis of these is one of the goals of qualitative research.

4 DIFFERENT WAYS OF PRESENTATION

The act of writing is problematic for the majority of sociologists. Here everyone has developed individual rituals, styles and procedures. What is troublesome are the two basic considerations: not being able to structure an event appropriately, and fear that what is presented could be untrue. Nevertheless, many sociologists adhere to an objective description of facts, and they find it difficult to accept that there is not a single correct and ultimately valid text, but that different texts have to be produced for different purposes (Becker 1986b). *En route* from experience to textual presentation it is even permissible to write different versions of a plausible text.

Van Maanen (1988) distinguishes three main forms of textual presentation. *Realistic presentation* is factual, written in the third person and dominated by a documentary style – the language of facts. The level of experience is played down. What is typical is foregrounded in the description, creating an objective reality. The researcher as author plays no role here: he or she functions as an impartial observer. Even self-interpretations of what is observed are avoided. What is produced is a single unambiguous description on the part of the researcher.

Confessional description has to do with a very personal style: the investigator is narrating from the field, with practical fieldwork experiences concerning access, experiences, feelings and, beyond that, how he or she was changed by the field. This is written in the first person, personal assumptions and prejudices are admitted, and a possible version – that of the investigator – is produced.

Impressionistic description is also highly personal. Here the researcher attempts to transport the audience into the world of what was investigated and to tell a gripping and extraordinary story from the field. What the investigator recalls as valuable in his or her activity is highlighted. The focus is on reliving the story, not on the interpretation or analysis. Only a very small part of the research issue is presented. The preferred textual form for this is the essay (Bude 1989). The frontier with literature is breached (see **3.3**, **5.21**).

We may observe the development that dissatisfaction with the traditional realistic presentation – dryly reporting results, but with no reference to the experiential side of research – the multiple experiences of the data-collection process, the vitality and colourfulness of the research issue, the symbolic worlds, everyday action and meaning-worlds of others, has led to the development of new modes of presentation: diaries (Malinowski 1967), the ethnological novel (e.g. Bowen 1964), poems (or ethnopoetry), literary presentations of experience in the fieldwork situation (Barley 1986). This has led to an enormous variety of such 'experiments' (Hirschauer and Amann 1997; Richardson 1994). The traditional medium of the written text offers only very limited possibilities of describing milieux or cultures which are authoritatively defined in such other forms as dance and music. Other means and media of expression are sought, such as audio reproduction and film presentation. The documentation of data or of analysis is achieved with the inclusion of a cassette or a CD-ROM. A more recent development, the production of 'hypertexts' on the Internet, also gives rise to new questions of writing: these are not characterized by classic internally closed content, but by their 'links' to other texts, or to involvement in many discussion threads (see **5.8**).

The different modes of presentation are also an expression of a variety of methodologies. The textuality of scientific texts is thereby made into an object of analysis. Such texts may be analysed, in respect of their rhetoric, for their creation of authority and credibility (e.g. Atkinson 1990; Knauth and Wolff 1990). Bazerman (1987), for example – using the example of rules for writing up psychological studies for publication in specialist journals – was able to demonstrate how the basic behaviourist assumptions of the discipline or of a particular school were documented in the modes of presentation. The relationship between theoretical concepts, textual presentation and argument therefore becomes an object of analysis (for example, using a range of authors: Geertz 1988; using Goffman's work: Atkinson 1989; further examples: *Sociological Theory* 1990).

Validation strategies

Essential textual strategies for validation in qualitative research are the disclosure of the procedure and the process of interpretation (its transparency), the presentation of the relevant data material, the reproduction of transcripts, field notes and so on (see **4.7**). The emphasis on transparency is important since the choice of data already constitutes an interpretation of the significance of what is reported. In theoretical works quotations and literary references fulfil a similar function. Moreover, diagrams, charts or illustrations for the visualization of theoretical relationships also convey the impression of rationality and may be analysed as strategies for persuasion.

Even if all of these requirements are met, there is still the problem of justifying the appropriateness of constructions. Geertz claims (1988: 140) that 'the burden of authorship cannot be evaded' (see **2.6**). The scientist is personally responsible for the quality of his or her work and bears the moral responsibility for taking care. The goal of this requirement is to make one's own authorship visible in a text, and to make clear one's own ideas, perspectives and competences. One cannot escape this burden by referring to methodological disagreements.

Texts are written for an audience who have to be convinced with the aid of credibly expressed arguments and analyses. The acceptability of a scientific text is dependent above all on the rules for research and text production that are recognized in the particular scientific community. Especially in the social sciences there is a clear bond to a specific audience. The relationship of the author to *his or her* scientific community functions, therefore, as a production factor and as a validation criterion for a scientific text (Reichertz 1992; see **4.7**). And so the reference to the context of the study, to its embedding in the specific practical circumstances and institutional frameworks where it was carried out, tells the reader why the text has this particular form (analysis, textual presentation). Validity is measured according to the relevance and appropriateness of the analysis in respect of knowledge of the area of study. In other words, we may ask: To what extent does this author's work contribute to an expansion of the framework for the discussion and interpretation of social reality?

If the 'reality of a description' is constituted through an interactive act, if both parties belong to the process – the rhetoric of the author and the inference of the reader/hearer – if it is not only the author's voice but also the recipient's ear that require understanding and explanation, then all attempts to justify or guarantee the validity, relevance or force of a description or an analysis – by the use of appropriate literary expressions, persuasive strategies or appealing to methodological premises – are ultimately doomed to failure. The 'success' of a work is seen as an achievement of the milieu in which it is competently received and discussed. On this process the author – as an author – has only a small influence.

FURTHER READING

Becker, H. S. (1986) *Writing for the Social Scientist: How to Start and Finish Your Thesis, Book or Article*. Chicago: Chicago University Press.

Clifford, J. and Marcus, G. E. (eds) (1986) *Writing Culture. The Poetics and Politics of Ethnography.* Berkeley, CA: University of California Press.

Van Maanen, J. (ed.) (1995) *Representation in Ethnography*. Thousand Oaks, CA: Sage.

Part 6

Qualitative Research in Context

Introduction

The theoretical and methodological possibilities and alternative forms of qualitative research that have been treated in the earlier parts of this book provide a comprehensive and well-tried resource which the researcher may use for issue-related, theory-driven and relevant studies. The practice of qualitative research not only takes place in different areas of reality; it must also react to contextual conditions of its own practice, to ethical questions, to problems of teaching and instruction and to the problems of its social application.

The contributions to this part again have been divided into subsections. The first (Part 6A) focuses on 'the use of qualitative research' in several respects. The use of qualitative research can be embedded in contexts of research ethics, of teaching and of utilization of result for practical purposes.

Dealing with matters of research ethics (see **6.1**) requires particular sensitivity in qualitative research. Through ethnographic procedures, it obtains profound insights into aspects of society that are otherwise relatively inaccessible. It has to deal with sensitive documents and materials, which can be used and abused for social control, and on occasions its subject-related procedures impinge upon the dignity, informational self-determination and interests of the person.

Qualitative research has always been particularly resistant to all attempts to reduce it to methodological directives and rules. One reason for this is that good studies always 'live' to a great extent on the basis of the researchers' personalities and the methods they use (cf. Part 2 of this book). This does not make it easy to translate research competence and attitudes into teaching. Nevertheless, the future of qualitative research will also depend on whether successful teaching methods for qualitative research can be found. General problems and examples of methods of teaching qualitative research will be dealt with in the relevant chapter (see **6.2**).

Communicating the results of qualitative research in contexts of social practice constitutes a third domain (see **6.3**), where it can itself exert only limited influence, but which – for this very reason – it must think about very intensively. The great proximity to everyday life and the 'thickness' of its procedures and results makes qualitative research particularly vulnerable to external trivialization and downgrading to the non-committal anecdote.

The second subsection of this part addresses qualitative research in the context of its future development (Part 6B). Three chapters discuss 'the future and challenges of qualitative research'. From different positions, their authors look critically at the present, past and expected future development of qualitative research. The future and the prospects for qualitative research are also discussed in the context of international trends and in the relationship of tension that exists between techniques and hermeneutics (see **6.4**). The challenges of qualitative research include the development of methodological procedures that are easy to use in practical contexts and commissioned research where time is at a premium (see **6.5**). In both chapters, attention is paid to the need to deal with the question of appropriate quality criteria (see **4.7**). In view of the large numbers of methods that have been developed and projects that have been completed, this part ends with a consideration of the role of theory development in present-day research, which, for Anselm Strauss, (see **2.1**) was a goal – if not the only one – of qualitative research (see **6.6**).

6.1   Research Ethics and Qualitative Research

Christel Hopf

1   INTRODUCTION – NORMATIVE AND LEGAL BASES

Under the keyword 'research ethics' it is usual in social sciences to group together all those ethical principles and rules in which it is determined – in a more or less binding and more or less consensual way – how the relationships between researchers on the one hand and those involved in sociological research on the other hand are to be handled. Typical questions, which are also regularly asked in qualitative research, include the following: the question of how voluntary was participation in the investigations, the question of guaranteeing anonymity and confidentiality, or the question of the admissibility of undercover forms of observation.

Whereas in American sociology a start was already made in the 1960s with establishing principles and rules of research ethics in the form of a comprehensive 'code of ethics',[1] in German sociology this only happened at the beginning of the 1990s. The members of the German Society for Sociology (DGS) and the Professional Association of German Sociologists, after comprehensive discussions within the organization, agreed on a code of ethics (cf. Ethik-Kodex 1993) in which – apart from questions of teaching, reviewing and the like – central questions of research ethics were also dealt with.

It is not, however, only professionally agreed principles and requirements that have to be considered in dealing with the norms governing one's own research practice: there are also the legal requirements. In Germany the state and federal data protection laws (for an overview cf. Gola and Schomerus 1997), governing the collection, storage, transmission and publication of sociological data, contain principles and regulations that are immediately relevant from the point of view of research ethics. What is fundamental here is the requirement to preserve the right to privacy, or to preserve 'the individual's right to determine personal information' (Gola and Schomerus 1997: 113), which has led to the many regulations dealing with the collection and analysis of sociological data. For example, the principle of informed consent not only derives from discussions of research ethics within sociology or psychology, but is also set down in law (cf. in this connection particularly §4 and §40 of the Federal Data Protection Act of 1990-BDS9).

In the United States, the UK and other countries, comparable ethical regulations for research exist. These are defined in the different codes of ethics of the specific professional and scientific organizations. Often they are also defined in a juridical form, on the basis of either laws or of administrative regulations.

In the context of the questions of research ethics that are discussed in the social scientific disciplines in different countries, philosophical problems play a role, too. The distinction of a deontological and a utilitarian ethic known from the philosophical discussion of ethics is taken up (see for an overview, for example, Beauchamp 1982) in order to position one's own research ethical options in this framework (see, for example, Kvale 1996: 121–123 or Birch et al. 2002: 5–9). It is asked: How far are one's own research ethical claims compulsory in the sense of Kant's ethics? Do utilitarian aspects play a decisive role in defining research ethic regulations or is it possible to argue for single deviations from the rules in a utilitarian way, for example with respect to the gain of knowledge? A closer look at different codes of ethics in the area of social sciences reveals that in the reality of research ethical regulations, mostly models of compromise are formulated. The compulsory character of specific regulations is highlighted, but deviations from the regulations are accepted in certain cases, if these serve the progress of knowledge and thus are founded in utility. One example for this can be found in the 'Code of Ethics' of the American Sociological Association (ASA) of 1997. In this code, the 'informed consent' as 'a basic ethical tenet of scientific research on human populations' (see Section 12) is acknowledged, but exceptions are accepted. These exceptions are only acceptable under certain conditions, but are defined in a utilitarian way, if 'the research could not practicably be carried out were informed consent to be required' (see section 2 of this chapter; see also **5.5**).

In what follows a selection of ethical and legal requirements will be presented, discussed and explored as to their research significance in the area of qualitative investigations. This will make it clear that questions of research ethics in qualitative research – in comparison to quantitative research – are more radical and also more difficult to solve. This is true both for the

implementation of the principle of informed consent and also for the guaranteeing of confidentiality and anonymity. For example, population surveys that are based on representative samples should not in general cause too much concern, even when they touch upon delicate matters. In subsequent research reports promises of confidentiality and anonymity may easily be kept, whereas the research reports on individual cases, communities or organizations – even when all the names involved are made anonymous and additional strategies for guaranteeing anonymity are used – can more easily lead to ethical problems and conflicts with the individuals involved in investigations (on this cf. Section 3; see also **5.1**).

2 THE PRINCIPLE OF INFORMED CONSENT

In the Code of Ethics of the German Society for Sociology and the Professional Association of German Sociologists this is described as follows:

> A general rule for participation in sociological investigations is that it is voluntary and that it takes place on the basis of the fullest possible information about the goals and methods of the particular piece of research. The principle of informed consent cannot always be applied in practice, for instance if comprehensive pre-information would distort the results of the research in an unjustifiable way. In such cases an attempt must be made to use other possible modes of informed consent. (Ethik-Kodex 1993: I B 2)

The group who developed the German Code of Ethics[2] related this formulation of the principle of informed consent to the requirement that the right to privacy of individuals involved in sociological investigations should always be protected. At the same time the possibility of some short-term deception, which might sometimes be necessary in social–psychological experiments, should not be barred from the outset. In such cases, as the above citation makes clear, other possibilities for informed consent should be used. What was intended here, in particular, was that temporarily deceived participants should be given the possibility, after subsequent explanation of the true purpose of the study, to withdraw the data collected – a possibility, incidentally, which is prescribed in German law (cf. BDSG 1990 §4).

The principle of voluntary participation in an investigation, and the requirement to inform potential participants as fully as possible in advance to enable them to decide appropriately about participation, exclude the possibility that groups or organizations could be deceived for an extended period about the identity and goals of social researchers who are observing 'undercover'. In such cases the principle of voluntary participation would be infringed in a serious manner that would be very hard to justify.

However, it should be noticed that 'undercover' research is less massively rejected in the 'Code of Ethics' of the ASA, even in the latest version of 1997. Paragraph 12.05(d) states: 'On rare occasions, sociologists may need to conceal their identity in order to undertake research that could not practically be carried out were they to be known as researchers.' In the 1960s and 1970s, the problems and risks linked to this issue were discussed very intensely within American sociology (see also Ryen 2004). The exception cited above is a consequence of these discussions. Thus one might not abandon at the outset, for example, a project to make an empirical study of organized crime (see, for example, Lofland 1961: 366). From the point of view of a deontological ethics (see also section 1 of this chapter), the exception accepted by the 'Code of Ethics' of the ASA can definitely not be justified. How can it be justified that the personal rights of a criminal should be less respected in sociology than those of an average citizen? According to utilitarian principles, however, one might be more liberal here. But the researcher has also to justify in this case why the study he or she wants to run is so valuable that it warrants breaking the rules (see also section 1 above).

Even when there is broad agreement in sociology on the rejection of undercover participant observation, the questions related to the principle of informed participation are still uncertain. In qualitative research – and particularly in primarily exploratory projects – it is therefore not always easy to give convincing and accurate information in advance about one's own research goals and research planning (on this and the following points, cf. Roth 1962; see also 5.1). In addition, it is conceivable that, even when comprehensive information is given about research goals and procedures, the information given will not be fully understood or will be wrongly interpreted by interviewees or participants.

In presenting one's own research plan one must therefore also allow for the perceptual, interpretative and value horizons of the groups under investigation (cf. Thorne 1980, and also the Ethik-Kodex 1993: I B4). The essential adjustment to the population under investigation can, however, be taken too far and lead to the suppression of offensive information which could endanger willingness to participate. For example, in a research group dealing with right-extremist orientations in young women we avoided using the term 'right-extremist' in the information on the planned study that we provided for experts and participants (cf. Projektgruppe 1996: 89ff.). Our impression was that the term 'right-extremist' led to strong defensive reactions, which we wished to avoid, thereby probably going to the limits of what was acceptable in terms of research ethics: indeed, we may well have exceeded those limits.

The fact that the principle of informed consent is in no sense easy to implement in qualitative research is also made clear in an article by Herbert Gans (1982) on the problems of participant observation. In this, he describes the fears with which fieldworkers are confronted. These also include the fear and uncertainty that relate to dishonesty toward the persons under investigation (cf. Gans 1982: 59f.). Even when those in the research field are informed appropriately and truthfully about the role of the researcher, elements of deception remain. The researcher 'pretends to participate emotionally when he does not; he observes even when he does not appear to be doing so, and like the formal interviewer, he asks questions with covert purposes of which his respondents are likely to be unaware. In short, psychologically, the participant observer is acting dishonestly; he is deceiving people about his feelings, and in observing when they do not know it, he is spying on them' (Gans 1982: 59). In the opinion of Herbert Gans, a consequence of this is that participant observers are confronted with feelings of guilt that they seek to diminish by over-identification with the informants (see 5.5). Whatever, in detail, the psychic consequences for the researchers might be, the problem of partial deception in participant observation is highly relevant. Here the limits that have to be set to the principle of informed consent become clear. At the same time, the problem of partial deception should sharpen our awareness of the social and psychological risks for the investigators that are associated with participant observation, and which make supervision and counselling essential elements of the research process.

3 THE PRINCIPLE OF DAMAGE AVOIDANCE

In the debates on research ethics there is no dissent on the requirement not to inflict damage on those involved in investigations. As with the principle of informed consent, the difficulties here are in the practical implementation and in the borderline cases.

In the Code of Ethics of the German Society for Sociology and the Professional Association of German Sociologists the principle of damage avoidance is described as follows:

> Persons who are observed, questioned or who are involved in some other way in investigations, for example in connection with the analysis of personal documents, shall not be subject to any disadvantages or dangers as a result of the research. All risks that exceed what is normal in everyday life must be explained to the parties concerned. The anonymity of interviewees or informants must be protected. (Ethik-Kodex 1993: I B 5)

Similar rules apply in many countries, either in codes of ethics in the realm of the social sciences or in laws or administrative regulations. In calculating possible impairment or damage resulting from social research, it is normal to proceed on the basis that those involved in sociological investigations – unlike those, for instance, in some kinds of medical research – are endangered less by the investigation itself than by the possible consequences of participation, particularly through breach of promises of confidentiality (cf. Tropp 1982: 399ff. for discussion of this). The obligation to keep promises of confidentiality belongs, to this extent, to the normative essentials of research ethics in sociology. Breaches of this obligation, as will be made clear in the following sections, may arise because of the release of personal data or as a result of sociological publications in which the informants, regions or institutions were not made sufficiently anonymous.

Release of personal data

Elmar Weingarten describes the case of a sociologist who was convicted in the 1980s by an American court. He had on several occasions ignored legal summonses and refused to make his field research notes available to the court (cf. Weingarten 1986: 220 for discussion of this and the following points). The background was that the sociologist in question – Mario Brajuha – was working on his doctoral dissertation, which was based on a workplace investigation in a restaurant. For this purpose – in the sense of the normal procedure for participant observation – he worked as a cook and a waiter in the restaurant in question and, in accordance with normal practice, had kept field notes on his experience. Towards the end of his employment the restaurant went up in flames and the police suspected arson – hence the interest in his records, which he refused to hand over. The trial ended in a settlement: the court did not insist that Brajuha hand over his notes, but he was required to pay a fine and costs amounting to several thousand dollars.

In principle, a case of this sort could also happen elsewhere. Sociologists in Germany – unlike priests or doctors, for example – have no right to withhold evidence and could therefore come under similar pressure from the police and the courts to hand over data. This is particularly relevant for sociologists working with deviant behaviour and criminality. In the German Code of Ethics that was cited above, consideration is given to this possibility and an attempt is made to give at least a moral justification of the right to withhold evidence: 'Sociologists, with reference to corresponding regulations for other professions, should be subject to the obligation to remain silent if there is reason to fear that, on the basis of information obtained in the course of sociological research, informants could be at risk of sanctions of whatever kind, including legal sanctions' (Ethik-Kodex 1993: I B 8).

Damage to informants through the release of information is possible not only in these striking ways but also in less drastic cases. Causes of this might be: inadequate security in the handling of original data (including sound recordings, or unencoded field notes), discussion of individual cases outside the work of the project, and neglect of the obligation to confidentiality, inadequate guaranteeing of anonymity in published documents and negligence in the electronic storage of unencoded data (for a collection of examples of this cf. Sieber 1992: 52ff.).

One of the results of modern data protection laws and recent debates on research ethics is that social research is much more intensively concerned today with guaranteeing promises of confidentiality and anonymity than was the case in the 1960s. In general terms, this has increased the volume of work in empirical research projects. In planning qualitative research projects it must also be considered that here it is more difficult to make data anonymous than in quantitative projects: large interview transcripts or observation reports that contain many more or less overt clues as to the identity of informants and the context of the investigation have to be made anonymous in such a way that no possible conclusions can be drawn about the persons, organizations and regions in the context of which the data collection took place, and at the same time in such a way that the information content is not so diminished that any analysis becomes pointless.

If one particular trend that can be observed today should continue, then in future even more care will have to be taken to make anonymous and to encode qualitative data. The requirement to pass on data for use in other research contexts and for central archiving, with which quantitative research has long had to deal, has in recent years also been increasingly directed at qualitative research (cf. Sieber 1992: 62f. for general discussion, and for qualitative research Kluge and Opitz 1999a). This has thrown up a large number of new organizational and ethical questions. Of these, the problems in the area of technology are of least importance, since in qualitative research anonymized reports of interviews and observations are often stored electronically. What is more difficult, on the other hand, is dealing with questions of research ethics and data protection law related to the dissemination of data. Informants must be asked for their agreement; this is given on the principle of informed consent and on the basis of the right to control personal information. There must also be a guarantee that the data truly contain no clue as to the organizational or regional context of the study. With qualitative projects that relate to particular organizations or regions this may well be difficult to realize, and may even be impossible. For this reason, in qualitative research one should approach with caution and scepticism the requirement to make text files available for central archiving and dissemination.

Problems of publication

It is possible to harm informants not only by exposing information about individuals, but also by talking about them as a group, in publications, in a way which they find harmful or which actually leads to some disadvantage for them.

A famous example of this is the so-called 'Springdale case' which will be described here briefly. In 1958 Arthur Vidich and Joseph Bensman published the results of a predominantly qualitative study of a small town in New York State (*Small Town in Mass Society*) – made anonymous under the name of 'Springdale'. The data on which the book was based had been collected by Vidich in the context of a research project at Cornell University, where, by the time of publication, he was no longer employed.

In terms of research ethics what Vidich and Bensman did was problematic from a number of different points of view (cf. the discussion in the journal *Human Organization*, vols 17–19, 1958–60). One of the problems was that anonymization was only partially successful. The individuals who were reported on in the study had indeed been given imaginary names. They were recognizable, however, on the basis of the particular descriptions of their functions (such as mayor, chief executive, and so on).

In general, people in 'Springdale' were upset and very annoyed – although this was not only because of the inadequate safeguarding of their anonymity but also because of the interpretations. It was the ideas on power structure in the community that seemed to cause particular annoyance, and also the claim that there was in Springdale a kind of 'invisible government' in which influential people who held no public office none the less determined the destiny of the small town (cf. Becker 1969: 260).

This incident unleashed a considerable controversy in the profession, which found its expression particularly in the journal *Human Organization*. Vidich and Bensman (1958, 1959) justified their conduct to their critics – for example William F. Whyte, who had voiced criticism in the journal's editorial – by pointing out that in investigations of organizations and communities negative reactions are to be expected if powerful groups and persons of respect figure in the research results. In the context of officially organized research and under the influence of public research funding these kinds of negative reactions have, unfortunately, become increasingly problematic. Here the following maxim applies: avoid annoyance and conflicts so that future funding will be available. But if one wishes, in sociology, to contribute to scientific progress and to address fundamental sociological problems, then one should not bow to this pressure but should preserve sufficient independence to be able to risk negative reactions and conflicts.

However illuminating the arguments of Vidich and Bensman may be from a scientific and political viewpoint, they ignore the legitimate demand of the individuals and institutions being investigated not to be harmed by the research process and research results. Pointing to scientific progress is of no further help in this, because it is rarely possible in the social sciences to reach agreement on which investigation will contribute to scientific progress and which will not. This depends both on the multiplicity of different paradigms in sociology – in theoretical and methodological approaches – and also on the fact that considerations of relevance and value always play a role in judging the contribution made by particular investigations to scientific progress. An investigation that is considered brilliant from a methodological viewpoint may none the less be considered unproductive, because the questions it deals with are felt to be irrelevant.

At a general level it is therefore impossible, in my opinion, to strike a rational balance between the contribution that a piece of research makes to scientific progress and its possible harmful effect, and, on the basis of this, to come to a decision whether to publish or not. One solution to this problem, which is difficult to implement in practice, might consist of giving those involved in the investigation the opportunity – as a matter of principle – of expressing their opinion on the planned content before any publication. What is not acceptable, in my opinion, is that questions of balancing costs against benefits – that is, weighing up possible damage against relevant knowledge-gain – should be left

to committees of research ethics, as is partly the case in the United States (cf. Sieber 1992: 75ff.). In view of the fact that in assessing the contribution that a sociological project has made to scientific progress political factors also play a role, there would be a danger that an ethical scrutiny of a piece of research would become a matter of political discipline.

NOTES

1 Cf. The Code of Ethics of the American Sociological Association (ASA 1969) *Toward a Code of Ethics,* which has been modified several times and voted on repeatedly – the last occasion being in 1997.
2 The group was made up as follows. From the German Society for Sociology: the then president Bernhard Schäfers, Dirk Käsler, who played an important role in initiating the debate on the Code of Ethics, and myself (at that time a member of the board and leader of the working party); from the Association of German Sociologists: the then president Siegfried Lamnek; and from the then still existing (East German) Society for Sociology: Hansgünter Meyer (until 1992 president of the society).

FURTHER READING

Becker, H. S. (1969) 'Problems in the Publication of Field Studies', in G. J. McCall and J. L. Simmsons (eds), *Issues in Participant Observation: A Text and Reader*. New York: Random House. pp. 260–270 (originally published 1964).

Ryen, A. (2004) 'Ethical Issues', in C. Seale, G. Gobo, J. F. Gubrium and D. Silverman (eds), *Qualitative Research Practice*. London: Sage. pp. 230–247.

Sieber, J. E. (1992) *Planning Ethically Responsible Research. A Guide for Students and Internal Review Boards*. Newbury Park, CA: Sage.

6.2 Teaching Qualitative Research

Uwe Flick and Martin Bauer

Qualitative research is taught today in a variety of contexts. In many places it has been accepted into the basic courses in methodological training, is sometimes taught as a subject in its own right as a supplement to such basic courses, and special courses are available as part of a higher qualification in qualitative research techniques for graduates in social sciences. There have hitherto been few explicit descriptions of how it should be taught, and few reports of experience which set out an individual approach or a range of ideas and practices in the teaching of qualitative research that could offer guidance to those who wish to design a course of this nature. The purpose of this chapter is to provide an outline of objectives and procedures for the teaching of qualitative research (methods) in these differing contexts. Section 3 offers a presentation of the approach of the London School of Economics, while section 4 uses an example from the Technical University of Berlin.

1 OBJECTIVES OF TEACHING QUALITATIVE METHODS

A variety of goals may be associated with the teaching of qualitative research – perhaps providing an overview of the increasingly heterogeneous field of qualitative approaches and procedures, or giving a detailed introduction into concrete techniques. In the few publications explicitly devoted to this topic (e.g. Glesne and Webb 1993; Strauss 1987, 1988; Webb and Glesne 1992), emphasis is given to the fact that courses in qualitative research differ sharply from other methods courses. The rationale for this, first and foremost, is that qualitative research can only be understood if it is taught in a way that includes practical procedures and source material. Here keywords such as 'learning by doing', 'learning in the field', 'learning with source material' take on a special significance. Since different qualitative methods (still) have something of the character of a *Kunstlehre* (art) – this is true of objective hermeneutics (see **5.16**) and also of Strauss's procedure (see **2.1**, **5.13**) – what is important in teaching is to strike the right balance between technique, attitude and the art of applying the method. Accordingly, a number of authors (e.g. Strauss 1988: 92) have recommended that seminars be designed as workshops that should be conducted with (sometimes significantly) fewer than 20 students (Glesne and Webb 1993: 260). Both types of goal – overview and practical 'hands on' experience – may best be achieved with a combination of different courses and types of courses.

- Survey courses (e.g. 'Introduction to qualitative research')

- Experience-oriented seminars (e.g. 'Methods of text-interpretation')
- Work-related courses (e.g. 'Setting up and carrying out interviews'); methods of interviewing and interpreting are best taught and learned in combination with practical applications and joint analysis of experience and problems. One way to achieve this is through systematic interview training.
- Seminars on the epistemological foundations of qualitative research (e.g. 'Constructivism – Variants and their implications for qualitative research', 'The justification of qualitative research').
- Issue-related teaching-research projects (study projects) that make it possible to work over an extended period, using one or more methods, on a particular question. Projects of this sort provide the framework for gaining practical experience which facilitates understanding of the possibilities and limitations of qualitative methods.

Webb and Glesne (1992: 786ff.) distinguish, by analogy, between introductory, research-design, theory-based and field-based research courses. The aim of this kind of teaching is to put students in the position

- to make a justified choice of methods;
- to understand the underlying principles of different procedures;
- to evaluate data in respect of their potential to provide evidence for particular questions;
- to interpret either pre-existing or the student's own research results; and finally
- to design and carry out one's own empirical investigations, in the framework of a graduate thesis and subsequent professional activity.

There are two basic ways to achieve these objectives. A rather detailed approach, which tends to put the analysis of available material in the foreground and focus on appropriate methods, should be distinguished from a process-oriented way which proceeds from the finding and framing of research questions, via case selection, data collection, transcription and analysis, to preparation of research reports. As a first venture with this second variant one might use, for example, a film such as Karin Brandauer's *Einstweilen wird es Mittag*, which is based on the study by Jahoda et al. (1933/1971,

cf. Jahoda 1995) of the unemployed in Marienthal. With the story of this film the essential steps, conflicts and problems of a qualitative study may readily be illustrated and discussed. In parallel, or as a supplement to this, the reading of the original study may be recommended (see **2.8**).

2 SPECIAL PROBLEMS IN TEACHING QUALITATIVE RESEARCH

In designing a teaching programme one question that arises is what literature should be used for basic orientation – for the teacher in designing the seminars, and for the students for further reading and private study. There is now a range of textbooks of differing levels offering an introduction into qualitative research (e.g. Flick 2002; Lamnek 1995; Mayring 1999; Silverman 2000; Strauss 1987; see Part 7 for an overview). For some approaches there has long been a need for systematic monographs suitable as introductions or textbooks. This is true of objective hermeneutics and also of cultural studies, which has recently become very influential in the area of mass media. It is also true of ethnography in the German-speaking world, although an English introduction is available in Hammersley and Atkinson (1983). Equally, for research involving narrative interviews there have hitherto been only a few good but rather short introductory articles (Fischer-Rosenthal and Rosenthal 1997a; Hermanns 1995), but there are no basic monographs that can be recommended. For introductory seminars the reading list has to be made up of articles, most of which deal with problems that are too specialized for the beginner. Up-to-date introductions, with detailed action-descriptions of procedure, are available for case-reconstruction research (Hildenbrand 1999) and conversation analysis (Deppermann 1999).

For other approaches, however, many textbooks are available – as, for example, in grounded theory (Glaser 1978, 1992; Glaser and Strauss 1967; Strauss 1987; Strauss and Corbin 1990). Here students sometimes encounter a problem in differentiating between the various terminologies and procedural variants that are to be found in textbooks that appeared at different stages in the development of the approach.

Webb and Glesne (1992) deal with a general problem encountered by students on courses involving qualitative research. The question is often asked: 'How many interviews do I have to conduct for them to be sufficient for a piece of scholarly research using qualitative methods?' Experience shows that this question can only be given a relative answer, 'It all depends ...' – depending on the research question, the data, the evidence needed, the level of generalization and finally the available resources. The impression that may arise of the arbitrariness of such decisions may be countered by appropriate examples. These should make it clear that, for example, in a comparative study what is decisive is less the number of interviews carried out than the dimensions under consideration (in the sense of theoretical sampling; see **4.4**), and the fact that from every group to be compared, more than a single case should be recorded.

What is also relevant are the difficulties encountered by many students (and researchers) in clarifying their own procedures and the sequence of steps that they followed. In addition to more general problems of scientific writing (cf. Becker 1986b; Narr and Stary 1999; Rückriem and Stary 1997), a particular problem that should be dealt with is how to present qualitative results and procedures (see **5.22**) and how to achieve credibility and authenticity (Flick 2002: ch. 19).

In the following section two examples of the teaching of qualitative research skills will be presented in more detail.

3 EDUCATION IN QUALITATIVE RESEARCH IN THE METHODOLOGY INSTITUTE OF THE LONDON SCHOOL OF ECONOMICS

At the London School of Economics and Political Science education and research on social science research methods are concentrated in the generously equipped Methodology Institute (LSE-Mi; Internet address: www.lse.ac.uk). The LSE-Mi was founded in 1994 as an interdisciplinary establishment to coordinate and strengthen, in the long term, postgraduate methodological training (research planning and design-construction, data collection, qualitative and quantitative statistical analysis) for doctoral students in all social science disciplines at the LSE.

One 15-week course entitled 'Text, image and sound in social research' forms the core of the training in qualitative methodology. Weekly lectures are supplemented by workshops (introduction to computer programs such as ATLAS.ti NUD•IST and so on; see **5.14**), courses on interview techniques and the 'advanced qualitative analysis' seminar. The working philosophy of the course is based on a structural view of research and distinguishes four dimensions of research activity: design (for example, single case or comparative study, person or time sampling), data types (for example, single interview, audiovisual data or observations), analytical procedures (coding, semiotic or content analysis), and epistemological interest (control and prognosis or emancipatory research). Each of the four dimensions includes a decision problem where elements can be combined and actually discovered beyond the dimensions. Every real research project therefore proceeds from a combination of elements: design principles are applied, one or more types of data are generated, these are analysed with particular procedures, pursuing a more general epistemological interest. A great deal of the unproductive polemic about qualitative versus quantitative methods is based on a confusion of these four dimensions of research activity: often, when one wants 'formalization', one looks in the drawer labelled 'data type'. In-depth interviews or ethnography are too hastily identified with an emancipatory epistemological interest, and the context of application is ignored, and so good intentions have the opposite effect (Bauer et al. 2000).

As the title 'Text, image, sound ...' already suggests, the course programme includes a range of data types. The methodological focus is broad, extending from interview procedures (see **5.2**, **5.3**) to textual materials, photography (see **5.6**), video and film materials (see **5.7**) and also sound and music as social data. For the analysis of all these types of data a range of analytical approaches is introduced: semiotics, rhetoric, discourse theory, narratology, classical content analysis and interpretation. The weekly cycle includes lectures and seminars, where active researchers and experts are sometimes also involved. In each of the weekly seminars one or two research papers that illustrate the lecture content are presented and discussed.

In spite of the many publications on qualitative methods in recent years there is still no textbook or handbook covering this particular programme with regard to data types, analytical methods and didactically processed examples.

The book that comes closest to the ideas of the course is that by Flick (2002), and this is required reading for all course participants. A 'home-grown' textbook that builds on the working philosophy of the LSE-Mi has also recently appeared (Bauer and Gaskell 2000). The lecture and seminar programme is as follows

A   Foundations

1   Overview of the course
2   Social research and epistemological interest
3   Corpus construction as a principle of qualitative selection

B   Data types

4   Field observation
5   Forms of interview
6   Group interviews
7   Sound and music as data
8   Photography and video/film

C   Analytical procedures

9   Semiotics
10 Classical content analysis: coding and indexing
11 Rhetorical analysis
12 Narratology

D   Problems

13 Problems of interpretation
14 Quality criteria for research: beyond sampling, reliability and validity
15 Final symposium

All course participants are assessed on the basis of the following five tasks.

The data portfolio

In the first weeks of the course lectures are interrupted, and before the academic discussion of data types and analytical procedures begins, every participant is required to produce his or her own portfolio with different types of data, if possible in the same subject area. One student who is interested in unemployment, for instance, may conduct several interviews, collect newspaper articles on the subject and perhaps carry out observations in a job centre. The report on what has been achieved will, on the one hand, describe the material from the point of view of how it was collected and of any systematic gaps, and, on the other hand, will describe personal experiences in data collection in the form of an unvarnished report of this field experience (borrowing the concept of 'confessional tales', Van Maanen 1995). As an end result there is every year a wealth of observations on large and small errors, realistic time demands and problems of research interaction, and these are discussed, in summary form, with all participants. This task increases problem-awareness and shows the relevance of research planning, self-reflection and self-monitoring on the part of the investigator.

The discursive essay

Mid-way through the lecture cycle all participants select a problem and work on this in a short essay of no more than 2,500 words. What is expected here is an argument supported by literary references, with main thesis, development and summary, on such themes as the function of numbers in research, the problem of engagement in social research, the contribution of design to the research process, a comparison of individual and group interviews as research methods.

Report to the final symposium

A further step is the symposium at the end of the course. Participants divide into four groups, each of which concentrates on one data type: observation and video/film, interview, textual materials, sound/music. In short reports aspects of these data types and analytical procedures are presented with a research example. In this three questions must be addressed:

1   Under what conditions is the particular data type or analytical method indicated?
2   What are the criteria of 'good research practice'?
3   What is 'good' about the particular research example?

Following the oral treatment of these three questions in the plenary session, participants put their reports on paper in a further short essay. The aim of this task is to make students aware of the question of indication and contraindication of method, and to avoid any monism of methods which would allow only one methodological approach for every conceivable research problem. Equally it is intended to raise the level of demand on qualitative methodology. Qualitative research can no longer persist in a negative attitude to 'positivistic research'. The mass of research practice now available requires the development of quality criteria analogous to sampling, reliability and validity in the research process (Flick 2002; Gaskell and Bauer 2000; Seale 1999a,b; see **4.7**).

Written examination

Every course ends with a final examination. After nine months, the course participants sit a three-hour written examination in which three questions out of ten have to be answered. For the first question an empirical research article from a leading international journal is prescribed. Participants are required to read the article in advance and then to write a methodological critique during the examination. The other two questions deal with themes similar to those of the discursive essay.

Empirical research project

Every participant completes the year with a short empirical research project, located and assessed in one of the related disciplines (for example, in social statistics, social policy, sociology, gender studies or social psychology), where knowledge from the methodological training is applied to a practical task.

4 EXAMPLE OF A TEACHING-RESEARCH PROJECT

The following illustration is of a two-semester course carried out in four-hour blocks with some 20 participants at the Technical University of Berlin. To provide a practical introduction into methods of data collection and analysis, the course includes a short research project that deals with the ideas on health of professionals in the field (doctors, nursing staff) in all its essential stages from determining and limiting the research questions to data collection and analysis. The didactic methods used include moderation techniques (mind mapping, small group work with working materials, and presentation of results to a plenary session;

cf. Weidenmann 1995). The essential problems of carrying out an interview-study (field access, see **5.1**; data protection, see **6.1**; interview variants, see **5.2**; conducting the interview, see **5.3**; coding and interpreting data, see **5.13**, **5.16**; presentation and generalization of results, see **5.22**) are covered in the form of short inputs with lists of further readings. The methods used in this example are the episodic interview (Flick 2002, 2000b) and the theoretical coding of Strauss (1987; see **5.13**). Practical tasks on the conduct of interviews take the form of role-plays and video-supported interview training sessions. This interview guide is further developed in an alternation between small group and whole group activities. Participants are given materials to structure this (cf. Figure 6.2.1 for an example).

In the first part of the course every participant conducts and transcribes (at least) one interview. The analysis of the collected data takes place in working groups in the second part. In addition to comparative interpretations students also prepare a short case description for each interview. As literature for an introduction to the content of this area a number of chapters from Flick (1998b) were used, and for methodology Flick (2002), Glaser and Strauss (1967) and Strauss (1987) served as a basis. Figure 6.2.2 provides an overview of the sequencing in the course.

The project is completed with an individual assignment which includes data and case analyses from the students' own interviews.

5 LEVELS AND CONTEXTS IN THE TEACHING OF QUALITATIVE RESEARCH

Courses in qualitative research are given in a number of different contexts, in each of which there may be specific problems in providing a well-founded type of training in the appropriate methods.

Qualitative research as a component of general methodological training

Frequently, in certain basic disciplines (sociology, education, psychology), one or more sessions on qualitative methods of data collection and analysis are planned into a general training programme in methods of empirical social

---

Interview Planning for an Episodic Interview

Interview planning includes suggestions for formulation (1) for the conduct of the interview (getting into the subject, question areas, questions, etc.) and (2) for the interview framework (data protection, general guidelines on questions and on the length and type of the conversation).

Working stages in the conduct of interviews

1 Choose moderator and rapporteur.
2 Overview of subjects of interest for the interview.
3 What themes are of central interest (1 up to a maximum of 4)?
4 What area of, for example, professional everyday life can provide information about the central theme(s)?
5 For every area formulate a narrative stimulus that could motivate the informant as clearly and unambiguously as possible to tell, for every topic under point 4, one or more stories related to the main themes (e.g. if you look back, what was your first experience or disagreement with ...? Could you tell me about this situation?).
6 For every area (max. 2–3) formulate questions about relationships etc. that could stimulate the informant as clearly and unambiguously as possible to fomulate his or her view of these relationships or concepts (e.g. What is ... for you? What do you associate with this term?).
7 Formulate keywords (max. 4) for important probing, i.e. on central aspects to which you would like to return if the informant does not deal with them.

Working stages in the interview framework

1 Consider what the interviewee should know in advance, to be well adjusted to the interview and to understand what it is about and what his or her role should be. Start with what the interviewee has perhaps already experienced when agreeing the time of the interview.
2 Formulate in keywords an appropriate introduction to the interview on the following aspects: purpose of the interview; tape-recording and data protection (after agreement, switch on the recorder at this point!); explanation of what the interview is about, e.g. a very personal view; explanation of how the conversation will proceed and how long it will probably last (the actual interview begins here).
3 Formulate in keywords the conclusion of the interview, e.g. Was anything important not dealt with? Feedback from interview partner.

Figure 6.2.1　Working material for developing a theme

research. The same may also be said of various textbooks in empirical social research (e.g. Bortz and Döring 1995; Diekmann 1995) insofar as they include chapters on this topic, but without building the methods into the overall logic of their presentation. One problem with this kind of approach to qualitative research is that in the course of two or three sessions there is no time to put across a deeper understanding of the methods and attitudes of qualitative research, let alone work on the relevant material. A second difficulty is that the teachers are often qualified in standardized procedures or specifically in statistics and have been appointed because of this qualification, the assumption being that they will also 'fit in' the qualitative methods. Sometimes students do at least have an opportunity to take supplementary 'empirical practical courses' using qualitative methods, where they can gain some experience of fieldwork and materials.

Special provision within an area of application

A second variant of training in qualitative research ties it to particular areas of application within the students' main study (such as clinical psychology, organizational psychology, and so on), as a kind of supplement or alternative to the methodological training provided in their main study. Here the problem often arises that the relevant courses are provided by teachers who are actually qualified and employed for other subjects (such as psychotherapists), and within a very restricted time-allocation, perhaps as a preparatory course for graduation theses in the field in question.

Teaching-Research Project: Professionals' Ideas on Health

Part I: Conduct of Interviews

1 Preliminary discussion: introduction

Orientation: Expectations and fears concerning the seminar
Small-group work: Use of a questionnaire and an interview outline
Input: Research process in qualitative research
Small-group work: Brainstorming on the research topic
Comparison and bundling of results of work
Input: Short introduction concerning 'ideas on health'
Formation of working groups

2 Introduction into the research topic

Short presentation of selected studies
Discussion on questions, procedures and results
Small-group work: Development and delimitation of the research questions
Comparison and bundling of research results
Input: On the role of research questions in qualitative research
Discussion
Input: Questions of access

3 Interview types and their indication

Input: Focused interview, narrative interview, episodic interview
Discussion of suitable procedures and selection
Small-group work: Interview planning
Comparison and bundling of results of work
Input: Data protection

4 Conduct of interviews I

Small-group work: Expectations and fears concerning the interview
Comparison and bundling of results of work
Input: Familiar problems in conducting interviews
Small-group work: Development of components of the guidelines
Comparison and bundling of results of work
Input: Sampling strategies in qualitative research

5 Conduct of interviews II

Interview training I (role-play with video, analysis in a plenary session)
Re-working and final editing of the guidelines
Interview partner: forming a pool, selection and allocation
Input: Interview documentation, recording and transcribing the interviews

6 Interview experiences

Report and analysis of the conduct of interviews in individual cases
Demonstration of extracts and feedback
Clarification of questions on transcription
Putting together first ideas and questions on interpretation
Looking toward the continuation programme in the following semester
Open questions

Part II: Interpretation of Interviews

7　Foundations and strategies of text interpretation

Stocktaking of available/transcribed interviews
Analysis of interview experiences
Small-group work: Introductory practice of text interpretation
Input: Foundations and strategies of text interpretation
Input: Rough structuring of the analysis
Small-group work: Production of a short description of every interview
Comparison and bundling of results of work: Continuing if necessary into the eighth session

8　Text analysis according to Strauss I

Input: Presentation of the study 'Awareness of dying' (Glaser and Strauss 1965b)
Input: Text analysis according to Strauss (1987 – grounded theory) I: open coding
Small-group work: Application to students' own interviews
Comparison and bundling of results of work

9　Text analysis according to Strauss II

Presentation of selected short descriptions
Input: Text analysis according to Strauss (grounded theory) II: axial coding
Small-group work: Application of the coding paradigm to students' own interviews
Comparison and bundling of results of work

10　Text analysis according to Strauss III

Small-group work: Application to students' own interviews
Comparison and bundling of results of work
Input: Text analysis according to Strauss (grounded theory) III: selective coding
Small-group work: Continuation of application to students' own interviews

11　Continuation and methodological alternative I: qualitative content analysis

Small-group work: Application of the coding paradigm to students' own interviews
Aim: Designation of the central phenomenon for students' own interviews
Linking to the coding paradigm
Stating the dimensions of the main concept
Comparison and bundling of results of work
Input: Methodological alternative I: qualitative content analysis

12　Continuation and methodological alternative II: hermeneutic procedures

Stock-taking of working results with students' own interviews
Small-group work: Application of the coding paradigm to case groups, e.g. professional groups (possibly differentiated according to gender)
Comparison and bundling of results of work
Input: Methodological alternative II: hermeneutic procedures

13　Quality criteria, generalization, presentation in qualitative research

Small-group work: Continuation of selective coding: formulation of a central category, related back to individual interviews
Comparison and bundling of results of work
Input: Quality criteria, generalization in qualitative research
Input: Modes of presentation for the results of qualitative research
Clarification of questions for the production of students' own assignment (case analyses)

Figure 6.2.2　Sequence of a teaching-research project

Postgraduate provision

In accordance with this situation many students in German-speaking countries – and Webb and Glesne (1992) report a similar situation in the United States – are confronted with the problem that they are inadequately prepared to write a dissertation using qualitative methodology and to undertake the work in the related research project. In view of this shortcoming there have been in recent years a large number of opportunities for further education in the area of qualitative research – ranging from commercial summer schools in objective hermeneutics to research workshops in biographical research, or doctoral lecture-programmes (for example, 'Biographical risks and new professional demands' at the Universities of Halle and Madgeburg: for an overview and further details see Part 7), to a new self-contained course of study on 'Qualitative methods in the social sciences' at the Free University of Berlin.

In this latter study programme, over three semesters a combination is offered of theoretical courses – such as a lecture cycle, a guided reading programme on symbolic interactionism (see 3.3) or ethnography (see 5.5) – project seminars and research workshops, which make possible theoretically reflected work on empirical material. Project seminars involve participants in the ongoing research work of their teachers. In research workshops participants join forces to undertake their own research projects under the guidance and supervision of their teachers (cf. Bohnsack 1998b).

Postgraduate courses of this type are so arranged that they bring together a range of courses that provide introductions and extensions of different theories and methods and combine these with practical materials analyses in regular research colloquia and workshops, thereby helping to eliminate the shortcomings of the basic courses of study. Similar goals are pursued in larger-scale research bodies through the setting up of methodological consultancy projects that also use qualitative methods (in the area of Public Health Research cf. Flick 2002: 276–277).

FURTHER READING

Bauer, M. and Gaskell, G. (eds) (2000) *Qualitative Researching with Text, Image and Sound – a Handbook*. London: Sage.

Glesne, C. and Webb, R. (1993) 'Teaching Qualitative Research – Who Does What?', *Qualitative Studies in Education*, 6 (3): 253–266.

Strauss, A. (1988) 'Teaching Qualitative Research Methods Courses: A Conversation with Anselm Strauss', *Qualitative Studies in Education*, 1 (1): 91–99.

6.3 Utilization of Qualitative Research

Ernst von Kardorff

1 SOCIAL-SCIENTIFIC KNOWLEDGE AND ITS UTILIZATION

The distinctiveness of qualitative research, its establishment within the social sciences as an independent and recognized domain of theory and methodology, and its broad spectrum of methodological and interpretative procedures for understanding social reality have not only come about because of the inherent dynamism of scientific development. Qualitative research has benefited generally from a secular development in modern societies in consequence of a 'social scientification' (Beck and Bonß 1989) of social knowledge and forms of social life (cf. Max Weber's hypothesis on the way to a methodical way of life). This extends from popular syntheses in the everyday world to 'correct' education and the setting up of relationships to curricula for in-service education of professionals and planning and decision-making in politics, administration and business (see **3.12**). The seepage of sociological knowledge into society is discussed from various points of view under the keyword 'utilization' and is studied in what Weiss (1983) called 'utilization research' (cf. Beck and Bonß 1984, 1989; Bonß and Hartmann 1985; Bosch et al. 1999; Wingens 1988).

After the loss of illusions about socio-technical control and the discovery that academic knowledge cannot always be automatically transferred into practice, there was talk of a crisis of utilization. In detail this is manifested in the fact that *social-scientific* knowledge is either not applied or is applied differently from the way its creators intended, that it is trivialized, used paradoxically and 'transformed', or else just 'disappears' in practice. Its direct effects in the direction of higher rationality in political decision-making are rather small in scale and difficult to prove (Wingens 1988; Wingens and Weyman 1988). Finally, its value is often judged by practitioners to be slight or ambivalent. This is equally true of both qualitative and quantitative research. What then are the particular types of utilization of qualitative research? What are the problems that arise? What contribution can qualitative research make to utilization research and to its own utilization?

2 MODES OF UTILIZATION OF QUALITATIVE RESEARCH

'Utilization' of qualitative research relates (1) to theories, concepts and views that have been accepted in various fields of use, (2) to research results that have led to reforms in particular fields and (3) to methods and procedures that have come to be used in different fields.

On the utilization of theories, concepts and views

A range of concepts from qualitative research have made a considerable career for themselves beyond the academic discipline in such fields of practice as social work, education, in-service professional education, medical care, psychiatry, the prison service and organizational reform. These includes such terms as 'social identity' (Mead 1934 and classical studies of the professional socialization of future doctors – Becker et al. 1961) or Goffman's concept of role-distance (1961b). A further example is the idea developed by Howard S. Becker (1963) and others of the 'deviant career' and 'labelling-theory', which has gained practical acceptance, for example, in juvenile court proceedings and expert reports, in teacher education, but also in the public debate about the causes of deviance. In this context we may also include the concept of stigma, treated by Erving Goffman (1963a; see **2.2**) under its interactive-strategic aspects, or his concept of the 'total institution' (1961a). These notions belong today to the standard language of specialist argument in the practice of pedagogy, social work, criminology or psychiatry, and in the fields of organizational analysis and the in-service education of professionals.

On the utilization of qualitative research results

The complex utilization of qualitative *research results* in fields of social practice may best be illustrated with an example.

In the investigations he carried out between 1954 and 1957 into psychiatric clinics, monasteries, prisons and merchant ships – published under the title *Asylums* – Erving Goffman (see **2.2**) was concerned with developing a sociological representation of the structure of the self (1961a: 11). Using inside views gained by means of observer participation he was able to show to what extent the features of the 'total institution', as a regulated daily routine with supervision and the absence of opportunity for privacy, determined the self-image and interaction patterns of the inmates of the respective institutions. The success and broad influence of these studies, which were intended as a contribution to sociological theory, can hardly be overestimated, particularly in psychiatric care and – to a lesser degree – in prison reform movements,

and for the first time the situation of patients was considered worthy of discussion (apart from René Spitz's psychological idea of hospitalism). What was most important for its broad reception – from the point of view of its uniquely qualitative approach – were the aspects of a reversal of perspective: the institution is seen through the eyes of the inmates and its effect on them, and is not described with reference to a normative understanding of its function or from the viewpoint of professional coding. In this way all those involved in attempting to adopt the alien perspective of the observer, who described the patients and the interactions between them and the staff in a reconstructive fashion, were able to look anew at familiar elements (on the sociological and political aspects of Goffman's reception, cf. von Kardorff 1991).

The acceptance of Goffman's analysis and his main concepts of 'total institution' and the 'moral career of the mentally ill' seem to be attributable to a kind of 'merging' and unplanned practical utilization, since Goffman's aim in these studies was theoretical. His studies had an influence on the debate about reforms in psychiatry and today are largely taken for granted in the inventory of (social-)psychiatric argumentation.

On the utilization of qualitative methods in different fields of practice

Here four fields of practice should, in particular, be mentioned: evaluation (see **3.12**), organizational analysis and development (see **3.11**), aspects of market research and the area of initial, further and in-service education (cf. also Dewe and Radtke 1989).

The following example of the utilization of sociological knowledge, taken from the further education of geriatric nurses (see Kondratowitz 1993), represents one type of primarily reflexive utilization of qualitative research. And it shows, in an exemplary way, how qualitative *methods* and *views* may be used in initial and further education.

In a longitudinal investigation of the further education of geriatric nurses – which aimed to promote the planning of patient-related nursing (von Kardorff 1987) – it became clear that using typical standard narratives about the daily routine of the home that were obtained by qualitative methods offered a possibility of breaking down resistance to changes in familiar action-routines. This breaking down occurred through a sociological reinterpretation of the metaphors of everyday professional burdens that were concealed in these standard narratives, such as the washing of inmates who were in need of attention. By contrasting the actors' model with its sociologically reconstructive analysis, practitioners can recognize alternative new modes of action and can recontextualize these for their everyday situation (cf. also section 5 below).

3 PROBLEMS IN THE UTILIZATION OF QUALITATIVE RESEARCH

The nature of knowledge from qualitative research

Even in research that is predominantly quantitative in its foundation and utilization-related, qualitative procedures have now won firm recognition for exploratory purposes, or for supplementation, reinforcement and differentiation. The use of the results of qualitative research, however, cannot be separated from its approach and from the research process itself. This depends upon the character of the knowledge generated by qualitative research: it tends to be hermeneutically circular rather than linear, horizontal rather than hierarchical, plural and specific rather than normative and universal, fragmentary, branching and interlocking rather than closed, open to alternative views rather than bound to results, and reflexive rather than dogmatic. This description does not, of course, imply that qualitative research is random or abandons its scientific and epistemological claims because of this openness: it demonstrates, with reference to the issues it investigates. To borrow a formulation of the sociologist Helga Nowotny (1999), which was actually applied to the relationship between science and society – 'It is like this. It could also be different.'

Problems of utilization

First, on account of its great proximity to the life-worlds of the areas it investigates, qualitative research has shown itself to be highly accessible in the sense that it has an element of familiarity and also of surprise. At the same time it is especially vulnerable to misunderstandings, since its results can be read not as an analysis but simply as a portrayal or, more negatively, as a 'genre picture' of social customs. This carries the risk that its results will not be taken seriously because they do not conform to lay opinions about science and its usual forms of presentation in tables and columns of figures.

Secondly, the research results about interviews, case studies and processes are sometimes very comprehensive and are seldom read in full by those who commission the assignment (see 6.5). This experience forces one into a results-based type of presentation (see 5.22) which makes invisible the course of social construction processes. The effect of qualitatively gained insights, however, reveals itself precisely in the course of (documented) feedback loops and focus groups (see 3.12).

Thirdly, even if qualitative research feels itself to be indebted programmatically to humanist and democratic ideals or to the disadvantaged (from William F. Whyte to Herbert Blumer, Howard Becker, Norman K. Denzin, and then to Egon Guba and Yvonna Lincoln – to mention only a few of its prominent protagonists), its results are in no sense humanist *per se*. Detailed knowledge of the investigated life-worlds of local (sub-)cultures, organizational milieux and commercial environments, and the biographies of quite normal people in their professional and private routines, do indeed contribute to a better understanding; but they can also be used for increased social control, disciplinary measures, clever integration into organizational targets and even for manipulation. This again relates to ethical aspects of research practice (see 6.1) and to its social responsibility.

4 THE CONTRIBUTION OF QUALITATIVE RESEARCH TO UTILIZATION RESEARCH

In general terms the conversion of scientific research results into practice or the utilization of scientific knowledge in a profession does not function according to the model of a deductive derivation schema for simply converting 'pure' scientifically obtained results to 'impure' utilization-related problem areas or fields of practice. This affects, to varying degrees, such different disciplines as the engineering sciences, meteorology and medicine, and also the social sciences and pedagogy. Here there is no primary difference in principle between whether one is dealing with experimentally obtained research results, whether they depend on quantitative collection and assessment procedures or whether they were obtained qualitatively. Utilization takes place in relation to a context and a situation, and relates to professional traditions, individual experiential knowledge and communicative routines: in this it does not generate an idio-syncratic type of knowledge.

Kroner and Wolff (1989) criticize traditional utilization research for *thinking about* the utiliza-tion of sociological knowledge rather than *dealing with* the utilization of this knowledge *by* members of society in concrete action situa-tions. It is precisely the ethnomethodological approaches, especially the 'studies of work' initiated by Harold Garfinkel (see **3.2**) and the various types of conversation analysis (see **5.17**), which have shown themselves to be productive here. They are able to demonstrate in what way sociological knowledge is 'built in' to the prac-tice of actors (see **3.2**) in practical contexts of action, such as their professional activity. Here it is a question of procedures for the social con-struction of scientifically supported professional activity which generate the 'utilization' of scientific elements (images, methods, knowledge) in their ongoing *execution*. Here we may speak in a dual sense of *reflexive utilization*: sociological knowledge is consciously applied as guiding, legitimizing or supporting knowledge as an ele-ment of construction in professional activity; and it is simultaneously used as reflexive knowl-edge for analysis and further development. This perspective of qualitative research on the uti-lization of scientific knowledge, through its dis-coveries, then provides reference points for the role of the social scientist in the reflexive utilization of this knowledge.

5 THE UTILIZATION OF QUALITATIVE RESEARCH AS CONSULTANCY – CONSULTANCY AS A UTILIZATION OF QUALITATIVE RESEARCH

Kroner and Wolff rightly see utilization as an 'independent social fact' (1989: 73). If knowl-edge of the professional *execution* of utilization by professionals, perhaps in the context of eval-uation studies (see **3.12**), is allowed to feed back into practice, this could constitute a basis for a

type of sociological consultancy based on qualitative research (and this in turn would have to be monitored). In this a reference point is provided in the shape of ideas on a 'clinical sociology', such as that proposed by Dewe and Radtke (1989; cf. also Dewe 1985 and 1991). In their view the task of this, using case studies from everyday professional life, would be to generalize or consolidate into a 'structural inter-pretation' what is typical about them:

> 'Clinical sociology' is interested neither in occu-pying only temporarily the situation of the actors, nor in bringing 'new' issue-related knowledge to the interpretation of a situation; its deliberate goal is rather to transfer the implicit knowledge available in a situation of professional activity to an explanation by the actors. (Dewe and Radtke 1989: 54)

In the first instance, this means that the task of this kind of consultant sociologist lies not in giving result-bound information about research findings – however these are dressed up didacti-cally – but in providing assistance in the recon-struction and reflection of action routines by the practitioners themselves, perhaps in a clinic. The alienating perspective of a qualitatively designed case study may serve as a mirror for practitioners which turns them into observers of their own everyday routines from the perspec-tive of observers momentarily liberated from the burden of activity and no longer from that of participants trapped by their own involvement; the *difference* between their familiar self-interpretation, generally confirmed by everyday practice and therefore seen as 'protected', and the image which is (ironically) broken by sur-prise or some defence-mechanism, or which is in any case reflexive, creates in itself a 'sociolog-ical view'. This change of perspective can then open up new areas of knowledge which evoke further interpretations on the part of the consultant/monitoring sociologist and elicit further reactions from the practitioners. The qualitative researcher then becomes, in the best case, a stimulus and catalyst for a learning organization (see **3.11**; Heiner 1998), by using qualitative analysis to guide the practitioners in the direction of a constant 'return to the data' (see **2.1**) as a source of knowledge. Utilization from this point of view becomes a common process of learning at the concrete interface between science and practice. More precisely, communication between the two separate 'cultures' of science and everyday life, with their structurally different forms of knowledge, becomes a practical requirement. The scientific experts (in this case qualitative researchers) become consultants and monitors of the professional experts. Expert knowledge, which has now also become a subject of qualitative investigations (cf. Hitzler et al. 1994), is not simply translated, but makes itself accessible to practice by means of the process of consultancy outlined here. 'Intercultural communication' between expert knowledge, practice knowledge and lay knowledge is therefore not primarily a problem of didactic translation or scientific correction of the activity of practitioners, but much more an independent work of construction based on dialogue (von Kardorff 1998b). The utilization of (qualitative) research could then become, as a form of practice, an 'applied (self-)enlightenment' by consultancy (Schmitz et al. 1989). The social sciences would then become 'sciences of potential' (Lepenies 1997) – precisely on account of the form of qualitative practice in consultancy and utilization.

FURTHER READING

Brown, R. H. (1989) *Social Science as Civic Discourse. Essays on the Invention, Legitimation, and Uses of Social Theory.* Chicago: University of Chicago Press.

Morse, J., Swanson, J. M. and Kunzel, A. J. (eds) (2001) *The Nature of Qualitative Evidence.* Thousand Oaks, CA: Sage. esp. Part V.

Torres, R. T., Preskill, S. H. and Piontek, M. E. (1996) *Evaluation Strategies for Communicating and Reporting. Enhancing Learning in Organizations.* London: Sage.

6.4   The Future Prospects of Qualitative Research

Hubert Knoblauch

1   INTRODUCTION

Even though it is highly risky to make statements about the future, in sociology we at least have the freedom to make statements about those who dare to make such predictions. Among these is Denzin (1997), for instance, who predicts that after the end of postmodernism qualitative research will contribute to a new 'scientific spirituality' and will thereby leave its mark on the morals of the society of the future. Traces of the religious prophesying that has entered many areas of society in North America are clearly visible in this statement. In Europe the predictions are much more modest and limit themselves to the future contribution of qualitative research to the canon of sociological methodologies. Optimists predict nothing less than a replacement of quantitative research which, in their eyes, is methodologically defective by reflexive social research. However, 'apocalyptic' voices can also be heard: qualitative research, they claim, is a transitory fashion that will be superseded and replaced by the next wave of fashion. Since it really has no clear

standards it will only have a future if it restricts itself to the exploratory clarification that precedes quantitative studies.

In order to be able to assess the future development of qualitative research it would certainly be helpful to consider its development so far. On the basis of this previous development it will then be possible to list a number of tendencies and *desiderata* for the future of qualitative research.

2   EXPANSION, ACCEPTANCE AND THE HERMENEUTIC INCLINATION OF QUALITATIVE RESEARCH

Even though qualitative research goes back to the beginnings of sociology, its present rise is due to a narrow sociological relationship with the breakdown of the supposed 'normative' consensus of the 'standardized middle-class society'. The rapid change in traditional community structures, the so-called pluralization of life-worlds and the increasing individualization of Western societies can no longer easily be represented with standardized methodologies.

One might say, in fact, that qualitative research is actually predestined to deal with the special features of late-modern society that are also characterized by such terms as privatization, de-traditionalization and reflexivization.

The reception of developments in qualitative research in Anglo-Saxon countries gave an important boost to their consequent later development in German-speaking countries. In the latter, great significance must be attached to the collections published by the group of Bielefeld sociologists which familiarized German readers with ethnomethodology (see 2.3, 3.2) and recent ethnographic approaches (see 5.5). During the 1980s qualitative research grew gradually and may be regarded as having become accepted during the course of the 1990s at both institutional and personal levels and by the scientific system.

The acceptance of qualitative research is also due to the fact that it has permeated an increasing number of areas within and also beyond sociology. It is certainly no exaggeration to claim that today almost every special discipline within sociology has its 'classical' qualitative studies, and that also in the neighbouring disciplines of social, cultural and humanitarian studies these not only have been received, but have left their mark on a major part of the spectrum of social science. Moreover qualitative research has also been taken up in other scientific disciplines such as psychology or linguistics. It may be a matter of surprise that it has also made inroads in the more strongly practical and applied disciplines such as economics, administrative studies, education, nursing and social work. These application-related disciplines offer promising opportunities for future development. We should make special mention of the areas of training and organizational development, but also the engineering sciences, which are today already making at least partial use of qualitative and, in particular, ethnographic methods.

Unlike in the Anglo-Saxon world, qualitative research in the German-speaking countries has a strong hermeneutic inclination in the processing of texts as raw data, which take the form either of interviews (see 5.2), natural language texts or documents produced by actors. This tendency was aptly described by Soeffner (1982) in the formulation 'social science as textual science'. Against the background of an independent tradition of hermeneutic text analysis and the theoretical sociological debate about

the notion of communication, a number of independent hermeneutic methodologies have developed – so far largely unnoticed at the international level – among which objective hermeneutics (see 5.16), sociological hermeneutics (see 3.5) and pictorial hermeneutics enjoy particular prominence (for an overview cf. Hitzler and Honer 1997).

This hermeneutic inclination in German-speaking countries had admittedly been at the expense of what is seen elsewhere as the main focus of qualitative research. In the Anglo-Saxon world it is associated primarily with ethnography (see 3.8, 5.5), and indeed the two are often equated (cf., for example, Vidich and Lyman 1994). In contrast, ethnography has played a subordinate role in German-speaking countries. Ethnographic studies have been carried out or systematically discussed by very few authors (e.g. Girtler 1980, 1984; Hildenbrand 1983), and it is only in the past few years that they have become more extensive (Hirschauer and Amann 1997; Knoblauch 1996b).

In order to be able to relate to international research, the development and recognition of ethnography should be a central concern of social research in the German-speaking world. Here there are good reasons for the assumption that ethnography developing in this way has great potential. In the first place, it is within the tradition of a theoretically and methodologically highly reflexive action-hermeneutics of a predominantly phenomenological provenance (see 3.1). And secondly, it focuses on a prominence of communication which is specific to German social theory. The natural relationship with independently developed hermeneutic methods also opens up the possibility of an innovative type of communicative social research, which would link together ethnographic methods and textual hermeneutic approaches in such a way that it could do justice to the increasing significance of communication.

From a technical point of view the emphasis on communication in qualitative research is accompanied and supported by the increasing use of audiovisual recording technologies, that is recorded tapes, cassette recorders and – to an increasing extent – video equipment. Admittedly the methodology of video analysis is still in its infancy (Heath 1997), and is therefore an important *desideratum* for qualitative research (see 5.7).

Looking at audiovisual data, we may distinguish between recordings of 'natural situations' and those that work with visual material created by the actors and produced out of aesthetic, political or economic interest (Ball and Smith 1992). Because this last-named type of data is often dealt with in the communication sciences, there are useful reciprocal influences between media research and qualitative research which could lead to the foundation of a timely methodology for empirical cultural analysis, and this would pay particular attention to popular culture and its marked visuality, or even multi-mediality (see **2.4**, **3.9**).

3 TECHNIQUE, QUALITY CRITERIA AND REFLEXIVE METHODOLOGY

The spread of qualitative research in the past 20 years was initially legitimized by its harsh criticism of quantitative research. Of course, more recently this confrontation has been increasingly downplayed, and indeed the two approaches are sometimes considered as complementary. The question remains, however, what form this complementarity might take: whereas some people see the two approaches as being of equal value, for others qualitative research serves merely to explore or extend the findings of quantitative research. More recently, however, hybrid or 'mixed' methodologies have emerged which combine both types of procedure (see **4.5**).

Within qualitative methodology the development of a hybrid methodology may also be expected, often concealed by the methodologically misleading concept of triangulation (see **4.6**). Here we are rarely concerned with corrective methods but rather with supplementary methods that deal with a range of research issues or aspects of issues. Ethnography in particular is predestined for such hybrid methodologies. Here it should also be borne in mind that ethnographies are fully compatible with formal and quantitative methods. Hybridization of methodologies is favoured by modern technology, which is accompanied by many types of formalization, standardization and automation that were previously only known from quantitative social research. Automation today focuses on the electronic analysis and interpretation of data. Software programs (see **5.14**; Part 7) are available not only for textual searches and administration but also for coding and code-based theory development (see **5.13**). Thereby they lead to a standardization of analysis that cannot easily be understood from outside. Because the coding processes are carried out automatically, these programs systematically miss the hermeneutic and classificatory requirements imposed on researchers, the disclosure and reflection of which make an important contribution to the analysis.

However problematic the use of this software may be, the increasing technologization of qualitative research has lead to a systematization of the research process that is summed up under the heading of data management. Even today computerization makes it possible to assemble visual and acoustic data in central locations, to record or exchange the data systematically. These technologies not only lead to the development of new types of cooperation between investigators. The use of new types of data, such as visual materials, also raises the question of appropriate forms for the presentation of scientific results. Without favouring the random selection of postmodern genres, visual and filmed modes will develop (see **5.22**) for the presentation of data and research results (ranging from the publication of visual and acoustic data on the Internet to video publications). This visualization of the presentation of scientific results and the increasing automation of data processing (for example, transcription, see **5.9**) will presumably also have implications for the approach to analysis, which may well move away from its written-logical base.

One of the fundamental problems of qualitative research is the evaluation of its results. Traditionally it has been thought that they tend to be 'impressionistic' and that intersubjective verification is rather cumbersome. To counter this, the idea is now advanced that traditional quality criteria (see **4.7**) such as reliability and validity are ill-suited to the evaluation of qualitative research. Instead, new quality criteria should be developed that permit a more appropriate evaluation of this type of research. Among these we find communicative validation, that is, obtaining the agreement of interviewees to research findings, procedural validity, which has to be guaranteed in the course of the research process, and such ethical criteria as trustworthiness, credibility and dependability (Flick 2002: 218–238). Other authors, however, are of the opinion that traditional quality criteria are indeed suited to the evaluation of qualitative methods and that it is only a question of defining reliability and validity in an appropriate fashion (Peräkylä 1997).

The adaptation of quality criteria to standardized social research may lead, however, to a loss of the specific contribution of qualitative research. It is therefore necessary for qualitative research to develop its own quality criteria. One indispensable precondition for this is the continuation of a qualitative methodology, related in particular to the so-called grounded theory (see **2.1**, **5.13**, **6.6**) that was developed by Strauss and Glaser. This counts among the few approaches to a scientific procedure which have made scientifically well-founded proposals using analytical induction, triangulation and comparative methodology and which have incorporated these proposals into a set of techniques, elaborated in detail, that make it possible to conduct a measure of methodological checking of their overt procedures.

Apart from this methodology there is also a more specific development towards what has been called 'praxeological' (Bohnsack 1999) or reflexive methodology. This is because a piece of research (no matter whether it is 'subjective' or 'structural/objective') directed at meaningfully acting or communicating individuals must take account, first, of their meaning orientations, knowledge and communicative procedures, and secondly of the relevance of what is being scientifically investigated from the point of view of the informants. A reflexive methodology therefore justifies the scientific relevance of the aspects being investigated against the background of the relevance system of the informants.

As has been demonstrated by research in the qualitative sociology of science (admittedly mostly with reference to the natural sciences), scientific practice is also largely determined by the methods of everyday action. Against this background it is, however, very surprising that qualitative methodology still follows the model of the scientist researching and discovering in isolation. We must therefore require of reflexive methodology that it makes the actual processes of qualitative research a subject of analysis and, at the same time, a research resource.

In sociological terms, however, it would be extremely naive to hope that any methodology could be determined, in a fluctuating social space, solely on the basis of abstract and ideal categories. The very attempt to develop methodologically controlled procedures is directly bound to the practices of existing scientific groups. This reflection on one's own research practice amounts to a further aspect of reflexive methodology. For this, apart from the processes of scientific politics that operate at the level of micro-politics, the institutional backgrounds must also be taken into account. It is a fact that in the area of qualitative research particular tendencies to institutionalization are found, which have an impact on the formation of study units, scientific and extra-scientific research institutes and other bodies (see Part 7). Because this institutionalization is normally related to a preference for particular methods and methodologies, one might also speak of 'schools' which – in parallel to the institutionalization – seek to implement a particular canon coloured by their own organization (that is, fixing of rules, orientation to 'foundation texts', methodological ideas; see **6.2**). Because of their loosely formed common public (in terms of journals, series of books, lectures), they all tend to take on the character of 'invisible colleges' rather than that of a more public forum. Because of their social invisibility, these various groups, schools and traditions are to a great extent confused and unorganized. Against this background three possibilities may be distinguished: (a) if the degree of transparency cannot be increased it will prove to be difficult for qualitative research to maintain its level of acceptance; (b) one or more approaches will show themselves to be acceptable to the scientific establishment and will therefore be able to impose their standards; (c) so that particular binding standards for qualitative research may be developed extending beyond individual schools, a common public will be created that will bring about one precondition: there will have to be a methodological pluralism which not only reluctantly approves of other approaches, but also recognizes that different approaches relate to different aspects of the research issues.

4   AFTER POSTMODERNITY

The postmodern debate that was mentioned at the outset brings to light two problems of social research: under the heading of a crisis of legitimization there is doubt as to whether the findings of scientific observers can have any particular claims to generality, intersubjectivity or objectivity. Qualitative researchers and their findings, it is claimed, are bound to a particular historical and social context. The fact that in the system of science there is a predominance of middle-class men from the Western cultural context is seen as an indication that even science can only deliver ethnocentric and particularist cultural findings whose claims to validity depend solely on their cultural hegemony.

Secondly, under the heading of a crisis of representation, doubts are expressed about whether in fact the observed culture can be portrayed in texts. This criticism relates, on the one hand, to a positivism which it detects in many qualitative approaches as an unvoiced assumption. In addition, it is directed at the claim that texts are able to reconstruct the social reality under investigation. Because the claim to representativity of scientific texts is called into question, their rhetorical, aesthetic and sometimes even fictional qualities become more prominent.

Undoubtedly this postmodern criticism in the Anglo-Saxon debate has made important contributions which have also had an impact among German scholars: it has led, for instance, to a recognition of female points of view (Ribbens and Edwards 1998; Warren 1988); the positions of widely differing ethnic groups are given increasing attention; and finally there is also a demand to experiment with new forms for the presentation of scientific research (Denzin 1997; see **3.3, 5.22**).

Admittedly, in German-language qualitative research the feminist position (see **3.10**) has hitherto received little attention – not to mention the position of ethnic groups. It is to be expected, however, that these positions will become more important in the course of time, but it can hardly be expected today that this development will continue to be related to what is characterized as 'postmodern'. For even in the United States a degree of weariness may already be detected. Marcus (1994: 573), for example,

speaks of a 'current exhaustion with the explicit rhetoric of postmodern debates', which sometimes leads to a paralysing form of relativism and a fear of analytical distinctions and logical arguments that is alien to science. And Lincoln and Denzin (1998: 583) claim that the postmodern era has expired: 'we are already in the post-"post" period – post-structuralism, post-postmodernism'.

Because postmodernism in Germany was never closely associated with qualitative research, the rapid demise of this 'epoch' will not have such profound effects. Among German scholars qualitative research will rather continue to be related to traditional and basic sociological concepts such as meaning, understanding or communication. However, precisely because even these terms are no longer uncontested, it will have to mark out its own position more clearly and promote its own theoretical foundation. In this way it could liberate itself from the role of being a mere aid to scientific discovery and make independent theoretical contributions to an empirically well-founded and interpretative analysis of modern society.

FURTHER READING

Flick, U. (2002) *An Introduction to Qualitative Research,* 2nd edn. Thousand Oaks, CA: Sage.

Lincoln, Y. S. and Denzin, N. K. (1998) 'The Fifth Moment', in Y. S. Lincoln and N. K. Denzin (eds), *The Landscape of Qualitative Research. Theories and Issues.* Thousand Oaks, CA: Sage. pp. 407–429.

Marcus, G. E. (1994) 'What Comes after "post". The Case of Ethnography', in N. K. Denzin and Y. S. Lincoln (eds), *Handbook of Qualitative Research.* Thousand Oaks, CA: Sage. pp. 563–574.

6.5   The Challenges of Qualitative Research

Christian Lüders

Qualitative social research and reconstructive methodologies have gained a remarkable degree of acceptance and recognition in the past 30 years. The reason for this growth is a large number of excellent empirical studies, which have not only established criteria from a methodological point of view but also had an important impact on the relevant disciplinary discourses. A significant contribution has been made by a series of publications on the methodology of qualitative research.

In spite of such uncontentious progress this degree of success remains surprising, since on close inspection it must be admitted that from the point of view of practical research and methodology a number of problems are still unsolved and the future development of the field is in no sense clearly defined. Here two sets of problems may immediately be identified: unsolved internal problems and outside expectations. Amongst the internal problems the most important are the lack of clarity about the value of standards in research practice, unanswered methodological questions, and gaps in the research issues. With regard to outside expectations it must be remembered that outside the universities and academic circles qualitative research has grown into an independent epistemological approach in many research and professional contexts. So far, however, the experience gathered there and the challenges of 'mainstream' publications in the methodological debate have gone largely unnoticed – at least in the German-speaking countries.

1   INTERNAL PROBLEMS

The value of standards for qualitative research

Even in 1991, the editors of the German *Handbook of Qualitative Social Research* (Flick et al. 1995/1991) were still demanding that qualitative research should succeed 'according to its own (sometimes still undeveloped) standards' (see Kardorff 1995: 4). Anyone who looks today at the specialist methodological literature is forced to admit that this demand has been met only too well. In general surveys today a whole range of criteria are proposed. To name but a few: intersubjective replicability, openness, explication, transparency, flexibility, issue-relatedness, theoretical saturation, exactness, reliability (see 4.7). These criteria are further developed and put into concrete terms in the various schools and methodological approaches (for example, the methodology of documentary interpretation: Bohnsack 1999).

For the vast majority of these proposals, however, it is true to say that mostly they remain general and that where they are made more concrete, the differences quickly become clear. This leads to the irritating state of affairs that although the list of standards for qualitative research has now become very long, there is as yet no binding consensus about what minimal standards must be adhered to in research practice. We may clarify this with an example: no one would seriously disagree with the idea that intersubjective transparency is an essential quality criterion in qualitative research. It is, however, impossible, both in the literature on the methodology of qualitative research and using available research reports, to determine in any binding way what this criterion relates to in concrete terms, and what this would imply for the conduct and representation of qualitative research. In this it is not only the heterogeneity of the proposals and the multiplicity of types of research practice that are an obstacle, but the fact that frequently one cannot avoid the impression that criteria of this sort are not taken particularly seriously. If we remain with the example of intersubjective in very many research reports one finds that data collected on the basis of the 'grounded theory' approach (see **2.1, 5.13**) have been coded and typologized in order to draw theoretical conclusions in the concluding chapter. If one were to take seriously the criterion of intersubjective it might be expected that at least somewhere in these studies there would be a description or exemplification from a single case study of how, in concrete terms, the coding was done, what codes and sub-codes were developed on the basis of what data, and how these were ultimately consolidated and given dimensions (for a detailed discussion cf. Kluge 1999; Kelle and Kluge 1999). This is missing, however, in the vast majority of cases. Much the same may be found in respect of most of their criteria (and a similar state of affairs may also be found in quantitative research).

In qualitative research meanwhile, instead of precision and replicability, a culture has developed of making research results appear plausible, which aims at establishing the author as a credible authority, in order to give the reader the feeling that the results could be plausible. In this way a rather unsatisfactory situation has arisen: at the level of research reports every author seeks to give an impression of internal, context-related plausibility. This occurs in most cases by means of assertions or through somewhat literary devices, so that external checking is rarely possible. If there are no outstanding contradictions or inconsistencies the leap of faith is normally sufficient. Of course, if one were to read these studies from the perspective of the criteria listed in the handbooks, they would all be seen as more or less deficient from a methodological viewpoint.

One might now argue that this kind of internal plausibility is sufficient and that hitherto it

has done no apparent damage to the development of qualitative research. Against this it might be said this only appears to be so from a limited internal perspective. Anyone who wished to 'sell' qualitative research and its results beyond the cartel of citation in university circles would encounter considerable resistance. This is nourished in part by prejudice against small numbers of cases, but it also represents a reaction to unsolved problems concerning its own standards and the experience that apparently almost anything is still methodologically possible under the label of qualitative research.

Open methodological questions

In many areas of its practice qualitative research can point to tried and tested strategies. Examples of this may be seen in the now very well-developed methodologies of biographical research (see **3.6, 5.11**), of documentary interpretation (see **5.4**), objective hermeneutics (see **5.16**), content analysis (see **5.12**) and others. What is characteristic of these methodologies is their use in a variety of practical research contexts and a well-documented methodological confrontation with the requirements, stages and implications of the procedure in question. At the same time, however, there is one type of research practice in which so far there has been almost no methodological reflection. Two very different examples will serve here to illustrate this kind of methodological gap.

Qualitative longitudinal studies have so far not been very numerous but have occasionally been carried out. If one wishes to reconstruct long-term processes such studies represent an indispensable tool-kit that is of great practical value in, for example, follow-up studies. Surprisingly, however, the methodological debate has not become involved in this topic. There are no answers to the simple question of how such studies should be structured (but cf. Strehmel 2000 on this point), from the matter of the methodological approaches down to the epistemological problem of whether a different case structure at time t_2 indicates a change in structure or whether it should rather be seen as a falsification of the reconstruction of the case at time t_1.

The following is a further example: any researcher who has been required to complete an empirical research project against a deadline knows about the time pressure associated with this and about the many problems of having to process large quantities of sometimes heterogeneous qualitative data. The interpretative or reconstructive strategies recommended in the textbooks are extremely time-consuming, so that in this form one can normally only analyse fully and in all their details a small number of cases that are strategically central to the project. For the remainder of the material *short cut strategies* (see **4.1**) have to be applied. But with regard to the related methodological questions one can only say that all participants are aware of the problem and that the methodological discussion is again elegantly silenced. There is no approved set of abbreviation strategies, nor are there any appropriate reference texts to which one could turn with a clear conscience. In most project reports one looks in vain for successful examples, and if one asks one's colleagues the information obtained is of limited value.

Even in those projects that rely on information technology to administer and code their data (cf. Kelle 1995, see **5.14**) using a database system suited to qualitative materials (e.g. MAXqda, ATLAS.ti, NUD•IST, Hyper Research, The Ethnograph; see Part 7), the guidelines are quite often limited to rudimentary forms of a simple enumeration of allocated codes and contents to be found in the material. Any abbreviation of the analysis in these projects comes down to attempts at least superficially to 'come to grips' with the large quantities of data. Not infrequently this leads to a situation where quasi-quantifying procedures replace interpretative approaches. This situation becomes even more critical in the particular case of commissioned projects, because many people who undertake projects see themselves as obliged to be able to present a reasonably acceptable number of cases as the basis of their study.

This list of methodological gaps could be considerably extended. Apart from the now almost routinely cited open questions of quality criteria (see **4.7**), the design of qualitative projects (see **4.1**) and the manifold problems of research ethics (see **6.1**), there is still a lack of agreed concepts and procedures for the production and analysis of ethnographic protocols, for strategies of qualitative secondary analyses (but cf. Kluge and Opitz 1999b on this), on the sensible interrelationship of qualitative and quantitative data (Erzberger 1998; Kelle and Erzberger 1999, see **4.5**), and on the triangulation of data resulting from different methodological approaches (see **4.6**). Even less widely discussed are trust and

data protection (Gläser 1999), the practice of which in many projects should immediately involve those responsible for data protection: interview transcripts, for example, are frequently stored on a hard disk with no security of access. In many projects there is no lockable safe where person-related data – and these are involved in most interviews – could be protected from break-in. In addition, research practice in the area of delinquency research, for example, demonstrates that researchers are regularly hearing events that are relevant under criminal law, so that it would be worth discussing how such information should be handled, particularly since researchers have no legal right to withhold evidence (see **6.1**).

Gaps in the areas of investigation

As with the methodological gaps outlined above, these areas of research that remain relatively unexplored are also, to a great extent, dependent on the researchers' own interests and the research contexts. Two areas in particular seem to have been insufficiently developed in German-speaking countries, and their importance should be uncontestable since for both there has been a vast amount of discussion in English-speaking countries, with countless publications, independent journals and institutions. We refer to the areas of *qualitative organizational research* (see **3.11**) and *qualitative evaluation research* (see **3.12**).

In both of these areas there are empirical studies and ongoing projects in German-speaking countries, but a cursory glance at the relevant handbooks and publishers' lists will immediately show that whereas the English literature offers a considerable number of methodological and theoretical texts (e.g. Clegg et al. 1996; Guba and Lincoln 1989; Patton 1990; Shaw 1999), in Germany there are almost no works of this sort (but cf. Heiner 1998).

2 EXTERNAL EXPECTATIONS OF QUALITATIVE RESEARCH

In German-speaking countries qualitative research has shown itself to be essentially – at least in its dominant self-justificatory discourse – a university, not to say academic, matter, with the result that only scarce consideration is given to many topics and challenges which are dealt with in journals, book series and manuals in the English-speaking world. At the same time, in many fields of research outside the universities, qualitative strategies have developed into an essential feature of research practice. In this one should think not only of the major extra-university research institutes and training establishments but also of the many types of knowledge generation in such professional fields as adult education, child care and youth-work, health management organizational development and so on. If one disregards the fact that the unanswered internal methodological questions inevitably still give external encouragement to the unchecked growth of strategies and a barrage of labels, so that one frequently has major problems in distinguishing what was research and what is better described as non-committal discussion which led the author to some idea or other, the official tasks for qualitative research projects imply, in most cases, a set of concrete methodological requirements. Qualitative research in these areas is currently moving on very thin – and slippery – ice, because there is a lack of convincing methodological responses to the expectations of those who commission particular projects. (In most cases these are organizations and political bodies at national, regional and local levels.)

Reliable descriptions

If one looks through qualitative research reports and methodological textbooks, what seems to be the primary task of qualitative research is to make contributions to the creation of an empirically supported theory. This may explain the high level of interest in such ideas as 'grounded theory'. Mere description, on the other hand, is seen rather as a debased or at best transient preliminary stage. Of course this orientation proves to be a pure illusion for most university projects, since the majority of such projects in no sense meet this demand; what is perhaps more important is that it would be extremely helpful, both for scientific work and theory-development, and also for politics, administration and professional work, to determine *what* something is *like*, *why* something develops the way it does, and *what* occurs *where* under particular circumstances. What would be needed, therefore, would primarily be valid *descriptive knowledge*,

under certain circumstances also conceptual knowledge, or the answer to the question of how something might be better done. In view of these expectations qualitative research would continue to have good prospects if the feeling were to develop that quantitative procedures only gloss over the surface. This is particularly true as virulent new problem situations arise. For this it is not necessary to have large numbers of affected parties. But in the case of questions focusing less on the investigation of new problem situations of addressees than with the responsible institutions and the processes taking place within them (whether they be hospitals, youth services, schools, psychiatric clinics, prisons, offices, political parties, and so on), for these in particular qualitative methods are required. In such cases qualitative research promises a deeper and more precise type of knowledge, with more detail about the complex processes. What is essential here, however, is that this knowledge is seen to be workable in the medium term, particularly for the consumer but also, under certain circumstances, for those who commissioned the research. That is to say, it must provide an apposite and, from the participants' point of view, transparent description of such matters as the current situation as a basis for the planning of infrastructure in a city district, the reorganization of a company or a reorientation of youth services (cf. Permien and Zink 1998).

This requirement, however, has many consequences particularly from the methodological viewpoint.

First, this interest in detailed descriptive knowledge has implications for the methods and methodological approaches. A clear interest in descriptive knowledge suggests, depending on the particular research question, particular strategies and renders others less plausible; theoretically well-founded designs are of less interest than empirically based contrasts that reveal the available spectrum and the options it contains. By analogy, it would make little sense to propose to funding agencies and consumers of results a rigid constructivist type of methodology when reconstructivist positions would correspond better to their requirements and expectations.

Second, the interest in descriptive knowledge regularly has to confront the problem of an 'appropriate' number of cases. It is, for example, completely inconceivable to try to 'sell' to a ministry the dysfunctional effects of a particular legal framework for professional practice on the basis of a detailed analysis of only four cases – however valid the analyses may be. In addition, the heterogeneity of institutional contexts, the pluralization of life-situations, frequently requires not only a degree of regional scattering but also, depending on the research questions, as systematic as possible a treatment of the differing conditions (for example, at least a consideration of different geographical locations, urban–rural differences, and different institutional structures). To comply with such expectations, even in relatively small projects something in the order of 40 to 60 cases, depending on the particular question, will be the norm.

At the same time, it is true to say that the results will be conditioned by particular deadlines: the scope for extensions is normally very precisely determined. In particular this must be seen against the background that the normal two to three year duration of a piece of research is already barely acceptable from the point of view of the client or user.

Third, the expectation that the research will produce detailed descriptive knowledge often leads to the problem of the *applicability* and *validity of the results* (see **4.7**). Here the interesting question is how, at an average level of abstraction and against the background of heterogeneous contexts, one can first of all *validate* and then *legitimately generalize* the data obtained. The most recent publications on typologizing have suggested important keywords in relation to this (cf. Kelle and Kluge 1999). A great deal of work is required, however, before the strategies suggested there can be applied in such a way that they can serve as a basis for outsiders to answer the simple question: 'Can we trust these data, and for what areas are they important?'

Fourth, in relation to these problems it has hitherto always been siginificant to point to the fact that the collection, processing and analysis of data is always under the control of the research team. In addition to allowing reference to the likely investment of time because of the amount of data to be processed, this also provides justification for the fact that the projects in question always involve full-time academic positions for at least two staff and that appropriate amounts of time have to be included in the planning. In addition, this argument facilitates access to further staffing resources, for instance scientific advisory bodies, method workshops and other types of quality assurance by colleagues. Experience shows that structures of this sort of collective consultancy can make important contributions to the validation, systematization and theoretical categorization of results.

In view of the growing shortage of financial resources, it is increasingly the case that additional arguments are needed for funding groups of research assistants. The funding for a project advisory council is quickly exhausted, and the purchase of a new computer with software for coding and analysis would be preferred to an additional research assistant's position. Interpretation groups or research workshops (and not only for training purposes), and making these a precondition for a *quality circle in research practice*, would be an important topic for methodological debate.

Knowledge transmission

A further problem area relevant to methodology arises from the specific context of utilization (see **6.3**). It is not only that the political administration and specialist practitioners would always prefer to have their results by yesterday. Every client is interested in having their research activities widely known. They are part of symbolic politics and as such are of major importance. This implies the rapid presentation even of interim findings, the quickest possible publication of the results of a project, the holding of workshops, appearance at hearings, assistance with inquiries, giving expert opinions, and much more besides. Inductively or abductively designed research strategies (see **4.3**), which are normal in qualitative projects, are in a relationship of considerable tension with these requirements.

At the same time it should not be forgotten that the client's time for reading is limited. A methodological consequence of this is that comprehensive results must quickly be made more concise. Exhaustive case studies, which are based on the idea that a wealth of detail both enhances credibility and also renders the proposed typologies and theoretical conclusions more plausible, are at best only possible for illustrative purposes. But how can case analyses be generalized and compressed in such a way that, on the one hand, they still meet scientific standards, and on the other hand are relevant to the contexts of utilization of political administration and professional practice? Behind this lies a more general problem of qualitative research: in view of its voluminous research reports, it runs the risk of being received only by tiny minorities.

This can also be expressed differently: the image of qualitative research depends essentially upon whether it can succeed in finding satisfactory answers to the external expectations and its internal open questions. If the success of recent years is to be consolidated, it will have to face these challenges.

FURTHER READING

Flick, U. (2002) *An Introduction to Qualitative Research,* 2nd edn. Thousand Oaks, CA: Sage.

Morse, J., Swanson, J. M. and Kunzel, A. J. (eds) (2001) *The Nature of Qualitative Evidence.* Thousand Oaks, CA: Sage.

Seale, C. (1999) *The Quality of Qualitative Research*. London: Sage.

6.6 The Art of Procedure, Methodological Innovation and Theory-formation in Qualitative Research

Alexandre Métraux

1 INTRODUCTION

In this chapter I shall develop a number of sometimes critical arguments on particular aspects of qualitative research. The key to the argument is in the approach of Anselm Strauss (see **2.1**, **5.13**), who, of course, should not be seen as a mirror of qualitative research in its entirety but who may, nevertheless, assume the role of paradigm. I am making no systematic claim, for the simple reason that the self-imposed brevity could not deliver the kind of order required by the needs of a system. This is reason enough to make statements about function, goals and limits of qualitative methods in social research in a case-related way, that is to say, in accordance with the paradigm associated with the name of Strauss.

2 THEORETICAL DEFICITS AND QUALITATIVE METHODS

When *The Discovery of Grounded Theory: Strategies for Qualitative Research* by Barney Glaser and Anselm Strauss appeared in 1967, it diagnosed in formal terms a substantial methodological opposition between procedures for theory-formation. This had initially less to do with the battle about the value and significance of qualitative and quantitative methods than with the plausibility of the different forms of hypothesis-generation and theory-formation. Two opposing views of hypothesis-generation were immediately noted in the opening section of the book: first the New York functionalism of Robert Merton and Paul Lazarsfeld and then the Chicago-based research tradition represented by scholars such as William Thomas, Florian Znaniecki, George H. Mead and Herbert Blumer (cf. Fisher and Strauss 1979 for discussion). For Glaser and Strauss this latter tradition was 'associated with down-to-earth qualitative research, a less than rigorous methodology, and an unintegrated presentation of theory' (Glaser and Strauss 1967: vii) – all matters that must have seemed abominable to functionalists and which prospective academics had to avoid if they were to protect their future careers. The opposition between the two schools, however, was not overstated because it had to do with the diagnosis of a *general shortcoming*: according to 'our conviction … neither of these traditions – nor any other in post-war sociology – has been successful at closing the embarrassing gap between theory and empirical research' (Glaser and Strauss 1967: vii). With the new start signalled by this book, however, the two authors exposed themselves to the (gentle) pressure to demonstrate the feasibility of a research style at the level of theory and also at the level of data collection by means of convincing results.

One further historical event must be mentioned: according to the view predominant at that time in US sociology, only a single wide-ranging thought-structure could be considered as a 'theory', whereas smaller-scale thought-structures – whatever they were – did not count as theories. A proponent of this view was Talcott Parsons, who devoted the whole of his life, following Max Weber, to the pursuit of a whole-society *grand theory* (cf., for example, Parsons 1937, and Parsons and Shils 1951). This apparently arbitrary convention became established as an academic diktat: since smaller-scale investigations apparently had (and could have) no theoretical value, the only possibility open to researchers was to distinguish themselves by improving the means of collecting and analysing data or by collecting new data, even without a theoretical compass (cf. Glaser and Strauss 1967: vii–viii and 1–2).

Apparently, therefore, the stimulus for the foundation of qualitative research did not derive from the antagonistic relationship into which methods were forced – the quantitative ones here and the qualitative there – but from a general disquiet about the general state of social research. If one considers the application of qualitative procedures in the different branches of social research,[1] and then reconstructs their history from the point of view of a redefinition of what might be called their 'theoretical worth', the rhetoric of the oppositions with their connotative loading (qualitative *versus* quantitative, explain *versus* describe) may be seen as a way of talking used *from the sidelines*, perhaps to gain the advantage over competing disciplines or to promote a particular project. What is true of Strauss, at least, is that he developed qualitative methods not out of any principled opposition to quantitatively operating social research but out of an interest in the development of a rigorous theory. It would therefore be advisable not to confuse the social ritual of methods with sociological methodology when the critical evaluation of qualitative methods is under consideration.

A third aspect merits brief discussion. The traditional distinction between the discovery and the justification context implies that the generation of hypotheses – where these are not derived from pre-existing superordinate material – may be related to individual psychic notions. Compared to the justification context, however, where we are concerned with falsification, verification and other such noble aspects of human knowledge, the discovery context shows itself as no more than a side issue. Who is likely to be interested in how a hypothesis came about if it has not been proved? But if it has been proved, then intuitions, thought-experiments and data collection are of little consequence – except perhaps as an anecdotal flourish – compared to the fact that the research has produced something that is demonstrably 'true'.

It may be the case, however, that this idea of the discovery context is short-sighted. Instead of the accidental intuition or a cognitively unquantifiable chance, the generation of hypotheses might be the result of some pre-structuring insight into reality. This is related to the fact that there are forms of experience-processing which may be evaluated for hypothesis-generation and therefore also for theory design. This collecting and evaluating, with reference to earlier developments in science, may be looked upon as an 'art': it might also remind us that chemistry was referred to as the 'art of separation' and that medicine is even today known as a 'healing art'. It was precisely this artistically formed, learnable and teachable *exposition* of sociological knowledge that an approach such as that of Strauss and Glaser was looking for. If one interprets this approach in the sense that the testing of grammatically well-formed statements about social facts does not take place in a vacuum but on the basis of systematically collected data, then any justification of so-called *grounded theory* or any other sociological theory is, of course, a trivial exercise. But if one bases an interpretation on the guiding principle that the collecting of *innovative* data happens *both before and after* the formulation of a set of hypotheses that claim to be new (cf. Glaser and Strauss 1967: 5, 21–26 and 31–43), this constitutes a landmark that is not trivial either historically or methodologically.

After these retrospective explanations I come to the conclusion that one can point to at least three sufficiently comprehensible reasons for the development of grounded theory.

1 Dissatisfaction with the style of sociological research, particularly in the time after 1945.
2 The desire to get back to theoretical creativity by reinterpreting the concept of theory that was dominant at that time.
3 The use of sociological experience in the construction of theories of whatever scope.[2]

3 THE ART OF PROCEDURE AND THEORY-FORMATION

As we have indicated, every proposal for a new method leads consistently to its being tried out. This testing puts the researcher into a situation in which ready-made rules are initially only of conditional value. With any claim to a procedural innovation there arises a set of circumstances in which errors cannot be excluded, heresies are probable and revisions are desirable. In competing with traditional approaches, however, untried innovations inevitably lose out.

In view of the *structure of the research process* (see **4.1**), however, one might ask whether the competitive disadvantage is real or only apparent. To explain this a brief digression is required. Research is carried out in order to examine, understand and explain unknown phenomena. The unknown, or an unsolved problem for informants in the research process (for example, the human genome – to cite a topical research object), or some fact that is partially contentious and therefore leads to considerable debate: all of these can have a disturbing effect on an experiment. A classic example from the history of medicine may help to illustrate the last of these possibilities. As Ludwik Fleck demonstrated, adherents of the old theory of infection regarded microscopically small pathogens as the cause of diseases. When it was shown that these pathogens were also found in healthy people, the original explanation was no longer sufficient: that one could make no further theoretical progress with the uncontested fact that the presence of these pathogens did *not* lead to an infectious disease. This did not mean that the first theory was abandoned. It was simply that attention had been drawn to an unknown mechanism which would probably never have been noticed if it had appeared without any prior work, that is, outside the theoretical framework of the original theory of pathogens (cf. Fleck 1935/1979).

The unknown, therefore, puts the machinery of research into action again or contributes to some acceleration. This sort of situation opens up a choice of strategic alternatives:

1 one can make an attempt to deal with the unknown with older already available methods; or
2 one can make a counter-attempt to cope with the unknown by means of some new methodological tool.

The first strategy centres on method; it is conceived out of methodological purism and rooted in the expectation that the unknown is so structured that it will not resist the use of the tested methods. In metaphorical terms we could say: a method-centred strategy assumes that a given key will open a lock that has so far proved to be obstinate, if only one turns the key at the right moment.

This kind of expectation is often detrimental to the research process: the available key will damage rather than open the lock. There now remains only the possibility of trying a problem-oriented strategy. But problem-oriented strategies lead to *bricolage*, whereby – in the same way as in a medical clinic – all possibilities are tried on the basis of considerations of opportunity, until a plausible result is achieved.

A brief glance at qualitative methods in social research will show that thoughts on the justification and qualification of methodological modelling are heterogeneous. The phenomenological approach proposed by Graumann and Métraux (1977) contains no indication as to how, for example, one might set up a field study, how to conduct observations or analyse data. The approach rather spells out four structural–analytical categories (physicality, environmentality, sociality and historicity) as a conceptual quadruplet which, because it seems to determine the situations of human behaviour and action, imposes an absolute limit on the expression of the smallest analytical unit in the field of social research (cf. Graumann and Métraux 1977: 47–49). According to this approach, the reflex mechanism (irrespective of the nervous system in which it is activated or the equipment used to objectivize it) is the object of neither qualitative nor quantitative social research, precisely because the above-mentioned limit for the formation of analytical units is transgressed. From this, of course, it does *not* follow that reflex mechanisms are unimportant manifestations of human behaviour and action, nor that they should not be considered in the social and behavioural sciences. But if reflex mechanisms are to be analysed, this should be done in the framework of those disciplines which, as it is sometimes expressed, play the role of ancillary sciences. The approach of Graumann and Métraux is therefore concerned with the way of *thinking* in social research and the *cognitive preconditions* for sociological concept-formation, while it reserves its position as far as concrete research activities are concerned.

The very detailed introduction to qualitative research produced by Strauss (1987) on the basis of many years of experience, particularly in medical sociology, proceeds somewhat differently. If one compares this introduction with the methodological programme for *grounded theory* which appeared 20 years earlier, it becomes clear that the more recent publication uses a range of examples to show how one should proceed at different points in a research project, whereas the 1967 book, although it does not comprise a plea for a particular sociological mode of *thought*, indulges in an almost excessive inductivism, where sufficiently comprehensive quantities of data would make visible the high frequencies and intersections that are presumably usable in theory-forming. (If individuals almost always behave in the same way in a particular environment, it may be assumed that we are dealing with a socially binding pattern; the accumulation of such observational data is then used, as suggested above, in the pre-structuring of a hypothesis or partial theory.)

The case is again different with introductions to content analysis (see **5.12**) using data from focus groups, from which it becomes clear what rules are used by different readers to limit the semantic bandwidth of sentences (cf., for example, Lisch and Kriz 1978). Introductions of this type, however, are data-specific and in principle not applicable to all possible data.

From this it follows that uncertainties, short-term methodological lapses and imponderabilities in work with qualitative methods cannot be ignored in the research process. The kind of methodological purism (that is, whatever does not satisfy a finite quantity of statistical criteria is not a finished scientific product) that is particularly popular among those with a markedly statistical way of thinking provokes a defence mechanism that inhibits innovation, irrespective of the fact that even the simplest measurements are dependent on the *formation* of units that are in no way *self*-defining: before the formal arithmetical system for measuring entities there lies the path of interpretation (cf. Ellis 1968: 22–23).

4 THE ACTORS' PERSPECTIVE

Qualitative research has sometimes been accused of attributing too much weight to the view of the actors under investigation, with the result that the objectivity requirement which is indispensable in any science is damaged by smuggling in a heterogeneous point of view. This accusation is based on a misunderstanding.

Let us assume that we need to explain in the most informative possible way certain interrelated sequences of actions in which a number of actors participate with various kinds of cooperation (as may be the case in universities, local authorities, hospitals and so on). In this process the collecting of information about the actors' motives, drives, expectations and the like proves to be an indispensable component of the research. It may then be assumed that a particular circumstance (such as a chronic illness) that is at the actors' focus of attention leads to different patterns of action and different behavioural strategies. A doctor, because of her professional type of socialization when confronted with a patient's illness that has been diagnosed as chronic, will behave differently compared to the patient himself, and the patient will behave differently compared to his relatives, the nursing staff or the members of the psychotherapeutic team. A description of the work-processes that take place (hospital care, organization of the patient's return home, home nursing) cannot be achieved without taking account (in the broadest sense) of the mental processes and conditions of the actors (cf. Fagerhaugh and Strauss 1977). But the description and the analytical dissection of events is therefore no less relevant than the description of, for instance, the morphology of the tulip or the anatomical dissection of the lung of a whale. It is an untenable idea that the anatomy of a whale's lung or the morphology of a tulip are objective simply because neither of the two research-objects has any autonomous mental life, and that the description of social events, in contrast, must be rejected as subjective because the 'research-objects' have a particular world-view, are differently motivated or pursue different interests.

We know, however, that explicit motives are not necessarily the ultimate reasons for action and that overt interests without knowledge on the part of actors may depend on covert drives. So long as social research does not accept without question the explanations the actors who are being investigated offer for their actions, the danger of subjectivism does not arise. If, for example, we do not take account of particular actors' views in the reconstruction of actions which these actors engage in after the diagnosis of a chronic illness, then it is precisely this *social* process that will prove difficult to understand (cf. Strauss 1978).

How far we extend the 'deep' analysis of actors' mental representations depends again on (a) the research question, (b) the requirements of the theory, and (c) the artistic production (or modelling) of adequate analytical procedures. Moreover it is precisely in dealing with the deep-structure analysis considered to be necessary that qualitative research must establish the crucial and the irrelevant factors. Some investigators believe that the analysis of linguistic utterances can also achieve everything that others believe can only be explained by participant observation. Others again believe that verbal data constitute too slender a basis and that paralinguistic, gestural, iconic and other types of data should also be included. But what was said above about the competition between qualitative and quantitative approaches is equally true of competition between rival approaches within qualitative research. Qualitative research is not helped if the social ritual of methods is equated or confused with sociological methodology. Ultimately nobody in research has a monopoly of any particular magic method.

Groups of outsiders, gender-specific phenomena, power-constellations and compelling institutional forces all have – and incidentally quite legitimately – a certain appeal for qualitative research. In the institutions in which researchers pursue their work social processes are inevitably also taking place, and the investigation of these

is no less attractive than other aspects of social life. It might therefore be rewarding to make qualitative research itself an object of investigation, with some explanatory and critical intention, and this would imply some modelling of methods to explain the unknown. It was for this kind of meta-social research that Anselm Strauss was ultimately also arguing.

NOTES

1 Apart from that contained in the present volume, a presentation of different approaches to qualitative research may be found in Flick et al. (1995).
2 Similar constellations of motives were always important for other authors, such as Cicourel (1964), Garfinkel (1967a) and Goffman (1961b) (to mention only a small number of sociologists of the same generation as Strauss).

FURTHER READING

Goffman, E. (1961) *Asylums. Essays on the Social Situation of Mental Patients and Other Inmates*. New York: Doubleday Anchor.

Maines, D. R. (ed.) (1991) *Social Organization and Social Process*. New York: Aldine de Gruyter.

Strauss, A. (1987) *Qualitative Analysis for Social Scientists*. Cambridge: Cambridge University Press.

Part 7

Resources

7.1 Resources for Qualitative Researchers

Heike Ohlbrecht

There is ample evidence, in the form of the large quantity of new specialist literature or developments in the World Wide Web, to suggest there is currently a great deal of movement in the world of qualitative research. This chapter will give a brief presentation of a selection of textbooks and manuals which provide an introduction to the themes of qualitative research or which are suitable for the extension of existing knowledge. Then, after a presentation of journals and book series, as well as a number of classic texts, we shall consider the explosive development of qualitative research on the Internet. Here one must expect constant change; many Internet sources are developing, some of which have only recently come into existence.

1 TEXTBOOKS AND HANDBOOKS

Textbooks

Flick, U. (2002) *An Introduction to Qualitative Research*, 2nd edition
This textbook provides a survey of theoretical positions and the most important methods of collecting and interpreting verbal and visual data. The research process, questions of qualitative research and field access are presented, and questions of the presentation of results and criteria for justifying validity are discussed. In the chapter on text interpretation, the procedures of text analysis are presented, including coding, categorization and sequential analysis. This book is particularly suitable as an introductory text.

Mason, J. (2002) *Qualitative Researching*, 2nd edition
Jennifer Mason is aiming in this book at interested students and scientists. There is a clear presentation of methodological problems, followed by the research process and different types of qualitative data. A special didactic feature of this book is the set of 'difficult questions' that are intended to give an introduction into the thought processes and the tradition of qualitative research. Different strategies and procedures are presented, making clear the diversity of qualitative research.

Kvale, S. (1996) *InterViews: An Introduction to Qualitative Research Interviewing* (2nd edition 2004)
This book is devoted to a thorough consideration of the qualitative interview – one of the central research procedures. The author provides both theoretical underpinnings and practical aspects of the interviewing process. After

examining the importance of the interview in the context of qualitative research a number of different theoretical backgrounds are discussed (phenomenology, hermeneutics, etc.). The author delivers practical insight with the 'seven stages of the interviewing process', from research design to conducting the interview, analysis and presentation of research results.

Strauss, A. and Corbin, J. (1990) *Basics of Qualitative Research. Techniques and Procedures for Developing Grounded Theory* (2nd edition 1998)
The formation of grounded theory is one of the most widely used procedures of qualitative research, and is presented here in a very clear and practical fashion, with many examples from different research fields. This book owes its particular attraction to its didactic step-by-step introduction, which also makes it readily accessible for beginners. For more advanced students additional new techniques are presented. The book is divided into three sections: section 1 provides a survey of the thoughts that underlie grounded theory; in section 2 special techniques and procedures (e.g. types of coding) are presented in more detail; and in section 3 additional procedures are explained and evaluation criteria are introduced.

Silverman, D. (1997) *Qualitative Research. Theory, Method and Practice*
This book assembles well-known international qualitative researchers. The contributors reflect on the analysis of each of the kinds of data – observation, texts, talk and interviews – and using particular examples of data analysis to advance analytic arguments. Illuminating both the theory and the practice of qualitative analysis, this book is a helpful resource for academics and students involved in qualitative research.

Handbooks

Denzin, N. K. and Lincoln, Y. S. (eds) (2000) *Handbook of Qualitative Research,* 2nd edition
This complex manual embraces primary theoretical considerations, paradigms of qualitative research, strategies and stages in the research process, as well as techniques for collection, analysis, interpretation and presentation. It includes a summary of the different research strategies, such as ethnography, phenomenology, grounded, biographical research, clinical research, and also an introduction to

such procedures as observation, document analysis and qualitative interviews, and the use of computers in the qualitative research process. The book concludes with a consideration of the future prospects of qualitative research.

Bauer, M. W. and Gaskell, G. (eds) (2000) *Qualitative Researching with Text, Image and Sound. A Practical Handbook*
In four complex sections, this practical handbook gives an overview of the current state of qualitative research. Part I is on the 'Construction of a Research Corpus', part II addresses 'Analytic Approaches for Text, Image and Sound', part III focuses on 'Computer Assistance', and part IV deals with 'Issues of Good Practice'. The book claims to provide essential reading for students and researchers across the social sciences.

Gubrium, J. F. and Holstein, J. (eds) (2001) *Handbook of Interviewing Research*
Interviewing is the predominant mode of research in the social sciences. The handbook offers a comprehensive examination of interviewing at the cutting edge of information technology. From interview theory to the nuts-and-bolts of the interview process, the coverage of this area is very broad and authoritative.

Atkinson, P., Coffey, A., Lofland, J. and Lofland, L. (2001) *Handbook of Ethnography*
This handbook gives in essays an overview of some of the intellectual contexts within which ethnographic research has been fostered, developed and debated. Ethnographic research in different fields is discussed and also ethnography as work, its reality and its implications, both for the doing of research and institutional support, are debated. This handbook establishes the central and complex place ethnography now occupies in the human disciplines.

Flick, U., Kardorff, E. von, Keupp, H., Rosenstiel, L. von and Wolff, S. (eds) (1995) *Handbuch Qualitative Sozialforschung*
This handbook provides a thorough survey of qualitative research beginning with perspectives and traditions, and continuing to theories and examples of classical studies, followed by stages in the research process and a summary presentation of a range of methods. This leads to a discussion of some of the more important applications of qualitative research. The book ends

with a section on questions of generalization and the validation of qualitative research.

2 JOURNALS AND BOOK SERIES

In the area of qualitative research the following journals and book series are of particular interest.

Journals

Journal of Narrative and Life History (editors McCabe, A. and Bamberg, M.), Lawrence Erlbaum Associates
The International Yearbook of Oral History and Life Stories (editors Thompson, P., Bertaux, D. and Passerini, L.), Oxford University Press
Quality and Quantity. International Journal of Methodology (editor Capecchi, V.), Kluwer Academic Publishers
Qualitative Sociology (editor Zussmann, R.), Kluwer Academic Publishers
Qualitative Inquiry (editors Denzin, N. K. and Lincoln, Y. S.), Sage
International Journal of Qualitative Studies in Education (editors Scheurich, J. and Foley, D.), Taylor & Francis
Qualitative Research (editors Atkinson, P. A. and Delamont, S.), Sage
Qualitative Health Research (editor Morse, J. M.), Sage
Research on Language and Social Interaction (editor Zimmerman, D. H.), Lawrence Erlbaum Associates
Qualitative Social Work (editors Ruckdeschel, R. and Shaw, I.), Sage
Qualitative Research in Psychology (editors Giles, D., Gough, B. and Packer, M.), Gower
Ethnography (editors Wacquant, L. and Willis, P.), Sage
Journal of Contemporary Ethnography (editor Maddox, G.), Sage
Field Methods (editor Bernard, R. H.), Sage
Narrative Inquiry (editors Bamberg, M. G. W. and McCabe, A.), John Benjamins

Book series

The *Qualitative Research Methods Series* from Sage publishers has been appearing since 1986 with contributions on various aspects of qualitative research, such as *Reliability and Validity in Qualitative Research* (Kirk and Miller 1986), *Interpretive Biography* (Denzin 1989d), *Understanding Ethnographic Texts* (Atkinson 1992), *Focus Groups as Qualitative Research* (Morgan 1988) and *Discourse Analysis* (Phillips and Hardy 2002).

The series *The Narrative Study of Lives*, edited by Josselson and Lieblich, has approved in six volumes since 1993.

Introducing Qualitative Methods is a series edited by David Silverman since 1998. *Qualitative Research in Information Systems* (Myers and Avison 2002), *Categories in Text and Talk* (Lepper 2000) or *Doing Conversation Analysis* (ten Have 1999) are topics of this particular series, as well as books on the quality of qualitative research (Seale 1999a) or the use of documents (Prior 2003).

A complete list of previous volumes in these three series published by Sage may be found at: http://www.sagepub.co.uk/.

The series *Understanding Social Research* edited by Alan Bryman, from Open University Press, deals with various aspects of qualitative research, for example *Ethnography* (Brewer 2000), *Qualitative Data Analysis – Explorations with Nvivo* (Gibbs 2002), *Biographical Research* (Roberts 2002).

3 CLASSIC STUDIES AND ARTICLES

Some examples of classic studies and articles in the qualitative research tradition are presented here. The examples chosen constitute productive stimuli for further studies and reveal a rich epistemological potential, so that one may justifiably speak of the establishment of a paradigm.

Symbolic interactionism

According to the theory of symbolic interactionism, individuals act by displaying to themselves and to others the symbolic meaning of their action. One central idea is the understanding of meaning, and the clarification of the term 'meaning' goes back to George Herbert Mead's main work *Mind, Self and Society* (1934).

Becker, H. S. (1963) *Outsiders. Studies in the Sociology of Deviance*
Goffman, E. (1959) *The Presentation of Self in Everyday Life*

Participant observation

A particular feature of this approach is the researcher's 'diving into' the field of investigation (Herbert Blumer) by participating in the contexts of everyday life (Goffman).

Park, R. (1939) *An Outline of the Principles of Society*
Whyte, W. F. (1955) *Street Corner Society. The Social Structure of an Italian Slum*

Ethnomethodology

According to ethnomethodology, social reality unfolds in everyday practical action, which implies that social order is to be seen as an ongoing result of meaning attribution and acts of interpretation.

Garfinkel, H. (1967a) *Studies in Ethnomethodology*

Conversation analysis

Conversation analysis was founded in the mid 1960s as a result of the work of Harvey Sacks. Sacks applied to conversations the ethnomethodological question concerning the methods actors use continuously to create social order.

Sacks, H. (1967) 'The Search for Help. No One to Turn To'

Harvey Sacks's lectures, which provide a rich source of analyses, reflections and ideas, are now available to a broad public after long being available only to a small circle of insiders.

Sacks, H. (1992) *Lectures on Conversation, Volumes I and II* (ed. G. Jefferson)

Objective hermeneutics

Objective hermeneutics is concerned with the reconstruction of the objective meaning-structure of a text. The specific approach represented by Oevermann (1999a,b) is characterized by him as a structuralist position that is obligatorily linked to a methodology based on the logic of reconstruction.

Oevermann, U. (1993) 'Die objektive Hermeneutik als unverzichtbare methodologische Grundlage für die Analyse von Subjektivität'

Community sociology

The study by William Isaac Thomas and Florian Znaniecki, *The Polish Peasant in Europe and America* (1918), is considered to be a landmark. It heralded the blossoming of empirical–theoretical research at the Department of Sociology in Chicago, which subsequently – as the Chicago School – exerted an enormous influence upon sociology. The sociological problem of migration is investigated here on the basis of the surge in immigration by Polish peasants in the first decade of the twentieth century.

Thomas, W. I. and Znaniecki, F. (1918) *The Polish Peasant in Europe and America*

Sociography

According to Jahoda (1989), the main task of sociography is to account for the social, local and temporal conditions of a given situation. One study of the effect of long-term unemployment on a village community, first published in 1933, became the basic text for sociographic research.

Jahoda, M., Lazarsfeld, P. F. and Zeisel, H. (1971) *Marienthal: The Sociography of an Unemployed Community*

Ethnography

In the second decade of the twentieth century, ethnology moved from extensive data collection to the intensive investigation of local contexts. The roots of ethnographic methods are in the anthropological and ethnological works of Bronislaw Malinowski and Franz Boas, and in the linguistic studies of Edward Sapir. The following text is representative of these:

Malinowski, B. (1935) *Coral Gardens and their Magic. A Study of the Methods of Tilling the Soil and Agricultural Rites in the Trobriand Islands*

Ethnopsychoanalysis

The empirical basis of ethnopsychoanalysis is the ethnopsychoanalytical conversation rather than the therapeutic setting of psychoanalysis. The core is the processing and analysis of subconscious transfer and counter-transfer relationships in the research field. A classic study of a psychoanalytically oriented type of social research is:

Parin, P. (1980b) *Fear Thy Neighbour as Thyself. Psychoanalysis and Society among the Anyi of West Africa*

Biographical research, analysis of narratives

The above-mentioned study by Thomas and Znaniecki is also important in biographical research as one of the earliest attempts to make biographical material accessible for sociological analysis. There was still a long route from the instrumental and illustrative use of biographical material to modern sociological biographical research. In Germany, Fritz Schütze, with the development of the narrative interview, was able to introduce a text-analytical method of biographical research that relates to the traditions of the Chicago School.

Riemann, G. and Schütze, F. (1987) 'Trajectory as a Basic Theoretical Concept for Analyzing Suffering and Disorderly Social Processes'

Rosenthal, G. (1993) 'Reconstruction of Life Stories. Principles of Selection in Generating Stories for Narrative Biographical Interviews'

Interpretations of film or photos and pictures

Film and television are exerting an increasingly strong influence on everyday life. Denzin analyses Hollywood films since these also regularly include a social reflection of societal experiences, values, norms, institutions or historical events.

Denzin, N. K. (1995) *The Cinematic Society. The Voyeur's Gaze*

Harper, D. (1987) *Working Knowledge. Skill and Community in a Small Shop*

Denzin, N. K. (2002) *Reading Race: Hollywood and the Cinema of Racial Violence*

Medical sociology

In the early 1960s Glaser and Strauss investigated the interaction between clinical personnel and dying patients. These empirical studies proved to be exemplary, and particularly for the methodological reception of grounded theory (see **2.1**).

Glaser, B. G. and Strauss, A. L. (1965b) *Awareness of Dying*

Corbin, J. M. and Strauss, A. L. (1988) *Unending Work and Care*

4 INTERNET SOURCES

The following selection contains an overview – with no claim to completeness – of the information available on the World Wide Web in the area of sociological qualitative research. The rapid development of the Internet makes any attempt to provide a complete overview impossible and, moreover, only temporarily valid

statements can be made. By the time this book is published some sources may already be outdated, some may have been supplemented or replaced and others may have appeared. What follows here therefore is a selection of Internet resources. Since every Internet source has its own specific possibilities and limitations, a networked use of the various links and sources is recommended.

Bibliography, citation of Internet sources

Because of its richness and density of information, its speed, international character, flexibility and interactivity, the Internet offers new perspectives to scientific research. The use of completely new communication media, such as mailing lists, online journals, chat rooms, Web rings and so on, makes it increasingly necessary to refer to these. As with the citation of printed literature, information about the author, title, place (Internet address = URL, or uniform resource locator) and date of publication has to be given with digital documents. The date of access is important to the extent that here, unlike printed media, one is dealing with a document that can include different versions at different times. For a reference as a citation or for inclusion in a list of literature there are a number of possibilities. At the time of writing there are no agreed standards. Recommendations for modes of formal citation of Internet sources may be found at *Electronic Reference Formats*: Recommended by the American Psychological Association (APA Style Guide)

http://www.apastyle.org/elecgeneral.html

Links and online journals

Sources of general information
The American Sociological Association
http://www.asanet.org

The British Sociological Association
http://www.britsoc.org.uk

Qualpage (resources for qualitative researchers)
http://www.qualitativeresearch.uga.edu/QualPage/
This offers a wide range of information in the field of qualitative research, such as lists of discussion fora, online journals, organizations and software. There is a detailed presentation of

different methods of qualitative research, such as biographical methods, ethnomethodology and conversation analysis, grounded theory, narrative inquiry and phenomenology.

International Institute for Qualitative Methodology.
   http://ualberta.ca/~iiqm/
This address leads to the homepage of the International Institute for Qualitative Research at the University of Alberta, giving information on workshops, conferences, publications and software programs for computer-assisted analysis of qualitative data, and more besides.

Qualitative Research in Information Systems
   http://www.auckland.ac.nz/msis/isworld/
Here there is an overview compiled by Michael D. Myers of various methods (grounded theory, hermeneutics, narration analysis, semiotics), techniques for data analysis, software programs, calls for papers and other topics. The references and links to qualitative research are comprehensive and informative.

Qualitative Research Resources on the Internet
   http://www.nova.edu/ssss/QR/qualres.html
This was compiled by Ronald Chenail and provides a detailed survey of Web pages, texts, workshops and other information on qualitative research.

The Qualitative Interest Group (QUIG)
   http://www.coe.uga.edu/quig/
Available here is an interesting and high-frequency mailing list and papers from the International Qualitative Research in Education Conference.

The Qualitative Research Webring
   http://www.webring.org/cgi-bin/webring?ring=qualres;list
Focuses on qualitative research and is of particular interest to graduate students and faculty who are interested in all aspects of qualitative research.

Online journals

There is a growing tendency for specialist periodicals and journals to have, in addition to their printed version, a (frequently shorter) online version. But recently there have appeared a range of dedicated online journals that promote specialist interactive exchange.

The Qualitative Report
   http://www.nova.edu/ssss/QR/index.html
Designed as an online journal of qualitative research and critical discussion, it sees itself as a forum for scientists, students and any others who are interested in qualitative research. It is open to different schools, critical commentaries and remarks, as well as new developments in the area of qualitative methods. It has been produced since 1990 by Ronald Chenail.

Qualitative Inquiry (QI)
   http://www.sagepub.co.uk/journals.aspx?pid=105751
Edited by Norman K. Denzin and Yvonna S. Lincoln and offering online journal information on the Internet.

Sociological Research Online (SRO)
   http://www.socresonline.org.uk
This is edited by Liz Stanley and Larry Ray. It is designed as a forum for theoretical, empirical and methodological questions of sociology related to current developments in politics, society and science. Abstracts and articles since 1996 are freely available.

Social Research UPDATE (SRU)
   http://www.soc.surrey.ac.uk/sru/sru.htm
This electronic journal is produced by the Department of Sociology of the University of Surrey, UK, and gives information about the latest developments in the area of qualitative research. Information and articles are freely available.

Ethnographic Journal
   http://www.pscw.uva.nl/emca/Journals.htm#ETHNOGRAPHIC
An online journal of ethnographic research.
ETHNO/CA News
   http://www2.fmg.uva.nl/emca/
ETHNO/CA News offer information on ethnomethodology and conversation analysis

International Journal of Qualitative Studies in Education
   http://www.tandf.co.uk/journals/online/0951-8398.asp
Edited by J. Scheurich and D. Foley, the journal provides information and abstracts since 1997. It is freely available online.

Social Scientific Research Methodology in Cyberspace
   http://www.socio.demon.co.uk/research-methodology.html

Forum: Qualitative Social Research (FQS) is a multilingual online journal for qualitative research. The main aim of *FQS* is to promote discussion and cooperation between qualitative researchers from different nations and social science disciplines.

http://www.qualitative-research.net/fqs/fqs.htm

*Computer-assisted analysis
of qualitative data*
QUALNET is a mailing list for the area of computer-assisted analysis of qualitative data. Its email address is:

LISTSERVE@SUVM.ACS.SYR.EDU

A project is running at the University of Surrey with the goal of contributing to the dissemination of software for computer-assisted analysis of qualitative data, establishing training courses and investigating this field. Information concerning this may be found at:

http://www.soc.surrey.ac.uk/caqdas

5 SOFTWARE PROGRAMS FOR COMPUTER-ASSISTED PROCESSING OF QUALITATIVE DATA

Software programs in the field of qualitative research are not only used for text searches and management but also – in the sense of a systematic text processing which includes a codified procedure – they may be used for theory-building. In this way, they surpass anything that conventional text-processing packages can achieve. We should, of course, point out that the software does not analyse data (this remains the task of the investigator) but provides support in the form of a tool. To describe IT programs for computer-assisted analysis of qualitative data, the label 'QDA-software' (= qualitative data analysis) has been generally accepted (cf. Kuckartz 1999). The available programs have developed with amazing speed in recent years, and a fuller treatment is available in the surveys of Kuckartz (1999) and Kelle (1995).

Before opting for a particular program (and currently around 25 are available), and therefore also a type of program,[1] one ought to consider the particular features and functions that are of value. An overview of the most important programs can readily be constructed from the Internet. Demo-versions of current programs

may be downloaded from the Internet at the URLs given below.

The Ethnograph
http://www.qualisresearch.com/
First developed by John Seidel and published in 1985, The Ethnograph was one of the first programs for computer-assisted analysis of qualitative data. The program has been continuously developed since then and is now in widespread use in many scientific disciplines. It is a classic cut-and-paste program and is therefore highly suitable for functions of selection, search, coding and processing of text-based data and for the production of memos.

Hyper Research
http://www.researchware.com
This is a software program for the coding of different data types and large data sets. It was developed in 1990 by S. Hess-Biber, T. S. Kinder and P. Dupuis. The main emphasis is on a deductive and case-oriented analytical procedure. It is a multi-media program which supports the analysis of qualitative data and facilitates networking/data-transfer to statistical programs.

NUD•IST
http://www.qsr-software.com
This program supports the process of searching for and organizing data, to facilitate theory-building. QSR, like ATLAS.ti, relates explicitly to grounded theory and supports its methods. A particular feature is the presentation of the system of categories in a hierarchical tree-structure that branches downward. Within this system relationships can be established. The program was developed by T. and L. Richards.

Code-a-Text
http://www.code-a-text.co.uk
This came about in the context of analysing conversations from therapy encounters and was developed by A. Cartwright. Code-a-Text is now used for the analysis of a range of text types. The multi-media version makes possible the analysis of videos and pictures. The publisher Sage/Scolari has specialized in the marketing and promotion, and detailed information on QDA software may be obtained from the following address:

http://www.scolari.com
As examples of the great variety of QDA software, two programs will be examined more closely: MAXqda and ATLAS.ti.

MAXqda

http://www.maxqda.de

MAXqda, the new program from the developers (Kuckartz) of WinMAX, is a powerful tool for the analysis of text-based qualitative data that is also setting new standards in user-friendliness.

MAXqda is available in German, English and Spanish. The program supports those researchers who are concerned with the analysis of non-numerical and unstructured data. Its fields of application range from the analysis of qualitative interviews, sociological fieldwork and media analyses to the analysis of open questions in the context of surveys. MAXqda is used in many scientific and practical fields: in sociology, political science, psychology and psychoanalysis, education, ethnology, criminology, social work, marketing and social planning. MAXqda supports the processes of text interpretation and theory-building. In texts it is possible to search, categorize, classify, code, evaluate and typologize without losing the typical complexity of the data.

The Internet address given above gives details of workshops in the UK and Germany that provide an introduction to the software program.

ATLAS.ti

http://www.atlasti.de/

What is fundamental for ATLAS.ti is the grounded theory approach and therefore the coding paradigm of Strauss (1987). The software program developed by Muhr is available in English and offers processing possibilities at both the textual and the conceptual level. From the initial text, for example an interview to be interpreted and the interpretations or codings that belong to it, a 'hermeneutic' unit is formed on the screen. The principal strategy of the program can be characterized as 'VISE': Visualization, Integration, Serendipity and Exploration. Textual locations can be marked, ordered, commented or related to one another for a better overview, and in this way form semantic networks. ATLAS.ti makes it possible to work with textual data and to analyse further media types such as graphics, audio and video. ATLAS.ti has also been widely adopted in a range of scientific disciplines. There is a mailing list[2] in English which permits users to exchange experiences. The homepage of ATLAS.ti lists dates for introductory workshops into the program, which take place, for example, in the USA, Canada, the UK and Germany.

Both programs, MAXqda and ATLAS.ti, offer a range of functions which are present on the screen and which, in addition to the search and code-allocation, do not allow the reference to the particular textual locations to be lost. The PC acquires a reference system of textual locations, categories, generic categories and codes which support the processes of analysis and interpretation of qualitative data. The programs both offer interfaces with other programs, such as SPSS (Statistical Package for the Social Sciences). There are differences in respect of coding levels, coding word-length, media types, visualization and the production of hierarchical links (see **5.14**).

6 UNIVERSITY TEACHING AND POSTGRADUATE EDUCATION

At the Methodology Institute of the London School of Economics and Political Science (LSE-Mi) education and research concentrate on sociological research methods. A 15-week course on 'Text, Image and Sound in Social Research' has its primary focus on training in qualitative methods (see **6.2**). The homepage of the LSE is:

http://www.lse.ac.uk

In Germany, the only course is for graduates at the Free University of Berlin in the form of a three-semester further study programme on 'Qualitative Methods in the Social Sciences', which can lead to a certificate. This course, which is only in German, includes teaching units on the main emphases, theoretical bases and classical studies of qualitative research, together with a treatment of the many ways of collecting and analysing data. Practical knowledge of research methods is developed in project seminars and research workshops.

Information about the content of the study programme, application procedure and other details may be found at:

http://www.fu-berlin.de/qlmethoden/

NOTES

1 For example, the following program types may be distinguished: code-and-retrieve programs/coding and search programs, code-based theory-builders, terminological and conceptual network-builders, rule-based theory-building systems, and so on.

2 The mailing list may be reached at ATLAS-TI@atlas.ti.de. The following message should be sent to listserve@atlasti.de: SUB ATLAS-TI, giving first name, last name and institution.

References

Abel, T. (1948) 'The Operation Called Verstehen', *American Journal of Sociology*, 54: 211–218.

Abu Lughod, L. (1991) 'Writing Against Culture', in R. G. Fox (ed.), *Recapturing Anthropology*. Santa Fe, NM: School of American Research. pp. 137–162.

Abu Lughod, L. (1993) *Writing Women's Worlds. Bedouin Stories*. Berkeley, CA: University of California Press.

Ackerman, N. W. and Jahoda, M. (1950) *Anti-Semitism and Emotional Disorder: A Psychoanalytic Interpretation* (Studies in Prejudice, Volume 5). New York: Harper and Brothers.

Adler, M. (1993) *Ethnopsychoanalyse. Das Unbewusste in Wissenschaft und Kultur*. Stuttgart: Schattauer.

Adler, P. A. and Adler, P. (1987a) 'The Past and the Future of Ethnography', *Journal of Contemporary Ethnography*, 1: 4–24.

Adler, P. A. and Adler, P. (1987b) *Membership Roles in Field Research*. Newbury Park, CA: Sage.

Adorno, T. W. (1969a) 'Einleitung zum Positivismusstreit in der deutschen Soziologie', in *Gesammelte Schriften*, Volume 8. Frankfurt a. M.: Suhrkamp. pp. 280–353.

Adorno, T. W. (1969b) 'Gesellschaftstheorie und empirische Forschung', in *Gesammelte Schriften*, Volume 8. Frankfurt a. M.: Suhrkamp. pp. 538–546.

Adorno, T. W. (1973) *Negative Dialectics*. New York: Seabury Press.

Adorno, T. W., Frenkel-Brunswik, D. H., Levinson, R. and Sanford, N. (1950) *The Authoritarian Personality. Studies in Prejudice* (edited by M. Horkheimer and S. H. Flowerman). New York: Norton Library.

Agar, M. (1991) 'The Right Brain Strikes Back', in N. G. Fielding and R. M. Lee (eds), *Using Computers in Qualitative Research*. Newbury Park, CA: Sage. pp. 181–194.

Agar, M. (1996) *The Professional Stranger*, 2nd edn. San Diego: Academic Press.

Agee, J. and Evans, W. (1960) *Let Us Now Praise Famous Men*. Boston, MA: Houghton Mifflin.

Albert, H. (1985) *Treatise on Critical Reason* (trans. M. V. Rorty). Princeton, NJ: Princeton University Press.

Alewyn, R. (1929) 'Das Problem der Generationen in der Geschichte', *Zeitschrift für deutsche Bildung*, 5: 519–527.

Allaire, Y. and Firsirotu, M. E. (1984) 'Theories of Organizational Culture', *Organization Studies*, 3: 193–226.

Altheide, D. L. and Johnson, J. M. (1980) *Bureaucratic Propaganda*. Boston, MA: Allyn and Bacon.

Amann, K. and Hirschauer, S. (1997) 'Die Befremdung der eigenen Kultur. Ein Programm', in S. Hirschauer and K. Amann (eds), *Die Befremdung der eigenen Kultur. Zur ethnographischen Herausforderung soziologischer Empirie*. Frankfurt a. M.: Suhrkamp. pp. 7–52.

Anderson, D. (1995) *Strand of System. The Philosophy of C. Peirce*. West Lafayette, IN: Purdue University Press.

Anderson, R. J. and Sharrock, W. W. (1984) 'Analytic Work: Aspects of the Organization of Conversational Data', *Journal for the Theory of Social Behaviour*, 14: 103–124.

Antaki, C. and Widdicombe, S. (eds) (1998) *Identities in Talk*. London: Sage.

Apel, K. O. (1967) *Der Denkweg von Charles Sanders Peirce*. Frankfurt a. M.: Suhrkamp.

Arbeitsgruppe Bielefelder Soziologen (eds) (1973) *Alltagswissen, Interaktion und gesellschaftliche Wirklichkeit*. Reinbek: Rowohlt (new edn 1980, Opladen: Westdeutscher Verlag).

Argelander, H. (1970) *Das Erstinterview in der Psychotherapie*. Darmstadt: Wissenschaftl. Buchgesellschaft.

ASA (1969) *Toward a Code of Ethics for Sociologists. The American Sociologist*, 3 (1968)/4 (1969): 316–318.

Amercian Sociological Association (ASA) (1997) *Code of Ethics* (Approved by ASA Membership in June 1997).

Aster, R., Merkens, H. and Repp, M. (eds) (1989) *Teilnehmende Beobachtung. Werkstattberichte und methodologische Reflexionen*. Frankfurt a. M.: Campus.

Atkinson, J. M. and Heritage, J. (eds) (1984) *Structures of Social Action – Studies in Conversation Analysis*. Cambridge: Cambridge University Press.

Atkinson, P. (1988) 'Ethnomethodology: A Critical Review', *Annual Review of Sociology*, 14: 411–465.

Atkinson, P. (1989) 'Goffman's Poetics', *Human Studies*, 12: 59–76.

Atkinson, P. (1990) *The Ethnographic Imagination. Textual Constructions of Reality*. London: Routledge.

Atkinson, P. (1992) *Understanding Ethnographic Texts* (Qualitative Research Methods Series). London: Sage.

Atkinson, P. and Coffey, A. (1997) 'Analysing Documentary Realities', in D. Silverman (ed.), *Qualitative Research. Theory, Method and Practice*. London: Sage. pp. 45–62.

Atkinson, P., Coffey, S. D., Lofland, J. and Lofland, L. (eds) (2001) *Handbook of Ethnography*. London: Sage.

Atteslander, P. (1996) 'Auf dem Wege zur lokalen Kultur. Einführende Gedanken', in W. F. Whyte, *Die*

Street Corner Society. Die Sozialstruktur eines Italienerviertels. Berlin: de Gruyter. pp. IX–XIV.

Attewell, P. (1974) 'Ethnomethodology since Garfinkel', *Theory and Society*, 1: 179–210.

Auer, P. (1986) 'Kontextualisierung', *Studium Linguistik*, 19: 22–47.

Aufenanger, S. and Lenssen, M. (eds) (1986) *Handlung und Sinnstruktur. Bedeutung und Anwendung der objektiven Hermeneutik.* Munich: Kindt.

Austin, J. L. (1962) *How to Do Things With Words.* Oxford: Clarendon Press.

Ayaß, R. (1997) *Das Wort zum Sonntag. Fallstudie einer kirchlichen Sendereihe.* Stuttgart: Kohlhammer.

Bachmann-Medick, D. (ed.) (1996) *Kultur als Text: die anthropologische Wende in der Literaturwissenschaft.* Frankfurt a. M.: Fischer.

Bahrdt, H. P. (1996) *Grundformen sozialer Situationen – Eine kleine Grammatik des Alltagslebens.* Munich: Beck.

Bakhtin, M. (1989) *Speech Genres and Other Essays.* Austin, TX: University of Texas Press.

Ball, M. S. and Smith, G. W. (1992) *Analysing Visual Data.* Newbury Park, CA: Sage.

Ball, S. J. (1990) 'Self-doubt and Soft Data: Social and Technical Trajectories in Ethnographic Fieldwork', *Qualitative Studies in Education*, 3: 157–171.

Ballstaedt, S.-P., Mandl, H., Schnotz, W. and Tergan, S.-O. (1981) *Texte verstehen, Texte gestalten.* Munich: Urban and Schwarzenberg.

Bamberg, M. G. (ed.) (1997) 'Oral Versions of Personal Experience: Three Decades of Narrative Analysis', *Special Issue of Journal of Narrative and Life History*, 7: 1–4.

Barley, N. (1986) *The Innocent Anthropologist: Notes from a Mud Hut.* Harmondsworth: Penguin Books.

Barthes, R. (1957/1972) *Mythologies.* New York: Hill and Wang.

Barthes, R. (1969) *Literatur oder Geschichte.* Frankfurt a. M.: Suhrkamp.

Barthes, R. (1976) *The Pleasure of the Text* (translated from the French by Richard Miller). London: Cape.

Barthes, R. (1977) *Image–Music–Text.* London: Fontana.

Barthes, R. (1981) *Camera Lucida.* New York: Hill and Wang.

Barton, A. H. and Lazarsfeld, P. F. (1955) 'Some Functions of Qualitative Analysis in Social Research', *Frankfurter Beiträge zur Soziologie I.* Frankfurt a. M.: Europäische Verlagsanstalt. pp. 321–361.

Bateson, G. and Mead, M. (1942) *Balinese Character: A Photographic Analysis.* New York: New York Academy of Sciences.

Bauer, M. W. and Gaskell, G. (eds) (2000) *Qualitative Researching with Text, Image and Sound: A Practical Handbook.* London: Sage.

Bauer, M. W., Gaskell, G. and Allum, N. C. (2000) 'Quality, Quantity and Knowledge Interests: Avoiding Confusions', in M. W. Bauer and G. Gaskell (eds), *Qualitative Researching with Text, Image and Sound – A Handbook.* London: Sage. pp. 3–17.

Baugh, J., Feagin, C., Guy, G. and Schiffrin, D. (eds) (1997) *Towards a Social Science of Language: A Festschrift for William Labov.* Amsterdam: John Benjamins.

Bazerman, Ch. (1987) 'Codifying the Social Scientific Style. The APA Publication Manual as a Behaviourist Rhetoric', in J. S. Nelson, A. Megill and D. N. McCloskey (eds), *The Rhetoric of the Human Sciences.* Madison, WI: University of Wisconsin Press. pp. 125–144.

Bazzi, D. (1996) 'Vom Ort des Notstands zur Gruppenhaut', *Tsantsa*, 1: 54–65.

Beach, W. (ed.) (1989) 'Special Issue on "Sequential Organization of Conversational Activities"', *Western Journal of Speech Communication*, 53: 2.

Beach, W. (ed.) (1996) *Conversations about Illness: Family Preoccupations with Bulimia.* Mahwah, NJ: Lawrence Erlbaum.

Beauchamp, T. L. (1982) *Philosophical Ethics. An Introduction to Moral Philosophy.* New York: McGraw Hill.

Beauvoir, S. de (1993) *The Second Sex* (translated and edited by H. M. Parshley; with a new introduction, bibliography, and chronology by David Campbell). New York: Alfred A. Knopf (first published 1953).

Beck, U. and Bonß, W. (1984) 'Soziologie und Modernisierung. Zur Ortsbestimmung der Verwendungsforschung', *Soziale Welt*, 25: 381–406.

Beck, U. and Bonß, W. (eds) (1989) *Weder Sozialtechnologie noch Aufklärung? Analysen zur Verwendung sozialwissenschaftlichen Wissens.* Frankfurt a. M.: Suhrkamp.

Becker, H. S. (1963) *Outsiders. Studies in the Sociology of Deviance.* New York: Free Press.

Becker, H. S. (1969) 'Problems in the Publication of Field Studies', in G. J. McCall and J. L. Simmsons (eds), *Issues in Participant Observation: A Text and Reader.* New York: Random House. pp. 260–270.

Becker, H. S. (1974) 'Photography and Sociology', *Studies in the Anthropology of Visual Communication*, 1: 3–26. (Reprinted in Becker, H. S. (1986) *Doing Things Together. Selected Papers.* Evanston, IL: Northwestern University Press.)

Becker, H. S. (1986a) *Doing Things Together. Selected Papers.* Evanston, IL: Northwestern University Press.

Becker, H. S. (1986b) *Writing for Social Scientists: How to Start and Finish Your Thesis, Book or Article.* Chicago: Chicago University Press.

Becker, H. S. (1998) *Tricks of the Trade.* Chicago: University of Chicago Press.

Becker, H. S., Geer, B., Hughes, E. C. and Strauss, A. L. (1961) *Boys in White. Student Culture in Medical School.* Chicago: Chicago University Press.

Becker-Schmidt, R., Brandes-Erlhoff, U., Karrer, M., Rumpf, M. and Schmidt, B. (1982*) Nicht wir haben die Minuten, die Minuten haben uns. Zeitprobleme und Zeiterfahrungen von Arbeitermüttern. Studie zum Projekt 'Probleme lohnabhängig arbeitender Mütter'.* Bonn: Verlag Neue Gesellschaft.

Becker-Schmidt, R. and Knapp, G.-A. (eds) (1995) *Das Geschlechterverhältnis als Gegenstand in den Sozialwissenschaften.* Frankfurt a. M: Campus.

Belgrad, J. (ed.) (1997) 'Politisches szenisch entschlüsseln. Tiefenhermeneutik als Verfahren politischer Analyse', *Politisches Lernen*, 15.

Belgrad, J., Görlich, B., König, H. D. and Schmid Noerr, G. (eds) (1987) *Zur Idee einer psychoanalytischen Sozialforschung. Dimensionen szenischen Verstehens.* Frankfurt a. M.: Fischer.

Benninghaus, H. (1994) *Einführung in die sozialwissenschaftliche Datenanalyse.* Munich: Oldenbourg.

Berg, E. and Fuchs, M. (eds) (1993) *Kultur, soziale Praxis, Text. Die Krise der ethnographischen Repräsentation.* Frankfurt a. M.: Suhrkamp.

Berger, J. and Mohr, J. (1975) *A Seventh Man.* New York: Viking.

Berger, P. L. and Kellner, H. (1982) *Sociology Reinterpreted. An Essay on Method and Vocation.* Harmondsworth: Penguin.

Berger, P. L. and Luckmann, T. (1966) *The Social Construction of Reality.* Garden City, NY: Doubleday.

Bergmann, J. R. (1981a) 'Frage und Frageparaphrase – Aspekte der redezuginternen und sequenziellen Organisation eines Äußerungsformats', in P. Winkler (ed.), *Methoden der Analyse von Face-to-Face-Situationen.* Stuttgart: Metzler. pp. 128–142.

Bergmann, J. R. (1981b) 'Ethnomethodologische Konversationsanalyse', in P. Schröder and P. Steger (eds), *Dialogforschung. Jahrbuch des Instituts für deutsche Sprache.* Düsseldorf: Schwann. pp. 9–51.

Bergmann, J. R. (1985) 'Flüchtigkeit und methodische Fixierung sozialer Wirklichkeit: Aufzeichnungen als Daten der interpretativen Soziologie', in W. Bonß and H. Hartman (eds), *Entzauberte Wissenschaf: Zur Relativität und Geltung soziologischer Forschung. Soziale Welt*, Special Issue 3, pp. 299–320.

Bergmann, J. R. (1988) 'Ethnomethodologie und Konversationsanalyse' Kurseinheit 1–3. *Studienbrief für die Fernuniversität Gesamthochschule Hagen.* Hagen: Fernuniversität.

Bergmann, J. R. (1991) 'Goffmans Soziologie des Gesprächs und seine ambivalente Beziehung zur Konversationsanalyse', in R. Hettlage and K. Lenz (eds), *Erving Goffman – ein soziologischer Klassiker der zweiten Generation.* Berne: Haupt. pp. 301–326.

Bergmann, J. R. (1993) *Discreet Indiscretions: The Social Organization of Gossip.* New York: Aldine de Gruyter.

Bergmann, J. R. and Luckmann, T. (eds) (1999) *Kommunikative Konstruktion von Moral.* Opladen: Westdeutscher Verlag.

Bergold, J. B. and Flick, U. (eds) (1987) *Ein-Sichten. Zugänge zur Sicht des Subjekts mittels qualitativer Forschung.* Tübingen: DGVT-Verlag.

Bergs-Winkels, D. (1998) *Weiterbildung in Zeiten organisationskultureller Revolution. Zwei Fallstudien.* Hamburg: Dr Kovac.

Bernard, H. R. (1988) *Research Methods in Cultural Anthropology.* Newbury Park, CA: Sage.

Berreby, D. (1995) 'Unabsolute Truths: Clifford Geertz', *New York Times Magazine*, 9 April, 44–47.

Bihl, G. (1995) *Werteorientierte Personalarbeit.* Munich: Beck.

Billig, M. (1987) *Arguing and Thinking: A Rhetorical Approach to Social Psychology.* Cambridge: Cambridge University Press.

Billig, M. (1991) *Ideology and Opinions.* London: Sage.

Billig, M., Condor, S., Gane, M., Middleton, D. and Radley, A. (1988) *Ideological Dilemmas: A Social Psychology of Everyday Thinking.* London: Sage.

Bion, W. R. (1962) *Learning from Experience.* London: Heinemann.

Birch, M., Miller, T., Mauthner, M. and Jessop, J. (2002) 'Introduction', in M. Mauthner, M. Birch, Jessop, J. and Miller, T. (eds), *Ethics in Qualitative Research.* London: Sage. pp. 1–13.

Blaikie, N. W. (1991) 'A Critique of the Use of Triangulation in Social Research', *Quality and Quantity*, 25: 115–136.

Blank, R. (1997) '"Ich habe andere Sorgen als Politik" – Qualitative Studie "Jugend '97"', in Jugendwerk der Deutschen Shell (eds), *Jugend '97. Zukunftsperspektiven, Gesellschaftliches Engagement, Politische Orientierungen.* Opladen: Leske and Budrich. pp. 33–77.

Bloor, M. (1997) 'Techniques of Validation in Qualitative Research: A Critical Commentary', in G. Miller and R. Dingwall (eds), *Context and Method in Qualitative Research.* London: Sage. pp. 37–50.

Blumenberg, H. (1981) *Wirklichkeiten in denen wir leben.* Stuttgart: Reclam.

Blumer, H. (1969) *Symbolic Interactionism. Perspective and Method.* Englewood Cliffs, NJ: Prentice Hall.

Blumer, H. (1981) 'George Herbert Mead', in B. Rhea (ed.), *The Future of the Sociological Classics.* Boston, MA: George Allen and Unwin. pp. 136–169.

Boccia Artieri, G. (1996) 'The Virtual Image Technology, Media, and the Construction of Visual Reality', *Visual Sociology*, 11: 56–61.

Boden, D. and Zimmerman, D. H. (eds) (1991) *Talk and Social Structure: Studies in Ethnomethodology and Conversation Analysis.* Cambridge: Polity Press.

Bogdan, R. and Ksander, M. (1980) 'Policy Data as a Social Process: A Qualitative Approach to Quantitative Data', *Human Organization*, 39: 302–309.

Bohnsack, R. (1989) *Generation, Milieu und Geschlecht – Ergebnisse aus Gruppendiskussionen mit Jugendlichen.* Opladen: Leske and Budrich.

Bohnsack, R. (1992) 'Dokumentarische Interpretation von Orientierungsmustern – Verstehen – Interpretieren – Typenbildung in wissenssoziologischer Analyse', in M. Meuser and R. Sackmann (eds), *Analyse sozialer Deutungsmuster.* Pfaffenweiler: Centaurus. pp. 139–160.

Bohnsack, R. (1997) 'Dokumentarische Methode', in R. Hitzler and A. Honer (eds), *Sozialwissenschaftliche Hermeneutik.* Opladen: Leske and Budrich. pp. 191–211.

Bohnsack, R. (1998a) 'Rekonstruktive Sozialforschung und der Grundbegriff des Orientierungsmusters', in D. Siefkes, P. Eulenhöfer, H. Stach and K. Städtler (eds), *Sozialgeschichte der Informatik – Kulturelle Praktiken und Orientierungen*. Wiesbaden: Deutscher Universitätsverlag. pp. 105–121.

Bohnsack, R. (1998b) *'Zusatzstudium "Qualitative Methoden in den Sozialwissenschaften" – Informationen für Studierende im achten Durchgang'*. Manuscript, Free University of Berlin.

Bohnsack, R. (1999) *Rekonstruktive Sozialforschung – Einführung in Methodologie und Praxis*. Opladen: Leske and Budrich.

Bohnsack, R., Loos, P., Schäffer, B., Städtler, K. and Wild, B. (1995) *Die Suche nach Gemeinsamkeit und die Gewalt der Gruppe – Hooligans, Musikgruppen und andere Jugendcliquen*. Opladen: Leske and Budrich.

Bohnsack, R. and Nohl, A.-M. (1998) 'Adoleszenz und Migration – Empirische Zugänge einer praxeologisch fundierten Wissenssoziologie', in R. Bohnsack and M. Marotzki (eds), *Biographieforschung und Kulturanalyse – Transdisziplinäre Zugänge qualitativer Forschung*. Opladen: Leske and Budrich. pp. 260–282.

Bolton, R. (ed.) (1989) *The Contest of Meaning: Critical Histories of Photography*. Cambridge, MA: MIT Press.

Bonfantini, M. (1988) 'Semiotik und Geschichte: eine Synthese jenseits des Marxismus'. *Zeitschrift für Semiotik*, 10: 85–95.

Bonß, W. and Hartmann, H. (eds) (1985) *Entzauberte Wissenschaft: Zur Relativität and Geltung soziologischer Forschung. Soziale Welt*, Special Issue 3.

Born, C., Krüger, H. and Lorenz-Meyer, D. (1996) *Der unentdeckte Wandel: Annäherung an das Verhältnis von Struktur und Norm im weiblichen Lebenslauf*. Berlin: Edition Sigma.

Bortz, J. and Döring, N. (1995) *Forschungsmethoden und Evaluation für Sozialwissenschaftler*, 2nd rev. edn. Berlin: Springer.

Bosch, A., Fehr, H., Kraetsch, C. and Schmidt, G. (eds) (1999) *Sozialwissenschaftliche Forschung und Praxis. Interdisziplinäre Sichtweisen*. Wiesbaden: Deutscher Universitätsverlag.

Böttger, A. (1998) 'Zur Bedeutung der Theorie im rekonstruktiven Interview'. Paper given at the Jahrestagung der Arbeitsgruppe 'Methoden der qualitativen Sozialforschung' in Frankfurt a. M., 8 May 1998.

Bourdieu, P. (1982) *Sozialer Sinn. Kritik der theoretischen Vernunft*. Frankfurt a. M.: Suhrkamp.

Bourdieu, P. (2000) *Distinction: A Social Critique of the Judgement of Taste*. London: Routledge.

Bourdieu, P., Chamboredon, J.-C. and Passeron, J.-C. (1991) *The Craft of Sociology*. Berlin: de Gruyter.

Bourgeois III, L. J. and Eisenhart, K. M. (1988) 'Strategic Decision Processes in High Velocity Environments: Four Cases in the Microcomputer Industry', *Management Science*, 7: 816–835.

Bowen, E. S. (1964) *Return to Laughter: An Anthropological Novel*. New York: Doubleday.

Boyer, L. B. (1980) 'Die Psychoanalyse in der Ethnologie', *Psyche*, 34: 694–715.

Boyer, L. B. (1983) 'Approaching Cross-Cultural Psychotherapy', *Journal of Psychoanalytic Anthropology*, 6: 237–245.

Boyer, L. B. and Grolnik, S. A. (eds) (1975) *The Psychoanalytic Study of Society*, Volume 1. Hillsdale, NJ: The Analytic Press.

Boyer, L. B. and Grolnik, S. A. (eds) (1988) *Essays in Honor of George Devereux* (The Psychoanalytic Study of Society, Volume 12). Hillsdale, NJ: The Analytic Press.

Boyer, L. B. and Grolnik, S. A. (eds) (1989) *Essays in Honor of Paul Parin* (The Psychoanalytic Study of Society, Volume 14). Hillsdale, NJ: The Analytic Press.

Brandstätter, H. (1978) 'Organisationsdiagnose', in A. Mayer (ed.), *Organisationspsychologie*. Stuttgart: Poeschel. pp. 43–71.

Brauner, H. (1978) *Die Phänomenologie Edmund Husserls und ihre Bedeutung für soziologische Theorien*. Meisenheim a. G.: Hain.

Breuer, F. (ed.) (1996) *Qualitative Psychologie*. Opladen: Westdeutscher Verlag.

Brewer, J. D. (2000) *Ethnography* (Understanding Social Research Series). Buckingham: Open University Press.

Bromley, R., Göttlich, U. and Winter, C. (eds) (1999) *Cultural Studies. Grundlagentexte zur Einführung*. Lüneburg: zu Klampen.

Brosius, G. (1988) *SPSS/PC and Basics und Graphics. Einführung und praktische Beispiele*. Hamburg: McGraw Hill.

Brown, M. E. (1994) *Soap Opera and Women's Talk. The Pleasure of Resistance*. Thousand Oaks, CA: Sage.

Brown, R. (1977) *A Poetic for Sociology – Toward a Logic of Discovery for the Human Sciences*. London: Cambridge University Press.

Bruce, G. (1992) 'Comments', in J. Svartvik (ed.), *Directions in Corpus Linguistics. Proceedings of the Nobel Symposium 82, Stockholm, August 4–8, 1991*. Berlin: de Gruyter. pp. 145–147.

Bruckner, P. and Finkielkraut, A. (1981) *Das Abenteuer gleich um die Ecke*. Munich: Hanser.

Bruner, E. (1984) 'Experience and Its Expressions', in V. M. Turner and E. N. Bruner (eds), *The Anthropology of Experience*. Urbana, IL: University of Illinois Press.

Bruner, J. (1987) 'Life as Narrative', *Social Research*, 54: 11–32.

Bruner, J. (1990) *Acts of Meaning*. Cambridge, MA: Harvard University Press.

Bruyn, S. T. (1966) *The Human Perspective in Sociology. The Methodology of Participant Observation*. Englewood Cliffs, NJ: Prentice Hall.

Bryk, A. (ed.) (1983) *Stakeholder-based Evaluation*. San Francisco: Jossey–Bass.

Bryman, A. (1988) *Quantity and Quality in Social Research*. London: Unwin Hyman.

Bude, H. (1984) 'Rekonstruktion von Lebenskonstruktionen – eine Antwort auf die Frage, was die

Biographieforschung bringt', in M. Kohli and
G. Robert (eds), *Biographie und soziale Wirklichkeit.
Neuere Beiträge und Forschungsperspektiven*. Stuttgart:
Metzler. pp. 7–28.

Bude, H. (1987) *Deutsche Karrieren – Lebenskonstruktionen sozialer Aufsteiger aus der Flakhelfer-
Generation*. Frankfurt a. M.: Suhrkamp.

Bude, H. (1988) 'Auflösung des Sozialen? Die
Verflüssigung der soziologischen "Gegenstandes"
im Fortgang des soziologischen Theorie', *Soziale
Welt*, 39: 4–17.

Bude, H. (1989) 'Der Essay als Form der Darstellung
sozialwissenschaftlicher Erkenntnisse', *Kölner
Zeitschrift für Soziologie und Sozialpsychologie*,
41: 526–539.

Bude, H. (1993) 'Die soziologische Erzählung', in
S. Jung and S. Müller-Doohm (eds), *"Wirklichkeit" im
Deutungsprozeß – Verstehen und Methoden in den
Kultur- und Sozialwissenschaften*. Frankfurt a. M.:
Suhrkamp. pp. 409–429.

Bude, H. (1995) *Das Altern einer Generation – Die
Jahrgänge 1938 bis 1948*. Frankfurt a. M.: Suhrkamp
(2nd edn 1997).

Bude, H. (1997) 'Die "Wir-Schicht" der Generation',
Berliner Journal für Soziologie, 7: 197–204.

Bude, H. (2000) 'Die biographische Relevanz der
Generation', in M. Kohli and M. Szydlik (eds),
Generationen in Familie und Gesellschaft. Opladen:
Leske and Budrich. pp. 19–35.

Bühler, K. (1934/1990) *Theory of Language: The
Representational Function of Language*. Amsterdam:
John Benjamins.

Bühler-Niederberger, D. (1985) 'Analytische Induktion
als Verfahren qualitativer Methodologie', *Zeitschrift
für Soziologie*, 14: 475–485.

Bühler-Niederberger, D. (1995) 'Analytische Induktion',
in U. Flick, E. von Kardorff, H. Keupp, L. von
Rosenstiel and S. Wolff (eds), *Handbuch Qualitative
Sozialforschung*. Munich: Psychologie Verlags Union.
pp. 446–450.

Bungard, W., Holling, H. and Schultz-Gambard, J. (1996)
Methoden der Arbeits- und Organisationspsychologie.
Weinheim: Beltz.

Burgess, R. G. (1982) 'Elements of Sampling in Field
Research', in R. G. Burgess (ed.), *Field Research: A
Sourcebook and Field Manual*. London: George Allen
and Unwin. pp. 76–78.

Burgess, R. G. (1991) 'Sponsors, Gatekeepers, Members,
and Friends', in W. B. Shaffir and R. A. Stebbins (eds),
*Experiencing Fieldwork. An Inside View of Qualitative
Research*. Newbury Park, CA: Sage. pp. 43–52.

Burke, P. (1993) *The Art of Conversation*. Cambridge:
Polity Press.

Burkitt, I. (1999) *Bodies of Thought: Embodiment,
Identity and Modernity*. London: Sage.

Burns, T. (1992) *Erving Goffman*. London: Routledge.

Burr, V. (1994) *An Introduction to Social Constructionism*.
London: Routledge.

Busse, D. (1994) 'Interpretation, Verstehen und
Gebrauch von Texten: Semantische und pragmatische

Aspekte der Textrezeption', in A. Böhm, A. Mengel
and T. Muhr (eds), *Texte verstehen. Konzepte,
Methoden, Werkzeuge*. Konstanz: Universitätsverlag.
pp. 49–80.

Büssing, A. (1995) 'Organisationsdiagnose', in
H. Schuler (ed.), *Lehrbuch der Organisationspsychologie*.
Berre: Huber. pp. 445–480.

Butler, J. P. (1990) *Gender Trouble: Feminism and the
Subversion of Identity*. New York: Routledge.

Butler, J. (1991) *Das Unbehagen der Geschlechter*.
Frankfurt a. M.: Suhrkamp.

Butler, J. (1993) 'Imitation and Gender Insub-
ordination', in C. Lemert (ed.), *Social Theory: The
Multicultural and Classic Readings*. Boulder, CO:
Westview. pp. 637–648.

Button, G. (ed.) (1991) *Ethnomethodology and the
Human Sciences*. Cambridge: Cambridge University
Press.

Button, G. (ed.) (1993) *Technology in Working Order.
Studies of Work, Interaction, and Technology*. London:
Routledge.

Button, G., Drew, P. and Heritage, J. (eds) (1986)
'Interaction and Language Use', *Human Studies*,
(4): 2–3.

Button, G. and Lee, J. R. (eds) (1987) *Talk and Social
Organisation*. Clevedon: Multilingual Matters.

Campbell, D. T. and Fiske, D. W. (1959) 'Convergent
and Discriminant Validation by the Multitrait-
Multimethod Matrix', *Psychological Bulletin*, 56:
81–105.

Carnap, R. (1928) *The Logical Structure of the World*.
Berkeley, CA: University of California Press.

Casagrande, J. B. (ed.) (1960) *In the Company of Man*.
New York: Harper and Row.

Cassirer, E. (1953–1996) *Philosophy of Symbolic Forms*,
4 vols. New Haven, CT: Yale University Press.

Chaflen, R. (1986) *Snapshot Versions of Life*. Bowling
Green, OH: Bowling Green University Press.

Chalmers, A. F. (1982) *What is This Thing Called
Science?* Brisbane: University of Queensland
Press.

Chamberlayne, P., Bornat, J. and Wengraf, T. (eds)
(2000) *The Turn to Biographical Methods in Social
Science. Comparative Issues and Examples*. London:
Routledge.

Charmaz, K. (1985) 'Rethinking Self and Feeling:
Review of '"On understanding emotion"' by
N. K. Denzin', *Contemporary Sociology*, 14: 552–555.

Charmaz, K. (1990) '"Discovering" Chronic Illness:
Using Grounded Theory', *Social Science and Medicine*,
30: 1161–1172.

Charmaz, K. (2000) 'Grounded Theory: Objectivist
and Constructivist Methods', in N. K. Denzin and
Y. S. Lincoln (eds), *Handbook of Qualitative Research*,
2nd edn. Thousand Oaks, CA: Sage. pp. 509–536.

Chelimsky, E. and Shadish, W. R. (eds) (1997) *Evaluation
for the 21st Century. A Handbook*. Thousand Oaks,
CA: Sage.

Chell, E. (1998) 'Critical Incident Technique', in
C. Cassell and G. Symon (eds), *Qualitative Methods*

and Analysis in Organizational Research. A Practical Guide. London: Sage. pp. 51–72.

Christie, R. and Jahoda, M. (eds) (1954) *Studies in the Scope and Method of 'The Authoritarian Personality'* (Continuities in Social Research, Volume 2). Glencoe, IL: Free Press.

Cicourel, A. V. (1964) *Method and Measurement in Sociology.* New York: Free Press of Glencoe.

Cicourel, A. V. (1968) *The Social Organization of Juvenile Justice.* New York: Wiley.

Cicourel, A. V. (1975) *Sprache in der sozialen Interaktion.* Munich: List.

Cicourel, A. V. and Jennings, K. H. (1974) *Language Use and School Performance.* New York: Academic Press.

Cicourel, A. V. and Kitsuse, J. I. (1963) *The Educational Decision-Makers.* Indianapolis: Bobbs–Merrill.

Clarke, A. E. (forthcoming) *Grounded Theorising after the Postmodernist Turn: Situation Analysis with Historical, Visual and Discursive Materials.*

Clarke, J., Cohen, P., Corrigan, P., Gerber, J., Hall, S., Hebdige, D., Jefferson, T., McCron, R., McRobbie, A., Murdock, G., Parker, H. and Roberts, B. (1979) 'Jugendkultur als Widerstand. Milieus, Rituale, Provokationen' (edited by R. Honneth, R. Lindner and R. Paris). Frankfurt a. M.: Syndikat.

Clegg, S., Hardy, C. and Nord, W. (eds) (1996) *Handbook of Organization Studies.* London: Sage.

Clifford, J. (1983) 'On Ethnographic Authority', *Representations*, 1 (2): 118–146.

Clifford, J. (1986a) 'Ethnographic Allegory', in J. Clifford and G. E. Marcus (eds), *Writing Culture: The Poetic and Politics of Ethnography. Experiments in Contemporary Anthropology.* Berkeley, CA: University of California Press. pp: 98–121.

Clifford, J. (1986b) 'Introduction: Partial Truths', in J. Clifford and G. E. Marcus (eds), *Writing Culture: The Poetic and Politics of Ethnography. Experiments in Contemporary Anthropology.* Berkeley, CA: University of California Press. pp. 1–26.

Clifford, J. (1988a) 'Ethnographic Authority', in J. Clifford (ed.), *The Predicament of Culture. Twentieth Century Ethnography Literature, and Art.* Cambridge, MA: Harvard University Press. pp. 21–45.

Clifford, J. (1988b) 'On Ethnographic Surrealism', in J. Clifford (ed.), *The Predicament of Culture. Twentieth Century Ethnography, Literature, and Art.* Cambridge, MA: Harvard University Press. pp. 117–151.

Clifford, J. and Marcus, G. E. (eds) (1986) *Writing Culture: The Poetic and Politics of Ethnography.* Berkeley, CA: University of California Press.

Clough, P. T. (1998) *The End(s) of Ethnography*, 2nd edn. New York: Peter Lang.

Coffey, A., Holbrook, B. and Atkinson, P. (1996) 'Qualitative Data Analysis: Technologies and Representations', *Sociological Research Online*, 1 (http://www.socresonline.org.uk/socresonline/1/1/4html).

Colby, A. and Kohlberg, L. (1987) *The Measurement of Moral Judgment*, 2 vols. Cambridge: Cambridge University Press.

Collier, J. Jr and Collier, M. (1986) *Visual Anthropology: Photography as a Research Method.* Albuquerque, NM: University of New Mexico Press.

Collins, R. (1980) 'Erving Goffman's Sociology: Social Origins of an American Structuralism', in J. Ditton (ed.), *The View from Goffman.* New York: Macmillan. pp. 170–209.

Comelli, G. (1985) 'Training als Beitrag zur Organisationsentwicklung. Handbuch der Weiterbildung für die Praxis, *Wirtschaft und Verwaltung.* Munich: Hanser.

Comelli, G. (1994) 'Teamentwicklung – Training von "family groups"', in L. M. Hofmann and E. Regnet (eds), *Innovative Weiterbildungskonzepte.* Göttingen: Verlag für Angewandte Psychologie. pp. 61–84.

Conrad, P. and Reinarz, S. (1984) 'Qualitative Computing: Approaches and Issues', *Qualitative Sociology*, 7: 34–60.

Converse, J. (1984) 'Strong Arguments and Weak Evidence: The Open/Closed Questioning Controversy of the 1940s', *Public Opinion Quarterly*, 48: 267–282.

Cook, G. (1990) 'Transcribing Infinity – Problems of Context Presentation', *Journal of Pragmatics*, 14: 1–24.

Cooley, C. H. (1902) *Human Nature and the Social Order.* New York: C. Scribner's Sons.

Cooley, C. H. and Mead, G. H. (1902/1967) *Human Nature and the Social Order.* New York: Schocken.

Corbin, J. M. and Strauss, A. L. (1988) *Unending Work and Care.* San Francisco: Jossey–Bass.

Corbin, J. M. and Strauss, A. L. (1990) 'Grounded Theory Research: Procedures, Canons and Evaluative Criteria', *Zeitschrift für Soziologie*, 19: 418–427.

Coulter, J. (1989) *Mind in Action.* Cambridge: Polity Press.

Coulter, J. (ed.) (1990) *Ethnomethodological Sociology.* Brookfield: Edward Elgar.

Couper-Kuhlen, E. and Selting, M. (eds) (1996) *Prosody in Conversation: Interactional Studies.* Cambridge: Cambridge University Press.

Crabtree, B. F. and Miller, W. L. (1992) 'A Template Approach to Text Analysis: Developing and Using Codebooks', in B. F. Crabtree and W. L. Miller (eds), *Doing Qualitative Research. Volume 3: Research Methods for Primary Care.* Newbury Park, CA: Sage. pp. 93–109.

Crapanzano, V. (1973) *The Hamadsa: A Study in Moroccan Ethnopsychiatry.* Berkeley, CA: University of California Press.

Crapanzano, V. (1983) *Tuhami: Portrait eines Marokkaners.* Stuttgart: Klett–Cotta.

Crapanzano, V. (1985) *Waiting: The Whites of South Africa.* London: Granada.

Crapanzano, V. (1986) 'Hermes Dilemma – The Masking of Subversion in Ethnographic Description', in J. Clifford and G. Marcus (eds), *Writing Culture – The Poetics and Politics of Ethnography.* Berkeley, CA: University of California Press. pp. 51–76.

Creswell, J. W. (1998) *Qualitative Inquiry and Research Design – Choosing Among Five Traditions*. Thousand Oaks, CA: Sage.

Cronbach, L. J. (1982) 'In Praise of Uncertainty', in P. Rossi (ed.), *New Directions for Program Evaluation Practice*. San Francisco: Jossey–Bass. pp. 49–66.

Cronbach, L. J. (1983) 'Ninety-five-Theses', in G. F. Madaus, M. Scriven and D. L. Stufflebeam (eds), *Evaluation Models*. Boston, MA: Kluwer–Nijhoff.

Czyzewski, M., Gülich, E., Hausendorf, H. and Kastner, M. (eds) (1995) *Nationale Selbst- und Fremdbilder im Gespräch: Kommunikative Prozesse nach der Wiedervereinigung Deutschlands und dem Systemwechsel in Ostmitteleuropa*. Opladen: Westdeutscher Verlag.

Dammann, R. (1991) *Die dialogische Praxis der Feldforschung. Der ethnographische Blick als Paradigma der Erkenntnisgewinnung*. Frankfurt a. M.: Campus.

D'Andrade, R. (1995) *The Development of Cognitive Anthropology*. Cambridge: Cambridge University Press.

Darnton, R. (1989) 'Ein Bourgeois bringt seine Welt in Ordnung: Die Stadt als Text', in R. Darnton, *Das große Katzenmassaker*. Munich: Hanser. pp. 125–168.

Dausien, B. (1996) *Biographie und Geschlecht – Zur biographischen Konstruktion sozialer Wirklichkeit in Frauenlebensgeschichten*. Bremen: Donat.

Davies, W. H. (1972) *Peirce's Epistemology*. The Hague: Martinus Nijhoff.

De Certeau, M. (1984) *The Practice of Everyday Life*. Berkeley, CA: University of California Press.

Delany, C. F. (1993) *Science, Knowledge and Mind: A Study in the Philosophy of C.S. Peirce*. Notre Dame, IN: University of Notre Dame Press.

Dennett, D. C. (1991) *Consciousness Explained*. Harmondsworth: Penguin.

Denzin, N. K. (1969) 'Symbolic Interactionism and Ethnomethodology: A Proposed Synthesis', *American Sociological Review*, 34: 922–934.

Denzin, N. K. (1971) 'The Logic of Naturalistic Inquiry'. *Social Forces*, 50: 166–181.

Denzin, N. K. (1977) 'Notes on the Criminogenic Hypothesis: A Case Study of the American Liquor Industry', *American Sociological Review*, 42: 905–920.

Denzin, N. K. (1978) *The Research Act. A Theoretical Introduction to Sociological Methods*. New York: McGraw Hill (2nd edn).

Denzin, N. K. (1979) 'The Interactionist Study of Social Organization: A Note on Method', *Symbolic Interaction*, 2: 59–72.

Denzin, N. K. (1982) 'On Time and Mind', *Studies in Symbolic Interaction*, 4: 35–42.

Denzin, N. K. (1983) 'A Note on Emotionality, Self and Interaction', *American Journal of Sociology*, 89: 402–409.

Denzin, N. K. (1984) *On Understanding Emotion*. San Francisco: Jossey–Bass.

Denzin, N. K. (1985a) 'Emotion as Lived Experience', *Symbolic Interaction*, 8: 223–240.

Denzin, N. K. (1985b) 'On the Phenomenology of Sexuality, Desire, and Violence', *Current Perspectives in Social Theory*, 6: 39–56.

Denzin, N. K. (1986) 'Reflections on the Ethnographer's Camera', *Current Perspectives in Social Theory*, 7: 105–123.

Denzin, N. K. (1987) 'On Semiotics and Symbolic Interactionism', *Symbolic Interaction*, 10: 1–19.

Denzin, N. K. (1988) 'Blue Velvet: Postmodern Contradictions', *Theory, Culture and Society*, 5: 461–473.

Denzin, N. K. (1989a) 'Review Symposium on Field Methods: Review of the Clinical Perspective in Fieldwork by Edgar Schein, Membership Roles in Field Research by P. A. Adler and P. Adler, and Semiotics and Fieldwork by P. K. Manning', *Journal of Contemporary Ethnography*, 18: 89–109.

Denzin, N. K. (1989b) *Interpretive Interactionism* (Applied Social Research Methods Series, Volume 16). Thousand Oaks, CA: Sage.

Denzin, N. K. (1989c) *The Research Act: A Theoretical Introduction to Sociological Methods*, 3rd edn. Englewood Cliffs, NJ: Prentice Hall.

Denzin, N. K. (1989d) *Interpretive Biography* (Qualitative Research Methods Series). London: Sage.

Denzin, N. K. (1990a) 'Presidential Address on The Sociological Imagination Revisited', *The Sociological Quarterly*, 31: 1–22.

Denzin, N. K. (1990b) 'Writing the Interpretive Postmodern Ethnography: Review Essay of "The Python Killer" by Vinigi L. Grottanelli and "In Sorcery's Shadow", by Paul Stoller and Cheryl Olkes', *Journal of Contemporary Ethnography*, 19: 231–236.

Denzin, N. K. (1991a) 'The Postmodern Sexual Order: Sex, Lies and Yuppie Love', *The Social Science Journal*, 28: 407–424.

Denzin, N. K. (1991b) 'Empiricist Cultural Studies in America: A Deconstructive Reading', *Current Perspectives in Social Theory*, 11: 17–39.

Denzin, N. K. (1992) *Symbolic Interactionism and Cultural Studies: The Politics of Interpretation*. Cambridge, MA: Blackwell.

Denzin, N. K. (1993) 'Rain Man in Las Vegas: Where is the Action for the Postmodern Self?', *Symbolic Interaction*, 16: 65–77.

Denzin, N. K. (1995) *The Cinematic Society. The Voyeur's Gaze*. New York: Sage.

Denzin, N. K. (1996a) 'Prophetic Pragmatism and the Postmodern: A Comment on Maines', *Symbolic Interaction*, 19: 341–355.

Denzin, N. K. (1996b) 'Sociology at the End of the Century', *The Sociological Quarterly*, 37: 743–752.

Denzin, N. K. (ed.) (1996c) *Cultural Studies. A Research Volume*. Greenwich, CT: JAI Press (annually since 1996).

Denzin, N. K. (1997) *Interpretive Ethnography. Ethnographic Practices for the 21st Century*. Thousand Oaks, CA: Sage.

Denzin, N. K. (1999) 'Interpretive Ethnography for the Next Century', *Journal of Contemporary Ethnography*, 28 (5): 510–519.

Denzin, N. K. (2000) 'The Practices and Politics of Interpretation', in N. K. Denzin and Y. S. Lincoln (eds),

Handbook of Qualitative Research. Thousand Oaks, CA: Sage. pp. 897–922.

Denzin, N. K. (2002) *Reading Race: Hollywood and the Cinema of Racial Violence*. London: Sage.

Denzin, N. K. and Lincoln, Y. S. (1994a) 'Introduction: Entering the Field of Qualitative Research', in N. K. Denzin and Y. S. Lincoln (eds), *Handbook of Qualitative Research*. London: Sage. pp. 1–17.

Denzin, N. K. and Lincoln, Y. S. (eds) (1994b) *Handbook of Qualitative Research*. Thousand Oaks, CA: Sage.

Denzin, N. K. and Lincoln, Y. S. (1994c) 'Strategies of Inquiry', in N. K. Denzin and Y. S. Lincoln (eds), *Handbook of Qualitative Research*. Thousand Oaks, CA: Sage. pp. 200–208.

Denzin, N. K. and Lincoln, Y. S. (eds) (2000) *Handbook of Qualitative Research*, 2nd edn. Thousand Oaks, CA: Sage.

Deppermann, A. (1999) *Gespräche analysieren: Eine Einführung in konversationsanalytische Methoden*. Opladen: Leske and Budrich.

Dern, D. P. (1997) 'Footprints and Fingerprints in Cyberspace: The Trail you Leave Behind', *ONLINE*, July.

Devereux, G. (1951) *Reality and Dream: Psychotherapy of a Plain Indian*. Madison, CT: International Universities Press.

Devereux, G. (1961) *Mohave Ethnopsychiatry: The Psychic Disturbances of an Indian Tribe*. Washington, DC: Smithsonian Institute Press.

Devereux, G. (1967) *From Anxiety to Method in the Behavioural Sciences*. The Hague: Mouton and Co.

Devereux, G. (1974) *Normal und Anormal*: *Aufsätze zur allgemeinen Ethnopsychiatrie*. Frankfurt a. M.: Suhrkamp.

Dewe, B. (1985) 'Soziologie als beratende Rekonstruktion. Zur Metapher des klinischen Soziologen', in W. Bonß and H. Hartmann (eds), *Entzauberte Wissenschaft: Zur Relativität und Geltung soziologischer Forschung. Soziale Welt*, Special Issue 3, pp. 351–390.

Dewe, B. (1991) *Beratende Wissenschaft*. Göttingen: Schwartz.

Dewe, B. and Radtke, F.-O. (1989) 'Klinische Soziologie – eine Leitfigur der Verwendung sozialwissenschaftlichen Wissens', in U. Beck and W. Bonß (eds), *Weder Sozialtechnologie noch Aufklärung?* Frankfurt a. M.: Suhrkamp. pp. 46–71.

Dewey, J. (1934) *Art as Experience*. New York: Minton, Balach, and Co.

Diederichsen, D. (1993) *Freiheit macht arm – Das Leben nach dem Rock´n´Roll 1990–93*. Cologne: Kiepenheuer and Witsch.

Diekmann, A. (1995) *Empirische Sozialforschung*. Reinbek: Rowohlt.

Diepold, P. (1996) 'Internet. Neue Chancen für die Lehre', in *Neue Medien in der Hochschullehre. Handbuch Hochschullehre Highlights*, Volume 2. Bonn: Raabe. pp. 1–22.

Dierkes, M. and Hähner, K. (1993) 'Sozio-ökonomischer Wandel und Unternehmensleitbilder', in B. Strümpel and M. Dierkes (eds), *Innovation und Beharrung der Arbeitspolitik*. Stuttgart: Schäffer-Poeschel. pp. 277–310.

Dilthey, W. (1968a) 'Über vergleichende Psychologie. Beiträge zum Studium der Individualität', in W. Dilthey, *Gesammelte Schriften, Volume V: Die geistige Welt. Einleitung in die Philosophie des Lebens*, 5th edn. Erste Hälfte. Abhandlungen zur Grundlegung der Geisteswissenschaften. Stuttgart: B. Teubner Verlagsanstalt. pp. 241–316.

Dilthey, W. (1968b) 'Die Entstehung der Hermeneutik', in W. Dilthey, *Gesammelte Schriften, Volume V: Die geistige Welt. Einleitung in die Philosophie des Lebens. Erste Hälfte. Abhandlungen zur Grundlegung der Geisteswissenschaften*, 5th edn. Stuttgart: B. Teubner Verlagsanstalt. pp. 317–338.

Dilthey, W. (1968c) 'Der Aufbau der geschichtlichen Welt in den Geisteswissenschaften', in W. Dilthey, *Gesammelte Schriften*, Volume 7, 5th edn. Stuttgart: B. Teubner Verlagsanstalt.

Dilthey, W. (1996) *Selected Works. Volume 4: Hermeneutics and the Study of History*. Princeton, NJ: Princeton University Press.

Dölling, I. and Krais, B. (eds) (1997) *Ein alltägliches Spiel – Geschlechterkonstruktion in der sozialen Praxis*. Frankfurt a. M.: Suhrkamp.

Douglas, J. D. (1967) *The Social Meaning of Suicide*. Princeton, NJ: Princeton University Press.

Douglas, J. D. (ed.) (1970) *Understanding Everyday Life: Toward the Reconstruction of Sociological Knowledge*. Chicago: Aldine.

Douglas, J. D. (1976) *Investigative Social Research*. Beverly Hills, CA: Sage.

Douglas, J. D. and Johnson, J. M. (eds) (1978) *Existential Sociology*. Cambridge: Cambridge University Press.

Douglas, M. (1973) *Natural Symbols: Explorations in Cosmology*. London: Barrie and Jenkins.

Drew, P. (1978) 'Accusations: The Occasioned Use of Members' Knowledge of "Religious Geography" in Describing Events', *Sociology*, 12: 1–22.

Drew, P. and Heritage, J. (eds) (1992) *Talk at Work: Interaction in Institutional Settings*. Cambridge: Cambridge University Press.

Drew, P. and Wootton, A. (1988) 'Introduction', in P. Drew and A. Wootton (eds), *Erving Goffman – Exploring the Interaction Order*. Cambridge: Polity Press. pp. 1–13.

Dreyfus, S. E. and Dreyfus, H. L. (1986) *Mind over Machine – The Power of Human Intuition and Expertise in the Era of the Computer*. Oxford: Blackwell.

Du Bois, J. W. (1991) 'Transcription Design Principles for Spoken Discourse Research', *Journal of Pragmatics*, 15: 71–106.

Du Gay, P. (ed.) (1997) *Production of Culture/Cultures of Production*. London: Sage.

Du Gay, P., Hall, S., Janes, L., Mackay, H. and Negus, K. (1997) *Doing Cultural Studies. The Story of the Sony Walkman*. London: Sage.

Duerr, H.-P. (ed.) (1987) *Authentizität und Betrug in der Ethnologie*. Frankfurt a. M.: Suhrkamp.

Duneier, M. (1999). *Sidewalk*. New York: Farrar Straus and Giroux.

Dunn, R. G. (1998) *Identity Crisis*. Minneapolis: University of Minnesota Press.

Duranti, A. (1997) *Linguistic Anthropology*. Cambridge: Cambridge University Press.

Eagleton, T. (1983) *Literary Theory: An Introduction*. Oxford: Blackwell.

Eagleton, T. (1991) *Ideology: An Introduction*. London: Verso.

Eagleton, T. (1996) *The Illusions of Postmodernism*. Oxford: Blackwell.

Easterlin, R. A. (1980) *Birth and Fortune – The Impact of Numbers on Personal Welfare*. New York: Basic Books.

Eberle, T. (1984) *Sinnkonstitution in Alltag und Wissenschaft: Der Beitrag der Phänomenologie an die Methodologie der Sozialwissenschaften*. Berne: Haupt.

Eberle, T. S. (1999) 'Die methodologische Grundlegung der interpretativen Sozialforschung durch die phänomenologische Lebensweltanalyse von Alfred Schütz', *Österreichische Zeitschrift für Soziologie*, 4: 65–90.

Eco, U. (1981) 'Guessing: from Aristotle to Sherlock Holmes', *Versus*, 3–19.

Edmondson, R. (1984) *Rhetoric in Sociology*. London: Macmillan.

Edwards, D. (1995) 'A Commentary on Discursive and Critical Psychology', *Culture and Psychology*, 1: 55–63.

Edwards, D. and Potter, J. (1992) *Discursive Psychology*. London: Sage.

Edwards, D. and Potter, J. (1993) 'Language and Causation: A Discursive Action Model of Description and Attribution', *Psychological Review*, 100: 23–41.

Edwards, E. (ed.) (1992) *Anthropology and Photography, 1860–1920*. New Haven, CT: Yale University Press.

Edwards, J. A. and Lampert, M. D. (eds) (1993) *Talking Data: Transcription and Coding in Discourse Research*. Hillsdale, NJ: Erlbaum.

Ehlich, K. (1993) 'HIAT – A Transcription System for Discourse Data', in J. A. Edwards and M. D. Lampert (eds), *Talking Data – Transcription and Coding in Discourse Research*. Hillsdale, NJ: Erlbaum. pp. 123–148.

Ehlich, K. and Rehbein, J. (1976) 'Halbinterpretative Arbeitstranskriptionen' (HIAT), *Linguistische Berichte*, 45: 21–41.

Eickelpasch, R. and Lehmann, B. (1983) *Soziologie ohne Gesellschaft? Probleme einer phänomenologischen Grundlegung der Soziologie*. Munich: Fink.

Eisenhardt, K. M. (1995) 'Building Theories from Case Study Research', in G. P. Huber and A. H. van de Ven (eds), *Longitudinal Field Research. Studying Processes of Organizational Change*. Thousand Oaks, CA: Sage. pp. 65–90.

Ellis, B. (1968) *Basic Concepts of Measurement*. Cambridge: Cambridge University Press.

Emerson, R., Fretz, R. and Shaw, L. (1995) *Writing Ethnographic Fieldnotes*. Chicago: Chicago University Press.

Engelmann, J. (ed.) (1999) *Die kleinen Unterschiede. Der Cultural Studies-Reader*. Frankfurt a. M.: Campus.

Engeström, Y. and Middleton, D. (eds) (1996) *Cognition and Communication at Work*. Cambridge: Cambridge University Press.

Engler, S. (1997) 'Zur Kombination von qualitativen und quantitativen Methoden', in B. Friebertshäuser and A. Prengel (eds), *Handbuch Qualitative Forschungsmethoden in der Erziehungswissenschaft*. Weinheim: Juventa. pp. 118–130.

Englisch, F. (1991) 'Bildanalyse in strukturalhermeneutischer Einstellung – Methodische Überlegungen und Anwendungsbeispiele', in D. Garz and K. Kraimer (eds), *Qualitativ-empirische Sozialforschung*. Opladen: Westdeutscher Verlag. pp. 133–176.

Erdheim, M. (1982) *Die gesellschaftliche Produktion von Unbewußtheit. Eine Einführung in den ethnopsychoanalytischen Prozeß*. Frankfurt a. M.: Suhrkamp.

Erdheim, M. (1988) *Psychoanalyse und Unbewußtheit in der Kultur. Aufsätze 1980–1987*. Frankfurt a. M.: Suhrkamp.

Erdheim, M. and Nadig, M. (1983) 'Ethnopsychoanalyse', in W. Mertens (ed.), *Psychoanalyse. Ein Handbuch in Schlüsselbegriffen*. Munich: Urban and Schwarzenberg. pp. 129–135.

Erzberger, C. (1998) *Zahlen und Wörter. Die Verbindung quantitativer und qualitativer Daten und Methoden im Forschungsprozeß*. Weinheim: Deutscher Studien Verlag.

Erzberger, C. and Kelle, U. (2001) 'Making Inferences in Mixed Methods: The Rules of Integration', in A. Tashakkori and C. Teddlie (eds), *Handbook of Mixed Methodology*. Thousand Oaks, CA: Sage.

Erzberger, C. and Prein, G. (1997) 'Triangulation: Validity and Empirically Based Hypothesis Construction', *Quality and Quantity*, 31: 141–154.

Esser, H. (1996) 'Die Definition der Situation', *Kölner Zeitschrift für Soziologie und Sozialpsychologie*, 48: 1–34.

Esser, H. (1999) 'Die Konstitution des Sinns', in A. Honer, R. Kurt and J. Reichertz (eds), *Diesseitsreligion*. Konstanz: UVK. pp. 135–150.

'Ethik-Kodex der Deutschen Gesellschaft für Soziologie und des Berufsverbandes Deutscher Soziologen', *DGS-Informationen*, 1/93: 13–19.

Ethnopsychoanalyse 1–6 (1990) Frankfurt a. M.: Brandes and Apsel.

Everitt, A. and Hardiker, P. (1996) *Evaluating for Good Practice*. London: Macmillan.

Ewald, W. (1985) *Portraits and Dreams: Photographs and Stories by Children of the Appalachians*. New York: Writers and Readers Publishing.

Fagerhaugh, S. Y. and Strauss, A. (1977) *Politics of Pain Management: Staff–Patient Interaction*. Menlo Park, CA: Addison–Wesley.

Fann, K. T. (1970) *Peirce's Theory of Abduction*. The Hague.

Fehr, B. J., Stetson, J. and Mizukawa, Y. (1990) 'A Bibliography for Ethnomethodology', in J. Coulter (ed.), *Ethnomethodological Sociology*. Brookfield: Edward Elgar. pp. 473–559.

Feldman, M. S. and March, J. G. (1981) 'Information in Organizations as Signal and Symbol', *Administrative Science Quarterly*, 26: 171–186.

Fengler, C. and Fengler, T. (1980) *Alltag in der Anstalt: Wenn Sozialpsychiatrie praktisch wird. Eine ethnomethodologische Untersuchung*. Rehburg-Loccum: Psychiatrie-Verlag.

Ferguson, M. and Golding, P. (eds) (1997) *Cultural Studies in Question*. Thousand Oaks, CA: Sage.

Festinger, L (1957) *A Theory of Cognitive Dissonance*. Stanford, CA: Stanford University Press.

Fetterman, D. M. (1989) *Ethnography: Step by Step*. Newbury Park, CA: Sage.

Fetterman, D. M. (1994) 'Empowerment Evaluation', *Evaluation Practice*, 15: 1–15.

Fetterman, D. M., Kaftarian, S. and Wandersman, A. (1996) *Empowerment Evaluation: Knowledge and Tools for Self-assessment and Accountability*. Thousand Oaks, CA: Sage.

Fielding, N. G. and Fielding, J. L. (1986) *Linking Data*. Beverly Hills, CA: Sage.

Fielding, N. G. and Lee, R. M. (1998) *Computer Analysis and Qualitative Research*. London: Sage.

Filmer, P., Phillipson, M., Silverman, D. and Walsh, D. (1972) *New Directions in Sociological Theory*. London: Collier–Macmillan.

Filstead, W. J. (ed.) (1970) *Qualitative Methodology. Firsthand Involvement with the Social World*. Chicago: Markham.

Fine, G. A. (1993) 'The Sad Demise, Mysterious Disappearance, and Glorious Triumph of Symbolic Interactionism', *Annual Review of Sociology*, 19: 61–87.

Fischer, W. (1982) *Time and Chronic Illness. A Study on the Social Constitution of Temporality*. Berkeley, CA: University of California Press.

Fischer-Rosenthal, W. and Rosenthal, G. (1997a) 'Narrationsanalyse biographischer Selbstpräsentationen', in R. Hitzler and A. Honer (eds), *Sozialwissenschaftliche Hermeneutik*. Opladen: Leske and Budrich. pp. 133–164.

Fischer-Rosenthal, W. and Rosenthal, G. (1997b) 'Warum Biographieanalyse und wie man sie macht', *Zeitschrift für Sozialisationsforschung und Erziehungssoziologie*, 17: 405–427.

Fish, S. (1980) *Is There a Text in This Class? – The Authority of Interpretative Communities*. Cambridge, MA: Harvard University Press.

Fisher, B. M. and Strauss, A. L. (1979) 'Interactionism', in T. Bottomore and R. Nisbet (eds), *A History of Sociological Analysis*. London: Heinemann. pp. 457–498.

Fiske, J. (1989) *Understanding Popular Culture*. London: Unwin Hyman.

Fiske, J. (1993) *Power Plays – Power Works*. London: Verso.

Fiske, J. (1994a) 'Audiencing: Cultural Practice and Cultural Studies', in N. K. Denzin and Y. Lincoln (eds), *Handbook of Qualitative Research*. London: Sage. pp. 189–198.

Fiske, J. (1994b) *Media Matters. Everyday Culture and Political Change*. Minneapolis: University of Minnesota Press.

Fleck, C. (2002) 'Introduction to the Transaction edition', in M. Jahoda, P. F. Lazarsfeld and H. Zeisel, *Marienthal: The Sociography of an Unemployed Community*. New Brunswick, NJ: Transaction Books. pp. vii–xxx.

Fleck, L. (1935/1979) *Genesis and Development of a Scientific Fact*. Chicago: University of Chicago Press.

Flick, U. (1989) *Vertrauen, Verwalten, Einweisen – Subjektive Vertrauenstheorien in sozialpsychiatrischer Beratung*. Wiesbaden: Deutscher Universitätsverlag.

Flick, U. (1992a) 'Entzauberung der Intuition. Triangulation von Methoden und Datenquellen als Strategie der Geltungsbegründung und Absicherung von Interpretationen', in J. Hoffmeyer-Zlotnik (ed.), *Analyse qualitativer Daten*. Opladen: Westdeutscher Verlag. pp. 11–55.

Flick, U. (1992b) 'Triangulation Revisited – Strategy of or Alternative to Validation of Qualitative Data', *Journal for the Theory of Social Behaviour*, 22: 175–197.

Flick, U. (1995) 'Stationen des qualitativen Forschungsprozesses', in U. Flick, E. von Kardorff, H. Keupp, L. von Rosenstiel and S. Wolff (eds), *Handbuch Qualitative Sozialforschung*. Munich: Psychologie Verlags Union. pp. 148–175.

Flick, U. (1996) *Psychologie des technisierten Alltags – Soziale Konstruktion und Repräsentation technischen Wandels in verschiedenen kulturellen Kontexten*. Opladen: Westdeutscher Verlag.

Flick, U. (1998a) *An Introduction to Qualitative Research*. Thousand Oaks, CA: Sage.

Flick, U. (ed.) (1998b) *Wann fühlen wir uns gesund? Subjektive Vorstellungen von Gesundheit und Krankheit*. Weinheim: Juventa.

Flick, U. (1998c) 'Triangulation – Geltungsbegründung oder Erkenntniszuwachs', *Zeitschrift für Soziologie der Erziehung und Sozialisation*, 18: 443–447.

Flick, U. (2000a) 'Konstruktion und Rekonstruktion – Methodologische Überlegungen zur Fallrekonstruktion', in K. Kraimer (ed.), *Die Fallrekonstruktion – Beiträge zur Wirklichkeitsdeutung sozialen Lebens*. Frankfurt a. M.: Suhrkamp. pp. 177–197.

Flick, U. (2000b) 'Episodic Interviewing', in M. Bauer and G. Gaskell (eds), *Qualitative Researching with Text, Image and Sound – A Handbook*. London: Sage. pp. 75–92.

Flick, U. (2000c) 'Qualitative Inquiries into Social Representations of Health', *Journal of Health Psychology*, 5: 309–318.

Flick, U. (2002) *An Introduction to Qualitative Research*, 2nd edn. Thousand Oaks, CA: Sage.

Flick, U., Hoose, B. and Sitta, P. (1998) 'Gesundheit und Krankheit gleich Saúde and Doenca? Gesundheitsvorstellungen bei Frauen in Deutschland und Portugal', in U. Flick (ed.), *Wann fühlen wir uns gesund? – Subjektive Vorstellungen von Gesundheit und Krankheit*. Weinheim: Juventa. pp. 141–159.

Flick, U., Kardorff, E. von, Keupp, H., Rosenstiel, L. von and Wolff, S. (eds) (1995) *Handbuch Qualitative Sozialforschung. Grundlagen, Konzepte, Methoden und Anwendungen*, 2nd edn. Munich: Psychologie Verlags Union.

Foley, D. E. (1990) *Learning Capitalist Culture: Deep in the Heart of Tejas*. Philadelphia: University of Pennsylvania Press.

Ford, N. A. (1998) 'A Blueprint for Negro Authors', in P. Liggins Hill (ed.), *Call and Response: The Riverside Anthology of the African American Literary Tradition*. New York: Houghton Mifflin (originally published in *Phylon*, 1950).

Foucault, M. (1978) *The History of Sexuality. Volume I: An Introduction*. Harmondsworth: Penguin.

Foucault, M. (1979) *Discipline and Punish: The Birth of the Prison*. Harmondsworth: Penguin.

Foucault, M. (1980) *Power/Knowledge: Selected Interviews and Other Writings 1972–1977*. Hassocks, Sussex: Harvester.

French, W. and Bell, C. (1977) *Organization Development*. Englewood Cliffs, NJ: Prentice Hall.

Frerichs, P. and Steinrücke, M. (1993) 'Klasse und Geschlecht als Strukturkategorien moderner Gesellschaften', in B. Aulenbacher and M. Goldmann (eds), *Transformationen im Geschlechterverhältnis – Beiträge zur industriellen und gesellschaftlichen Entwicklung*. Frankfurt a. M.: Campus. pp. 231–245.

Freter, H.-J., Hollstein, B. and Werle, M. (1991) 'Integration qualitativer und quantitativer Verfahrensweisen – Methodologie und Forschungspraxis', *ZUMA-Nachrichten*, 29: 98–114.

Freud, S. (1893–95/1955) 'Studies on Hysteria', in *The Standard Edition of the Complete Psychological Work of Sigmund Freud*, Volume II. London: The Hogarth Press.

Freud, S. (1905/1958) 'Three Essays on the Theory of Sexuality', in *The Standard Edition of the Complete Psychological Works of Sigmund Freud*, Volume VII. London: The Hogarth Press. pp. 123–245.

Freud, S. (1908/1959) ' "Civilized" Sexual Morality and Modern Nervous Illness', in *The Standard Edition of the Complete Psychological Works of Sigmund Freud*, Volume IX. London: The Hogarth Press. pp. 177–204.

Freud, S. (1912/1958) 'Recommendations to Physicians Practising Psycho-Analysis', in *The Standard Edition of the Complete Psychological Works of Sigmund Freud*, Volume XII. London: The Hogarth Press. pp. 109–120.

Freud, S. (1920–22/1955) 'Psycho-analysis', in *The Standard Edition of the Complete Psychological Works of Sigmund Freud*, Volume XVIII. London: The Hogarth Press. pp. 235–254.

Freud, S. (1930/1961) 'Civilization and its Discontents', in *The Standard Edition of the Complete Psychological Works of Sigmund Freud*, Volume XXI. London: The Hogarth Press. pp. 57–145.

Freundlieb, A. and Wolff, S. (1999) 'Evaluation', in J. Pelikan and S. Wolff (eds), *Das gesundheitsfördernde Krankenhaus*. Weinheim, Munich: Juventa. pp. 80–91.

Frevert, U. (1995) *'Mann und Weib, und Weib und Mann' – Geschlechter-Differenzen in der Moderne*. Munich: Beck.

Friebertshäuser, B. (1996) 'Feldforschende Zugänge zu sozialen Handlungsfeldern. Möglichkeiten und Grenzen ethnographischer Feldforschung', *Neue Praxis*, 26: 75–86.

Friebertshäuser, B. (1997) 'Interviewtechniken – ein Überblick', in B. Friebertshäuser and A. Prengel (eds), *Handbuch Qualitative Forschungsmethoden in der Erziehungswissenschaft*. Weinheim: Juventa. pp. 371–395.

Friedlander, F. and Brown, L. D. (1974) 'Organization development', *Annual Review of Psychology*, 25: 313–341.

Friedrichs, J. (1973/1983) *Methoden empirischer Sozialforschung*. Opladen: Westdeutscher Verlag.

Fröhlich, G. and Mörth, I. (eds) (1998) *Symbolische Anthropologie der Moderne. Kulturanalysen nach Clifford Geertz*. Frankfurt a. M.: Campus.

Fryer, D. (1986) 'The Social Psychology of the Invisible: An Interview with Marie Jahoda', *New Ideas in Psychology*, 4: 107–118.

Fryer, D. (In press) 'Marie Jahoda: Community and Applied Social Psychologist', Special Issue (Guest edited by D. Fryer), *Journal of Community & Applied Social Psychology*.

Fuchs, W. (1984) *Biographische Forschung. Eine Einführung in Praxis und Methoden*. Opladen: Westdeutscher Verlag.

Fühlau, J. (1982) *Die Sprachlosigkeit der Inhaltsanalyse. Linguistische Bemerkungen zu einer sozialwissenschaftlichen Analyse*. Tübingen: Narr.

Fuhs, B. (1997) 'Fotografie und qualitative Forschung. Zur Verwendung fotografischer Quellen in den Erziehungswissenschaften', in B. Friebertshäuser and A. Prengel (eds), *Handbuch Qualitative Forschungsmethoden in der Erziehungswissenschaft*. Weinheim: Juventa. pp. 265–285.

Fuller, R. and Petch, A. (1995) *Practitioner Research: The Reflexive Social Worker*. Buckingham: Open University Press.

Gadamer, H. G. (1975) *Truth and Method*. New York: Seabury Press.

Gans, H. (1982) 'The Participant Observer as a Human Being: Observations on the personal aspects of

Fieldwork', in R. G. Burgess (ed.), *Field Research: A Sourcebook and Field Manual*. London: Allen and Unwin (originally published 1968). pp. 53–61.

Garfinkel, H. (1952) '*The Perception of the Other: A Study in Social Order*'. PhD dissertation. Boston, MA: Harvard University.

Garfinkel, H. (1961) 'Aspects of Common-Sense-Knowledge of Social Structures', in *Transactions of the Fourth World Congress of Sociology*, Volume IV. London: International Sociological Association. pp. 51–65.

Garfinkel, H. (1963) 'A Conception Of, and Experiments With, "Trust" as a Condition of Stable Concerted Actions', in O. J. Harvey (ed.), *Motivation and Social Interaction*. New York: Free Press. pp. 187–238.

Garfinkel, H. (1967a) *Studies in Ethnomethodology*. Englewood Cliffs, NJ: Prentice Hall.

Garfinkel, H. (1967b) '"Good" Organizational Reasons for "Bad" Clinical Records', in H. Garfinkel, *Studies in Ethnomethodology*. Englewood Cliffs, NJ: Prentice Hall. pp. 186–207.

Garfinkel, H. (1974) 'The Origins of the Term "ethnomethodology"', in R. Turner (ed.), *Ethnomethodology: Selected Readings*. Harmondsworth: Penguin. pp. 15–18.

Garfinkel, H. (ed.) (1986) *Ethnomethodological Studies of Work*. London: Routledge and Kegan Paul.

Garfinkel, H. (1991) 'Respecification: Evidence for Locally Produced, Naturally Accountable Phenomena of Order, Logic, Reason, Meaning, Method, etc. in and as of the Essential Haecceity of Immortal Ordinary Society, (I): An Announcement of Studies', in G. Button (ed.), *Ethnomethodology and the Human Sciences*. Cambridge: Cambridge University Press. pp. 11–19.

Garfinkel, H. (1996) 'Ethnomethodology's Program', *Social Psychology Quarterly*, 59: 5–21.

Garfinkel, H., Lynch, M. and Livingston, E. (1981) 'The Work of a Discovering Science Construed with Materials from the Optically Discovered Pulsar', *Philosophy of the Social Sciences*, 11: 131–158.

Garfinkel, H. and Sacks, H. (1970) 'On Formal Structures of Practical Actions', in J. C. McKinney and E. A. Tiryakian (eds), *Theoretical Sociology. Perspectives and Development*. New York: Appleton–Century–Crofts. pp. 337–366.

Garfinkel, H. and Wieder, D. L. (1992) 'Two Incommensurable, Asymmetrically Alternate Technologies of Social Analysis', in G. Watson and R. M. Seiler (eds), *Text in Context. Contributions to Ethnomethodology*. Newbury Park, CA: Sage. pp. 175–206.

Garz, D. and Kraimer, K. (1991) 'Qualitativ-empirische Sozialforschung im Aufbruch', in D. Garz and K. Kraimer (eds), *Qualitativ-empirische Sozialforschung*. Opladen: Westdeutscher Verlag. pp. 1–34.

Garz, D. and Kraimer, K. (eds) (1994a) *Die Welt als Text. Zur Theorie, Kritik und Praxis der objektiven Hermeneutik*. Frankfurt a. M.: Suhrkamp.

Garz, D. and Kraimer, K. (1994b) 'Die Welt als Text. Zum Projekt einer hermeneutisch-rekonstruktiven Sozialwissenschaft', in D. Garz and K. Kraimer (eds), *Die Welt als Text. Theorie, Kritik und Praxis der objektiven Hermeneutik*. Frankfurt a. M.: Suhrkamp. pp. 7–21.

Gaskell G. and Bauer, M. W. (2000) 'Towards Public Accountability: Beyond Sampling, Reliability and Validity', in M. W. Bauer and G. Gaskell (eds), *Qualitative Researching with Text, Image and Sound – A Handbook*. London: Sage. pp. 336–350.

Gawatz, R. and Nowak, P. (eds) (1993) *Soziale Konstruktionen von Gesundheit*. Ulm: Universitätsverlag.

Gebauer, G. and Flick, U. (1998) '*Die Aufführung der Gesellschaft in Spielen. Projektantrag im Rahmen des Sonderforschungsbereiches "Kulturen des Performativen"*'. Manuscript, Berlin.

Gebauer, G. and Wulf, C. (1995) *Mimesis: Culture, Art, Society*. Berkeley, CA: University of California Press.

Gebert, D. (1978) *Organisation und Umwelt*. Stuttgart: Kohlhammer.

Gebert, D. (1995) 'Interventionen in Organisationen', in H. Schuler (ed.), *Lehrbuch der Organisationspsychologie*. Berne: Huber. pp. 481–494.

Gebert, D. and Rosenstiel, L. von (1996) *Organisationspsychologie*. Stuttgart: Kohlhammer.

Geer, B. (1964) 'First Days in the Field. A Chronicle of Research in Progress', in P. E. Hammond (ed.), *Sociologists at Work – Essays on the Craft of Social Research*. New York: Basic Books. pp. 322–344.

Geertz, C. (1959) 'Ritual and Social Change: A Javanese Example', *American Anthropologist*, 61: 991–1012.

Geertz, C. (1966) 'Religion As a Cultural System', in M. Banton (ed.), *Anthropological Approaches to the Study of Religion*. London: Tavistock Publications. pp. 1–46.

Geertz, C. (1968) *Islam Observed. Religious Development in Morocco and Indonesia*. Chicago: University of Chicago Press.

Geertz, C. (1972) 'Deep Play: Notes on the Balinese Cockfight', *Daedalus*, 101: 1–37.

Geertz, C. (1973a) *The Interpretation of Cultures*. New York: Basic Books.

Geertz, C. (1973b) 'Thick Description: Toward an Interpretative Theory of Culture', in C. Geertz, *The Interpretation of Cultures*. New York: Basic Books. pp. 3–30.

Geertz, C. (1980) *Negara – The Theatre State in Nineteenth-Century Bali*. Princeton, NJ: Princeton University Press.

Geertz, C. (1983a) 'Blurred Genres – The Refiguration of Social Thought', in C. Geertz, *Local Knowledge – Further Essays in Interpretative Anthropology*. New York: Basic Books. pp. 19–35.

Geertz, C. (1983b) 'Local Knowledge – Fact and Law in Comparative Perspective', in C. Geertz, *Local Knowledge – Further Essays in Interpretative Anthropology*. New York: Basic Books. pp. 167–234.

Geertz, C. (1983c) 'Introduction', in C. Geertz, *Local Knowledge – Further Essays in Interpretative Anthropology*. New York: Basic Books. pp. 3–18.

Geertz, C. (1984a) 'Distinguished Lecture – Anti Anti-Relativism', *American Anthropologist*, 86: 603–613.

Geertz, C. (1984b) 'From the Native's Point of View', in R. Shweder and R. LeVine (eds), *Culture Theory*. Cambridge: Cambridge University Press. pp. 123–136.

Geertz, C. (1988) *Works and Lives. The Anthropologist as Author*. Stanford, CA: Stanford University Press.

Geertz, C. (1995) *After the Fact – Two Countries, Four Decades, One Anthropologist*. Cambridge, MA: Harvard University Press.

Geertz, C. (1998) 'The World in Pieces', *FOCAAL*, 32: 91–117.

Geertz, C. (2000) *Available Light. Anthropological Reflexions on Philosophical Topics*. Princeton, NJ: Princeton University Press.

Gehrie, M. J. (1989) 'Psychoanalytic Anthropology: The Analogous Tasks of the Psychoanalyst and the Ethnographer', *The Psychoanalytic Study of Society*, 14: 41–69.

Gephardt, R. P. Jr (1988) *Ethnostatistics: Qualitative Foundations for Quantitative Research*. Newbury Park, CA: Sage.

Gerbner, G., Holsti, O. R., Krippendorff, K., Paisley, W. J. and Stone, P. J. (eds) (1969) *The Analysis of Communication Content*. New York: Wiley.

Gerdes, K. (ed.) (1979) *Explorative Sozialforschung*. Stuttgart: Enke.

Gergen, K. J. (1973) 'Social Psychology as History', *Journal of Personality and Social Psychology*, 26: 309–320.

Gergen, K. J. (1985) 'The Social Constructionist Movement in Modern Psychology', *American Psychologist*, 40: 266–275.

Gergen, K. J. (1988) 'If Persons Are Texts', in S. B. Messer, L. A. Sass and R. L. Woolfolk (eds), *Hermeneutics and Psychological Theory. Interpretive Perspectives on Personality, Psychotherapy, and Psychopathology*. Brunswick, NJ: Rutgers University Press. pp. 28–51.

Gergen, K. J. (1991) *The Saturated Self: Dilemmas of Identity in Contemporary Life*. New York: Basic Books.

Gergen, K. J. (1994) *Realities and Relationships. Soundings in Social Construction*. Cambridge, MA: Harvard University Press.

Gergen, K. J. (1999) *An Invitation to Social Construction*. London: Sage.

Gerhardt, U. (1986) *Patientenkarrieren. Eine medizin-soziologische Studie*. Frankfurt a. M.: Suhrkamp.

Gerhardt, U. (1995) 'Typenbildung', in U. Flick, E. von Kardorff, H. Keupp, L. von Rosenstiel and S. Wolff (eds), *Handbuch Qualitative Sozialforschung. Grundlagen, Konzepte, Methoden und Anwendungen*, 2nd edn. Weinheim: Psychologie Verlags Union. pp. 435–439.

Gibbs, G. (2002) *Qualitative Data Analysis – Explorations with Nvivo* (Understanding, Social Research Series). Buckingham: Open University Press.

Giddens, A. (1981) *A Contemporary Critique of Historical Materialism*. Berkeley, CA: University of California Press.

Giddens, A. (1984) *The Constitution of Society. Outline of the Theory of Structuration*. Cambridge: Polity Press.

Giddens, A. (1993) *New Rules of Sociological Method: A Positive Critique of Interpretative Sociologies*. Stanford, CA: Stanford University Press.

Gieseke, W. (1998) *Die besten Tools zum Web-Surfen*. Bonne: International Thomson.

Gildemeister, R. and Robert, G. (1999) 'Vergeschlecht-lichung – Entgrenzung – Revergeschlechtlichung – Geschlechterdifferenzierende Arbeitsteilung zwischen Rationalisierung der Arbeitswelt und "postindus-triellem Haushaltssektor"', in S. Hradil (ed.), *Verhandlungen des 29. Kongresses der Deutschen Gesellschaft für Soziologie in Freiburg i. Br. 1998*. Frankfurt a. M.: Campus. pp. 787–803.

Gildemeister, R. and Wetterer, A. (1992) 'Wie Geschlechter gemacht werden – Die soziale Konstruktion der Zweigeschlechtlichkeit und ihre Reifizierung in der Frauenforschung', in G.-A. Knapp and A. Wetterer (eds), *Traditionen Brüche – Entwicklungen feministischer Theorie*. Freiburg: Kore. pp. 201–254.

Gillespie, M. (1995) *Television, Ethnicity and Cultural Change*. London: Routledge.

Girtler, R. (1980) *Polizei-Alltag*. Opladen: Westdeutscher Verlag.

Girtler, R. (1984) *Methoden der qualitativen Sozial-forschung. Anleitung zur Feldarbeit*. Vienna: Böhlau.

Girtler, R. (1989) 'Die "teilnehmende unstrukturierte Beobachtung" – ihr Vorteil bei der Erforschung des sozialen Handelns und des in ihm enthaltenen Sinns', in R. Aster, H. Merkens and M. Repp (eds), *Teilnehmende Beobachtung*. Frankfurt a. M.: Campus. pp. 299–320.

Glaser, B. G. (1978) *Theoretical Sensitivity: Advances in the Methodology of Grounded Theory*. Mill Valley, CA: Sociology Press.

Glaser, B. G. (1992) *Basics of Grounded Theory Analysis: Emergence vs. Forcing*. Mill Valley, CA: Sociology Press.

Glaser, B. G. and Strauss, A. L. (1965a) 'Discovery of Substantive Theory: A Basic Strategy Underlying Qualitative Research', *The American Behavioral Scientist*, 8: 5–12.

Glaser, B. G. and Strauss, A. L. (1965b) *Awareness of Dying*. Chicago: Aldine.

Glaser, B. G. and Strauss, A. L. (1967) *The Discovery of Grounded Theory. Strategies for Qualitative Research*. Chicago: Aldine.

Glaser, B. G. and Strauss, A. L. (1968) *Time for Dying*. Chicago: Aldine.

Gläser, J. (1999) 'Datenschutzrechtliche und ethische Probleme beim Publizieren von Fallstudien: Informantenschutz und "Objektschutz"', *Soziologie*, 28: 32–47.

Glasersfeld, E. von (1992) 'Aspekte des Konstruk-tivismus: Vico, Berkeley, Piaget', in G. Rusch and S. J. Schmidt (eds), *Konstruktivismus: Geschichte und Anwendung*. Frankfurt a. M.: Suhrkamp. pp. 20–33.

Glasersfeld, E. von (1995) *Radical Constructivism. A Way of Knowing and Learning*. London: The Falmer Press.

Glesne, C. and Webb, R. (1993) 'Teaching Qualitative Research – Who Does What?', *Qualitative Studies in Education*, 6: 253–266.

Goffman, E. (1959) *The Presentation of Self in Everyday Life*. New York: Doubleday.

Goffman, E. (1961a) *Encounters: Two Studies in the Sociology of Intervention*. Indianapolis: Bobbs–Merrill.

Goffman, E. (1961b) *Asylums. Essays on the Social Situation of Mental Patients and Other Inmates*. New York: Doubleday Anchor.

Goffman, E. (1963a) *Stigma. Notes on the Management of Spoiled Identity*. Englewood Cliffs, NJ: Prentice Hall.

Goffman, E. (1963b) *Behaviour in Public Places. Notes on the Social Organization of Gatherings*. New York: Free Press.

Goffman, E. (1967) *Interaction Ritual: Essays on Face-to-Face Behaviour*. New York: Doubleday.

Goffman, E. (1969) *Strategic Interaction*. Philadelphia: University of Pennsylvania Press.

Goffman, E. (1971) *Relations in Public. Microstudies of the Public Order*. New York: Harper and Row.

Goffman, E. (1974) *Frame Analysis – An Essay on the Organization of Experience*. New York: Harper and Row.

Goffman, E. (1976) 'Replies and Responses', *Language in Society*, 5: 257–331.

Goffman, E. (1977) 'The Arrangement between the Sexes', *Theory and Society*, 4: 301–331.

Goffman, E. (1979) *Gender Advertisements*. New York: Harper and Row.

Goffman, E. (1981) *Forms of Talk*. Philadelphia: University of Pennsylvania Press.

Goffman, E. (1983) 'The Interaction Order', *American Sociological Review*, 48: 1–17.

Goffman, E. (1989) 'On Fieldwork' (transcribed and edited by Lyn H. Lofland), *Journal of Contemporary Ethnography*, 18: 123–132.

Gola, P. and Schomerus, R. (1997) *Bundesdatens chutzgesetz (BDSG) mit Erläuterungen*, Munich: C. H. Beck'sche Verlagsbuchhandlung.

Goodenough, W. H. (1964) 'Cultural anthropology and Linguistics', in D. Hymes (ed.), *Language in Culture and Society*. New York: Harper (first published 1957). pp. 36–39.

Goodman, N. (1978) *Ways of Worldmaking*. Indianapolis: Hackett.

Gouldner, A. W. (1954) *Patterns of Industrial Bureaucracy*. Glencoe, IL: Free Press.

Gouldner, A. W. (1971) *The Coming Crisis of Western Sociology*. London: Heinemann.

Grady, J. (1996) 'The Scope of Visual Sociology', *Visual Sociology*, 11 (2), 10–24.

Graf-Deserno, S. and Deserno, H. (1998) *Entwicklungs-schancen in der Institution. Psychoanalytische Team-supervision*. Frankfurt a. M.: Fischer.

Gramsci, A. (1991) *Gefängnishefte in 10 Bänden*. Hamburg: Argument.

Grathoff, R. (1989) *Milieu und Lebenswelt*. Frankfurt a. M.: Suhrkamp.

Graumann, C. F. and Métraux, A. (1977) 'Die phänomenologische Orientierung in der Psychologie', in K. A. Schneewind (ed.), *Wissenschaftstheoretische Grundlagen der Psychologie*. Munich: Ernst Reinhardt. pp. 27–35.

Greenblatt, S. (1997) 'The Touch of the Real', *Representations*, 59: 14–29.

Greif, S. (1978) 'Intelligenzabbau und Dequalifizierung durch Industriearbeit?', in M. Frese, S. Greif and N. Semmer (eds), *Industrielle Psychopathologie*. Berne: Huber. pp. 232–256.

Greif, S., Holling, H. and Nicholson, N. (1989) *Arbeits- und Organisationspsychologie*. Munich: Psychologie Verlags Union.

Grills, S. (ed.) (1998) *Doing Ethnographic Research. Fieldwork Settings*. Thousand Oaks, CA: Sage.

Groeben, N. (1990) 'Subjective Theories and the Explanation of Human Action', in G. R. Semin and K. J. Gergen (eds), *Everyday Understanding. Social and Scientific Implications*. London: Sage. pp. 19–44.

Groeben, N., Wahl, D., Schlee, J. and Scheele, B. (1988) *Forschungsprogramm Subjektive Theorien. Eine Einführung in die Psychologie des reflexiven Subjekts*. Tübingen: Francke.

Gross, P. (1994) *Die Multioptionsgesellschaft*. Frankfurt a. M.: Suhrkamp.

Gross, P. (1999) *Ich-Jagd*. Frankfurt a. M.: Suhrkamp.

Grossberg, L. (1992) *We Gotta Get Out of This Place. Popular Conservatism and Postmodern Culture*. New York: Routledge.

Grossberg, L. (1995) 'What's in a Name (One More Time)', *Taboo*, 1 (Spring): 1–37.

Grundmann, M. (ed.) (1999) *Konstruktivistische Sozialisationsforschung*. Frankfurt a. M.: Suhrkamp.

Grüneisen, V. and Hoff, E. (1977) *Familienerziehung und Lebenssituation*. Weinheim: Beltz.

Gstettner, P. (1995) 'Handlungsforschung', in U. Flick, E. von Kardorff, H. Keupp, L. von Rosenstiel and S. Wolff (eds), *Handbuch qualitative Sozialforschung*, 2nd edn. Weinheim: Psychologie Verlags Union. pp. 266–268.

Guba, E. G. and Lincoln, Y. S. (1989) *Fourth Generation Evaluation*. Newbury Park, CA: Sage.

Gubrium, J. F. and Buckholdt, D. R. (1979) 'The Production of Hard Data in Human Service Organization', *Pacific Sociological Review*, 22: 115–136.

Gubrium, J. F. and Holstein, J. A. (1997) *The New Language of Qualitative Method*. New York: Oxford University Press.

Gubrium, J. F. and Holstein, J. (eds) (2001) *Handbook of Interviewing Research*. Thousand Oaks, CA: Sage.

Gumbrecht, U. and Pfeiffer, K. L. (eds) (1986) *Stil – Geschichten und Funktionen eines kulturwissenschaftlichen Diskurselementes*. Frankfurt a. M.: Suhrkamp.

Gumperz, J. (1982) *Discourse Strategies – Studies in Interactional Sociolinguistics*. Cambridge: Cambridge University Press.

Gumperz, J. (1992) 'Contextualization Revisited', in P. Auer and A. Diluzio (eds), *The Contextualization of Language*. Amsterdam: John Benjamins. pp. 39–53.

Gumperz, J. and Cook-Gumpertz, J. (1981) 'Ethnic Differences in Communicative Style', in C. A. Ferguson and S. H. Heath (eds), *Language in the USA*. Cambridge: Cambridge University Press. pp. 430–445.

Gumperz, J. and Hymes, D. (eds) (1972) *Directions in Sociolinguistics: The Ethnography of Communication*. New York: Holt, Rinehart and Winston.

Günthner, S. (1993) *Diskursstrategien in der interkulturellen Kommunikation: Analysen deutsch-chinesischer Gespräche*. Tübingen: Niemeyer.

Günthner, S. and Knoblauch, H. (1996) 'Die Analyse kommunikativer Gattungen in Alltagsinteraktionen', in S. Michaelis and D. Tophinke (eds), *Texte – Konstitution – Verarbeitung – Typik*. Munich: Lincom. pp. 36–57.

Gurwitsch, A. (1964) *The Field of Conciousness*. Pittsburgh: Duquesne University Press.

Gurwitsch, A. (1976) *Die mitmenschlichen Begegnungen in der Milieuwelt*. Berlin: de Gruyter.

Gurwitsch, A. (1977/1979) *Human Encounters in the Social World*. Pittsburgh: Duquesne University Press.

Gusfield, J. (1976) 'The Literary Rhetoric of Science: Comedy and Pathos in Drinking Driver Research', *American Sociological Review*, 41: 16–34.

Habermas, J. (1970) *Zur Logik der Sozialwissenschaften*. Frankfurt a. M.: Suhrkamp (first published 1967).

Habermas, J. (1971) *Knowledge and Human Interest* (trans. J. J. Shapiro). Boston: Beacon Press.

Hacking, I. (1999) *The Social Construction of What?* Cambridge, MA: Harvard University Press.

Hagaman, D. (1996) *How I Learned Not to be a Photojournalist*. Lexington, KY: University of Kentucky Press.

Hahn, A. (1997) 'Geheimnis', in C. Wulf (ed.), *Vom Menschen – Handbuch Historische Anthropologie*. Weinheim: Beltz. pp. 1105–1118.

Hall, S. (1980) 'Encoding/Decoding', in S. Hall, D. Hobson, A. Lowe and P. Willis (eds), *Culture, Media, Language*. London: Unwin Hyman. pp. 128–138.

Hall, S. (1990) 'The Emergence of Cultural Studies and the Crisis of the Humanities', *October*, 53: 11–23.

Hall, S. (1991) 'The Local and the Global: Globalization and Ethnicity', in A. D. King (ed.), *Culture Globalization and the World-System*. London: Macmillan. pp. 19–39.

Hall, S. (1992) 'The Question of Cultural Identity', in S. Hall, D. Held and T. McGrew (eds), *Modernity and Its Futures*. Milton Keynes: Polity Press/The Open University. pp. 273–316.

Hall, S. (1994) *Rassismus und kulturelle Identität*. Ausgewählte Schriften 2. Hamburg: Argument.

Hall, S. (1996a) 'Introduction', in S. Hall, D. Held, D. Hubert and K. Thompson (eds), *Modernity: An Introduction to Modern Societies*. Cambridge, MA: Blackwell. pp. 3–18.

Hall, S. (1996b) 'New Ethnicities', in D. Morley, K. Chen and S. Hall (eds), *Critical Dialogues in Cultural Studies*. London: Routledge. pp. 441–444.

Hall, S. (1996c) 'The West and the Rest: Discourse and Power', in S. Hall, D. Held, D. Hubert and K. Thompson (eds), *Modernity: An Introduction to Modern Societies*. Cambridge, MA: Blackwell. pp. 184–228.

Hall, S. (1996d) '"What is this 'Black' in Black Popular Culture?"', in D. Morley, K. Chen and S. Hall (eds), *Critical Dialogues in Cultural Studies*. London: Routledge. pp. 465–475.

Hall, S. (1996e) 'Cultural Studies. Two Paradigms', in J. Storey (ed.), *What is Cultural Studies? A Reader*. London: Arnold. pp. 31–48.

Hall, S. (1996f) 'Who Needs "Identity"?', in S. Hall and P. du Gay (eds), *Questions of Cultural Identity*. London: Sage: 1–17.

Hall, S. (ed.) (1997) *Representation: Cultural Representations and Signifying Practices*. London: Sage.

Hall, S. and Jefferson, T. (eds) (1976) *Resistance through Rituals. Youth Subcultures in Post-war Britain*. London: Hutchinson.

Halliday, M. A. (1978) *Language as Social Semiotic*. London: Edward Arnold.

Hammersley, M. (1990) *Reading Ethnographic Research. A Critical Guide*. London: Longman.

Hammersley, M. and Atkinson, P. (1983) *Ethnography – Principles in Practice*. London: Tavistock.

Hannerz, U. (1992) *Cultural Complexity. Studies in the Social Organization of Meaning*. New York: Columbia University Press.

Hannerz, U. (1995) '"Kultur" in einer vernetzten Welt. Zur Revision eines ethnologischen Begriffs', in W. Kaschuba (ed.), *Kulturen, Identitäten, Diskurse. Perspektiven europäischer Ethnologie*. Berlin: Akademie. pp. 64–84.

Hanson, N. R. (1965) 'Notes toward a Logic of Discovery', in J. R. Bernstein (ed.), *Perspectives on Peirce*. New Haven, CT. pp. 42–65.

Haraway, D. (1995) 'Primatologie ist Politik mit anderen Mitteln', in B. Orland and E. Scheich (eds), *Das Geschlecht der Natur – Feministische Beiträge zur Geschichte und Theorie der Naturwissenschaften*. Frankfurt a. M.: Suhrkamp. pp. 136–198.

Hargreaves, D. H., Hester, S. K. and Mellor, F. J. (1981) *Abweichendes Verhalten im Unterricht*. Weinheim: Beltz (first published 1975).

Harper, D. (1987) *Working Knowledge: Skill and Community in a Small Shop*. Chicago: University of Chicago Press.

Harper, D. (1992) 'Small N's and Community Case Studies', in C. C. Ragin and H. S. Becker (eds), *What Is a Case? Exploring the Foundations of Social Inquiry*. Cambridge: Cambridge University Press. pp. 139–158.

Harper, D. (1994) 'On the Authority of the Image: Visual Methods at the Crossroads', in N. K. Denzin and Y. S. Lincoln (eds), *Handbook of Qualitative Research*. Thousand Oaks, CA: Sage. pp. 403–412.

Harper, D. (1997) 'Visualizing Structure: Reading Surfaces of Social Life', *Qualitative Sociology*, 20: 57–77.

Harper, D. (2000) 'Reimagining Visual Methods: Galileo to Neuromancer', in N. Denzin and Y. S. Lincoln (eds), *Handbook of Qualitative Research*, 2nd edn. London: Sage. pp. 717–732.

Harré, R. (1992) 'The Discursive Creation of Human Psychology', *Symbolic Interaction*, 15: 515–527.

Harré, R. and Gillett, G. (1994) *The Discursive Mind*. London: Sage.

Harré, R. and Secord, P. F. (1972) *The Explanation of Social Behaviour*. Oxford: Blackwell.

Hartley, J. F. (1994) 'Case Studies in Organizational Research', in C. Cassell and G. Symon (eds), *Qualitative Methods in Organizational Research. A Practical Guide*. London: Sage. pp. 208–229.

Hartmann, H. (1988) 'Sozialreportagen und Gesellschaftsbild', in H.-G. Soeffner (ed.), *Kultur und Alltag. Soziale Welt*, Special Issue 5, pp. 342–352.

Hauschild, T. (1981) 'Ethno-Psychoanalyse. Symboltheorien an der Grenze zweier Wissenschaften', in W. Schmied-Kowarzik and J. Stagl (eds), *Grundfragen der Ethnologie*. Berlin: Reimers. pp. 151–168.

Hausen, K. and Nowotny, H. (eds) (1986) *Wie männlich ist die Wissenschaft?* Frankfurt a. M.: Suhrkamp.

Hausendorf, H. (1992) *Gespräch als System. Linguistische Aspekte einer Soziologie der Interaktion*. Opladen: Westdeutscher Verlag.

Have, P. ten (1999) *Doing Conversation Analysis: A Practical Guide* (Introducing Qualitative Methods Series). London: Sage.

Have, P. ten and Psathas, G. (eds) (1995) *Situated Order: Studies in the Social Organisation of Talk and Embodied Activities*. Washington, DC: University Press of America.

Hawkes, T. (1977) *Structuralism and Semiotics*. London: Methuen.

Heald, S. and Deluz, A. (eds) (1994) *Anthropology and Psychoanalysis. An Encounter through Culture*. London: Routledge.

Heath, C. (1986) *Body Movement and Speech in Medical Interaction*. Cambridge: Cambridge University Press.

Heath, C. (1997) 'The Analysis of Activities in Face to Face Interaction Using Video', in D. Silverman (ed.), *Qualitative Research*. London: Sage. pp. 183–199.

Hebdige, D. (1979) *Subculture. The Meaning of Style*. London: Methuen.

Heiner, M. (ed.) (1988a) *Praxisforschung in der sozialen Arbeit*. Freiburg: Lambertus.

Heiner, M. (ed.) (1988b) *Selbstevaluation in der sozialen Arbeit*. Freiburg: Lambertus.

Heiner, M. (ed.) (1998) *Experimentierende Evaluation. Ansätze zur Entwicklung lernender Organisationen*. Weinheim: Juventa.

Heinrichs, H. J. (1993) 'Über Ethnopsychoanalyse, Ethnopsychiatrie und Ethno-Hermeneutik', in W. Schmied-Kowarzik and J. Stagl (eds), *Grundfragen der Ethnologie*. Berlin: Reimers. pp. 359–380.

Heinz, W., Kelle, U., Zinn, J. and Witzel, A. (1998) 'Vocational Training and Career Development in Germany. Results from a Longitudinal Study', *International Journal of Behavioral Development*, 22: 77–101.

Heinze, T., Klusemann, H.-W. and Soeffner, H.-G. (eds) (1980) *Interpretationen einer Bildungsgeschichte*. Bensheim: päd.-extra-Buchverlag.

Helm, D. T., Anderson, W. T., Meehan, A. J. and Rawls, A. W. (eds) (1989) *Interactional Order: New Directions in the Study of Social Order*. New York: Irvington.

Helmers, S. (1993) 'Beiträge der Ethnologie zur Unternehmenskultur', in M. Dierkes, L. von Rosenstiel and U. Steger (eds), *Unternehmenskultur in Theorie und Praxis*. Frankfurt a. M.: Campus. pp. 147–187.

Henriques, J., Hollway, W., Urwin, C., Venn, C. and Walkerdine, V. (1998) *Changing the Subject: Psychology, Social Regulation and Subjectivity* (Reissued edition). London: Routledge.

Heppner, G., Osterhoff, J., Schiersmann, C. and Schmidt, C. (1990) *Computer? 'Interessieren tät's mich schon, aber …' – Wie sich Mädchen in der Schule mit Neuen Technologien auseinandersetzen*. Bielefeld: Kleine-Verlag.

Heritage, J. C. (1984) *Garfinkel and Ethnomethodology*. Cambridge: Polity Press.

Heritage, J. C. (1987) 'Ethnomethodology', in A. Giddens and J. H. Turner (eds), *Social Theory Today*. Cambridge: Polity Press. pp. 224–272.

Hermanns, H. (1995) 'Narratives Interview', in U. Flick, E. von Kardorff, H. Keupp, L. von Rosenstiel and S. Wolff (eds), *Handbuch Qualitative Sozialforschung*. Munich: Psychologie Verlags Union. pp. 182–185.

Hertz, R. and Imber, J. B. (eds) (1997) *Studying Elites Using Qualitative Methods*. Thousand Oaks, CA: Sage.

Herwartz-Emden, L. (1986) *Türkische Familien und Berliner Schule. Die deutsche Schule im Spiegel von Einstellungen, Erwartungen und Erfahrungen türkischer Eltern. Eine empirische Untersuchung*. Berlin: Express.

Hesse-Biber, S. and Dupuis, P. (1995) 'Hypothesis Testing in Computer-aided Qualitative Data Analysis', in U. Kelle (ed.), *Computer-aided Qualitative Data Analysis. Theory, Methods and Practice*. London: Sage. pp. 129–135.

Hester, S. and Eglin, P. (eds) (1997) *Culture in Action: Studies in Membership Categorization Analysis*. Washington, DC: International Institute for Ethnomethodology and Conversation Analysis and University Press of America.

Hilbert, R. A. (1992) *The Classical Roots of Ethnomethodology: Durkheim, Weber, and Garfinkel*. Chapel Hill, NC: University of North Carolina Press.

Hildenbrand, B. (1983) *Alltag und Krankheit. Ethnographie einer Familie*. Stuttgart: Klett.

Hildenbrand, B. (1995) 'Fallrekonstruktive Forschung', in U. Flick, E. von Kardorff, H. Keupp, L. von

Rosenstiel and S. Wolff (eds), *Handbuch Qualitative Sozialforschung*, 2nd edn. Weinheim: Beltz. pp. 256–259.

Hildenbrand, B. (1999) *Fallrekonstruktive Familienforschung – Anleitungen für die Praxis*. Opladen: Leske and Budrich.

Hildenbrand, B. and Walter, J. (1988) '"Gemeinsames Erzählen" und Prozesse der Wirklichkeitskonstruktion in familiengeschichtlichen Gesprächen', *Zeitschrift für Soziologie*, 17: 203–217.

Hirschauer, S. (1993) *Die soziale Konstruktion der Transsexualität – Über die Medizin und den Geschlechtswechsel*. Frankfurt a. M.: Suhrkamp.

Hirschauer, S. (1994) 'Die soziale Fortpflanzung der Zweigeschlechtlichkeit', *Kölner Zeitschrift für Soziologie und Sozialpsychologie*, 46: 668–692.

Hirschauer, S. (1995) 'Dekonstruktion und Rekonstruktion – Plädoyer für die Erforschung des Bekannten', in U. Pasero and F. Braun (eds), *Konstruktion von Geschlecht*. Pfaffenweiler: Centaurus. pp. 67– 88.

Hirschauer, S. and Amann, K. (eds) (1997) *Die Befremdung der eigenen Kultur. Zur ethnographischen Herausforderung soziologischer Empirie*. Frankfurt a. M.: Suhrkamp.

Hitzler, R. (1991) 'Dummheit als Methode', in D. Garz and K. Kreimer (eds), *Qualitativ-empirische Sozialforschung*. Opladen: Westdeutscher Verlag. pp. 295–318.

Hitzler, R. (1993) 'Die Wahl der Qual', *Zeitschrift für Sexualforschung*, 3/93: 228–242.

Hitzler, R. (1995) 'Ehe trotz Bonn?', in G. Matjan (ed.), *Individualisierung und Politik (Kurswechsel Buch)*. Vienna: Sonderzahl. pp. 56–62.

Hitzler, R. (1997) 'Perspektivenwechsel'. *Soziologie*, pp. 5–18.

Hitzler, R. (1999a) 'Konsequenzen der Situationsdefinition', in R. Hitzler, J. Reichertz and N. Schröer (eds), *Hermeneutische Wissenssoziologie*. Konstanz: UVK. pp. 289–308.

Hitzler, R. (1999b) 'Welten erkunden', *Soziale Welt*, 4: 473–482.

Hitzler, R., Behring, A., Göschl, A. and Lustig, S. (1996) 'Signale der Sicherheit', in H. Knoblauch (ed.), *Kommunikative Lebenswelten*. Konstanz: UVK. pp. 177–197.

Hitzler, R. and Honer, A. (1984) 'Lebenswelt, Milieu, Situation', *Kölner Zeitschrift für Soziologie und Sozialpsychologie*, 36: 56–74.

Hitzler, R. and Honer, A. (1988) 'Der lebensweltliche Forschungsansatz', *Neue Praxis*, 18: 496–501.

Hitzler, R. and Honer, A. (1991) 'Qualitative Verfahren zur Lebensweltanalyse', in U. Flick, E. von Kardorff, H. Keupp, L. von Rosenstiel and S. Wolff (eds), *Handbuch qualitative Sozialforschung. Grundlagen, Konzepte, Methoden und Anwendungen*. Munich: Psychologie Verlags Union. pp. 382–385.

Hitzler, R. and Honer, A. (1994) 'Bastelexistenz', in U. Beck and E. Beck-Gernsheim (eds), *Riskante Freiheiten*. Frankfurt a. M.: Suhrkamp. pp. 307–315.

Hitzler, R. and Honer, A. (eds) (1997) *Sozialwissenschaftliche Hermeneutik*. Opladen: Leske and Budrich.

Hitzler, R., Honer, A. and Maeder, C. (eds) (1994) *Expertenwissen – die institutionalisierte Kompetenz*. Opladen: Westdeutscher Verlag.

Hitzler, R. and Pfadenhauer, M. (1998) 'Let Your Body Take Control! Zur ethnographischen Kulturanalyse der Techno-Szene', in R. Bohnsack and W. Marotzki (eds), *Biographieforschung und Kulturanalyse*. Opladen: Leske and Budrich. pp. 75–92.

Hitzler, R., Reichertz, J, and Schröer, N. (eds) (1999) *Hermeneutische Wissenssoziologie. Standpunkte zur Theorie der Interpretation*. Konstanz: Universitätsverlag Konstanz.

Hochschild, A. R. (1992) *Das gekaufte Herz*. Frankfurt a. M.: Campus.

Hodder, I. (1994) 'The Interpretation of Documents and Material Culture', in N. K. Denzin and Y. S. Lincoln (eds), *Handbook of Qualitative Research*. Thousand Oaks, CA: Sage. pp. 393–402.

Hoffmann, F. (1989) 'Erfassung, Bewertung und Gestaltung von Unternehmenskulturen. Von der Kulturtheorie zu einem anwendungsorientierten Ansatz', *Zeitschrift für Führung und Organisation*, 3: 168–173.

Hoffmann-Riem, C. (1980) 'Die Sozialforschung einer interpretativen Soziologie. Der Datengewinn', *Kölner Zeitschrift für Soziologie und Sozialpsychologie*, 32: 339–372.

Hoggart, R. (1957) *The Uses of Literacy*. London: Chatto and Windus.

Hollander, A. N. den (1965) 'Soziale Beschreibung als Problem', *Kölner Zeitschrift für Soziologie und Sozialpsychologie*, 17: 201–233.

Holstein, J. A. and Gubrium, J. F. (1995) *The Active Interview* (Qualitative Research Methods Series No. 37). Thousand Oaks, CA: Sage.

Holstein, J. A. and Gubrium, J. F. (2000) *The Self We Live By: Narrative Identity in a Postmodern World*. New York: Oxford University Press.

Honegger, C. (1991) *Die Ordnung der Geschlechter – Die Wissenschaften vom Menschen und das Weib 1750–1850*. Frankfurt a. M.: Campus.

Honer, A. (1985) 'Beschreibung einer Lebens-Welt. Zur Empirie des Bodybuilding', *Zeitschrift für Soziologie*, 14: 31–139.

Honer, A. (1993) *Lebensweltliche Ethnographie. Ein explorativ-interpretativer Forschungsansatz am Beispiel von Heimwerker-Wissen*. Wiesbaden: DUV.

Honer, A. (1994a) 'Aspekte des Selbermachens. Aus der kleinen Lebens-Welt des Heimwerkers', in R. Richter (eds), *Sinnbasteln*. Vienna: Böhlau. pp. 138–149.

Honer, A. (1994b) 'Das explorative Interview', *Schweizerische Zeitschrift für Soziologie*, pp. 623–640.

Honer, A. (1999) 'Bausteine zu einer lebensweltorientierten Wissenssoziologie', in R. Hitzler, J. Reichertz and N. Schröer (eds), *Hermeneutische Wissenssoziologie*. Konstanz: UVK. pp. 51–67.

Hopf, C. (1978) 'Die Pseudo-Exploration – Überlegungen zur Technik qualitativer Interviews in der Sozialforschung', *Zeitschrift für Soziologie*, 7: 97–115.

Hopf, C. (1983) 'Die Hypothesenprüfung als Aufgabe qualitativer Sozialforschung', *ASI-News*, 6: 33–55.

Hopf, C. (1991) 'Zwischen Betrug und Wahrhaftigkeit. Fragen der Forschungsethik in der Soziologie', *Soziologie*, 2: 174–191.

Hopf, C. (1996) 'Hypothesenprüfung und qualitative Sozialforschung', in R. Strobl and A. Böttger (eds), *Wahre Geschichten? Zu Theorie und Praxis qualitativer Interviews*. Baden-Baden: Nomos. pp. 9–21.

Hopf, C. (1998) 'Attachment Experiences and Aggressions Against Minorities', *Social Thought and Research*, 21 (1–2): 133–149.

Hopf, C., Rieker, P., Sanden-Markus, M. and Schmidt, C. (1995) *Familie und Rechtsextremismus. Familiale Sozialisation und rechtsextreme Orientierungen junger Männer*. Weinheim: Juventa.

Hopf, C. and Schmidt, C. (eds) (1993) *Zum Verhältnis von innerfamilialen sozialen Erfahrungen, Persönlichkeitsentwicklung und politischen Orientierungen. Dokumentation und Erörterung des methodischen Vorgehens in einer Studie zu diesem Thema*. Hildesheim: Vervielfältigtes Manuskript.

Hopper, P. J. (1997) 'Dualism in the Study of Narrative: A Note on Labov and Waletzky', *Journal of Narrative and Life History*, 7: 75–82.

Hopper, R. (ed.) (1990/91) 'Special Issue on "Ethnography and Conversation Analysis"', *Research on Language and Social Interaction*, 24 (2–3).

Horkheimer, M. (1932/1988) *Geschichte und Psychologie*. Collected Works, Volume 3. Frankfurt a. M.: Fischer. pp. 48–69.

Horkheimer, M. and Adorno, T. (1972) *Dialectic of Enlightenment*. New York: Seabury Press.

Horn, K., Beier, C. and Wolf, M. (1983) *Krankheit, Konflikt und soziale Kontrolle. Eine empirische Untersuchung subjektiver Sinnstrukturen*. Opladen: Westdeutscher Verlag.

Hornby, P. and Symon, G. (1994) 'Tracer Studies', in C. G. Cassell and C. Symon (eds), *Qualitative Methods in Organizational Research. A Practical Guide*. London: Sage. pp. 157–186.

Hornsby-Smith, M. (1993) 'Gaining Access', in N. Gilbert (eds), *Researching Social Life*. London: Sage. pp. 52–67.

House, E. (1980) *Evaluating with Validity*. Beverly Hills, CA: Sage.

House, E. (1993) *Professional Evaluation: Social Impact and Political Consequences*. Newbury Park, CA: Sage.

House, E. (1994) 'The Future of Perfect Evaluation', *Evaluation Practice*, 15: 239–248.

Huber, G. L. (ed.) (1992) *Qualitative Analyse. Computereinsatz in der Sozialforschung*. Munich: Oldenburg Verlag.

Huberman, A. M. and Miles, M. B. (1994) 'Data Management and Analysis', in N. K. Denzin and Y. S. Lincoln (eds), *Handbook of Qualitative Research*. Thousand Oaks, CA: Sage. pp. 428–444.

Humphreys, L. (1970) *Tearoom Trade*. London: Duckworth.

Husserl, E. (1936/1978) *The Crisis of European Sciences and Transcendental Phenomenology: An Introduction to Phenomenological Philosophy*. Evanston, IL: Northwestern University Press.

Hutchby, I. and Wooffitt, R. (1998) *Conversation Analysis: Principles, Practices and Applications*. Cambridge: Polity Press.

Inglies, F. (2000) *Clifford Geertz. Culture, Custom and Ethics*. Cambridge: Polity Press.

Irigaray, L. (1987) *Zur Geschlechterdifferenz – Interviews u. Vorträge*. Vienna: Wiener Frauenbuchverlag.

Irle, M. (1963) *Soziale Systeme*. Göttingen: Hogrefe.

Iser, W. (1978) *The Act of Reading*. London: Methuen.

Jackson, M. (1998) *Minima Ethnographica: Intersubjectivity and the Anthropological Project*. Chicago: University of Chicago Press.

Jaeger, H. (1977) 'Generationen in der Geschichte', *Geschichte und Gesellschaft*, 3: 429–452.

Jahoda, M. (1961) 'A Social-psychological Approach to the Study of Culture', *Human Relations*, 14: 23–30.

Jahoda, M. (1977) *Freud and the Dilemmas of Psychology*. London: The Hogarth Press.

Jahoda, M. (1979) 'The Impact of Unemployment in the 1930s and the 1970s', *Bulletin of the British Psychological Society*, 32: 309–314.

Jahoda, M. (1980/81) 'Aus den Anfängen der sozialwissenschaftlichen Forschung in Österreich', *Zeitgeschichte*, 8: 133–141.

Jahoda, M. (1983) 'The Emergence of Social Psychology in Vienna: An Exercise in Long-term Memory', *British Journal of Social Psychology*, 22: 343–349.

Jahoda, M. (1987) 'Unemployed Men at Work (1938)', in D. Fryer and P. Ullah (eds), *Unemployed People: Social and Psychological Perspectives*. Milton Keynes: Open University Press. pp. 1–73.

Jahoda, M. (1989) 'Why a Non-reductionistic Social Psychology is Almost Too Difficult to be Tackled but Too Fascinating to be Left Alone', *British Journal of Social Psychology*, 28: 71–78.

Jahoda, M. (1992) 'Reflections on Marienthal and After', *Journal of Occupational and Organizational Psychology*, 65: 355–358.

Jahoda, M. (1995) 'Jahoda, M., Lazarsfeld, P. and Zeisel, H., "Die Arbeitslosen von Marienthal"', in U. Flick, E. von Kardorff, H. Keupp, L. von Rosenstiel and S. Wolff (eds), *Handbuch Qualitative Sozialforschung – Grundlagen, Konzepte, Methoden und Anwendungen*. Weinheim: Beltz Psychologie Verlags Union. pp. 119–122.

Jahoda, M. and Cook, S. W. (1952) 'Security Measures and Freedom of Thought: An Exploratory Study of the Impact of Loyalty and Security Programs', *The Yale Law Journal*, 61: 295–333.

Jahoda, M., Deutsch, M. and Cook, S. W. (1951) *Research Methods in Social Relations, with Especial Reference to Prejudice*. New York: The Dryden Press (2nd one-volume edn, 1959).

Jahoda, M., Lazarsfeld, P. F. and Zeisel, H. (1933/1971) *Marienthal: The Sociology of an Unemployed Community*. Chicago: Aldine–Atherton.

James, W. (1890) *Principles of Psychology*. New York: Holt.

Jameson, F. (1976) 'On Goffman's Frame Analysis', *Theory and Society*, 3: 119–133.

Jaques, E. (1951) *The Changing Culture of a Factory*. London: Tavistock.

Jefferson, G. (1972) 'Side Sequences', in D. Sudnow (ed.), *Studies in Social Interaction*. New York: Free Press. pp. 294–338.

Jefferson, G. (1988) 'On the Sequential Organization of Troubles-talk in Ordinary Conversation', *Social Problems*, 35: 418–441.

Jick, T. (1983) 'Mixing Qualitative and Quantitative Methods: Triangulation in Action', in J. von Maanen (ed.), *Qualitative Methodology*. London: Sage. pp. 135–148.

Johnson, J. C. (1990) *Selecting Ethnographic Informants*. Newbury Park, CA: Sage.

Jorgensen, D. L. (1989) *Participant Observation. A Methodology for Human Studies* (Applied Social Research Methods Series, Volume 15). Newbury Park, CA: Sage.

Jugendwerk der Deutschen Shell (eds) (1981) *Jugend '81. Lebensentwürfe, Alltagskulturen, Zukunftsbilder*. Volume 2. Hamburg: Jugendwerk der Deutschen Shell.

Jugendwerk der Deutschen Shell (eds) (1985) *Jugendliche und Erwachsene 85*, 5 vols. Opladen: Leske and Budrich.

Jugendwerk der Deutschen Shell (eds) (1991) *Jugend '92. Lebenslagen, Orientierungen und Entwicklungsperspektiven im vereinigten Deutschland. Volume 1: Gesamtdarstellung und Biographische Porträts*. Opladen: Leske and Budrich.

Jugendwerk der Deutschen Shell (eds) (1997) *Jugend '97. Zukunftsperspektiven, Gesellschaftliches Engagement, Politische Orientierungen*. Opladen: Leske and Budrich.

Jung, P. (1987) 'Selbstorganisationsleistungen zur Gestaltung der betrieblichen Mikroorganisationen', *Zeitschrift für Organisationspsychologie*, 56: 313–319.

Kahn, R. L. (1977) 'Organisationsentwicklung: Einige Probleme und Vorschläge', in B. Sievers (ed.), *Organisationsentwicklung als Problem*. Stuttgart: Klett. pp. 281–301.

Kallmeyer, W. (ed.) (1994) *Kommunikation in der Stadt*, Teile 1–4. Berlin: de Gruyter.

Kallmeyer, W. (1997) 'Vom Nutzen des technologischen Wandels in der Sprachwissenschaft – Gesprächsanalyse und automatische Sprachverarbeitung', *Zeitschrift für Literaturwissenschaft und Linguistik*, 27: 124–152.

Kallmeyer, W. and Schütze, F. (1976) 'Konversationsanalyse', *Studium Linguistik*, 1: 1–28.

Kallmeyer, W. and Schütze, F. (1977) 'Zur Konstitution von Kommunikationsschemata der Sachverhaltsdarstellung', in D. Wegener (ed.), *Gesprächsanalysen*. Hamburg: Buske. pp. 159–274.

Kardorff, E. von (1987) 'Die Verwendung sozialwissenschaftlichen Wissens in der Fortbildung für Altenpfleger', in U. Dallinger (ed.), *Die Arbeit mit älteren Menschen*. Kassel: ASG. pp. 35–57.

Kardorff, E. von (1988) 'Praxisforschung als Forschung der Praxis', in M. Heiner (ed.), *Praxisforschung in der sozialen Arbeit*. Freiburg: Lambertus. pp. 77–100.

Kardorff, E. von (1991) 'Goffmans Anregungen für soziologische Handlungsfelder', in R. Hettlage and K. Lenz (eds), *Erving Goffman – ein soziologischer Klassiker der zweiten Generation*. Berne: Haupt. pp. 327–354.

Kardorff, E. von (1995) 'Qualitative Sozialforschung – Versuch einer Standortbestimmung', in U. Flick, E. von Kardorff, H. Keupp, L. von Rosenstiel and S. Wolff (eds), *Handbuch Qualitative Sozialforschung. Grundlagen, Konzepte, Methoden und Anwendungen*. Munich: Psychologie Verlags Union. pp. 3–8.

Kardorff, E. von (1998a) 'Evaluation', in S. Grubitzsch and K. Weber (eds), *Psychologische Grundbegriffe. Ein Handbuch*. Reinbek: Rowohlt. pp. 151–154.

Kardorff, E. von (1998b) 'Laien- und Expertenkulturen – Probleme transkultureller Kommunikation am Beispiel von Therapie und Rehabilitation', in I. Ionach (ed.), *Sprache und Sprechen*, Volume 34. Munich: Reinhardt-Verlag. pp. 77–89.

Kardorff, E. von (2000) 'Qualitative Forschung in der Rehabilitation', in U. Koch and J. Bengel (eds), *Handbuch der Rehabilitationswissenschaften*. Berlin: Springer. pp. 409–427.

Karp, D. A. (1980) 'Observing Behaviour in Public Places – Problems and Strategies', in W. B. Saffir, R. A. Stebbins and A. Turowetz (eds), *Fieldwork Experience – Qualitative Approaches to Social Research*. New York: St Martin's Press. pp. 82–97.

Kaschube, J. (1993) 'Betrachtung der Unternehmens- und Organisationskulturforschung aus (organisations)-psychologischer Sicht', in M. Dierkes, L. von Rosenstiel and U. Steger (eds), *Unternehmenskultur in Theorie und Praxis*. Frankfurt a. M.: Campus. pp. 90–146.

Kaufmann, F.-X. (1993) 'Generationsbeziehungen und Generationsverhältnisse im Wohlfahrtsstaat', in K. Lüscher and F. Schultheis (eds), *Generationenbeziehungen in 'postmodernen' Gesellschaften*. Konstanz: Universitätsverlag. pp. 95–108.

Kayales, C. (1998) *Gottesbilder von Frauen auf den Philippinen: Die Bedeutung der Subjektivität für eine interkulturelle Hermeneutik*. Münster: Lit.-Verlag.

kea (4/1992) *Zeitschrift für Kulturwissenschaft*, Book 4: Writing Culture.

Kelle, U. (1994) *Empirisch begründete Theoriebildung – Zur Logik und Methodologie interpretativer Sozialforschung*. Weinheim: Deutscher Studienverlag.

Kelle, U. (ed.) (1995) *Computer-Aided Qualitative Data Analysis. Theory, Methods and Practice*. London: Sage.

Kelle, U. (1996) 'Die Bedeutung theoretischen Vorwissens in der Methodologie der Grounded Theory', in R. Strobl and A. Böttger (eds), *Wahre Geschichten? Zu Theorie und Praxis qualitativer Interviews*. Baden-Baden: Nomos. pp. 24–45.

Kelle, U. (1997a) 'Theory Building in Qualitative Research and Computer Programs for the Management of Textual Data', *Sociological Research Online*, 2 (http://www.socresonline.org.uk/socresonline/2/2/1.html).

Kelle, U. (1997b) 'Computer-aided Methods for Typification in Qualitative Social Research', in R. Klar and O. Opitz (eds), *Classification and Knowledge Organization*. Berlin: Springer Verlag. pp. 342–354.

Kelle, U. and Erzberger, C. (1999) 'Integration qualitativer und quantitativer Methoden: methodologische Modelle und ihre Bedeutung für die Forschungspraxis', *Kölner Zeitschrift für Soziologie und Sozialpsychologie*, 51, 509–531.

Kelle, U. and Kluge, S. (1999) *Vom Einzelfall zum Typus. Fallvergleich und Fallkontrastierung in der qualitativen Sozialforschung*. Opladen: Leske and Budrich.

Kelle, U., Kluge, S. and Prein, G. (1993) *Strategien der Geltungssicherung in der qualitativen Sozialforschung. Zur Validitätsproblematik im interpretativen Paradigma*. Arbeitspapier Nr. 24 des Sfb 186. Bremen: Universität.

Kelle, U. and Laurie, H. (1995) 'Computer Use in Qualitative Research and Issues of Validity', in U. Kelle (ed.), *Computer-aided Qualitative Data Analysis. Theory, Methods and Practice*. London: Sage. pp. 19–28.

Kelle, U. and Zinn, J. (1998) 'School-to-Work Transition and Occupational Careers – Results from a Longitudinal Study in Germany', in T. Lange (ed.), *Understanding the School-to-Work Transition*. New York: Nova Science Publishing. pp. 71–90.

Keppler, A. (1985) *Information und Präsentation. Zur politischen Berichterstattung im Fernsehen*. Tübingen: Niemeyer.

Keppler, A. (1994) *Tischgespräche. Über Formen kommunikativer Vergemeinschaftung am Beispiel der Konversation in Familien*. Frankfurt a. M.: Suhrkamp.

Kessler, S. J. and McKenna, W. (1978) *Gender – An Ethnomethodological Approach*. New York: Wiley.

Ketner, K. L. (ed.) (1995) *Peirce and Contemporary Thought*. New York: Fordham University Press.

Kets de Vries, M. F. and Miller, D. (1986) 'Personality, Culture, and Organization', *Academy of Management Review*, 11: 266–279.

Keupp, H. (ed.) (1994) *Zugänge zum Subjekt. Perspektiven einer reflexiven Sozialpsychologie*. Frankfurt a. M.: Suhrkamp.

Kieser, A. (1988) 'Von der Morgenansprache zum "Gemeinsamen HP-Frühstück". Zur Funktion von Werten, Mythen, Ritualen und Symbolen. "Organisationskulturen" in der Zunft und in modernen Unternehmen', in E. Dülfer (ed.), *Organisationskultur*. Stuttgart: Poeschl. pp. 207–225.

Kieser, A. and Kubicek, H. (1977) *Organisation*. Berlin: de Gruyter.

Kirchhöfer, D. (1998) *Aufwachsen in Ostdeutschland. Langzeitstudie über die Tagesläufe 10– bis 14 jähriger Kinder*. Weinheim: Juventa.

Kirk, J. and Miller, M. L. (1986) *Reliability and Validity in Qualitative Research* (Qualitative Research Methods Series). London: Sage.

Kitsuse, J. I. and Cicourel, A. V. (1963) 'A Note on the Use of Official Statistics', *Social Problems*, 11: 131–139.

Kitzinger, J. (1994) 'The Methodology of Focus Groups – The Importance of Interaction between Research Participants', *Sociology of Health and Illness*, 16: 103–121.

Klein, S. (1991) *Der Einfluß von Werten auf die Gestaltung von Organisationen*. Berlin: Duncker and Humboldt.

Klinger, C. (1990) 'Bis hierher und wie weiter? Überlegungen zur feministischen Wissenschafts- und Rationalitätskritik', in M. Krüll (ed.), *Wege aus der männlichen Wissenschaft – Perspektiven feministischer Erkenntnistheorie*. Pfaffenweiler: Centaurus. pp. 21–56.

Kluge, S. (1999) *Empirisch begründete Typenbildung. Zur Konstruktion von Typen und Typologien in der qualitativen Sozialforschung*. Opladen: Leske and Budrich.

Kluge, S. and Opitz, D. (1999a) *Die Archivierung qualitativer Daten am Sonderforschungsbereich 186 der Universität Bremen*. Vortrag. Munich: Jahrestagung der Arbeitsgruppe 'Methoden der qualitativen Sozialforschung' der Deutschen Gesellschaft für Soziologie (DGS – 7/8. May).

Kluge, S. and Opitz, D. (1999b) 'Die Archivierung qualitativer Interviewdaten. Forschungsethik und Datenschutz als Barrieren für Sekundäranalysen?', *Soziologie*, 28: 48–63.

Knapp, G.-A. (1988) 'Die vergessene Differenz', *Feministische Studien*, 6: 12–31.

Knauth, B. and Wolff, S. (1990) 'Realität für alle praktischen Zwecke: Die Sicherstellung von Tatsächlichkeit in psychiatrischen Gerichtsgutachten', *Zeitschrift für Rechtssoziologie*, 11: 211–233.

Knauth, B. and Wolff, S. (1991) 'Zur Fruchtbarkeit der Konversationsanalyse für die Untersuchung schriftlicher Texte', *Zeitschrift für Soziologie*, 20: 36–49.

Knoblauch, H. (1988) '"Wenn Engel reisen …". Kaffeefahrten und Altenkultur', *Soziale Welt*, Special Issue 6, *Kultur und Alltag*: 397–411.

Knoblauch, H. (1991a) *Die Welt der Wünschelrutengänger und Pendler*. Frankfurt a. M.: Campus.

Knoblauch, H. (1991b) 'The Taming of Foes: The Avoidance of Asymmetry in Informal Discussions', in I. Markova and K. Foppa (eds), *Asymmetries in Dialogue*. Hertfordshire: Harvester. pp. 166–194.

Knoblauch, H. (1994a) 'Vom moralischen Kreuzzug zur Sozialtechnologie. Die Nichtrauchkampagne in Kalifornien', in R. Hitzler, A. Honer and C. Maeder (eds), *Expertenwissen.* Opladen: Westdeutscher Verlag. pp. 248–267.

Knoblauch, H. A. (1994b) 'Erving Goffmans Reich der Interaktion', in E. Goffman, *Interaktion und Geschlecht.* Herausgegeben und eingeleitet von H. A. Knoblauch. Mit einem Nachwort von H. Kotthoff. Frankfurt a. M.: Campus. pp. 7–49.

Knoblauch, H. (1995) *Kommunikationskultur. Die kommunikative Konstruktion kultureller Kontexte.* Berlin: de Gruyter.

Knoblauch, H. (1996a) 'Soziologie als strenge Wissenschaft?', in G. Preyer, G. Peter and A. Ulfig (eds), *Protosoziologie im Kontext.* Würzburg: Königshausen and Neumann. pp. 93–105.

Knoblauch, H. (ed.) (1996b) *Kommunikative Lebenswelten. Zur Ethnographie einer geschwätzigen Gesellschaft.* Konstanz: Universitätsverlag.

Knoblauch, H. (1996c) 'Arbeit als Interaktion: Informationsgesellschaft, Post-Fordismus und Kommunikationsarbeit', *Soziale Welt*, 47: 344–362.

Knoblauch, H. (1997) 'Zwischen den Geschlechtern? In-Szenierung, Organisation und Identität des Transvestismus', in S. Hirschauer and K. Amann (eds), *Die Befremdung der eigenen Kultur.* Frankfurt a. M.: Suhrkamp. pp. 84–113.

Knoblauch, H. (1998) 'Transzendenzerfahrung und symbolische Kommunikation', in H. Tyrell, V. Krech and H. Knoblauch (eds), *Religion als Kommunikation.* Würzburg: Ergon. pp. 147–186.

Knoblauch, H. (2002) 'Communication, Contexts and Culture. A Communicative Constructivist Approach to Intercultural Communication', in A. di Luzio, S. Günthner and F. Orletti (eds), *Culture in Communication. Analyses of Intercultural Situations.* Amsterdam: John Benjamins. pp. 3–33.

Knorr-Cetina, K. (1981) *The Manufacture of Knowledge – An Essay on the Constructivist and Contextual Nature of Science.* Oxford: Pergamon Press.

Knorr-Cetina, K. (with: Amann, K., Hirschauer, S. and Schmidt, K.-H.) (1988) 'Das naturwissenschaftliche Labor als Ort der "Verdichtung" von Gesellschaft', *Zeitschrift für Soziologie*, 17: 85–101.

Knorr-Cetina, K. (1989) 'Spielarten des Konstruktivismus – Einige Notizen und Anmerkungen', *Soziale Welt*, 40: 86–96.

Knorr-Cetina, K. and Mulkay, M. (eds) (1983) *Science Observed: Perspectives on the Social Study of Science.* London: Sage.

Koch-Straube, U. (1997) *Fremde Welt Pflegeheim. Eine ethnographische Studie.* Berne: Hans Huber.

Kohl, K.-H. (1992) 'Geordnete Erfahrung. Wissenschaftliche Darstellungsformen und literarischer Diskurs in der Ethnologie', in J. Matthes (ed.), *Zwischen den Kulturen? Die Sozialwissenschaften vor dem Problem des Kulturvergleichs. Soziale Welt*, Special Issue 8, pp. 363–374.

Kohlstruck, M. (1997) *Zwischen Erinnerung und Geschichte – Der Nationalsozialismus und die jungen Deutschen.* Berlin: Metropol.

Kondratowitz, H.-J. v. (1993) *Verwendung gerontologischen Wissens in der Kommune.* Berlin: DZA.

König, E. and Zedler, P. (eds) (1995) *Bilanz qualitativer Forschung. Volume I: Grundlagen qualitativer Forschung.* Weinheim: Deutscher Studien Verlag.

König, H. D. (1990) 'High Noon im Mittelmeer. Die Reinszenierung des Mythos des Westens auf der politischen Bühne', in W. Kempf (ed.), *Medienkrieg oder 'Der Fall Nicaragua'. Politpsychologische Analysen über US-Propaganda und psychologische Kriegführung.* Berlin: Argument. pp. 169–187.

König, H. D. (1993) 'Die Methode der tiefenhermeneutischen Kultursoziologie', in T. Jung and S. Müller-Doohm (eds), *"Wirklichkeit" im Deutungsprozeß. Verstehen und Methoden in den Kultur- und Sozialwissenschaften.* Frankfurt a. M.: Suhrkamp. pp. 190–222.

König, H. D. (1995a) 'Der in dem Film *Basic Instinct* inszenierte Geschlechterkampf', in S. Müller-Doohm and K. Neumann-Braun (eds), *Kulturinszenierungen.* Frankfurt a. M.: Suhrkamp. pp. 141–164.

König, H. D. (1995b) 'Die Holocaust-Überlebende und der grinsende Neonazi. Tiefenhermeneutische Rekonstruktion einer Szenensequenz aus dem Bonengel-Film *Beruf Neonazi*', in H. D. König. (ed.), *Mediale Inszenierungen rechter Gewalt*, Special issue *Psychosozial*, 18: 13–25.

König, H. D. (1995c) 'Ein Neonazi in Auschwitz. Tiefenhermeneutische Rekonstruktion einer Filmsequenz aus Bonengels *Beruf Neonazi* und ihre Wirkung im kulturellen Klima der Postmoderne', in H. D. König (ed.), *Sozialpsychologie des Rechtsextremismus.* Frankfurt a. M.: Suhrkamp. pp. 372–415.

König, H. D. (1996a) 'Hitler als charismatischer Massenführer. Tiefenhermeneutische Fallrekonstruktion zweier Sequenzen aus dem Film Triumph des Willens und ihre sozialisationstheoretische Bedeutung', in H. D. König (ed.), *Sozialpsychologie des Rechtsextremismus.* Frankfurt a. M.: Suhrkamp. pp. 41–82.

König, H. D. (1996b) 'Todessehnsüchte und letztes Aufbegehren. Eine tiefenhermeneutische Rekonstruktion des Endspiels', in H. D. König (ed.), *Neue Versuche, Becketts Endspiel zu verstehen. Sozialwissenschaftliches Interpretieren nach Adorno.* Frankfurt a. M.: Suhrkamp. pp. 250–313.

König, H. D. (1996c) 'Methodologie und Methode der tiefenhermeneutischen Kultursoziologie in der Perspektive von Adornos Verständnis kritischer Sozialforschung', in H. D. König (ed.), *Neue Versuche, Becketts Endspiel zu verstehen. Sozialwissenschaftliches Interpretieren nach Adorno.* Frankfurt a. M.: Suhrkamp. pp. 314–387.

König, H.-D. (ed.) (1996d) *Neue Versuche, Becketts Endspiel zu verstehen. Sozialwissenschaftliches Interpretieren nach Adorno.* Frankfurt a. M.: Suhrkamp.

König, H. D. (1997a) '"Ich trage heute einen Judenstern in der Form eines Hakenkreuzes!" Tiefenhermeneutische Biographieforschung am Beispiel von Bonengels Dokumentarfilm *Beruf Neonazi'*, in 'Politisches szenisch entschlüsseln. Tiefenhermeneutik als Verfahren politischer Analyse', Special issue, *Politisches Lernen*, 3–4/97: 141–176.

König, H. D. (1997b) '"Ihr seid Ihr selbst und müßt Euch selber befreien!" Ideologiekritische und sozialpsychologische Rekonstruktion der Rede eines Neonazis vor Jugendlichen in Cottbus', in R. Heim and H. D. König (ed.), 'Generation, Unbewußtes und politische Kultur', Special issue, *Psychosozial*, 20: 69–90.

König, H. D. (1997c) 'Tiefenhermeneutik als Methode kultursoziologischer Forschung', in R. Hitzler and A. Honer (eds), *Sozialwissenschaftliche Hermeneutik*. Leverkusen: Leske and Budrich. pp. 213–241.

König, H. D. (ed.) (1998) *Sozialpsychologie des Rechtsextremismus*. Frankfurt a. M.: Suhrkamp.

Koselleck, R. (1978) 'Einleitung', in O. Brunner, W. Conze and R. Koselleck (eds), *Geschichtliche Grundbegriffe – Historisches Lexikon zur politisch-sozialen Sprache in Deutschland*, Volume 1: XIII–XXVII. Stuttgart: Klett–Cotta.

Kowal, S. and O'Connell, D. C. (1995) 'Notation und Transkription in der Gesprächsforschung', *KODIKAS/ CODE. Ars Semiotica: An International Journal of Semiotics*, 18: 113–138.

Kowal, S. and O'Connell, D. C. (2003a) Datenerhebung und Transkription, in Rickheit, G., Herrman, T. and Deutsch, W. (eds), Psycholinguistik/ Psycholinguistics: Ein internationales Handbuch/ An International Handbook. Berlin: de Gruyter. pp. 92–106.

Kowal, S. and O'Connell, D. C. (2003b) Die Transkription mündlicher Äußerungen, in Herrmann T. and Grabowski, J. (eds), *Enzyklopädie der Psychologie*, Series III: Sprache, Volume 1: *Sprachproduktion*. Göttingen: Hogrefe. pp. 101–120.

Kracauer, S. (1952) 'The Challenge of Qualitative Content Analysis', *Public Opinion Quarterly*, 16: 631–642.

Kraus, W. (1995) 'Qualitative Evaluationsforschung', in U. Flick, E. von Kardorff, H. Keupp, L. von Rosenstiel and S. Wolff (eds), *Handbuch Qualitative Sozialforschung*, 2nd edn. Weinheim: Psychologie Verlags Union. pp. 412–415.

Kress, G. and Leeuwen, T. von (1996) *Reading Images. The Grammar of Visual Design*. London: Routledge.

Krippendorff, K. (1980) *Content Analysis. An Introduction to its Methodology*. Beverly Hills, CA: Sage.

Kroeber, A. L. and Parsons, T. (1958) 'The Concepts of Culture and Social System', *American Sociologist*, 23: 582–583.

Kroner, W. and Wolff, S. (1989) 'Pädagogik am Berg. Verwendung sozialwissenschaftlichen Wissens als Handlungsproblem vor Ort', in U. Beck and W. Bonß (eds), *Weder Sozialtechnologie noch Aufklärung?* Frankfurt a. M.: Suhrkamp. pp. 72–121.

Krueger, R. A. (1988) *Focus Groups – A Practical Guide for Applied Research*. Newbury Park, CA: Sage.

Kubicek, H. (1984) 'Führungsgrundsätze als Organisationsmythen und die Notwendigkeit von Entmythologisierungsversuchen', *Zeitschrift für Betriebswirtschaft*, 54: 4–29.

Kubik, G. (1993) 'Die mukanda-Erfahrung. Zur Psychologie der Initiation der Jungen im Ostangola-Kulturraum', in M.-J. van de Loo and M. Reinhart (eds), *Kinder. Ethnologische Forschungen in fünf Kontinenten*. Munich: Trickster. pp. 309–347.

Kubik, G. (1994) 'Ethnicity, Cultural Identity and the Psychology of Culture Contact', in G. Béhague (ed.), *Music and Black Ethnicity. The Caribbean and South America*. New Brunswick, NJ: Transaction Books. pp. 17–46.

Kuckartz, U. (1995) 'Case-oriented Quantification', in U. Kelle (ed.), *Computer-Aided Qualitative Data Analysis*. London: Sage. pp. 158–166.

Kuckartz, U. (1997) 'Qualitative Daten computergestützt auswerten: Methoden, Techniken, Software', in B. Friebertshäuser and A. Prengel (eds), *Handbuch qualitative Methoden in der Erziehungswissenschaft*. Weinheim: Juventa. pp. 584–595.

Kuckartz, U. (1999) *Computergestützte Analyse qualitativer Daten*. Opladen: Westdeutscher Verlag.

Kühlmann, T. M. and Franke, J. (1989) 'Organisationsdiagnose', in E. Roth (ed.), *Organisationspsychologie. Enzyklopädie der Psychologie*, Volume 3. Göttingen: Hogrefe. pp. 631–651.

Kuhn, Th. S. (1970) *The Structure of Scientific Revolutions*, 2nd edn. Chicago: University of Chicago Press.

Kuper, A. (1973) *Among the Anthropologists. History and Context in Anthropology*. New York: Pica Press.

Kvale, S. (1989) 'To Validate is to Question', in S. Kvale (ed.), *Issues of Validity in Qualitative Research*. Lund: Studienlitteratur. pp. 73–92.

Kvale, S. (1995a) 'Validierung: Von der Beobachtung zu Kommunikation und Handeln', in U. Flick, E. von Kardorff, H. Keupp, L. von Rosenstiel and S. Wolff (eds), *Handbuch Qualitative Sozialforschung*, 2nd edn. Weinheim: Psychologie Verlags Union. pp. 427–431.

Kvale, S. (1995b) 'The Social Construction of Validity', *Qualitative Inquiry*, 1: 19–40.

Kvale, S. (1996) *InterViews. An Introduction to Qualitative Research Interviewing*. Thousand Oaks, CA: Sage (2nd edn 2004).

Labov, W. and Waletzky, J. (1967/1997) 'Narrative Analysis: Oral Versions of Personal Experience', *Journal of Narrative and Life History*, 7: 3–38.

Lachmund, J. and Stollberg, G. (eds) (1992) *The Social Construction of Illness. Illness and Medical Knowledge in Past and Present*. Stuttgart: Steiner.

Lamnek, S. (1995) *Qualitative Sozialforschung*, 3rd corr. edn. *Volume 1: Methodologie. Volume 2: Methoden und Techniken*. Weinheim: Beltz, Psychologie Verlags Union.

Lamnek, S. (1998) *Gruppendiskussion – Theorie und Praxis*. Weinheim: Psychologie Verlags Union.

Langer, S. K. (1957) *Philosophy in a New Key. A Study in the Symbolism of Reason, Rite and Art*. Cambridge: Cambridge University Press.

Laqueur, T. W. (1990) *Making Sex: Body and Gender from the Greeks to Freud*. Cambridge, MA: Harvard University Press.

Latour, B. and Woolgar, S. (1979) *Laboratory Life. The Social Construction of Scientific Facts*. Beverly Hills, CA: Sage.

Lau, T. (1992) *Die heiligen Narren. Punk 1976 – 1986*. Berlin: de Gruyter.

Lau, T. and Wolff, S. (1983) 'Der Einstieg in das Untersuchungsfeld als soziologischer Lernprozeß', *Kölner Zeitschrift für Soziologie und Sozialpsychologie*, 35: 417–437.

Lautman, J. and Lécuyer, B.-P. (eds) (1998) *Paul Lazarsfeld 1901–1976. La Sociologie de Vienne à New York*. Paris: Editions L'Hamattan.

Lechinsky, A. (1988) 'Lebenslaufforschung – ein neues Paradigma sozial- und erziehungswissenschaftlicher Forschung', *Zeitschrift für Pädagogik*, 34: 19–23.

LeCompte, M. D. and Preissle, J. (1993) *Ethnography and Qualitative Design in Educational Research*, 2nd edn. San Diego: Academic Press.

Lee, R. M. (1993) *Doing Research On Sensitive Topics*. London: Sage.

Lee, R. M. and Fielding, N. G. (1996) 'Qualitative Data Analysis: Representations of a Technology. A Comment on Coffey, Holbrook and Atkinson', *Sociological Research Online*, (1) 4 (http://www.socresonline.org.uk/socresonline/1/4/lf.html).

Leech, G., Myers, G. and Thomas, J. (eds) (1995) *Spoken English on Computer – Transcription, Mark-up, and Application*. Harlow: Longman.

Legewie, H. (1987) 'Interpretation und Validierung biographischer Interviews', in G. Jüttemann and H. Thomae (eds), *Biographie und Psychologie*. Heidelberg: Springer-Verlag. pp. 138–150.

Legewie, H., Jaeggi, E., Böhm, A., Boehnke, K. and Faas, A. (1989) *Längerfristige psychische Folgen von Umweltbelastungen*. Berlin: Institut für Psychologie der Technischen Universität (Endbericht zum Forschungsprojekt FIP 2/17).

Legge, K. (1984) *Evaluating Planned Organizational Change*. London: Academic Press.

Leggewie, C. (1995) *Die 89er – Porträt einer Generation*. Hamburg: Hoffmann and Campe.

Leisering, L. (1992) *Sozialstaat und demographischer Wandel – Wechselwirkungen, Generationsverhältnisse, politisch-institutionelle Steuerung*. Frankfurt a. M.: Campus.

Leithäuser, T. and Volmerg, B. (1988) *Psychoanalyse in der Sozialforschung. Eine Einführung am Beispiel einer Sozialpsychologie der Arbeit*. Opladen: Westdeutscher Verlag.

Lemert, C. (1997) *Postmodernism Is Not What You Think*. Malden, MA: Blackwell.

Lenz, K. (1991) 'Goffman – ein Strukturalist?', in R. Hettlage and K. Lenz (eds), *Erving Goffman – ein soziologischer Klassiker der zweiten Generation*. Berne: Haupt. pp. 243–300.

Lepenies, W. (1988) *Between Literature and Science: The Rise of Sociology*. Cambridge: Cambridge University Press.

Lepenies, W. (1997) 'Die Sozialwissenschaften nach dem Ende der Geschichte', in W. Lepenies (ed.), *Benimm und Erkenntnis. Zwei Vorträge*. Frankfurt a. M.: Suhrkamp. pp. 51–100.

Lepper, G. (2000) *Categories in Text and Talk. A Practical Introduction to Categorization Analysis* (Introducing Qualitative Methods Series). London: Sage.

Leuzinger, M. (1998) 'Qualitative und quantitative Einzelfallforschung. Versuch einer Brückenbildung zwischen klinischer "Junktim-Forschung" und nachträglicher "extraklinischer" Psychotherapieforschung', *Psychotherapieforum*, 6: 102–117.

Levenstein, A. (1912) *Die Arbeiterfrage*. Munich: Reinhardt.

Levinson, S. C. (1983) *Pragmatics*. Cambridge: Cambridge University Press.

Lévi-Strauss, C. (1978) *Strukturale Anthropologie I*. Frankfurt a. M.: Suhrkamp.

Lévi-Strauss, C. (1981) *Die elementaren Strukturen der Verwandtschaft*. Frankfurt a. M.: Suhrkamp.

Lewin, K. (1947) 'Frontiers in Group Dynamics', *Human Relations*, 1: 5–41.

Lewin, K. (1948) *Resolving Social Conflicts*. New York: Harper.

Lewin, M. (1986) *Psychologische Forschung im Umriß*. Berlin: Springer Verlag.

Lewis, O. (1967) *La Vida: A Puerto Rican Family in the Culture of Poverty – San Juan and New York*. London: Secker and Warburg.

Leymann, H. (1993) *Mobbing. Psychoterror am Arbeitsplatz und wie man sich dagegen wehren kann*. Reinbek: Rowohlt.

Lichtenberg, G. C. (1983) 'Sudelbücher (1765–1799)', in G. C. Lichtenberg, *Schriften und Briefe,* Volume I. Frankfurt a. M.: Insel. pp. 63–526.

Liebau, E. (1987) *Gesellschaftliches Subjekt und Erziehung*. Weinheim: Beltz.

Liebes, T. and Katz, E. (1990) *The Export of Meaning. Cross-cultural Readings of Dallas*. Oxford: Oxford University Press.

Lincoln, Y. S. (1994) 'Tracks towards a Postmodern Politics of Evaluation', *Evaluation Practice*, 15: 299–310.

Lincoln, Y. S. and Denzin, N. K. (1998) 'The Fifth Moment', in Y. S. Lincoln and N. K. Denzin (eds), *The Landscape of Qualitative Research. Theories and Issues*. Thousand Oaks, CA: Sage. pp. 407–429.

Lincoln, Y. S. and Guba, E. G. (1985) *Naturalistic Inquiry*. Beverly Hills, CA: Sage.

Lindemann, G. (1993) *Das paradoxe Geschlecht – Transsexualität im Spannungsfeld von Körper, Leib und Gefühl.* Frankfurt a. M.: Suhrkamp.

Lindner, R. (1981) 'Die Angst des Forschers vor dem Feld', *Zeitschrift für Volkskunde,* 77: 51–70.

Lindner, R. (1990) *Die Entdeckung der Stadtkultur. Soziologie aus der Erfahrung der Reportage.* Frankfurt a. M.: Suhrkamp.

Lindsay, J. and O'Connell, D. C. (1995) 'How Do Transcribers Deal with Audio Recordings of Spoken Discourse?', *Journal of Psycholinguistic Research,* 24: 101–115.

Linell, P. (1998) *Approaching Dialogue: Talk, Interaction and Contexts in Dialogical Perspectives.* Amsterdam: John Benjamins.

Lisch, R. and Kriz, J. (1978) *Grundlagen und Modelle der Inhaltsanalyse.* Reinbek: Rowohlt.

Lissmann, U. (1997) *Inhaltsanalyse von Texten.* Landau: Verlag Empirische Pädagogik.

List, E. (1983) *Alltagsrationalität und soziologischer Diskurs: Erkenntnis- und wissenschaftstheoretische Implikationen der Ethnomethodologie.* Frankfurt a. M.: Campus.

Livingston, E. (1986) *The Ethnomethodological Foundations of Mathematics.* London: Routledge and Kegan Paul.

Lofland, J. (1961) 'Comment on "Initial Interaction of Newcomers in Alcoholics Anonymous"', *Social Problems,* 8: 365–367.

Lofland, J. F. and Lejeune, R. A. (1960) 'Initial Interaction of Newcomers in Alcoholics Anonymous: A Field Experiment in Class Symbols and Socialization'. *Social Problems,* 8: 102–111.

Lofland, J. and Lofland, L. H. (1984) *Analyzing Social Settings: A Guide to Qualitative Observation and Analysis.* Belmont, CA: Wadsworth.

Lonkila, M. (1995) 'Grounded Theory as an Emerging Paradigm for Computer-assisted Qualitative Data Analysis', in U. Kelle (ed.), *Computer-aided Qualitative Data Analysis. Theory, Methods and Practice.* London: Sage. pp. 41–51.

Loos, P. and Schäffer, B. (2000) *Das Gruppendiskussionsverfahren – Theoretische Grundlagen und empirische Anwendung.* Opladen: Leske and Budrich.

Lorenzer, A. (1970) *Sprachzerstörung und Rekonstruktion.* Frankfurt a. M.: Suhrkamp.

Lorenzer, A. (1971) 'Symbol, Interaktion und Praxis', in A. Lorenzer et al. (eds), *Psychoanalyse als Sozialwissenschaft.* Frankfurt a. M.: Suhrkamp.

Lorenzer, A. (1972) *Zur Begründung einer materialistischen Sozialisationstheorie.* Frankfurt a. M.: Suhrkamp.

Lorenzer, A. (1974) *Die Wahrheit der psychoanalytischen Erkenntnis. Ein historisch-materialistischer Entwurf.* Frankfurt a. M.: Suhrkamp.

Lorenzer, A. (1981a) *Das Konzil der Buchhalter. Die Zerstörung der Sinnlichkeit. Eine Religionskritik.* Frankfurt a. M.: Fischer.

Lorenzer, A. (1981b) 'Zum Beispiel "Der Malteser Falke". Analyse der psychoanalytischen Untersuchung literarischer Texte', in B. Urban and W. Kudszus (eds), *Psychoanalytische und psychopathologische Literaturinterpretation.* Darmstadt: Wissenschaftliche Buchgesellschaft. pp. 23–46.

Lorenzer, A. (1986) 'Tiefenhermeneutische Kulturanalyse', in H. D. König, A. Lorenzer, H. Lüdde, S. Naghol, U. Prokop, G. Schmid-Noerr and A. Eggert (eds), *Kultur-Analysen. Psychoanalytische Studien zur Kultur.* Frankfurt a. M.: Fischer. pp. 11–98.

Lorenzer, A. (1990) 'Verführung zur Selbstpreisgabe – psychoanalytisch-tiefenhermeneutische Analyse des Gedichtes von Rudolf Alexander Schröder', *Kulturanalysen,* 2: 261–277.

Lotringer, S. (1983) *New Yorker Gespräche.* Berlin: Merve.

Lübbe, H. (1983) 'Der Nationalsozialismus im deutschen Nachkriegsbewußtsein', *Historische Zeitschrift,* 236: 579–599.

Luckmann, B. (1970) 'The Small Life-Worlds of Modern Man', *Social Research,* 4: 580–596.

Luckmann, T. (ed.) (1978) *Phenomenology and Sociology.* Harmondsworth: Penguin.

Luckmann, T. (1979) 'Phänomenologie und Soziologie', in W. Sprondel and R. Grathoff (eds), *Alfred Schütz und die Idee des Alltags in den Sozialwissenschaften.* Stuttgart: Enke. pp. 196–206.

Luckmann, T. (1983) *Life-World and Social Realities.* London: Heinemann.

Luckmann, T. (1986) 'Grundformen der gesellschaftlichen Vermittlung des Wissens: Kommunikative Gattungen', *Kölner Zeitschrift für Soziologie und Sozialpsychologie,* Special Issue 27: 191–211.

Luckmann, T. (1989) 'Kultur und Kommunikation', in M. Haller, H.-J. Hoffmann-Nowottny and W. Zapf (eds), *Kultur und Gesellschaft* (Verhandlungen des Soziologentags in Zürich 1988). Frankfurt a. M.: Campus. pp. 33–45.

Luckmann, T. (1990) 'Lebenswelt: Modebegriff oder Forschungsprogramm', *Grundlagen der Weiterbildung,* 1: 9–13.

Luckmann, T. (1992) *Theorie des sozialen Handelns.* Berlin: de Gruyter.

Luckmann, T. (1993) 'Schützsche Protosoziologie?', in A. Bäumer and M. Benedikt (eds), *Gelehrtenrepublik – Lebenswelt.* Vienna: Passagen. pp. 321–326.

Luckmann, T. and Gross, P. (1977) 'Analys Kommunikation und Interaktion als Zugang zum Problem der Konstitution sozialwissenschaftlicher Daten', in H.-U. Bielefeld (ed.), *Soziolinguistik und Empirie.* Wiesbaden: Athenaion. pp. 198–207.

Lüders, C. (1995) 'Von der teilnehmenden Beobachtung zur ethnographischen Beschreibung', in E. König and P. Zedler (eds) *Bilanz qualitativer Forschung. Volume II: Methoden.* Weinheim: Deutscher Studien Verlag. pp. 311–342.

Lüders, C. (1996) 'Between Stories – Neue Horizonte der qualitativen Sozialforschung?' Review of N. K. Denzin and Y. S. Lincoln (eds), *Handbook of*

Qualitative Research, in *SozialWissenschaftliche Literaturrundschau*, 19: 19–29.

Lüders, C. and Reichertz, J. (1986) 'Wissenschaftliche Praxis ist, wenn alles funktioniert und keiner weiß warum. Bemerkungen zur Entwicklung qualitativer Sozialforschung', *Sozialwissenschaftliche Literaturrundschau*, 12: 90–102.

Lueger, M. and Schmitz, Ch. (1984) *Das offene Interview. Theorie – Erhebung – Rekonstruktion latenter Strukturen*. Vienna: Service-Fachverlag an der Wirtschaftsuniversität Wien.

Luhmann, N. (1972) 'Einfache Sozialsysteme', *Zeitschrift für Soziologie*, 1: 85–107.

Luhmann, N. (1990a) *Soziologische Aufklärung 5 – Konstruktivistische Perspektiven*. Opladen: Westdeutscher Verlag.

Luhmann, N. (1990b) *Die Wissenschaft der Gesellschaft*. Frankfurt a. M.: Suhrkamp.

Luhmann, N. (1997) *Die Gesellschaft der Gesellschaft*. Frankfurt a. M.: Suhrkamp.

Lunt, P. and Livingstone, S. (1996) 'Rethinking the Focus Group in Media Research', *Journal of Communication*, 46: 79–98.

Lutz, B., Hartmann, M. and Hirsch-Kreinsen, H. (eds) (1996) *Produzieren im 21. Jahrhundert*. Frankfurt a. M.: Campus.

Lynch, M. (1985) *Art and Artifact in Laboratory Science: A Study of Shop Work and Shop Talk in a Research Laboratory*. London: Routledge and Kegan Paul.

Lynch, M. (1993) *Scientific Practice and Ordinary Action: Ethnomethodology and Social Studies of Science*. Cambridge: Cambridge University Press.

Lynch, M., Livingston, E. and Garfinkel, H. (1983) 'Temporal Order in Laboratory Work', in K. Knorr-Cetina and M. Mulkay (eds), *Science Observed. Perspectives in the Social Study of Science*. Beverly Hills, CA: Sage. pp. 207–238.

Lyotard, F. (1993) *The Postmodern Condition: A Report on Knowledge*. Minneapolis: University of Minnesota Press.

MacWhinney, B. (1995) *The CHILDES project – Tools for Analyzing Talk*, 2nd edn. Hillsdale, NJ: Erlbaum.

Madaus, L. G. F., Scriven, M. and Stufflebeam, D. L. (eds) (1983) *Evaluation Models*. Boston: Kluwer–Nijhoff.

Mahnkopf, B. (1985) *Verbürgerlichung. Die Legende vom Ende des Proletariats*. Frankfurt a. M.: Campus.

Mai, T. V. (1983) *Vietnam: Un Peuple, Des Voix*. Paris: Pierre Horay.

Maier, C. (1996) *Das Leuchten der Papaya: Ein Bericht von den Trobriandern in Melanesien*. Hamburg: Europ. Verlagsanstalt.

Mainiero, L. A. (1994) *Liebe im Büro – Flirts, Intrigen und Karrieren am Arbeitsplatz*. Stuttgart: Kreuz.

Malinowski, B. (1935) *Coral Gardens and Their Magic. A Study of the Methods of Tilling the Soil and Agricultural Rites in the Trobriand Islands*. New York: American Book Company.

Malinowski, B. (1967) *A Diary in the Strict Sense of the Term* London: Routledge and Kegan Paul.

Mangold, W. (1960) *Gegenstand und Methode des Gruppendiskussionsverfahrens*. Frankfurt a. M.: Europäische Verlagsanstalt.

Mangold, W. (1973) 'Gruppendiskussionen', in R. König (eds), *Handbuch der empirischen Sozialforschung*, 3rd edn, Volume 2. Stuttgart: Enke.

Mann, C. and Stewart, F. (2002) *Internet Communication and Qualitative Research*. London: Sage.

Mannheim, K. (1952a) 'On the Interpretation of Weltanschauung', in K. Mannheim, *Essays on the Sociology of Knowledge*, London: Routledge and Kegan Paul.

Mannheim, K. (1952b) 'The Problem of Generations', in K. Mannheim, *Essays on the Sociology of Knowledge*. London: Routledge and Kegan Paul. pp. 276–320.

Mannheim, K. (1982) *Structures of Thinking*. London: Routledge.

Manning, K. (1997) 'Authenticity in Constructivist Inquiry: Methodological Considerations without Prescriptions', *Qualitative Inquiry*, 3: 93–115.

Manning, P. (1992) *Erving Goffman and Modern Sociology*. Stanford, CA: Polity Press.

Marcus, G. E. (1986) 'Contemporary Problems of Ethnography in the Modern World System', in J. Clifford and G. E. Marcus (eds), *Writing Culture. The Poetics and Politics of Ethnography*. Berkeley, CA: University of California Press. pp. 165–193.

Marcus, G. E (1994) 'What Comes after "Post". The Case of Ethnography', in N. K. Denzin and Y. S. Lincoln (eds), *Handbook of Qualitative Research*. Thousand Oaks, CA: Sage. pp. 563–574.

Marcus, G. E. and Fischer, M. M. (1986) *Anthropology as Cultural Critique. An Experimental Moment in the Human Sciences*. Chicago: University of Chicago Press.

Margolis, E. (1998) 'Picturing Labor: A Visual Ethnography of the Coal Mine Labor Process', *Visual Sociology*, 13: 5–36.

Marotzki, W. (1995a) 'Qualitative Bildungsforschung', in E. König and P. Zedler (eds), *Bilanz qualitativer Forschung. Band I: Grundlagen qualitativer Forschung*. Weinheim: Deutscher Studien Verlag. pp. 99–134.

Marotzki, W. (1995b) 'Forschungsmethoden der erziehungswissenschaftlichen Biographieforschung', in H. H. Krüger and W. Marotzki (eds), *Erziehungswissenschaftliche Biographieforschung*. Opladen: Leske und Budrich. pp. 55–89.

Marotzki, W. (1997a) 'Morphologie eines Bildungsprozesses. Eine mikrologische Studie', in D. Nittel and W. Marotzki (eds), *Berufslaufbahn und biographische Lernstrategien. Eine Fallstudie über Pädagogen in der Privatwirtschaft*. Hohengehren: Schneider. pp. 83–117.

Marotzki, W. (1997b) 'Biographieanalyse als mikrologische Zeitdiagnose. Eine methodologisch inspirierte Relektüre der Schriften Walter Benjamins', in B. Frischmann and G. Mohr (eds), *Erziehungswissenschaft – Bildung – Philosophie*. Weinheim: Deutscher Studien Verlag. pp. 131–148.

Marshall, C. and Rossman, G. B. (1995) *Designing Qualitative Research*, 2nd edn. Thousand Oaks, CA: Sage.

Marx, W. (1987) *Die Phänomenologie Edmund Husserls*. Munich: Fink.

Maso, I. (2001) 'Phenomenology and Ethnography', in P. Atkinson, A. Coffey, S. Delamont, J. Lofland and L. Lofland (eds), *Handbook of Ethnography*. London: Sage. pp. 136–144.

Mason, J. (2002) *Qualitative Researching*, 2nd edn. London: Sage.

Matthes, J. (1985) 'Die Soziologen und ihre Wirklichkeit – Anmerkungen zum Wirklichkeitsverhältnis der Soziologie', in W. Bonß and H. Hartmann (eds), *Entzauberte Wissenschaft: Zur Relativität und Geltung soziologischer Forschung. Soziale Welt*, Special Issue 3, pp. 49–64.

Matthiesen, U. (1983) *Das Dickicht der Lebenswelt und die Theorie des kommunikativen Handelns*. Munich: Fink.

Mauthner, M., Birch, M., Jessop, J. and Miller, T. (eds) (2002) *Ethics in Qualitative Research*. London: Sage.

Maxwell, J. A. (1996) *Qualitative Research Design – An Interactive Approach*. Thousand Oaks, CA: Sage.

Mayer, K. U. (1990) 'Lebensverläufe und sozialer Wandel. Anmerkungen zu einem Forschungsprogramm', in K. U. Mayer (eds), *Lebensverläufe und sozialer Wandel. Kölner Zeitschrift für Soziologie und Sozialpsychologie*, Special Issue 31, pp. 7–21.

Maynard, D. W. (ed.) (1988) 'Special issue on "Language, Interaction, and Social Problems"', *Social Problems* 35 (4).

Maynard, D. W. and Clayman, S. (1991) 'The Diversity of Ethnomethodology', *Annual Review of Sociology*, 17: 385–418.

Mayntz, R. (1985) 'On the Use and Non-use of Methodological Rules in Social Research', in U. Gerhardt and M. E. Wadsworth (eds), *Stress and Stigma*. Frankfurt a. M.: Campus. pp. 39–52.

Mayntz, R., Holm, K. and Hübner, P. (1969) *Einführung in die Methoden der empirischen Sozialforschung*. Cologne: Westdeutscher Verlag.

Mayring, P. (1999) *Einführung in die qualitative Sozialforschung. Eine Anleitung zu qualitativem Denken*, 4th edn. Munich: Psychologie Verlags Union.

Mayring, P. (2000a) 'Qualitative Content Analysis', *Forum: Qualitative Social Research*, 1 (2) (http://www.qualitative-research.net/fqs).

Mayring, P. (2000b) *Qualitative Inhaltsanalyse. Grundlagen und Techniken*, 7th edn. Weinheim: Deutscher Studien Verlag.

Mayring, P. (2002a) 'Qualitative Content Analysis – Research Instrument or Mode of Interpretation?', in M. Kiegelmann (ed.), *The Role of the Researcher in Qualitative Psychology*. Tübingen: Verlag Ingeborg Huber. pp. 139–148.

Mayring, P. (2002b) 'Qualitative Approaches in Research on Learning and Instruction', in B. Ralle and I. Eilks (eds), *Research in Chemical Education – What Does it Mean?* Aachen: Shaker Verlag. pp. 111–118.

Mayring, P., König, J. and Birk, N. (1996) 'Computerunterstützte Qualitative Inhaltsanalyse von Berufsbiographien arbeitsloser LehrerInnen in den Neuen Bundesländern', in W. Bos and C. Tarnai (eds), *Computergestützte Inhaltsanalyse in der Empirischen Pädagogik, Psychologie und Soziologie*. Münster: Waxmann. pp. 105–120.

McCabe, C. (1974) 'Realism and the Cinema: Notes on Some Brechtian Themes', in C. McCabe, *Theoretical Essays*. Manchester: Manchester University Press. pp. 34–39.

McCall, G. J. and Simmons, J. L. (eds) (1969) *Issues in Participant Observation: A Text and Reader*. Reading, MA: Addison–Wesley.

McHoul, A. W. (1982) *Telling How Texts Talk*. Oxford: Blackwell.

McRobbie, A. (1980) 'Settling Accounts with Subcultures', *Screen Education*, 34: 37–49.

McRobbie, A. (1998) *British Fashion Design. Rag Trade or Image Industry?* London: Routledge.

Mead, G. H. (1934) *Mind, Self and Society from the Standpoint of a Social Behaviourist*. Chicago: University of Chicago Press.

Mead, M. (1958) *Mann und Weib. Das Verhältnis der Geschlechter in einer sich wandelnden Welt*. Reinbek: Rowohlt.

Mehan, H. and Wood, H. (1975) *The Reality of Ethnomethodology*. New York: Wiley.

Meier, C. (1997) *Arbeitsbesprechungen: Interaktionsstruktur, Interaktionsdynamik und Konsequenzen einer sozialen Form*. Opladen: Westdeutscher Verlag.

Meier, C. (1998) 'Zur Untersuchung von Arbeits- und Interaktionsprozessen anhand von Videoaufzeichnungen', *Arbeit. Zeitschrift für Arbeitsforschung, Arbeitsgestaltung und Arbeitspolitik*, 7: 257–275.

Meinefeld, W. (1995) *Realität und Konstruktion – Erkenntnistheoretische Grundlagen einer Methodologie der empirischen Sozialforschung*. Opladen: Leske and Budrich.

Meinefeld, W. (1997) 'Ex-ante Hypothesen in der Qualitativen Sozialforschung: zwischen "fehl am Platz" und "unverzichtbar"'. *Zeitschrift für Soziologie*, 26: 22–34.

Menschik-Bendele, J. and Ottomeyer, K. (1998) *Sozialpsychologie des Rechtsradikalismus. Entstehung und Veränderung eines Syndroms*. Opladen: Leske and Budrich.

Merkens, H. (1986) 'Vorwissen und Hypothesenbildung beim Prozeß des Beobachtens – Überlegungen zu den Grenzen der Beobachtung in der Arbeitsmigrantenforschung', in H. P. Hoffmeyer-Zlotnik (ed.), *Qualitative Methoden der Datenerhebung in der Arbeitsmigrantenforschung*. Mannheim: Forschung Raum und Gesellschaft e.V. pp. 78–108.

Merkens, H. (1997) 'Stichproben bei qualitativen Studien', in B. Friebertshäuser and A. Prengel (eds),

Handbuch qualitative Forschungsmethoden in der Erziehungswissenschaft. Weinheim: Juventa. pp. 97–106.

Merten, K. (1983) *Inhaltsanalyse. Einführung in Theorie, Methode und Praxis.* Opladen: Westdeutscher Verlag.

Mertens, W. and Lang, H.-J. (1991) *Die Seele im Unternehmen.* Berlin: Springer.

Merton, R. K. (1967) *On Theoretical Sociology.* New York: Free Press.

Merton, R. K. (1968) 'The Bearing of Empirical Research on Sociological Theory', in R. K. Merton (ed.), *Social Theory and Social Structure.* New York: Free Press. pp. 156–171.

Merton, R. K. (1987) 'The Focused Interview and Focus Groups – Continuities and Discontinuities', *Public Opinion Quarterly*, 51: 550–556.

Merton, R. K., Fiske, M. and Kendall, P. L. (1956) *The Focused Interview. A Manual of Problems and Procedures.* Glencoe, IL: Free Press.

Merton, R. K. and Kendall, P. (1945/46) 'The Focused Interview', *American Journal of Sociology*, 51: 541–557.

Meuser, M. (1998) *Geschlecht und Männlichkeit – Soziologische Theorie und kulturelle Deutungsmuster.* Opladen: Leske and Budrich.

Meuser, M. and Nagel, U. (1991) 'ExpertInneninterviews – vielfach erprobt, wenig bedacht. Ein Beitrag zur qualitativen Methodendiskussion', in D. Garz and K. Kraimer (eds), *Qualitativ-empirische Sozialforschung.* Opladen: Westdeutscher Verlag. pp. 441–468.

Meyer, M. W. and Rowan, B. (1977) 'Institutional Organizations: Formal Structure as Myth and Ceremony', *American Journal of Sociology*, 83: 340–363.

Mikos, L. (1994) *Fernsehen im Erleben der Zuschauer.* Munich: Quintessenz.

Miles, M. B. and Huberman, A. M. (1994) *Qualitative Data Analysis – An Expanded Sourcebook*, 2nd edn. Thousand Oaks, CA: Sage.

Miller, G. (1997) 'Contextualizing Texts: Studying Organizational Text', in G. Miller and R. Dingwall (eds), *Context and Method in Qualitative Research.* London: Sage. pp. 77–91.

Mills, C. W. (1963) *Power, Politics, and People: The Collected Essays of C. Wright Mills, edited with an Introduction by Irving Louis Horowitz.* New York: Ballantine.

Mintzberg, H. (1973) *The Nature of Managerial Work.* New York: Wiley.

Mishler, E. G. (1986) *Research Interviewing. Context and Narrative.* Cambridge, MA: Harvard University Press.

Mitterer, J. (1999) 'Realismus oder Konstruktivismus? – Wahrheit oder Beliebigkeit?', *Zeitschrift für Erziehungswissenschaft*, 2: 485–498.

Modelmog, I. (1991) 'Empirische Sozialforschung als Phantasietätigkeit', *Ethik und Sozialwissenschaften*, 2: 521–532.

Moerman, M. (1974) 'Accomplishing Ethnicity', in R. Turner (ed.), *Ethnomethodology.* Harmondsworth: Penguin. pp. 34–68.

Moerman, M. (1988) *Talking Culture – Ethnography and Conversation Analysis.* Philadelphia: University of Pennsylvania Press.

Möhring, P. and Apsel, R. (eds) (1995) *Interkulturelle psychoanalytische Therapie.* Frankfurt a. M.: Brandes and Apsel.

Morgan, D. L. (1988) *Focus Groups as Qualitative Research* (Qualitative Research Methods Series). Newbury Park, CA: Sage.

Morgan, D. L. and Krueger, R. A. (1993) 'When to Use Focus Groups and Why?', in D. L. Morgan (ed.), *Successful Focus Groups.* Newbury Park, CA: Sage. pp. 3–20.

Morgan, G. (1986) *Images of Organization.* Thousand Oaks, CA: Sage.

Morgenthaler, F. (1978) *Technik. Zur Dialektik der psychoanalytischen Praxis.* Frankfurt a. M.: Syndikat.

Morley, D. (1980) *The Nationwide Audience. Structure and Decoding.* London: British Film Institute.

Morley, D. (1991) 'Where the Global Meets the Local. Aufzeichnungen aus dem Wohnzimmer', *Montage*, 6: 5–35.

Morley, D. (1992) *Television, Audiences and Cultural Studies.* London: Routledge.

Morley, D. (1996) 'Medienpublika aus der Sicht der Cultural Studies', in U. Hasenbrink and F. Krotz (eds), *Die Zuschauer als Fernsehregisseure – Zum Verständnis individueller Nutzungs- und Rezeptionsmuster.* Baden-Baden: Nomos. pp. 37–51.

Moro, M. R. (1994) *Parents en exil. Psychopathologie et migration.* Paris: Presses Universitaires de France.

Moro, M. R. (1998) *Psychiatrie transculturelle des enfants des migrants.* Paris: Dunod.

Morrill, C., Buller, D. B., Buller, M. K. and Larkey, L. L. (1999) 'Toward an Organizational Perspective on Identifying and Managing Formal Gatekeepers', *Qualitative Sociology*, 22: 51–72.

Morrison, K. (1981) 'Some properties of "telling-order designs" in didactive inquiry', *Philosophy of the Social Sciences*, 11: 245–262.

Morse, J. M. (1994) 'Designing Funded Qualitative Research', in N. K. Denzin and Y. S. Lincoln (eds), *Handbook of Qualitative Research.* Thousand Oaks, CA: Sage. pp. 220–235.

Moscovici, S. (1961) *La Psychanalyse, son image et son public.* Paris: Presses Universitaires de France (2nd edn. 1976).

Moscovici, S. (1984) 'The phenomenon of social representations', in R. M. Farr and S. Moscovici (eds), *Social Representations.* Cambridge: Cambridge University Press. pp. 3–69.

Moser, H. (1995) *Grundlagen der Praxisforschung.* Freiburg: Lambertus.

Mostyn, B. (1985) 'The Content Analysis of Qualitative Research Data: A Dynamic Approach', in M. Brenner, J. Brown and D. Cauter (eds), *The Research Interview.* London: Academic Press. pp. 115–145.

Muensterberger, W. (1970) *Man and His Culture; Psychoanalytic Anthropology after Totem and Taboo.* New York: Taplinger.

Mühlfeld, C., Windolf, P., Lampert, N. and Krüger, H. (1981) 'Auswertungsprobleme offener Interviews', *Soziale Welt*, 32: 325–352.

Muhr, T. (1997) *ATLAS.ti – Qualitative Data Analysis, Management, Model Building* (manual for software). London: Scolari Sage.

Mulkay, M. (1985) *The World and the Word*. London: George Allen and Unwin.

Müller, P. J. (ed.) (1977) *Die Analyse prozeß-produzierter Daten*. Stuttgart: Klett–Cotta.

Müller, W. (1978) 'Der Lebenslauf von Geburtskohorten', in M. Kohli (ed.), *Soziologie des Lebenslaufs*. Berlin: Luchterhand. pp. 54–77.

Müller-Böling, D. (1992) 'Organisationsforschung, Methodik der empirischen', in E. Frese (ed.), *Handwörterbuch der Organisation*. Stuttgart: Schäffer–Poeschel. pp. 1491–1505.

Musolf, G. R. (1998) *Structure and Agency in Everyday Life: An Introduction to Social Psychology*. Dix Hills, NY: General Hall.

Myers, M. D. and Avison, D. (2002) *Qualitative Research in Information Systems* (Introducing Qualitative Methods Series). London: Sage.

Nadig, M. (1986) *Die verborgene Kultur der Frau. Ethnopsychoanalytische Gespräche mit Bäuerinnen in Mexiko. Subjektivität und Gesellschaft im Alltag von Otomi-Frauen*. Frankfurt a. M.: Fischer.

Nadig, M. (1992) 'Der ethnologische Weg zur Erkenntnis. Das weibliche Subjekt in der feministischen Wissenschaft', in G. A. Knapp and A. Wetterer (eds), *Traditionen – Brüche. Entwicklungen feministischer Theorie*. Freiburg: Kore. pp. 151–200.

Nadig, M. and Erdheim, M. (1980) 'Die Zerstörung der wissenschaftlichen Erfahrung durch das akademische Milieu. Ethnopsychoanalytische Überlegungen zur Aggressivität in der Wissenschaft', *Berliner Hefte*, 15: 35–52.

Narr, W. D. and Stary, J. (eds) (1999) *Lust und Last des wissenschaftlichen Schreibens: Hochschullehrerinnen und Hochschullehrer geben Studierenden Tips*. Frankfurt a. M.: Suhrkamp.

Nathan, T. (1977) *Ideologie, Sexualität und Neurose: Eine Abhandlung zur ethnopsychoanalytischen Klinik*. Frankfurt a. M.: Suhrkamp.

Nathan, T. (1988) *Psychoanalyse paienne. Essays éthpsychoanalytiques*. Paris: Dunod.

Nathan, T. (1995) *L'Influence qui guérit*. Paris: Jacob.

Nathan, T. and Stengers, I. (1995) *Médecins et sorciers: manifeste pour une psychopathologie scientifique, le médecin et le charlatan*. Le Plessis-Robinson: Synthélabo.

Neuberger, O. (1985) *Arbeit*. Stuttgart: Enke.

Neuberger, O. (1988a) 'Führung (ist) symbolisiert'. Manuscript, Universität Augsburg.

Neuberger, O. (1988b) *Was ist denn da so komisch?* Weinheim: Psychologie Heute TB.

Neuberger, O. (1989a) 'Organisationstheorien', in E. Roth (ed.), *Organisationspsychologie. Enzyklopädie der Psychologie*, Volume 3. Göttingen: Hogrefe. pp. 205–250.

Neuberger, O. (1989b) 'Symbolisierung', *Organisationen. Augsburger Beiträge zur Organisationspsychologie und Personalwesen*, 4: 24–36.

Neuberger, O. (1995a) *Mikropolitik*. Stuttgart: Enke.

Neuberger, O. (1995b) 'Unternehmenskultur', in U. Flick, E. von Kardorff, H. Keupp, L. von Rosenstiel and S. Wolff (eds), *Handbuch Qualitative Sozialforschung*. Munich: Beltz/PVU. pp. 302–304.

Neuberger, O. and Kompa, A. (1987) *Wir, die Firma*. Weinheim: Beltz.

Nicholson, L. (1994) 'Interpreting Gender', *Signs. Journal for Women in Culture and Society*, 20: 79–103.

Nickel, B., Berger, M., Schmidt, P. and Plies, K. (1995) 'Qualitative Sampling in a Multi-Method Survey. Practical Problems of Method Triangulation in Sexual Behaviour Research', *Quality and Quantity*, 29: 223–240.

Nickl, M. (1998) 'Web Sites – die Entstehung neuer Textstrukturen', in S. Bollmann and C. Heibach (eds), *Kursbuch Internet, Anschlüsse an Wirtschaft und Politik, Wissenschaft und Kultur*. Reinbek: Rowohlt. pp. 388–400.

Nießen, M. (1977) *Gruppendiskussion – Interpretative Methodologie – Methodenbegründung – Anwendung*. Munich: Fink.

Nightingale, V. (1996) *Studying Audiences. The Shock of the Real*. London: Routledge.

Ninck Gbeassor, D. (1999) *Überlebenskunst in Überlebenswelten*. Ethnopsychologische Betreuung von Asylsuchenden. Berlin: Reimer.

Nisbet, R. A. (1976) *Sociology as an Art Form*. London: Heinemann.

Nora, P. (1996) 'Generation', in P. Nora (ed.), *Realms of Memory – The Construction of the French Past. Volume 1: Conflicts and Divisions*. New York: Columbia University Press. pp. 499–531.

Nowotny, H. (1999) *Es ist so. Es könnte auch anders sein*. Frankfurt a. M.: Suhrkamp.

Obeyesekere, G. (1990) *The Work of Culture: Transformation in Psychoanalysis and Anthropology*. Chicago: Chicago University Press.

Ochs, E. (1979) 'Transcription as Theory', in E. Ochs and B. B. Schieffelin (eds), *Developmental Pragmatics*. New York: Academic Press. pp. 43–72.

Ochs, E., Schegloff, E. A. and Thompson, S. A. (eds) (1997) *Interaction and Grammar*. Cambridge: Cambridge University Press.

O'Connell, D. C. and Kowal, S. (1994) 'The Transcriber as Language User', in G. Bartelt (ed.), *The Dynamics of Language Processes: Essays in Honor of Hans W. Dechert*. Tübingen: Gunter Narr. pp. 119–142.

O'Connell, D. C. and Kowal, S. (1995a) 'Basic Principles of Transcription', in J. A. Smith, R. Harré and L. Van Langenhove (eds), *Rethinking Methods in Psychology*. London: Sage. pp. 93–105.

O'Connell, D. C. and Kowal, S. (1995b) 'Transcription Systems for Spoken Discourse', in J. Verschueren, J.-O. Oestman and J. Blommaert (eds), *Handbook of Pragmatics*. Amsterdam: John Benjamins. pp. 646–656.

Oevermann, U. (1984) 'Il n'y a pas de probléme de déscription dans les sciences sociales'. Manuscript, Frankfurt a. M.

Oevermann, U. (1987) *Über Abduktion.* Tonbandmitschnitt seines Vortrages auf der Semiotik-Tagung, Essen.

Oevermann, U. (1993) 'Die objektive Hermeneutik als unverzichtbare methodologische Grundlage für die Analyse von Subjektivität. Zugleich eine Kritik der Tiefenhermeneutik', in T. Jung and S. Müller-Doohm (eds), *Wirklichkeit im Deutungsprozeß. Verstehen in den Kultur- und Sozialwissenschaften.* Frankfurt a. M.: Suhrkamp. pp. 106–189.

Oevermann, U. (1996) 'Konzeptualisierung von Anwendungsmöglichkeiten und praktischen Arbeitsfeldern der objektiven Hermeneutik. Manifest der objektiv hermeneutischen Sozialforschung'. Manuscript, Frankfurt a. M.

Oevermann, U. (1997) 'Literarische Verdichtung als soziologische Erkenntnisquelle: Szenische Realisierung der Strukturlogik professionalisierten ärztlichen Handelns in A. Schnitzlers Professor Bernhardi', in M. Wicke (ed.), *Konfigurationen lebensweltlicher Strukturphänomene.* Opladen: Westdeutscher Verlag. pp. 276–335.

Oevermann, U. (1999a) 'Zur Klärung der Begriffe Regel, Norm und Normalität in der Analyse von Bewußtseinsformationen'. Manuscript, Frankfurt a. M.

Oevermann, U. (1999b) 'Strukturale Soziologie und Rekonstruktionsmethodologie', in W. Glatzer (ed.), *Ansichten der Gesellschaft.* Opladen: Leske and Budrich. pp. 72–85.

Oevermann, U., Allert, T. and Konau, E. (1980) 'Zur Logik der Interpretation von Interviewtexten. Fallanalyse anhand eines Interviews mit einer Fernstudentin', in T. Heinze, H.-W. Klusemann and H.-G. Soeffner (eds), *Interpretationen einer Bildungsgeschichte.* Bensheim: päd.-extra-Buchverlag. pp. 15–69.

Oevermann, U., Allert, T., Konau, E. and Krambeck, J. (1979) 'Die Methodologie einer "objektiven Hermeneutik" und ihre allgemeine forschungslogische Bedeutung in den Sozialwissenschaften', in H.-G. Soeffner (ed.), *Interpretative Verfahren in den Sozial- und Textwissenschaften.* Stuttgart: Metzler. pp. 352–433.

Ong, W. J. (1982) *Orality and Literacy. The Technologizing of the Word.* London: Methuen.

Opp, K.-D. (1984) 'Wissenschaftstheoretische Grundlagen der empirischen Sozialforschung', in E. Roth and K. Heidenreich (eds), *Sozialwissenschaftliche Methoden – Lehr- und Handbuch für Forschung und Praxis.* Munich: Oldenbourg. pp. 47–71.

Ortner, S. B. (1972) 'On Key Symbols', *American Anthropologist,* 27: 1338–1346.

Ortner, S. B. (1984) 'Theory in Anthropology since the Sixties', *Comparative Studies of Society and History,* 26: 126–166.

Ortner, S. B. (1997) 'Introduction', *Representations,* 59: 1–13.

Oser, F. and Althoff, W. (1992) *Moralische Selbstbestimmung. Modelle der Entwicklung und Erziehung im Wertebereich.* Stuttgart: Klett–Cotta.

Ostrow, J. M. (1990) 'The Availability of Difference: Clifford Geertz on Problems of Ethnographic Research and Interpretation', *Qualitative Studies in Education,* 3: 61–69.

Oswald, H. (1984) 'In Memoriam Erving Goffman', *Kölner Zeitschrift für Soziologie und Sozialpsychologie,* 36: 210–213.

Ottomeyer, K. (1997) *Kriegstrauma, Identität und Vorurteil.* Klagenfurt: Drava.

Parin, P. (1965) 'Orale Eigenschaften des Ich bei Westafrikanern', *Schweizerische Zeitschrift für Psychologie und ihre Anwendungen,* 24: 342–347.

Parin, P. (1976) 'Das Mikroskop der vergleichenden Psychoanalyse und die Makrosozietät', *Psyche,* 30: 1–25.

Parin, P. (1977) 'Das Ich und die Anpassungs-Mechanismen', *Psyche,* 31: 481–515.

Parin, P. (1980) *Fear the Neighbour as Thyself: Psychoanalysis and Society among the Anyi of West Africa.* Chicago: University of Chicago Press.

Parin, P. (1989) 'Zur Kritik der Gesellschaftskritik im Deutungsprozeß', *Psyche,* 43: 98–119.

Parin, P. (1992) *Der Widerspruch im Subjekt. Ethnopsychoanalytische Studien.* Hamburg: Europäische Verlagsanstalt.

Parin, P., Morgenthaler, F. and Parin-Matthèy, G. (1971) *Fürchte deinen Nächsten wie dich selbst. Psychoanalyse und Gesellschaft am Modell der Agni in Westafrika.* Frankfurt a. M.: Suhrkamp.

Parin, P., Morgenthaler, F. and Parin-Matthèy, G. (1993) *Die Weißen denken zuviel. Psychoanalytische Untersuchungen bei den Dogon in Westafrika. Mit einem neuen Vorwort von Paul Parin und Goldy Parin-Matthèy,* 4th edn. Hamburg: Europäische Verlagsanstalt.

Parin, P. and Parin-Matthèy, G. (1988) *Subjekt im Widerspruch.* Frankfurt a. M.: Athenäum Verlag.

Parin, P. and Parin-Matthèy, G. (1992) 'Das Ich und die Anpassungsmechanismen', in P. Parin (ed.), *Der Widerspruch im Subjekt. Ethnopsychoanalytische Studien.* Hamburg: Europäische Verlagsanstalt.

Park, R. (1939) *An Outline of the Principles of Sociology.* New York: Free Press.

Park, R. E. (1950) 'Human Migration and the Marginal Man', in R. E. Park (ed.), *Race and Culture. Collected Papers, Volume 1.* Glencoe, IL: Free Press. pp. 345–356.

Parker, I. (1992) *Discourse Dynamics: Critical Analysis for Social and Individual Psychology.* London: Routledge.

Parker, I. (1994) 'Discourse analysis', in P. Banister, E. Burman, I. Parker, M. Taylor and C. Tindall, *Qualitative Methods in Psychology: A Research Guide.* Buckingham: Open University Press. pp. 92–107.

Parker, I. (1997) 'Discursive Psychology', in D. Fox and I. Prilleltensky (eds), *Critical Psychology: An Introduction.* London: Sage. pp. 284–298.

Parker, I. (1999) 'Critical Psychology: Critical Links', *Annual Review of Critical Psychology*, 1: 5–20.

Parker, I. and Burman, E. (1993) 'Against Discursive Imperialism, Empiricism and Constructionism: Thirty-two Problems with Discourse Analysis', in E. Burman and I. Parker (eds), *Discourse Analytic Research: Repertoires and Readings of Texts in Action*. London: Routledge. pp. 155–172.

Parker, I. and the Bolton Discourse Network (1999) *Critical Textwork: Varieties of Discourse and Analysis*. Buckingham: Open University Press.

Parker, K. A. (1998) *The Continuity of Peirce's Thought*. New York: Vanderbilt University Press.

Parsons, T. (1937) *The Structure of Social Action*. New York: Free Press.

Parsons, T. and Shils, E. A. (1951) *Towards a General Theory of Action*. Harward, MA: Harward University Press.

Pasero, U. (1995) 'Dethematisierung von Geschlecht', in U. Pasero and F. Braun (eds), *Konstruktion von Geschlecht*. Pfaffenweiler: Centaurus. pp. 50–66.

Patton, M. (1998) 'Discovering Process Use', *Evaluation*, 4 (2): 225–233.

Patton, M. Q. (1990) *Qualitative Evaluation and Research Methods*, 2nd edn. Newbury Park, CA: Sage.

Patton, M. Q. (1997) *Utilization-Focused Evaluation. The New Century Text*, 3rd edn. Thousand Oaks, CA: Sage.

Patzelt, W. J. (1987) *Grundlagen der Ethnomethodologie: Theorie, Empirie und politikwissenschaftlicher Nutzen einer Soziologie des Alltags*. Munich: Fink.

Pawlowsky, P. and Bäumer, J. (1993) 'Funktionen und Wirkungen beruflicher Weiterbildung', in B. Strümpel and M. Dierkes (eds), *Beharrung und Wandel in der Arbeitspolitik*. Stuttgart: Poeschel. pp. 69–120.

Peckhaus, V. (1999) 'Abduktion und Heuristik', in J. Nida-Rümelin (ed.), *Rationality, Realism, Revision. Vorträge des 3. internationalen Kongresses der Gesellschaft für Analytische Philosophie vom 15. bis zum 18 September 1997*. Berlin: de Gruyter.

Pedrina, F. (1999) *Kultur, Migration und Psychoanalyse: therapeutische Konsequenzen theoretischer Konzepte*. Tübingen: Diskord.

Peirce, C. S. (1929) 'Guessing', *Hound and Horn*, 2: 267–282.

Peirce, C. S. (1931–35) *The Collected Papers of C. S. Peirce*, 8 vols. Cambridge, MA: Harvard University Press.

Peirce, C. S. (1960a) *Collected Papers Volume V: Pragmatism and Pragmaticism*. Cambridge, MA: Harvard University Press.

Peirce, C. S. (1960b) *Collected Papers Volume VII: Science and Philosophy*. Cambridge, MA: Harvard University Press.

Peirce, C. S. (1973) *Lectures on Pragmatism – Vorlesungen über Pragmatismus. Herausgegeben mit Einleitung und Anmerkungen von Elisabeth Walther*. Hamburg: Felix Meiner Verlag.

Peirce, C. S. (1976) *The New Elements of Mathematics*, 4 vols. Mouton: The Hague.

Peirce, C. S. (1986) *Semiotische Schriften, Volume 1: Herausgegeben und übersetzt von Christian Kloesel und Helmut Pape*. Frankfurt a. M.: Suhrkamp.

Peirce, C. S. (1992) *Reasoning and the Logic of Things* (ed. K. L. Ketner). Cambridge, MA: Harvard University Press.

Peltzer, K. (1995) *Psychology and Health in African Cultures. Examples of Ethnopsychotherapeutic Practice*. Frankfurt a. M.: IKO-Verlag für Interkulturelle Kommunikation.

Peräkylä, A. (1995) *AIDS Counselling: Institutional Interaction and Clinical Practice*. Cambridge: Cambridge University Press.

Peräkylä, A. (1997) 'Reliability and Validity in Research Based on Tapes and Transcripts', in D. Silverman (ed.), *Qualitative Research*. London: Sage. pp. 199–220.

Permien, H. and Zink, G. (1998) *Endstation Straße? Straßenkarrieren aus der Sicht von Jugendlichen*. Munich: Deutsches Jugendinstitut.

Peters, T. J. and Waterman, R. H. (1982) *In Search of Excellence: Lessons from America's Best-Run Companies*. New York: Harper and Row.

Petersen, J. (1926) *Die Wesensbestimmung der deutschen Romantik. Einführung in die moderne Literaturwissenschaft*. Leipzig: Quelle and Meyer.

Peukert, H. (1984) 'Über die Zukunft der Bildung', *Frankfurter Hefte, FH-extra*, 6: 129–137.

Phillips, N. and Hardy, C. (2002) *Discourse Analysis – Investigating Processes of Social Construction* (Qualitative Research Methods Series). Thousand Oaks, CA: Sage.

Piaget, J. (1937) *La Construction du réel chez l'enfant*. Neuchâtel: Delachaux and Niestlé.

Platt, J. (1981) 'Evidence and Proof in Documentary Research'. *Sociological Review*, 29: 31–66.

Platt, J. (1992) 'Cases of Cases ... of Cases', in C. C. Ragin and H. S. Becker (eds), *What is a Case – Exploring the Foundations of Social Inquiry*. Cambridge: Cambridge University Press. pp. 21–52.

Plessner, H. (1970) *Philosophische Anthropologie*. Frankfurt a. M.: Suhrkamp.

Plessner, H. (1974) 'Husserl in Göttingen', in H. Plessner (ed.), *Diesseits der Utopie*. Frankfurt a M.: Suhrkamp. pp. 143–159.

Plessner, H. (1982) 'Lachen und Weinen', in H. Plessner (ed.), *Gesammelte Schriften VII*. Frankfurt a. M.: Suhrkamp. pp. 201–387.

Plessner, H. (1983) 'Mit anderen Augen', in H. Plessner (ed.), *Gesammelte Schriften VIII*. Frankfurt a. M.: Suhrkamp. pp. 88–104.

Plessner, H. (1985) 'Soziale Rolle und menschliche Natur', in H. Plessner (ed.), *Gesammelte Schriften X*. Frankfurt a. M.: Suhrkamp. pp. 227–240.

Pollner, M. (1987) *Mundane Reasoning – Reality in Everyday and Sociological Discourse*. Cambridge: Cambridge University Press.

Pollner, M. (1991) 'Left of Ethnomethodology: The Rise and Decline of Radical Reflexivity', *American Sociological Review*, 56: 370–380.

Pollock, F. (ed.) (1955) *Gruppenexperiment – Ein Studienbericht. Frankfurter Beiträge zur Soziologie*, Volume 2. Frankfurt a. M.: Europäische Verlagsanstalt.

Pomerantz, A. (1984) 'Agreeing and Disagreeing with Assessments: Some Features of Preferred/ Dispreferred Turn Shapes', in J. M. Atkinson and J. C. Heritage (eds), *Structures of Social Action*. Cambridge: Cambridge University Press. pp. 57–101.

Pomerantz, A. (ed.) (1993) Special Issue on 'New Directions in Conversation Analysis', *Text*, 13 (2).

Popitz, H. (1972) *Der Begriff der sozialen Rolle als Element der soziologischen Theorie*. Tübingen: Mohr (Siebeck).

Popper, K. (1934) *The Logic of Scientific Discovery*. London: Routledge.

Potter, J. (1996) *Representing Reality – Discourse, Rhetoric and Social Construction*. London: Sage.

Potter, J. and Wetherell, M. (1987) *Discourse and Social Psychology: Beyond Attitudes and Behaviour*. London: Sage.

Potter, J. and Wetherell, M. (1998) 'Social Representation, Discourse Analysis and Racism', in U. Flick (ed.), *Psychology of the Social. Representations in Knowledge and Language*. Cambridge: Cambridge University Press. pp. 138–155.

Prein, G., Kelle, U. and Kluge, S. (1993) *Strategien zur Integration quantitativer und qualitativer Auswertungsverfahren*. Universität Bremen, Sfb 186. Arbeitspapier Nr 19.

Prior, L. (2003) *Using Documents in Social Research* (Introducing Qualitative Methods Series). London: Sage.

Projektgruppe 'Soziale Beziehungen in der Familie, geschlechtsspezifische Sozialisation und die Herausbildung rechtsextremer Orientierungen' (1996) *Dokumentation und Erläuterung des methodischen Vorgehens*. Hildesheim: Institut für Sozialwissenschaften der Universität Hildesheim.

Psathas, G. (ed.) (1973) *Phenomenological Sociology*. New York: Wiley.

Psathas, G. (ed.) (1979) *Everyday Language: Studies in Ethnomethodology*. New York: Irvington.

Psathas, G. (1989) *Phenomenology and Sociology*. Lanham, MD: University Press of America.

Psathas, G. (ed.) (1995) 'Ethnomethodology: Discussions and Contributions', *Human Studies, Special Issue*, 18: 2–3.

Psathas, G. and Anderson, T. (1990) 'The "practices" of transcription in conversation analysis', *Semiotica*, 78: 75–99.

Ragin, C. C. (1992) 'Introduction: Cases of What is a Case', in Ragin, C. C. and Becker, H. S. (eds), *What is a Case? Exploring the Foundations of Social Inquiry*. Cambridge: Cambridge University Press. pp. 1–18.

Ragin, C. C. (1994) *Constructing Social Research*. Thousand Oaks, CA: Pine Forge Press.

Ragin, C. C. and Becker, H. S. (eds) (1992) *What Is a Case? Exploring the Foundations of Social Inquiry*. Cambridge: Cambridge University Press.

Reck, U. (1991) 'Imitation und Mimesis – Eine Dokumentation', *Kunstforum*, 114: 69–85.

Redder, A. and Ehlich, K. (eds) (1994) *Gesprochene Sprache – Transkripte und Tondokumente*. Tübingen: Niemeyer.

Redfield, R. (1948) 'The Art of Social Science', *American Journal of Sociology*, 54: 181–190.

Refisch, H. (1997) *Freundschaft und Führung oder Haben Die Freunde, Chef?* Munich: Unveröffentlichte Dissertation, LMU.

Reiche, R. (1995) 'Von innen nach außen? Sackgassen im Diskurs über Psychoanalyse und Gesellschaft', *Psyche*, 49: 227–258.

Reichenbach, H. (1938) *Experience and Prediction*. Chicago: University of Chicago Press.

Reichertz, J. (1986) *Probleme qualitativer Sozialforschung*. Frankfurt a. M.: Campus.

Reichertz, J. (1988) 'Der Hermeneutiker als Autor – Das Problem der Darstellbarkeit hermeneutischer Fallrekonstruktionen', *Grounded*, pp. 29–49.

Reichertz, J. (1989) 'Hermeneutische Auslegung von Feldprotokollen? – Verdrießliches über ein beliebtes Forschungsmittel', in R. Aster, H. Merkens and M. Repp (eds), *Teilnehmende Beobachtung. Werkstattberichte und methodologische Reflexionen*. Frankfurt a. M.: Campus. pp. 84–102.

Reichertz, J. (1991a) *Aufklärungsarbeit – Kriminalpolizisten und Feldforscher bei der Arbeit*. Stuttgart: Enke.

Reichertz, J. (1991b) 'Folgern Sherlock Holmes oder Mr. Dupin abduktiv?', *Kodikas/Code*, 4: 345–367.

Reichertz, J. (1992) 'Beschreiben oder Zeigen – Über das Verfassen Ethnographischer Berichte', *Soziale Welt*, 43: 331–350.

Reichertz, J. (1997) 'Plädoyer für das Ende einer Methodologiedebatte bis zur letzten Konsequenz', in T. Sutter (ed.), *Beobachtung verstehen – Verstehen beobachten*. Opladen: Westdeutscher Verlag. pp. 98–133.

Reichmayr, J. (1995) *Einführung in die Ethnopsychoanalyse. Geschichte Theorien und Methoden*. Frankfurt a. M.: Fischer.

Reichmayr, J. (ed.) (2000) 'Biobibliographisches Lexikon der Ethnopsychoanalyse' (http://www.uni-klu.ac.at/lex epsa).

Ribbens, J. and Edwards, R. (eds) (1998) *Feminist Dilemmas in Qualitative Research. Public Knowledge and Private Lives*. London: Sage.

Richards, L. and Richards, T. (1991) 'The Transformation of Qualitative Method: Computational Paradigms and Research Processes', in R. M. Lee and N. G. Fielding (eds), *Using Computers in Qualitative Research*. London: Sage. pp. 38–53.

Richards, T. and Richards, L. (1994) 'Using Computers in Qualitative Research', in N. K. Denzin and Y. S. Lincoln (eds), *Handbook of Qualitative Research*. Thousand Oaks, CA: Sage. pp. 445–460.

Richardson, L. (1994) 'Writing. A Method of Inquiry', in N. K. Denzin and Y. S. Lincoln (eds), *Handbook of Qualitative Research*. Thousand Oaks, CA: Sage. pp. 516–529.

Richardson, S. A., Snell Dohrendwend, B. and Klein, D. (1979) *Interviewing: Its Forms and Functions*. New York: Basic Books

Richter, H. (1988) 'Transkription', in U. Ammon, N. Dittmar and K. J. Mattheier (eds), *Sociolinguistics/ Soziolinguistik – An International Handbook of the Science of Language and Society/Ein internationales Handbuch zur Wissenschaft von Sprache und Gesellschaft*. Berlin: de Gruyter. pp. 966–972.

Ricoeur, P. (1981a) 'Mimesis and Representation', *Annals of Scholarship*, 2: 15–32.

Ricoeur, P. (1981b) 'The Narrative Function', in P. Ricoeur (ed.), *Hermeneutics and the Human Sciences*. Cambridge: Cambridge University Press. pp. 274–295.

Ricoeur, P. (1984) *Time and Narrative*, Volume 1. Chicago: University of Chicago Press.

Riedel, M. (1969) *Wandel des Generationenproblems in der modernen Gesellschaft*. Düsseldorf: Diederichs.

Rieger, J. (1996) 'Photographing Social Change', *Visual Sociology*, 11: 5–49.

Rieker, P. (1997) *Ethnozentrismus bei jungen Männern*. Weinheim: Juventa.

Riemann, G. (1987) *Das Fremdwerden der eigenen Biographie. Narrative Interviews mit psychiatrischen Patienten*. Munich: Fink.

Riis, J. A. (1971) *How the Other Half Lives*. New York: Dover (first published 1890).

Ritsert, J. (1964) 'Zur Gestalt der Ideologie in der Populärliteratur über den Zweiten Weltkrieg', *Soziale Welt*, 15: 244.

Ritsert, J. (1972) *Inhaltsanalyse und Ideologiekritik. Ein Versuch über kritische Sozialforschung*. Frankfurt a. M.: Athenäum.

Roberts, B. (1975) 'Naturalistic Research into Sub-cultures and Deviance: An account of a sociological tendency', in T. Jefferson (ed.), *Resistance through Rituals*. Birmingham: CCCS. pp. 243–252.

Roberts, B. (2002) *Biographical Research* (Understanding Social Research Series). Buckingham: Open University Press.

Robillard, A. B. (1999) *Meaning of a disability: The Lived Experience of Paralysis*. Philadelphia: Temple University Press.

Rodriguez-Rabanal, C. (1990) *Überleben im Slum: psychosoziale Probleme peruanischer Elendsviertel*. Frankfurt a. M.: Suhrkamp.

Roethlisberger, F. J. and Dickson, W. J. (1939) *Management and the Worker*. Cambridge, MA: Harvard University Press.

Rogers, M. F. (1992) 'They All Were Passing: Agnes, Garfinkel, and Company', *Gender and Society*, 6: 169–191.

Roller, E., Mathes, R. and Eckert, T. (1995) 'Hermeneutic-Classificatory Content Analysis', in U. Kelle (ed.), *Computer-Aided Qualitative Data Analysis*. London: Sage. pp. 167–176.

Rorty, R. (1979) *Philosophy and the Mirror of Nature*. Princeton, NJ: Princeton University Press.

Rose, N. (1985) *The Psychological Complex: Psychology, Politics and Society in England, 1869–1939*. London: Routledge and Kegan Paul.

Roseberry, W. (1982) 'Balinese Cockfights and the Seduction of Anthropology', *Social Research*, 49: 1013–1028.

Rosen, M. (1988) 'You Asked for It, Christmas at the Bosses' Expense', *Journal of Management Studies*, 25: 463–480.

Rosenstiel, L. von (2000) *Grundlagen der Organisationspsychologie: Basiswissen und Anwendungshinweise*, 4th edn. Stuttgart: Poeschel.

Rosenstiel, L. von, Einsiedler, H. E., Streich, R. and Rau, S. (1987) *Motivation durch Mitwirkung*. Stuttgart: Schäffer.

Rosenstiel, L. von, Nerdinger, F. and Spieß, E. (1991) *Was morgen alles anders läuft*. Düsseldorf: Econ.

Rosenthal, G. (1993) Reconstruction of Life Stories. Principles of Selection in Generating Stories for Narrative Biographical Interviews (*The Narrative Study of Lives*). London: Sage. 1 (1): 59–91.

Rosenthal, G. (1995) *Erlebte und erzählte Lebensgeschichte*. Frankfurt a. M.: Campus.

Rosenthal, G. (ed.) (1998) *The Holocaust in Three-Generations. Families of Victims and Perpetrators of the Nazi-Regime*. London: Cassell.

Rosenthal, G. (2004) 'Biographical Research', in C. Seale, G. Gobo, J. F. Gubrium and D. Silverman (eds), *Qualitative Research Practice*. London: Sage. pp. 48–64.

Rosler, M. (1989) 'In, Around and Afterthoughts (On Documentary Photography)', in R. Bolton (ed.), *The Contest of Meaning: Critical Histories of Photography*. Cambridge, MA: MIT Press.

Rossi, P. H. and Freeman, H. E. (1993) *Evaluation. A Systematic Approach*. Beverly Hills, CA: Sage.

Roth, C. (1998) 'Kulturschock, Macht und Erkenntnis. Zur Auseinandersetzung mit Grenzen in der ethnologischen Forschungssituation', in S. Schröter (ed.), *Körper und Identitäten. Ethnologische Ansätze zur Konstruktion von Geschlecht*. Hamburg: Lit. pp. 169–185.

Roth, J. (1962) 'Comments on "Secret Observation"', *Social Problems*, 9: 278–280.

Rückriem, G. and Stary, J. (1997) 'Wissenschaftlich arbeiten – Subjektive Ratschläge für ein objektives Problem', in B. Friebertshäuser and A. Prengel (eds), *Handbuch qualitative Methoden in der Erziehungswissenschaft*. Weinheim: Juventa. pp. 831–847.

Rühl, M. (1976) 'Vom Gegenstand der Inhaltsanalyse', *Rundfunk und Fernsehen*, 24: 367–378.

Rust, H. (1980) 'Qualitative Inhaltsanalyse – begriffslose Willkür oder wissenschaftliche Methode? Ein theoretischer Entwurf', *Publizistik*, 25: 5–23.

Ryan, G. W. and Bernard, H. R. (2000) 'Data Management and Analysis Methods', in N. K. Denzin and Y. S. Lincoln (eds), *Handbook of Qualitative Research*, 2nd edn. Thousand Oaks, CA: Sage. pp. 769–802.

Ryave, A. L. and Schenkein, J. N. (1974) 'Notes on the Art of Walking', in R. Turner (ed.), *Ethnomethodology*. Harmondsworth: Penguin. pp. 265–274.

Ryder, N. B. (1965) 'The Cohort as a Concept in the Study of Social Change', *American Sociological Review*, 30: 843–861.

Ryen, A. (2004) 'Ethical issues', in C. Seale, G. Gobo, J. F. Gubrium and D. Silverman (eds), *Qualitative Research Practice*. London: Sage. pp. 230–247.

Ryle, G. (1971) *Essays, 1929–1968*, (Volume 2 of Collected Papers). London: Hutchinson.

Sackmann, R. (1998) *Konkurrierende Generationen auf dem Arbeitsmarkt – Altersstrukturierung in Arbeitsmarkt und Sozialpolitik*. Opladen: Westdeutscher Verlag.

Sacks, H. (1963) 'Sociological Description', *Berkeley Journal of Sociology*, 1: 1–16.

Sacks, H. (1967) 'The Search for Help. No One to Turn to', in E. Schneidmann (ed.), *Essays in Self Destruction*. New York: Science House. pp. 203–223.

Sacks, H. (1972) 'On the Analyzability of Stories by Children', in J. J. Gumperz and D. Hymes (eds), *Directions in Sociolinguistics: The Ethnography of Communication*. New York: Holt, Rinehart and Winston. pp. 325–345.

Sacks, H. (1984) 'Notes on Methodology', in J. M. Atkinson and J. C. Heritage (eds), *Structures of Social Action*. Cambridge: Cambridge University Press. pp. 21–27.

Sacks, H. (1992) *Lectures on Conversation, Volumes I and II* (edited by G. Jefferson with introductions by E. A. Schegloff). Oxford: Blackwell.

Sacks, H., Schegloff, E. A. and Jefferson, G. (1974) 'A Simplest Systematics for the Organization of Turn-taking for Conversation', *Language*, 50: 696–735 (reprint 1978).

Saffir, W. B., Stebbins, R. A. and Turowetz, A. (eds) (1980) *Fieldwork Experience – Qualitative Approaches to Social Research*. New York: St Martin's Press.

Safranski, R. (1997) *Ein Meister aus Deutschland. Heidegger und seine Zeit*. Frankfurt a. M.: Fischer.

Saller, V. (1993) 'Von der Ethnopsychoanalyse zur interkulturellen Therapie', *Lucifer – Amor. Zeitschrift zur Geschichte der Psychoanalyse*, 12: 99–123.

Sanders, J. R. (ed.) (1999) *Handbuch der Evaluationsstandards*. Joint Committee on Standards for Educational Evaluation. Opladen: Leske and Budrich.

Sartre, J.-P. (1981) *The Family Idiot: Gustave Flaubert, 1821–1857*. Chicago: University of Chicago Press.

Sartre, J.-P. (1983) *Between Existentialism and Marxism/ Jean-Paul Sartre* (translated from the French by John Matthews). London: Verso.

Saussure, F. de (1974) *Course in General Linguistics*. London: Fontana.

Schafer, R. (1981) *A New Language for Psychoanalysis*. London: Yale University Press.

Schatzman, L. and Strauss, A. L. (1973) *Field Research: Strategies for a Natural Sociology*. Englewood Cliffs, NJ: Prentice Hall.

Scheele, B. and Groeben, N. (1988) *Dialog-Konsens-Methoden zur Rekonstruktion Subjektiver Theorien*. Tübingen: Francke.

Scheff, T. J. (1966) *Being Mentally Ill. A Sociological Theory*. Chicago: Aldine.

Scheff, T. J. (1994) *Bloody Revenge. Emotions, Nationalism and War*. Boulder, CO: Westview.

Schegloff, E. A. (1968) 'Sequencing in Conversational Openings', *American Anthropologist*, 70: 1075–1095.

Schegloff, E. A. (1988) 'Description in the Social Sciences I: Talk-in-interaction', *IPrA Papers in Pragmatics*, 2: 1–24.

Schegloff, E. A. (1997) '"Narrative Analysis" Thirty Years Later', *Journal of Narrative and Life History*, 7: 97–106.

Schegloff, E. A. and Sacks, H. (1973) 'Opening Up Closings', *Semiotica*, 7: 289–327.

Schein, E. H. (1984) 'Coming to a New Awareness of Organizational Culture', *Sloan Management Review*, 3–16.

Schein, E. H. (1985) *Organizational Culture and Leadership*. San Francisco: Jossey–Bass.

Schein, E. H. (1990) 'Organizational Culture', *American Psychologist*, 45: 109–119.

Scheler, M. (1923/1974) *Centennial Essays*. The Hague: Nijhoff.

Schelsky, H. (1981) 'Die Generationen der Bundesrepublik', in W. Scheel (ed.), *Die andere deutsche Frage*. Stuttgart: Klett–Cotta. pp. 178–198.

Schenkein, J. (ed.) (1978) *Studies in the Organization of Conversational Interaction*. New York: Academic Press.

Scheuch, E. K. (1973) 'Das Interview in der Sozialforschung', in R. König (ed.), *Handbuch der empirischen Sozialforschung*, Volume 2. Stuttgart: Enke. pp. 66–190.

Schiebinger, L. (1993) *Nature's Body: Gender in the Making of Modern Science*. Boston: Beacon Press.

Schmid Noerr, G. (1987) 'Der Wanderer über dem Abgrund. Eine Interpretation des Liedes "Gute Nacht" aus dem Zyklus "Winterreise" von Franz Schubert und Wilhelm Müller. Zum Verstehen von Musik und Sprache', in J. Belgrad, B. Görlich, H. D. König and G. Schmid Noerr (eds), *Zur Idee einer psychoanalytischen Sozialforschung. Dimensionen szenischen Verstehens*. Frankfurt a. M.: Fischer. pp. 367–397.

Schmid Noerr, G. and Eggert, A. (1986) 'Die Herausforderung der Corrida. Vom latenten Sinn eines profanen Rituals', in H. D. König, A. Lorenzer, H. Lüdde, S. Naghol, U. Prokop, G. Schmid-Noerr and A. Eggert (eds), *Kultur-Analysen. Psychoanalytische Studien zur Kultur*. Frankfurt a. M.: Fischer. pp. 99–162.

Schmidt, C. (1997) '"Am Material": Auswertungstechniken für Leitfadeninterviews', in B. Friebertshäuser and A. Prengel (eds), *Handbuch qualitative Forschungmethoden in der Erziehungswissenschaft*. Weinheim: Juventa. pp. 544–568.

Schmidt, S. J. (1998) *Die Zähmung des Blicks. Konstruktivismus – Empirie – Wissenschaft*. Frankfurt a. M.: Suhrkamp.

Schmitt, R. (1992) *Die Schwellensteher. Sprachliche Präsenz und sozialer Austausch in einem Kiosk*. Tübingen: Narr.

Schmitz, E., Bude, H. and Otto, C. (1989) 'Beratung als Praxisform "angewandter Aufklärung"', in U. Beck and W. Bonß (eds), *Weder Sozialtechnologie noch Aufklärung?* Frankfurt a. M.: Suhrkamp. pp. 122–148.

Schmitz, U. (1997) 'Schriftliche Texte in multimedialen Kontexten', in R. Weingarten (ed.), *Sprachwandel durch Computer*. Opladen: Westdeutscher Verlag. pp. 131–158.

Schneider, G. (1987) *Interaktion auf der Intensivstation. Zum Umgang des Pflegepersonals mit hilflosen Patienten*. Berlin: Papyrus.

Schneider, W. L. (1994) *Die Beobachtung von Kommunikation: Zur kommunikativen Konstruktion sozialen Handelns*. Opladen: Westdeutscher Verlag.

Schnell, R., Hill, P. B. and Esser, E. (1999) *Methoden der empirischen Sozialforschung*. Munich: Oldenbourg.

Scholl, W., Pelz, J. and Rade, J. (1996) *Computervermittelte Kommunikation in der Wissenschaft*. Münster: Waxmann.

Schönhammer, R. (1985) 'Stichwort "Manipulation" – Zur Exploration und Analyse eines heiklen Aspektes alltäglicher ("impliziter") Führungsphilosophie', *Zeitschrift für Arbeits- und Organisationspsychologie*, 1: 2–14.

Schreyögg, G. (1992) 'Organisationskultur', in E. Frese (ed.), *Handwörterbuch der Organisation*. Stuttgart: Pöschel. pp. 1525–1537.

Schröder, K. C. (1994) 'Audience Semiotics, Interpretive Communities and the "Ethnographic Turn" in Media Research', *Media, Culture and Society*, 16: 333–347.

Schröer, N. (ed.) (1994) *Interpretative Sozialforschung. Auf dem Weg zu einer hermeneutischen Wissenssoziologie*. Opladen: Westdeutscher Verlag.

Schröer, N. (1997) 'Wissenssoziologische Hermeneutik', in R. Hitzler and A. Honer (eds), *Sozialwissenschaftliche Hermeneutik*. Opladen: Westdeutscher Verlag. pp. 109–132.

Schründer-Lenzen, A. (1997) 'Triangulation und idealtypisches Verstehen in der (Re-)Konstruktion subjektiver Theorien', in B. Friebertshäuser and A. Prengel (eds), *Handbuch Qualitative Forschungsmethoden in der Erziehungswissenschaft*. Weinheim: Juventa. pp. 107–117.

Schütz, A. (1932/1967) *The Phenomenology of the Social World*. Evanston, IL: Northwestern University Press.

Schütz, A. (1962) *Collected Papers. Volume I: Studies in Social Theory*. The Hague: Nijhoff.

Schütz, A. (1964) *Collected Papers. Volume II: Studies in Social Theory*. The Hague: Nijhoff.

Schütz, A. (1966) *Collected Papers Volume III: Studies in Phenomenological Philosophy*. The Hague: Nijhoff.

Schütz, A. (1978) *The Theory of Social Action. The Correspondence of Alfred Schutz and Talcott Parsons* (edited by Richard Grathoff). Bloomington, IN: Indiana University Press.

Schütz, A. and Luckmann, T. (1973) *Structures of the Life-World*, Volume I. Evanston, IL: Northwestern University Press.

Schütz, A. and Luckmann, T. (1989) *Structures of the Life-World*, Volume II. Evanston, IL: Northwestern University Press.

Schütze, F. (1976) 'Zur Hervorlockung und Analyse von Erzählungen thematisch relevanter Geschichten im Rahmen soziologischer Feldforschung', in Arbeitsgruppe Bielefelder Soziologen (eds), *Kommunikative Sozialforschung*. Munich: Fink. pp. 159–260.

Schütze, F. (1977) 'Die Technik des narrativen Interviews in Interaktionsfeldstudien – dargestellt an einem Projekt zur Erforschung von kommunalen Machtstrukturen'. Manuscript, University of Bielefeld, Faculty of Sociology.

Schütze, F. (1983) 'Biographieforschung und narratives Interview', *Neue Praxis*, 3: 283–293.

Schütze, F. (1987) 'Das narrative Interview in Interaktionsfeldstudien', I. *Studienbrief der Fernuniversität Hagen*. Kurseinheit 1. FB Erziehungs-, Sozial- und Geisteswissenschaften. Hagen: Fernuniversität.

Schütze, F. (1994) 'Das Paradoxe in Felix' Leben als Ausdruck eines "wilden" Wandlungsprozesses', in H.-Ch. Koller and R. Kokemohr (eds), *Lebensgeschichte als Text. Zur biographischen Artikulation problematischer Bildungsprozesse*. Weinheim: Deutscher Studienverlag. pp. 13–60.

Schwartz, H. and Jacobs, J. (1979) *Qualitative Sociology. A Method to the Madness*. New York: Free Press.

Scott, J. A. (1990) *Matter of Record*. Cambridge: Polity Press.

Scott, M. B. and Lyman, S. M. (1968) 'Accounts', *American Sociological Review*, 33: 46–62.

Seale, C. (1999a) *The Quality of Qualitative Research* (Introducing Qualitative Methods Series). London: Sage.

Seale, C. (1999b) 'Quality in Qualitative Research', *Qualitative Inquiry*, 5: 465–478.

Sebeok, T. and Umiker-Sebeok, J. (1985) '"Sie kennen ja meine Methode." Ein Vergleich von Ch. S. Peirce und Sherlock Holmes', in U. Eco and T. Sebeok (eds), *Der Zirkel oder: Im Zeichen der Drei*. Munich: Hanser. pp. 28–87.

Seidel, J. and Kelle, U. (1995) 'Different Functions of Coding in the Analysis of Textual Data', in U. Kelle (ed.), *Computer-aided Qualitative Data Analysis. Theory, Methods and Practice*. London: Sage. pp. 52–61.

Selting, M. (2000) 'Probleme der Transkription verbalen und paraverbalen/prosodischen Verhaltens', in G. Antos, K. Brinker, W. Heinemann and S. Sager (eds), *Text- und Gesprächslinguistik – Ein internationales Handbuch zeitgenössischer Forschung. 20 Halbband: Gesprächslinguistik [Linguistics of Text and Conversation – An International Handbook of Contemporary Research. Volume 2: Linguistics of Conversation.]* Berlin: de Gruyter.

Selting, M., Auer, P., Barden, B., Bergmann, J., Couper-Kuhlen, E., Günthner, S., Meier, C., Quasthoff, U., Schlobinski, P. and Uhmann, S. (1998) 'Gesprächs-analytisches Transkriptionssystem (GAT)' *Linguistische Berichte*, 91–122.

Shaffir, W. B. and Stebbins, R. A. (1991) *Experiencing Fieldwork. An Inside View of Qualitative Research*. Newbury Park, CA: Sage.

Shaffir, W. B., Stebbins, R. A. and Turowetz, A. (eds) (1980) *Fieldwork Experience. Approaches to Social Research*. New York: St Martin's Press.

Shankman, P. (1984) 'The Thick and the Thin – On the Interpretative Theoretical Program of Clifford Geertz', *Current Anthropology*, 25: 261–279.

Sharrock, W. and Anderson, B. (1986) *The Ethnomethodologists*. Chichester: Horwood, Tavistock.

Shaw, I. F. (1999) *Qualitative Evaluation*. London: Sage.

Shaw, I. F. and Lishman, J. (eds) (1999) *Evaluation and Social Work Practice*. London: Sage.

Shotter, J. (1990) *Knowing of the Third Kind*. Utrecht: ISOR.

Shotter, J. and Gergen, K. J. (eds) (1989) *Texts of Identity*. London: Sage.

Sieber, J. E. (1992) *Planning Ethically Responsible Research. A Guide for Students and Internal Review Boards*. Newbury Park, CA: Sage.

Sievers, B. (1977) *Organisationsentwicklung als Problem*. Stuttgart: Klett.

Signer, D. (1994) *Konstruktionen des Unbewußten. Die Agni in Westafrika aus ethnopsychoanalytischer und poststrukturalistischer Sicht*. Vienna: Passagen.

Silverman, D. (1985) *Qualitative Methodology and Sociology*. Aldershot: Gower.

Silverman, D. (1993) *Interpreting Qualitative Data. Methods for Analysing Talk, Text and Interaction*. London: Sage.

Silverman, D. (1997) *Qualitative Research. Theory, Method and Practice*. London: Sage.

Silverman, D. (1998) *Harvey Sacks. Social Science and Conversation Analysis*. New York: Oxford University Press.

Silverman, D. (2000) *Doing Qualitative Research – A Practical Handbook*. London: Sage.

Simmel, G. (1902/1985) 'Weibliche Kultur', in H.-J. Dahme and K. C. Köhnke (eds), *Schriften zur Philosophie und Soziologie der Geschlechter*. Frankfurt a. M.: Suhrkamp. pp. 159–176.

Simmel, G. (1984) *Das Individuum und die Freiheit*. Berlin: Wagenbach (Neuausgabe: Brücke und Tür).

Slack, R. S. (1998) 'On the Potentialities and Problems of a WWW-based Natural Sociology', *Sociological Research Online*, 3 (2) (http://www.soc.surrey.ac.uk/socresonline/3/2/3.html).

Smircich, L. (1983) 'Concepts of Culture and Organizational Analysis', *Administrative Science Quarterly*, 28: 339–358.

Smith, B. H. (1981) 'Narrative Versions, Narrative Theories', in W. J. Mitchell (ed.), *On Narrative*. Chicago: University of Chicago Press. pp. 209–232.

Smith, D. E. (1974) 'The Social Construction of Documentary Reality', *Sociological Inquiry*, 44: 257–268.

Smith, D. E. (1978) 'K is Mentally Ill. The Anatomy of a Factual Account', *Sociology*, 12: 23–53.

Smith, D. E. (1984) 'Textually Mediated Social Organization', *International Social Science Journal*, 36: 59–75.

Smith, D. E. (1986) 'The Active Text. Texts as Constituents of Social Relations', in D. E. Smith (ed.), *Texts, Facts and Femininity*. Boston, MA: Northeastern University Press. pp. 120–158.

Smith, J. A., Harré, R. and Van Langenhove, L. (1995) 'Introduction', in J. A. Smith, R. Harré and L. Van Langenhove (eds), *Rethinking Methods in Psychology*. London: Sage. pp. 1–8.

Smith, J. K. (1984) 'The Problem of Criteria for Judging Interpretive Inquiry', *Educational Evaluation and Policy Analysis*, 6: 379–391.

Smythe, D. (1994) 'The Material Reality Under Monopoly Capitalism is That All Non-Sleeping Time of Most of the Population is Work Time', in T. Guback (ed.), *Counterclockwise. Perspectives on Communication from Dallas Smythe*. Boulder, CO: Westview. pp. 263–299.

Sociological Theory (1990) 8, No. 2: Special Section: 'Writing the Social Text'.

Soeffner, H.-G. (1982) 'Statt einer Einleitung: Prämissen einer sozialwissenschaftlichen Hermeneutik', in H.-G. Soeffner (ed.), *Beiträge zur empirischen Sprachsoziologie*. Tübingen: Narr. pp. 9–48.

Soeffner, H.-G. (1985) 'Anmerkungen zu gemeinsamen Standards standardisierter und nichtstandardisierter Verfahren in der Sozialforschung', in M. Kaase and M. Küchler (eds), *Herausforderungen der Empirischen Sozialforschung*. Mannheim: ZUMA. pp. 109–126.

Soeffner, H.-G. (ed.) (1988) 'Kultur und Alltag', *Soziale Welt*, Special issue 6 (Göttingen: Schwartz).

Soeffner, H.-G. (1989) *Auslegung des Alltags – Der Alltag der Auslegung*. Frankfurt a. M.: Suhrkamp.

Soeffner, H.-G. (1991) '"Trajectory" – das geplante Fragment', *BIOS*, 4: 1–12.

Soeffner, H.-G. (1995) 'The Art of Experienced Analysis: Anselm Strauss and His Theory of Action', *Mind, Culture and Activity*, 2: 29–32.

Soeffner, H.-G. (1997) *The Order of Rituals: The Interpretation of Everyday Life*. New Brunswick, NJ: Transaction Books.

Soeffner, H.-G. and Hitzler, R. (1994a) 'Hermeneutik als Haltung und Handlung – Über methodisch kontrolliertes Verstehen', in N. Schröer (ed.), *Interpretative Sozialforschung*. Opladen: Westdeutscher Verlag. pp. 28–54.

Soeffner, H.-G. and Hitzler, R. (1994b) 'Qualitatives Vorgehen – Interpretation', in T. Herrmann and W. H. Tack (eds), *Enzyklopädie der Psychologie. Methodologische Grundlagen der Psychologie. Forschungsmethoden der Psychologie I*. Göttingen: Hogrefe. pp. 98–136.

Sokal, A. (1996) 'Transgressing the Boundaries. Towards a Transformative Hermeneutics of Quantum Gravity', *Social Text*, 46/47: 217–252.

Sola Pool, I. de (1957) 'A Critique of the Twentieth Anniversary Issue', *Public Opinion Quarterly*, 21: 14ff.

Solomon-Godeau, A. (1991) *Photography at the Dock: Essays on Photographic History, Institutions and Practices*. Minneapolis, MN: University of Minnesota Press.

Spöhring, Walter (1989) *Qualitative Sozialforschung*. Stuttgart: Teubner.

Spradley, J. P. (1979) *The Ethnographic Interview*. New York: Holt, Rinehart and Winston.

Spradley, J. P. (1980) *Participant Observation*. New York: Holt, Rinehart and Winston.

Srubar, I. (1981) 'Max Scheler: Eine wissenssoziologische Alternative', in N. Stehr and V. Meja (eds), *Wissenssoziologie. Kölner Zeitschrift für Soziologie und Sozialpsychologie*, Special issue, pp. 343–359.

Srubar, I. (1988) *Kosmion. Die Genese der pragmatischen Lebenswelttheorie von Alfred Schütz und ihr anthropologischer Hintergrund*. Frankfurt a. M.: Suhrkamp.

Stagl, J. (1986) 'Kulturanthropologie und Kultursoziologie'. *Kölner Zeitschrift für Soziologie und Sozialpsychologie*, Special issue 27 'Kultur und Gesellschaft', pp. 75–91.

Stake, R. E. (1995) *The Art of Case Study Research*. Thousand Oaks, CA: Sage.

Stake, R. E. (1997) 'Advocacy in Evaluation. A Necessary Evil?', in E. Chelimsky and W. R. Shadish (eds), *Evaluation for the 21st Century*. Thousand Oaks, CA: Sage. pp. 470–476.

Star, S. L. (1997) 'Anselm Strauss: An Appreciation', *Sociological Research Online*, 2: 1–8.

Stark, W. (1996) *Empowerment*. Freiburg: Lambertus.

Stary, J. and Kretschmer, H. (1994) *Umgang mit wissenschaftlicher Literatur. Eine Arbeitshilfe für das sozial- und geisteswissenschaftliche Studium*. Frankfurt a. M.: Cornelsen Scriptor.

Stehr, N. (1991) 'The Power of Scientific Knowledge – and Its Limits', *Canadian Review of Sociology and Anthropology*, 29: 460–482.

Stehr, N. (1994) *Arbeit, Eigentum und Wissen. Zur Theorie von Wissensgesellschaften*. Frankfurt a. M.: Suhrkamp.

Steiger, R. (1995) 'First Children and Family Dynamics', *Visual Sociology*, 10: 28–49.

Steinke, I. (1999) *Kriterien qualitativer Forschung. Ansätze zur Bewertung qualitativ-empirischer Sozialforschung*. Weinheim: Juventa.

Stiftung für die Rechte zukünftiger Generationen (eds) (1998) *30 Jahre 68er. Warum wir Jungen sie nicht mehr brauchen*. Freiburg: Kore.

Stonequist, E. V. (1961) *The Marginal Man*. New York: Russel & Russel (originally published 1937, Charles Scribner's Sons).

Strauss, A. L. (1968) *Spiegel und Masken. Die Suche nach Identität*. Frankfurt a. M.: Suhrkamp.

Strauss, A. L. (1978) *Negotiations: Varieties, Contexts, Processes, and Social Order*. San Francisco: Jossey–Bass.

Strauss, A. L. (1987) *Qualitative Analysis for Social Scientists*. Cambridge: Cambridge University Press.

Strauss, A. L. (1988) 'Teaching Qualitative Research Methods Courses: A Conversation with Anselm Strauss', *Qualitative Studies in Education*, 1: 91–99.

Strauss, A. L. (1991) *Creating Sociological Awareness*. New Brunswick, NJ: Transaction Books.

Strauss, A. L. (1993a) 'Intellectual Biography: Sources and Influences'. Manuscript.

Strauss, A. L. (1993b) *Continual Permutations of Action*. New York: Aldine de Gruyter.

Strauss, A. L. (1995a) 'Analysis Through Microscopic Examination'. Manuscript.

Strauss, A. L. (1995b) 'Anselm Strauss im Gespräch mit H. Legewie und Barbara Schervier-Legewie', *Journal für Psychologie*, 3: 64–75.

Strauss, A. L. and Corbin, J. (1990) *Basics of Qualitative Research Techniques and Procedures for Developing Grounded Theory*. Newbury Park, CA: Sage (2nd edn 1998).

Streeck, J. and Hartge, U. (1992) 'Previews: Gestures at the transition place', in P. Auer and A. Di Luzio (eds), *The Contextualization of Language*. Amsterdam: John Benjamins. pp. 135–158.

Strehmel, P. (2000) 'Qualitative Längsschnittanalyse', *Zeitschrift für Soziologie der Erziehung und Sozialisation*, 20: 98–100.

Strobl, R. (1998) 'Der Stellenwert theoretischer Vorannahmen in der theoriebildenden qualitativen Forschung', Paper given at the Jahrestagung der Arbeitsgruppe 'Methoden der qualitativen Sozialforschung' in Frankfurt a. M., 8 May 1998.

Stufflebeam, D. (1994) 'Empowerment Evaluation, Objectivist Evaluation, and Evaluation Standards: Where the Future of Evaluation Should Not Go and Where it Needs to Go', *Evaluation Practice*, 15: 321–338.

Suchman, L. (1987) *Plans and Situated Actions. The Problem of Human–Machine Communication*. Cambridge: Cambridge University Press.

Sudnow, D. (1965) 'Normal Crises', *Social Problems*, 12: 255–276.

Sudnow, D. (1967) *Passing On. The Social Organization of Dying*. Englewood Cliffs, NJ: Prentice Hall.

Sudnow, D. (ed.) (1972) *Studies in Social Interaction*. New York: Free Press.

Sudnow, D. (1978) *Ways of the Hand: The Organization of Improvised Conduct*. London: Routledge and Kegan Paul.

Sudnow, D. (1979) *Talk's Body: A Meditation between Two Keyboards*. New York: Alfred Knopf.

Sutter, H. (1997) *Bildungsprozesse des Subjekts. Eine Rekonstruktion von U. Oevermanns Theorie- und Forschungsprogramms*. Opladen: Westdeutscher Verlag.

Sutter, T. (ed.) (1997) *Beobachtung verstehen, Verstehen beobachten*. Opladen: Westdeutscher Verlag.

Szyperski, N. and Müller-Böling, D. (1981) 'Zur technologischen Orientierung der empirischen Forschung', in E. Witte (ed.), *Der praktische*

Nutzen empirischer Forschung. Tübingen: Mohr. pp. 159–188.

Tagg, J. (1988) *The Burden of Representation: Essays on Photographies and Histories*. Basingstoke: Macmillan.

Tashakkori, A. and Teddlie, C. (1998) *Mixed Methodology. Combining Qualitative and Quantitative Approaches* (Applied Social Research Methods Series, Volume 46). London: Sage.

Taubitz, H. (1990) *Die Unternehmenskultur der Deutschen Bundespost*. Heidelberg: Decker.

Taylor, S. J. and Bogdan, R. (1980) 'Defending Illusions – The Institution's Struggle for Survival', *Human Organization*, 39: 209–218.

Taylor, S. J. and Bogdan, R. (1984) *Introduction to Qualitative Research Methods: The Search for Meanings*. New York: Wiley (2nd edn 1998).

Terhart, E. (1981) 'Intuition – Interpretation – Argumentation. Zum Problem der Geltungs-begründung von Interpretationen', *Zeitschrift für Pädagogik*, 27: 769–793.

Terhart, E. (1995) 'Kontrolle von Interpretationen', in E. König and P. Zedler (eds), *Bilanz qualitativer Forschung. Volume 1: Grundlagen qualitativer Forschung*. Weinheim: Deutscher Studien Verlag. pp. 373–297.

Tesch, R. (1990) *Qualitative Research. Analysis Types and Software Tools*. New York: Falmer Press.

Thomas, W. I. and Znaniecki, F. (1918) *The Polish Peasant in Europe and America*, Volumes 1 and 2. Chicago: University of Chicago Press.

Thompson, E. P. (1961) 'The Long Revolution', *New Left Review*, 9/10: 24–39.

Thompson, E. P. (1963) *The Making of the English Working Class*. London: Victor Gollancz.

Thompson, M. (1979) *Rubbish Theory. The Creation and Destruction of Value*. Oxford: Oxford University Press.

Thorne, B. (1980) '"You still takin' notes?" Fieldwork and problems of informed consent', *Social Problems*, 27: 284–297.

Thorne, B. (1993) *Gender Play. Girls and Boys in School*. New Brunswick, NJ: Rutgers University Press.

Titscher, S., Meyer, M., Wodak, R. and Vetter, E. (2000) *Methods of Text and Discourse Analysis*. London: Sage.

Todorov, T. (1989) 'Fictions et verités', *L'Homme*, 29: 7–33.

Torres, R. T., Preskill, S. H. and Piontek, M. E. (1996) *Evaluation Strategies for Communicating and Reporting. Enhancing Learning in Organizations*. London: Sage.

Toulmin, S. (1990) *Cosmopolis: The Hidden Agenda of Modernity*. New York: Free Press.

Travers, M. (1997) *The Reality of Law: Work and Talk in a Firm of Criminal Lawyers*. Dartmouth: Ashgate.

Trescher, H. G. (1985) *Theorie und Praxis der psychoana-lytischen Pädagogik*. Mainz: Grünewald.

Trice, H. M. and Beyer, J. (1985) 'Using Six Organizational Rites to Change Culture', in R. Kilmann (ed.), *Gaining Control of the Corporate Culture*. San Francisco: Jossey–Bass. pp. 370–399.

Trinh, T. M. (1989) *Woman, Native, Other: Writing Postcoloniality and Feminism*. Bloomington, IN: Indiana University Press.

Trinh, T. M. (1991) *When the Moon Waxes Red: Representation, Gender and Cultural Politics*. New York: Routledge.

Trinh, T. M. (1992) *Framer Framed*. New York: Routledge.

Tripet, L. (1990) *Wo steht das verlorene Haus meines Vaters?* Afrikanische Analysen. Freiburg: Kore.

Tropp, R. A. (1982) 'A Regulatory Perspective on Social Science Research', in T. L. Beauchamp, R. R. Faden, R. J. Wallace Jr and L. Walters (eds), *Ethical Issues in Social Science Research*. Baltimore, MD: Johns Hopkins University Press. pp. 391–415.

Türk, K. (1992) 'Organisationssoziologie', in E. Frese (ed.), *Handwörterbuch der Organisation*. Stuttgart: Schäffer-Poeschel. pp. 1633–1648.

Turner, R. (1962) 'Role-taking: Process versus confor-mity', in A. M. Rose (ed.), *Human Behaviour and Social Processes*. London: Routledge and Kegan Paul. pp. 20–40.

Turner, R. (ed.) (1974) *Ethnomethodology: Selected Readings*. Harmondsworth: Penguin.

Turner, S. (1977) 'Complex Organizations as Savage Tribes', *Journal for the Theory of Social Behaviour*, 7: 99–125.

Tursman, R. (1987) *Peirce's Theory of Scientific Discovery*. Bloomington, IN: Indiana University Press.

Ulich, D., Haußer, K., Mayring, P., Strehmel, P., Kandler, M. and Degenhardt, B. (1985) *Psychologie der Krisenbewältigung. Eine Längsschnittuntersuchung mit Arbeitslosen*. Weinheim: Beltz.

Ulich, E. (1994) *Arbeitspsychologie*. Stuttgart: Schäffer-Poeschel.

Ulmer, B. (1988) 'Konversionserzählungen als rekon-struktive Gattung', *Zeitschrift für Soziologie*, 17: 19–33.

Valle, T. de (1993) *Gendered Anthropology*. London: Routledge.

van der Does, S., Edelaar, I., Gooskens, M. and van Mierlo, M. (1992) 'Reading Images: A Study of a Dutch Neighborhood'. *Visual Sociology*, 7: 4–68.

Van Dijk, T. A. (1980) *Macrostructures*. Hillsdale, NJ: Erlbaum.

Van Dijk, T. (1997) 'The Study of Discourse', in T. Van Dijk (ed.), *Discourse as Structure and Process. Discourse Studies: A Multidisciplinary Introduction*, Volume 1. London: Sage. pp. 1–34.

Van Maanen, J. (1988) *Tales of the Field: On Writing Ethnography*. Chicago: University of Chicago Press.

Van Maanen, J. (ed.) (1995) *Representation in Ethnography*. Thousand Oaks, CA: Sage.

Vaughan, D. (1992) 'Theory Elaboration: The Heuristics of Case Analysis', in C. C. Ragin and H. S. Becker (eds), *What Is a Case? Exploring the Foundations of Social Inquiry*. Cambridge: Cambridge University Press. pp. 173–202.

Veyne, P. (1984) *Writing History: Essay on Epistemology*. Middletown, CT: Wesleyan University Press.

Vidich, A. and Bensman, J. (1958) *Small Town in Mass Society*. Princeton, NJ: Princeton University Press.

Vidich, A. and Bensman, J. (Winter 1958/59) 'Commentary on: "Freedom and Responsibility in Research"', *Human Organization*, 17: 2–5.

Vidich, A. J. and Lyman, S. M. (1994) 'Qualitative Methods. Their History in Sociology and Anthropology', in N. K. Denzin and Y. S. Lincoln (eds), *Handbook of Qualitative Research*. Thousand Oaks, CA: Sage. pp. 23–52.

Vogel, B. (1995) '"Wenn der Eisberg zu schmelzen beginnt …". Einige Reflexionen über den Stellenwert und die Probleme des Experteninterviews in der Praxis der empirischen Sozialforschung', in C. Brinkmann, A. Deeke and B. Völkel (eds), *Experteninterviews in der Arbeitsmarktforschung*. Institut für Arbeitsmarkt und Berufsforschung der Bundesanstalt für Arbeit, BetrAB 191. pp. 73–83.

Völter, B. (1998) 'An anti-fascist "legend"?: The Kaufmann family', in G. Rosenthal (ed.), *The Holocaust in Three-Generations. Families of Victims and Perpetrators of the Nazi-Regime*. London: Cassell. pp. 215–239.

Vorderer, P. and Groeben, N. (eds) (1987) *Textanalyse als Kognitionskritik? Möglichkeiten und Grenzen ideologiekritischer Inhaltsanalyse*. Tübingen: Narr.

Voß, A. (1992) *Betteln und Spenden – Eine soziologische Studie über Rituale freiwilliger Armenunterstützung ihre historischen und aktuellen Formen sowie ihre sozialen Leistungen*. Berlin: de Gruyter.

Walkerdine, V. (1991) *Schoolgirl Fictions*. London: Verso.

Walton, J. (1992) 'Making the Theoretical Case', in C. C. Ragin and H. S. Becker (eds), *What Is a Case? Exploring the Foundations of Social Inquiry*. Cambridge: Cambridge University Press. pp. 121–137.

Warren, C. A. (1988) *Gender Issues in Field Research*. Newbury Park, CA: Sage.

Wartenberg, G. (1971) *Logischer Sozialismus – Die Transformation der Kantschen Transzendentalphilosophie durch Ch. S. Peirce*. Frankfurt a. M.: Suhrkamp.

Watson, G. and Seiler, R. M. (eds) (1992) *Text in Context. Contributions to Ethnomethodology*. Newbury Park, CA: Sage.

Watson, R. (1997) 'Ethnomethodology and Textual Analysis', in D. Silverman (ed.), *Qualitative Research. Theory, Method and Practice*. London: Sage. pp. 80–98.

Webb, E. J., Campbell, D. T., Schwartz, R D. and Sechrest, L. (1966) *Unobtrusive Measures: Nonreactive Research in the Social Sciences*. Chicago: Rand McNally.

Webb, R. B. and Glesne, C. (1992) 'Teaching Qualitative Research', in M. LeCompte, W. L. Milroy and J. Preissle (eds), *The Handbook of Qualitative Research in Education*. New York: Academic Press. pp. 771–814.

Weber, M. (1949a) 'The Meaning of "Ethical Neutrality" in Sociology and Economics', in M. Weber, *The Methodology of the Social Sciences*. New York: Free Press. pp. 1–47.

Weber, M. (1949b) '"Objectivity" in Social Science and Social Policy', in M. Weber, *The Methodology of the Social Sciences*. New York: Free Press. pp. 49–112.

Weber, M. (1972/1978) *Economy and Society: An Outline of Interpretive Sociology*. Berkeley, CA: University of California Press.

Weidenmann, B. (1995) *Erfolgreiche Kurse und Seminare. Professionelles Lernen mit Erwachsenen*. Weinheim: Beltz.

Weidmann, R. (1990) *Rituale im Krankenhaus*. Wiesbaden: Dt. Univ.-Verlag.

Weilenmann, M. (1992) 'Das Unbewußte im Rechtsprozeß. Eine ethnopsychoanalytische Studien über Burundi'. *Journal*, 29, Psychoanalytisches Sem. Zürich. pp. 26–55.

Weingarten, E. (1986) 'Das sozialwissenschaftliche Experiment – verdeckte und teilnehmende Beobachtung', in H. Helmchen and R. Winau (eds), *Versuche mit Menschen in Medizin, Humanwissenschaft und Politik*. Berlin: de Gruyter. pp. 220–234.

Weingarten, E., Sack, F. and Schenkein, J. (eds) (1976) *Ethnomethodologie: Beiträge zu einer Soziologie des Alltagshandelns*. Frankfurt a. M.: Suhrkamp.

Weishaupt, H. (1995) 'Qualitative Forschung als Forschungstradition – Eine Analyse von Projektbeschreibungen der Forschungsdokumentation Sozialwissenschaften (FORIS)', in E. König and P. Zedler (eds), *Bilanz qualitativer Forschung, Volume I: Grundlagen qualitativer Forschung*. Weinheim: DSV. pp. 75–96.

Weiss, C. (1983) 'Three Terms in Search of Reconceptualization: Knowledge, Utilization and Decision-Making', in B. Holzner, K. Knorr and H. Strasser (eds), *Realizing Social Science Knowledge*. Vienna: Physika-Verlag.

Weiss, C. H. (1998) *Evaluation: Methods for Studying Policies and Programs*. New York: Prentice Hall.

Weiss, F. (1991) *Die dreisten Frauen. Ethnopsychoanalytische Gespräche in Papua Neuguinea*. Frankfurt a. M.: Campus.

Weitzman, E. A. and Miles, M. B. (1995) *Computer Programs for Qualitative Data Analysis*. Newbury Park, CA: Sage.

Wellmer, A. (1985) *Zur Dialektik von Moderne und Postmoderne – Vernunftkritik nach Adorno*. Frankfurt a. M.: Suhrkamp.

Welter-Enderlin, R. and Hildenbrand, B. (1996) *Systemische Therapie als Begegnung*. Stuttgart: Klett–Cotta.

Welz, F. (1996) *Kritik der Lebenswelt*. Opladen: Westdeutscher Verlag.

West, C. and Zimmerman, D. H. (1991) 'Doing Gender', in J. Lorber and S. A. Farrell (eds), *The Social Construction of Gender*. Newbury Park, CA: Sage. pp. 13–37.

Wetherell, M. and Potter, J. (1992) *Mapping the Language of Racism: Discourse and the Legitimation of Exploitation*. Hemel Hempstead: Harverster Wheatsheaf.

Wever, U. and Besig, H.-M. (1995) *Unternehmenskommunikation als Lernprozeß*. Frankfurt a. M.: Campus.

Whyte, W. F. (1955) *Street Corner Society. The Social Structure of an Italian Slum*, Enlarged edition. Chicago: University of Chicago Press.

Widmer, J. (1991) 'Goffman und die Ethnomethodologie', in R. Hettlage and K. Lenz (eds), *Erving Goffman – ein soziologischer Klassiker der zweiten Generation*. Berne: Haupt. pp. 211–242.

Wiedemann, P. (1995) 'Gegenstandsnahe Theoriebildung', in U. Flick, E. von Kardorff, H. Keupp, L. von Rosenstiel and S. Wolff (eds), *Handbuch qualitative Sozialforschung*. Munich: Psychologie Verlags Union. pp. 211–242.

Wieder, D. L. (1974) *Language and Social Reality: The Case of Telling the Convict Code*. The Hague: Mouton.

Wieviorka, M. (1992) 'Case Studies: History or Sociology?', in Ch. C. Ragin and H. S. Becker (eds), *What Is a Case? Exploring the Foundations of Social Inquiry*. Cambridge: Cambridge University Press. pp. 159–172.

Wikan, U. (1990) *Managing Turbulent Hearts – A Balinese Formula for Living*. Chicago: University of Chicago Press.

Wiley, N. (1994) *The Semiotic Self*. Chicago: University of Chicago Press.

Willems, H. (1997) *Rahmen und Habitus – Zum theoretischen und methodischen Ansatz Erving Goffmans*. Frankfurt a. M.: Suhrkamp.

Williams, F., Rice, R. E. and Rogers, E. M. (1988) *Research Methods and the New Media*. New York: Free Press.

Williams, R. (1958) *Culture and Society, 1780–1950*. London: Chatto and Windus.

Williams, R. (1977) *Marxism and Literature*. Oxford: Oxford University Press.

Williams, R. (1988) 'Understanding Goffman's Methods', in P. Drew and A. Wootton (eds), *Erving Goffman – Exploring the Interaction Order*. Cambridge: Polity Press. pp. 64–88.

Willis, P. (1975) *The Main Reality. Final Report on the SSRC Project Entitled 'The Transition from School to Work'*. Birmingham: CCCS.

Willis, P. (1976) 'The Man in the Iron Cage: Notes on Method', *Working Papers in Cultural Studies*, 9: 135–143.

Willis, P. (1977) *Learning to Labour – How Working Class Kids get Working Class Jobs*. Westmead, Farnborough, Hants: Saxon House.

Willis, P. (1978) *Profane Culture*. London: Routledge and Kegan Paul.

Willis, P. (1990) *Common Culture. Symbolic Work at Play in the Everyday Cultures of the Young*. Milton Keynes: Open University Press.

Willis, P. (1997) 'TIES: Theoretically Informed Ethnographic Study', in S. Nugent and C. Shore (eds), *Anthropology and Cultural Studies*. London: University of Chicago Press. pp. 182–192.

Wilson, T. P. (1970) 'Conceptions of Interaction and Forms of Sociological Explanation', *American Sociological Review*, 35: 697–710.

Wingens, M. (1988) *Soziologisches Wissen und politische Praxis*. Frankfurt a. M.: Campus.

Wingens, M. and Weyman, A. (1988) *Die Verwendung soziologischen Wissens in der bildungspolitischen Diskussion*. Pfaffenweiler: Centaurus.

Winnicott, D. W. (1997) *Playing and Reality*. London: Routledge.

Winograd, T. and Flores, F. (1986) *Understanding Computers and Cognition*. Chicago: Ablex.

Winter, R. (1995) *Der produktive Zuschauer. Medienaneignung als kultureller und ästhetischer Prozeß*. Munich: Quintessenz.

Winter, R. (2001) *Die Kunst des Eigensinns. Cultural Studies als Kritik der Macht*. Weilerswist: Velbrück Wissenschaft.

Wirth, U. (1995) 'Abduktion und ihre Anwendungen', *Zeitschrift für Semiotik*, 17: 405–424.

Wittgenstein, L. (1958) *Philosophical Investigations*. New York: Macmillan.

Wittkowski, J. (1994) *Das Interview in der Psychologie. Interviewtechnik und Codierung von Interviewmaterial*. Opladen: Westdeutscher Verlag.

Wittmann, H. H. (1985) *Evaluation*. Berne: Huber.

Witzel, A. (1982) *Verfahren der qualitativen Sozialforschung. Überblick und Alternativen*. Frankfurt a.M.: Campus.

Witzel, A. (1985) 'Das problemzentrierte Interview', in G. Jüttemann (ed.), *Qualitative Forschung in der Psychologie*. Weinheim: Beltz. pp. 227–255.

Witzel, A. (1996) 'Auswertung problemzentrierter Interviews', in R. Strobl and A. Böttger (eds), *Wahre Geschichten? Zu Theorie und Praxis qualitativer Interviews*. Baden-Baden: Nomos. pp. 49–76.

Wohlrab-Sahr, M. (1992) *Biographische Unsicherheit. Formen weiblicher Identität in der "reflexiven Moderne": Das Beispiel der Zeitarbeiterinnen*. Opladen: Leske and Budrich.

Wolcott, H. F. (1995) *The Art of Fieldwork*. Walnut Creek: Altamira Press.

Wolff, K. H. (1976) *Surrender and Catch: Experience and Inquiry Today*. Dordrecht and Boston: D. Reidel.

Wolff, S. (1980) *Der rhetorische Charakter der Sozialen Ordnung*. Berlin: Dunker and Humboldt.

Wolff, S. (1992) 'Die Anatomie der Dichten Beschreibung – Clifford Geertz als Autor', in J. Matthes (ed.), *Zwischen den Kulturen? Die Sozialwissenschaften vor dem Problem des Kulturvergleichs. Soziale Welt*, Special Issue 8, pp. 339–361.

Wolff, S. (1995) *Text und Schuld. Die Rhetorik psychiatrischer Gerichtsgutachten*. Berlin: de Gruyter.

Wolff, S. and Müller, H. (1997) *Kompetente Skepsis. Eine konversationsanalytische Untersuchung zur Glaubwürdigkeit in Strafverfahren*. Opladen: Westdeutscher Verlag.

Wooffitt, R. (1992) *Telling Tales of the Unexpected: The Organization of Factual Discourse*. Hemel Hempstead: Harvester Wheatsheaf.

Woolgar, S. (1980) 'Discovery: Logic and Sequence in a Scientific Text', in K. D. Knorr, W. Krohn and R. Whitley (eds), *The Social Process of Scientific*

Investigation. Sociology of the Sciences Yearbook, Volume IV. Dordrecht: Reidel. pp. 239–268.

Worth, S. (1981) *Studying Visual Communication*. Philadelphia: Temple University Press.

Wottawa, H. and Thierau, H. (1998) *Lehrbuch Evaluation*, 2nd edn. Berne: Huber.

Wundt, W. (1928) *Elements of Folk Psychology*. London: Allen and Unwin.

Würker, A. (1993) *Das Verhängnis der Wünsche. Unbewußte Lebensentwürfe in Erzählungen E. T. A. Hoffmanns*. Frankfurt a. M.: Fischer.

Yanow, D. (1999) *Conducting Interpretive Policy Analysis*. London: Sage.

Zavala, A., Locke, E. A., Van Cott, H. P. and Fleishman, E. A. (1965) *The Analysis of Helicopter Pilot Performance*. Washington, DC: American Institutes for Research.

Zeiher, H. J. and Zeiher, H. (1998) *Orte und Zeiten der Kinder. Soziales Leben im Alltag von Großstadtkindern*, 2nd edn. Weinheim: Juventa.

Zimbardo, P. G. (1988) *Psychology and Life*, 12th edn. Glenview, IL: Scott, Foresman.

Zimmerman, D. H. (1974) 'Fact as a Practical Accomplishment', in R. Turner (ed.), *Ethnomethodology*. Harmondsworth: Penguin. pp. 128–143.

Zinser, H. (1984) 'Die Wiedereinsetzung des Subjektes: Von der psychoanalytischen Ethnologie zur Ethnopsychoanalyse', *Kölner Zeitschrift für Soziologie und Sozialpsychologie, Sonderheft*, 26: 101–112.

Author Index

Subject Index